MEDIA GRAPHIC PRODUCTION

Second Custom Edition

Taken from:

Adobe® After Effects® CS3 Professional Studio Techniques
by Mark Christiansen

After Effects CS3 Professional for Windows and Macintosh: Visual QuickPro Guide
by Antony Bolante

3ds max® 4 Media Animation
by John P. Chismar

Inside 3ds max® 4
edited by Kim Lee

3ds max® 6 Fundamentals
by Ted Boardman

Adobe® After Effects® 6.5 Studio Techniques
by Mark Christiansen

Custom Publishing

New York Boston San Francisco
London Toronto Sydney Tokyo Singapore Madrid
Mexico City Munich Paris Cape Town Hong Kong Montreal

Cover image: courtesy of PhotoDisc/Getty Images.

Excerpts taken from:

Adobe® After Effects® CS3 Professional Studio Techniques
by Mark Christiansen
Copyright © 2008 by Mark Christiansen
Published by Peachpit Press, a Pearson Education Company
Berkeley, California 94710

After Effects CS3 Professional for Windows and Macintosh: Visual QuickPro Guide
by Antony Bolante
Copyright © 2008 by Antony Bolante
Published by Peachpit Press, a Pearson Education Company

3ds max® 4 Media Animation
by John P. Chismar
Copyright © 2001 by New Riders Publishing
Published by New Riders Publishing, a Pearson Education Company
Indianapolis, Indiana 46290

Inside 3ds max® 4
edited by Kim Lee
Copyright © 2002 by New Riders Publishing
Published by New Riders Publishing, a Pearson Education Company

3ds max® 6 Fundamentals
by Ted Boardman
Copyright © 2004 by New Riders Publishing
Published by Peachpit Press, a Pearson Education Company

Adobe® After Effects® 6.5 Studio Techniques
by Mark Christiansen
Copyright © 2005 Adobe Systems Incorporated
Published by Peachpit Press, a Pearson Education Company

Printed in the United States of America

10 11 12 13 V0CR 13 12 11 10

2008120081

KW

Pearson Custom Publishing is a division of

www.pearsonhighered.com

ISBN 10: 0-555-05164-1
ISBN 13: 978-0-555-05164-1

Acknowledgment

Many thanks to Paul Ashlin of the Rancho Cordova, California campus, ITT Technical Institute for his editorial review and selection of this textbook.

TABLE OF CONTENTS

Chapter 5 The Timeline and Layers 139

Taken from Christiansen and Bolante

PART I

INTRODUCTION

1

The Production Process

What Is Media Animation?

Media animation is the rapidly growing industry that provides graphic content for television, film, print, Internet, and every other multimedia format imaginable. The industry demands original content under tight deadlines. In this fast-paced industry where the speed of the technology pushes your skills to the edge, people working in the field need a deep understanding of the tools available to them, and they must know how to create cutting-edge effects on-the-fly.

Many animators in the corporate world complain that the "powers that be" think the animator clicks a "Make Animation" button and a wonderful animation manifests itself. It's true that those in management often misunderstand the term computer animation; they don't understand the amount of work that is actually involved. Because of this misunderstanding, the animator must be prepared, must have the ability to create any type of animation or effect that is expected of them, and must be able to edit and change their work quickly.

Preparation and Planning

Before creating the first 3D element of a project, you should have a few basic organizational details settled. This ensures that all those involved know their responsibilities and have a good idea of the scope of the project and the time frame in which elements are to be completed.

Even the smallest projects with only one or two members of the staff benefit from a good plan going into production. When the project has more than a few collaborators, the planning stages become paramount to developing a solid outline that each team member can refer to as the work progresses.

It is unrealistic to think that after developing a good plan of attack, nothing will change. 3D projects often seem to be in a constant state of change for a variety of reasons. However, the changes will be much less disruptive to the overall goals if those goals are spelled out for all involved.

Do not skip this step in the creation process to save time; doing so will be an exercise in false economy.

The Chain of Command

Critical communication paths between those who order the work, those who create the content, and those who present to the client must be established with each having an understanding of the available talent and resources.

Communications between the client and production stall, whether that is designers in-house or the actual client, will be something that will develop over time and constantly evolve as the whole visualization process matures. However, educating the client about the general process involved in creating the visualizations can smooth these communications The client need not know specifically how scenes are created, but should know what types of requests will take time and which can be done quickly.

Letting the in-house client sit in on a half-day, hands-on training session with the 3D software can help him understand that there is no magic "make art" button on the computer and ran give him better insight to some of the difficulties the production staff faces.

Regular short meetings between the production staff, and the in-house "clients" can keep each team up-to-date on processes that either increase or hinder productivity from either side.

Needs Assessment

An important step in productivity is determining the scope and quality of work required to satisfy the client's expectations within the confines of time and budget.

Not every job that goes out the door requires photorealistic-quality images to communicate the important messages to the client. Feature films certainly need all the cutting-edge refinements technology has to offer, but public-service announcements to be shown on regional television might not have the same budget considerations and you will have to determine where you can trim production costs with the least effect on quality.

Flexible stages of production can help you avoid costly changes that require you to start from scratch. If modeling and details are too high early in the design development or if complete materials with high-resolution maps are applied to models, for example, it might focus unnecessary attention on decisions that are better left for later.

A better approach might be to rough out models much the same way a stone sculptor would and then go back to add details as they become necessary.

You could use highly compressed stand-in maps while developing the scenes to allow for faster test rendering, for instance, and then replace those with the quality maps near the end of the project.

Storyboarding

Storyboarding is the process of creating a graphic outline that illustrates the story and provides cues to production issues before any work begins on the project.

Storyboards can range from simple sketches to airbrushed or hand-painted panels that could be classified as works of art in their own right (see **Figure 1.1**).

For rendered still images, as an architectural visualization artist might require, the storyboard panels could contain the camera angles, direction, and notes describing specific colors or materials. Lighting scenarios and notes about the quality of lighting might prove to be helpful in storyboards, too.

Animation storyboards could contain the same information plus added notes and sketches referring to action in the scene, One storyboard panel per major action change in the animation motion would be a good place to start.

You might even include additional information pertaining to timing codes and dialogue or sound effects in the margins of the panels.

If a storyboard is short and to the point, you can use just sheets of paper with several panels. For more complex projects, however, a large corkboard with individual panel sheets pinned in place gives a quick overview and is easy to change. Avoid the temptation to use sticky notepads—you might come back from lunch to find that a change in temperature or a breeze has caused your storyboard to scatter across the room like so many fall leaves in a storm.

The importance is not so much on the quality of the artwork of storyboards, but on how clearly it explains the scope and scheduling of the project.

Figure 1.1 High-quality storyboard panels by Andrew Paquette.

Execution

Another crucial component of high productivity is planning the use of available talent and tools. Meet with team members and management to discuss some of the following topics before getting into actual production.

Choose a Team with Both Desire and Talent

Familiarize a broad range of personnel with the creation process and cultivate a pool or artists with a strong desire to apply the extra effort required to become proficient.

Forcing staff to become directly involved in the processes they are not comfortable with—be it modeling, lighting, materials, or animation—leads to bad office politics and pulls good talent from areas where they can be more productive.

Set Up a Productive Working Environment

Provide and maintain current and powerful computer systems. Hardware is a fixed-cost item and can be passed through the office, first as rendering stations, and then as clerical machines for years to come.

Do not, however, buy new hardware as the sole method of increasing productivity until you have mastered the art of scene optimization. Using new hardware as a fix for poor production practices is a waste of resources and time.

In a production office, pay particular attention to seating, lighting, and input devices. For example, a mouse and a tablet at each workstation can minimize stress and injury during long work sessions.

A clean, stable network system for network rendering can increase production (while requiring very little cost and maintenance).

Make sure that team members have an understanding of all the tools available to them before deciding on a production process. With a little practice, it will become habit to choose the right tool for the right job and you will avoid many of the pit falls that come with forcing a tool to do a job for which it is not appropriate.

Know When to Stop

Focus on the elements of 3D production that will most impact the output and leave the rest by the wayside. For example, radiosity rendering might not add enough to your story line to justify the extra time involved in setting up or rendering (see **Figure 1.2**).

Figure 1.2 The image on the left, by the author, is of low quality and was made from scratch in about 4 hours. The image on the right, by Frances Gainer Davey, is very high quality and required about 16 hours to model the interior with furniture and accessories merged from other files.

Do not use the technology for the sake of the technology alone.

Upon reaching a certain level of quality or communication value, it is important to be able to stop and move on to the next task. Perfection is an unobtainable goal—always worth striving for, but only up to the point where it becomes a burden on production.

Integration and Output

You might be called upon to simultaneously create content tor multiple uses. For example, you might be creating a computer game, but you will need higher-quality scenes for the marketing trailers and you might need even higher-quality still images.

Don't forget that more than one software package might be used to generate content. Therefore, you need appropriate converters and workflow methods to remain compatible throughout the project.

The Project/The Elements

The first step in creating a successful workflow is to examine the project and establish a list of the necessary elements. Artists from both the broadcast and the film industries might be faced with totally different artistic and technical challenges with each new project. One client might need digital set extensions involving camera tracking, while another might need hundreds of digital characters and clothing. No matter what the scenario is, someone must sit down and go over every shot and determine what elements are needed and how they should best be created.

Typically this decision making process will be a collaborative effort including a director, producer(s), and visual effects supervisor(s). In cases involving a smaller production staff, the role of the visual effects supervisor will be filled by either the project lead, the technical director, or the lead artist—and, in some cases, all of these. Regardless of the number of people or their titles, the important thing is that individuals strong in a combination of both artistic and technical skills be involved to consider both the artistic integrity of the finished product and the feasibility of the methods employed to achieve them. Although the methods by which a particular element is realized might change over the course of actual production, it is important at this point to determine which, if any, of the elements required are impractical to achieve in their current form.

Sometimes the results of these meetings Will require a rewrite of the script, a change in the storyboards, or a reworking of preproduction designs. Ultimately, after every aspect of the project has been analyzed and agreed upon, a shot-by-shot list should be compiled detailing the element requirements. It is at this time that the individual(s) fulfilling the role of visual effects supervisor must decide what talent and tools are needed to do the job.

The Artists

Regardless of what the marketing departments at software and hardware companies say, the quality of the final work does not come down to the tool but rather to the talent of the artists. Ultimately, it is the artists that drive the industry, and perhaps the hardest part of putting together a successful production workflow is finding the right artists. Regardless of whether the artists are on staff or freelance, their individual skills and talents should complement the type of work needed.

Essentially, artists can be put into one of two categories: those who have a strong, interest and, hopefully talent, in multiple disciplines, making them a kind of jack of all trades; and those who prefer to specialize in only one or two areas. The type and size of the production company will obviously have an influence over which type of artists are available. Generally the two most apparent production strategies favor the two types of artist. Larger production companies, most apparent in film, seem to favor the specialized/departmentalized approach with many specialized artists working only on specific pieces of a project. One of the higher-profile examples of this is Industrial Light & Magic, where 3D modelers do nothing but model and character animators do nothing but animate. The results of this approach certainly speak for themselves.

However, the other approach, which is certainly proven viable by smaller companies every day, involves a workflow in which artists might need to wear multiple hats on a project. These artists might model, texture, and rig a character, while another might handle lighting, particles, and rendering. Ultimately, many factors influence the approach that best fits the project, including budget, schedule, and, last but certainly not least, available talent.

Geography

In many cases, the particular mix of talent deemed necessary for the success of a project might not be readily at hand, in house, in state, or even in country. Ideally, most projects would certainly benefit from having their entire team located under one roof. In fact, for many projects, the immediacy of having artists available for spur-of-the-moment creative meetings with directors, project leaders, and art directors is a must. The added benefits of synergy between artists are another strong reason for having the talent all working in-house.

However, the influence of the Internet and the increasing access to high bandwidth for many companies and artists cannot be denied. Depending on the specifics of the project, allowing artists to work remotely can definitely be a viable and possibly economical option. Assuming a fast enough Internet connection on both sides, some factors that will influence the decision between onsite and remote include the following:

- Is the artist a known quantity?
- Has the artist worked with this team or production company before?
- How well is the artist able to communicate with and receive direction from the director?
- How closely will the remote artist(s) need to work with others in house?
- If the artists are specializing in a certain area, will there need to be a lot of back-and-forth adjustments to files between artists? For example, a character rigger might experience a significant number of back-and-forth adjustments as the rigs are tested by the animator, so working remotely could slow production unacceptably. On the other hand, if a cinematic full-motion video (FMV) sequence is needed for the opening of a game, the artist(s) might not be closely tied to the actual game production at all; in that case, the remote approach could definitely work.
- What is the balance between schedule and budget? It might be significantly cheaper to let someone work remotely

without the burden of transportation and lodging costs that might be necessary to bring that talent on site. Of course, this must be balanced with any possible adverse effect to the project schedule.

Ultimately, it will come down to the comfort level of the director/producer in the ability, speed, and professionalism of the given artist.

If a remote approach is needed, certain obvious infrastructure issues will need to be implemented onsite. These include possible FTP site setup, a project Web site for artists, strict naming conventions, and availability to the artist of any third-party or proprietary tools or plug-ins needed for the project. Another obvious but often-overlooked issue is whether the remote artist is using the same exact version of the software.

Schedule

Working out a realistic project schedule is obviously of paramount importance, followed closely by actually adhering to the schedule during production. In setting up a schedule, many variables must be taken into consideration. The first is to understand the eight different phases required in 3D production. Typically these are as follows:

- Layout/previs
- Modeling
- Texturing/mapping
- Rigging/animation setup
- Animation
- Lighting
- Rendering
- Compositing

✔ Note

> It is important to note that it is typical for the approval process to be closely tied to these phases. This is covered in the next section.

Now is probably a good time to point out just how dependant all the phases are on the others, not just in a schedule sense. None of these phases can operate in a vacuum without taking into consideration the technical issues of the others. For example, how a modeler builds a model will influence the ease or difficulty of the texturing/mapping phase and the rigging phase. Additionally, artists rigging a character must work closely with the animators to produce a rig that is easy to animate and capable of the action required. Lighting will affect the look of textures, and how a shot is rendered will affect how smooth the compositing phase proceeds.

For some of these phases (modeling, texturing/mapping, animation, and lighting), it is obvious, even for intermediate users, from their names what kind of work is involved. Let's look at a few of the phases that readers new to production might be unfamiliar with.

Layout/Previs

During the layout/previs (or previsualization) phase, the project will be blocked out in 3D. This is often done using very low-resolution models, often barely more than primitives. It is here that the director can see any potential timing or staging problems before full-blown production commences. Animation during this phase is typically very rough and basic. Optionally, if the project requires the integration of CG elements with live-action backplates, as in this book, this phase also might require camera matchmoving to execute the actual layout/previs. Otherwise, in an all CG shot, lighting issues and camera issues such as lens and animation can be worked out quickly, relative to the action being previsualized.

Rigging/Animation Setup

The rigging phase is more common to 3D character work but can also include other types of animation setup. Typically this phase will be handled by artists in the role of technical director (TD). A character TD will usually be charged with creating the skeletons and IK setups for a character, along with any custom animation controls required by the animators. Using 3ds max 4, this would include creating complex IK hierarchies, creating manipulators or custom attribute controls, skinning/enveloping the character model, writing custom scripts (possibly using MAXScript), and setting up morph controls for facial animation. Optionally, this might also include setting up any clothing or hair controls. For noncharacter work this phase could include setting up any mechanical hierarchies and controls, particle systems, and any other custom scripts necessary lor the other phases of the project.

Rendering

The rendering phase in production is usually a bit more involved than merely clicking the Render button. Artists or TDs will usually need to have a good understanding of the compositing process to set up render passes or elements that are needed by the compositors. Often the same individuals who handle the lighting phase might be involved in the rendering phase. This is also the phase in which individuals known commonly as render wranglers will oversee any distributed rendering on a render farm using 3ds max Network Rendering features.

For the gaming industry today, in which most of the 3D work is destined to be rendered by a real-time gaming engine on a client's computer, this phase can be replaced with (or renamed) Export to Game Engine. Often this is handled by programmers rather than 3D artists.

Compositing

Finally, the compositing phase is where it all comes together. This is where the final look of the work is tweaked. Traditionally, this work is done using 2D compositing packages such as combustion, flame, or inferno, or in other popular third-party compositing packages such as After Effects, Digital Fusion, or Shake. Recently, however, the industry has begun to incorporate new tools that enable compositors to maintain much of the flexibility of the 3D realm while working with 2D image files. This functionality is most obviously seen with the integration features found between 3ds max and combustion. Regardless of which platform a project is composited on, the compositing phase allows for faster and more flexible tweaking of the final look than would be afforded by re-rendering in 3D. Ultimately, it is a workflow step that is popular not only for large production companies, but also for individuals working on a smaller scale.

This phase, along with the modeling, texturing/mapping, animation, and lighting phases, is not new to the process of creating 3D animation. However, it is important to understand that to complete a project within the confines of schedules typical to 3D production, it is often necessary to have a schedule set up in which the different phases can overlap. The example schedule spreadsheet shown in **Figure 1.3** illustrates this overlap.

Notice that the modeling phase has been further divided into two areas of expertise, character modeling and (general) modeling,

Example 3d Schedule Overview

Scene #	Week 1	Week 2	Week 3	Week 4	Week 5	Week 6	Week 7	Week 8
	modeling	modeling						
	character modeling	character modeling						
		texture/mapping	texture/mapping	texture/mapping				
		Rigging/Setup	Rigging/Setup					
1			animation	animation				
				character animatior	character animation	character animation		
			fx	fx	fx			
					lighting	lighting		
						Rendering	Rendering	
							Compositing	Compositing

Figure 1.3 Example schedule spreadsheet.

and that a similar division has been made to the animation phase. Regardless of how you need to categorize the different parts of the process, the important thing to do is to organize it in a way to keep the workload as even as possible given the number of artists on the project. This example schedule assumes that multiple models need to be built over the course of two weeks. The artists working on modeling can begin work on another scene after the second week of production. Meanwhile, texture/mapping artists and riggers/TDs can begin working on models that have been completed after the first week.

It is easy to see how this kind of schedule would be suitable for a production company based on the specialization model of distributed labor. However, this can also work for shops that employ artists that are proficient in multiple disciplines. The only difference is that more careful planning will be necessary to make sure that the schedules for a particular artist's strengths are not in conflict. For example, you could easily have the same artist fill the roles of texture artist and lighting artist. Of course, this schedule is only a rough guideline because every production will necessitate a custom approach. The three ingredients that are key to producing a similar workable, realistic schedule are listed here:

- Knowing how many artists are available and what their strengths are
- Being able to make realistic estimates of how long a given task will take to complete
- Not forgetting about the client approval process

The first point should be relatively easy to put together. The second is probably the hardest especially when dealing with reasonably unseasoned production artists. However, this can be difficult for even seasoned pros when faced with design/technical issues that they do not have extensive experience with. Sometimes there is just no way to accurately estimate how long something will take until you try to do it. This is why the research and development (R&D) phase exists. Not all projects will have enough time or budget for an R&D phase, but if you find yourself blessed with one, use it wisely.

Either way, you should remember to ask yourself a few basic things and make some assumptions when trying to estimate time needed for a given task:

- How fast/proficient are you or the artist?
- How familiar are you with the technology (when dealing with new techniques such as new plugins or hardware)?
- Assume that the software *will* crash.
- Assume that you *will* find bugs or shortcomings in the software that you were unaware of.

I realize that these last two points might seem a bit pessimistic or even humorous, but, as the saying goes, "That's the nature of the beast." That's the reason for writing this book. Although many workarounds are covered in this book based on artists learning what works the hard way, you will no doubt discover issues not covered within these pages that will require an adjustment of your production schedule, hopefully in a positive sense.

Approvals

The client approval process can sometimes prove to be the slowest phase of a production and must be accounted lot early. Although it's nut always the case, clients are often uneducated in the realities of 3D production. In their defense, it really isn't their problem; it's ours. However, it is important early in the planning stage to implement a strict approval process and set ground rules covering how many and what kind of changes can be made at a given phase of production. Obviously, it is preferable to get final approvals or client sign-offs on 3D models while still in the modeling phase of the schedule rather than during the rendering phase.

However, there must also be a limit set for how many times a client may request changes at a given stage, especially if the client is new to the 3D production process. Often, if left to their own devices, clients can ask an artist to tweak a model or a scene for so long that it starts to eat into the time allotted for other scenes or phases. In the end it is usually the artist who pays, linding him or herself working around the clock to make up for misspent time. Other times the production company will be forced to hire extra artists near the end of production to get the project out the door. Although this scenario seems ubiquitous in everything from film work to games, an awareness of the issue can certainly lessen the impact, on the project.

Changes

If there is any one truth shared in life and in working in 3D, it is that the only constant is change. There will *always* be changes to your work, no matter how well-crafted you believe your work might be. Although we are hopefully all artists at heart, and whether we are working on a game, Web site, commercial, movie, architectural walkthrough, or product display, remember the phrase quoted at the end of this book's Introduction: "This is commerce, not art." We will undoubtedly all become personally attached to whatever piece we are working on, but remember that we are being paid (hopefully) to please a client. And because, in theory, "the customer is always right," your workflow, like the artist's, must be designed to facilitate and adapt to changes at any point of the project.

Luckily for us the underlying architecture of the 3ds max software is reasonably flexible and capable of allowing the artist to make changes earlier in the pipeline without losing all later work. This can be achieved with hopefully minimal suffering on the part of the artist through careful technical planning and use of certain features of the software.

However, there certainly are varying degrees of feasibility when it comes to making changes. Obviously, it is impractical to change the design of a character if the existing character models have made it all the way to the final animation stage. Knowledge of what changes are feasible given the software and workflow is necessary in preparing or briefing a client early on as to what can be changed and when it can be changed. Of course, this is tied closely to the topic on approvals covered earlier.

The Tools

Because this is primarily a book focused on the technical/tool side of the process, we will be looking at some of the ways to take advantage of certain features of max that will facilitate a good workflow. Bear in mind that the following suggestions might not be ideal for your particular project, but they will hopefully inspire alternate approaches that might be more suitable.

Assuming a workflow pipeline in which many artists will need to access files created or modified by others, here are some guidelines taken in the order of a generic production, starting first with general advice common to all phases.

General

- Agree on a standard file-naming convention and centralized storage location.
- Take the time to name objects in a file intelligently and consistently, whether it is a model, a texture, a light, a bone, or a glow effect.
- Get in a habit of saving incrementally. This can be done easily with the plus (+) button located in the Save As dialog box.
- If you're unsure of the results of a procedure that you plan to perform, use the Hold feature often. The Hold feature is located in the Edit drop-down menu. Remember that executing a Hold will actually save your scene to a temporary file that gets overwritten every time you use it. However, even if max crashes, you can retrieve last Hold file by using the Fetch feature.
- Learn some basic MAXScript. It's not hard, it will make your life easier, and it just might open a whole new world for you.
- Whenever possible, create selection sets for models, rigs, lights, and so on. This makes hiding and unhiding things much easier, which will speed up productivity.
- Use the Pop-Up Notes feature to include important comments for other artists that will appear when they open your file. This is especially important if you need to hand your work off to someone else to complete.

Layout/Previs

- If time permits, always do a previs.
- Create the previs as accurately as possible in terms of timing, camera moves, and overall action. Don't overwork the previs. It's more important to see if the overall pacing of a scene is correct at this stage than it is to see if a character is bending its knees correctly.
- If possible, build the previs to the same scale as the real scene is intended to be built. This way you might be able to swap in models and animation using the previs file as a base, and therefore avoid totally rebuilding everything that was worked out in the previs.

Modeling

- Whenever possible, avoid collapsing an object's Modifier Stack. This will maintain the object's history and allow for easier changes. Of course, at some points you must collapse the stack. Therefore, you will need to save incremental files so that you can get back to any stage of the modeling process, if necessary. In many cases you will ultimately want to collapse the Modifier Stack to cut down on CPU/memory overhead for phases such as rigging or texturing. In this case, save a separate uncollapsed version of the model for safe keeping.
- Set up hotkeys or custom Quad menus to speed up productivity.

- Agree upon a standard scene scale, especially if many artists will be building models for the same project.
- If Xrefs will be used in production, use the master model to make low-res proxy versions to speed the animation process.

Texturing/Mapping

- If at all possible, use individual modifiers to assign Material IDs to sub-object selections and to apply mapping coordinates. This enables you to easily go back and make changes without having to dig into one editable mesh, poly, or patch entry. It also makes your work transferable because the modifiers can be copied to other objects. This is especially useful if the animation phase needs to begin before the texture/mapping phase is completed.
- When picking bitmap files for use in a material, consider whether others will be opening the file and whether they will be able to access the same map paths. If centralized storage is configured in your production environment, try to use UNC paths so that every machine can see the same pith.
- Name materials and maps intelligently.
- Create material libraries to facilitate the use of your materials in other scene files.

Rigging/Animation Setup

- Get in a habit of giving bones unique names and/or a prefix for the particular character. For example, if your character is called Jester, name your bones jester-bone01, Jester-bone02, and so on. This way, if the character needs to be merged into another file with other characters, you can avoid same-name conflicts and the confusion that goes with it. Make sure to do the same for any helper or manipulator objects used.
- If you know that your rig will he merged into other files, be aware that, when using constraints, the object you are constraining to will be merged even if it is not selected in the object merge list. This can cause problems, especially if you are constraining object to part of another rig. You might want to create a temporary proxy object For your constraints for merging purposes.
- Talk to the animators at length to get a good idea of what kind of motion they will need the rig to be capable of. Be prepared to cater to their needs. Remember that the most complex rig is useless if the animator cannot use it easily. The best rigs/setups hide the complex technical aspect from the animators and let them just worry about the art of animation, not the technology.

Animation

- If applicable, use the capabilities of controller lists to allow animation to be added in layers. This will make trying out alternate animation performances easier without having to change existing keyframes.
- Use the RAM Player whenever possible to compare and examine animations. It's much more flexible than the Media Player that comes with Windows.
- When feasible, use the Xref features of max to include externally referenced models in your scene. Although this feature does work with the Skin modifier now, typically using Xrefs involves bringing in prop objects that will not be deformed. Remember that you can use the proxy feature of Xrefs to animate with the low-res version of the models,

which will speed things up especially in heavy scene files.

Lighting

- Name lights intelligently, especially when you know that they might be merged into other scene files.
- If possible, work closely with the texture/mapping artists and the rendering artists.

Rendering

- Use UNC paths wherever possible, especially when using network rendering.
- Whenever it will speed up production, render out separate passes (elements) for compositing purposes. If something can be done faster on the compositing side, then do it, especially if you think that changes or tweaks are likely.
- If you really want or need to use a post effect from the max side, such as a glow, render it as a separate pass also.

Compositing

- Make sure to sit down with the artists who will be doing the compositing and make a checklist for yourself of everything the artists will need. Do not take anything for granted. A few of the things that you should not forget to discuss are Alpha Channels, frame rates and counts, pixel aspect ratios and frame resolution, image file formats, and compression types, if applicable.
- Don't use the compositing phase as a crutch for 3D. Just because a project will be implementing a compositing phase doesn't mean that the 3D artists can get sloppy or lazy. Only so much can be tweaked or fixed in compositing. Remember that compositing is supposed to add the icing to the cake, not fix the baking stage.

Summary

These are just a few guidelines that are important to consider. As you progress through the production portions of this book, you will see some of these points discussed in greater detail. Ultimately, the success of a given pipeline will increase as the artist gains experience and discovers what techniques work better, faster, and are more reliable.

2

THE ROLE OF COMPOSITING

Up to now, the topic of 3d production has been the primary focus of this book with a brief mention of compositing in the workflow chain. Compositing has the ability to combine elements such as live footage, 3d animation, 3d objects, render elements, 2d images and text to create a visual effects or scenes. Only in recent history has it been possible to use the computer to do this process. How were these visual effects achieved before the arrival of the computer as a compositing tool?

The Cult of Magic

Back in the early days of magic, before you could go to your local bookstore or magic shop and buy a copy of David Pogue's *Magic for Dummies* (Hungry Minds), magic was a dark art practiced by masters sequestered in private clubs and learned by a handful of apprentices. The roots of the word "magic" refer to the Magi, the members of the Zoroastrian priesthood. I don't suppose it gets much more sequestered than that.

Figure 2.1 *Trip to the Moon* is sometimes called the first visual effects film.

✔ Note

One of the great novels of the decade is Michael Chabon's *The Amazing Adventures of Kavalier and Clay* (Random House). If you enjoy stories about magic in the days of Houdini, stories about the birth of comics, or just an extremely well-written novel, I highly recommend this Pulitzer Prize winner.

Visual effects, those skillful re-creations of reality, have been an art form since the beginning of filmmaking; just watch 1900's *Trip to the Moon* by George Meliés (**Figure 2.1**). In fact, the earliest films capitalized on two phenomena above all others: the startling realism of the medium and the ability to make up scenes that were impossible to create any other way.

Figure2.2 The Lumière brothers, Louis Lumière famously declared, "The cinema is an invention without a future."

✔ Note

The earliest public motion picture display by the Lumière brothers (**Figure 2.2**) reputedly included footage of a train pulling into a station that had the poor naive audience diving to the floor in panic, believing a real train was headed their way. Louis Lumière evidently grew quickly tired of this spectacle, famously declaring a short time later, "The cinema is an invention without a future."

But until the 1990s, special effects post-production for movies was a craft known only to a few hundred practitioners worldwide, and the dark art of its practices (often photo-chemical, sometimes crude, sometimes sophisticated, almost always labor-intensive and fraught with treacherously little room for error) was largely known only to them, passed on in a

Figure 2.3 A torture device? Only according to your point of view. An optical printer such as this one was the sole means of compositing film prior to the digital age.

guild-like fashion to those few apprentices who found their way to this strange specialization (**Figure 2.3**).

Enter the color desktop computer, then Adobe Photoshop, then After Effects, and suddenly anyone with a few thousand bucks for equipment, or access to borrow it, could have a go at creating a visual effects shot. And have a go people did, creating visionary low-budget videos (as well as hundreds of *Star Wars* tribute films) and growing the professional visual effects community exponentially.

A 2004 survey by an Adobe product manager turned up some 250 Hollywood features that had relied on After Effects. Stu Maschwitz, author of Chapter 15, Learning to See," led the Rebel Mac group at Industrial Light + Magic for several years in the 1990s; their use of After Effects on big-budget, Academy-nominated effects films was largely unpublicized, mostly due to the perception (even among film studios) that only "big iron" was up to work of that caliber.

Yet the old cultish altitudes in many way, prevailed. Sure, lot of kids proved that they could produce a convincing lightsaber battle on the family computer, but try to learn how to create an elaborate effects shot by reading up on it and you got smoke, mirrors, vagaries, and what has quickly become a cliché of *Cinefex* magazine (once the source for ill kinds of nitty-gritty details): the use of "proprietary software." Visual effects work might as well have been magic because it seemed to be made up of a bunch of exacting techniques crafted by super-geniuses and jealously guarded as trade secrets.

This book aims to demystify the realm of visual effects, focusing on the skill of re-creating reality with After Effects, of fooling viewers into thinking they are seeing a shot that was taken with a camera all at once.

Think of this book as a basic magic manual, teaching you the visual equivalents of hiding a card or palming a coin. If your goal is to be the David Blaine of compositing, you must master the basics that come up again and again, those effects that are often a key part of the most original and fantastic movie sequences.

Truly Challenging

Ironically, visual effects artists themselves often fail to notice how complicated it is to craft a shot; until you step back a little bit, all you notice is that you spent long days of hard work making subtle corrections to dozens of takes of a few seconds of film. The individual steps now seem almost unremarkable and trivial, but a complex shot might consist of thousands of such steps, many of which were at some point surprising and revelatory to each of us.

Also, each visual effects shot seems to be unique, and in many ways, it is. Explaining the exact steps to create one shot may be of little use when it comes time to create the next one. Some bread-and-butter effects, however, are done at every studio and are no one's trade secret. These come up all the time, sometimes as a component of a larger and more complex shot, sometimes as the main focus of a simple shot. Every compositing artist should know how to do them.

This book is about those kinds of effects; ultimately, it is about the process of building them up to create a shot that is greater than the sum of its parts and fools the eye of the viewer.

All visual effects can be broken down into comprehensible components (although, to comprehend some of the components might very well also require an understanding of wave dynamics or Fourier transforms). Moreover, very few (even simple) effects can be called complete without being broken down much further than the novice artist typically wants to go with them.

This brings us to the keys to creating the best visual effects, those that are often pretty close to invisible and call no attention to themselves whatsoever. They do not detract from the story, but enhance it, and only later on do you wonder, "How the heck did they do thay?"

The Keys

You do it by following some simple guidelines—simple, yet so important in delineating your success or failure as an effects composition. The keys are

- **Get reference**. You can't re-create what you can't see clearly and in great detail. Great artists recognize many features of the world that the untrained eye fails to see.
- **Simpler is often better**. Effects compo siting is complicated enough without overcomplicating it with convoluted processes and needless extra steps. A robust effects pipeline is typically made up of the simplest available solutions, and it's usually worth the extra effort to simplify your workflow however you can. Occam's Razor, which states that the simplest solution or explanation is often the best one, applies in spades here.
- **Break it down**. This, more than anything else, addresses the biggest error made by beginners: They try to solve problems using a single solution, applied globally to the whole shot or one of its elements. For example, beginning artists tend not to look at individual color channels when matching foreground and background colors. You must be willing to examine the individual red, green, and blue channels and adjust them separately to match

overall color effectively. And if this advice applies to something so fundamental as color matching, you'd, better believe it applies to more complex effects.

- **It's not good enough**. This sounds discouraging, doesn't it? What you must take away is the spirit, rather than the literal truth of this statement, and always strive for the best result possible.

If you let your guard down and settle for "good enough," someone's going to say it . . .

✔ **Note**

The willingness to go beyond the one-button solution and break apart a shot into adjustable components is what will make your shots stand out. Otherwise you're just relying on luck to overcome laziness.

"That Looks Fake"

Can't you just hear that flat condemnation, uttered with no subtlety or restraint by the teenage kid sitting behind you at the multiplex? That kid is sometimes wrong (I've heard this label slapped on a shot that I knew had no visual effects), but you can hardly argue with the sentiment if your goal is to fool the skeptical viewer.

A little bit of that petulant teen lives in all of us. Ideally the statement will evolve to "That looks fake because . . ." with you able to complete the phrase using your eyes, your observations of the world and those of your colleagues, and information from a source like this book.

A somewhat more civilized version of that rude teenager shows up at dailies on a feature film effects project, but with the title of Visual Effects Supervisor. Here's how dailies generally go: At the start of a workday, a bunch of people get some coffee, go into a dark screening room, watch a shot more times in a minute or two than the average audience will watch it in a lifetime (unless of course it's a shot from *Star Wars*), and you are told why it doesn't look right, It sounds like a harsh way to start the day, but actually, this is absolutely where the real process of doing great work is rooted.

Relentless dissatisfaction is one of the keys to successful visual effects. Try not to confuse it with actual discouragement, no matter how harsh your own (or someone else's) criticism. If it doesn't look right to you, it doesn't mean you're a bad artist; it simply means you have the taste and discrimination to know the difference (a wise statement I first heard from my former colleague Paul Topolos, now at Pixar).

What Compositing Can (and Can't) Do

The type of full visual effects pipeline used to produce a big-budget feature film contains many roles and specializations; depending on your point of view and on the shot in question, the compositor's role can be the most crucial or the most denigrated. Typically, with the possible exception of a colorist, the compositor is the last one to touch the shot before it goes in the movie, so it's an important job if only for that reason.

To a large extent, a composite is only as good as the sum of its elements. The best compositors have a reputation for producing gold out of dross, building a great looking shot despite poorly shot plates and slapdash 3D elements. But compositors still need elements to do their work, and poorly shot or created elements typically lead to an equally poor result.

If you're still learning how to composite, you may be creating all of your elements yourself. That's great, because compositors benefit from understanding the disciplines that feed into the shot. For example, it's essential that you understand how the camera gathers images so you can mimic the reality created by a camera. If you're comfortable as a 3D animator, those skills will help you navigate the 3D capabilities of After Effects, and you will learn how much time you can save fine-tuning your shots in 2D rather than tweaking them endlessly in numerous 3D renders.

As a compositor, you have to know about these other disciplines, because to some extent you're re-creating their results from scratch, and you have far more room to cheat and make up your own rules. A cameraman cannot go further than the limits of what a camera can do, but you can. And one dirty secret is that sometimes you must cheat actual reality to make your shot believable.

3

Real-World Case Study

John Chismar has been creating Media Graphics for NBC since 1994. The primary tool he uses for producing this media content is 3ds Max. In this real-world case study, Mr. Chismar takes the reader through the media production process at NBC with a project you may have seen used by NBC for the 2000 Presidential Election Campaign.

NBC News 2000

I had worked in news graphics long enough to know that when the U.S. 2000 elections were right around the corner, it could mean only one thing: a whole lot of work. Turns out that none of us could have accurately foreseen the amount of work that lay on the road ahead. Knowing that the presidential race was close, something in the back of my head said, "Recount," but I didn't have time to think of what to do after Election Day; I needed to focus on creating what we knew we needed.

In the weeks leading up to out election coverage, I was working closely with Lori Neuhardt, MSNBC'S Creative Director, and Vince Diga, designer, on the Newsfront project. We were working under tight schedules to wrap up the creation of Newsfront and then start the Decision 2000 animations. Sam Mandragona, NBC's Executive Creative Director, was kind enough to call me every two or three days to make sure I could start the project on time.

While I was working on Newsfront, Sam stopped by to chat about the Decision 2000 project. He brought a Xerox of a pencil sketch storyboard that had been drawn by Tony Franquera, NBC's Associate Creative Director, on the train during his commute to work. It looked pretty straightforward (see **Figure 3.1**), but I had concerns about having enough action to fill the 20 seconds of animation in one camera shot. We decided to conquer that hurdle when it rose in front of us.

Before I started the animation, I asked Sam if he could have someone colorize the storyboards to give me a better idea of the desired feel. He assured me he was on it and headed back across the river to 30 Rock (NBC NY—30 Rockefeller Center).

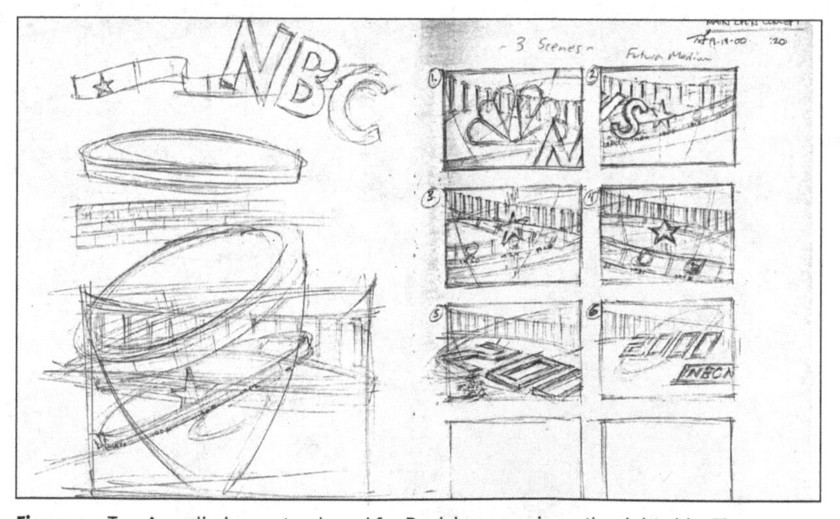

Figure 3.1 Tony's preliminary storyboard for Decision 2000 is on the right side. The sketches on the left were the result of my project planning session with Sam.

Making the Preliminary Studies

The day after I wrapped up the Newsfront animation, I started to sink my heels into Decision 2000. I examined the pencil sketch storyboard and began to collect my thoughts. Sam had told me they wanted the animation to have dark colors and glasslike materials. The pencil strokes told me one thing clearly: There were going to be glass rings. Two to three weeks before I needed to have the animation finished, I started to develop it.

RingsA01.max

To help me visualize the glass ring concept, I created my first scene in 3ds max, mostly to develop a mood for the scene and to begin creating the "glass" materials. The first scene I created was RW1\scenes\ringsA01.max (shown in **Figure 3.2**).

RingsA01.max is a simple scene with a few colored Omni lights, a camera, and four Tube primitives linked in a hierarchy with Noise Rotation Controllers assigned to them. You can watch the rendered animation by viewing RW1\ringsA01.mov. Four glass rings rotate and refract through one another as they turn randomly.

The visual effect, although dark, is quite complex and interesting. It may or may not be a big surprise that this was an extremely simple scene to create. In the Material Editor, you can see the settings for the

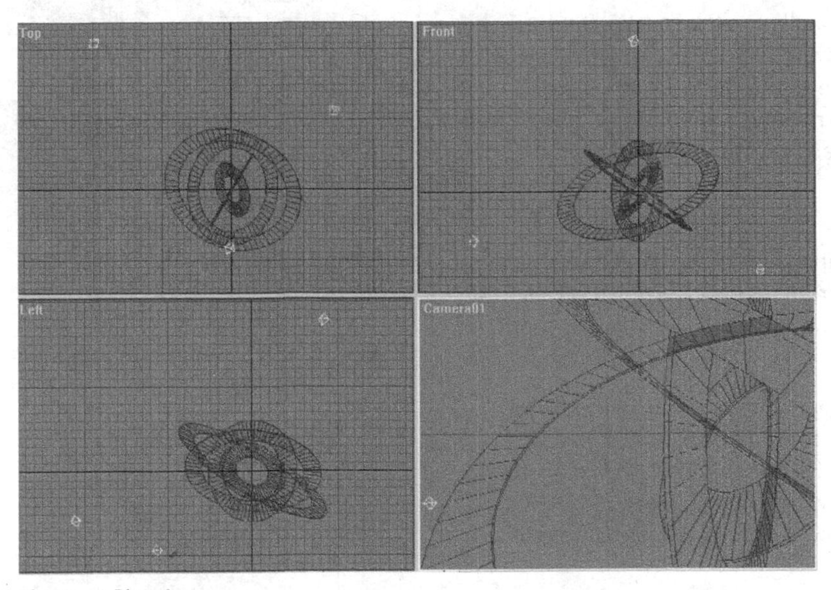

Figure 3.2 RingsA01.max.

Material #1 material (see **Figure 3.3**). (Bad John for not naming your materials!)

The material is 100% transparent (signified by the Opacity value of 0), so no color is derived from the Ambient or Diffuse channels of the material. The specular highlights are both white, and the First Specular Layer highlight has some Anisotropy applied for a more metallic look. The blue and orange color that appears on the rings as they rotate is obtained from the colored Omni lights in the scene.

The refraction is created with a Raytrace Retraction Map applied to the material. The default settings are applied. I did, however, change the Index of the Refraction: value to .75 in the Extended Parameters rollout of the material. To obtain the Index of Refraction setting, I generally refer to the list in the Help menu (shown in **Figure 3.4**).

Glass is usually a setting of 1.5, but because my rings were flat objects, that setting didn't work quite as dramatically as I desired. Through trial and error, I found that .75 was a much better setting.

✔ Tip

- You can animate the Index of Refraction value from its lowest value 0 through 10 to see what value works best in your scene.

I was happy with the result of this scene, and I kept it in my back pocket in case I needed it. I still didn't have the color storyboards in work with, so I wasn't sure if it was what was desired; I knew it was close though.

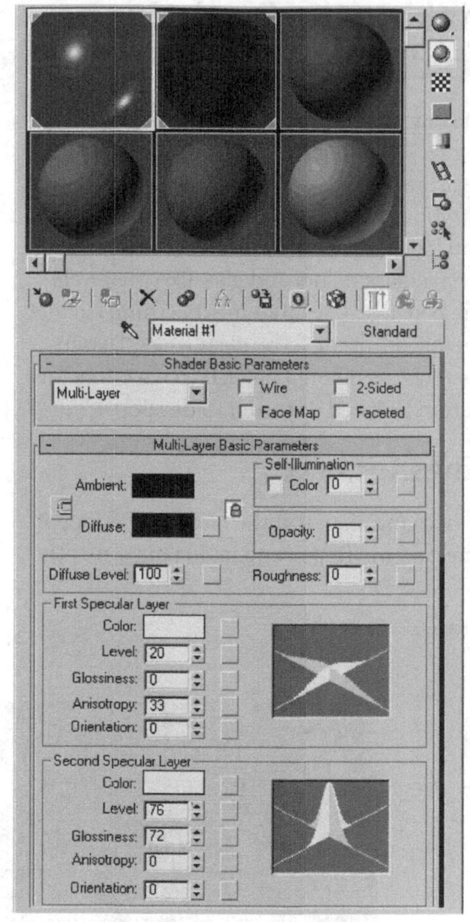

Figure 3.3 The Material Editor settings for Material #1.

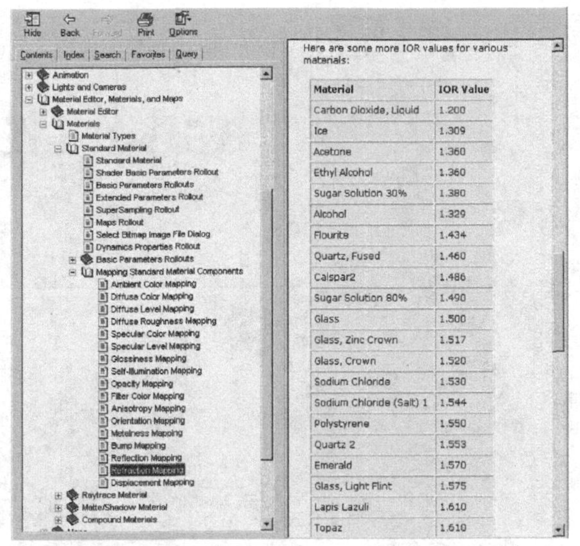

Figure 3.4 The 3ds max User Reference with the Refraction Mapping help open.

RingsB01.max

Beacuse I was happy with the rendered result of the ringsA01.max file, I decided to push it a little further. Tony's pencil storyboard shows the colonnade that surrounds the scene. I built the columns with as low a polygon count as I could and placed them in a scene similar to ringsA01.max. The result can be viewed in RW1\scenes\ringsB01.max (shown in **Figure 3.5**). You can watch the rendered animation by viewing RW1\ringB01.mov.

The ring's material is the same, but the Index of Refraction was changed to a more modest value of .9. The pillar objects in the scene have a very simple blue plastic material applied. The floor that the pillars are resting on has the same material as the pillars except a Flat Mirror reflection was added to reflect the pillars slightly.

When I finished this animation, I called Joe Dettmore, MSNBC's Assistant Creative Director, to have him view the results, Joe and I discussed the rendered animations and how we could use this refraction effect on an upcoming project if it wasn't used on Decision 2000. While I waited for the color storyboards, I started to familiarize myself with the Decision 2000 logo object that I had created a while back.

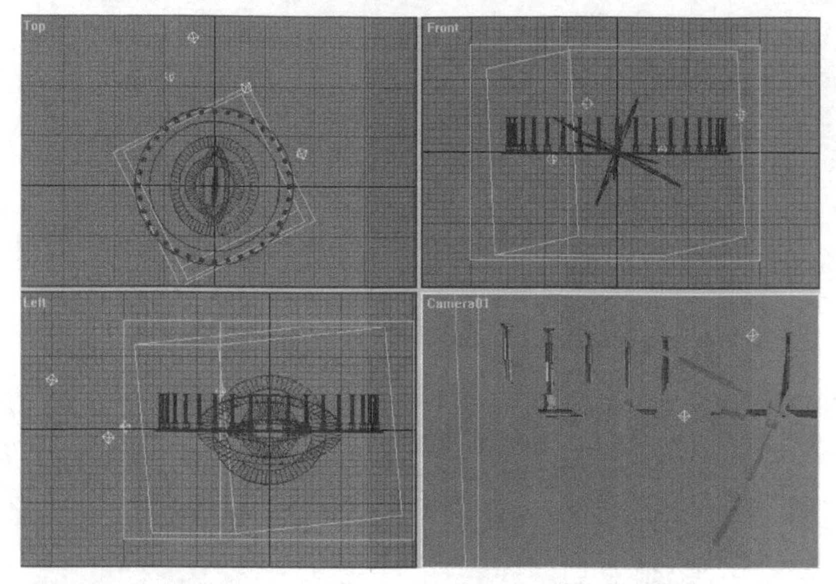

Figure 3.5 RingB01.max.

Working with the Storyboard

Two weeks before my deadline, Sam and Tony stopped by with a color storyboard of sorts (see **Figure 3.6**).

From the beginning, we were planning for the animation to be three shots long, meaning there would be three scenes, and we would transition from one to the next with dissolves. Tony's storyboard was basically the first shot of this sequence. Along with this color storyboard, they brought along other backgrounds and preliminary images they had been working on at 30 Rock (see **Figure 3.7**).

Looking at these images, I could see that I had the color scheme down fairly close.

Figure 3.6 The color storyboard for Decision 2000.

Figure 3.7 Preliminary back-ground images created at 30 Rock.

But the newer storyboard didn't contain as many rings as I had first predicted.

Sam, Toni, Joe, and I sat in my office and discussed what should happen with the animation. Finally, we had everyone in one room and ready to talk about the project in detail. We spoke a lot about the presidential ring that is symbolized by the gold ring on Tony's storyboard This ring was going to have the picture of every president chronologically texture mapped around it. As we progressed through the animation, we would see apparently random sections of the ring progressing to the more recent presidents.

Sam and Toni brought up the fact that they wanted to see the Presidential seal somewhere in the animation as well. Joe chimed in and asked me to play those ray-traced refracted tube object animations I created. As the animations looped out on my monitor, it was unanimous that these rings should become the Presidential seal. Now we all had a rough idea of what I needed to create. All that was left was for me to make sense of it all.

Before we wrapped up the meeting, we agreed that there should be four shots in the animation instead of three. The first shot would be the establishing shut that showcased the Presidential seal and colonnade; this would allow viewers to get a grasp on where they were. The second shot would be the presidential ring. The third shot would be the peacock and U.S. Capitol dome, and the fourth shot would be the Decision 2000 logo. It sounded simple. I was left to actually do it all in less than two weeks.

Creating Shot 1

I decided to work on the animation from start to finish. So I started with the first shot, the Presidential seal and colonnade (see **Figure 3.8**). Before I could complete the shot, however, I needed to build a clean and appropriate Presidential seal.

Figure 3.8 A frame from shot I.

This proved to be one of the biggest hurdles of the project. But if I could just complete the Presidential seal, I could then build the rest of the scene around it.

The Presidential Seal

What was the quickest way to make a clean Presidential seal? That was the question. The text and stars were the easy part. What concerned me most were the eagle and shield. I scanned the seal from a cover of a book about the presidency. I tried to clean up the color artwork to make a black and white bump or displacement map. The moirè pattern of the scan made it nearly impossible to quickly create the map I needed. I then loaded the book cover scan as the Viewport background to try to build the object as a mesh. I didn't get far (see **Figure 3.9**) before I realized it would take forever to do that as well.

After about a day or day and a half, I still hadn't accomplished anything. I was working over the weekend. It was Sunday afternoon, and I was anxious to have something finished for Monday morning. I decided to go for a walk.

When I left my room, I ran into Christo Manco, a designer on our team. He was working the weekend as well. It didn't take long before I was ferociously grumbling about my predicament. Because Christo is usually the person who traces the logos in illustrator for use in 3D, I joked that he might have a lot of tracing on his hands. He glanced up at me and said, "Tsukasa has a CD with all those government seals on it."

Too bad Tsukasa had left MSNBC a few months back for a warmer job in Miami. But that got me thinking. "Was the CD really *his* or did we have one at MSNBC as well?"

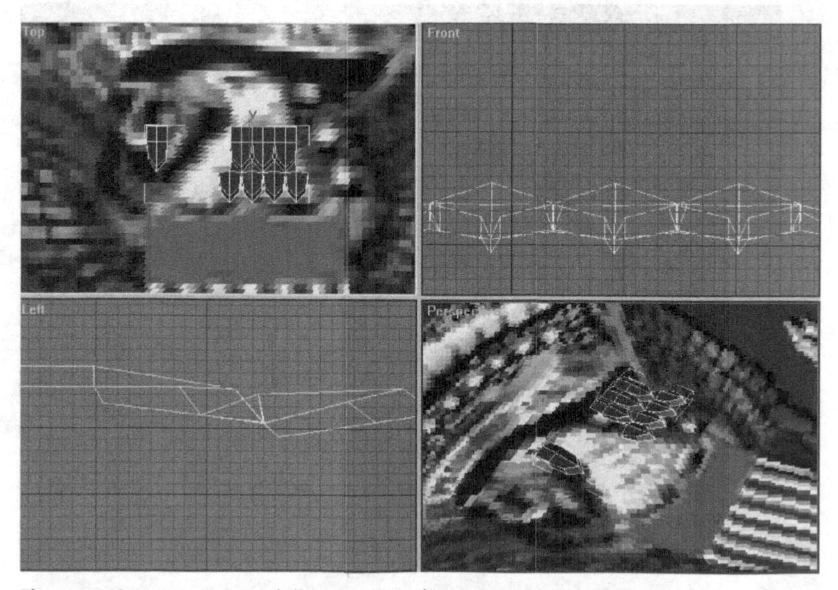

Figure 3.9 An attempt at modeling the eagle (those things are feathers).

I raided the closet where we keep all our digital archives and came across a CD that I thought might have it. I put it into my workstation, but the CD wouldn't read on a PC. So I went to a Mac system and loaded the CD. Voilá! There was in fact an Illustrator file of the Presidential seal! Now all I had to do was load it into 3ds max, clean it up a bit, and extrude it.

Nah. It couldn't be that simple. After I imported the Illustrator file of the presidential seal into 3ds max, I started to break it up into sections (head, wings, claws and so on) to be Cleaned up. However, the 5,997 vertices of the seal shape intimidated me (see **Figure 3.10**), and after creating only the head and beak, I gave up and opted for a much simpler solution.

Finally, I realized I could use the Illustrator file of the seal to generate the bump map I wanted In the first place! Why didn't I think of that sooner? When I loaded the Illustrator file into Photoshop, it gave me the image I needed. I simply cropped out

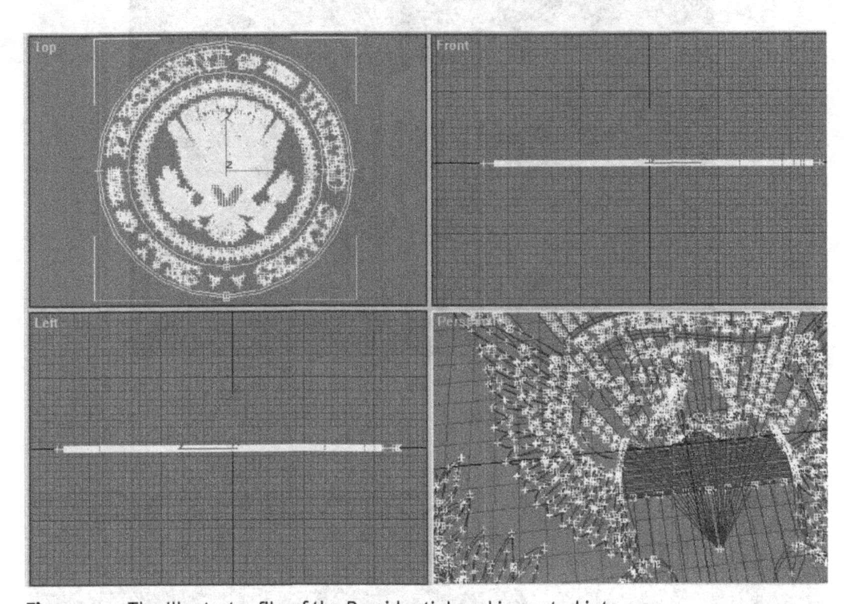

Figure 3.10 The Illustrator file of the Presidential seal imported into max.

the eagle portion and saved it as a jpg (see **Figure 3.11**). I named this image bird2good.jpg.

To give the seal a little life in the first shot, Joe, Sam, Toni, and I decided that the shield should have a little color. To apply it, I needed to generate two more texture maps using bird2good.jpg as the template; the texture maps were bird2goodcolor.jpg and bird2good-colormatte.jpg. They're shown in **Figure 3.12**.

Figure 3.11 Bird2good.jpg.

Figure 3.12 Bird2good-color-matte.jpg (left) and bird2good-color.jpg (right).

Using the refraction material we discussed earlier as a base, I added the new maps I had Created from the Illustrator file. **Figure 3.13** shows the RingBird material's settings. This material generated the precise result I wanted (see **Figure 3.14**). You can't imagine how elated I was when this object and material was finished. From start to finish, it took me two and a half days to complete the objects and materials for the Presidential seal.

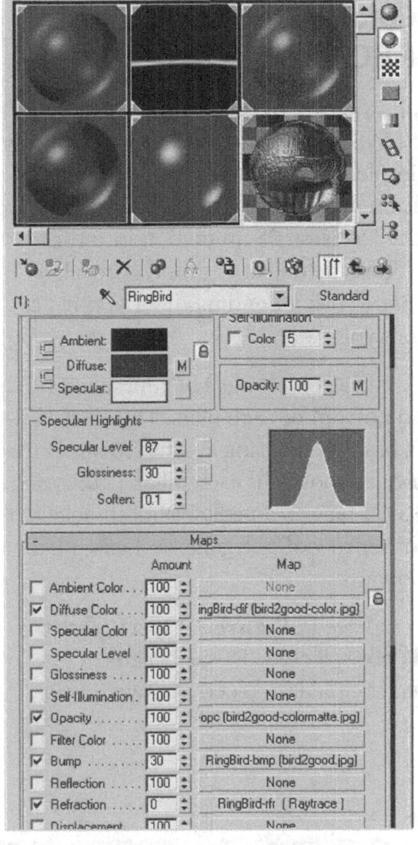

Figure 3.13 The Material Editor showing the RingBird material settings (at lower right).

Figure 3.14 The rendered object with the RingBird material applied.

The Colonnade and NBC NEWS Type

The construction of the colonnade and the NBC NEWS type (shown in **Figure 3.15** was very simple. As a tribute to the Decision 98 animation, I merged the NBC NEWS type from the Decision 98 animation into the scene. The type object is simply a beveled type Shape with a Bend modifier applied to arch the type.

To create the colonnade, I box modeled the top and bottom of each pillar. The round pillar was built by creating a lathe. To apply the lengthwise grooves in each pillar, I collapsed the pillar lathe into an editable mesh, selected every other row of polygons, and extruded them inward.

As you ran see in **Figure 3.15**, every tenth pillar is not selected. This is because I grouped the pillar objects into two groups. This way I could hide the pillars selected In **Figure 3.15** but still have every tenth pillar visible as a reference when I was animating. This allowed realtime views to play back more accurately. However, later in production, I think I just selected each pillar, right-clicked it, chose Properties, and activated Display as Box. This accomplished the same thing by reducing each pillar into a box shape in the view, and it reduced the number of polygons in the scene.

The Environment

The environment is generally one of the hardest things to get right when you're building "high profile" animations. Usually nobody, including myself, can make up his or her mind as to what looks best. At the time, the only thing I knew for sure was what Tony had in mind. So I copied his storyboard and created a bright blue

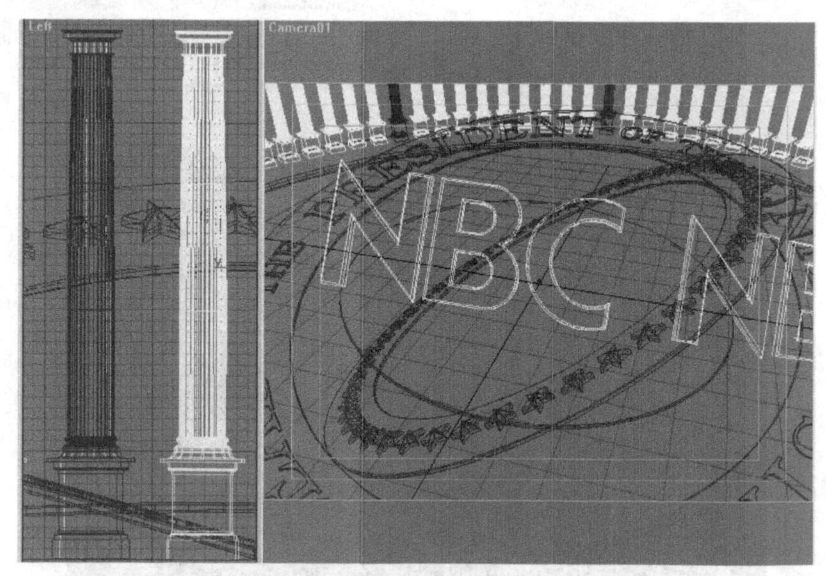

Figure 3.15 The colonnade objects (left) and NBC NEWS object (right).

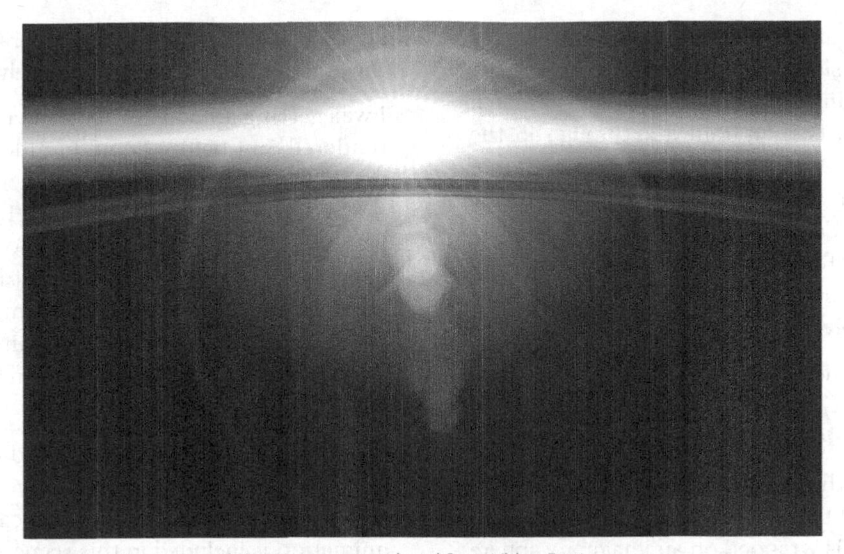

Figure 3.16 Frame 60 of shot A01.max rendered from Video Post.

horizon line over a black background (see **Figure 3.16**).

Included on the CD is the file RW1\scenes\shotA01.max. This file has all the elements I used to create the environment for the scene and the camera motion. Also in the scene is the PillarFloor object, which the colonnade stood on. This was added as a reference of perspective. To see a wireframe animation of the first shot with all the objects, view RW1\wire_shotA.avi.

To create the blue horizon line, I applied a Gradient Ramp to the Environment map channel. If you load RW1\scenes\shotA01.max and open the Material Editor in the second material preview slot, you will see the Env map (shown in **Figure 3.17**).

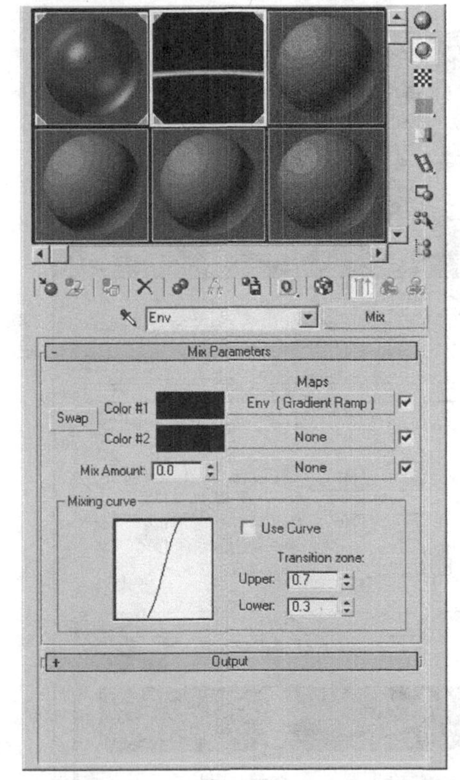

Figure 3.17 The Material Editor with the Env map selected at frame 100.

Notice that the Gradient Ramp is in the Color #1 slot of a Mix map. This is because the beginning of the shot shows the scene in darkness. Then in frames 25 through 45, the blue horizon appears. To accomplish the transition from black to the horizon, I mixed between Color #2 (black) and Color #1 (the Gradient Ramp) between frames 25 and 45. If you scrub the time slider, you can watch the dissolve.

To examine the Gradient Ramp, you can click the Gradient Ramp button in the Mix map (see **Figure 3.18**).

Because the Gradient Ramp uses the Spherical Environment mapping, the gradient is wrapped on an imaginary sphere around the scene. When the camera moves, the gradient will move appropriately.

I was getting anxious to see something rendered, but before I could render, I needed to add a flare to the horizon. I opened Video Post and applied a Lens Effects Flare (see **Figure 3.19**). To my recollection, either I used the default flare, or I loaded one that came with 3ds max. I made some modifications and animated some of the parameters (as shown in **Figure 3.20**).

The animated flare is also included with the RW1\scenes\shotA0l.max file for your examination purposes. Also, the actual camera animation is included in this scene as well.

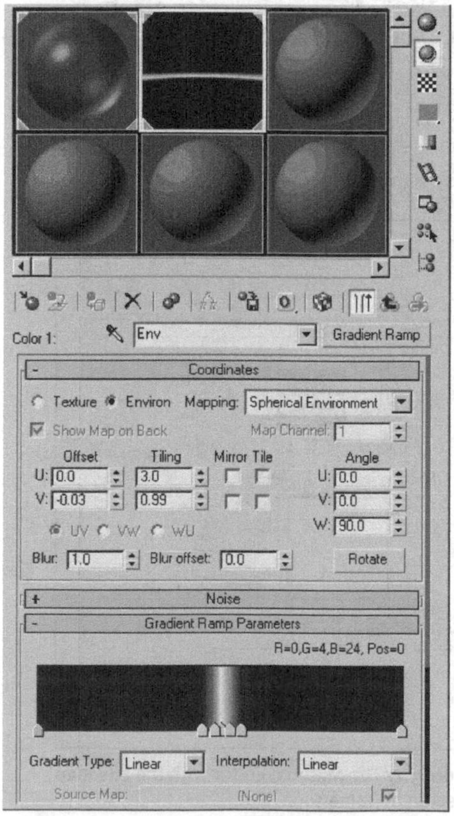

Figure 3.18 The Gradient Ramp for the blue horizon.

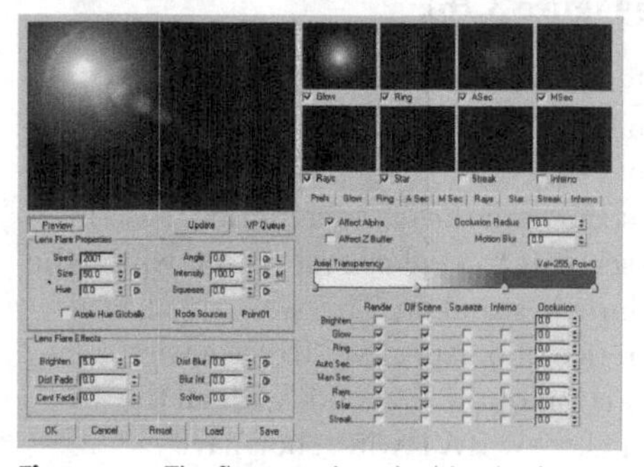

Figure 3.19 The flare used on the blue horizon.

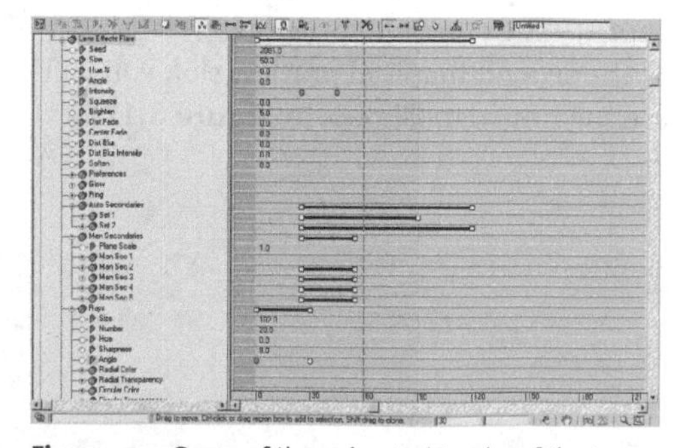

Figure 3.20 Some of the animated tracks of the Lens Effects Flare.

The NBC NEWS Shooters

The first shot was created in two passes. The first pass included the Presidential seal, the colonnade, the NBC NEWS type, and the environment—pretty much everything. In the second pass, I added the red, white, and blue shooters that pass above and below the NBC NEWS type. These two passes were then composited in Discreet Combustion. The reason I rendered it in two layers was that I was sure management liked everything except for the shooters. This way, if I needed to change the shooters, I wouldn't have to re-render everything.

The shooter file is included on the CD as well. You can find it at RW1\scenes\shotA0lshooter.max. **Figure 3.21** shows that file.

The shooter objects are Torus primitives with an animated Slice value by which they "write on." At the tips of each shooter is a Point helper. This Point helper is the source for a Lens Effects Flare event in Video Post. The flare is basically just a red glow. The Lens Effects Flare settings are in Video Post of the shotA0lshooter.max file for purposes of examination.

A Few Extra Thoughts

Sometimes projects this large and important go through very big changes relatively quickly. Often Sam will want will to see my progress as often as once a day. Because Sam and I do not work in the same building (or state for that matter), I email tests back and forth to him. Four of these tests are on the CD: RW1\td2kl.mov through td2k4.mov

I refer to these test animations again when discussing the other shots. However, right now I want you to view td2k1.mov. Notice that the eagle's shield doesn't have any red, white, and blue coloring and that a ring appears behind NBC NEWS. These two things don't appear that way in the final

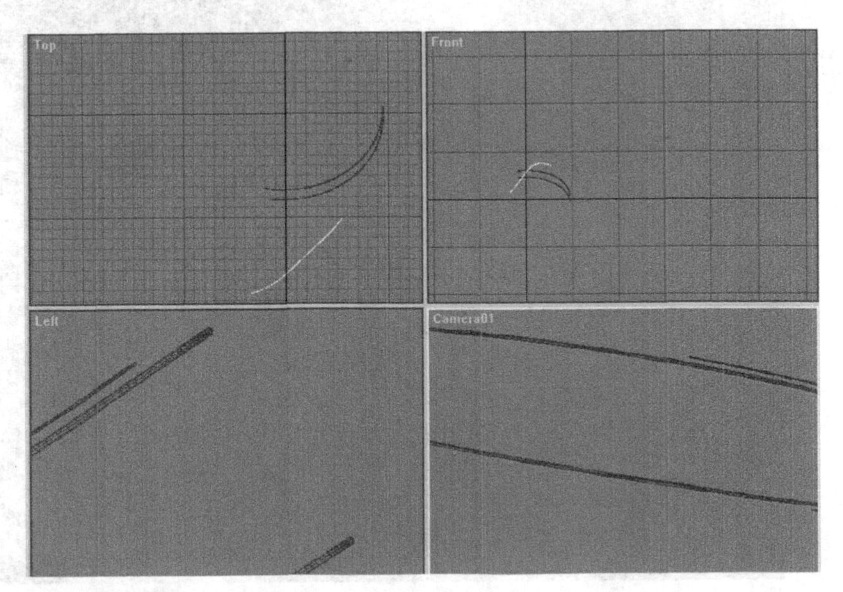

Figure 3.21 ShotA01 shooter.max.

animation. This was the way the scene appeared when I first made it. It went through a few changes before it was considered final. If you view the other tests, you will see the final first pass of the first shot, but the shooter objects do not appear on any of them.

Creating Shot 2

Generally speaking, the second shot (see **Figure 3.22**) of the animation was easy to create because most of the objects already existed. The only new object I needed to introduce to the scene was the ring with each president's face. By viewing the test animations RW1\td2k1.mov–td2k4.mov you can see the iterations this object went through.

The Ring

At first I kept the appearance of the ring close to what Tony originally illustrated in his storyboard: a gold ring. As the production of the scene progressed though, we decided that blue was the best color for the ring. However, we were still debating about the appearance of the ring. The design we settled on is shown in **Figure 3.23**.

Each facet of the ring had a flat front screen on which a president's head was to be textured. The back plate was arched to create interesting refractions as it moved through the scene. Although this was the design we chose, we were unsure how to finish it. If you watch the test animations again you will see little red bars underscoring and separating the president's heads. Those red bars were one of the design elements we were considering. In the end, we decided to go with the little NBC NEWS type and the simple stroked lines shown in **Figure 3.22**.

Figure 3.22 Shot 2 of the Decision 2000 animation.

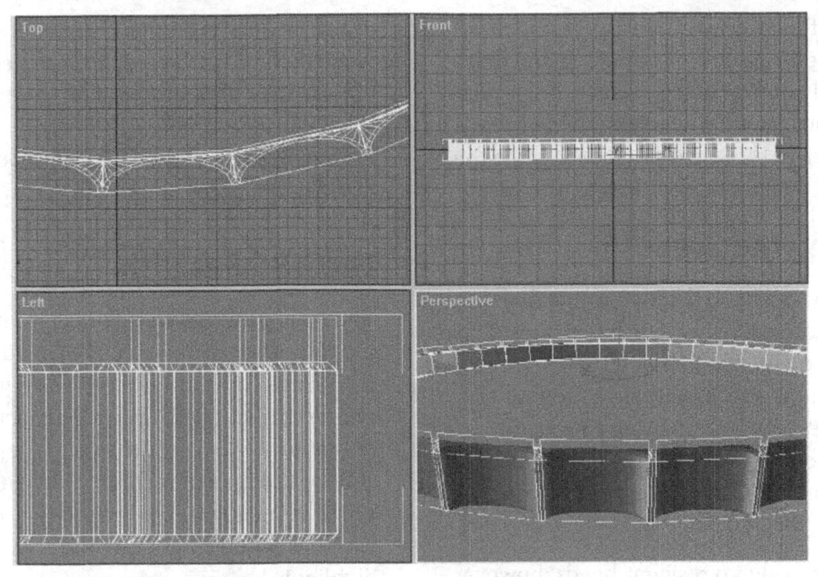

Figure 3.23 The ring object used in the final animation.

The Presidents' Heads

When it came to acquiring the headshots of the presidents, I turned to Matt Wisner, the MSNBC Graphics Department's research point person. He was kind enough to round up at least one headshot for each president of this wonderful United States. I then started the long process of adding each image to a carefully measured strip in Photoshop (see **Figure 3.24**).

Along with applying the headshots to this extremely long and narrow image, I needed to keep track of the alpha channel in order to key all the heads off the map. It is these still images of the presidents' heads that you see in the test animations on the CD.

Joe and I discussed the possibility of putting moving video on the foreground of the ring to add more drama to the animation. We decided hands down to make that a reality. Joe took on the daunting task of rotoscoping moving talking head video of the presidents. (The term *rotoscoped* refers to a matte that was hand drawn for each frame of video to key the head off the background.) Only five presidents needed to be rotoscoped. Joe spent a weekend accomplishing this on the Quantel Hal, a proprietary compositing system.

Figure 3.24 A portion of the presidents' heads strip.

When Joe finished with his work to the presidents, I applied them to the object. The ring in the final animation still had the other presidents' heads as still images mapped on them, but because of the angle at which you see the ring in the final rendering, they can't be seen.

Finishing the Scene

This shot was finished a lot like the first shot was completed, in multiple passes. The first pass consisted of most all the objects; the second pass included the little rows of NBC NEWS type and the thin line scoring the top and bottom of the ring. You can see a wireframe of the first pass by viewing RW1\wire_shotB.avi.

The moving video p resident heads, however, were not rendered in the first pass. I was afraid that if something went wrong with the video and the matte, hours of rendering would be ruined. So I rendered the presidents separately as a third pass.

Speaking of hours of rendering, while I was working on this project, I kept 10 machines rendering around the clock. Certain shots in this animation took two days to render, using all 10 of those computers. As for the specs on those computers, well, it's a grab bag. Engineering hooked me up with anything available that resembled a speedy processor. So the computers ranged from single 600MHz machines to dual 800+ machines.

When all the passes had been rendered, I composited them in Combustion. To composite, I used an elliptical selection to select the perimeter of the image. I then used that selection to apply a slight blur to the perimeter of the image. It's very subtle, but it creates a nice blurred peripheral vision effect.

Creating Shot 3

Shot 3 didn't require as much attention as the first two shots did because, once again, most of the objects were already created. Shot 3, however, introduced two objects that have not yet been seen in this sequence: the peacock (see **Figure 3.25**) and the U.S. Capitol dome (see **Figure 3.26**).

The NBC Peacock

The NBC peacock was an object I had used in other animations. I created it a few years back; I like it because everything is rounded, so it picks up great reflections and refractions. The color the peacock picks up is from the Specular color of the submaterials. This means the only time the color is visible is when a light creates a specular highlight.

If you watch the test animations on the CD in file RW1\td2k1.mov–td2k4.mov, you can see the evolution of the peacock as I worked on the animation. Shot 3 in td2kl.mov was basically a place filler; I just needed something very rough to illustrate my intentions. In td2k3.mov, you will see a more refined peacock. Sam thought the peacock was too big in the picture and too thick, so I made those changes. When I re-rendered the scene, I just wrote over the old image files. In td2k3.mov, you can see the new changes I made (early part of the scene) and the old peacock (later part of the scene). At the time I constructed that test animation, the network had only rendered that many new frames. In td2k4.mov, you could see a version of the peacock much closer to the final.

The U.S. Capitol Dome

There isn't much of interest to point out about the dome. Basically I removed it from a complete capitol-building model that we purchased from a stock object company.

Figure 3.25 The NBC peacock from shot.3 of the Decision 2000 animation.

Figure 3.26 The U.S. Capitol from shot 3 of the Decision 2000 animation.

The Presidential Seal

In shot 3, we see the U.S. Capitol dome rise through a hole in the Presidential seal. As far as I know, it doesn't symbolize anything. It just looked cool, and we had to gel the Capitol in somehow. If you watch RW1\wire_shotC.avi, you can see the hole in the center of the Presidential seal open up, and the dome moves up through it. The following are the steps I used to animate the hole in the seal. Open RW1\scenes\shotC01.max (shown in **Figure 3.27**) to see it.

Looking at the Ring-Inner object, you can see that a small hole was beveled in the center of the object. I still needed to enlarge the hole. If I collapsed the stack and used a sub-object transform on the mesh to enlarge the hole, the size of the bevel would have been affected as well. To avoid this problem, I opted for a much cleaner process.

I applied a transform to the center circle of the shape before I applied the bevel modifier in the stack. If you were to select the Ring-Inner object and activate the Editable Spline object in the stack, you would see that the center vertices are selected and much further apart than they appeal when all the modifiers are applied (see **Figure 3.28**).

I left the vertex sub-object level active and applied an XForm modifier. I then animated the scale track of the XForm modifier between frames 90 and 160. On top of the XForm modifier (which was acting on the vertex sub-object level of the circle spline), I applied a bevel modifier. Therefore, the size of the hole was changed before the Bevel modifier was applied; so the bevel will remain the same size throughout the whole animation.

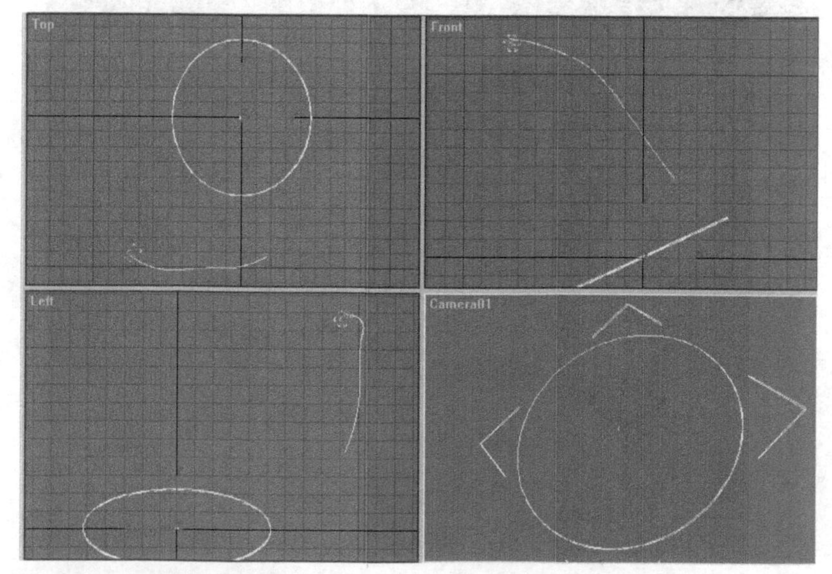

Figure 3.27 ShotC01.max.

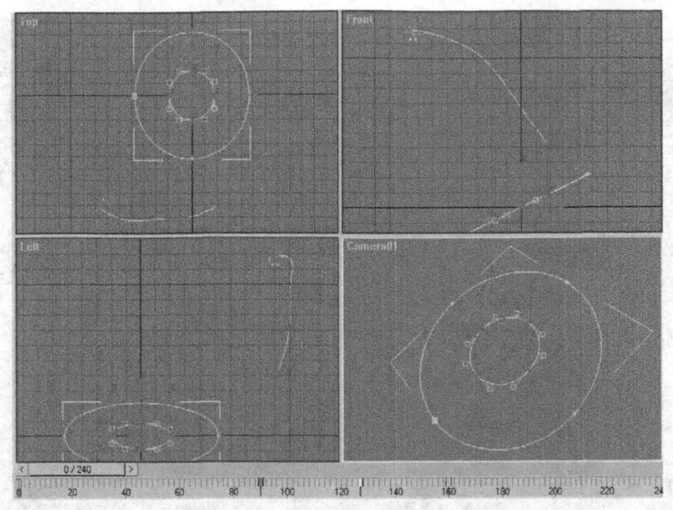

Figure 3.28 The Editable Spline object in the stack is selected.

Creating Shot 4

Often when I am working on an animation this large, it seems there is very little time to work on the most important part: the logo. I had only about two weeks to create the entire animation from start to finish. However, one thing worked to my advantage on this project: I had built the logo a few months back because the news folks were already covering certain aspects of the story. **Figure 3.29** shows that logo.

The Logo Resolve

If you examine the test animations I created (in RW1\td2k2.mov–td2k4.mov), you will see many different variations of the logo resolve. I tried very hard to animate the logo and the Presidential seal environment all in one pass. I couldn't get a shot of the environment that I thought was interesting enough and that, at the same time, allowed all the individual pieces of the logo to fly easily. The reason I wanted it to all be in one pass was that I wanted the refractions to be accurately calculated.

In the end, I decided to cheat and render the scene in multiple passes: the background pass and the individual logo element passes. If you view RW1\wire_shotDb.avi, you will see a wireframe of the background animation. Notice that the hole in the Presidential seal closes up again.

The Materials

Rendering the logo in pieces has one great advantage: You have the ability to color correct, add effects, and apply 2D shadows to all the individual layers in Combustion (see **Figure 3.30**). Generally, when I render my 3D animations, I immediately take the rendered output into Combustion and add contrast and saturation to the images. It adds a little extra punch.

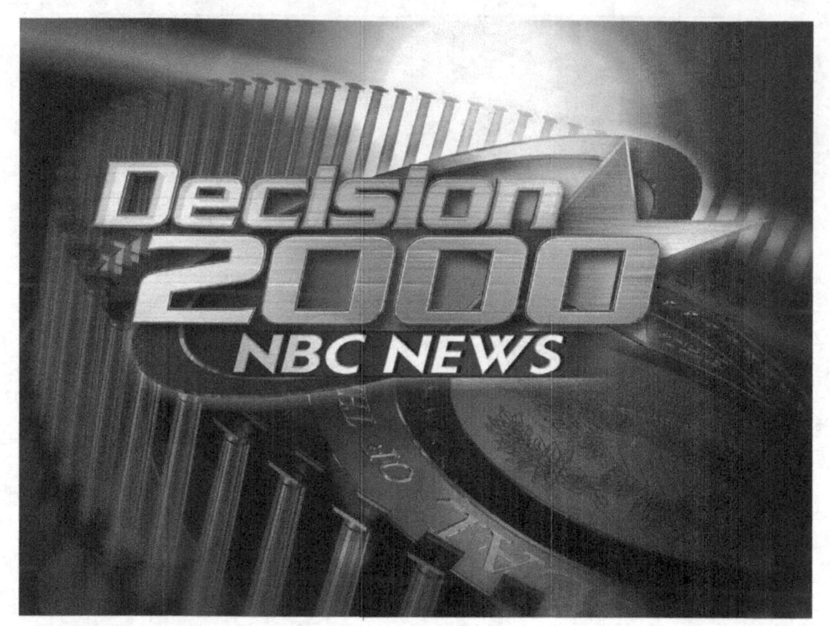

Figure 3.29 Shot 4 from the Decision 2000 animation.

Figure 3.30 The brushed glass material on the Decision 2000 logo.

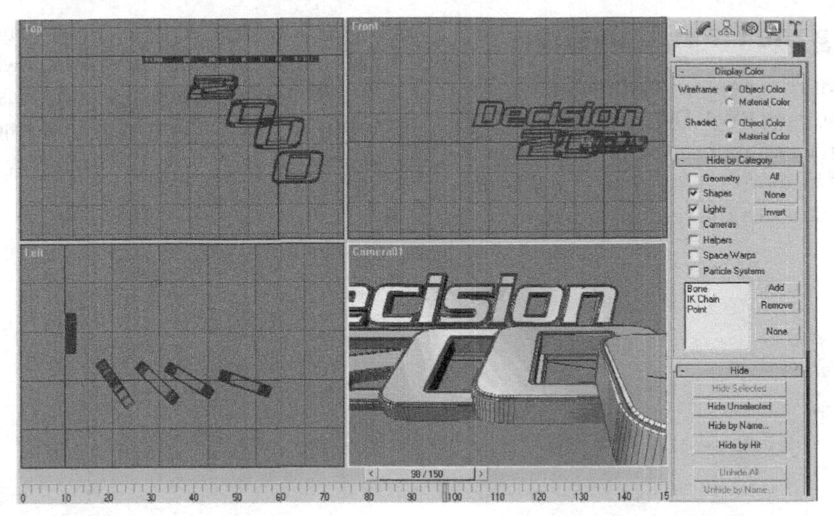

Figure 3.31 ShotDLogo01.max.

Open RW1\scenes\shotDLogo01.max (see **Figure 3.31**). If you play the animation, you should see the Decision 2000 type fly in as it does in the final animation. If you want to examine the materials on the type, open the Material Editor. You will notice that there are 10 materials with the name "decision." However, each one has a different capitalized letter (for example, Decision, dEcision, deCision, and so on). The capitalized letter signifies the object it is applied to. Each letter in the word "Decision" mixes from a clear glass refractive material to the gold-brushed glass material at a different time, which means each one needs individual materials.

In this example, the renderer and the ray-traced refractions of the clear glass material use AshDback0000.ifl as the environment. This IFL simply points to AshDback.jpg, whereas originally it pointed to the full rendered background sequence. The "brushed" look is caused by the stretched Cellular map in the bump and specular map channels (it's stretched because of the low ".02" X: Tiling setting).

The type looks complex partly because of the number of bevels I managed to place onto the object. On top of that, there are two different sub-materials on the bevels alone (D2-eb and D2-fb). If you want to view the different sub-materials and see where they are placed on the objects, examine the 2000 material. You can uncheck the On/Off boxes and render only selected sub-materials on the 2000 type. Try rendering those tests at approximately frame 100.

Viewing the Final Animation

If you want to see the entire finished animation, view RW1\Decision2k.mov. This animation was supposed to air in its entirety twice and in shorter 3- to 10-second versions as well. Thanks to the recount situation, my animation received much more play than I ever imagined. I was very pleased with how the animation turned out, and I was very happy to hear that many people enjoyed it as well.

PART 

COMPOSITING

COMPOSITING IN AFTER EFFECTS

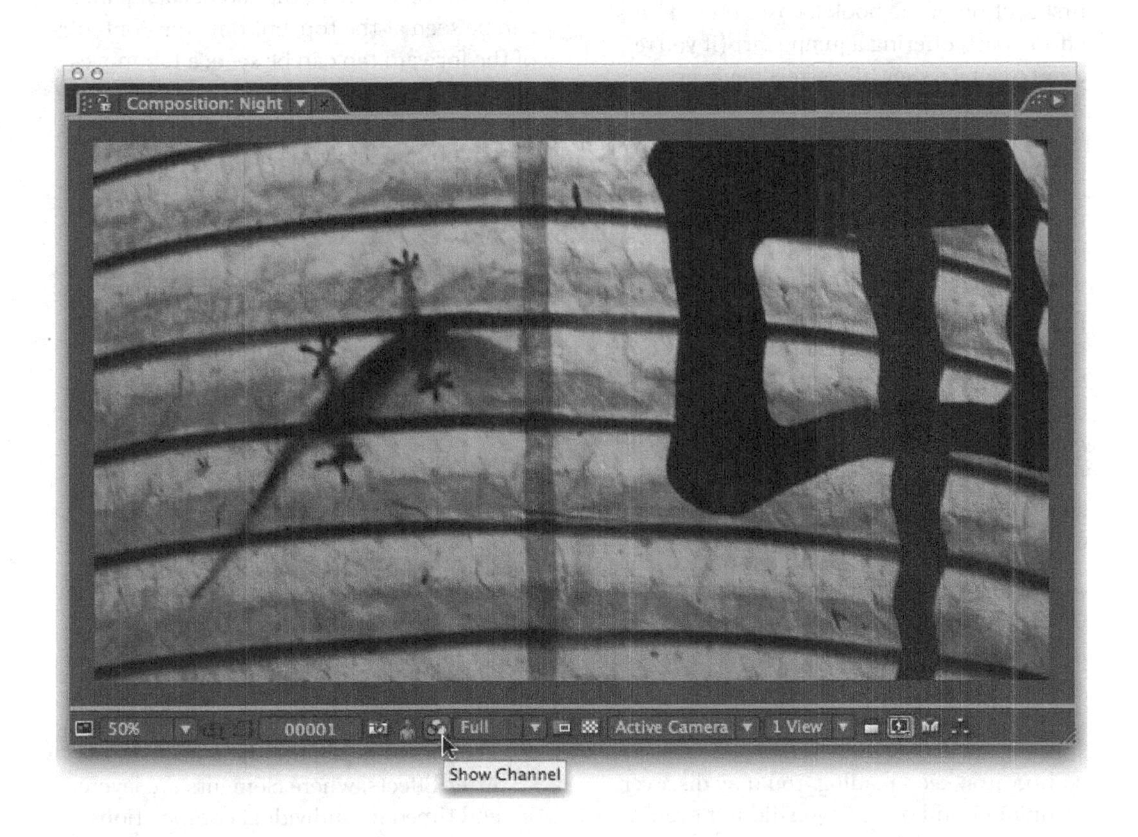

Good surfing is power, speed, and flow.
The rest of it doesn't matter to me at all.

–Gary Elkerton, Australian surfer

Compositing in After Effects

This is a book about visual effects compositing in general, and about Adobe After Effects in particular. If you use After Effects, the goal is to help you composite believable shots from elements that were not shot together, and to do it with less effort. This first section of the book focuses on the "less effort" part, offering a jump-start (if you're new) or a refresher (if you're already an After Effects artist) on the After Effects workflow.

"Workflow" is essentially the methodology used to get things done. A successful compositor obviously needs to get a lot of stuff done, as even a simple A over B shot is comprised of many, many combinations of artistic and engineering decisions. The less effort expended on each individual decision, the freer you are to experiment and make changes, and that's what it's really all about. Iteration, maybe more than anything else, separates great effects shots from mediocre ones.

And so, this chapter focuses on how to get things done in After Effects as effortlessly as possible. This first chapter assumes you already know your way around the basics of After Effects and are ready to learn to work smarter. So, even if you're an experienced compositor, keep reading. You may discover techniques and options you did not even know were available to you. I encourage you to look through this chapter carefully for new ideas about working with After Effects.

✔ Notes

If this book opens at too advanced a level for you, check out *Adobe After Effects CS3 Professional Classroom in a Book* (Adobe Press), a helpful beginner's resource.

Workspaces and Panels

Figure 4.1 shows the Standard workspace that appears when you first open After Effects CS3. The interface consists of one main *application window* containing *panel groups*, separated by *dividers*. Each group contains one or more *panels*. If a group contains multiple panels, the tab of each panel can be seen at the top, but only the contents of the forward tab can be seen; a tab moves forward when you select it. Some panels are viewers; these include a pull-down menu in the tab that lets you choose what is displayed.

✔ Tip

- **Figure 4.1** uses darker user interface colors than are displayed in After Effects by default. The User Interface Brightness control resides in Preferences > User Interface Colors.

The heart of After Effects can be found by choosing the Minimal workspace (**Figure 4.2**), either using the pulldown menu at the upper right of the Tools panel or via the Window > Workspace menu. This reveals two panels only:

- The Composition panel is a viewer, where you examine the shot.
- The Timeline panel is the true heart of After Effects, where elements are layered and timed for individual compositions (or shots). A project may have many of these open at any given time, and a whole composition can appear as a layer in another composition.

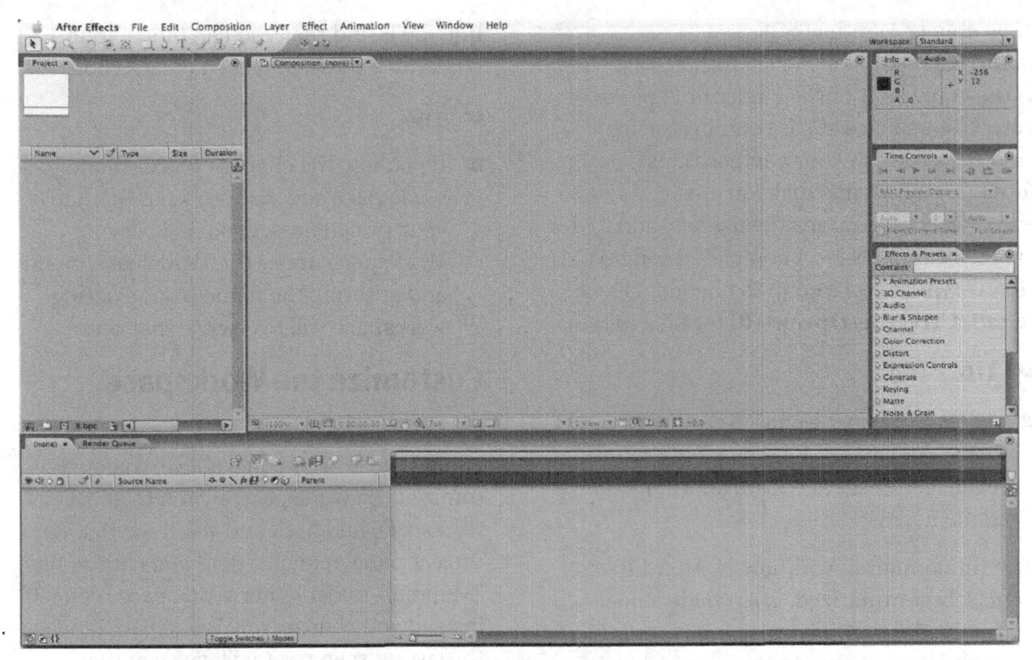

Figure 4.1 The Standard workspace layout is all contained in a single application window. The frame containing the Project panel (A) is currently active, as indicated by the yellow highlight around the panel's border. Dividers such as the long one (B) between the Composition panel and the smaller panels at the right separate the frames. The tab of the Composition viewer (C) includes a pull-down menu for choosing a particular composition, and a lock icon for keeping that composition forward regardless of what else is clicked.

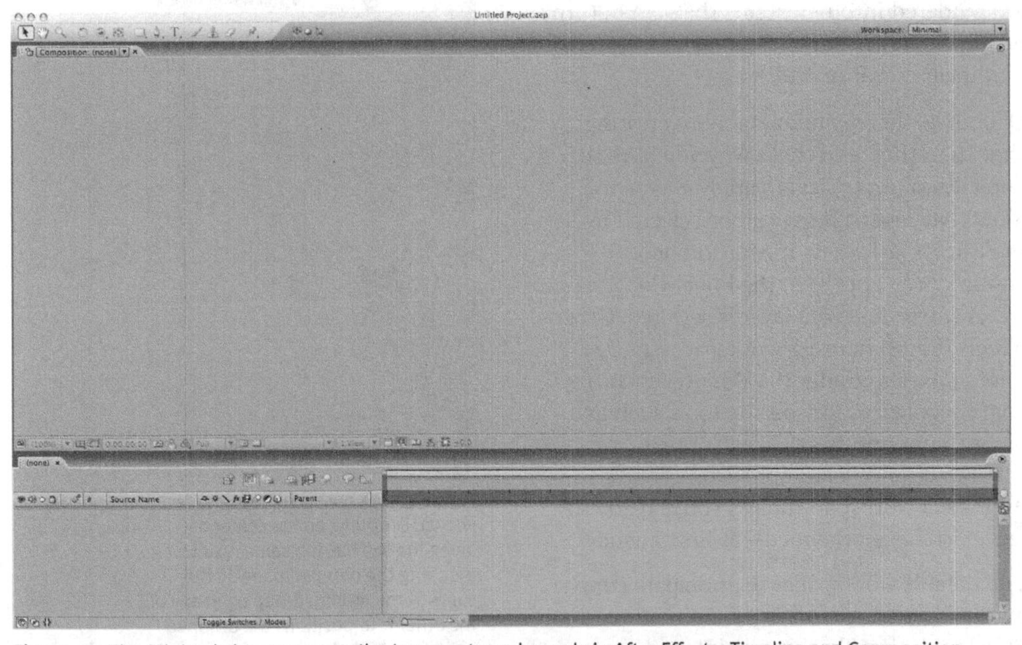

Figure 4.2 The Minimal view serves up the two most used panels in After Effects: Timeline and Composition.

Now choose Window > Project (**Cmd/Ctrl+0**) to add the Project panel. This is the equivalent of the Finder or Explorer of your system software. It contains the file resources used in your compositions (source footage, stills, solids that you create, audio, even the compositions themselves) and folders to contain them. A completed composition is typically placed in the Render Queue (**Cmd/Ctrl+Alt/Option+0**) for final output.

✔ Tip

- All available panels in After Effects are listed under the Window menu; some even list preset keyboard shortcuts for rapid access.

The fundamental workflow of After Effects, concisely summarized, is to create a new composition, typically containing items from the Project panel, which you add to the Timeline so that they appear in the Composition panel. Saving the project doesn't affect the items in the Project panel; the compositions made using these elements are rendered into new items that can in turn be imported or sent elsewhere (such as to a nonlinear editor or NLE).

Of course, there is much more to creating a shot than that, and that's why you have this book. It's quite typical to apply effects to individual layers; these can be selected in the Effects & Presets menu, and once applied, they appear in the Effect Controls panel when the given layer is selected. Other panels (found in other workspaces, or by selecting them under the Window menu) contain controls for specific tools such as paint (Paint and Brush Tips), or text (Character and Paragraph). Don't enable the All Panels workspace unless you're ready to feel a little overwhelmed—at first, anyhow.

The default workspaces to anticipate common usages of After Effects: Animation, Effects, Motion Tracking, Paint, and Text, but you'll find that you can (and should) customize these, and even create your own.

✔ Tip

- If you like the changes you've made to a workspace and want to keep them in your preferences, choosing New Workspace under the Workspace menu and entering the name of an existing workspace will overwrite that one.

Customize the Workspace

By choosing the Minimal workspace and adding the Project panel above, you customized the workspace; switch to another workspace and back and you'll see that the Project panel remains, until you choose Reset "Minimal" under either Workspace menu. If instead you choose New Workspace, and save the layout, then reset will give you that.

When you added the Project panel it probably appeared at the lower left, next to the Timeline. You might choose to move it some-

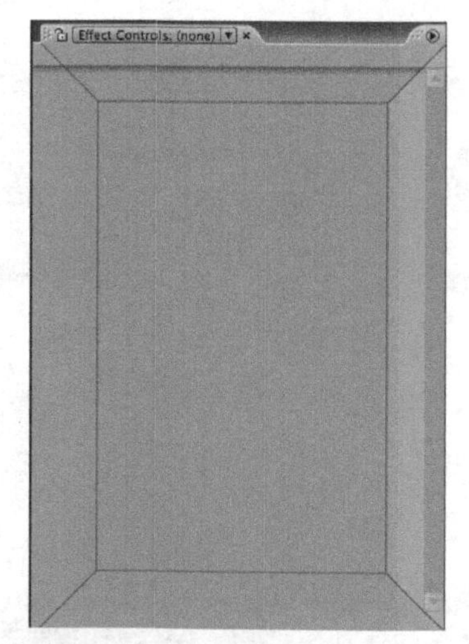

Figure 4.3 Six possible drop areas are shown. Dropping on the center or along the top has the same result: grouping the dropped panel in the same frame as Info; dropping in any of the other four positions the dropped panel just to that side of Info.

where else, such as the upper left or right. To do so, click and drag its tab around the screen. As you move it over another panel, purple geometric shapes like those in **Figure 4.3** appear. These are the *drop zones*. The *docking zones* along the edges let you place a panel adjacent—for example, to the left of the Composition panel. The *grouping zones* in the center group panels together in one frame.

Drag a panel to one edge of the application window and aqua colored bands appear along the edge; the panel will occupy that entire side when dropped there (**Figure 4.4**).

Special arrowed icons appear when you move the cursor between two or more panel groups, allowing you to resize adjacent panels. I don't habitually resize panels this way because of one of my favorite After Effects shortcuts, the Tilde key (~), which toggles the currently active panel (with a yellow borderline) to occupy the entire application window. This shortcut makes small and large monitors more usable when you want to focus on one big thing, typically lots of layers and keyframes in the Timeline or a zoomed-in shot in the Composition or Layer viewers.

✔ Close-Up

Maximixe the screen When you tear off a panel and move it to a second monitor as a floating window, you may notice that it lacks the Zoom button along the top to send the window to full screen.

The shortcut ***Ctrl***+\ (***Cmd***+\) can zoom the window instead. If the selected floating window is not occupying the full borders of the screen (or has been moved or offset), pressing the shortcut keys maximizes the window. If you press again, the shortcut toggles off the top menu bar, filling the entire screen with the window.

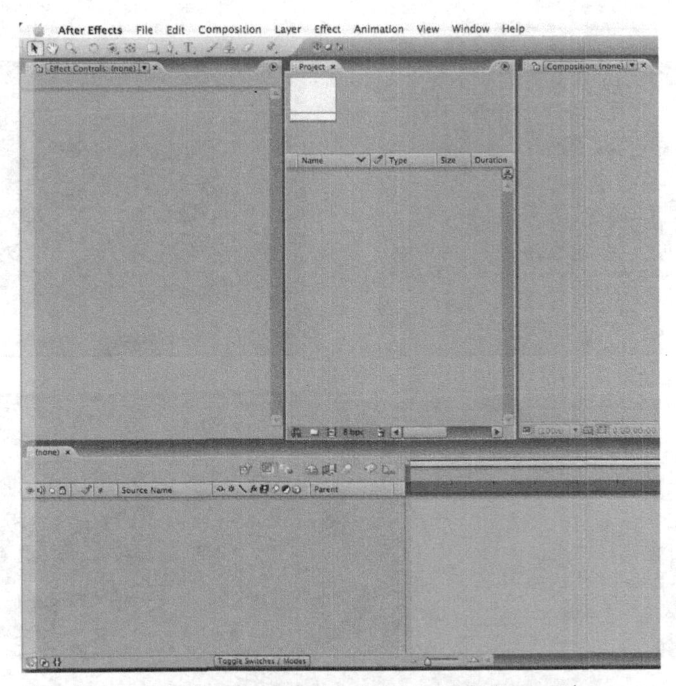

Figure 4.4 More radical rearrangement of your workspace can be accomplished by making a panel occupy one entire side of the workspace, as shown.

This also works with the main UI window; if you don't like seeing the top of your monitor taken up by the After Effects menu bar, you can use **Ctrl+** (**Cmd+**) to maximize the entire UI.

It is not uncommon these days to preview to a monitor that shares at least one dimension with your footage. For example, I often work with HD footage (1920×1080) on a set of 1920×1200 monitors. To see my Composition panel at 100% on one of those monitors, I make it a floating window and then use this shortcut.

As is noted later, you can always RAM Preview in full-screen mode by checking the Full Screen box in the Time Controls.

Figures 4.5 a–c show a few workspaces that I like for various monitor configurations; these could even help you decide which is best for you for After Effects, one big monitor or multiple smaller ones. More methods for customizing views are explored in later chapters.

✔ **Tip**

- You can tear off any panel and make it float by holding down the **Ctrl/Cmd** key as you drag it away; my personal preference is to tear off the Render Queue, as in **Figure 4.5a**, because I only use it at specific times, and I can toggle it on and off via its shortcut (**Alt+Ctrl+0/Opt+Cmd+0**).

Make Use of the Interface

The ideal workflow is an effortless one, and so we now turn our attention to how best to perform steps repeated many, many times in a normal After Effects workday.

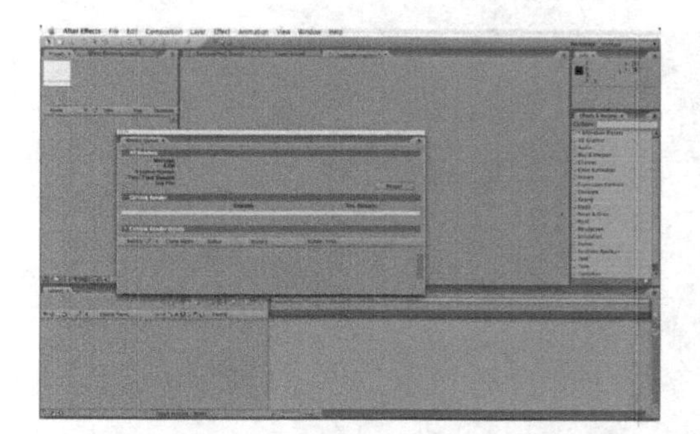

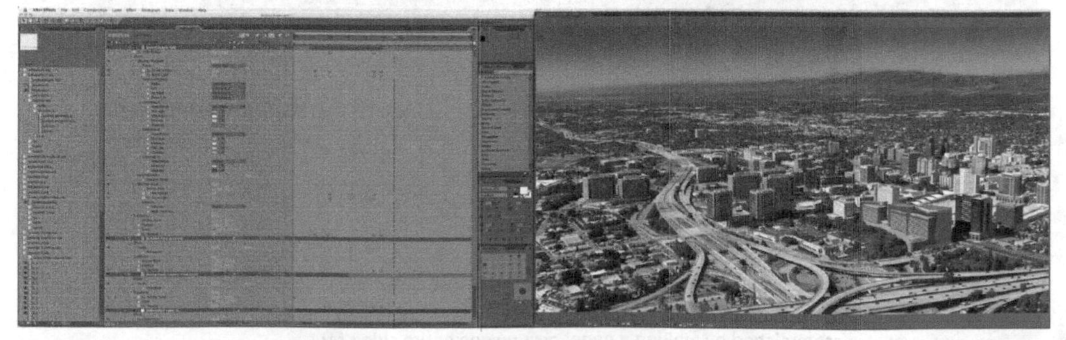

Figures 4.5a, b, and c Different monitors setups require different workspaces, whether for a laptop (a), 30-inch display (b), or two HD-resolution monitors side by side (c).

Organize your Source

Getting a source file from a disk or server into After Effects is no big deal. You can use File > Import > File. With several sources in various locations, File > Import > Multiple Files reopens this dialog until you cancel, a good option for image sequences. It doesn't matter which specific image in a sequence you select; they are all imported provided you select only one. However, by holding the **Shift** or **Ctrl** (**Cmd**) key as you select more than one frame, you can:

- specify a subset of frames to be imported in a sequence.
- select frames from more than one sequence in the same folder; a Multiple Sequences checkbox appears to make certain this is really what you want to do.
- specify sets of frames from multiple sequences (a combination of the above two modes).

✔ Tip

- The Force alphabetical order option which appears when a sequence is available adds placeholder files for any numbered stills missing from the sequence; this allows you to set up using a temporary render (say, a sequence containing only the first and last frame) before a full sequence is rendered.

Thus the Import dialog doesn't group multiple sequences together for you.

The most popular shortcut for importing is to drag footage directly into After Effects from a Finder or Explorer window, and dragging anywhere in the workspace will do it. To drag a sequence into After Effects, drag in the folder containing the sequence while holding the **Ctrl** (**Cmd**) key.

Want to get re-hired repeatedly as a freelancer, or be the most valued member in your organization? Organizing your projects well makes you a valued member of the team.

An ordinary project uses some source footage, a main composition, a couple of pre-comps, some reference footage, and at least one solid layer. For this project, you could employ project organization along the lines of that shown in **Figure 4.6**; each type of item resides in its own folder. Only the main composition resides in the root area of the project, and its main components are organized according to how they are used. An artist unfamiliar with the project—including you yourself, several months or even years in the future—can investigate it in this hierarchical fashion.

✔ Tip

- A folder of still images will import as a sequence when dragged in, but if you actually wanted the folder and individual stills, hold the Option/Alt key while dragging.

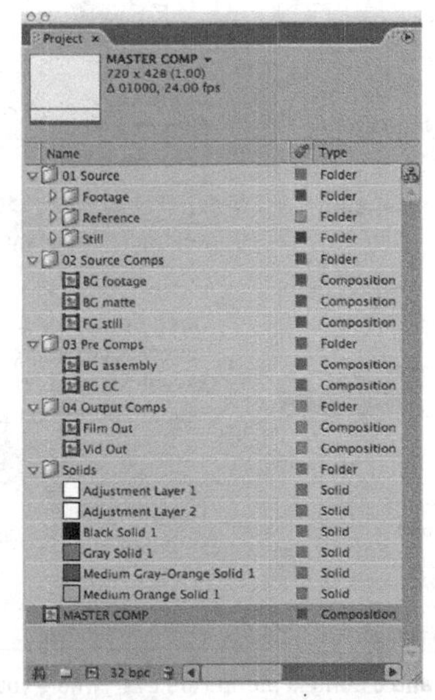

Figure 4.6 Even with a modest project it's pleasing to the eye and mind to keep things well organized.

Context-Clicks (and Keyboard Shortcuts)

Between keyboard shortcuts and context menus, an advanced user rarely visits the After Effects menu bar. The saved mouse movement and clicks may not seem like much at first, but once you learn to work this way, convenience is king.

Throughout the book are references to *context-clicking* on interface items. You could also call this "right-clicking" although certain devices, such as a Wacom tablet or one-button Mac mouse, don't have a right mouse button. Without detailing each individual context menu, **Figures 4.7a-c** contain a few of the most useful.

Context-click on a panel to see its panel menu (or use the little triangular icon on the upper right tab of each panel). These contain options also available via the top menus or on the panels themselves, but some of these are among the least discoverable features in After Effects, such as View Options for each viewer panel.

Redundancy, often considered a bad thing in logical design, is an often overlooked advantage of the After Effects interface; because features are available in multiple ways you can find them more easily and develop your own preference for how you access them.

✔ Notes

On a Mac without a right mouse button, such as a MacBook Pro, you must hold

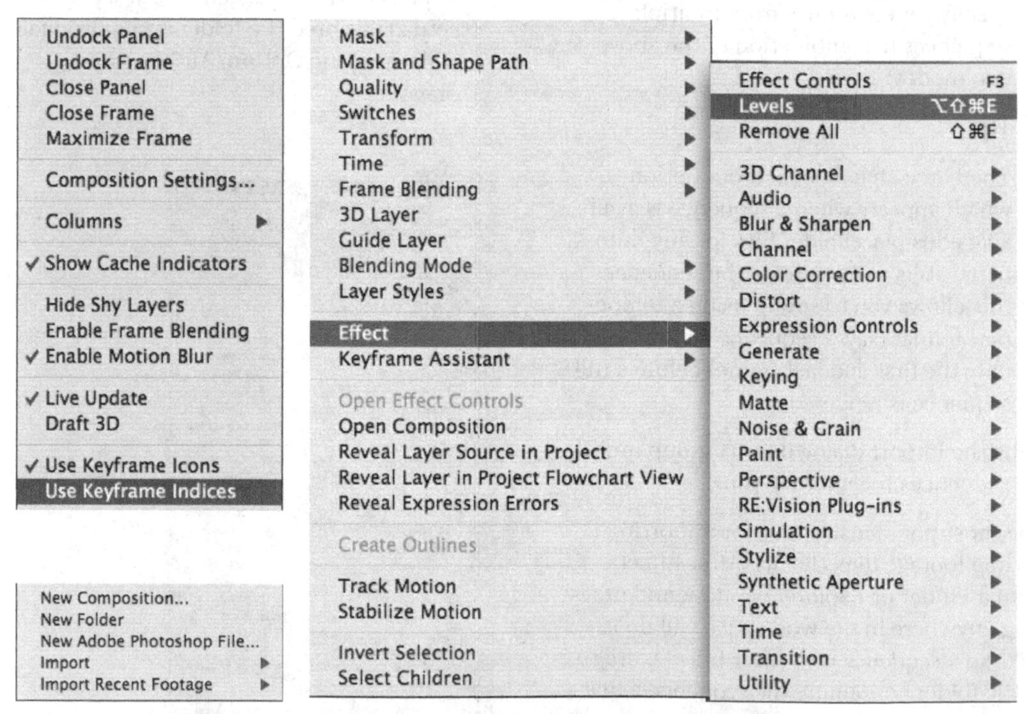

Figures 4.7a, b, and c Context menus are everywhere your cursor is, and for that reason, very effective. Context-click the tab of the Timeline panel (a), and you will see very different selections than if you context-click a layer in that panel (b), or the empty space below the layers (c). Depending on whether a layer is a camera, a solid, or footage, different options will appear.

the Control key while clicking in order to context-click.

Missing Footage

After Effects links to source footage files that can be anywhere, so footage essential to your comps will become unlinked as things are moved around (**Figure 4.8**). Assuming you can still locate a given source file, re-link it as follows:

- Double-click the missing footage item in the Project panel
- Context-click the missing footage, choose Replace Footage, and then choose File
- Highlight the missing footage, and press **Ctrl+H/Cmd+H**

These all activate the Replace Footage File dialog, where you choose the missing footage item (or, alternatively, an alternate file of your choosing).

✔ Notes

On larger and more ambitious projects shared by several artists, it is typical to create a project template that anticipates a certain workflow, so that items are easy to find in predictable locations.

You may receive a warning upon opening a project that files are missing, but this warning does not indicate which files it has flagged. To identify missing source files in your project, click the binoculars icon beneath the Project panel and, leaving the text field blank, check Find Missing Footage and click OK. Repeat as needed (this feature lacks a shortcut).

If a file you attempt to re-link or import is gray and cannot be highlighted in the import dialogs, the file is somehow not recognized by After Effects. Typically, adding a missing three-character extension will solve this, although certain formats do not read equally well on Mac and Windows (for example, Mac-generated PICT); see the Source Formats section later in this chapter for the most useful and universal file types to use.

After Effects has no mechanism to manage media should several items from various directories become unlinked. Therefore, keep source items grouped together in as few places as is practical; for example, I typically place all locally stored project footage in a Source folder with Footage and Stills subfolders.

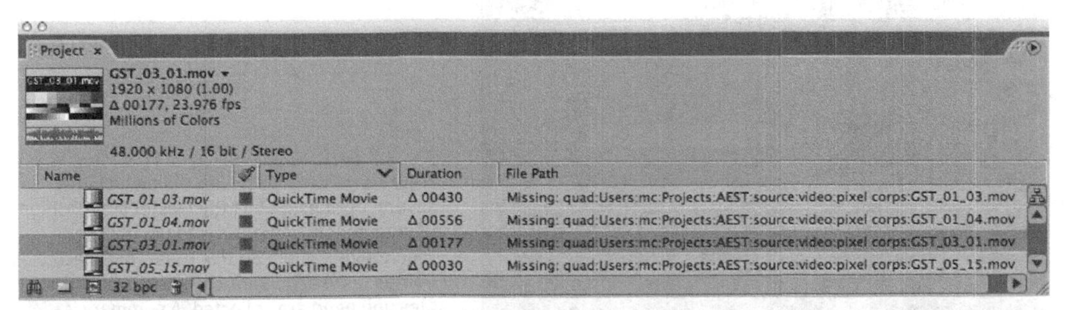

Figure 4.8 Missing footage appears with a small color bar icon. In the File Path column, After Effects also displays the path where the file was expected to be, which can help when searching on a drive or network for a missing, unlinked file.

✔ Tip

- After Effects will typically discover adjacent files in the same directory as the first missing file you replace and offer to re-link them, one more good reason to keep things well organized. For advice on organizing backups, see the next section, "Collect, Combine, Consolidate."

✔ Tip

- To simply reload footage instead of replacing it, context-click the item in question and choose Reload Footage (or use **Ctrl+Alt+L/Cmd+Option+L**).

Collect, Combine, Consolidate

If you need to move a project along with all of its linked source, and the source isn't neatly contained in one location, or you're only using a sub-set of what's there, you can employ File > Collect Files. This command supports multi-machine Watch Folder rendering but is also useful for backup, as it allows you to create a new folder that contains a copy of the project and all of its source files (**Figure 4.9**).

✔ Close-Up

Edit and Replace Source You notice a change needed to source material in your project created or edited in another application. ***Ctrl+E/Cmd+E*** opens a file from the Project in whatever application created it (according to its file type). When changes are made and saved in the other application, After Effects updates using the result, but only if you save over the same file (if instead you choose Save As, you must replace the source).

You can reduce the number of source files collected using the Collect Source Files menu; for example, select the master composition for a finished project and choose For Selected Comps; After Effects collects only the footage needed to create that comp.

To combine two After Effects projects before collecting files, import one into the other, or import both into a new project. The imported project appears in its own folder (**Figure 4.10**) with the complete organization of its Project palette intact. Therefore, if you've been organizing your projects as is encouraged here, you will have redundant folders to re-integrate manually.

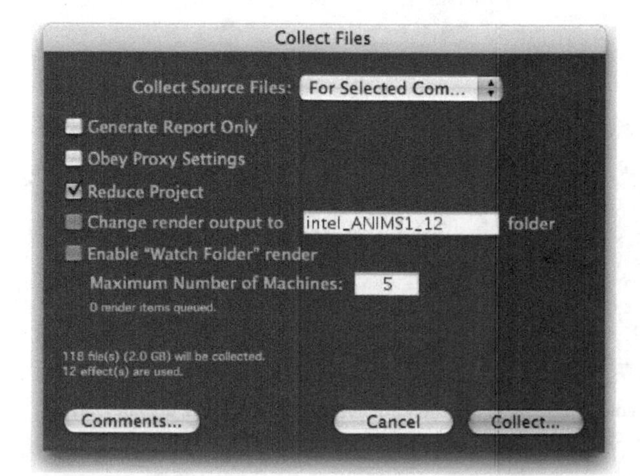

Figure 4.9 The Collect Files dialog includes several options. Select the master composition (if your shot has one) prior to Collect Files, then toggle Collect Source Files: For Selected Comps (as well as Reduce Project). Only the files you need are collected. A summary is shown in the lower-left corner, and you can add comments.

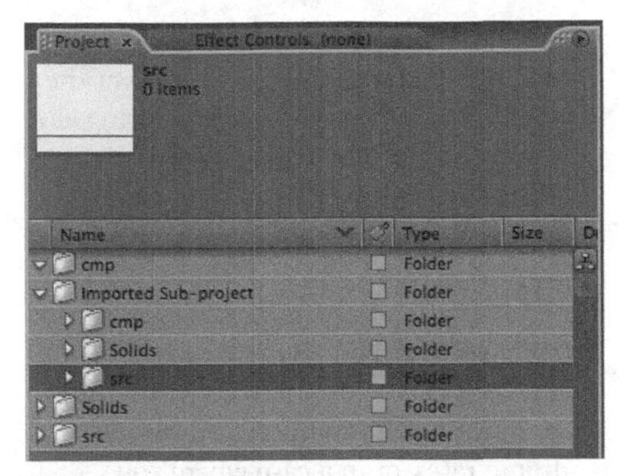

Figure 4.10 The imported project folder contains subdirectories that are redundant to those in the master composition. After Effects offers no built-in quick fix to reorganize these, but this book does; look for rd_MergeProjects.jsx on the book disc, by Adobe employee Jeff Almasol, which merges folders in the subfolder and folders of the same names in the master project.

✔ Notes

When you use Collect Files, source files are re-organized using the folder organization of the Project itself. Any image sequence will be placed into its own subfolder.

Select the main compositions in your project and choose File > Reduce Project; After Effects eliminates project items not used in the selected comps. You even get a warning dialog telling you how many items were removed (**Figure 4.11**).

File > Consolidate All Footage looks for two or more instances of a source file and combines them, choosing the first instance, top to bottom, in the Project. File > Remove Unused Footage rids a project of footage not included in any composition.

✔ Tip

- Consolidate All Footage always keeps the first instance of any redundant source in the project; therefore, to specify a particular folder to be eliminated, you can add the letter "z" before it's name to send it to the bottom of the Project list.

Advanced Save Options

Because After Effects projects are saved unique to the elements they contain, there are a few unique options for saving them that are worth knowing about.

File > Increment and Save attaches a version number to your saved project, or increments whatever number is already there, at the end of the file name before the .aep extension. It turns out that projects evolve in versions; sometimes a new version coincides with a new day's work, but in other cases you might want to try some risky, destructive edits in quick succession. After Effects projects are typically relatively small (unless they include a lot of paint strokes!) so there's little harm in saving a new version before trying something new.

✔ Tip

- If you habitually use Increment and Save, you can also freely use File > Revert to automatically return the project to its condition when it was incremented, rather than worrying about how many undo operations ago that was.

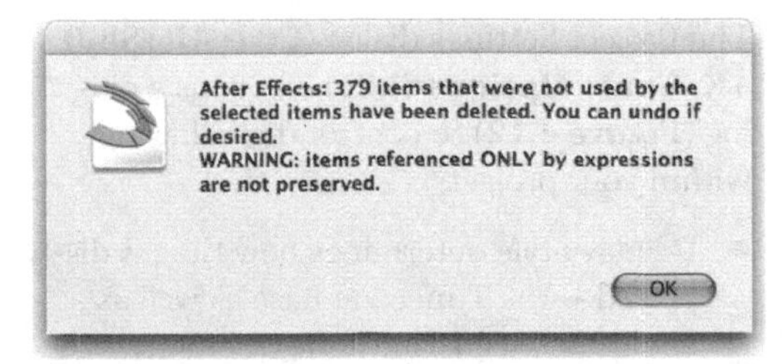

Figure 4.11 A warning, but no real cause for alarm. Reduce Project removes items from the project (not from the source disk). The admonition regarding expressions applies only if a property's expression links to a separate, otherwise unused composition (a somewhat rare case).

After Effects has a well-earned reputation for stability, but beyond crashes, other bad things can kill a project file—power outages, accidental shut-downs, hardware failures—and even the most talented artist can forget to save when engrossed in a tricky shot.

Preferences > Auto-Save contains the toggle option to automatically save projects as you work on them. It saves the number of versions you specify (5 by default) using your specified interval (default is 20 minutes). A folder called After Effects Auto-Save is created in the same folder as the project file, and the maximum number of versions for the open project has been reached, the oldest (lowest-numbered) version is deleted. The interval clock only runs when you are actually working, should you forget and leave a project open during lunch hour.

Project, Footage, and Composition Settings

After Effects is optimized to anticipate the settings you need so that the defaults often work for the novice; however, the settings are there for good reason. Artists who don't know them well typically find themselves fighting unnecessary uphill battles, kludging compromise solutions.

Project Settings

The Project Settings dialog (**Ctrl+Alt+Shift+K/Cmd+ Option+Shift+K**) opens a dialog (**Figure 4.12**) to control the following within your project:

- Display Style determines how time is displayed —the Timecode Base as well as a choice between Timecode or Frames
- Color Settings include the project-wide color depth (8, 16, or 32 bits per channel), as well as the Working Space and linear light handling.
- Audio Settings allow you to lower the default 48 kHz sample rate, to lower the memory overhead if you are working at a lower sample rate. In previous versions of After Effects, this was a Preference setting (applied to all projects).

✔ **Tip**

- Why set Timecode Base to anything but Auto? It can be useful to compare times or durations for items with differing frame rates, or in a case where you absolutely know that everything must conform to a particular rate.

✔ **Tip**

- To specify a particular frame, or even timecode, for a given composition, you

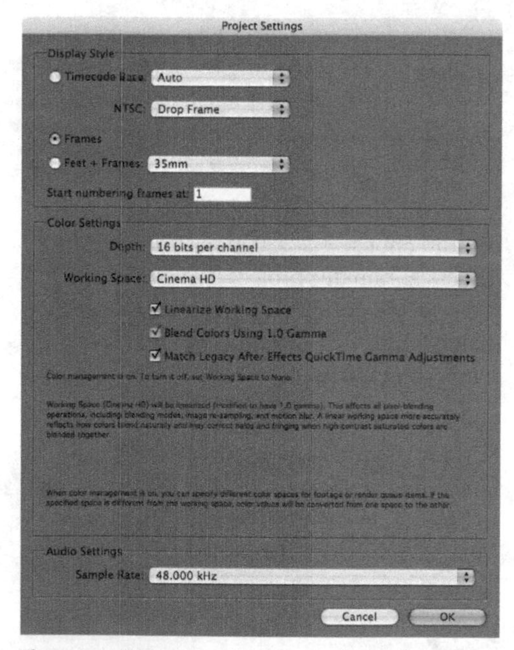

Figure 4.12 Time is displayed according to the Display Style section of File > Project Settings. Color Settings are covered in detail in Chapter 16, which explores how Depth and Working Space change the look of your footage, and how to use these settings.

can do so in the Start Frame field in Composition Settings (**Ctrl+K/Cmd+K**).

The Auto setting for Timecode Base is useful as it allows you to freely mix footage of varying frame rates without forcing you to choose one underlying frame rate to display for the entire project. Timecode Base only controls how timecode is displayed in the Timeline, it doesn't change the timing of footage—if the setting doesn't match the frame rate of the composition, values will round off to the nearest number, which is not generally what you want.

After Effects displays timecode by default, but particularly if you're working in film, you may want to choose Frames instead, as it's typical to refer to "frame 97" rather than "at 4:01." It's also typical to start numbering frames at 1, rather than the After Effects default of 0, but you can choose any number you want. The truly old-school option is to use Feet + Frames (which applies to actual reels of physical film, that format which is quickly becoming obsolete).

Even when the Frames option is active, the Timecode Base of an individual composition is displayed beside the frame counter in the Timeline (**Figure 4.13**).

Interpret Footage

This book generally eschews the practice of walking through After Effects menus, but sometimes the UI perfectly encapsulates a given set of production challenges. The

00047 (24.00 fps)

Figure 4.13 The Timeline provides a constant reminder (in parentheses) of what frame rate is being used in the current project, regardless of how time is displayed (in this case, in frames, which tends to be standard for film work while timecode is more often used for video).

Interpret Footage dialog is one such case, a section-by-section checklist of all the decisions to be made about imported footage:

- Alpha interpretation
- Frame Rate
- Fields and Pulldown
- Pixel Aspect Ratio (under Other Options)
- Color Management (under More Options with certain file types and the new Color Management tab)

To bring up the Interpret Footage dialog for a given clip, select it in the Project panel and press **Ctrl+F/Cmd+F** or context-click and select Interpret Footage > Main.

Alpha

To be a good compositor, you must thoroughly understand alpha channels. **Figure 4.14** shows the most visible symptom of a misinterpreted alpha channel: fringing.

For those getting started, here are a couple pointers and reminders:

- If the alpha channel type is unclear, click Guess in the Interpretation dialog that shows up when importing footage with alpha. This often, but not always, yields a correct setting.
- Preferences > Import contains a default alpha channel preference. Beware of setting this to anything besides Ask User until you are certain you know what you are doing and that your project isn't likely to have unexpected variables.

For the rest of the information on alpha channels and how they operate in After Effects, see Chapter 7.

✔ Notes

To try the Figure 4.14 example for yourself, import premultipliedAlpha.tif from

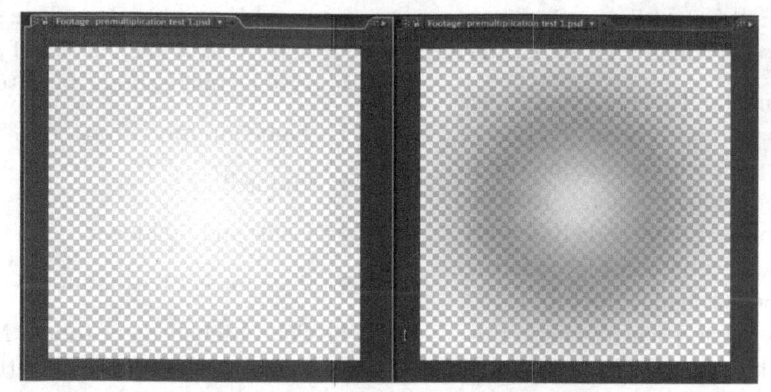

Figure 4.14 It's easy to distinguish a properly interpreted (left) from an incorrect alpha channel (right) if you're looking carefully. The giveaway is fringing, caused in this case by the failure to remove the background color from the edge pixels by unmultiplying them (with black). The left image is premultiplied, the right is straight.

the CH01 folder; try changing each from the correct Premultiplied setting to the incorrect (in this case) Straight setting.

Frame Rate

Footage appears herky-jerky in a composition with the intended frame rate? After Effects may be misinterpreting the frame rate. Misinterpreted frame rate is typically an issue with image sequences only, because unlike QuickTime, the files themselves contain no embedded frame rate.

✔ Tip

- You can change the default Frames Per Second setting for Sequence Footage under Preferences > Import.

✔ Close-Up

Why Sequences for Moving Footage? While movie formats such as QuickTime (.mov) or Windows Media (.avi) are convenient, it is typical to render and import image sequences in a video effects production environment because

- A bad frame in a sequence can (typically) be replaced; a bad frame frame will (typically) make a movie unusable, perhaps costing hours of rendering or transfer time
- It's easy to replace a section of an image sequence precisely; simply over-write specific numbered frames
- Still image formats are more universal, particularly cross-platform (see Source Formats, below, for which ones are preferable and why)
- HD or film resolution movie files are huge and cumbersome to move or edit

Adobe's handling of image sequences isn't entirely ideal; neither the After Effects Import dialog nor Bridge groups them together automatically, so it's up to you to notice if a single folder contains multiple image sequences. There is also no mechanism to import part of a sequence; to work with a range of images from a sequence, especially long ones with thousands of images, it is often best to choose the range you need and copy it, or symbolic links to it, into a separate folder.

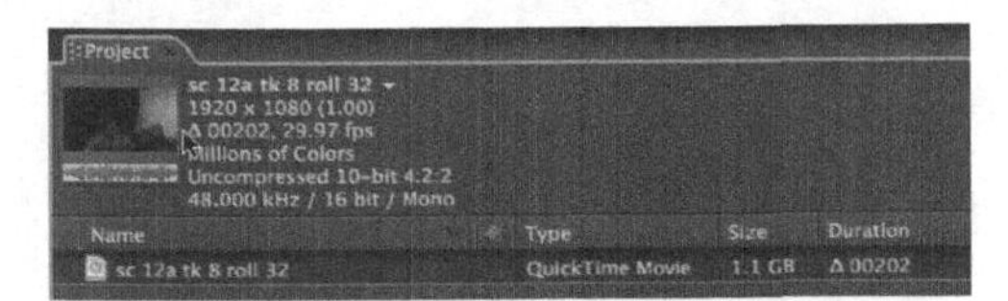

Figure 4.15 Useful information about any selected footage item can be found atop the Project panel. To see and select specific comps in which it is used, click the carat to the right of the file name. The selected file itself also shows size, type, and source location.

Therefore, when importing still image sequences to use as moving footage, remember

- Just because Project Settings contain the proper frame rate (e.g. 24 fps for a feature film project), image sequences may still import at 30 fps (the default).
- You can assign any frame rate to any moving footage, even overriding the rate specified in a QuickTime or Windows Media file.

Keep in mind that when a clip is selected in the Project panel, its current frame rate, duration, and other information is displayed at the top of the panel (**Figure 4.15**).

Figure 4.16 The ellipse travels horizontally at high speed, creating clear interlaced fields. This describes two frames' worth of motion via every other vertical pixel of a single frame.

Fields, Pulldown, Pixel Aspect Ratio

One surprise for the digital video novice is that moving images are often not made up of whole frames containing square pixels like the still images we're all used to; instead, a video frame is often interlaced into two fields, and its pixels are stored non-square, all in order to enable faster and more efficient playback.

Fields combine two frames into one by interlacing them together, vertically alternating one horizontal line of pixels from the first with one from the second. The result is half the image detail but twice the motion detail. **Figure 4.16** details this principle in action.

Figure 4.17 shows how a frame of footage with heavy motion and interlacing looks with Separate Fields set to Off. It's okay to roll this way if you're not doing any compositing, transformation, paint/masking, or distortion (color correction is okay); otherwise, it's best to match the Separate Fields setting to that of the footage, causing After Effects to recognize the interlace frame as two separate frames of video.

Figure 4.17 The foreground pickup truck spells trouble if you're planning on doing much more than a simple color correction; fields were not removed for this clip. If you see a problem like this, check your Interpret Footage settings immediately.

✔ Notes

Both legacies discussed here (interlacing and non-square pixels) carry over from standard definition (SD) formats (NTSC and PAL) into newer high definition (HD) formats because they enable higher throughput and smaller file sizes.

Pulldown uses fields to run 24 fps film footage smoothly at 29.97 fps by repeating one field every five frames. This creates a pattern that After Effects can accurately guess if there is sufficient motion in the first few frames of the footage. If not, the backup option (which still works) is trial-and-error, trying each initial pattern listed under Remove Pulldown until the field artifacts disappear in a 23.976 fps comp. There are two basic types of pulldown (3:2 and 24Pa), each with five potential initial patterns.

✔ Notes

3:2 pulldown is the traditional format designed to make footage that originated at 24 fps play smoothly at 29.97 fps; telecine conversions from film to television use this. 24P Advance Pulldown was introduced to allow the best possible recovery of the original 24 frames by grouping them together; the pattern allows the interlaced frame to be discarded because it is always bookended by two whole frames.

Pixel Aspect Ratio (PAR) is another compromise intended to maximize image detail while minimizing frame size. The pixels in the image are displayed non-square on the broadcast monitor, with extra detail on one axis compensating for its lack on the other.

Your computer monitor, of course, displays square pixels, so any clip with a non-square PAR will look odd if displayed without compensating for the difference. Therefore, After Effects includes a toggle below the viewer panels to stretch the footage so that its proportions look correct (**Figure 4.18**) while the footage or composition itself isn't changed.

With some digital formats such as DV, field order and pixel aspect are standardized and set automatically in After Effects. With other formats, it's best to know the correct field order and pixel aspect as specified by the camera or software that generated the image.

✔ Notes

To accustom yourself with non-square pixels and how they appear in After

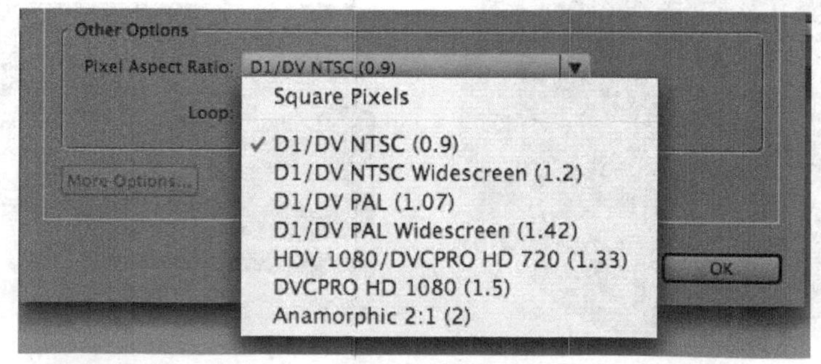

Figure 4.18 Listed are the non-square pixel video formats parsed by After Effects. Those with values above 1.0 use pixels that are wider than they are tall, making the image appear anamorphic—a.k.a. too skinny—when displayed using square pixels, without compensation.

Effects, try opening d1circle.tif from the CH01 folder and experiment with the PAR toggle in any viewer panel (Composition, Layer, or Footage).

Source Formats

After Effects is capable of importing and exporting a wide array of footage formats, yet only a small subset of these recur typically in visual effects production. **Table 4.1** contains a run-down of common raster image formats, and some advantages and disadvantages of each.

Which formats will you use most? Probably TIFF and JPEG.

TIFF offers lossless LZW compression, giving it an advantage over Photoshop, especially when you consider that TIFF can even store multiple layers, each with its own transparency. Other formats with lossless compression such as TGA don't support multiple bit-depths and layers like TIFF does. PNG is more limited and slower, but the file sizes are smaller.

✔ Notes

One oddity of the PNG format is that it specifies that an alpha channel is saved and interpreted as Straight, with no explicit option to change the default.

JPEG is a lossy 8-bit format, but it's so useful for storing anything that doesn't have to be final high-quality that it has to be mentioned here. It is fast, standard everywhere and if you keep the quality at 7 or above (on the 0-9 scale used by After Effects), it's not always immediately obvious that there is any compression at all.

✔ Tip

- To get the benefits of JPEG with options for higher bit depth, transparency and more, check out JPEG-2000, which was meant to supersede JPEG, then was not widely released due to apprehension about patent issues: http://jpeg.org/jpeg2000

For film and computer graphics, it is normal to pass around CIN and DPX files (essentially the same format) and EXR, designed (and open-sourced) by ILM specifically to handle HDR renders with multiple channels of data (and these can be customized to contain useful information such as Z depth and motion data). More on these formats is found in Chapter 16, which also includes

Table 4.1 Raster Image Formats and Their Advantages

Format	Bit Depth	Lossless Compression	Lossy Compression	Alpha Channel	Output Format
TIFF	8/16/32 bit	Y	N	Y (multiple via layers)	Y
PNG	8/16	Y	N	Y (straight only)	Y
CIN/DPX	10	N	N	N	Y (Cineon 4.5 or DPX, see Cineon Settings)
CRW	12	N	N	N	N
EXR (non-native)	16/32	Y	N	Y	Y (downloadable plug-in)
JPG	8	N	Y	N	Y

information on working with Camera Raw CRW images.

✔ Tip

- Multi-channel OpenEXR plug-ins for After Effects, along with sample files and information on how to use them, can be found at http://www.fnordware.com/OpenEXR; they are also included on the book's disk.

Photoshop Files

Although PSD files do not include even lossless compression, they do add a few features that allow you to work more easily between Photoshop and After Effects, making them highly useful in specific cases.

Although PSD and TIFF files are virtually indistinguishable when opened in Photoshop, only PSD can be imported as an After Effects composition. This is extremely useful for working with a matte painting or design that has been refined in Photoshop, but may want further tweaking when it is put into motion in After Effects. In the Import File dialog, choose Composition or Composition (Cropped Layers) using the Import As pulldown menu (**Figure 4.19**).

You can create a PSD file directly in After Effects (File > New > Adobe Photoshop File). Its dimensions will match that of the most recently opened composition, including title-safe and action-safe guides, and it is automatically included in your After Effects project.

Photoshop CS3 includes video layers; for the first time, not only can Photoshop work with moving images, but the PSD format can store them. This gives you new access to Photoshop's paint tools, which are fundamentally unique from those in After Effects.

✔ Tip

- You can even create a new Photoshop layer in the context of a composition by choosing Layer > New > Adobe Photoshop File.

Composition Settings

It's normal to think that to begin working in After Effects, after you've imported some footage, you select Composition > New Composition and choose a preset in the Composition Settings dialog, along with the appropriate duration. I rarely do this.

To ensure that composition settings are exactly as they should be with the least effort, try one of the following:

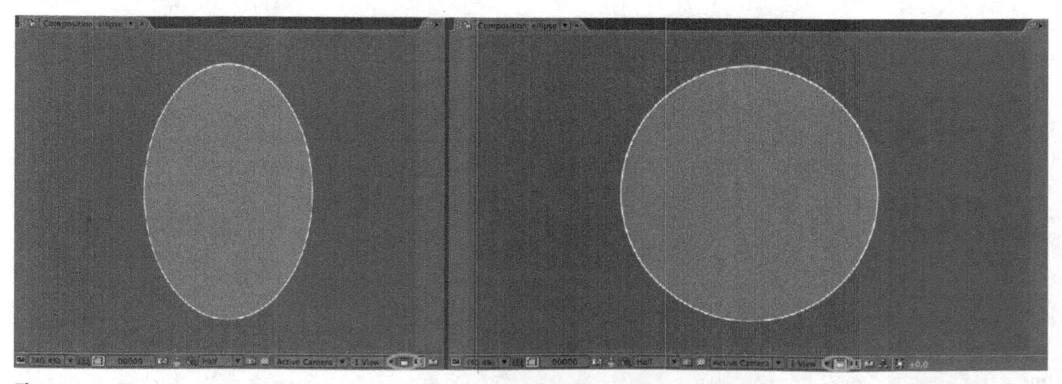

Figure 4.19 The same non-square pixel D1 aspect source, displayed with Pixel Aspect Ratio Correction toggled off (left) and on (right). The toggle for each is highlighted in green.

- Use a prebuilt project template that includes compositions whose settings are already correct; duplicate and rename an existing template composition.
- Create a new composition by dragging its main footage (often the background plate) to the Create a New Composition icon (**Figure 4.20**).

✔ Notes

The term "plate" stretches back to the earliest days of optical compositing (and indeed, of photography itself) and refers to the source footage, typically the background onto which foreground elements are composited.

The latter method automatically matches the pixel dimensions, Pixel Aspect Ratio, Frame Rate, and Duration all of which are crucial to get correct (although Duration is negotiable as long as it is not too short.)

✔ Tip

- If there's no factory preset for footage you'll use repeatedly, by all means create your own and save it using the small icon adjacent to the Preset pulldown menu (**Figure 4.21**).

Figure 4.20 Drag a source clip to the highlighted icon at the bottom of the Project panel to create a new composition with the clip's duration, pixel dimensions, pixel aspect, and frame rate. It's a reasonably foolproof way to match composition settings to a particular plate footage source.

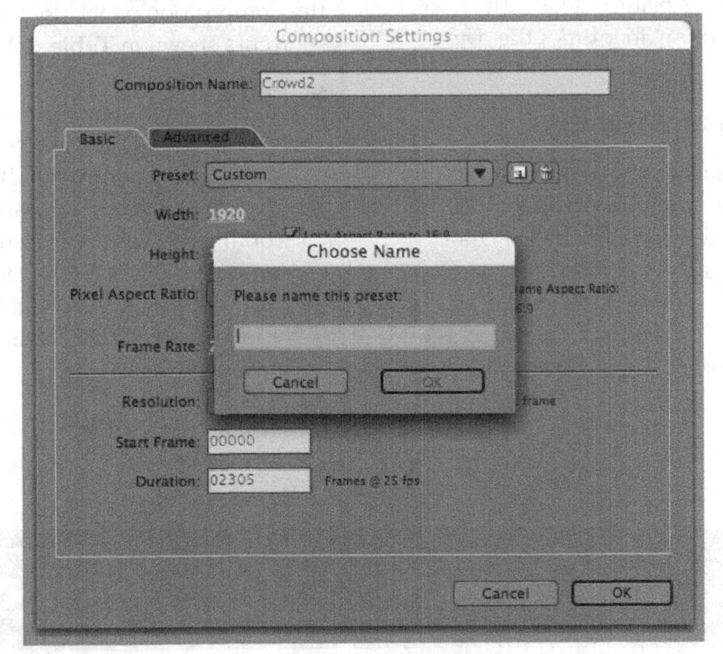

Figure 4.21 No preset matches what you need for your project? Create and save your own.

The Advanced tab in the Composition Settings dialog pertains to options for temporal and spatial settings and motion blur and 3D (Chapter 15, "The Camera and Optics").

Previews and Viewers

How exactly does a professional work with footage in After Effects? This section offers some of the habits of highly effective compositors, to paraphrase a popular productivity guru. These strategies are particularly helpful when working with typically large format footage such as 2K film plates.

✔ Notes

A 2K plate is the minimum typical horizontal film resolution: approximately 2000 pixels, or more precisely 2048 pixels in width. HD video, at 1920 pixels horizontal resolution, can also be considered a 2K format. Films are increasingly made with 4K effects plates—double the horizontal resolution, four times the overall pixels.

Resolution and Quality

There are several other effective ways to speed up previews and interactivity without ever setting a layer to Draft quality. Draft creates inaccurate previews by actually rounding off the numbers in calculating a mathematically precise operation such as a color key. Moreover, it is inconvenient, given the lack of a global toggle for layer quality (other than in the Render Queue).

To speed and lengthen previews, here are the methods I use, in rough order of preference:

- Lower viewer Resolution to Half, or in extreme cases, Quarter (**Figure 4.22**)
- Set a Region of Interest (ROI) if there are areas of frame that don't need attention
- Use Shift+RAM Preview to skip frames (default setting of 1 skips every second frame—details in "Caching and Previewing," below)

Half resolution allows four times as much data to fill a RAM preview, and Shift+RAM Preview allows twice that much data. Thus a half-resolution preview of every other frame should be at least 8 times faster than at full resolution and motion, which can be saved for fine tuning and final render preparation.

To quickly change the display resolution in the Composition panel, use the keyboard shortcuts shown in **Table 4.2**.

✔ Notes

Preferences > Display includes an toggle called Auto-Zoom When Resolution Changes. It's fine if you can get used to working this way; unfortunately, it's more common to want to change the Magnification (zoom) and want the resolution to match that setting, which this preference doesn't do.

Figure 4.22 Keep the resolution (highlighted, right) matched to the current magnification setting (highlighted, left) to prevent over-rendering the current view (wasting your time) and slow RAM Previews.

Table 4.2 Display Resolution/ Size Shortcuts

Resolution/Size	Keyboard Shortcut
Full	Ctrl+J/Cmd+J
Half	Ctrl+Shift+J/Cmd+Shift+J
Quarter	Ctrl+Shift+Alt+J/Cmd+Shift+Option+J
Fit in viewer	Shift+/
Fit up to 100%	Alt+/ / Option+/

Hold down the **Spacebar** or activate the Hand tool (**H**) to move your view of a clip around. To zoom in and out, you can use

- **Ctrl+=/Cmd+= and Ctrl+-/Cmd+-**
- Zoom tool (**Z**); press **Alt/Option** to zoom out
- Comma and period keys
- Use a mouse with a scroll wheel; with the cursor over a viewer, the wheel zooms in and out

✔ Tip

- With the cursor over a specific area of the frame, hold the **Option/Alt** key as you adjust the scroll wheel, and the viewer zooms around that point.

When focusing only on a particular section of the image, use the Region of Interest (ROI) tool (**Figure 4.23**), which lets you draw a rectangular preview region. Only the layer data needed to render that area is calculated and buffered, lengthening RAM previews.

✔ Notes

After Effects is a frame-based renderer; it generally calculates the entire frame even when you specify an ROI. Truthfully, it's quite a bit smarter than that, often ignoring elements entirely outside the ROI, but it won't deliver the speed boost of the equivalent feature in a scanline/ tile-based renderer like Shake or Nuke.

Responsiveness

One major gotcha in After Effects is that UI interaction itself can be slowed down by the heavy processor activity of a big shot—so much so, in some cases, that even a simple attempt to drag a slider or move a layer

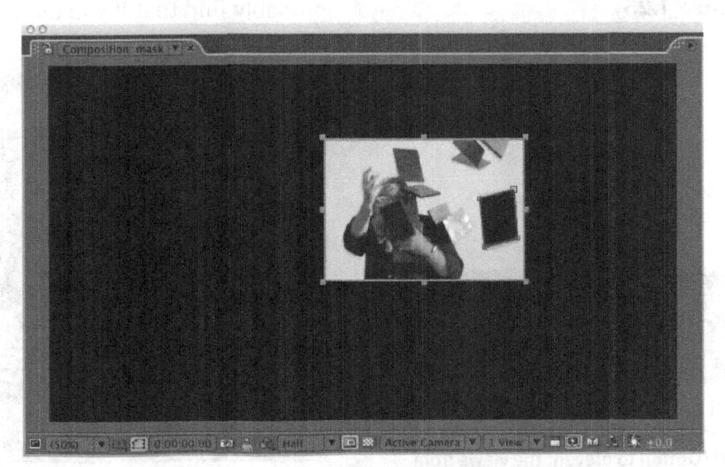

Figure 4.23 Region of Interest crops the active view region. You can even Crop Comp to Region of Interest (in the Composition menu) should a crop be exactly what you want.

position stutters to the point of non-interactivity. Here's a quick triage to solve the problem:

- **Enable OpenGL.** Preferences > Previews includes an Enable OpenGL toggle, which is off by default and unavailable on some systems. With it on, you can choose OpenGL-Interactive to get extra speed when, for example, positioning layers in 3D space. It only helps in specific cases, but in those cases it can make a huge difference for interactive setup.
- **Deactivate Live Update (Figure 4.24).** On by default, this toggle enables real-time update in the viewers as you adjust controls. Deactivate it and updates occur only when you release the mouse.
- **Hold Option/Alt as you make adjustments.** With Live Update on, this prevents views from updating. Deactivate Live Update and the behavior is inverted; the modifier keys instead enable real-time updates.
- **Activate Caps Lock.** If you don't mind working "blind" for periods of time, the caps lock key prevents updates to any viewer (**Figure 4.25**).

Figure 4.24 When Live Update is active, Composition and Layer panels update in real time as adjustments are made. Hold **Alt/Option** to prevent the views from updating (layers display as wireframes); with Live Update deactivated, this modifier causes the view to update in real time.

In general, the more responsive you can make your user interface, the better will be the result because you can make more decisions in a shorter period of time. Just leave time to double-check the result if you are in the habit of disabling viewers.

OpenGL in After Effects

OpenGL allows After Effects to use the graphics processor unit (GPU) to render elements in a composition, rather than the central processor unit (CPU), which is where all final-quality rendering is typically done. You get speedier interaction, particularly with 3D layers (a majority of OpenGL specifications apply to 3D), but the way the scene is drawn isn't as robust or as accurate; motion blur, for example, won't look right, and while the CPU has up to about 3 GB of RAM to use to create an image, the GPU can only have a fraction of that (at this writing all of my machines have 256 MB of VRAM, or graphics memory).

Thus you would only want to render with OpenGL enabled if it gave you a particular stylized look you wanted; instead, you will probably find that if you use it at all, it's

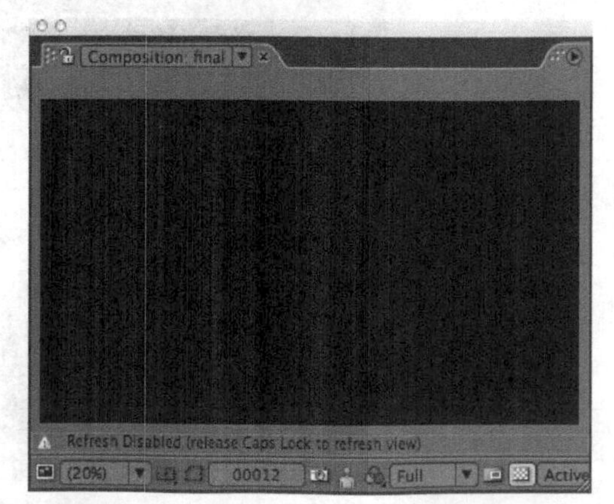

Figure 4.25 Caps Lock prevents view windows from updates; a prominent red border reminds you that it's on.

most useful for setting up a complex 3D scene quickly.

OpenGL is disabled by default in After Effects because it can introduce instability (crashes). You can discover what OpenGL features are available on your system, and enable it in Preferences > Previews; click OpenGL Info to see a list of capabilities and which are supported (**Figure 4.26**).

Once you've enabled the feature, you can choose it in the Fast Previews pulldown menu along the bottom of the Composition viewer. There are two OpenGL options, Interactive and Always On; the former will help you with fast scene setup, especially in a complicated 3D scene, and the latter will give you the look of OpenGL at all times as you work.

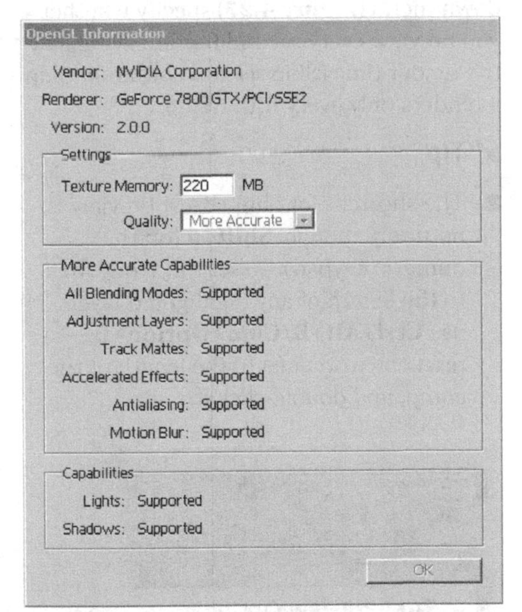

Figure 4.26 Clicking OpenGL Info in Preferences > Previews opens this dialog. Texture Memory should be set approximately 40 MB below the total on Windows, as shown; on Mac, the correct memory setting is entered automatically. OpenGL is not supported on all versions of OS X 10.4, regardless of what card is installed.

✔ Tip

- Even if OpenGL is set to Always On, it is not employed in a RAM Preview. To preview with OpenGL, advance frames by dragging the CTI, using **Page Up/Page Down**, or by pressing the **Spacebar**. Spacebar previews become faster on the second pass, once texture data has buffered onto the display card.

✔ Notes

OpenGL can for various reasons become disabled even if your card fully supports it; it is not supported on OS X 10.4, regardless of hardware. If After Effects crashes with an OpenGL error, the feature will be disabled (un-checked in Preferences) the next time you start the application. If After Effects crashes on startup, you can remove OpenGL.aex from the plug-ins folder, and if that solves the crash problem, you should update the system OpenGL drivers before moving the plug-in back.

Multiprocessing

New to After Effects CS3 is a Multiprocessing option that runs multiple processes to render more than one frame at a time. Off by default, you enable it via a toggle in Preferences > Multiprocessing; this dialog box contains only the single checkbox, accompanied by a long Description section.

This is one case where it's actually worthwhile to read the Description section. Not only is it customized for the system on which it appears, specifying how many processors are available and how they will be used, but it contains the following key tip (which reads the same on every system):

Each background process requires at least 400 MB of RAM. Reduce the Maximum RAM Cache Size in the Memory and Cache preferences to free RAM for the background processes.

In other words, lowering After Effects' RAM usage can greatly enhance performance. Assuming you heed this advice, there is no good reason not to enable Multiprocessing if your system supports it; previews and renders alike can be 80 to 100% faster per extra processor.

✔ **Tip**

- Nucleo Pro 2, from GridIron Software, goes even further to harness extra processor power, allowing you to cache precomps and pre-render individual layers in the background. Even with Multiprocessing now a part of After Effects, it can really help maximize what a single system can do with CS3.

Caching and Previewing

The more Timeline footage you can cache into physical memory, the better. After Effects does this automatically as you navigate from frame to frame (**Page Up/Page Down**) or load a RAM preview (**0** on the numeric keypad). The green line atop the Timeline shows which frames are loaded.

Given that After Effects can only use a bit less than 3 GB of physical memory per session, you can do better. To extend the cache from physical memory (RAM) to physical media (ideally a high-speed local drive), enable Disk Cache in Preferences > Memory & Cache. This locks away a portion of your drive for use only by After Effects. A blue line shows frames loaded in the Disk Cache.

When you activate Enable Disk Cache, you must also specify a disk location; if in doubt just create a local folder with an intuitive name like AE Scratch. Even the default 2 GB (2000 MB) setting greatly extends available cache without occupying permanent disk space.

✔ **Tip**

- For maximum performance, no drive should be full beyond 90% of capacity.

Two main questions usually come up regarding the Disk Cache:

- How can I make the application cache as much as possible?
- How do I preserve the cache once it is loaded?

The goal with caching, of course, is to get as close to real-time performance as possible. Disk Cache saves the time required to re-render a frame, but doesn't necessarily deliver real-time playback, and often is not invoked when you might think it should be.

If refined motion is not critical, use Shift+RAM Preview. Options in the pull-down menu (**Figure 4.27**) specify whether you preview every second frame, saving half the render time (Skip set to 1) or more (Skip 4 renders only every fifth frame, etc.).

✔ **Tip**

- The shortcut for Shift+RAM Preview is, naturally enough, **Shift+0** (on the numeric keypad). To set the Work Area to the length of any highlighted layers, use **Ctrl+Alt+B/Cmd+Option+B**—to reset the work area to the length of the comp, and double-click it.

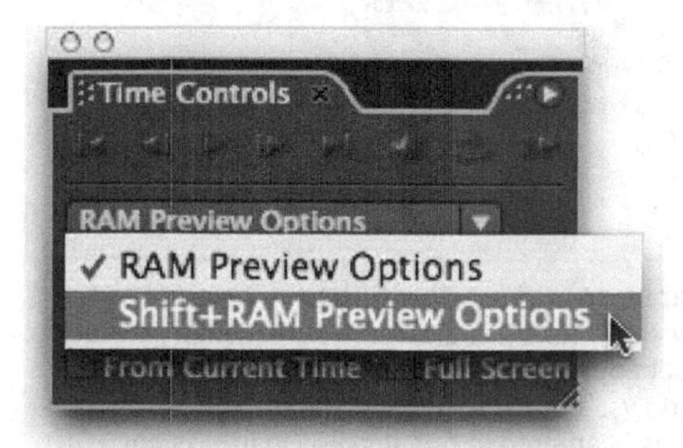

Figure 4.27 The panel menu of Time Controls toggles RAM Preview and Shift+RAM Preview options.

Preview Settings

Sometimes a feature is hidden in plain sight, and so it is with Time Controls for a lot of people. Therefore allow me to point out additional options for RAM previews:

- **Frame Rate and Resolution.** It's normal to leave them on Auto, but these settings ensure that previews are always consistent.
- **Loop options.** Hidden among the playback icons atop Time Controls is a toggle controlling how previews loop. Use this to disable looping, or amaze your friends and supervisors with the "ping pong" option.
- **From Current Time** (Time Controls panel). Toggle it on and the work area is ignored; previews begin at the current time and roll through to the end of the comp.
- **Full Screen** (Time Controls panel). Self-explanatory and rarely used.
- **Preferences > Video Preview** lets you specify an Output Device and how it is used (**Figure 4.28**). If you have a miniDV, DVCPro HD, or FireWire device attached with its own monitor, you can preview there even if the aspect ratio doesn't match (note the toggle to enable this). Third-party devices, such as PCI cards from Kona and Blackmagic, are supported as well.

✔ Tip

To update an external preview device, press /.

Customized Viewers

Custom, contrasting backgrounds are essential to a lot of effects work, such as keying and masking. You can customize the background color of the Composition viewer (**Ctrl+Shift+B/Cmd+Shift+B** or Composition > Background Color) or toggle the Transparency Grid icon beneath the Composition panel to evaluate edges in sharp relief.

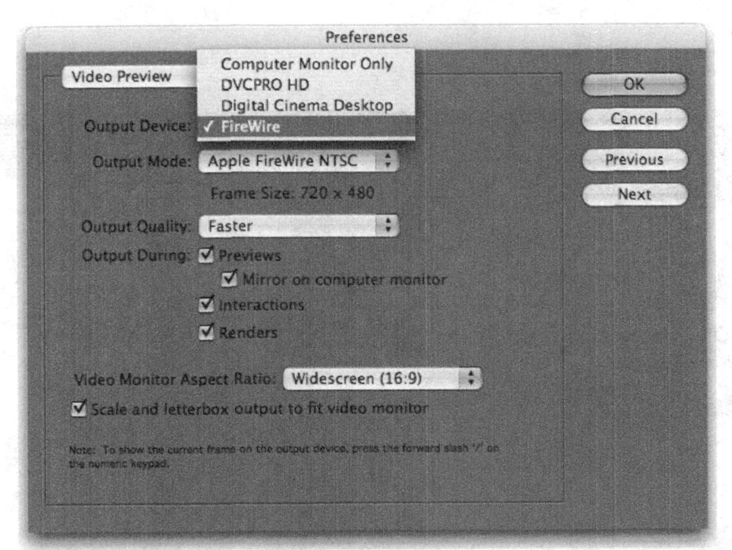

Figure 4.28 The items listed under Output Device in Preferences > Video Preview change according to the I/O and display hardware is installed on the system.

What a lot of people don't consider is that guide layers enable a completely customizable background that will never show up in a render, nor when nested into another comp. You can insert background or reference footage, or create a custom gradient background (**Figure 4.29**). To make any layer a guide layer, context-click it in the Timeline and choose Guide Layer (Layer > Guide Layer).

✔ Tip

- To create a basic gradient background, apply the Ramp effect to a solid layer.

Several other modes and toggles are available in the viewer panels. Some are familiar from other Adobe applications:

- **View > Show Grid (Ctrl+"/Cmd+")** displays an overlay grid.
- **View > Show Rulers (Ctrl+R/Cmd+R)** not only displays pixel measurements of the viewer, it includes guides, which have several uses to compose an image.
- **Title/Action Safe** overlays determine the boundaries of the frame as well as its center point.

All of the above features can be accessed by a single pulldown menu beneath the viewer panel (the one that looks like a crosshair). To pull out a guide, choose Show Rulers and then drag from either the horizontal or vertical ruler. To change where the origin point (0 on each ruler) is, drag the crosshair from the corner between the two rulers.

Other Adobe conventions are View > Show Rulers (**Ctrl+R/Cmd+R**) and the various Guides options under the View menu. I don't make use of guides much in After Effects, but I like the fact that, for example, when you create a new Photoshop file with After Effects, it includes guides showing the safe areas.

✔ Tip

- Use Preferences > Grids & Guides to customize your grid; the size, subdivisions and color are all fair game, and it's even

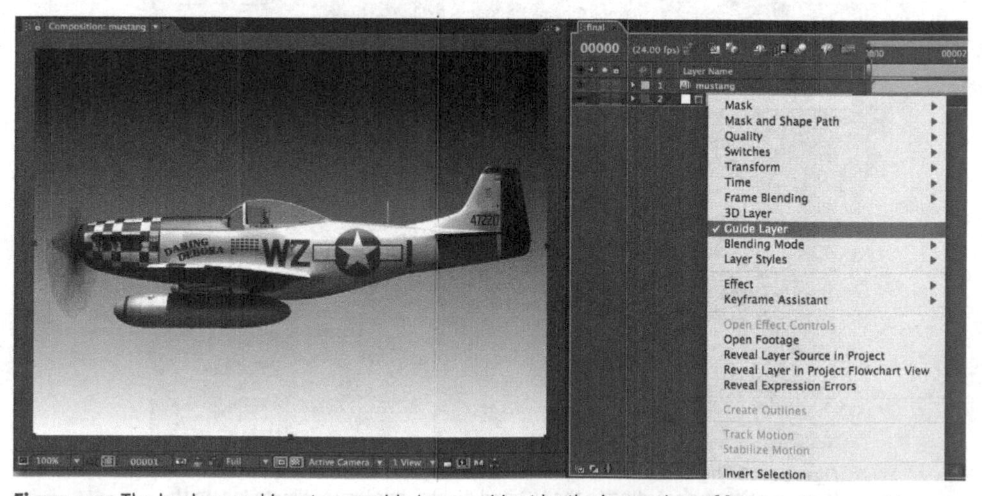

Figure 4.29 The background is set as a guide layer, evident by the icon, a box of four small cyan guides, that appears beside the layer name.

possible to replace lines with dashes or dots for a lighter touch. You can also customize the Safe Margins in the Title/Action Safe overlay, even setting them to 0% to use only the center crosshair if you prefer.

To toggle visibility of individual Layer Controls such as masks, keyframes, and motion paths, use View > View Options (**Ctrl+Alt+U/Cmd+Option+U**), or just hide them all using View > Hide Layer Controls (**Ctrl+Shift+H/Cmd+Shift+H**). There is also a toggle (next to Grid & Guide Options along the bottom of the viewer).

Throughout this book I encourage you to develop the habit of studying footage one color channel at a time. The Show Channel icon exists for this purpose, along with the corresponding keyboard shortcuts **Alt/Option+1** through **Alt/Option+4** (R, G, B, and A, respectively). An outline in the color of the selected channel helpfully appears around the viewer boundary (**Figure 4.30**).

Effects & Presets

After Effects contains a lot of *effects*. These are filters (as they would be called in Photoshop) or processes that affect the appearance of a layer (or entire comp). Some provide bread-and-butter processes you probably use all the time, such as adjusting color with Levels or applying a blur. Others may be too esoteric or outdated ever to find their way into your workflow. A few are entirely unique to After Effects, including

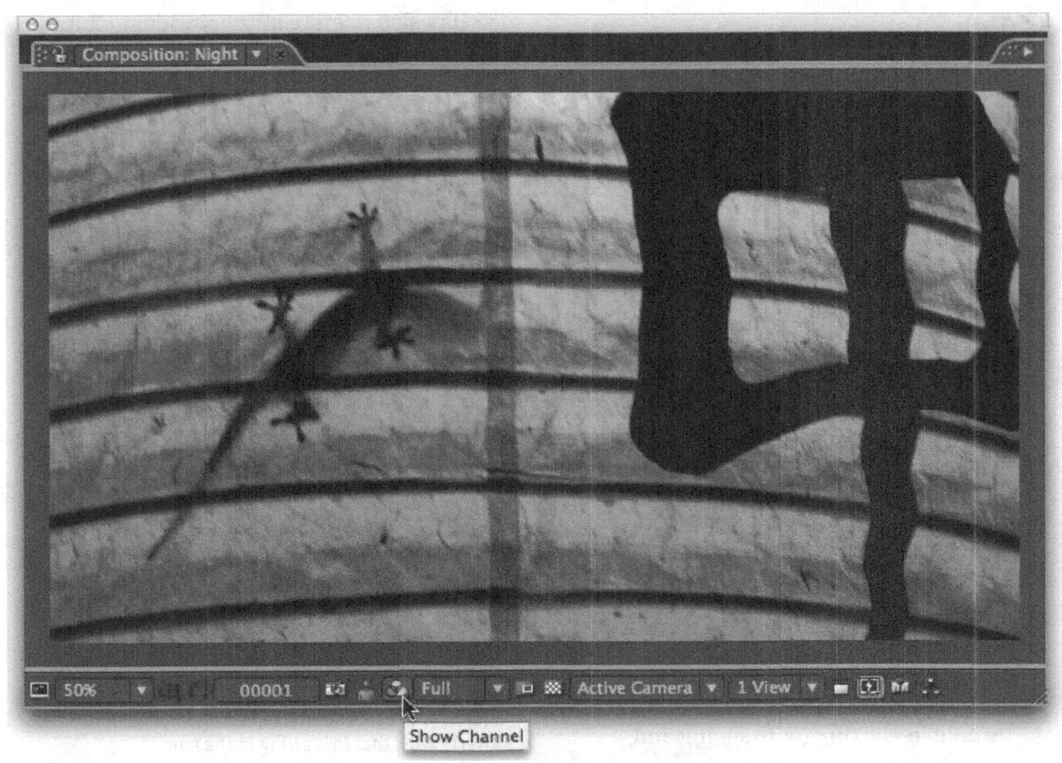

Figure 4.30 The green border indicates that only the green channel is displayed.

new ones developed by third-party (non-Adobe) software companies, with new ones coming along all the time.

At this writing I count about 200 effects plug-ins that ship with the application, and far more than that available on the open market. This book only covers a subsection of those 200, although it does so in depth, in many cases. The bottom line is

- It's likely that you'll use less than 10% of these effects something like 80–90% of the time, so there is no need to feel overwhelmed. You don't need to understand them all in order to use the most powerful ones.
- After Effects artists sometimes get a bad rap for using (or even buying) a plug-in to achieve an effect that can be done without it, if you know how.

✔ Tip

- Are you a MacIntel user with plug-ins from the pre-CS3 era? They won't work natively in After Effects CS3, but you can enable them by toggling Open in Rosetta in the Get Info dialog for Adobe After Effects CS3.app (in the Finder).

Thus, where possible, this book goes deeply enough into the most essential effects plug-ins that it should help you understand which are the most useful and how you can use them together to create effects you might not have thought possible.

There are three basic ways to apply an effect to a layer:

- Choose it in the Effect menu
- Context-click the layer and choose it in the Effect context menu
- Choose it in the Effects & Presets panel, by double-clicking (or dragging and dropping) it.

The Effects & Presets panel is the most versatile method. It has options to display effects without their categories (**Figure 4.31**), as well as a search field to help you look for a specific effect by name, or for all the effects whose names include a specific word, such as "blur" or "channel."

The Effects & Presets Panel

Each item in the Effects & Presets panel includes icon showing that it is one of the following types:

- an 8, 16 or 32 bit pixel effect (the highest possible bit depth is shown)
- an Animation Preset
- an Audio effect
- Missing

Effects that are capable of supporting 16 or 32 bits also operate at the standard 8 bits

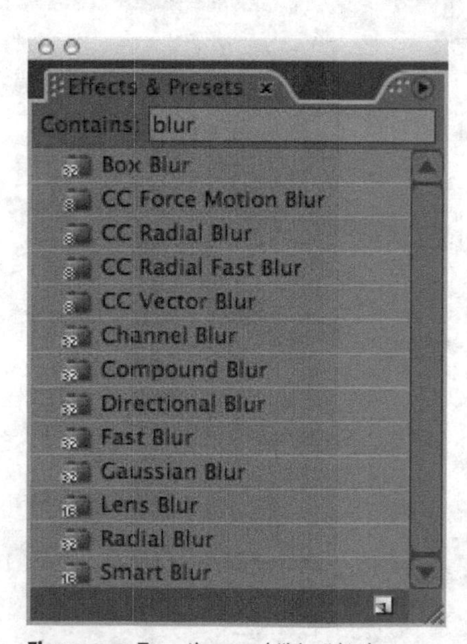

Figure 4.31 Type the word "blur" in the Effects & Presets search field and only effects with that text string in the name appear.

per channel. Chapter 16 contains more about the difference between bit depths and how to work with them.

The panel menu for Effects & Presets offers other unique ways to list its contents, options not available with standard menus, including the following toggles:

- Show only the effects that match the current project's bit depth (if 16 or 32 bpc)
- Alphabetical or Finder Folder order (as an alternative to the standard Categories found in the standard Effect menus
- Show Animation Presets

Animation Presets are sets of effects with custom default settings. You can use the ones that ship with After Effects or create your own. You can even browse the built-in ones from Adobe by choosing Browse Presets in the wing menu (or under the Animation menu); this opens the root folder containing them in Bridge, where selecting an individual .ffx file will also display an animated preview.

✔ Tip

- Having trouble finding an item in Effects & Presets? Make sure you haven't set a display toggle in the panel menu that hides some of its contents—for example, Show 32 bpc-capable Effects Only mode, which excludes the majority of effects

✔ Notes

An animation preset file is recognizable by its .ffx file suffix; they can be found in the Plug-ins folder, within the same folder where the application itself is found (on Windows, this is a shortcut to the folder, which is stored one level deeper in the Support Files folder).

Animation presets are particularly useful when you're working with a team and sharing standardized practices. To save your own, in the Effect Controls window or the Timeline select whatever effects and properties you want to save and choose Animation > Save Animation Preset.

You can save an Animation Preset wherever you like, but for it to show up in the Effects & Presets palette automatically, save it to the Presets folder (the default location, found in the folder where the application itself resides). In a studio situation, a preset can be distributed to a number of users simply by placing it in this folder. The next time they restart After Effects or update the palette (using the Refresh List command in the wing menu), the preset is listed, ready for use.

Output: The Render Queue

The Render Queue is the main exit for your After Effects compositions. Although relatively intuitive, it contains some great features that are easy to miss, as well as a gotcha or two.

✔ Tip

- You drag footage directly to the Render Queue, no comp required. After Effects makes one for you, rendering the footage as-is, which is efficient for quick file conversions (i.e. converting an image sequence to a Quicktime movie, or vice versa).

To place an item in the Render Queue, you can

- Use one of two keyboard shortcuts: **Ctrl+M** (**Cmd+M**) and the one I always tend to use, **Ctrl+Shift+/** (**Cmd+Shift+/**)

- Drag items from Project to the Render Queue
- Select Composition > Add to Render Queue

There are two key sections for each Render Queue item: Render Settings and Output Module. You can click on each to adjust settings manually, but as soon as you find yourself rendering more than one item with the same settings, you should choose, or as is likely necessary, create a template to save yourself one more opportunity for careless errors (the bane of the compositor's existence).

✔ Tip

- The output path you choose for the first of your active Render Queue items then becomes the default for the rest of them, should you wish to render several items to the same location.

Render Settings: Pre-flight Checklist

Most of the items in the top Composition section of the Render Settings dialog (accessed by clicking on the current setting itself) correspond to settings in your composition and Timeline. Current Settings for each category uses whatever settings are used in the comp, but you can instead override with specific settings for Quality, Resolution, Proxies, Effects, Solo Switches, Guide Layers, and the Color Depth. There is even a checkbox to use the OpenGL renderer instead of the standard software method, if you like that look.

✔ Notes

Most Render Settings are straightforward, offering either a Current or an override setting.

The Time Sampling section (center) has all to do with frames, fields, and overall frame rate and time span. Here you can introduce (or re-introduce) field order and pulldown to broadcast footage, control motion blur and frame blending (both further described in the next chapter).

In the bottom section, Options, After Effects defaults Use Storage Overflow toggled on; if your main render disk becomes full, the render doesn't have to fail if you have specified overflow volumes in Preferences > Output (**Figure 4.32**).

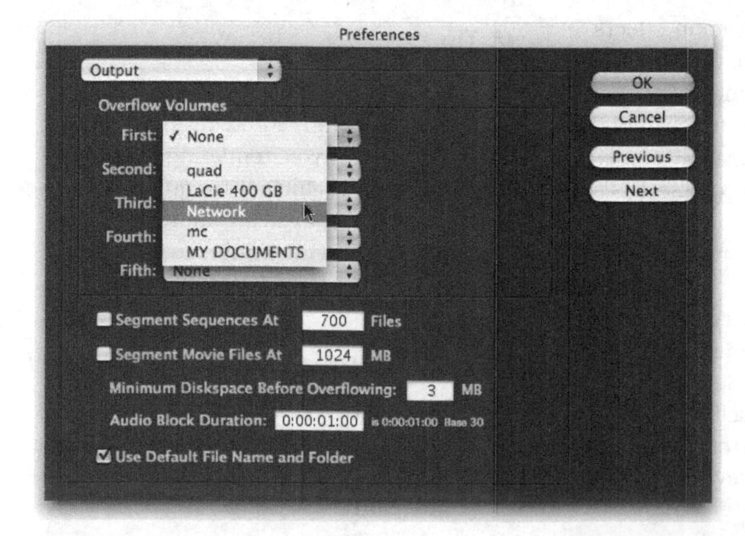

Figure 4.32 Storage overflow is insurance against failed planning; it's certainly preferable to a failed overnight render.

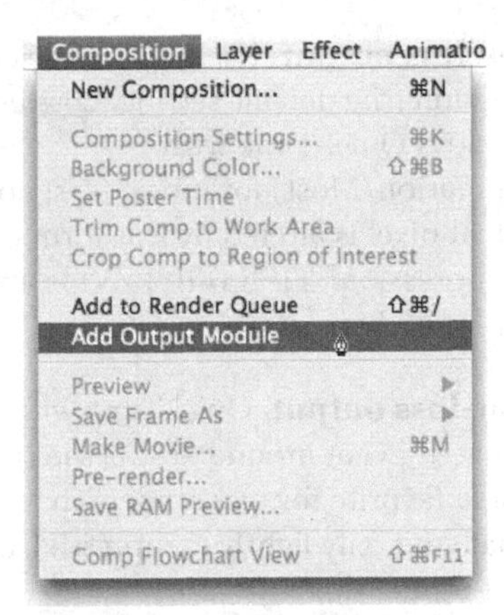

Figure 4.33 It's easy to miss that you can add multiple Output Modules to a single render queue item, via Composition > Add Output Module. This can be an immense timesaver.

✔ Tip

- When rendering a still sequence, you can enable the Skip Existing Files toggle in Render Settings, and After Effects checks whether a frame already exists before rendering it.

Render Settings, then, functions as a preflight checklist of the decisions needed to make a composition look as it should before the image is saved to disk; the actual save operation is handled in the Output Modules.

Output Modules: Making Movies

Output Modules do one thing only: convert a rendered frame into a particular video (or still) format with a given name. Included are options for which video and audio channels are included and at what size (or for audio, sample rate).

✔ Tip

- To render at a smaller size, it's best in most cases to scale down using a Stretch setting in the Output Module rather than a Resolution setting in the Render Settings (unless speeding up the render is more important than quality).

Output Module appears beneath Render Settings, item by item, because the visual order represents the order in which things actually happen. In this case, Render Settings are applied prior to frame actually being written using Output Module settings.

Several elegant and easily missed problem-solving tools are embedded in the Output Modules:

- You can add multiple Output Modules per Render Queue item (**Figure 4.33**).
- You can edit multiple Output Modules to a different preset by Shift-selecting the Output Modules themselves, rather than the Render Queue items (**Figure 4.34**).
- You can custom-number an image sequence beginning with the integer of your choice (**Figure 4.35**).

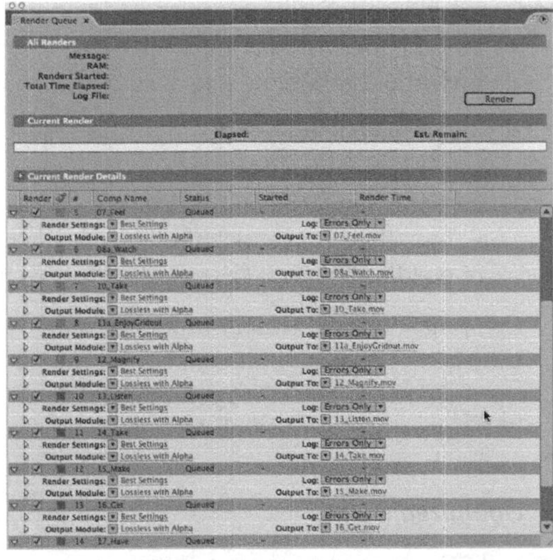

Figure 4.34 Select the first Output Module in the group and Shift-select the last, then change any of the selected ones and they all follow.

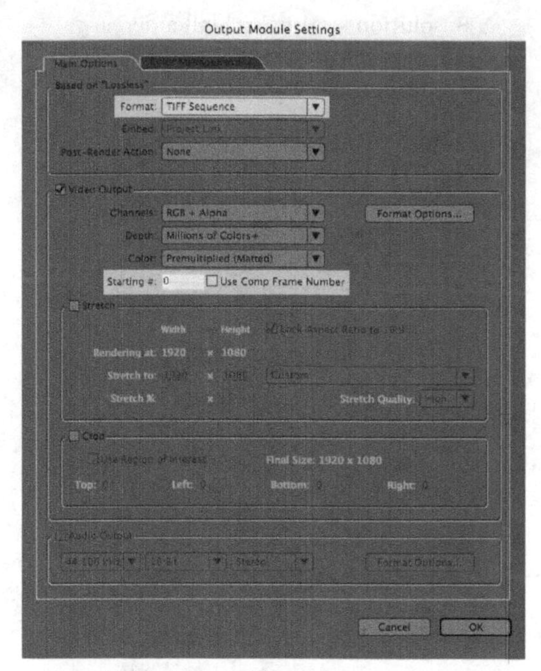

Figure 4.35 Custom-number a frame sequence by setting Use Comp Frame Number.

- Working with non-square pixels or letterboxing? Stretching and cropping output lets you change the pixel aspect without having to re-render.
- Post-Render Actions are available to import or replace the source composition.
- A numbered image sequence must contain a string like [###] somewhere within its name (replaced, in this example, with a three-digit sequential number, one digit of padding for each # symbol).

Creating your own Output Modules using the Make Template option at the bottom of the pulldown menu saves you the trouble of having to think of most of these options each time you render.

Optimized Output

Following are some suggested output settings (Render Settings and Output Modules) for specific situations:

- **Lossless output.** Use inter-frame compression (the default setting, Lossless, employs QuickTime with Animation/Most) for movie files; no individual pixel is altered by this form of "compression." TIFF with LZW is a good bet for still images.
- **Low-loss output.** QuickTime with Photo-JPEG at around 75% is the traditional favorite for test renders that are small and only lightly compressed, and that render quickly.
- **Online review.** This is a fast-changing area, but whatever format you choose, it is likely better to compress it outside of After Effects for multiple-pass encoding, which is key to your success with a format like H.264 or MPEG formats.
- **DV/HDV**. These are heavily compressed formats. You are stuck with them if you are shooting or delivering with them, but you don't need to use them at any other point in your process. Heed Stu Maschwitz's repeated advice in *The DV Rebel's Guide* (Peachpit Press, 2006); render once only: the final, directly from the source.

Obviously, there is much more to choosing your output settings than is covered here, including which source and delivery formats are demanded for your particular project.

✔ Notes

Photo-JPEG is universally available, even in older versions of QuickTime. Plus, at 100% it provides 4:4:4 chroma sampling, and at 75%, 4:2:2 (see Chapter 16 for more on chroma). New at this writing is Apple ProRes 422, introduced as part of Final Cut Pro 6, and delivering far less loss than Photo-JPEG without the compromises of H.264. Note that not all

QuickTime compressors are not available with QuickTime for Windows.

Study a Shot like an Effects Artist

Seasoned visual effects supervisors miss nothing. The most trained eyes do not even need to see a clip twice to spot problems. In dailies on a feature film, nonetheless, a shot may loop for several minutes while the whole team gangs up on it, picking it apart. This is how shots in feature films can end up looking so good.

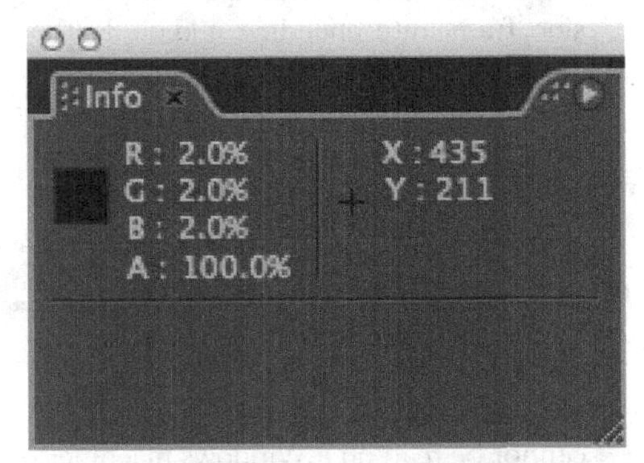

Figure 4.36 Whoops! The background level was meant to be black, but a glance at the Info palette with the cursor is over the background shows that it is actually 2% gray.

✔ Notes

Although After Effects cannot delivery multi-pass encoding via the Render Queue (despite the inclusion of Adobe Media Encoder for formats such as H.264) the Production Premium and Master Collection include it in Premiere Pro, via Adobe Media Encoder.

You can and should scrutinize your shot just as carefully in After Effects. Specifically, throughout this book I encourage you to get in the following habits:

- Check the Info palette (**Figure 4.36**)
- Loop or rock and roll previews (**Figure 4.37**).

✔ Close-Up

Naming Conventions Part of growing a studio is devising a naming scheme that keeps projects and renders organized. It's generally considered good form to

- Use standard Unix naming conventions (replacing spaces with underscores, intercaps, dashes, or dots).
- Put the version number at the end of the project name and the output file, and have them match. To add a version

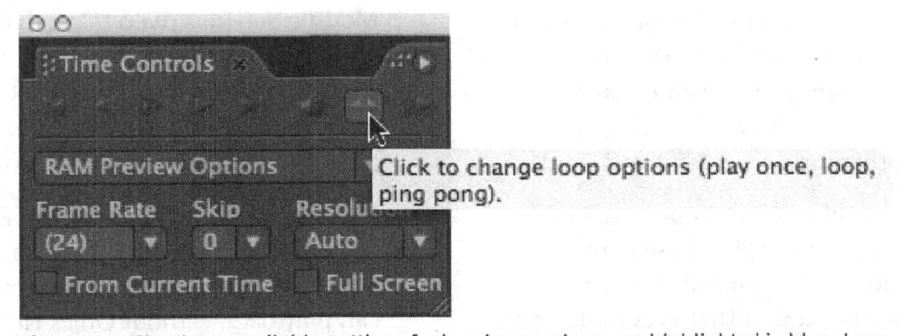

Figure 4.37 The three available settings for looping previews are highlighted in blue: Loop (the default, top), Ping-pong (center), or Play Through Once (bottom); toggle these by clicking on the icon.

number to a numbered sequence, you can name the image sequence file something like foo_bar_[####]_v01.tif for version 1.

- Padding the numbers (adding zeros at the beginning) helps keep things in order as the overall number moves into multiple digits.
- After Effects doesn't like long file names; those above 32 digits are truncated in the Project panel and Timeline. Nonetheless, it's best to be explicit in the name about what is being rendered, e.g. pirates_precomp_colorkey03_forFinal_[####].tif

- Zoom in to examine individual pixels, especially along any composited edges.
- Examine footage channel by channel.
- Slam the gamma and flash the blacks; details on how to use Levels on an adjustment layer like an investigative spotlight on your shot are included in Chapter 14, "Color Correction."
- Review your shot like the "bad cop," determined that there is something wrong that you cannot initially see, and try not to be hard on yourself when you find it.
- Approach your project like a computer programmer, trying to minimize the probability of a careless error (a "bug") invalidating the effort. Compositing and programming are more closely related than you might think; each consists of many logical decisions that hinge upon one another for a successful end result.

When I teach this subject in person, I add reminders of practices like these constantly. If you can do this for yourself, I guarantee beneficial results: a shot that is completed in fewer takes, with more of your own unique artistry in it. And that's what it's all about.

✔ Close-Up

What, exactly, is a QuickTime movie? QuickTime is the most ubiquitous and universal playback format among video professionals, despite that it's an Apple format, not even installed by default on Windows. Not only that, but not all Mac-based media encoders for QuickTime are even available on Windows. Say what?

- While still formats tend to offer a particular encoding option as part of the format itself, QuickTime is simply a container file that can hold arbitrary tracks of video, audio, still files, and more. Any of these tracks can have unique compression, frame rate, encoding, and bit depth. Sometimes, a given video or audio format is not available on a different machine or platform, even when it doesn't involve compression making QuickTime less universal than would be ideal.
- For example, Uncompressed 10-bit 4:2:2 is a useful Mac-only format; despite that the image is encoded but not compressed, as of this writing, the format cannot be read on a Windows machine; the movie will appear blank if played back.
- The type of video encoding used when rendering a QuickTime is specified in Format Options under the Output Module Settings dialog. The dialog box is labeled Compression Settings and the pulldown menu Compression Type, but some choices involve encoding, not compression; the same goes for Audio.
- Other moving image formats that seem to be related to QuickTime, such as .MP4 and .M4V, are more like sub-sets of it; they can play back without QuickTime Player installed, but they offer a more limited range of encoding and compression.

Importing Footage into a Project

Think of an After Effects project as a musical score. Just as a score refers to instruments and indicates how they should be played, your project lists the files you want to use and how you want to use them. When you've finished creating your project, you can output an animation as a movie file or an image sequence. The important thing to remember is that the project contains only references to the source files, not the files themselves. The project contains neither the sources nor the end result, any more than a sheet of music contains a tuba or a recording of the concert. For this reason, a project file takes up little drive space.

Source files, on the other hand, consume considerably more storage. You need both the project and the source files to preview or output your animation, just as a composer needs the orchestra to hear a work in progress or, ultimately, to perform it in concert. Non-linear editing systems (such as Adobe Premiere Pro and Apple Final Cut Pro) also work by referring to source files. Thus, if you're familiar with those programs, you have a head start on the concept of using file references in a project.

In the remainder of this chapter, you'll learn how to create a project and import various types of footage. The chapter covers the specifics of importing still images, motion footage, audio, and even other projects. In fact, After Effects ships with a number of astonishingly useful preset project templates. And that's not all: After Effects arrives accompanied by a full-fledged asset management program, Adobe Bridge.

Don't be intimidated by the length or depth of the chapter. Importing different types of footage into your project is a simple and straightforward process. As you go through the chapter, take just what you need. As you begin to incorporate a wider range of formats in your work, revisit sections to learn the idiosyncrasies of those particular formats. To revisit the musical metaphor, if a project is like a score, start by composing for an ensemble, and then build up to an orchestra.

Creating and Saving Projects

Creating a project is especially simple in After Effects, which doesn't prompt you to select project settings. As you'll see in the next chapter, most settings you specify are associated with compositions within the project.

You save After Effects projects as you would save a file in just about any program. But to more easily track changes to your work, you can instruct After Effects to save each successive version of a project using an incremental naming scheme.

Although you don't have to actively specify project settings when you start a project, you can change the default values at any time by choosing File > Project Settings. In the Project Settings dialog box, you can change the project's time display style, the sample rate at which audio is processed, and color settings—which includes a color depth setting as well as new color management options. You can find out more about these settings in the After Effects Help system.

To create a new project:

- *Do one of the following*:
  - Launch After Effects.
  - With After Effects running, choose File > New > New Project (**Figure 4.38**).

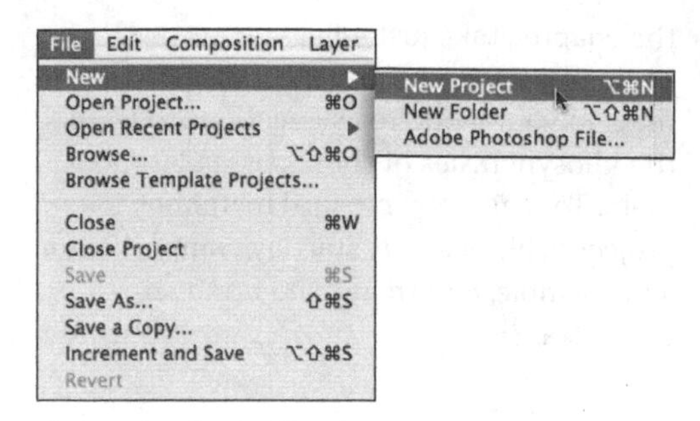

Figure 4.38 Choose File > New > New Project.

If a project is open, After Effects prompts you to save it. Otherwise, a new Project panel appears (**Figure 4.39**).

To save using incremental project names automatically:

- After the project has been saved, choose File > Increment and Save, or press Command-Opt-Shift-S (Mac) or Ctrl-Alt-Shift-S (Windows).

After Effects saves a copy of the project, appending a number to the filename that increases incrementally with each successive Increment and Save command.

✔ Tips

- A project's name appears at the top of the main application window, not the Project panel. When a project has unsaved changes, an asterisk (*) appears next to the project's name.
- You can instruct After Effects to save the current project at an interval you specify by choosing After Effects > Preferences > Auto-Save (Mac) or Edit > Preferences > Auto-Save (Windows) and specifying how frequently After Effects saves.
- As you might expect, the File menu also includes Save, Copy, and Revert to Last Saved commands.

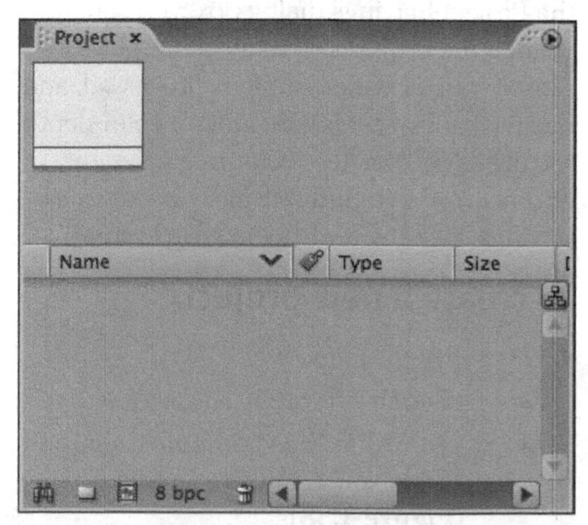

Figure 4.39 A new, untitled Project panel appears.

Opening and Closing Projects

In After Effects, you can have only one project open at a time. Opening another project closes the current project. However, closing the Project panel doesn't close the project; it merely removes the Project panel from the workspace.

As you learned in this chapter's introduction, an After Effects project contains footage items that refer to files on your system. When you reopen a project, After Effects must locate the source files to which each footage item refers. If After Effects can't locate a source file, the project considers it missing (**Figure 4.40**). (In Premiere Pro and other non-linear editing programs, missing footage is called *offline*.) The names of missing footage items appear in italics in the Project panel (**Figure 4.41**), and a placeholder consisting of colored bars temporarily replaces the source footage. You can continue working with the project, or you can locate the source footage.

✔ Tips

- To open a project you worked on recently, choose File > Open Recent Projects and choose the name of the project in the submenu.

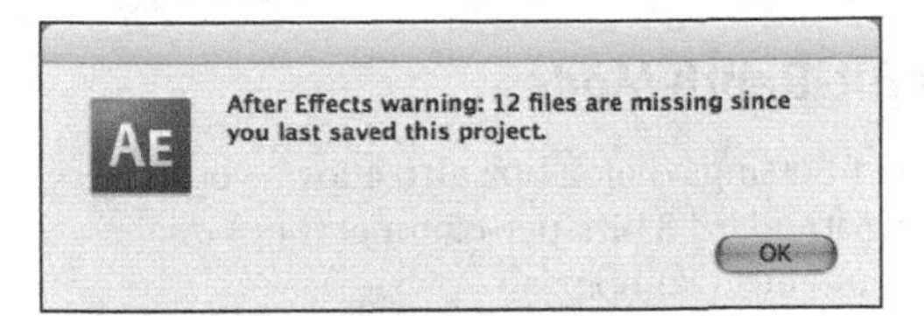

Figure 4.40 After Effects alerts you if it can't locate source files.

- With After Effects running, press Shift-Command-Opt-P (Mac) or Shift-Ctrl-Alt-P (Windows) to open the most recently opened project (think *p* for *previous project*).
- After Effects ships with a number of incredibly useful and inspiring preset project templates. See the section "Importing with Adobe Bridge," later in this chapter, for details.

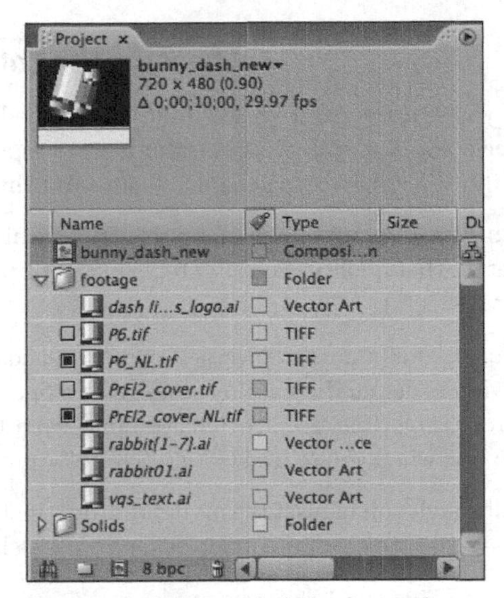

Figure 4.41 The names of missing footage items appear in italics, and the source footage is temporarily replaced by a color bar placeholder.

Importing Files

After Effects allows you to import a wide variety of still images, motion footage, and audio, as well as projects from After Effects and Premiere Pro. The procedures for importing footage are essentially variations on a theme, so you should get the hang of them quickly.

Although you may be tempted to speed through some sections in this part of the chapter, make sure you understand how the methods differ for each file type. Depending on the file, you may need to invoke the Interpret Footage command, which contains special handling options such as how to set the duration of stills or the frame rate of motion footage. The Interpret Footage command also lets you properly handle other aspects of footage, such as the alpha channel, field order, and pixel aspect ratio. If you're already familiar with these concepts, go directly to the numbered tasks; if not, check out the sidebars in this chapter for some technical grounding.

You'll find that you can often use several methods to import footage: menu bar, keyboard shortcuts, or context menu. You can even drag and drop from the desktop. Once you know your options, you can choose the method that best fits your needs or preferences.

The maximum resolution for import and export is 30,000 × 30,000 pixels. However, the PICT format is limited to 4,000 × 4,000 pixels and BMP to 16,000 × 30,000 pixels.

As you've already learned, After Effects Professional lets you import images with 16 bits per channel (bpc) and 32 bpc—an indispensable capability if you're doing high-end work.

The maximum image size and bit depth are limited by the amount of RAM available to After Effects (see the sidebar "Wham, Bam—Thank You, RAM").

After Effects supports an extensive and growing list of file formats, depending on your

Choosing the Color Bit-Depth Mode

If you're using After Effects Professional, the Project Settings dialog box also allows you to set the color bit-depth mode. In addition to supporting standard 8 bits-per-channel (bpc) images, After Effects Pro lets you process images using 16 and even 32 bpc.

This means your images not only can have higher color fidelity from the start, but they also retain that quality even after repeated color processing (for example, from transfer modes and effects).

But naturally, greater precision comes at a cost. For example, processing color in 16 bpc is twice as demanding as processing it in 8 bpc—that is, doing so requires twice the RAM and processing time. To save time, you may want to work in 8 bpc initially and then switch to 16 bpc when you're ready for critical color processing.

Although you can set the bit depth from the Project Settings dialog box, it's more convenient to toggle the bit-depth mode by Option/Alt-clicking the bit depth display in the Project panel.

platform. Photoshop and other third-party plug-ins can also expand the possibilities.

To import a file or files:

1. *Do one of the following*:

   ▲ Choose File > Import > File to import one item.

   ▲ Choose File > Import > Multiple Files to import several items (**Figure 4.42**).

The Import File or Import Multiple Files dialog box appears (**Figure 4.43**).

2. To expand or reduce the list of files, choose an option for Enable (**Figure 4.44**):

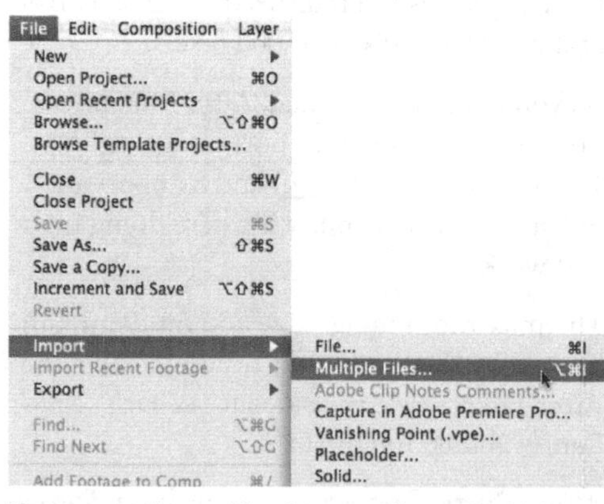

Figure 4.42 Choose File > Import > File or > Multiple Files.

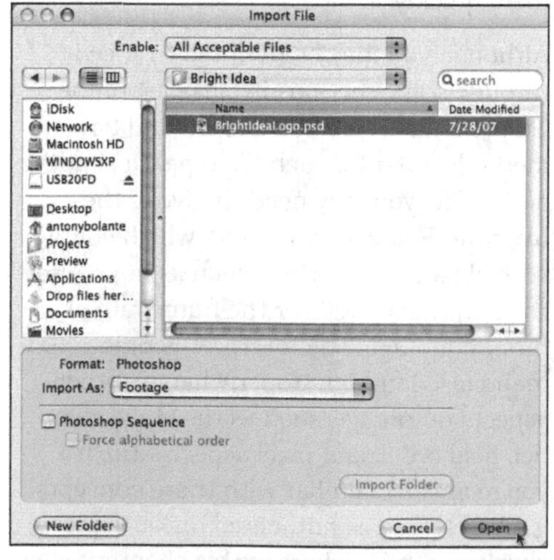

Figure 4.43 The Import File or Import Multiple Files dialog box appears.

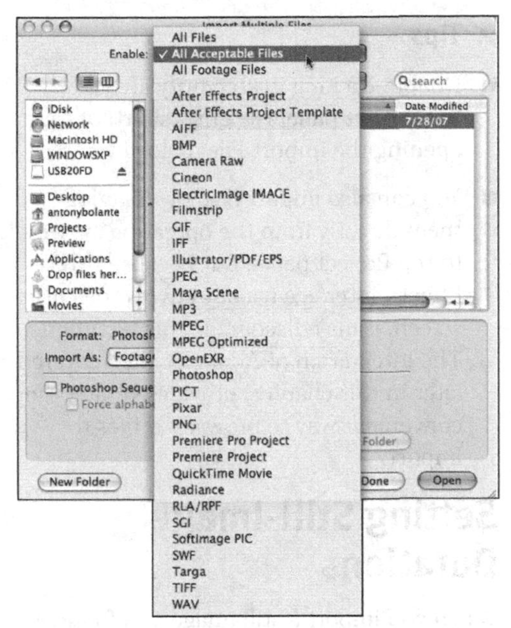

Figure 4.44 To sift the list of files, specify an option in the Enable pull-down menu.

All Files—Enables all files in the list, including files of an unrecognized file type

All Acceptable Files—Enables only file types supported by After Effects

All Footage Files—Enables only files that can be imported as footage items and excludes otherwise acceptable file types (such as After Effects or Premiere Pro project files)

AAF, AE Project, and so on—Enables only files of the same file type you select

Enabled files can be selected for import, whereas other files are unavailable and appear grayed out.

3. In the Import File or Import Multiple Files dialog box, choose Footage from the Import As pull-down menu.

   To import files as compositions or to import projects, see the corresponding sections later in this chapter.

4. Select the file you want to import, and then click Open (**Figure 4.45**).

   To select a range of files in the same folder, click the file at the beginning of the range to select it, Shift-click the end of the range, and then click Open.

   To select multiple noncontiguous files in the same folder, Command/Ctrl-click multiple files, and then click Open.

5. If prompted, specify other options for each file you import (such as its alpha channel type or how to import a layered file).

   The options for particular file types are discussed later in this chapter.

6. If you chose to import multiple files in step 1, repeat the subsequent steps until

Wham, Bam—Thank You, RAM

Here's the formula for calculating how much RAM an image requires:

Width in pixels × height in pixels × 4 bytes = RAM needed to display image

So, the largest file allowed would require 3.35 GB of RAM (30,000 × 30,000 × 4 bytes)—ouch!

A tall image used as an end credit roll for video output provides a less extreme example, as you can see:

720 × 30,000 × 4 bytes = 82.4 MB of RAM

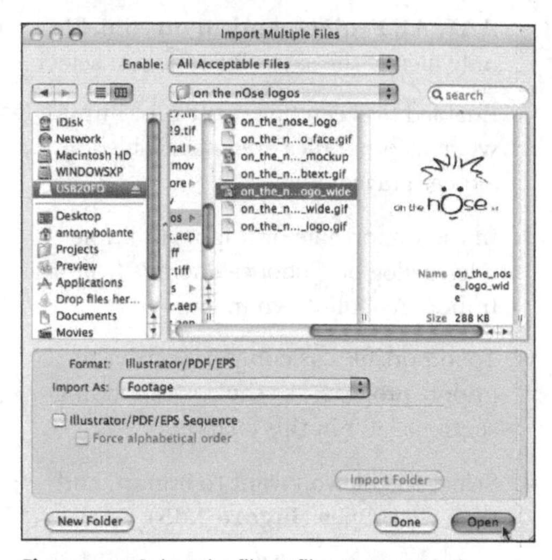

Figure 4.45 Select the file or files you want to import and click Open.

you've imported all the files you want to use; then, click Done to close the Import Multiple Files dialog box (**Figure 4.46**).

The file(s) appear as item(s) in the Project panel (**Figure 4.47**).

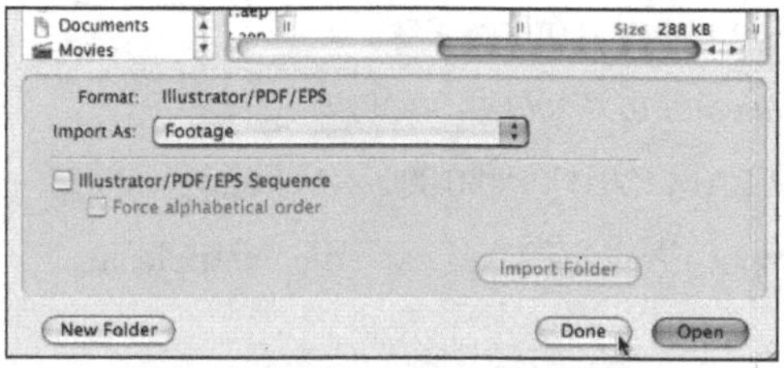

Figure 4.46 If you chose to import multiple files, click Done to close the dialog box.

✔ Tips

- Double-clicking in an empty area of the Project panel is a great shortcut for opening the Import File dialog box.
- You can also import files by dragging them directly from the operating system to the Project panel. But because After Effects' interface usually covers the entire screen, it may discourage this technique. The integration of Adobe Bridge (covered later in this chapter) provides yet another convenient way to browse for files to import.

Setting Still-Image Durations

When you import a still image as a footage file and make it a layer in a composition, you can set its duration to any length. By default, the duration of a still image matches the duration of the composition. However, you can also manually set the default duration for still images. Doing so comes in handy

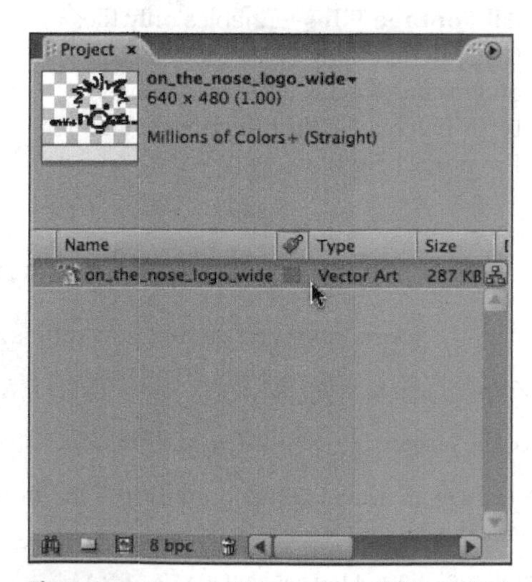

Figure 4.47 Imported items appear in the Project panel as footage files.

when you plan to use several stills for the same duration, such as a series of title cards for a credit sequence. Of course, you can always change the duration (or trim) of the layer later.

To change the default duration of still images:

1. Choose After Effects > Preferences > Import (Mac) or Edit > Preferences > Import (Windows) (**Figure 4.48**).

   The Import panel of the Preferences dialog box appears (**Figure 4.49**).
2. In the Still Footage section, *do one of the following* (**Figure 4.50**):
   - ▲ Select Length of Composition to make the still-images' duration the same as that of the composition you're adding them to.
   - ▲ Select the radio button next to the Time field and enter a default duration for imported still images.
3. Click OK to set the changes and exit the Preferences dialog box.

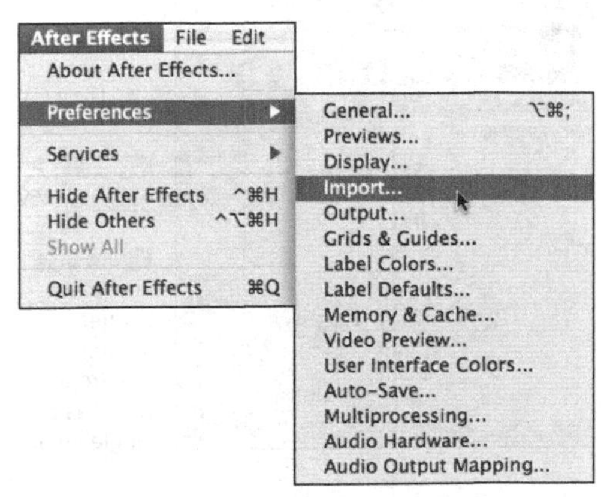

Figure 4.48 Choose After Effects › Preferences › Import (Mac) or Edit › Preferences › Import (Windows).

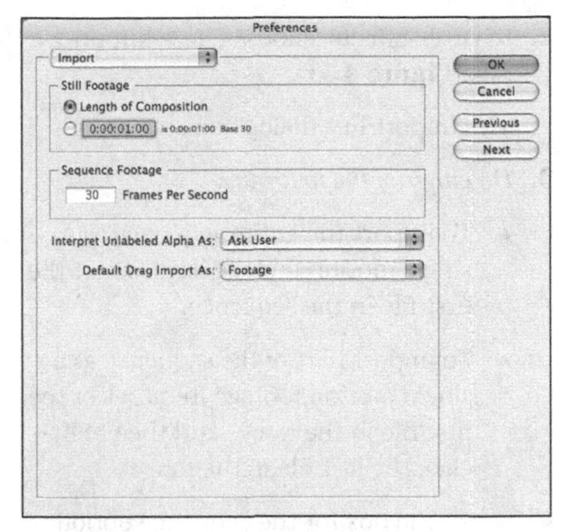

Figure 4.49 The Import panel of the Preferences dialog box appears.

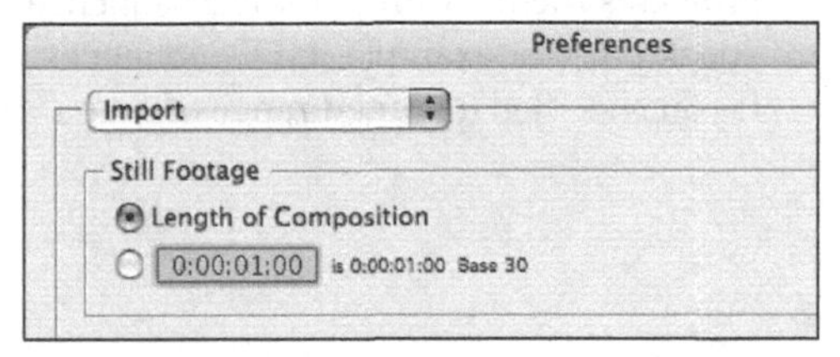

Figure 4.50 Set the default duration of still images to the duration of the composition or enter a custom duration.

Importing Still-Image Sequences

Many programs (including After Effects) can export motion footage not as a single movie file, but as a series of still images, or a *still-image sequence*. You can import all or part of a still-image sequence as a single motion footage item.

To import a still-image sequence:

1. Make sure all the still-image files in the sequence follow a consistent numeric or alphabetical filename pattern and are contained in the same folder.

2. In After Effects, choose File > Import > File (**Figure 4.51**).

   The Import File dialog box appears.

3. *Do either of the following:*

   ▲ To import the entire sequence as a single motion footage item, select the first file in the sequence.

   ▲ To import part of the sequence as a single motion footage item, select the first file in the range, and then Shift-click the last file in the range.

4. Select the box for the Sequence option (**Figure 4.52**).

   The Import File dialog box automatically indicates the file format for the Sequence check box (for example, TIFF Sequence). If you specified a limited range of sequence to import, the dialog box also displays the range next to the Sequence check box.

5. Click Open to import the file sequence and close the dialog box.

   The image file sequence appears as a single footage item in the Project panel (**Figure 4.53**).

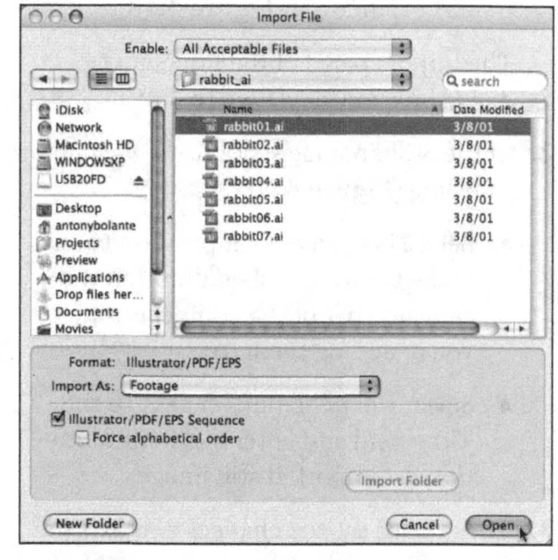

Figure 4.52 In the Import dialog box, select the first image in the sequence, and select the Sequence option.

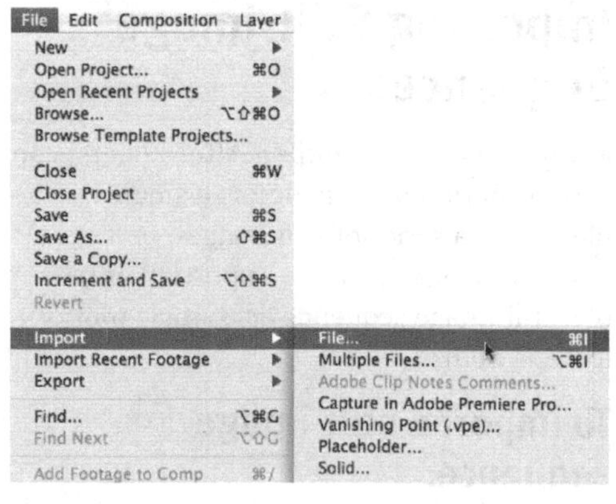

Figure 4.51 In After Effects, choose File > Import > File.

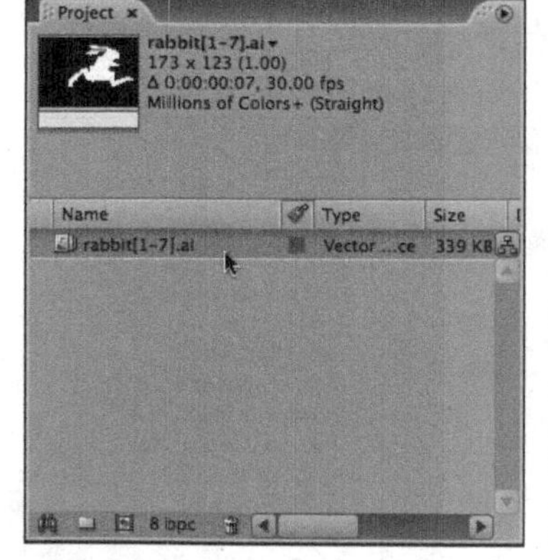

Figure 4.53 The image sequence appears in the Project panel as a single item.

To set the default frame rate for still-image sequences:

1. Choose After Effects > Preferences > Import (Mac) or Edit > Preferences > Import (Windows) (**Figure 4.54**).

   The Import panel of the Preferences dialog box appears.

2. In the Sequence Footage section of the Preferences dialog box, enter a frame rate (**Figure 4.55**).

3. Click OK to set the default frame rate and close the Preferences dialog box.

✔ Tip

- Dragging a folder of stills from the operating system is another way to import the folder's contents as an image sequence. (To import separate footage items within a folder, Option/Alt-drag the folder to the Project panel.)

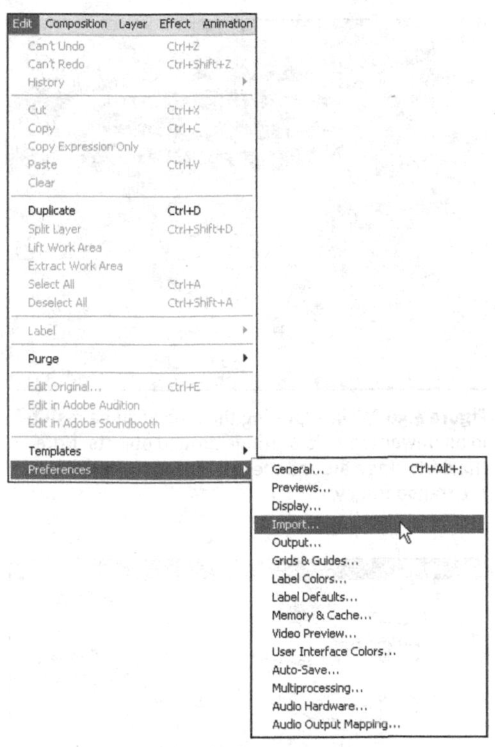

Figure 4.54 Choose After Effects › Preferences › Import (Mac) or Edit › Preferences › Import (Windows).

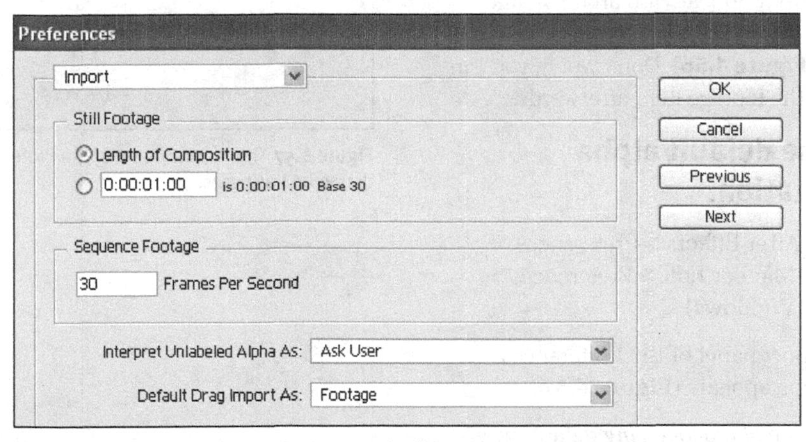

Figure 4.55 Enter a frame rate for imported still-image sequences.

Importing Files with Alpha Channels

A file's transparency information can be saved in two ways: as straight alpha or as premultiplied alpha. Both types store transparency information in an alpha channel. But in a file with a premultiplied alpha channel, the visible channels also take transparency into account. In semitransparent areas (including smooth edges), the RGB channels are mixed—or *multiplied*—with the background color (usually black or white).

When you import a file containing an alpha channel, After Effects tries to detect a label (encoded in the file) that indicates whether the alpha is straight or premultiplied and processes, or interprets, it accordingly. But if the alpha is unlabeled, After Effects interprets it according to a default you set in the Preferences dialog box. Alternatively, you can have After Effects prompt you with an Interpret Footage dialog box where you select how to interpret the alpha manually.

If the alpha channel is interpreted incorrectly, the footage may appear with an unwanted black or white halo or fringe around the edges of objects (**Figure 4.56**). Don't worry, you can reinterpret the footage item afterwards.

Figure 4.56 Misinterpreting the type of alpha results in an unwanted halo or fringe around objects. Note the dark fringe around the letters and the darkness in the transparency.

To set the default alpha interpretation:

1. Choose After Effects > Preferences > Import (Mac) or Edit > Preferences > Import (Windows).

   The Import panel of the Preferences dialog box appears (**Figure 4.57**).

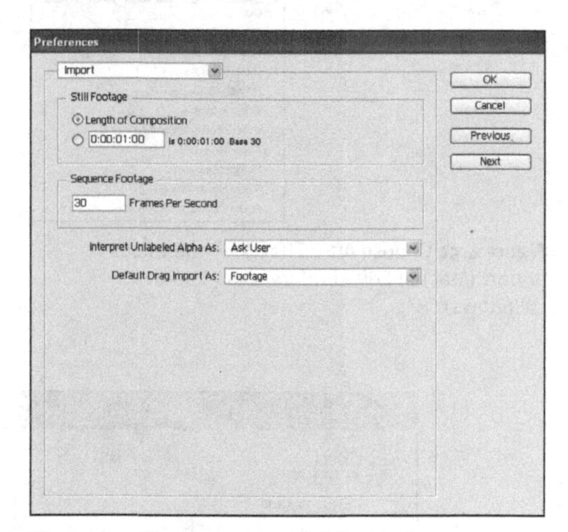

Figure 4.57 The Import panel of the Preferences dialog box appears.

2. *Choose one of the following* default interpretation methods from the Interpret

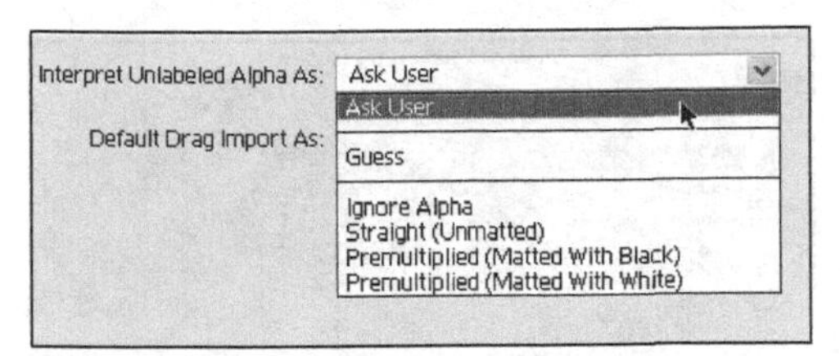

Figure 4.58 Choose a default interpretation method from the pull-down menu.

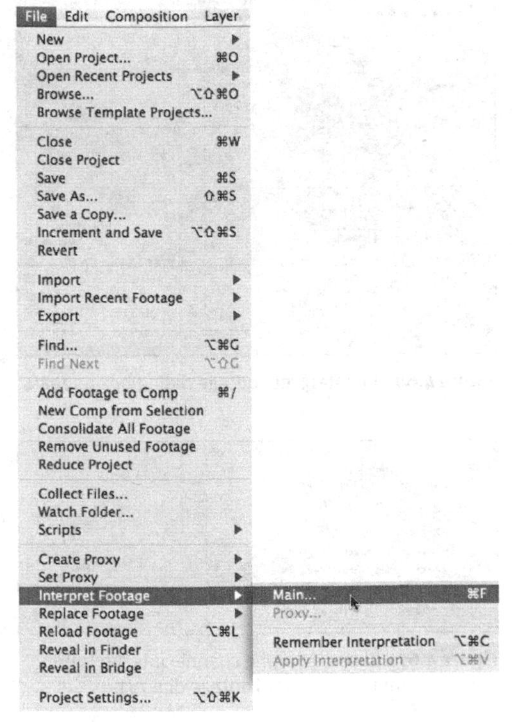

Figure 4.59 Choose File › Interpret Footage › Main.

Unlabeled Alpha As pull-down menu (**Figure 4.58**):

Ask User—You're prompted to choose an interpretation method each time you import footage with an unlabeled alpha channel.

Guess—After Effects attempts to automatically detect the file's alpha channel type. If After Effects can't make a confident guess, it beeps at you.

Ignore Alpha—After Effects disregards the alpha channel of imported images.

Straight (Unmatted)—After Effects interprets the alpha channel as straight alpha. Choose this option for a single Photoshop layer with an alpha or layer mask.

Premultiplied (Matted With Black)—After Effects interprets the alpha channel as premultiplied with black.

Premultiplied (Matted With White)—After Effects interprets the alpha channel as premultiplied with white. Choose this option to import merged Photoshop layers that use transparency.

3. Click OK to close the Preferences dialog box.

To set the alpha channel interpretation for a file in a project:

1. In the Project panel, select a file containing an alpha channel.
2. Choose File > Interpret Footage > Main (**Figure 4.59**).

   The Interpret Footage dialog box appears (**Figure 4.60**).

continues on next page

3. In the Alpha section of the Interpret Footage dialog box, choose an interpretation method (**Figure 4.61**).

   If the options are grayed out, the footage doesn't contain an alpha channel.

4. Click OK to close the Interpret Footage dialog box.

✔ Tips

- If an unexpected fringe or halo appears around the edges of a composited image, you should change the alpha interpretation.
- Internally, After Effects works in 32-bit depth (when a project is set to 8-bpc mode; see "Choosing the Color Bit-Depth Mode" earlier in this chapter). If a footage item's color space is less than this—as with a grayscale image—After Effects converts it to 32-bit depth when it displays. Similarly, if the footage doesn't contain an alpha channel, After Effects automatically supplies a full white alpha channel (which defines the image as fully opaque and visible).

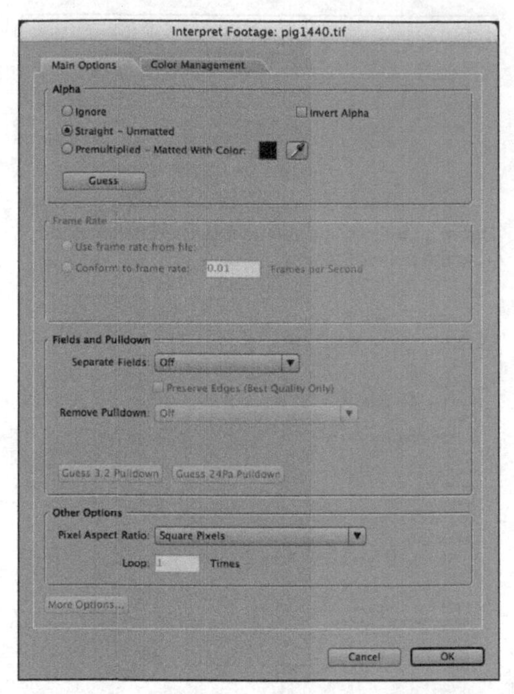

Figure 4.60 The Interpret Footage dialog box appears.

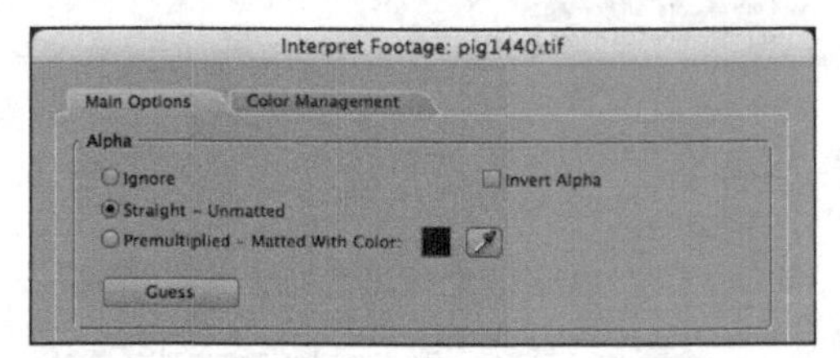

Figure 4.61 Choose an alpha channel interpretation method from the Interpret Footage dialog box.

Figure 4.62 You can import a layered file so that the layers are merged into a single footage item that uses the source document's dimensions.

Figure 4.63 You can also import an individual layer using either the dimensions of the document (in this case, 720 x 486) . . .

Figure 4.64 . . . or the minimum dimensions to contain the layer's image (this layer is 228 x 142).

Importing a Layered File as a Single Footage Item

When you import a layered Photoshop or Illustrator file as a footage item, you can either import all the layers as a single merged item or import layers individually. Importing the merged file results in a footage item with the same dimensions of the source file (**Figure 4.62**).

However, when you import individual layers, you have a choice. You can import the layer at the document's dimensions so that the layer appears as it did in the context of the other layers (**Figure 4.63**). On the other hand, you can choose to use the layer's dimensions—that is, the size of the layer only regardless of the document's size (**Figure 4.64**).

When importing a Photoshop layer that has layer styles, you can specify whether to merge the layer styles into the footage or to ignore them.

After Effects can also import all the layers assembled just as they were in Photoshop or Illustrator; you'll learn that technique in the following section.

To import a Photoshop or Illustrator file or layer as a single footage item:

1. Choose File > Import > File.

   The Import File dialog box appears.

2. Locate and select a Photoshop or Illustrator file.

3. Make sure Footage is selected in the Import As pull-down menu, and then click Open (**Figure 4.65**).

   The Import Photoshop/Illustrator dialog box appears. The dialog box has the same name as the file you're importing.

4. In the dialog box's Import Kind pull-down menu, make sure Footage is selected.

5. In the Layer Options area, *do either of the following* (**Figure 4.66**):

   ▲ Choose Merged Layers to import all layers in the file as a single footage item in After Effects.

   ▲ Select Choose Layer. Then, in the pull-down menu, choose a layer to import.

6. If you chose a single layer in step 5, specify the following options (**Figure 4.67**):

   Merge Layer Styles—Includes a Photoshop file's layer styles in the imported footage item under the property heading "Layer Styles."

   Ignore Layer Styles—Excludes a Photoshop file's layer styles from the imported footage item.

   Layer Size—Choosing this option in the pull-down menu imports the layer at its native size. Choose this option when you plan to use the layer outside the context of the other layers in the file.

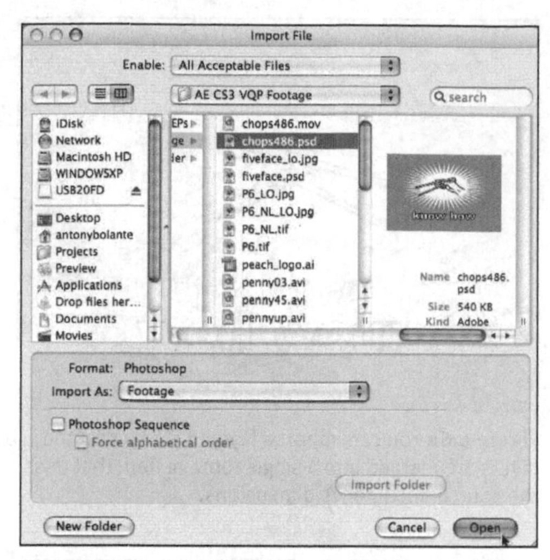

Figure 4.65 In the Import File dialog box, locate a Photoshop or Illustrator file and be sure Footage is selected in the Import As pull-down menu.

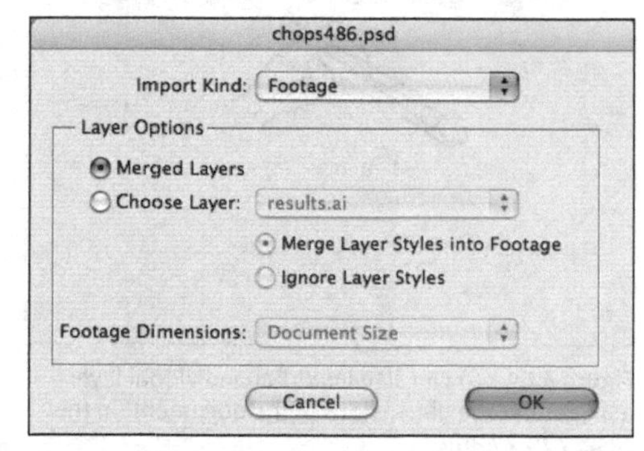

Figure 4.66 You can choose to import a single layer of a Photoshop or Illustrator file or to import merged layers.

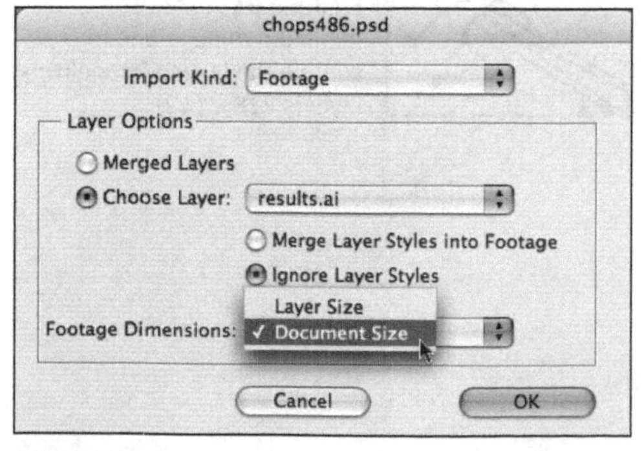

Figure 4.67 If you chose to import a single layer, specify whether to merge or ignore a Photoshop layer's layer style, and choose an option in the Footage Dimensions pull-down menu.

Document Size—Choosing this option in the pull-down menu imports the layer using the frame size of the document that contains the layer. Choose this option to maintain the layer's size and position relative to the document as a whole.

7. Click OK to close the dialog box.

A footage item appears in the Project panel. When you import a single layer, the name of the footage item is the name of the layer followed by the name of the Photoshop or Illustrator file. When you import merged layers, the name of the footage item is the name of the Photoshop or Illustrator file (**Figure 4.68**).

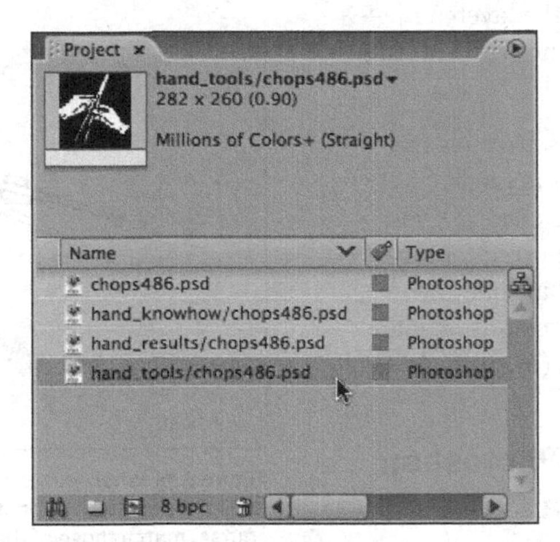

Figure 4.68 In the Project panel, single and merged Photoshop or Illustrator layers are clearly named.

Photoshop Styles and Text

After Effects retains practically every aspect of Photoshop files, including text and layer styles (such as drop shadow, inner glow, and so on). Initially, text and layer styles aren't fully editable—but you can remedy that with a simple menu command. Once you make Photoshop text a full-fledged After Effects text layer, you can employ all of After Effects' typesetting and text animation capabilities. By making layer styles After Effects-native, you can modify and animate layer styles as you would any other layer property (covered in Chapter 5).

In After Effects' timeline, select the layer that contains text imported from Photoshop and choose Layer > Convert to Editable Text. Similarly, you can select a layer that uses Photoshop layer styles and choose Layer > Layer Styles > Convert to Editable Styles.

Importing a Layered File as a Composition

One of After Effects' greatest strengths is its ability to import a layered Photoshop or Illustrator file as a ready-made composition—which consists of footage items arranged in time and space. After Effects not only imports all the layers as footage items but also arranges the layers in a composition of the same dimensions. In essence, the composition replicates the layered file—suddenly transported into the world of After Effects (**Figure 4.69**).

As when you import layers separately (see "Importing a Layered File as a Single Footage Item," earlier in this chapter), you can choose whether the imported footage items (conveniently located in their own folder) use their native dimensions or share the new comp's dimensions (**Figures 4.70** and **4.71**).

To import an Adobe Photoshop or Illustrator file as a composition:

1. Choose File > Import > File (**Figure 4.72**).

   The Import File dialog box appears.

Figure 4.69 After Effects can convert a layered file into a composition containing the same layers. This way, you can manipulate each layer individually in After Effects.

Figure 4.70 When you choose Composition-Cropped Layers, the imported footage includes the image only—in this case, the footage's dimensions are 314 × 125.

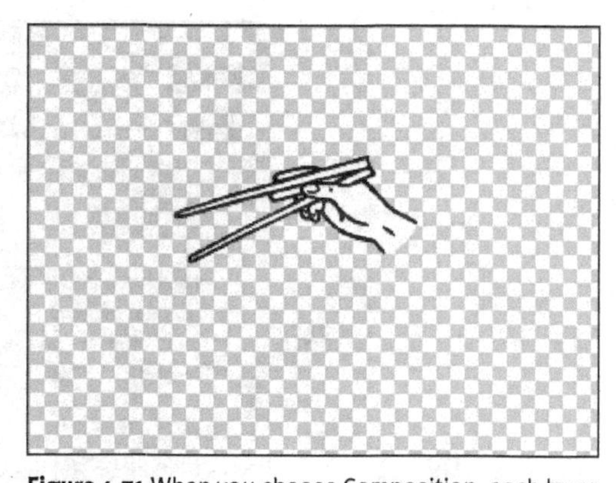

Figure 4.71 When you choose Composition, each layer uses the source document's dimensions—which, of course, match those of the imported composition. In this example, the source file's and comp's dimensions are 720 × 846.

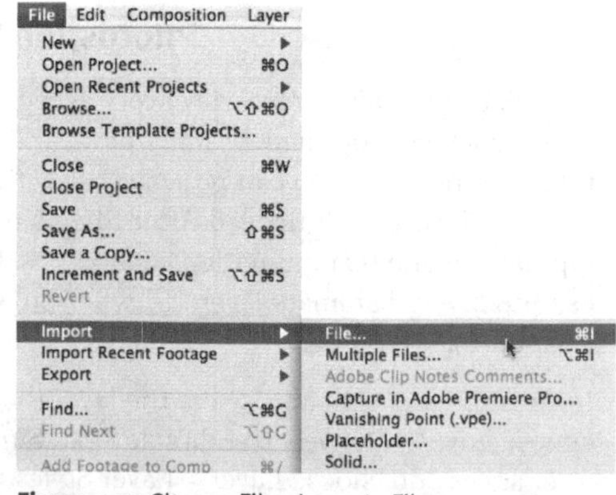

Figure 4.72 Choose File › Import › File.

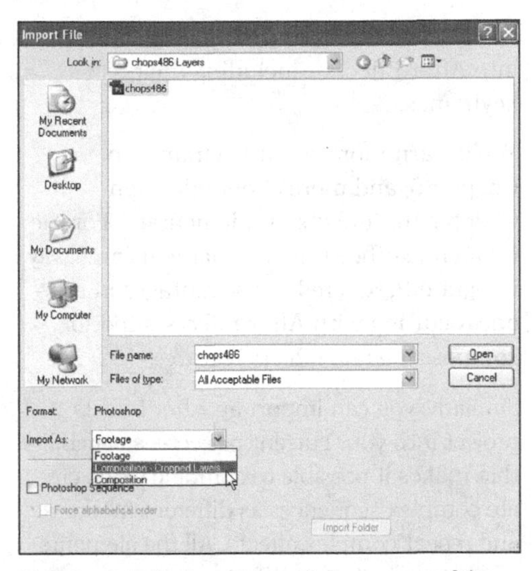

Figure 4.73 In the Import As pull-down menu of the Import File dialog box, choose the appropriate option.

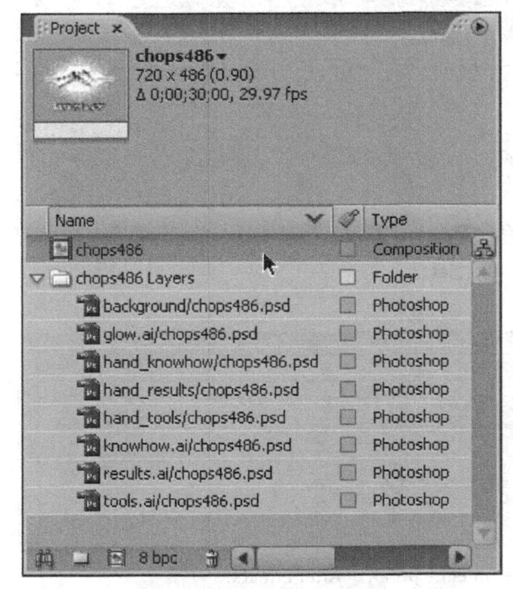

Figure 4.74 The Photoshop file appears both as a composition and as a folder containing individual layers.

2. Select an Adobe Photoshop or Illustrator file.
3. In the Import As pull-down menu, *choose either of the following* (**Figure 4.73**):

   Composition - Cropped Layers—Imports each source layer at its native size.

   Composition—Imports each source layer at the document's size.
4. Click Import.

   In the Project panel, the imported Photoshop or Illustrator file appears both as a composition and as a folder containing the individual layers imported as separate footage items (**Figure 4.74**).

✔ Tip

- After Effects imports Photoshop clipping groups as nested compositions within the main composition of the Photoshop file. After Effects automatically applies the Preserve Underlying Transparency option to each layer in the clipping group.

Importing Premiere Pro and After Effects Projects

Because After Effects can import projects from Premiere Pro, it's simple to move work from Adobe's non-linear editor for treatment in the company's advanced animation/compositing/effects program (and vice versa).

Each sequence in the Premiere Pro project appears in After Effects as a composition (in which each clip is a layer) and a folder of clips. In the composition, After Effects preserves the clip order, duration, and In and Out points, as well as marker and transition locations (**Figures 4.75 and 4.76**). Because Premiere Pro includes many After Effects filters, any effects shared by the two programs will also be transferred from Premiere Pro into After Effects—including their keyframes.

You'll learn more about keyframes in Chapter 5; and more about effects in Chapter 16, "Effects Fundamentals." For the moment, suffice it to say that you can easily integrate Premiere Pro's advantages in non-linear editing with After Effects' superior compositing and effects features.

Similarly, you can import an After Effects project into your current project—a capability that makes it possible to combine work, create complex sequences as different modules, and repeat complex effects. All the elements of an imported After Effects project are contained in a folder in the current project.

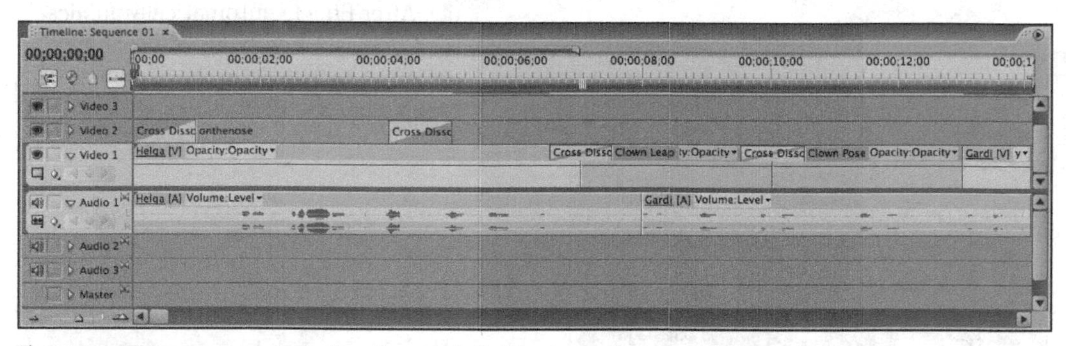

Figure 4.75 When you compare the Timeline panel of a Premiere project...

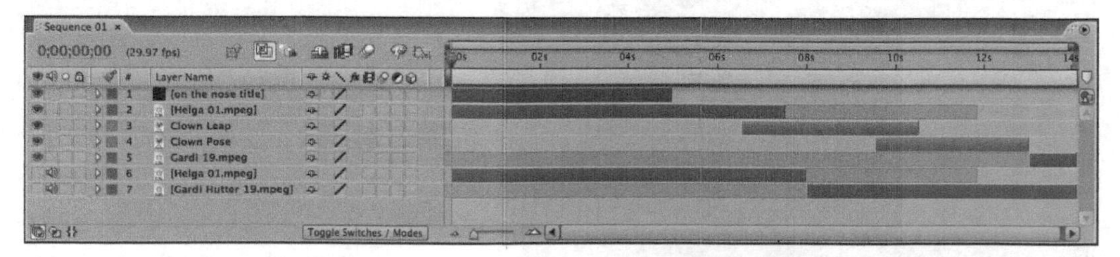

Figure 4.76 ...you can see how clips translate into layers in the Timeline panel of After Effects.

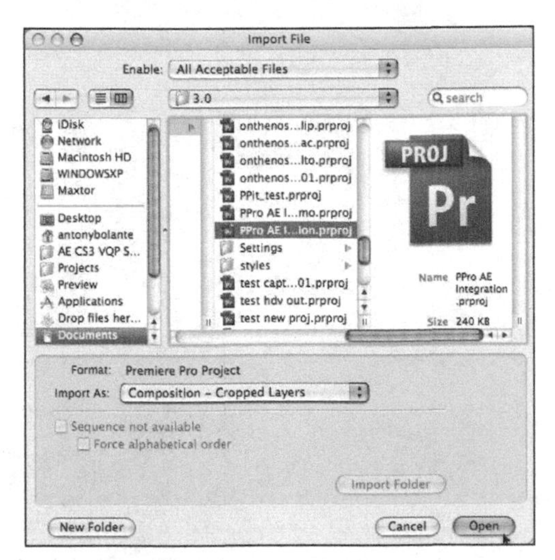

Figure 4.77 In the Import File dialog box, locate a Premiere Pro project and click Open.

Figure 4.78 Specify the Premiere Pro sequences you want to import as compositions in After Effects, and select whether you want to include audio.

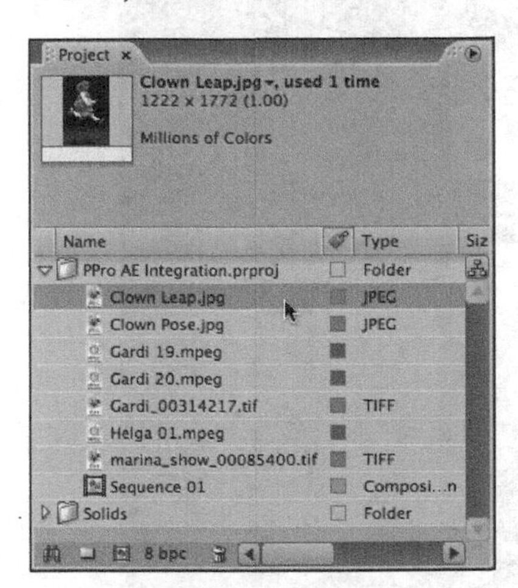

Figure 4.79 An imported Premiere Pro sequence appears in the Project panel as a composition. Clips appear as footage items, and bins appear as folders.

To import an Adobe Premiere Pro project:

1. Choose File > Import > File.

   The Import File dialog box appears.

2. Select a Premiere Pro project file (**Figure 4.77**).

   After Effects recognizes the file type automatically and selects Composition from the Import As pull-down menu.

3. Click Open.

   An Import Project dialog box appears.

4. Select the Premiere Pro sequences you want to import as compositions (**Figure 4.78**).

5. To import the audio clips in the selected sequences as audio footage items, select Import Audio. Leave the option unselected to omit the audio.

   The Premiere Pro project appears in the Project panel as a composition. Clips appear as footage items, and bins appear as folders (**Figure 4.79**). An After Effects project appears in the Project panel as a folder containing compositions and footage items.

✔ Tips

- The Dynamic Link feature allows an After Effects project to appear as a clip in a Premiere Pro sequence and reflect any changes you make without an intermediate rendering step.
- You can embed any movie exported from After Effects with a *program link*—which, as its name implies, is a link to the program that created it. This way, it's easy to reopen the project that created the movie.

Importing with Adobe Bridge

Chances are, you've accumulated a seemingly countless number of assets on your hard disks. It can be a chore to find the one you need. Fortunately, After Effects and other Adobe programs ship with a companion program—a research assistant, if you will—called Adobe Bridge.

Bridge facilitates asset management by providing a convenient way to search for, sift, and preview files. Bridge also lets you see information embedded in the file, or *metadata*. You can even apply your own metadata, label, rating, and keywords to a file, adding ways to distinguish the needle from the rest of the haystack (**Figure 4.80**).

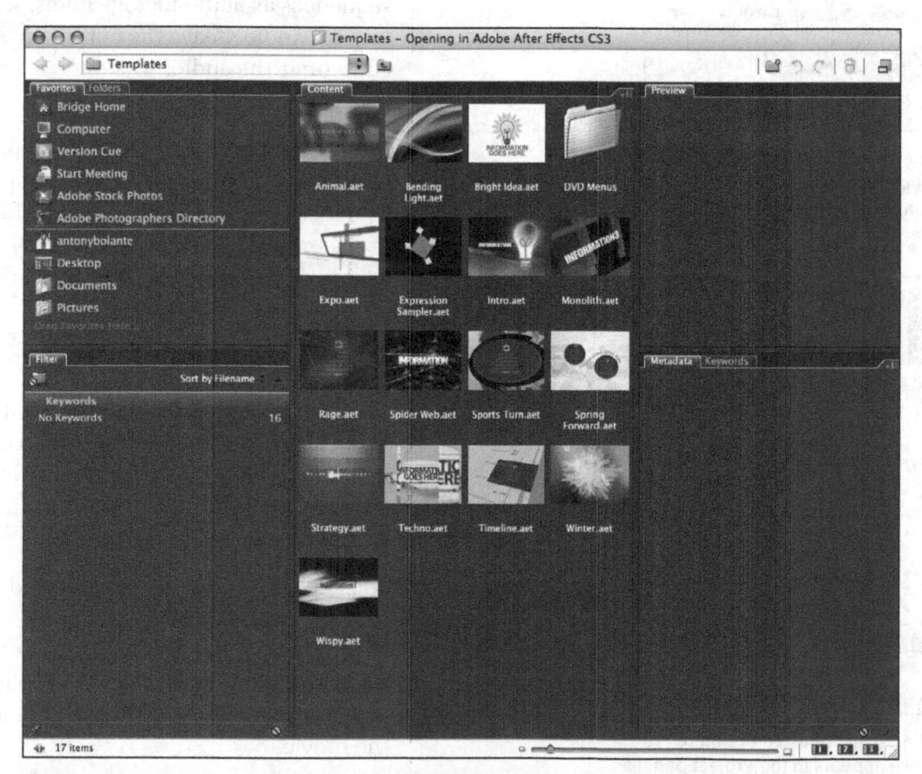

Figure 4.80 Bridge is a companion program that facilitates file management. It can help you locate and preview the file you need, including preset projects (selected here)...

Bridge also provides a great access point to numerous preset project templates. Even if you don't use these ready-made projects as templates per se, they demonstrate useful techniques and provide inspiration for your own work (**Figure 4.81**).

Naturally, this book can't cover all the features of another full-fledged program; this section focuses on browsing and importing using Bridge. Fortunately, you should get the hang of Bridge's familiar and intuitive interface with a little experimentation and a quick visit to its Help system.

Figure 4.81 ...that you can use as a template or simply as an instructional tool or source of inspiration.

To import a file or project template using Bridge:

1. *Do either of the following:*
   - ▲ To open any file, choose File > Browse.
   - ▲ To navigate to project templates directly, choose File > Browse Template Projects (**Figure 4.82**).

   After Effects launches its companion program, Adobe Bridge.

2. To navigate to the file you want to view, *do either of the following:*
   - ▲ Use the navigation tools at upper right of the Bridge window to select a disk volume or folder (**Figure 4.83**).
   - ▲ Select an item in the Favorites or Folders tab (**Figure 4.84**).

   The selected item's content appears in Bridge's large main panel. You can also open a folder by double-clicking it in the main panel. (The appearance of items in the main panel depends on the position of the icon size and viewing mode, which you can set using controls at lower right of the window.)

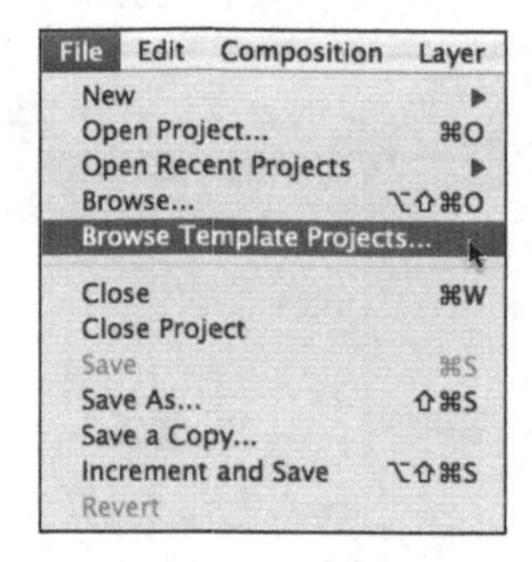

Figure 4.82 To find any file using Bridge, choose File › Browse; to go straight to project templates, choose File › Browse Template Projects (shown here).

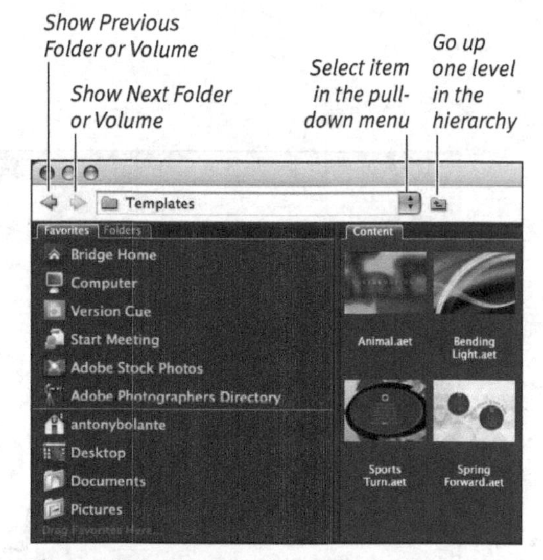

Figure 4.83 In Bridge, navigate using the browser-style navigation tools at the top of the window...

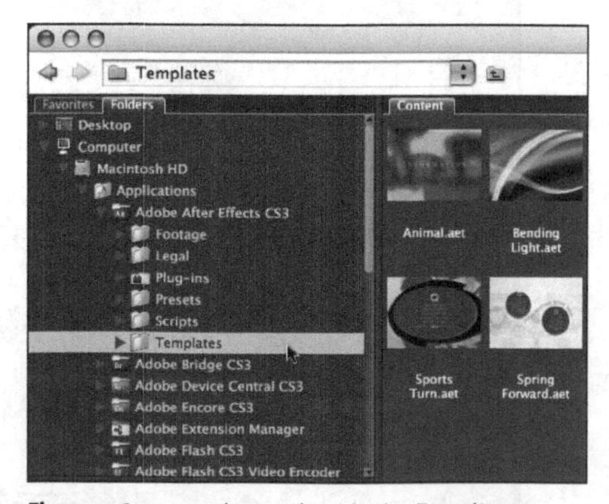

Figure 4.84 ...or select an item in the Favorites or Folders tab.

Figure 4.85 The selected item appears in the Preview tab; additional information appears in the Metadata and Keywords tabs.

3. To view a preview image and other information about the item, select the item.

   The item's image appears in Bridge's Preview tab. Motion footage and templates include standard playback controls. The item's metadata and keywords appear in the corresponding tabbed areas (**Figure 4.85**).

4. In the Bridge's main panel, double-click the item you want to import (**Figure 4.86**).

   After Effects may prompt you to specify options according to the type of item you import. (Refer to the section in this chapter pertaining to the file type.) The item appears in After Effects' Project panel (**Figure 4.87**).

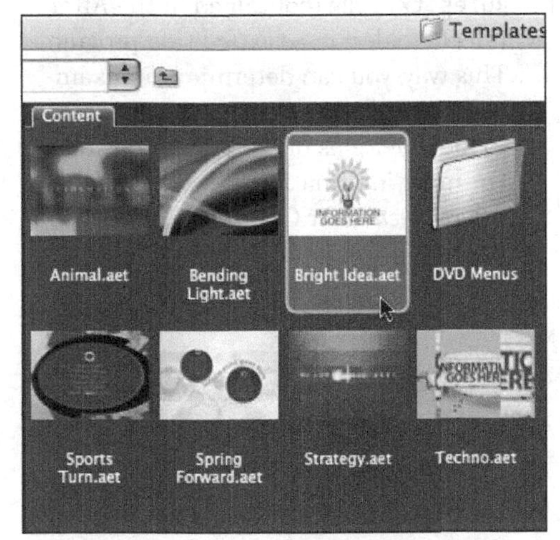

Figure 4.86 Double-clicking the item in Bridge's main panel...

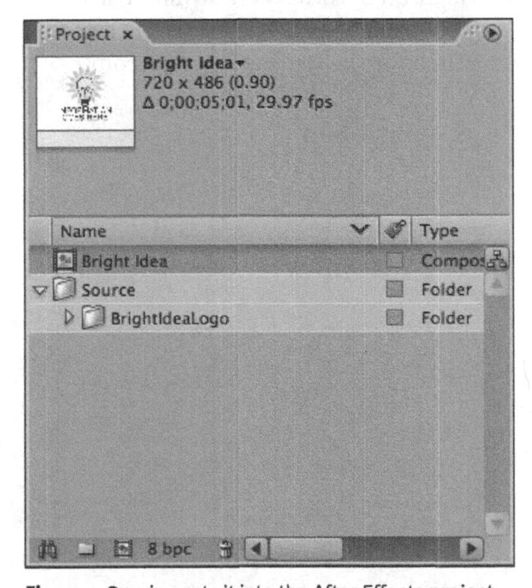

Figure 4.87 ...imports it into the After Effects project.

Motion Footage

The procedures for importing motion footage varies little from the procedures for importing other file types. But just as footage with alpha channels must be interpreted correctly, motion footage items possess unique attributes that must be processed properly. In the following sections, you'll use the Interpret Footage dialog box to specify how After Effects handles frame rate, field order, and pixel aspect ratio. This way, you can avoid or correct some of the most common problems that arise from misinterpreting motion footage. You'll also use the Interpret Footage dialog box to loop a footage item (without having to add it to a composition multiple times).

You can also use the Interpret Footage dialog to remove 3:2 pulldown and 24Pa pulldown from video transferred from film, expand an item's luminance levels, and specify EPS options. In After Effects CS3, the Interpret Footage dialog box includes new Color Management options. For a detailed explanation of these more advanced settings, consult the After Effects Help system or search for the topic at Peachpit.com.

✔ Tips

- You import audio-only files into an After Effects project just as you would any other file. Video footage that has audio can be imported as a single footage item.
- If your final output is destined for computer display only (not video display) or if it will be displayed at less than full screen size, you should deinterlace the video before you import it. Doing so spares you from separating fields in After Effects and from processing unnecessary information.
- In the sections to follow, you'll use the Interpret Footage dialog box to help After Effects properly interpret a footage item's attributes. You can copy the settings from one item by choosing File > Interpret Footage > Remember Interpolation, and apply it to another item by selecting it and choosing File > Interpret Footage > Apply Interpolation.
- You can customize the rules After Effects uses to interpret footage automatically by modifying the `Interpretation Rules.txt` file (contained in the After Effects folder) in a text-editing program. This way, you can determine, for example, the default pixel aspect ratio applied to footage items of certain dimensions. For more information, see the *Adobe After Effects* User Guide and Help system.

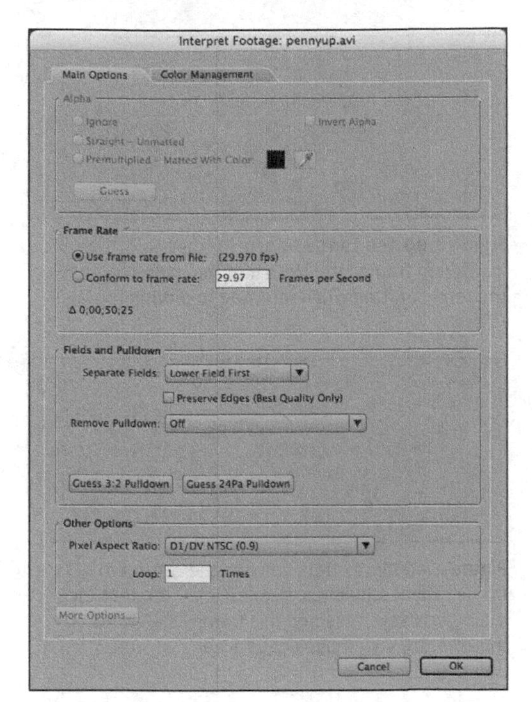

Figure 4.88 The Interpret Footage dialog box contains controls to set the frame rate of footage.

Setting the Frame Rate

Generally, you use the footage's native frame rate, which also matches the frame rate of the composition. Sometimes, however, you'll want to specify a frame rate for a footage item manually.

Because features like time stretch (see Chapter 5, "Layer Editing") and time remapping provide finer control over a layer's playback speed, it's more common to set the frame rate for image sequences than for movie files.

For example, some animations are designed to play back at 10 fps. If you interpreted such a sequence to match a 30-fps composition, 30 frames would play back in one second—three times as fast as they were intended to play. Manually specifying a 10-fps frame rate for a still-image sequence of 30 frames would result in a duration of three seconds when played in a 30-fps composition.

Conversely, many programs can't render interlaced video frames. Sometimes animators choose to render 60 fps, which can be interpreted at a higher frame rate and interlaced at output.

To set the frame rate for footage:

1. In the Project panel, select a footage item.
2. Choose File > Interpret Footage > Main, or press Command/Ctrl-F.

   The Interpret Footage dialog box appears (**Figure 4.88**).

3. For motion footage, *choose one of the following* options in the Frame Rate section (**Figure 4.89**):
   - ▲ **Use frame rate from file**—Uses the native frame rate of the footage item.
   - ▲ **Conform to frame rate**—Lets you enter a custom frame rate for the footage.

   Using a frame rate that differs from the original changes the playback speed of the movie.
4. For image sequences, enter a frame rate next to "Assume this frame rate" in the Frame Rate section of the Interpret Footage dialog box (**Figure 4.90**).
5. Click OK to close the Interpret Footage dialog box.

✔ Tip

- To interpret 60-fps animation sequences for output as interlaced fields, enter 59.94 in the "Assume this frame rate" field and use the footage item in a full-frame, 29.97-fps composition. Be sure to field-render the output. See Chapter 16, "Complex Projects," for more about rendering compositions.

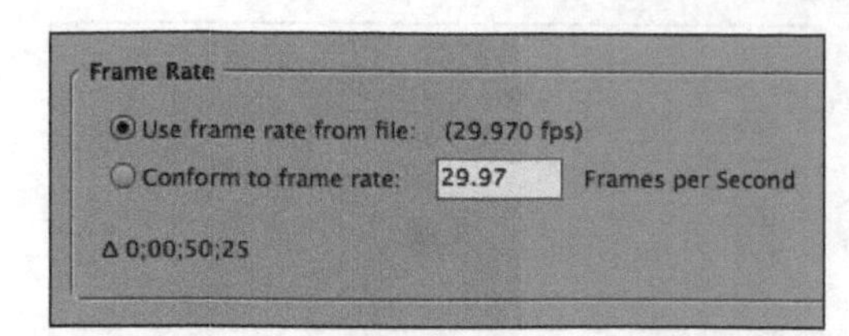

Figure 4.89 You can set movie footage to conform to a different frame rate. Note that the dialog box uses the term conform when referring to motion footage.

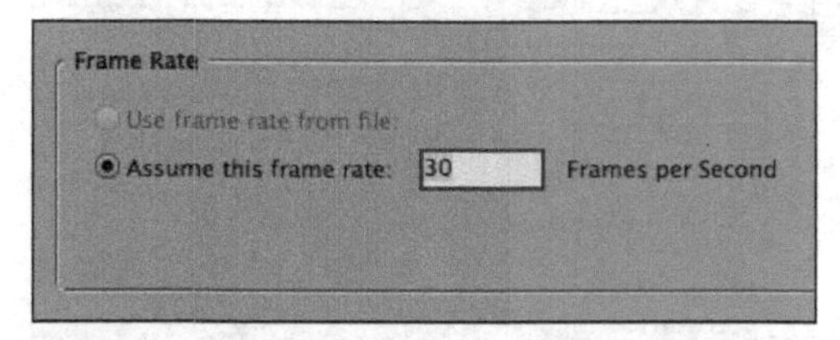

Figure 4.90 More often, you use the control to set the frame rate of still-image sequences. Note that the dialog box says "Assume this frame rate" when interpreting still-image sequences.

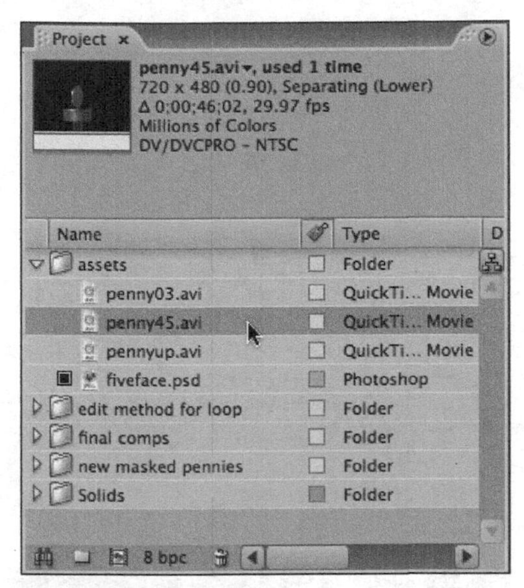

Figure 4.91 Select a footage item that uses interlaced video fields.

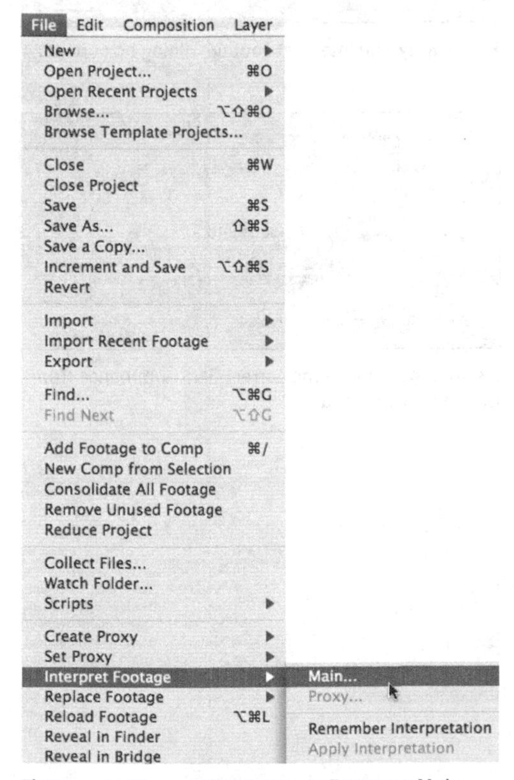

Figure 4.92 Choose File › Interpret Footage › Main.

Interpreting Interlaced Video

Depending on the format, the vertically stacked lines of video are displayed using either a progressive scan or as interlaced fields. Simply put, progressive video displays each line of video in succession, from top to bottom. In contrast, interlaced video divides each frame into two fields, which contain every other line of the image. The playback device presents one field first, and then the other to complete the frame.

When you import interlaced video, After Effects must correctly interpret the field order to play back the video accurately. If the fields are presented in the wrong order, movement appears staggered.

To interpret fields in video footage:

1. In the Project panel, select an interlaced video or field-rendered footage item (**Figure 4.91**).
2. Choose File > Interpret Footage > Main (**Figure 4.92**), or press Command/Ctrl-F.

   The Interpret Footage dialog box opens (**Figure 4.93**).

3. In the Fields and Pull-Down section, *select one of the following* options from the Separate Fields pull-down menu (**Figure 4.94**):

   Off—After Effects won't separate fields. Use this option for footage that doesn't contain interlaced video fields.

   Upper Field First—The fields of upper-field dominant source files will be separated correctly.

   Lower Field First—The fields of lower-field dominant source files will be separated correctly.

4. Click OK to close the Interpret Footage dialog box.

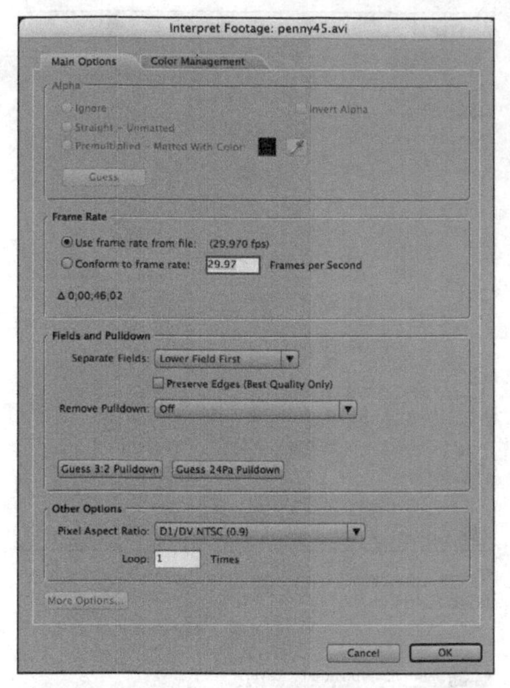

Figure 4.93 The Interpret Footage dialog box opens.

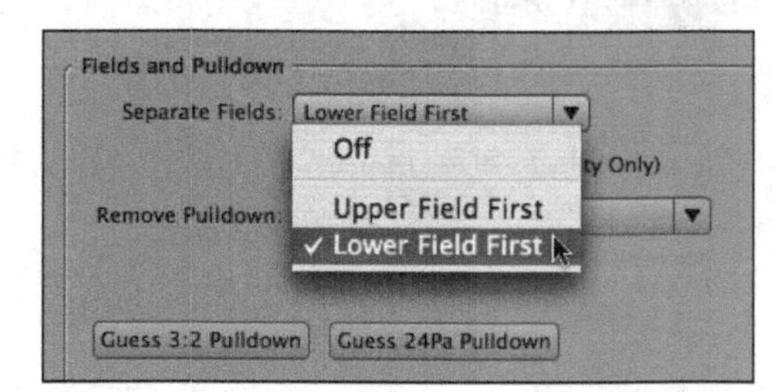

Figure 4.94 Choose the correct field dominance from the pull-down menu.

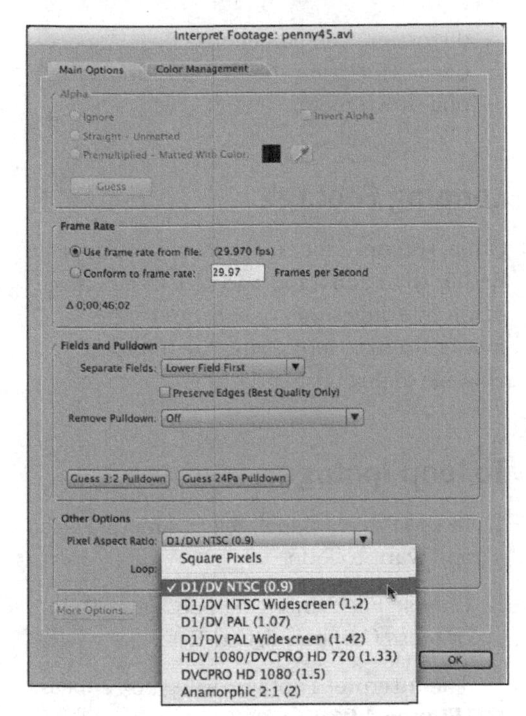

Figure 4.95 In the Interpret Footage dialog box, choose the appropriate pixel aspect ratio. Most computer monitors use square pixels to represent an image with a 4:3 aspect ratio.

Pixel Aspect Ratios

Generally, computer systems display images using square pixels (a 1:1 pixel aspect ratio, or 1.0 PAR). However, many formats, including common standards like D1 and DV, use nonsquare pixels to represent images. If you display nonsquare pixels on a square-pixel monitor, the image appears distorted. Luckily, After Effects can compensate for the difference between standards so you can use both in the same composition and output them without distortion.

After Effects automatically interprets D1 (720 × 486) and DV (720 × 480) footage to compensate correctly for their pixel aspect ratios. Nevertheless, you should check to see that your footage is interpreted correctly, and you should understand how to set the PAR for other standards. (You can even manually customize how the program automatically interprets footage; see the Help system for more about editing the interpretation rules file.)

To interpret the pixel aspect ratio:

1. In the Project panel, select a footage item.
2. Choose File > Interpret Footage > Main, or press Command/Ctrl-F.

   The Interpret Footage dialog box appears.
3. In the Other Options section, choose the appropriate Pixel Aspect Ratio setting for your footage (**Figure 4.95**):

   Square Pixels—1.0 PAR. Use for footage with a frame size of 640 × 480 or 648 × 486 and a 4:3 image aspect ratio.

   D1/DV NTSC—.9 PAR. Use for footage with a frame size of 720 × 486 (D1) or 720 × 480 (DV) and a 4:3 image aspect ratio.

D1/DV NTSC Widescreen—1.2 PAR. Use for footage with a frame size of 720 × 486 (D1) or 720 × 480 (DV) to achieve a 16:9 image aspect ratio in standard definition.

D1/DV PAL—1.0666 PAR. Use for footage with a 720 × 576 (PAL) frame size and a 4:3 image aspect ratio.

D1/DV PAL Widescreen—1.422 PAR. Use for footage with a 720 × 576 (PAL) frame size and a 16:9 image aspect ratio in standard definition.

Anamorphic 2:1—2.0 PAR. Use for footage shot with a 2:1 anamorphic film lens.

D4/D16 Standard—.9481481 PAR. Use for footage with a 1440 × 1024 or 2880 × 2048 image size and a 4:3 image aspect ratio.

D4/D16 Anamorphic—1.8962962 PAR. Use for footage with a 1440 × 1024 or 2880 × 2048 image size and an 8:3 image aspect ratio.

✔ Tips

- If you import a square-pixel image that uses a frame size common to D1 (720 × 486) or DV (720 × 480), After Effects automatically (and incorrectly) interprets that image as using nonsquare pixels. This happens because After Effects' default interpretation rules are set to assume images that use these dimensions use a PAR of .9. Use the Interpret Footage dialog box to change the pixel aspect ratio setting.
- To preview compositions that use nonsquare pixel aspect ratios without distortion, you can choose Pixel Aspect Correction from the Composition panel's pull-down menu.

Looping Footage

Often, you need footage to loop continuously. Rather than add a footage item to a composition multiple times, you can set the footage item to loop using the Interpret Footage dialog box.

To loop footage:

1. In the Project panel, select a footage item you want to loop.
2. Choose File > Interpret Footage > Main, or press Command/Ctrl-F.

   The Interpret Footage dialog box appears (**Figure 4.96**).
3. In the Other Options section, enter the number of times you want the footage to loop (**Figure 4.97**).

   You can only enter integers for complete cycles, not decimals for partial cycles. When you add the footage item to a composition as a layer, its duration reflects the Loop setting.

✔ Tip

- The Loop setting loops the content of the footage, not the movement of a layer—it's useful for turning an animation of two steps into a long walk, for example. You can't use this setting to repeat animated properties. For that, you'll need to use keyframes (Chapter 5) or expressions.

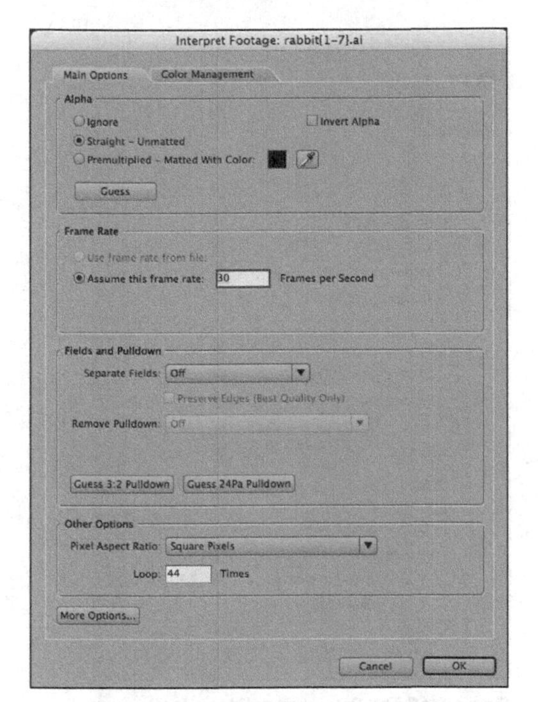

Figure 4.96 The Interpret Footage dialog box contains controls that allow you to loop a footage item (without repeating it in the composition).

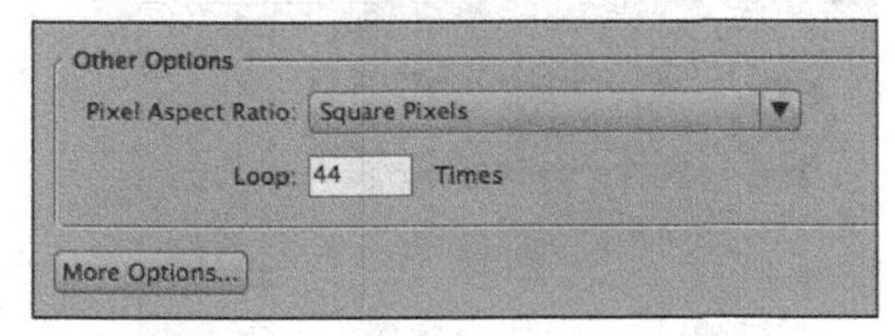

Figure 4.97 Enter the number of times you want the footage item to loop.

Managing Footage

As you saw in the previous chapter, the Project panel is basically a list of all your footage and compositions. The more complex the project, the lengthier and more unwieldy this list becomes. As the receptacle of this essential information, the Project panel can resemble either a cluttered junk drawer or a neat filing cabinet, a cardboard box filled with books or the Library of Congress. In this chapter, you'll learn how to use the Project panel to organize and sort the items contained in your project. You'll also learn about other aspects of asset management—such as how to replace missing footage, and how to use placeholders and proxies to temporarily stand in for footage items. As always, taking a little time to prepare will save you a lot of time in the long run.

This chapter also introduces you to the Footage panel, which lets you not only see your footage but really scrutinize it. Most of the controls in the Footage panel are also found in the Composition and Layer panels, which means that learning these controls now will go a long way toward providing the grounding you need later.

Displaying Information in the Project Panel

The Project panel (**Figure 4.98**) furnishes you with several ways to manage your footage and compositions. Icons that resemble those used on the desktop (Mac) or Explorer (Windows) provide an easy means of distinguishing between footage types. You can also view more detailed information about items in the Project panel, organize items into folders, and sort items according to categories. Depending on your needs, you can rearrange, resize, hide, or reveal the categories. And if you still need help locating an item, you can find it using the Project panel's Find button. There's also a button that lets you access a flowchart view of your project—but that explanation will wait for later when it will make more sense.

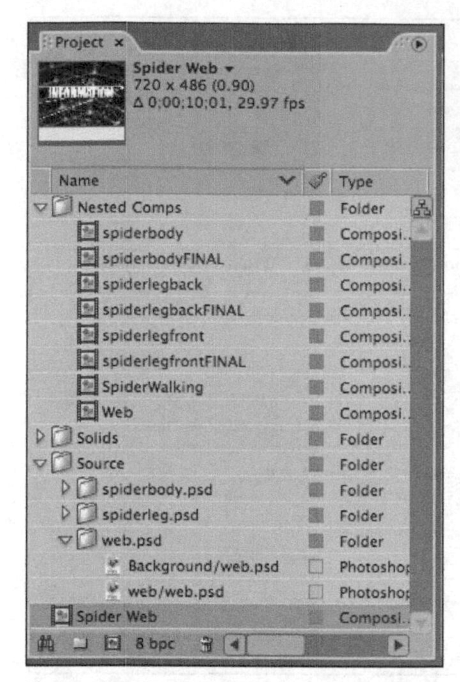

Figure 4.98 The Project panel doesn't simply list items; it helps you identify, sort, and organize them.

To display information about a footage item or composition:

◆ In the Project panel, click a footage item to select it.

  At the top of the Project panel, a thumbnail image of the footage item appears. Next to the thumbnail image, the name of the footage item appears, as well as information about the footage itself, such as frame size, color depth, codec, and so on (**Figure 4.99**).

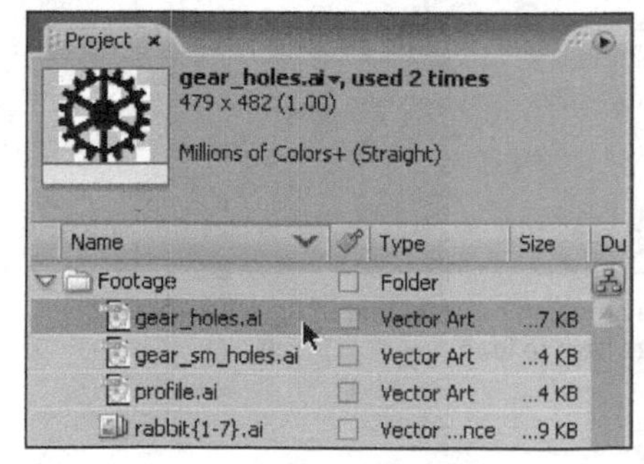

Figure 4.99 When you select an item in the Project panel, information about the selected item appears at the top of the panel.

✔ Tips

- By default, the thumbnail image displays transparency as black. To make transparent areas appear as a checkerboard pattern, choose Thumbnail Transparency Grid in the Project panel's pull-down menu.
- Option/Alt-clicking an item displays its file-type extension in addition to the usual information.

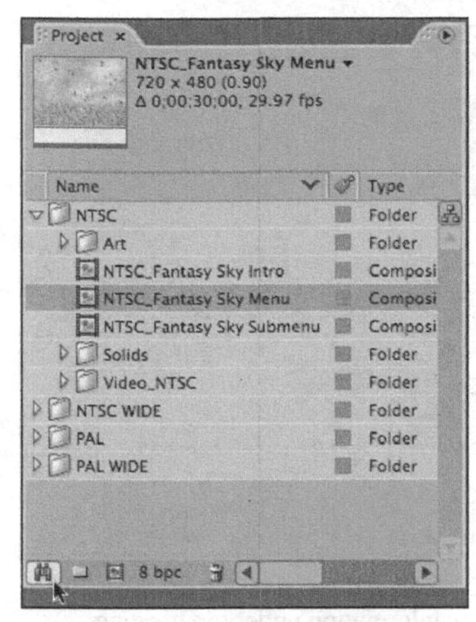

Figure 4.100 In the Project panel, click the Find button.

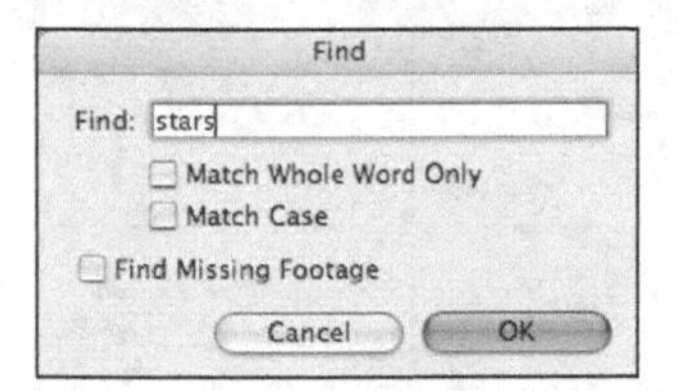

Figure 4.101 In the Find dialog box, enter all or part of the name of the item you're looking for, and select the options you want.

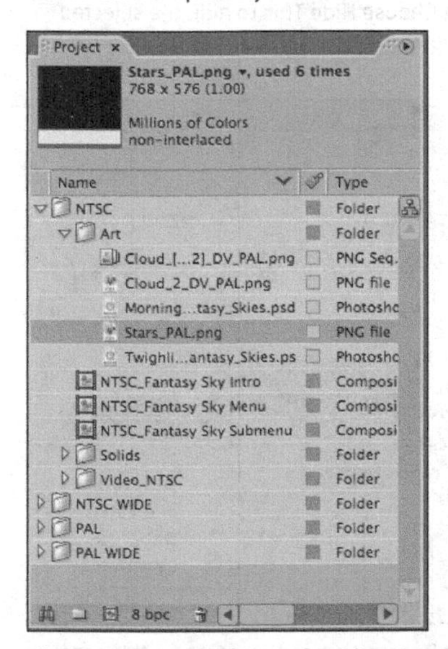

Figure 4.102 The first item matching the criteria you specified appears selected in the Project panel.

Finding Items in a Project

The Project panel includes a handy Find button to help you unearth items from your project that you've lost track of. Use it, and you'll never need to search through folders again.

To find an item in the Project panel:

1. In the Project panel, click the Find button (**Figure 4.100**).

   A Find dialog box appears.

2. Enter all or part of the name of the item you're looking for in the Find field (**Figure 4.101**).

   You can modify the search parameters by choosing the options described in the next step.

3. In the Find dialog box, select the options you want to use to modify your search:

   Match Whole Word Only—To locate only items that match the entire word you entered in the Find field.

   Match Case—To locate items that include the Find field's content, taking letter case into account. For example, a search for *Background* (with an uppercase *B*) won't locate an item called *background* (with a lowercase *b*).

   Find Missing Footage—To locate missing footage—that is, items that have lost their reference to a source file.

4. Click OK to search for the item.

   The first item that matches the criteria you specified appears selected in the Project panel (**Figure 4.102**).

✔ Tip

- Option/Alt-click the Find button to find the next item that matches the most recent Find criteria.

Sorting Footage in the Project Panel

By default, items in the Project panel are sorted by name, but you can sort the list by an assortment of other criteria, such as file type, size, duration, and so on. You can hide the column headings you don't want to use and rearrange their order. You can even assign a custom heading.

To sort footage items in the Project panel:

◆ In the Project panel, click a heading panel to sort the footage items according to the name, label, type, size, duration, file path, date, or comment (**Figure 4.103**).

To hide or display a heading panel in the Project panel:

1. In the Project panel, Control-click/right-click a heading panel.

   A context menu appears.

2. Choose an option:

   ▲ To hide the selected heading panel, choose Hide This (**Figure 4.104**). (This choice isn't available for the Name heading panel.)

   ▲ To hide any heading panel, choose Columns and a heading panel name to deselect it (**Figure 4.105**).

   ▲ To show a hidden heading panel, choose Columns and a heading panel name to select it.

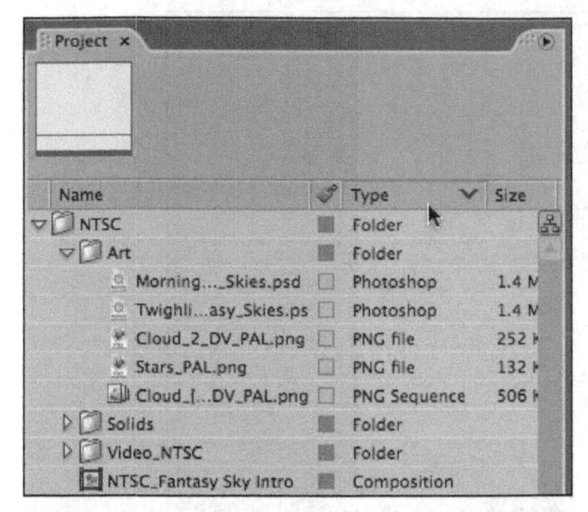

Figure 4.103 Click a heading panel to sort the items according to the information under the heading.

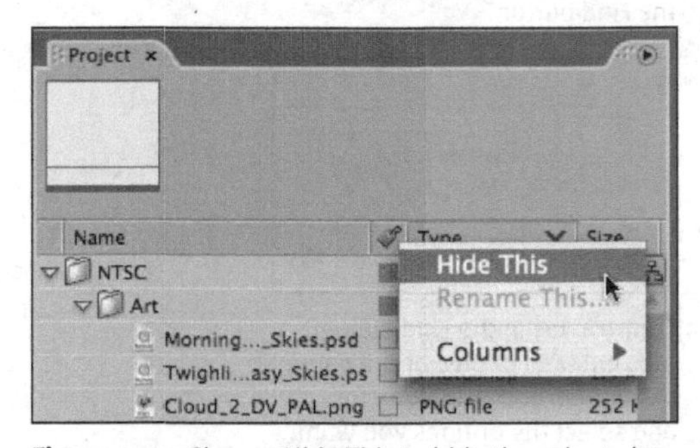

Figure 4.104 Choose Hide This to hide the selected heading panel.

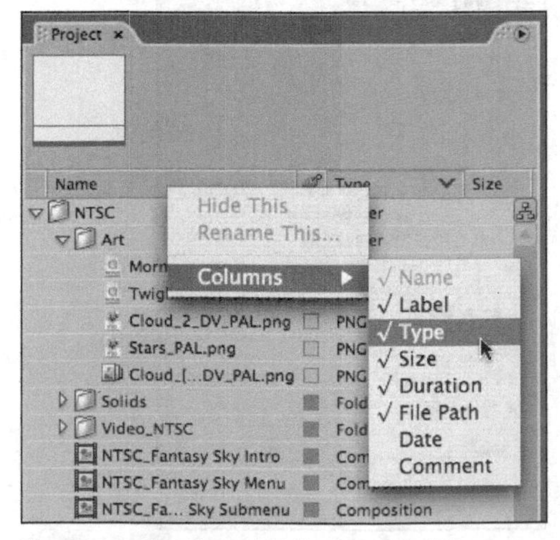

Figure 4.105 Deselect a heading name (in this case, the Type column).

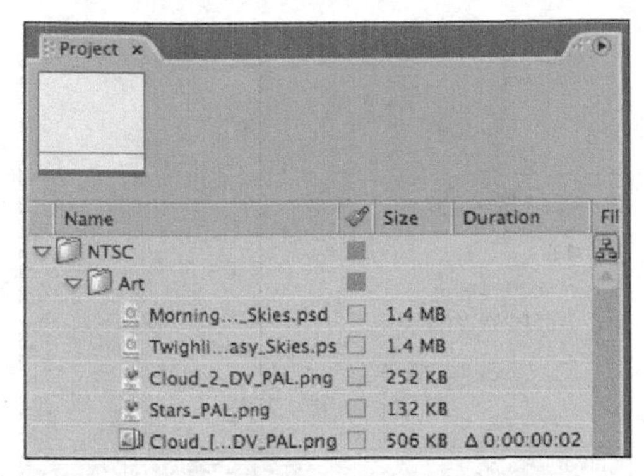

Figure 4.106 The heading and the column beneath it are hidden from view.

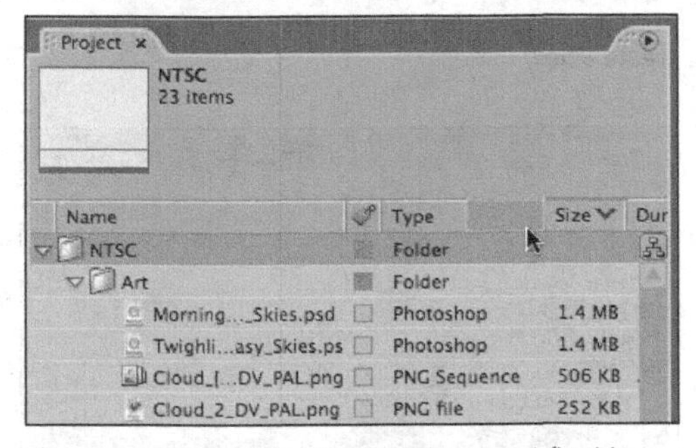

Figure 4.107 Drag the entire heading panel (in this case, the Size column) to the right or left...

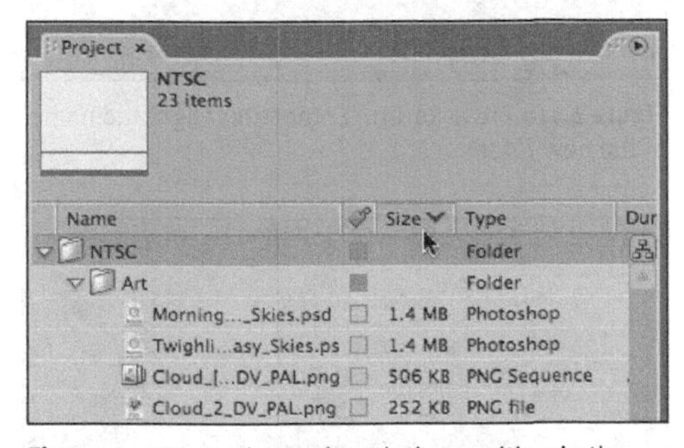

Figure 4.108 ...to change its relative position in the Project panel. Here, the Size column has been moved to the left of the Type column.

Depending on your choice, you can hide or display heading panels and the columns beneath them (**Figure 4.106**).

To reorder headings in the Project panel:

1. If necessary, resize the Project panel and make sure it displays the headings you want to rearrange.
2. Drag the heading panel(s) to the right or left to change the relative position of the heading columns (**Figures 4.107** and **4.108**).

✓ Tips

- You can rename the Comment heading by Control-clicking/right-clicking it and choosing Rename This in the context menu.
- By default, each type of footage is associated with a color label. You can sort items by label color, or reassign label colors in the Label Defaults panel of the Preferences dialog box. The timeline also represents layers using the color label.

Organizing Footage in Folders

As you learned earlier in the chapter, footage can be imported into the Project panel as items contained in a folder. Of course, you can also create your own folders to organize items in the project. Folders look and work much like they do on your operating system (particularly on the Mac's desktop). Clicking the triangle next to the folder's icon toggles the folder open and closed. The triangle spins clockwise to reveal the folder's contents in outline fashion; the triangle spins counterclockwise to collapse the outline, hiding the folder's contents. However, the folder can't open in its own window.

To create a folder in the Project panel:

1. In the Project panel, *do one of the following*:
   - ▲ Choose File > New > New Folder.
   - ▲ Click the folder icon at the bottom (**Figure 4.109**).

   An untitled folder appears in the Project panel.
2. Press Return/Enter to highlight the name of the folder (**Figure 4.110**).
3. Type a name for the folder (**Figure 4.111**).
4. Press Return/Enter to apply the name to the folder.

   The folder is sorted with other items according to the currently selected column heading.

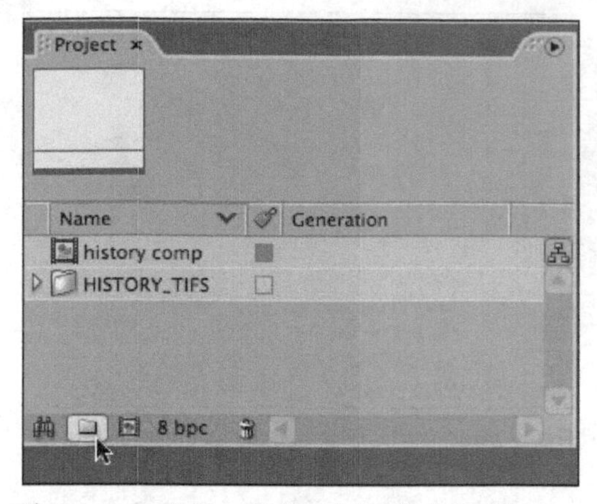

Figure 4.109 Clicking the New Folder button at the bottom of the Project panel is the easiest way to create a new folder.

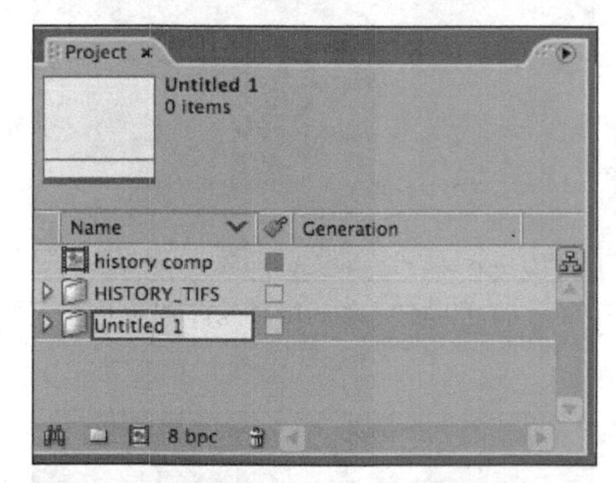

Figure 4.110 Press Return/Enter to highlight the name of the new folder...

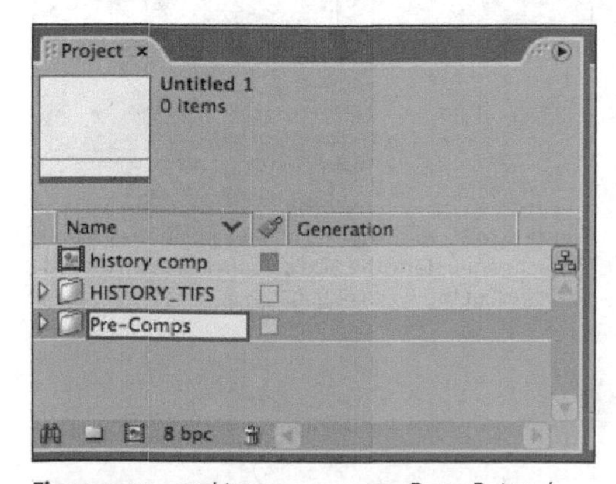

Figure 4.111 ...and type a new name. Press Return/Enter to apply the name.

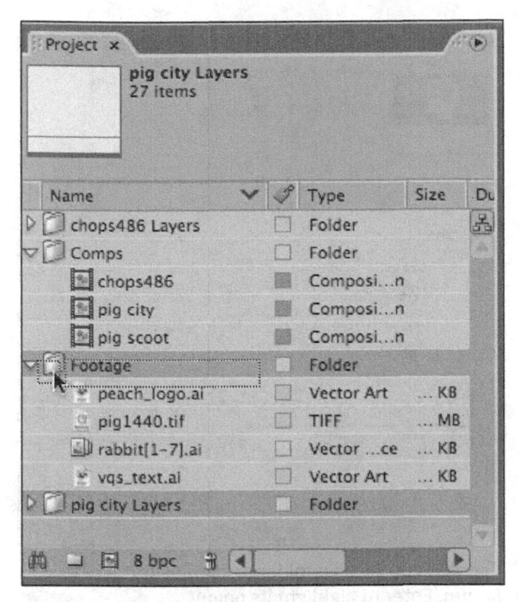

Figure 4.112 You can drag selected items directly into a folder.

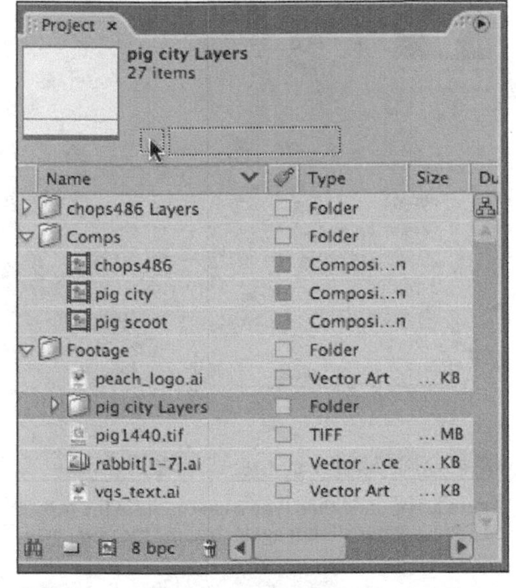

Figure 4.113 To move items out of a folder, drag them from the folder to the top of the Project panel.

To organize footage items in folders:

In the Project panel, do one of the following:

- To move items into a folder, select and drag items into the folder (**Figure 4.112**).
- To move items out of a folder, select and drag items from the folder to the gray area at the top of the Project panel (**Figure 4.113**).

Renaming and Removing Items

You can rename any footage item in the project panel. However, you'll notice that renaming items doesn't work quite like on your operating system; you have to use the Return/Enter key.

Just as important as organizing the elements you need is disposing of the elements you don't need. You can remove individual items or have After Effects automatically discard the items that haven't been used in a composition.

To rename folders or compositions in the Project panel:

1. In the Project panel, select a folder or composition.
2. Press Return/Enter.

   The name of the item appears highlighted (**Figure 4.114**).
3. Enter a name for the folder or composition (**Figure 4.115**).
4. Press Return/Enter.

   The new name of the item is no longer highlighted and becomes the current name.

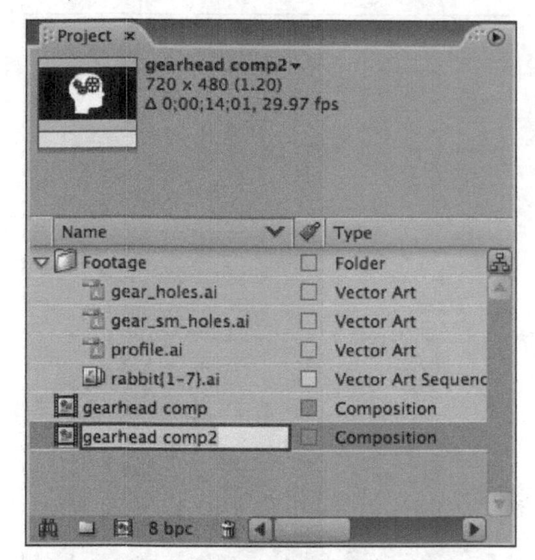

Figure 4.114 Select a folder or composition, press Return/Enter to highlight its name...

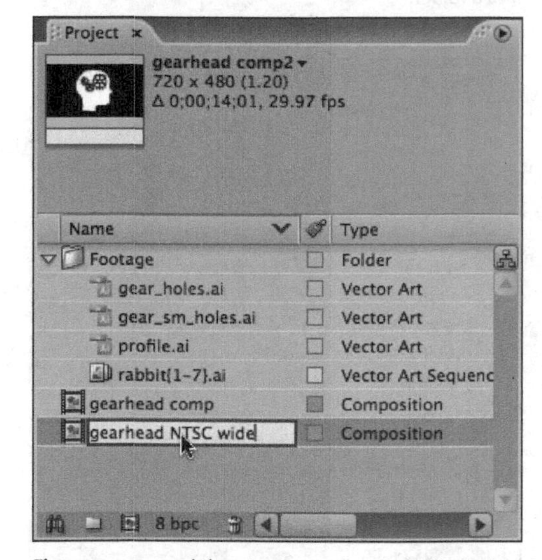

Figure 4.115 ...and then type a new name in the text box. Press Return/Enter again to apply the new name.

Figure 4.116 Click the Delete button at the bottom of the Project panel to delete selected items.

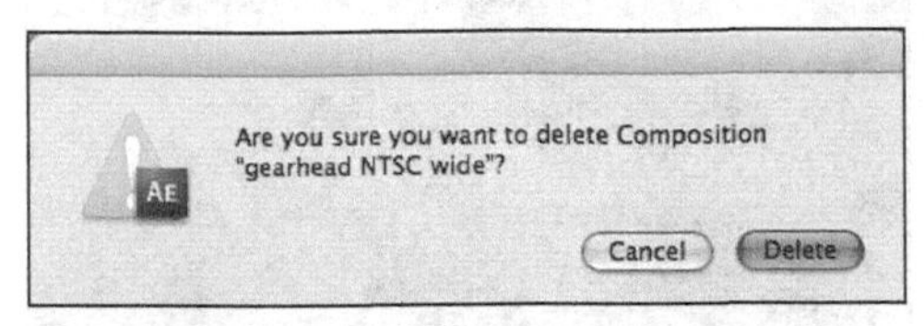

Figure 4.117 After Effects warns you if you attempt to delete an item that is in use.

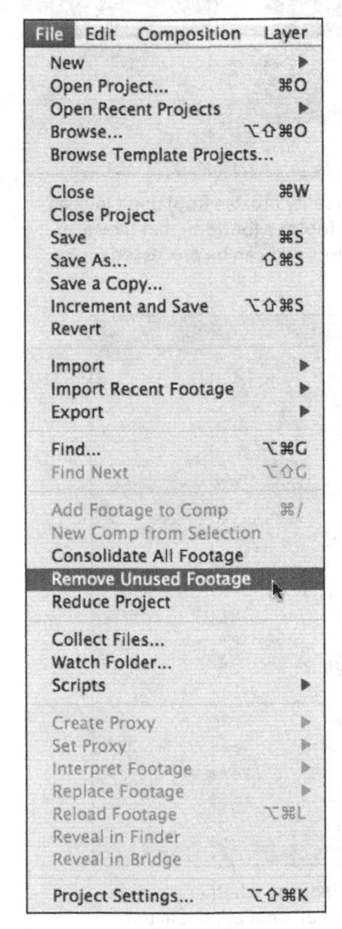

Figure 4.118 Choose File › Remove Unused Footage to remove items that aren't used in a composition.

To remove items from a project:

1. In the Project panel, select one or more items.
2. *Do one of the following*:
   - ▲ Press Delete.
   - ▲ Click the Delete button at the bottom of the Project panel (**Figure 4.116**).
   - ▲ Drag the items to the Delete button at the bottom of the Project panel.

   If any of the items are compositions or are being used in a composition, After Effects asks you to confirm that you want to delete the items (**Figure 4.117**).
3. If After Effects prompts you to confirm your choice, click Delete to remove the footage from the project or Cancel to cancel the command and retain the footage in the project.

   The footage is removed from the project and all compositions in the project.

To remove unused footage from a project:

- ◆ Choose File > Remove Unused Footage (**Figure 4.118**).

  All footage items that aren't currently used in a composition are removed from the project.

✔ Tip

- ■ Other commands aid in project "housekeeping," especially as a project nears completion. The Consolidate All Footage removes duplicate items; Reduce Project removes unselected comps and unused footage; and Collect Files copies the project's requisite files to a single location for archiving or moving to another workstation.

Proxies

A *proxy* is a low-resolution version of the actual footage (**Figure 4.119**). If you're familiar with nonlinear editing applications, you might compare using proxies to using low-quality clips for offline editing (the rough cutting phase, which often utilizes relatively low-quality copies of footage). Low-quality files take less time to process, allowing you to work more quickly. Proxies may also be necessary if you have to work on a less powerful workstation—one with less RAM, for example—than you'll finish on. When you're ready, you can replace the low-quality stand-ins with the high-quality original footage.

Figure 4.119 Low-quality proxies (top) don't look as good as the actual footage (bottom), but they also have smaller file sizes and can be processed faster.

Icons next to each item in the Project panel provide an easy way to determine whether source footage or its proxy is currently in use (**Figure 4.120**). A box containing a black square ■ indicates that the proxy is currently in use; the name of the proxy appears in bold text. An empty box □ indicates that a proxy has been assigned but that source footage is currently in use. If there is no icon, this means no proxy has been assigned to the footage item.

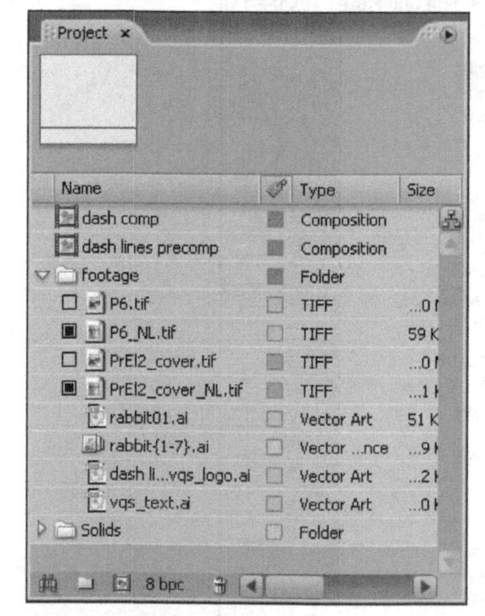

Figure 4.120 Icons indicate whether a proxy is in use or assigned to an item but not in use.

Proxies aren't effective for every circumstance, however. Although they can save time when you're animating motion, other effects—such as keying—can only be properly adjusted when using the footage at output quality.

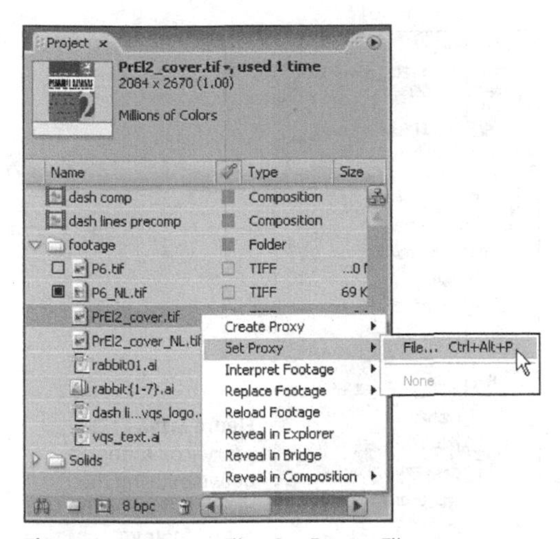

Figure 4.121 Choose File › Set Proxy › File.

To assign a proxy to a footage item:

1. In the Project panel, select a footage item to which you want to apply a proxy.
2. *Do either of the following:*
   - ▲ Choose File > Set Proxy > File.
   - ▲ Control-click/right-click the item, and choose Set Proxy > File in the context menu (**Figure 4.121**).

   The Set Proxy File dialog box appears.
3. Locate the file you want to assign as the proxy (**Figure 4.122**).
4. Click Open to select the file and close the dialog box.

   In the Project panel, a proxy icon appears next to the footage item, indicating that a proxy is currently in use (**Figure 4.123**).

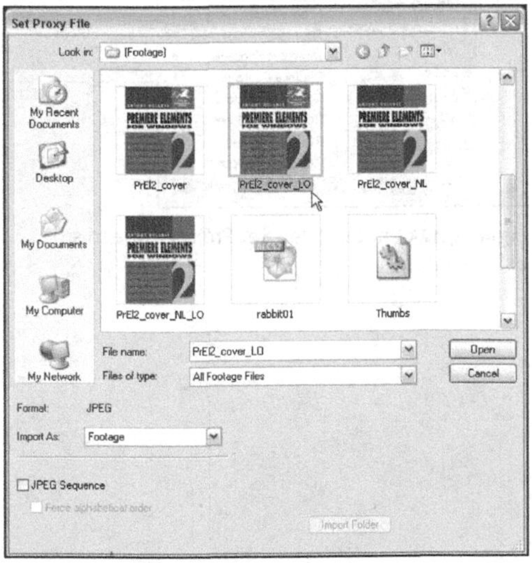

Figure 4.122 In the Set Proxy File dialog box, choose a file to act as a proxy for the actual footage.

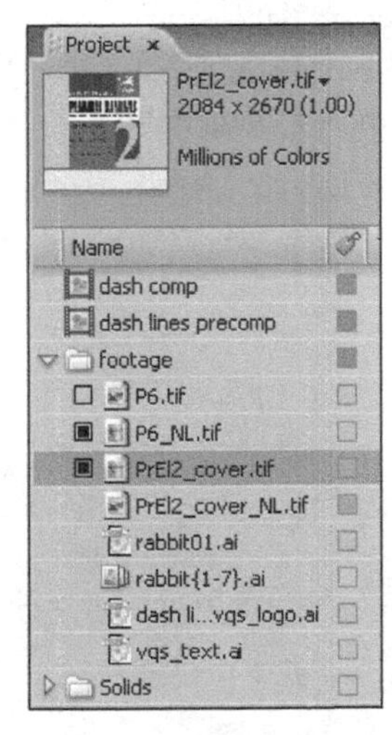

Figure 4.123 A black box appears next to the item, indicating that a proxy is in use.

To toggle between using a proxy and the original footage:

◆ In the Project panel, click the proxy icon to the left of a footage item to toggle between using the assigned proxy and using the original footage (**Figure 4.124**).

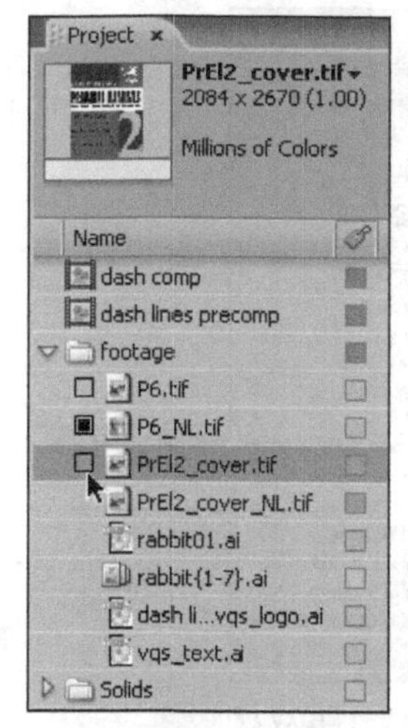

Figure 4.124 Click the proxy icon to toggle between using the proxy and using the actual footage.

To stop using a proxy:

1. In the Project panel, select a footage item that has been assigned a proxy.
2. *Do either of the following*:
   ▲ Choose File > Set Proxy > None.
   ▲ Control-click/right-click the item, and choose Set Proxy > None in the context menu (**Figure 4.125**).

   To the left of the footage item's name in the Project panel, the proxy icon disappears.

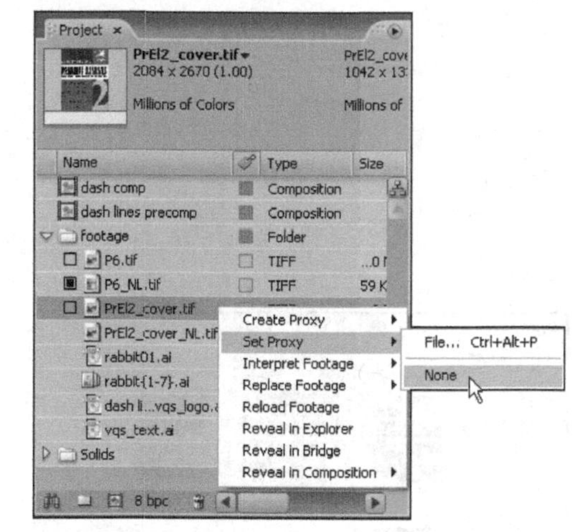

Figure 4.125 Choose File › Set Proxy › None to stop using a proxy.

✔ Tip

■ As pointed out earlier, After Effects automatically creates placeholders for missing footage. You can also create a placeholder manually, and then replace it with the actual footage item when it becomes available. You create placeholders by choosing File > Import > Placeholder.

Figure 4.126 Still images always open in an After Effects Footage panel.

Figure 4.127 By default, motion footage opens in a window according to the file type.

Figure 4.128 However, Option/Alt-double-clicking motion footage opens it in an After Effects Footage panel.

Viewing Footage

When you open an item in the Project panel, it appears either in an After Effects Footage panel or in the player native to its file type, depending on the file type and your preference.

Still images always open in an After Effects Footage panel. Motion footage and audio items, in contrast, open in the appropriate media player by default. For example, .mov files open in a QuickTime footage window; .avi files open in a Video for Windows footage window. However, you can opt to open them in an After Effects Footage panel instead.

Whereas a media player lets you play back motion and audio footage right away and at the full frame rate, the Footage panel relies on After Effects' frame rendering mechanism (explained fully in Chapter 6, "Playback, Previews, and RAM"). Therefore, the Footage panel won't necessarily play a movie at the full frame rate and won't play audio without rendering a preview. The Footage panel does offer a number of other viewing options (covered in the section "The Footage Panel," later in this chapter).

To view a footage item:

- In the Project panel, double-click a footage item.

  Still images open in a Footage panel (**Figure 4.126**); movie files open in the appropriate movie player (**Figures 4.127** and **4.128**).

To open a movie file in an After Effects Footage panel:

- In the Project panel, Option/Alt-double-click a movie footage item.

  The movie file opens in an After Effects Footage panel (**Figure 4.129**).

✔ Tips

- Some .avi files—including those using Microsoft's DirectX DV codec and files over 2 GB—will open only in an After Effects Footage panel.
- You can open any footage item in its native application by choosing Edit > Edit Original. Any changes you make to it are updated in After Effects. If not, choose File > Reload Footage.

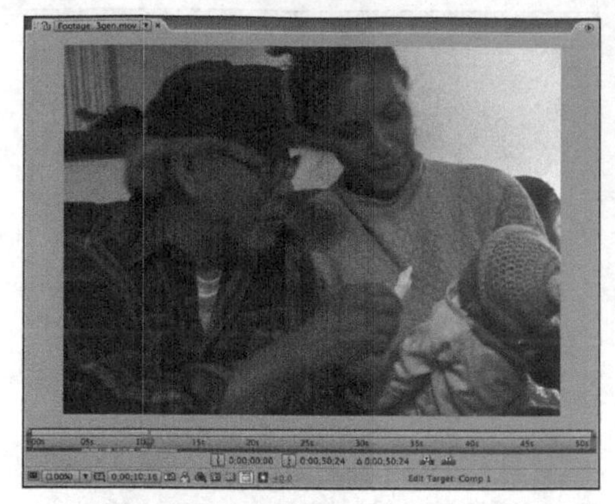

Figure 4.129 Audio files are also easier to preview in their own Footage panel.

The Footage Panel

An After Effects Footage panel has a variety of controls for viewing footage. As you might expect, it lets you play back and cue motion footage. You can magnify or reduce your view of the image, or see its individual channels. You can also show rulers, set guides, and superimpose a grid or video-safe zones. There is also a snapshot feature that lets you save and recall a frame of footage that you can use for reference (**Figure 4.130**).

As you'll see in the chapters to follow, you can also find all of these Footage panel controls in the Composition and Layer panels. If some of the controls don't seem useful now, be patient: They'll come in handy later.

The following sections cover these shared controls. Later chapters cover only the features unique to the Composition and Layer panels. Chapter 5, discusses in detail the Footage panel's controls for editing motion footage.

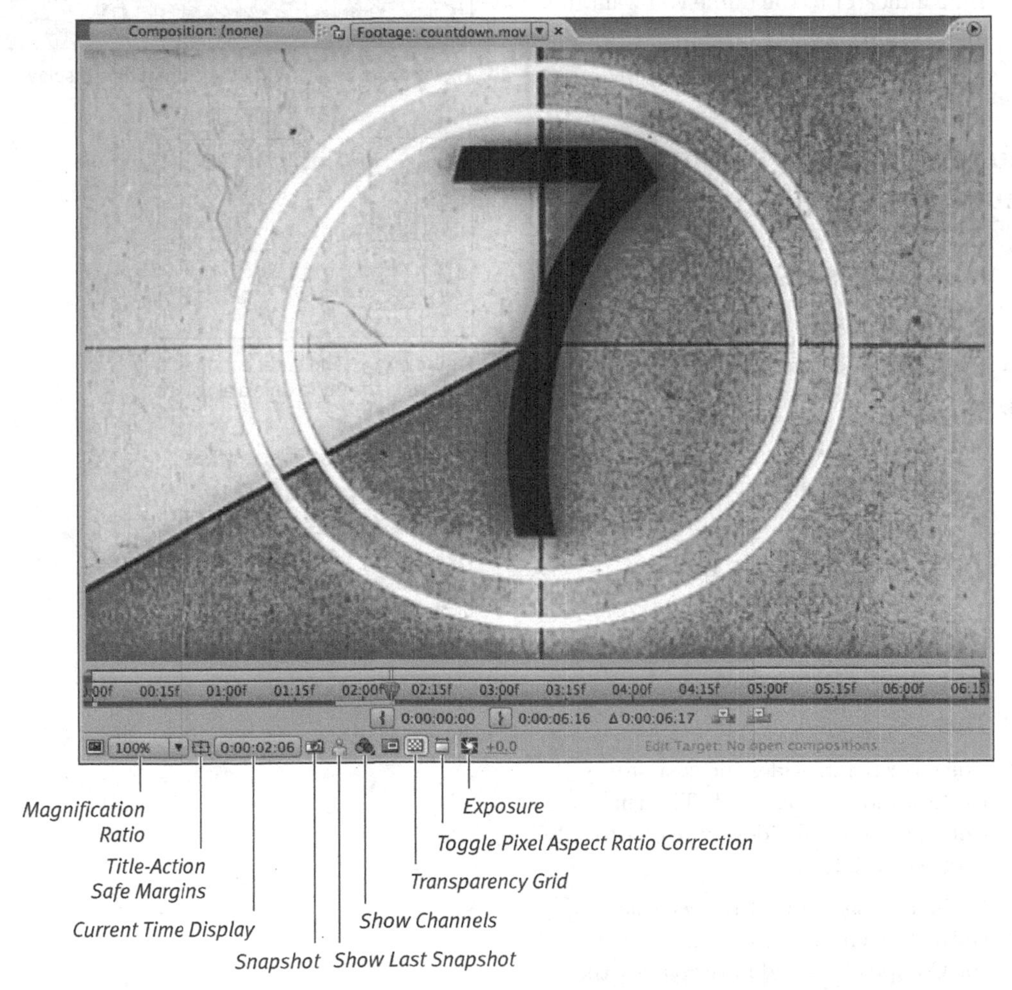

Figure 4.130 The following sections cover several features of the Footage panel that are shared by the Composition and Layer panels.

Cueing Motion Footage

Motion footage appears in the Footage, Composition, and Layer panels with a time ruler, current time indicator, and current time display. You can use the controls to view a specific frame or to play back the footage without sound.

To view a frame of motion footage by dragging:

- ◆ In the Footage panel, drag the current time indicator to the frame you want to view (**Figure 4.131**).

  The Footage panel displays the image at the current frame and the frame number.

To cue a frame of motion footage numerically:

1. In the Footage panel, click the current time display (**Figure 4.132**).

   The Go To Time dialog box opens.

2. Enter a time (**Figure 4.133**).
3. Click OK.

   The current time display and the image in the Footage panel show the frame you specified.

To play motion footage:

- ◆ Make sure the Footage, Composition, or Layer panel is active. Press the spacebar to start and stop playback.

✔ Tips

- ■ The spacebar provides the easiest way to start and stop playback. The Time Controls panel provides more control (**Figure 4.134**).
- ■ In the Footage panel, the time ruler shows the length of the source file; in the Composition and Layer panels, the time ruler corresponds to the length of the composition.

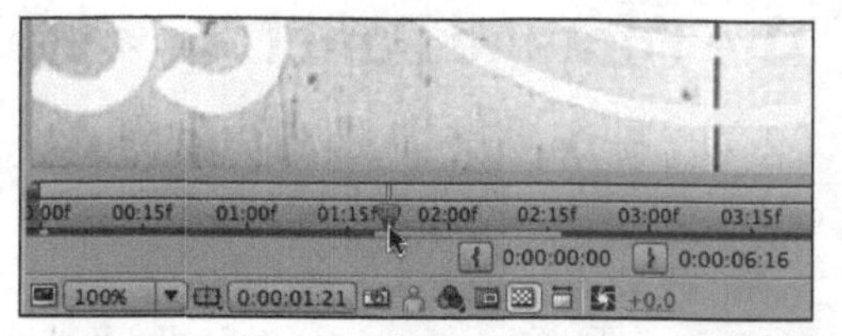

Figure 4.131 Drag the current time indicator to cue the footage to a particular frame.

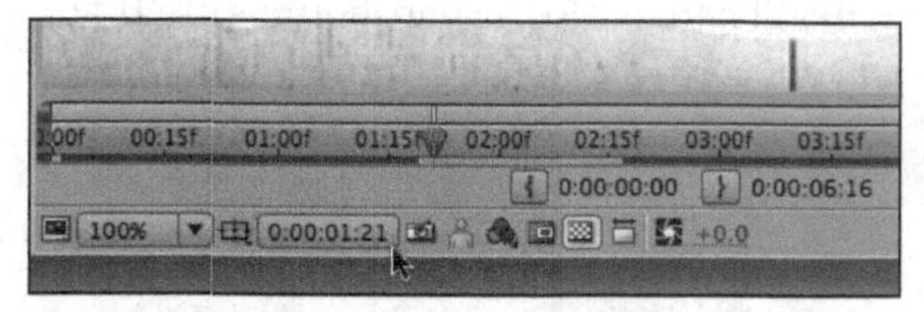

Figure 4.132 You can click the current time display...

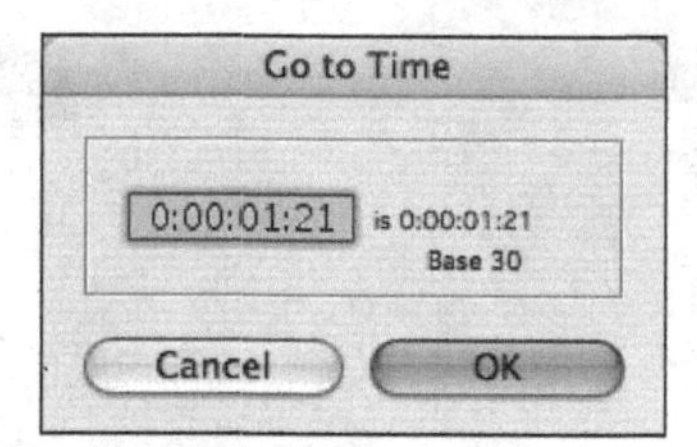

Figure 4.133 ...and enter a frame number in the Go To Time dialog box.

Figure 4.134 The Time Controls panel provides a complete set of playback options.

Figure 4.135 Choose a magnification from the pop-up menu.

Figure 4.136 The Footage panel displays the image at the magnification you specified.

Magnifying an Image

Sometimes, you'll want to magnify your footage view so that you can closely examine a detail of the image. Other times, you'll want to reduce magnification because viewing footage at 100 percent scale takes up too much screen space. After Effects lets you change the magnification ratio to suit your needs. However, keep in mind that this is for viewing purposes only: The actual scale of the footage doesn't change. You may be surprised to discover that no matter how much you magnify the image in the Footage panel, scroll bars don't appear. To view different parts of a magnified image, use the Hand tool instead.

To change the magnification of the Footage or Composition panel:

- In the Footage panel, press and hold the Magnification Ratio pop-up menu to choose a magnification (**Figure 4.135**).

  When you release the mouse button, the Footage panel uses the magnification ratio you selected (**Figure 4.136**).

To change the visible area of a magnified image in the Footage or Composition panel:

1. Select the Hand tool by *doing either of the following*:
   - ▲ In the Tools panel, click the Hand tool (**Figure 4.137**).
   - ▲ With the Selection tool active (the default tool), position the mouse pointer over the image in the Footage or Composition panel, and press the spacebar.

   The mouse changes to the hand icon (**Figure 4.138**).
2. Drag the hand to change the visible area of the image (**Figure 4.139**).

✔ Tip

- The Display pane of the Preferences dialog box includes the option Auto-zoom When Resolution Changes. Selecting this option makes the image's magnification change when you change the Comp panel's resolution setting. Note that the Footage and Layer panels don't include a resolution option.

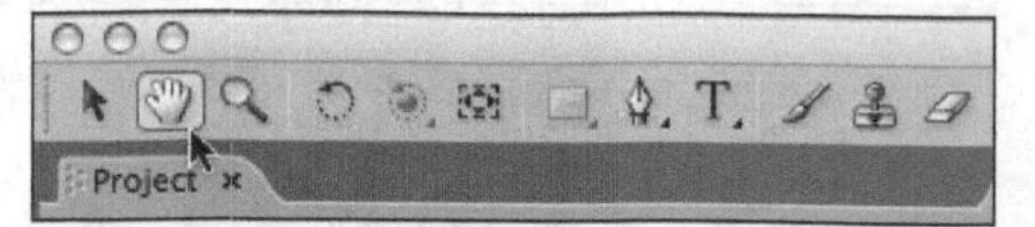

Figure 4.137 In the Tools panel, select the Hand tool...

Figure 4.138 ...or position the Selection tool over the image and press the spacebar to toggle it to the Hand tool.

Figure 4.139 Drag the image with the Hand tool to move other areas into view.

Figure 4.140 Choose whether you want to view safe zones or grids in the Grids and Guides pull-down menu.

Figure 4.141 You can view Title Safe and Action Safe zones...

Viewing Safe Zones and Grids

You can superimpose a grid or video-safe zones over an image to better judge its placement. Obviously, these simple visual guides aren't included in the final output. In addition, because video-safe zones indicate the viewable area of standard video monitors, you should display safe zones for images that match television's 4:3 aspect ratio.

To show video-safe zones and grids:

◆ In the Footage panel's Grid and Guides pull-down menu, choose the options you want (**Figure 4.140**):

  Title/Action Safe (Figure 4.141)

  Proportional Grid (Figure 4.142)

  Grid (Figure 4.143)

  You can display any combination of zones and guides at the same time.

✓ Tip

- You can change the safe zones from the standard setting and change the color, style, and spacing of grid lines in the Grids & Guides pane of the Preferences dialog box.

Figure 4.142 ...a proportional grid...

Figure 4.143 ...or a standard grid.

Displaying Rulers and Guides

Like Adobe Photoshop and Illustrator, After Effects lets you view rulers as well as set guides to help you arrange and align images. As usual, you can change the zero point of the rulers and toggle the rulers and guides on and off.

To toggle rulers on and off:

Do either of the following:

- In a Footage, Comp, or Layer panel's Grid and Guides pull-down menu, choose Rulers (**Figure 4.144**).
- With a Footage, Comp, or Layer panel active, press Command/Ctrl-R to toggle the rulers on and off.

To set the zero point of rulers:

1. If the rulers aren't visible, make them visible using one of the techniques described in the previous task.
2. Position the pointer at the crosshair at the intersection of the rulers in the upper-left corner of the Footage, Composition, or Layer panel.

   The pointer becomes a crosshair (**Figure 4.145**).
3. Drag the crosshair into the image area.

   Horizontal and vertical lines indicate the position of the mouse (**Figure 4.146**).
4. Release the mouse to set the zero point (**Figure 4.147**).

   The rulers use the zero point you selected.

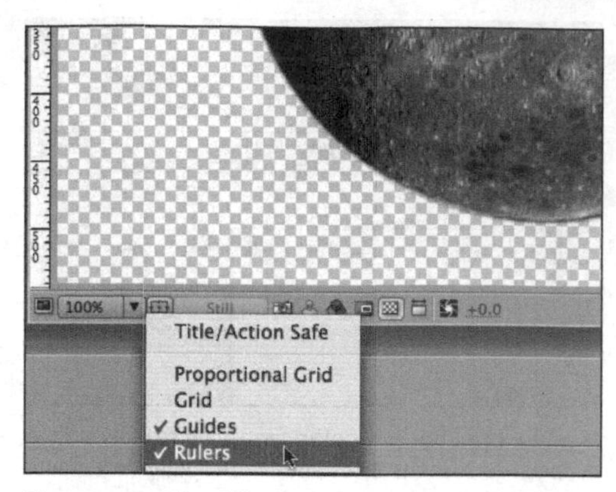

Figure 4.144 After Effects uses the same keyboard shortcut to show and hide rulers—Command/Ctrl-R—as Photoshop.

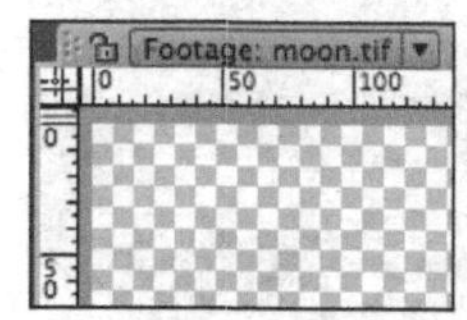

Figure 4.145 When you position the pointer at the intersection of the rulers, it becomes a crosshair icon.

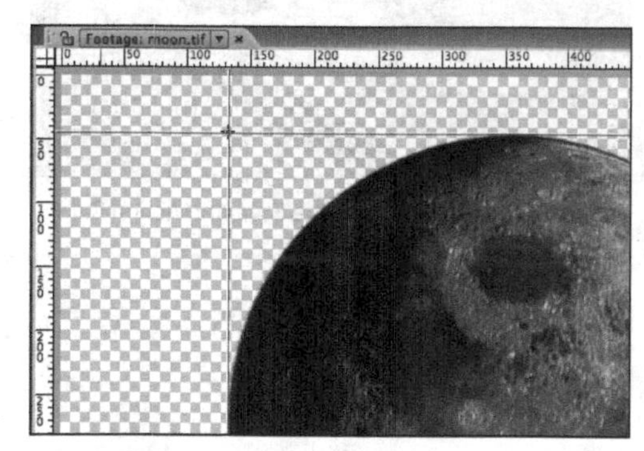

Figure 4.146 Drag the crosshair at the intersection of the rulers into the image area...

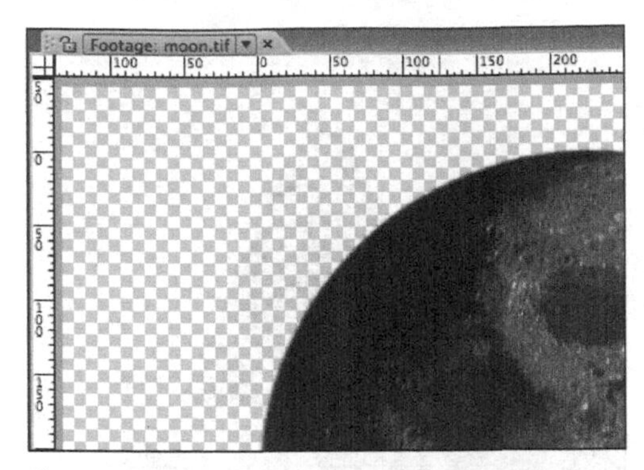

Figure 4.147 ...and release to set the zero point of the rulers.

Figure 4.148 Drag from a ruler into the image area to add a guide.

To reset the zero point of the rulers:

- Double-click the crosshair at the intersection of the horizontal and vertical rulers.

  The rulers' zero point is reset to the upper-left corner of the image.

✔ Tip

- Need to know the exact ruler coordinates of the mouse pointer? Use the Info panel.

To set guides:

1. If the rulers aren't visible, make them visible by pressing Command/Ctrl-R.
2. Position the pointer inside the horizontal or vertical ruler.

   The pointer changes into a Move Guide icon ✥.
3. Drag into the image area (**Figure 4.148**).

   A line indicates the position of the new guide.
4. Release the mouse to set the guide.

To reposition or remove a guide:

Do one of the following:

- To reposition the guide, drag it to a new position.
- To remove the guide, drag it off the image area.

✔ Tips

- You can hide, lock, clear, and have objects snap to guides by choosing the appropriate command in the View menu.
- You can customize the default settings for safe zones, grids, and guides in the Grids & Guides pane of the Preferences dialog box.

Viewing Snapshots

As you work, you'll often need to closely compare different frames. In After Effects, you can take a snapshot of a frame to store for later viewing. Then, with the click of a button, you can temporarily replace the current image in a Footage, Composition, or Layer panel with the snapshot image. The snapshot doesn't really replace anything; it's just used for quick reference—like holding a shirt up to yourself in a mirror to compare it with the one you're wearing. Toggling between the current frame and the snapshot makes it easier to see the differences.

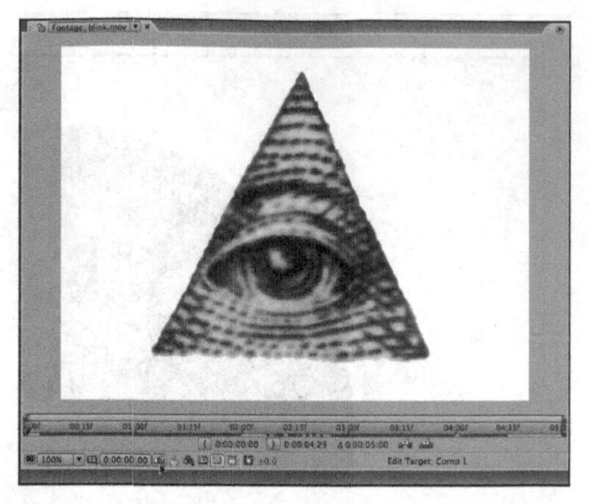

Figure 4.149 Click the Snapshot button to store the current image as a snapshot.

To take a snapshot:

1. If necessary, cue the footage to the frame you want to use as a reference snapshot.
2. Click the Snapshot button (**Figure 4.149**), or press Shift-F5.

   The current frame becomes the snapshot, and the Show Last Snapshot button becomes available.

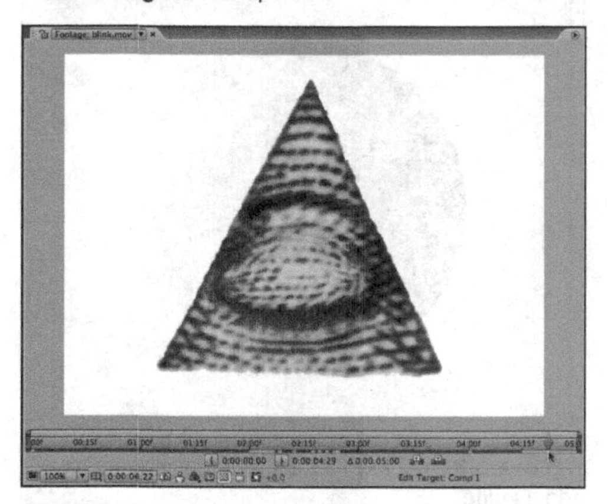

Figure 4.150 Cue to a new frame...

To view the most recent snapshot:

1. If necessary, cue the footage to the frame you want to compare to the snapshot (**Figure 4.150**).
2. Click and hold the Show Last Snapshot button, or press F5.

   As long as you hold down the mouse, the window displays the snapshot (**Figure 4.151**); when you release the mouse, the window displays the current frame.

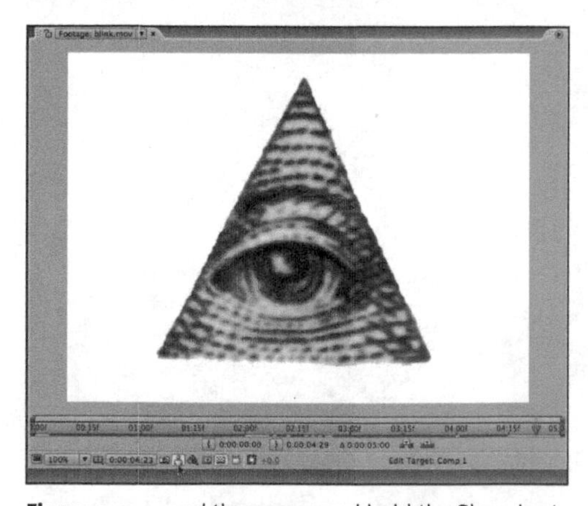

Figure 4.151 ...and then press and hold the Show Last Snapshot button to replace the current image temporarily with the snapshot. Release the Show Last Snapshot button to see the current frame again.

✔ Tips

- If a window uses a different aspect ratio than that of the snapshot, the snapshot is resized to fit into the window.

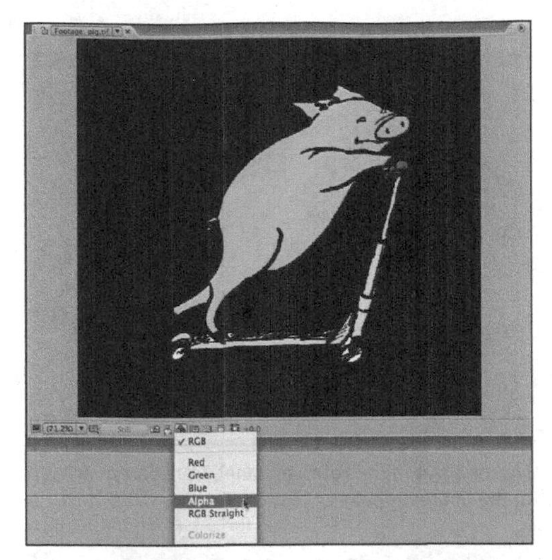

Figure 4.152 Click the Show Channel button, and then select the channel you want to view.

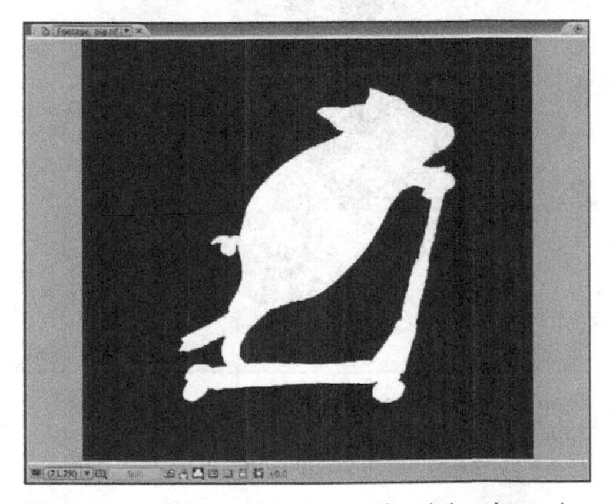
Figure 4.153 Choose Alpha to see the alpha channel.

Figure 4.154 To see the selected channel in color, select Colorize from the pull-down menu.

- Snapshots are stored in memory. If After Effects requires the memory that is used by a snapshot, it will discard the snapshot.

Viewing Channels

The Footage, Composition, and Layer panels allow you to view the individual red, green, blue, and alpha channels of an image. Color channels appear as grayscale images in which the degree of white corresponds to the color value. You can also view the color channel using its own color. The alpha channel appears as a grayscale image as well, where the degree of white corresponds to opacity. You can even view the unmultiplied color channels—that is, the color channels without the alpha taken into account.

To show individual channels:

1. In a Footage, Composition, or Layer panel, click the Show Channel button, and then choose the channel you want to view (Figure 4.152):

   RGB —Shows the normal image with visible channels combined.

   Red , **Green** , or **Blue** —Shows the selected channel as a grayscale.

   Alpha —Shows the alpha channel (transparency information) as a grayscale. If active, the transparency grid is disabled while Alpha is selected (**Figure 4.153**). See the next section, "Viewing Transparency."

   RGB Straight —Shows the unmultiplied RGB channels. If active, the transparency grid is disabled while RGB Straight is selected.

2. To show the selected channel depicted in color, select Colorize (**Figure 4.154**).

The Channel pull-down menu's icon changes according to the current selection.

Viewing Transparency

You've learned that the footage items you import can retain almost every aspect of their source files, including transparency. In the Footage panel, transparency always appears as black (**Figure 4.155**). However, if the black background isn't convenient, you can toggle the transparent areas to appear as a checkerboard pattern, or *transparency grid* (**Figure 4.156**).

Like many of the other buttons in the Footage panel, the Toggle Transparency Grid button is also available in the Layer and Composition panels. However, in contrast to the Footage panel, you can set the Composition panel's background to any color. The next chapter revisits viewing transparency and other unique aspects of the Composition panel.

To toggle the transparency grid:

- In the Footage, Composition, or Layer panel, click the Toggle Transparency Grid button (**Figure 4.157**).

  When the Toggle Transparency Grid button is selected, transparent areas appear as a checkerboard pattern; when the button isn't selected, transparent areas appear black in a Footage or Layer panel. In a Composition panel, transparent areas appear as the color you set.

✔ Tip

- The transparency grid is disabled whenever you select the Alpha or RGB Straight viewing option in the Show Channel pull-down menu (covered in the section "Viewing Channels," earlier in this chapter).

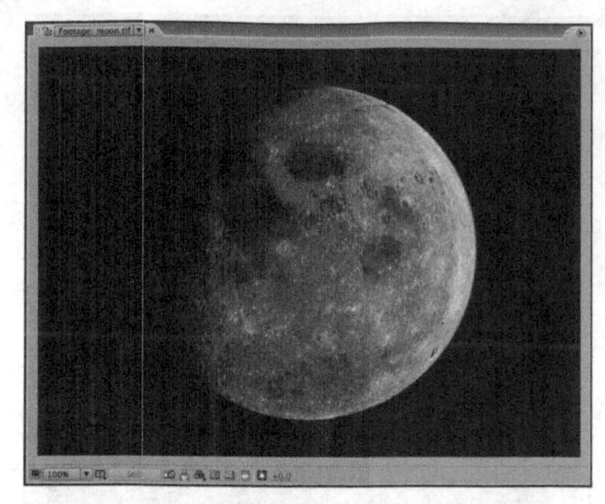

Figure 4.155 In the Footage panel, transparent areas of the image appear as black.

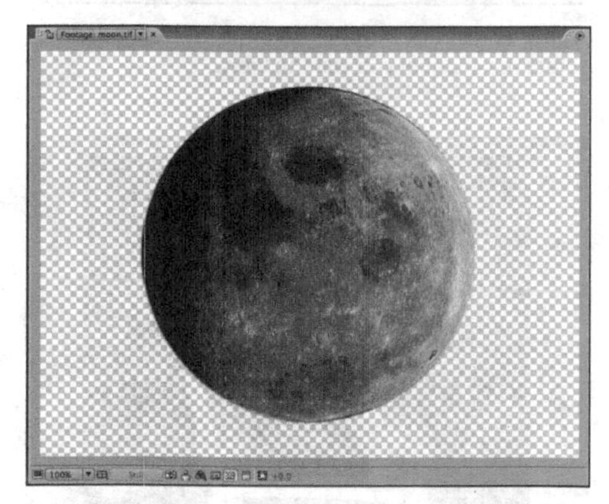

Figure 4.156 You can also make transparent areas appear as a checkerboard pattern, or transparency grid. This also works in the Composition and Layer panels.

Figure 4.157 Click the Toggle Transparency Grid button to toggle between showing transparent areas as black (in the Footage panel, or as the specified background color in the Composition panel) and showing them as a checkerboard pattern.

Correcting for Pixel Aspect Ratios

You've learned the importance of correctly interpreting an image's pixel aspect ratio (PAR) to prevent the image from appearing distorted. But even properly interpreted footage and comps that use a nonsquare PAR result in an image that looks distorted on a typical computer display (**Figure 4.158**). Fortunately, After Effects can compensate for the distortion due to PAR (**Figure 4.159**). As After Effects warns you when you use the Toggle Pixel Aspect Ratio Correction button, correcting the image this way is for viewing purposes only; it doesn't affect the image's actual scale. And because correcting an image requires some processing, it will take slightly longer to render frames.

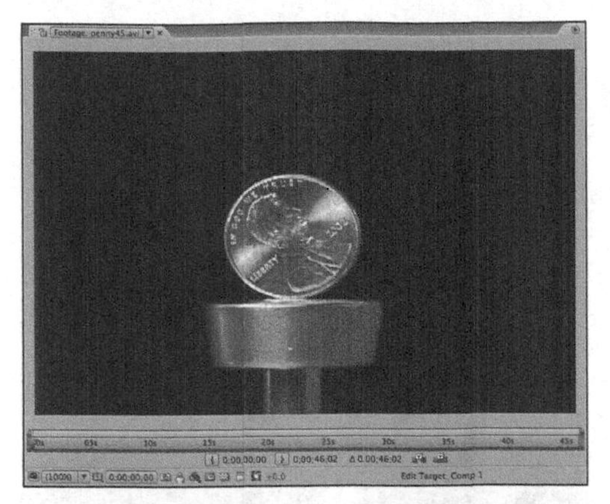

Figure 4.158 This footage uses a PAR of .9, so it appears slightly vertically squashed (or horizontally stretched) when displayed using square pixels.

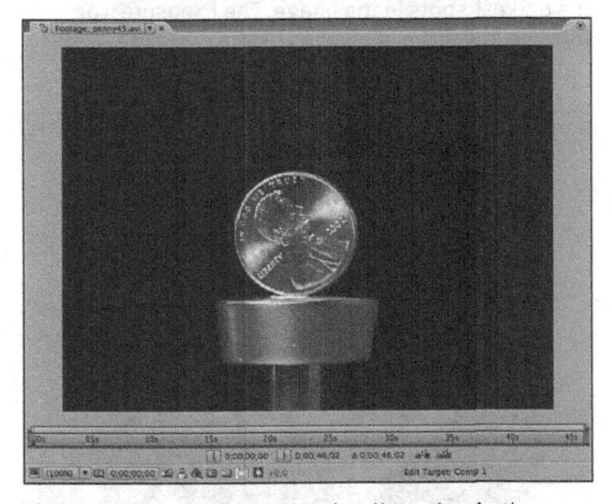

Figure 4.159 You can correct the distortion in the Layer, Composition, and Footage panels.

To toggle pixel aspect correction:

1. In a Footage, Composition, or Layer panel, click the Toggle Pixel Aspect Ratio Correction button to select it (**Figure 4.160**).

   If this is the first time you've used the button during this session, After Effects reminds you how PAR correction works and prompts you to specify whether you want to see the warning once per session or never again.

2. Select an option in the dialog box, and click OK.

   If the image's PAR doesn't match your computer monitor's PAR, After Effects scales the image so that it no longer appears distorted.

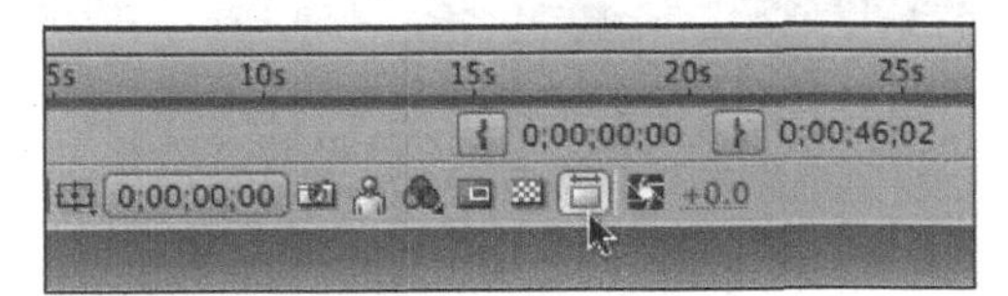

Figure 4.160 Click the Toggle Pixel Aspect Ratio Correction button.

Adjusting Exposure

Starting with After Effects CS3, Footage, Comp and Layer panels have controls for the view's exposure. Just as increasing the exposure in a camera results in a brighter photograph, increasing the view's exposure value makes its image appear brighter. The exposure setting affects the view only. Even if you adjust it in a Layer or Comp panel, it won't affect the output image (to alter the output image, add effects). However, the exposure setting does help you evaluate an image's brightness and is particularly useful in identifying an image's brightest and darkest areas.

Figure 4.161 Changing a view's Exposure value doesn't alter the source or output image; it helps you evaluate its brightness. Here, increasing the Exposure identifies the darkest spots in the image. The Exposure icon turns yellow when you set a custom exposure.

To adjust a view's exposure:

- In a Footage, Composition, or Layer panel, set the Adjust Exposure value next to the Reset Exposure button.

  Decreasing the value makes the image darker; increasing the value makes the image brighter (**Figure 4.161**). Setting the value to anything but 0 makes the Reset Exposure button's icon appear yellow.

To toggle exposure between a custom value and zero:

- In a Footage, Composition, or Layer panel, click the Reset Exposure button.

  Clicking the button when its icon is yellow makes the icon black and resets the exposure value to zero (**Figure 4.162**). Clicking the button again sets the exposure value to the most recent custom setting and makes the icon yellow.

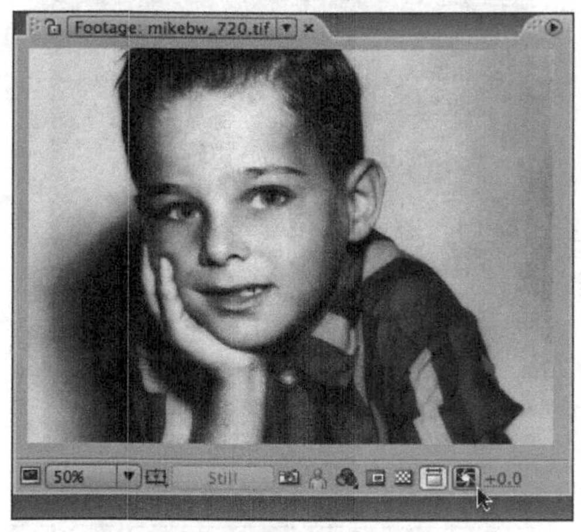

Figure 4.162 Clicking the Reset Exposure button toggles the image back to an exposure value of 0. Click it again to show the last custom setting.

The Timeline and Layers

I've been a long time coming, and I'll be a long time gone. You've got your whole life to do something, and that's not very long.

–Ani DiFranco
(American singer, songwriter, and guitarist)

The Timeline

The Timeline is After Effects' killer application. More than any other feature, it extends After Effects unique versatility to a wide range of work. With the Timeline at the center of the compositing process, you can time elements and animations precisely as you control their appearance.

✔ Note

The Timeline makes render order explicit if you know how to view it. 2D layers render beginning with the lowest in the stack and ending with the top, while properties of each layer (visible by twirling down) render in top-to-bottom order.

The Timeline panel is also a user-friendly part of the application, albeit one packed with hidden powers. By mastering its usage, you can streamline your workflow a great deal, setting the stage for more advanced work.

One major source of these hidden powers is the Timeline's set of keyboard shortcuts and context menus. These are not extras to be investigated once you're a veteran, but small productivity enhancers that you can learn gradually all the time. They actively build your momentum and confidence as an After Effects artist.

Organization

The Timeline is a dynamic environment; as you work with it, you constantly alter not only its contents, but also your view of the environment itself. Its building blocks are layers organized into columns, and you determine which layers or columns are visible at any given time.

Column Views

You can context-click on any column heading to see and toggle available columns in the Timeline, but there are smarter ways to configure these than toggling all the time. A minimal setup is shown in **Figure 5.1**. You can then augment or change the setup with the following tools:

- **Lower-left icons:** Most (but not quite all) of the extra data you need is available

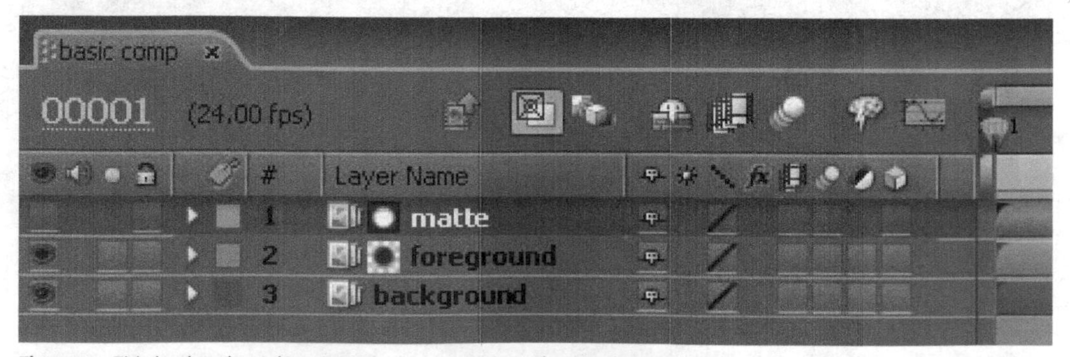

Figure 5.1 This basic column layout works when screen real estate is at a premium. The columns shown are useful virtually all of the time, and most of the rest are only a shortcut away.

Figure 5.2 These icons at the lower left of the Timeline expand (or collapse) the most used columns: Layer Switches, Transfer Controls, and the various timing controls. The button to the right corresponds to the first two, toggling between them.

via the three toggles found at the lower left of the Timeline (**Figure 5.2**).

- **Layer Switches/Transfer Controls:** Save horizontal space (if you need it) using a built-in toggle between the modes represented by the first two lower-left icons. When only one of them is enabled, the F4 key or the Toggle Switches / Modes button which appears below the column will swap them.

✔ **Tip**

- If both Layer Switches and Transfer Controls are displayed, the F4 toggle hides both of them, maximizing horizontal space.

- **Time Stretch:** The third lower-left icon toggles the timing columns (In, Out, Duration, and Stretch) together. It's easy to forget these even exist, given that layer Duration and In/Out are usually set to the layer bar itself, and Stretch isn't the usual way to retime a layer except in specific instances (detailed in "Manipulate Time," ahead).
- **Layer/Source:** You can (and often should) give a layer a custom name by selecting it, pressing Return, typing, and deselecting. The column heading switches from Source Name to Layer Name; click it to toggle them. Items in brackets in Layer Name mode still have the Source Name.

✔ **Tip**

- The general convention to rename an item anywhere in After Effects is to highlight it and press Return, instead of clicking and hovering (as can be done in the operating system).

- **Parent:** On by default with no shortcut, this one is most likely to be visible when it's not needed. Not parenting in this comp? Context-click the column title and choose Hide This from the resulting menu.
- **AV Features/Keys:** AV Features are usually too useful to hide, and Keys comes along for free; its controls are embedded beneath AV Features when the layer is twirled down. Unless you are really desperate, leave these alone.

Unless your monitor is huge or you're not doing much keyframing, the game is to preserve horizontal space for keyframe data by keeping only the relevant controls visible.

Comments and Color

Ever try to make sense of someone else's project? You can make it easier for others—and even yourself—by color-coding layers and compositions, so everyone can see at a glance how comps are organized (**Figure 5.3**). Or, if you're creating a template or other project to hand off to others, or use again in the future, you can append comments to whole layers as well as specific points on the Timeline.

✔ **Tip**

- After Effects colors and their names can be edited in Preferences > Label Colors; version CS3 includes 16 unique color labels. Therefore the same label can have a different color on another system.

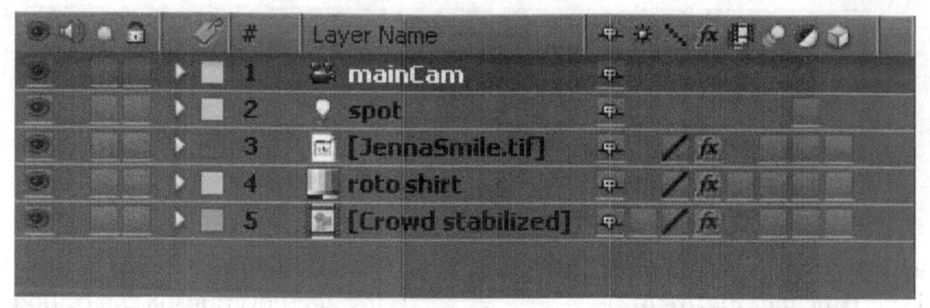

Figure 5.3 Each type of layer has a unique color, making it easy to discern among them.

Preferences > Label Defaults assigns specific colors to nine basic item types.

Colors are assigned to specific types of layers according to Preferences > Label Defaults. Additionally, you may wish to call out special types of layers, such as track mattes and adjustment layers, with specific colors of your own choosing.

Comments are generally the least used column in the Timeline, but they let you offer full contextual explanations of the comp setup, with no character limit (although you may have to twirl down some properties to reveal the scroll bar). However, if the column is not made visible, neither are the comments.

✔ Note

Included in the Redefinery folder on the book's disc is a script called rd_Commentron.jsx. It takes advantage of the long-text handling ability of the Comments fields in the Timeline and Project panels by duplicating information that is truncated in other fields, such as example, layer, and footage names that exceed 31 characters or other useful information.

Comments attached to layer markers are visible in the Layer view, where they require no extra space. To add one, highlight a target layer at a specific time and press the * key on the numeric keypad; a layer marker appears at the current time. Double-click it to open the Marker dialog. Add text to the Comment field and if the layer bar is visible, the result appears right on top of it.

Solo, Lock, and Shy

Several toggles on the A/V Features and Switches columns pertain to how layers are edited and viewed (or, in the case of audio, heard) as you work.

✔ Tip

- New in After Effects CS3, you can add text to comp markers (**Figure 5.4**).

The round, white icon (**Figure 5.5**) in A/V Features is the Solo switch. Solo a layer, and you see only it; render a comp with a layer toggled solo, and the Solo Switches menu in Render Settings determines whether it outputs that way. By default, whatever visibility settings you have in the comp, including solo layers, are what render.

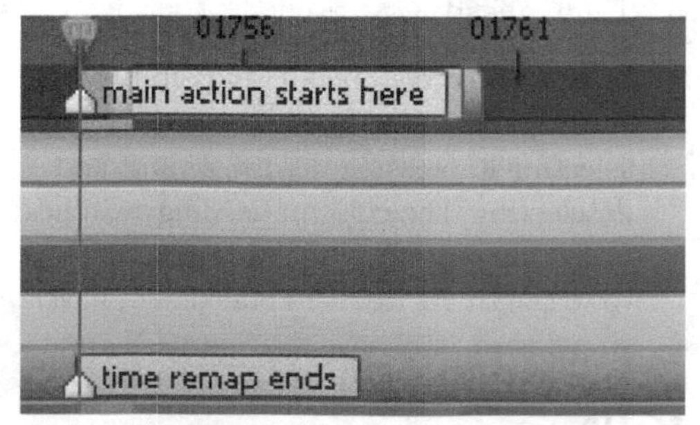

Figure 5.4 Comments can be added to layer or comp markers. In this case the layer marker is aligned to the comp marker, easy to do by holding down the Shift key to snap as you drag.

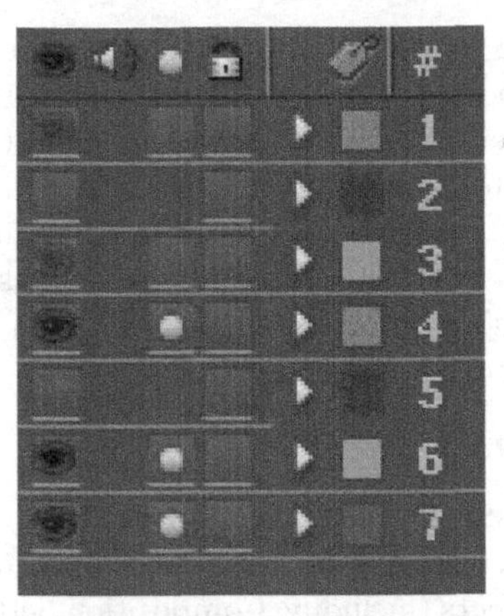

Figure 5.5 Three layers are solo, and the others behave as if deactivated; by default, the comp will also render this way.

✔ Tip

- To change the visibility (rather than the solo state) of selected layers, use Layer > Switches > Hide Other Video.

The Lock toggle is useful in situations when you know a layer is done and should not be touched; a locked layer can't even be selected, let alone edited.

✔ Tip

- To unlock a number of layers at once, use Layer > Switches > Unlock All Layers **(Ctrl+Shift+L/Cmd+Shift+L).**

Shy is a more elusive feature; toggle a layer to shy and nothing happens, until you also activate the Shy toggle for the entire composition (**Figure 5.6**). All shy layers disappear from the Timeline, although they still display in the comp itself, as before. This is a great way to keep only the layers you need in front of you.

✔ Note

Shy layers can greatly reduce clutter in the Timeline, but if you ever lose a layer, take a close look at the Index numbers. If any are out of sequence, the missing number belongs to a layer that is now shy.

Navigation and Shortcuts

More than anywhere else in After Effects, the Timeline is *the* place where keyboard shortcuts—lots of them—allow you, the expert, to make changes via a single keyboard shortcut or a single click of the mouse, where a beginner might require several mouse clicks, or might not know that a given feature existed at all.

Time Navigation

Many users—particularly editors—learn time navigation shortcuts right away. Others primarily drag the Current Time Indicator, which can quickly become tedious. Here are some useful time navigation shortcuts:

- The **Home, End, Page Up,** and **Page Down** keys correspond to moving to the first or last frame of the composition, one frame backward, and one frame

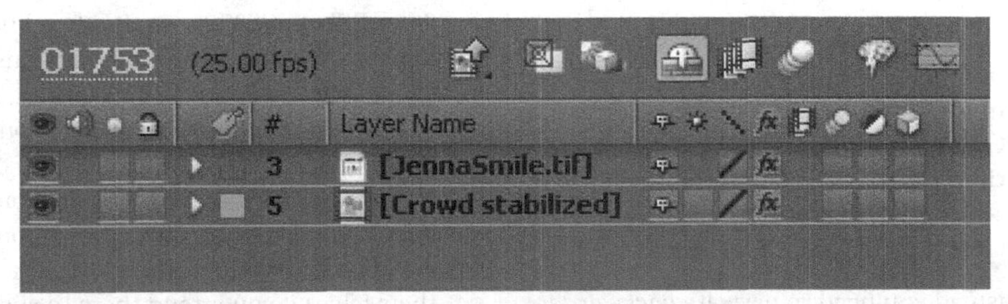

Figure 5.6 Layers 1, 2, and 4 from Figure 5.3 are shy; they still display in the comp viewer if visible, but I've made them invisible in the Timeline to leave only the layers I'm currently editing.

forward, respectively. Laptop users in particular may prefer **Ctrl/Cmd+left and right arrow** as an alternative to **Page Up** and **Page Down.**

- **Shift+Page Up** and **Shift+Page Down** skip ten frames backward or forward, respectively.

✔ Note

There's no need to add punctuation when entering time values into a number field in After Effects. 1000 is ten seconds (10:00) in Timecode mode or frame 1000 in Frames mode.

- **Shift+Home** and **Shift+End** navigate to the Work Area In and Out points, which can be set with the **B** and **N** keys, respectively. The **I** and **O** keys navigate to the beginning and end frames of the comp.
- Click on the current time status at the upper left of the Timeline to open the Go to Time dialog (press **Alt+Shift+J/Opt+Shift+J**).

✔ Tip

- Go to Time used to have the shortcut Ctrl+Shift+G/Cmd+Shift+G, but Shape layers claimed this one for grouping shapes, so that After Effects would be consistent with other Adobe applications such as Illustrator. Think of the new shortcut **(Alt+Shift+J/Opt+Shift+J)** as "Jump" to help yourself remember it.

- To navigate an arbitrary but precise number of frames or seconds (say, 48 frames following the current time), in the Go to Time dialog, replace the current time with your increment in the format +48, click OK, and After Effects calculates the increment for you.

If instead you need to navigate *backward* in time 48 frames, you can't simply enter –48 in the Go to Time dialog. If you do, you're transported to negative 48 (frames or seconds, either of which probably moves the indicator right off the Timeline—very confusing). Instead, you must use the format "+–48" to enter the offset; think of it as adding a negative number, rather than subtracting. It's weird, but it works.

✔ Tip

- The add-a-negative number offset now operates in most number fields in After Effects (including Composition Settings).

Make Layers Behave

I was reviewing film-outs of shots from *The Day After Tomorrow* with the other artists at The Orphanage when my shot began to loop; it looked out a window at stragglers making their way across a snow-covered plaza and featured a beautiful matte painting by Mike Pangrazio. About two-thirds through the shot came a subtle pop. At some point, the shot had been lengthened, and a layer of noise and dirt I had included at approximately 3% transparency (for the window itself) had remained shorter in a sub-composition.

This is a primary reason some effects artists don't like to work with a timeline-based application; in other compositing programs, such as Shake, this would not inadvertently happen because static elements don't have a length unless you specify one.

After Effects CS3 is more fluid and flexible in this respect than previous versions. Static elements such as stills and solids no longer have a fixed beginning or end, so you can always drag to extend them, and by default they extend the full length of the composition. If you lengthen the composition, however, you must still lengthen the layers themselves if you intend them to span the comp.

✔ Note

To avoid the gotcha in which a layer ends up too short for its host composition when either is edited, some users prefer to make all of their comps longer (in duration) than they ever expect to need, and manage timing using only the Work Area settings.

To add a layer beginning at a specific time, drag the element to the layer area; a second Time Indicator appears that moves with your cursor (horizontally). This determines the layer's start frame. If other layers are present and visible, you can also place it in layer order.

Here are some other useful tips and shortcuts:

- Navigate to the previous or next keyframe (or layer marker) by pressing **J** and **K**, respectively. This works for any visible keyframe or layer marker.

✔ Tips

- The keyboard shortcut **Ctrl+/ (Cmd+/)** adds selected items as the top layer(s) of the active composition.
- To trim a composition's Duration to the current Work Area, choose Composition > Trim Comp to Work Area.
- It can be annoying that the Work Area controls both preview and render frame ranges, because the two are often used exclusively of one another. By employing a separate "Render Final" composition that contains the Work Area for the final render, you can mess with your other composition Work Areas as much as you want without affecting the render range.

- To reset the Work Area to the length of the composition, double-click it; to set it to the exact length of the currently active layer, press **Ctrl+Alt+B/Cmd+Option+B.**
- Besides clicking on a layer to select it, you can enter the layer's index number using the numeric keypad.
- To select an adjacent layer without touching the mouse, use **Ctrl+Up Arrow (Cmd+Up Arrow)** to select the next layer up, and **Down Arrow** to select the next layer down.
- Add the **Alt** (**Option**) key to move a layer up or down in the stack, which you can also do with **Ctrl+]** and **Ctrl+[** (as in other Adobe applications). **Ctrl+Shift+]** moves a layer to the top of the stack and **Ctrl+Shift+[** moves it to the bottom.
- You can invert the layers currently selected: Context-click on a selected layer, and choose Invert Selection. (Locked layers are not selected, but Shy layers are selected even if invisible.)
- Duplicate any layer (or virtually any selected item) using **Ctrl+D (Cmd+D)**. If you duplicate a layer and its track matte (Chapter 7), they remain paired in layer order, above the source layers.
- For various reasons you might instead wish to split a layer (**Ctrl+Shift+D/ Cmd+Shift+D**); the source ends and the duplicate continues from the current time. This is useful, for example, when you need one layer to straddle another in 2D order.

✔ Note

There is even a preference controlling whether split layers are created above or below the source layer (Preferences > General; the toggle is labeled Create Split Layers Above Original Layer).

- To move a layer In point to the current time, use the **[** key, or press **]** to move the Out point. Add the **Alt** (**Option**) key to *set the current frame* as the In or Out point, trimming the layer.

- To slide a trimmed layer, preserving the In and Out points but translating the footage and its layer markers (but *not* keyframes), drag using the double-ended arrow you see over the area outside the In and Out points; it is visible when the layer has already been trimmed, making an edit handle available.
- To nudge a layer forward or backward in time (including its keyframes) use **Alt+Page Up/Page Down** (**Option+Page Up/Page Down**; hold **Option/Alt** with **Home** and **End** to move the layer's In point to the beginning of the comp, or the Out point to the end).

Often, you may add elements whose size or pixel aspect doesn't match those of the composition, yet which are meant to fill the frame (or one axis). No need to break open the Scale controls and guess; you can use the Fit to Comp shortcuts (which are included in the Layer > Transform menu).

✔ Tip

- Double-click a keyframe and some rather cool hidden options present themselves for positioning and scaling relative to the comp (**Figure 5.7**).

The standard Fit to Comp, **Ctrl+Alt+F** (**Cmd+Option+F**) can be dangerous in that it ignores the aspect ratio of the layer, stretching X and Y scale individually to match each to the comp itself.

More commonly useful are the shortcuts for Fit to Comp on a single axis (X or Y), which retain the aspect ratio to scale the non-dominant axis. You can Fit to Comp Width (**Ctrl+Alt+Shift+H/ Cmd+Option+Shift+H**), or Fit to Comp

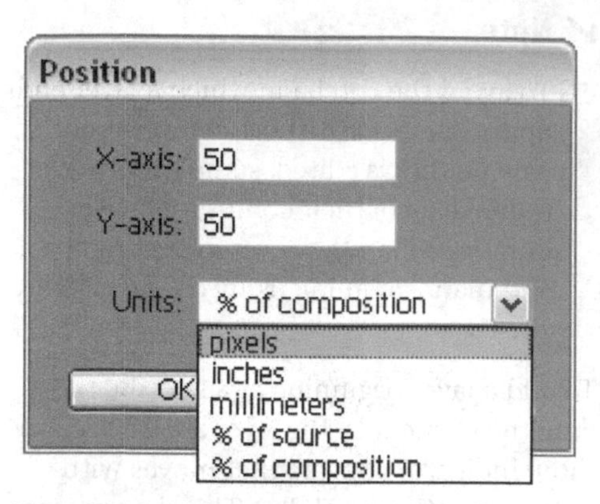

Figure 5.7 Need to position that layer relative to the composition, or to its source size? Double-click the keyframe and make use of this dialog; it's useful for other types of keyframes as well.

Height (twisting your fingers around **Ctrl+Alt+Shift+G/Cmd+Option+Shift+G**).

Timeline View Options

After Effects offers some useful workflow enhancements to help you work with keyframe data. These will help you work with timing more quickly, accurately and confidently.

- The **;** key toggles between a fully zoomed-in view of the current frame and a fully zoomed-out view of the whole Timeline.
- The slider at the bottom of the Timeline zooms in and out more selectively (**Figure 5.8**).
- If your mouse includes a scroll wheel, there's a cooler option: Not only can you scroll up and down the layer stack and

Figure 5.8 Absent a mouse scroll wheel, this click-and-drag interface at the bottom of the Timeline panel is probably the fastest method of zooming in and out.

Shift-scroll left and right in a zoomed Timeline view, but Alt-scrolling (Option-scrolling) dynamically zooms you in and out of time. Shift-scrolling navigates back and forth. Position your cursor over the Timeline panel to try these.

✔ Tip

- The scroll wheel also zooms in and out of viewer panels when the cursor is placed over them, no modifier or selection needed.

At the right edge of the Timeline is the Comp button (**Figure 5.9a**), which brings forward the Composition view associated with that Timeline. The Composition panel has a corresponding Timeline button (**Figure 5.9b**). Neither of these is strictly necessary, however; if you need to make either panel appear, or toggle between the two of them, use the backslash (\) key.

✔ Tip

- The Current Time Indicator is capable of going where your Timeline panel cannot: to time frames previous to the first frame of the composition or beyond the last frame (usually because the trimmed area of a layer extends there). In such cases, the indicator disappears from the Timeline entirely. Have no fear. Clicking in the Time Ruler to place the indicator or using any of the time shortcuts outlined above recovers it.

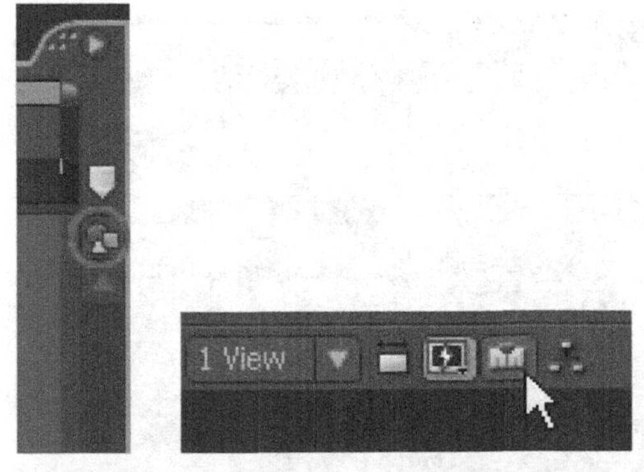

Figure 5.9 Need to locate the Timeline related to the displayed composition, or vice versa? The shortcut for each is here, or simply use the \ on your keyboard. Also in this group is the Comp marker bin; drag comp markers from here.

Just above the Comp button is the Comp marker bin, where you can drag out a marker to a point on your Timeline. Markers are numbered sequentially, but new in CS3, you can double-click them to add names instead.

✔ Tip

- Hold down the Shift key as you drag the Current Time Indicator to snap current time to comp or layer markers or visible keyframes.

  To add a specific numbered comp marker, press Shift and one of the numbers at the top of your keyboard (not the numeric keypad): 1 through 0.

Replace a Layer or Composition

You can easily replace the source of a layer with an alternate take or a different element in the Project panel, keeping all of its settings and keyframes. Highlight the layer to be replaced in the Timeline and hold down the Alt (Option) key while dragging the new source to the Timeline. Or even easier, select both the existing layer and the new source and then press **Ctrl+Alt+/** (**Cmd+Option+/**).

You can even Alt/Option-drag one composition over another in the Project panel to replace its usage throughout the project.

✔ Note

Beware when replacing with source material of a different size or aspect; mask values are relative and scale to the dimensions of the new layer, but other values (transforms and effects settings) are absolute and, generally speaking, do not.

Animation Methods

Twirl down any layer in the Timeline, and the Transform controls are revealed. Transforms are spatial data related to Position, Anchor Point, Scale, Rotation, and, um, Opacity. Opacity isn't really spatial transform data, but it's essential enough to be included with the spatial data.

- The keyboard shortcuts to reveal individual transforms are the first letter of each type: **P, A, S, R,** and, um, **T**—Opacity is the oddball again, because O is already in use as the Out point of a layer (mentioned above). Think of Opaci-"T."
- To reveal additional properties, hold down **Shift** when typing the letter shortcut; you can also toggle a property to hide in this manner.

A *property* in After Effects is a data channel under a twirled-down layer. Typically a property can be animated and has a stopwatch icon beside it which, when clicked, sets a keyframe at the current time.

That by itself is simple enough. But there are, in fact, many different ways to animate a property in After Effects (**Figure 5.10**).

Suppose you wanted to move a layer 200 pixels along the X axis over 24 frames. After setting the first keyframe and moving the time indicator forward 24 frames, you could

- Drag the layer to the new position in the Composition viewer (holding the Shift key to constrain it to one axis)
- **Shift+Right Arrow** 20 times to move the layer exactly 200 pixels
- Enter the new value in the Timeline by highlighting the X Position numerical value and typing in the new number
- Drag the X Position numerical value to the right until it is 200 pixels higher (perhaps holding Shift to increment by ten pixels)
- Enter a numerical offset by highlighting the X Position numerical value and typing +200 (as was done with time, above)

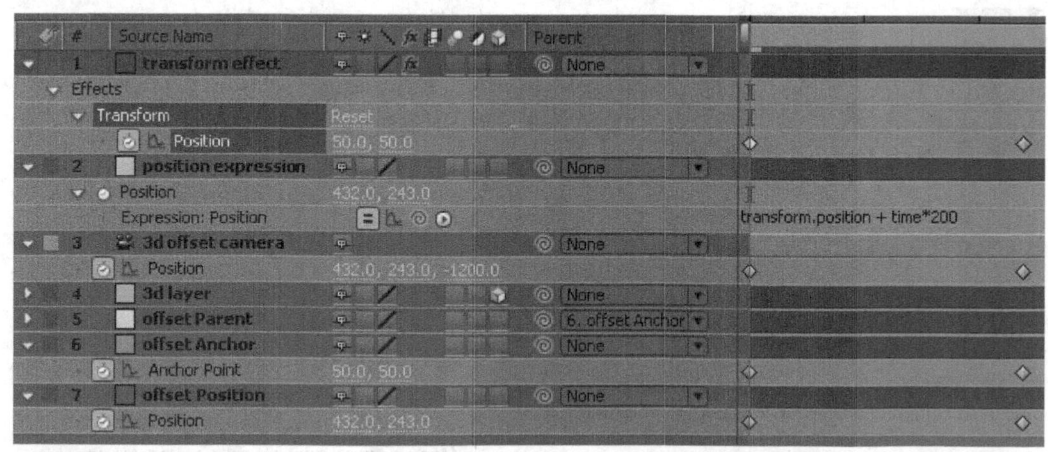

Figure 5.10 Each layer moves 200 pixels along the X axis over 24 frames; look carefully and you can see that each employs a unique method.

- Copy and paste the Position keyframe from another layer, or another point in time (assuming one exists)

And those are just the options to keyframe-animate that one property. You could also create the same animation without keyframing Position values, by

- Keyframing the anchor point in the opposite direction (negative 200 pixel X value) over 24 frames
- Enabling 3D for the layer, adding a 50mm camera, and animating the camera moving 200 pixels, again in the negative X direction
- Parenting the layer to another layer with the transform animation
- Replacing the layer with a nested composition that already contains the layer and transform
- Assigning an expression to the Position channel that performs the animation without keyframes

✔ Note

Don't worry, you won't be tested on these. This list is here to spark your imagination and perhaps provide animation ideas you hadn't considered.

If that's not crazy enough, you could even

- Apply the Transform effect to the layer and animate the effect's Position value
- Animate in real time via the cursor using Motion Sketch (I did say "crazy")
- Paste in a path (perhaps using a Mask or a Path from Photoshop or Illustrator) to the Position channel, adjusting timing as needed (this method defaults to creating a two-second animation)—again, crazy, but possible

✔ Note

The Transform effect allows you to specify when transforms occur relative to effects. Normal transforms occur before effects, but this plug-in lets you interleave them with effects without precomping.

Some of these options are clearly designed for other specific and most likely, more complex situations, such as parenting (under "Parent Hierarchy" later in this chapter) and expressions.

Note that there is even a variety of ways to enter values while animating. You can

- Drag with the Selection tool (shortcut: **V**)
- Drag the Pan Behind tool to move the anchor point (shortcut: **Y**)
- Drag the Rotate tool (shortcut: **W**, which the documentation even points out is for "wotate")

✔ Tip

- When dragging text in the Timeline or Effect Controls, hold down Shift to increment values at ten times the normal amount, or hold down **Ctrl+Alt (Cmd+Option)** to increment at one tenth the standard increment (usually a whole integer value, but this depends on the slider range, which you can edit; context-click the value in Effect Controls and choose Edit Value to adjust it).

You can also work directly with these values in the Timeline, whether by highlighting and entering values, or simply by dragging the value without highlighting. Try it.

Keyframes and the Graph Editor

The purpose of the Graph Editor is to give you maximum control over fine-tuning a

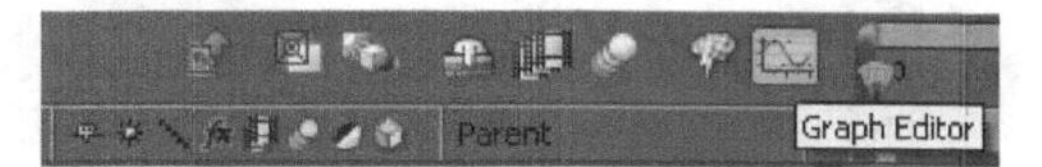

Figure 5.11 This icon activates the Graph Editor.

keyframe animation, whether it consists of one animated property or several. If you're adjusting one property, you can take complete control of its animation; if several, you get a thorough comparison of timings.

Make Use of the Graph Editor

The simplest way to get started with the Graph Editor is to examine a sample project and to try messing around with it. To demonstrate the many features of this tool set, 02_graphEditor.aep in the accompanying disc's Chapter02 directory contains a simple animation, "bouncing ball 2d." A ball bounces across the frame, with a little bit of squash and stretch animation occurring from where it hits the bottom of the boundary

To enable the Graph Editor, click its icon in the Timeline (**Figure 5.11**).

A grid appears in the area previously occupied by the layer bars. At the bottom of this grid are the Graph Editor controls, labeled in **Figure 5.12**.

Show Properties

By default, if nothing is selected, nothing displays; what you see depends on the settings in the Show Properties menu (the eye icon lower left). Three toggles in this menu control how animation curves are displayed:

- Show Selected Properties displays animation data only for selected properties
- Show Animated Properties displays all animated properties in a selected layer, whether they are selected or not
- Show Graph Editor Set displays properties whose Graph Editor Set toggle (next to the stopwatch and labeled I in Figure 5.12) is enabled

✔ Tip

- It's easy to turn on Show Selected Properties and disable the other two, but the opposite configuration (disabling that Show Selected Properties and turning on the others), is a more powerful (less annoying) way to work because properties don't inadvertently appear and disappear as you work.

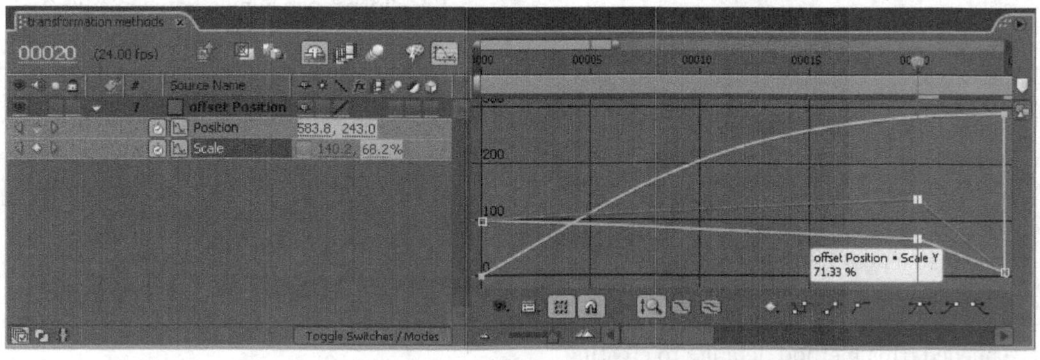

Figure 5.12 Components of the Graph Editor: (A) Show Properties, (B) Graph Options, (C) Show Transform Box, (D) Snap, (E) Zoom controls, (F) Keyframe controls, (G) Ease controls, (H) properties graphs, and (I) Graph Editor Set toggles.

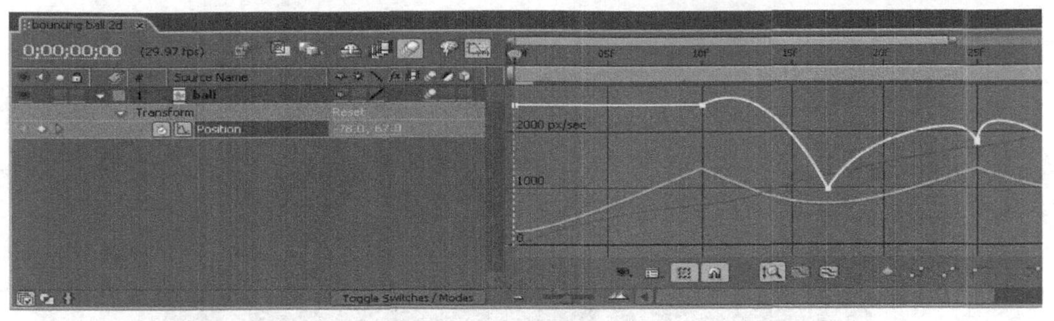

Figure 5.13 The 2D version of the bouncing ball animation is shown with the Speed graph active and the Value graph shown as a Reference graph.

You may already have your own preference, but I consider Graph Editor Set to be the most versatile option. By specifying what properties you want to see, you ensure that only they are displayed, and you can freely mix and match selections from various layers without having to keep everything carefully selected.

Graph Options

The real power of the Graph Editor has to do with how data is displayed, and there are options for displaying data that even advanced users miss. The Graph Options menu (labeled B in Figure 5.12) controls which components of the properties are displayed. For example, display only the Position data for ball and you might see something like the keyframe data in **Figure 5.13**.

Enable Show Reference Graph in the Graph Options and the actual spatial animation is displayed as curves, even though you normally edit motion paths in the viewer, and the Speed graph (the rate at which the layer animates) in the Graph Editor. For a bouncing ball animation, both contain vital information; as you edit speed to speed the ball toward the ground and slow it down in midair, you can move your cursor over the Value graph to see exactly where the ball is at a particular frame.

✔ Note

Auto Select Graph Type selects Speed graphs for spatial properties and Value graphs for all others.

Switch to Edit Value Graph and you can actually grab a vertex belonging to a given axis and change its value. What you cannot do is offset it in time from the other axes; any temporal changes you make to a keyframe on X are also made to Y and Z.

✔ Note

The Separate XYZ Position preset (in Animation Presets, in the Effects & Presets panel) uses expressions to set up separate spatial channels that can be timed independently of one another. This, however, can make life more complicated because it contains its own spatial properties which link to Position, and you must animate those to get the benefit.

The main use of the Reference graph is to get a property value at a specific time, which you can do by moving the cursor over the curve or simply by checking the Reference graph values displayed in gray at the right end of the Graph Editor (while values of the active graph are displayed left). If this is too much information at any

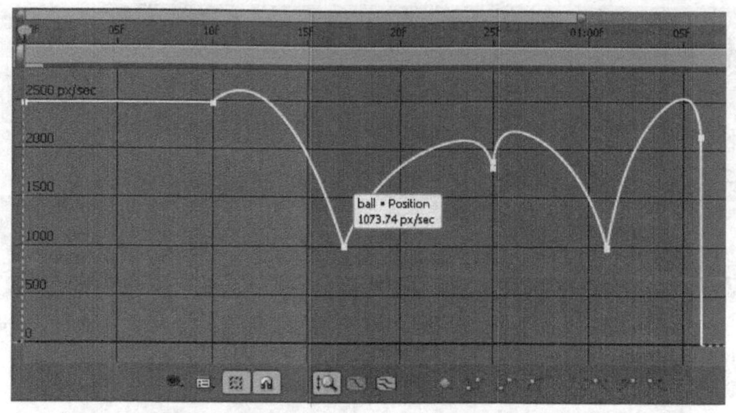

Figure 5.14 A Reference graph as in Figure 5.13 can be overkill, cluttering the view if more than one property is active. The Speed graph shows rates of transition; in this case, each bounce of the ball is an abrupt shift in speed.

point, toggle the Reference graph off (**Figure 5.14**).

At the bottom of the Graph Options menu is the Allow Keyframes Between Frames toggle. With this off, keyframes that you drag snap to precise frame values (as you would expect); turn it on and you can drag a keyframe to any point in time, should you need a keyframe to occur between frames. For example, you might want the moment when the ball hits not to be visible to match timing from a live shot. When you scale a set of keyframes using the Transform Box, keyframes will often fall in between frames whether or not this option is enabled.

✔ Tip

- Show Graph Tool Tips is worth leaving on most of the time; values are displayed for any curve under the mouse, whether or not a keyframe occurs at that point in time.

The Transform Box

The Transform Box lets you edit keyframe values in all kinds of wacky ways. Toggle on Show Transform Box and select more than one keyframe, and a white box with vertices surrounds the selected frames. Drag the handle at the right side left or right to speed or slow the entire animation, respectively, while the relative timing remains the same. Just as with mask transforms—covered in Chapter 7—dragging inside the box translates a set of keyframes, dragging the corners scales values. Additionally

- To offset the center of the Transform Box and thus the scale pivot, first drag the anchor to the desired pivot point, then (this is the important extra point) Ctrl-drag/Cmd-drag.
- To reverse keyframes, drag left/right beyond the opposite edge of the box (or simply context-click and choose Keyframe Assistant > Time-Reverse Keyframes).
- To scale the box proportionally, Shift-drag on a corner. To taper values at one end, Ctrl+Alt-drag (Cmd+ Option-drag) on a corner (**Figure 5.15**). To move one side of the box up or down, Ctrl+Alt+Shift-drag (Cmd+Option+Shift-drag) on a corner. You can even skew the contents of the box by Alt-dragging (Option-dragging) on a corner handle.

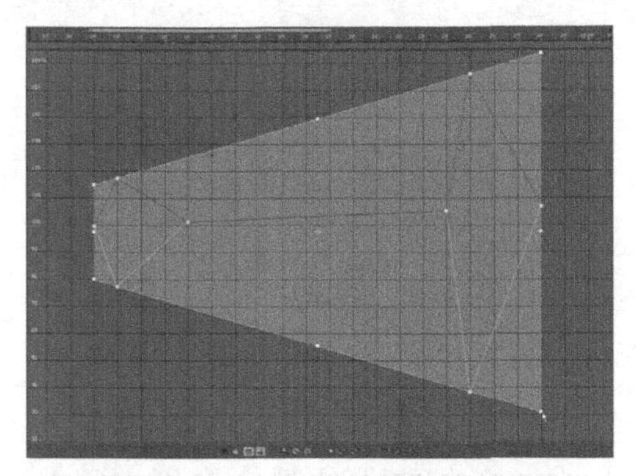

Figure 5.15 The Transform Box makes it possible to scale values proportionally. By Ctrl+Alt-dragging (Cmd+Option-dragging) on a corner, you can taper or expand values at one end of the selection area.

✔ Notes

Take note of the second set of "Show" options – layer In/Out points, audio waveforms, layer markers and expressions, all features of the Layer view (most of them described in this chapter) can also be displayed in the Graph Editor to help avoid excessive toggling.

The Snap button causes any keyframe you drag to snap to virtually any other visible marker in the Graph Editor, but it does not snap to whole frame values with Allow Keyframes Between Frames enabled.

✔ Close-Up

Flips and Flops After Effects includes a Flop, as well as a Flip and a Flip + Flop in Animation Presets > Image – Utilities (search on any of these in the Effects & Presets panel). To "flop" a shot means to invert it horizontally, on the Y axis (a "flip" occurs on the X axis). The preset employs the Transform effect, which unfortunately is not compatible with 32 bpc mode; you can instead toggle Constrain Proportions for Scale and add a minus sign beside the X value (Figure 5.16).

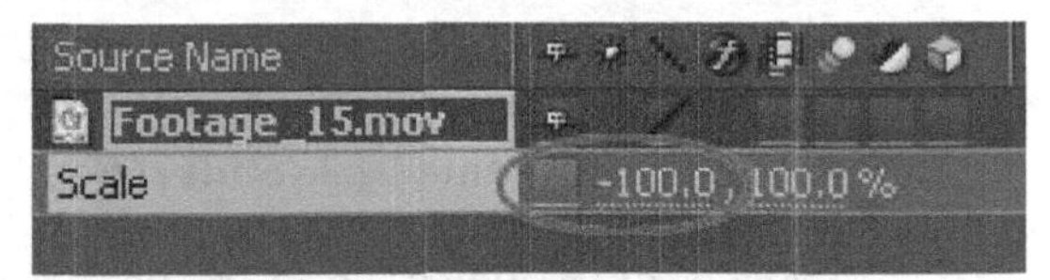

Figure 5.16 To flop a shot, be sure to uncheck Constrain Proportions before setting the X value to –100%.

Temporal Data and Eases

By default, After Effects offers linear temporal transitions between keyframes; a property proceeds from keyframe A to keyframe B at a steady rate, then from keyframe B to keyframe C at a separate but still steady rate, with an abrupt change of pace.

Experienced animators, anthropologists and economists alike recognize how rarely anything in nature proceeds in a linear fashion; natural motion is mostly arcs and curves. Think of a camera push: with a real camera operator moving that camera, a push starts and stops gently due to inertia and the human body, gradually moving at a more or less steady rate only at the middle of the transition. Thus the Easy Ease feature is your friend.

✔ Notes

Spatial interpretations, however, do not default to linear unless you enable Default Spatial Interpretation to Linear in Preferences > General. By default, a Bézier shape eases spatial transitions.

Easy Ease

Part of After Effects since around the time rapper Easy E was laid to rest (coincidence? Only a handful of guys named Dave know the truth), Easy Ease keyframe assistants ease transitions as follows:

- Context-click a keyframe and choose one of the Easy Ease options under the Keyframe Assistant submenu.

- Use keyboard shortcuts: **F9** applies Bézier interpolation, creating eases in and out of a keyframe, while **Shift+F9** creates an ease into the keyframe only, and **Ctrl+Shift+F9 (Cmd+Shift+F9)** creates an ease out, maintaining a linear transition in.

✔ Warning

Mac users beware: The F9 key is used by the system for the Exposé feature, revealing all open panels in all applications. You can change or disable this feature in System Preferences > Dashboard & Exposé.

- Click one of the Easy Ease buttons at the lower right of the Graph Editor (the ones that depict s-curved graph lines leading in and out of vertices).

For a camera push, you might add eases to the first and final frames, perhaps also adding intermediate keyframes with eases (disrupting the move to make it feel even more human and organic).

Figures 5.17a and **b** show the difference between a default linear camera push and one to which eases have been applied. The keyframes change from linear to Bézier type, and rate of motion is described by a curve instead of a straight line. You can (and often should) freely customize an ease using the Graph Editor. Select any keyframe and yellow Bézier handles extend to its left and

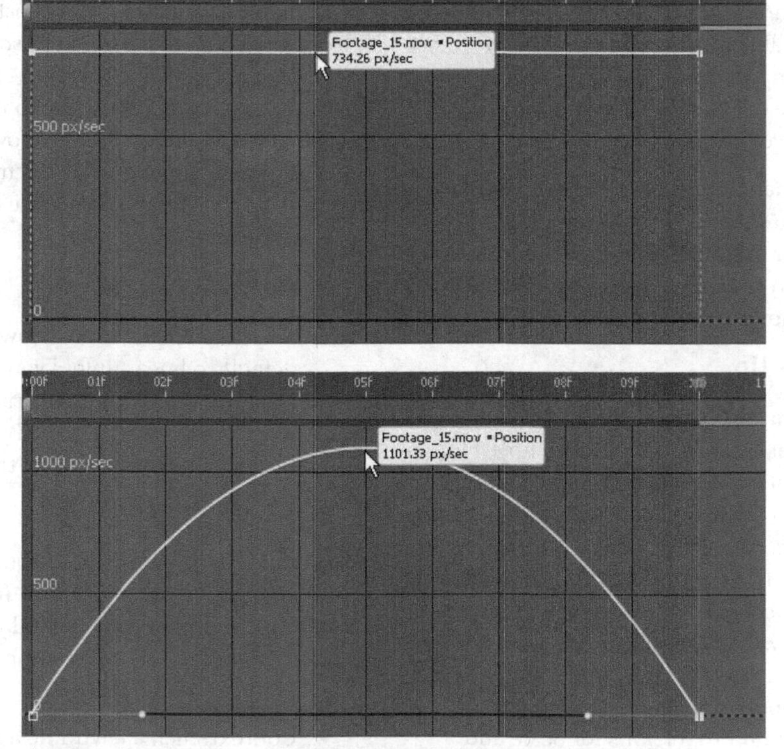

Figures 5.17a and b With no eases, the Speed graph for Position is flat, moving at a steady rate (a). Add eases (b), and it arcs from 0 (at the beginning and end of the move) to a higher value at the center peak of the ease.

right. To increase an ease, drag the yellow handle away from the keyframe; or inward toward the keyframe to reduce it. You don't even need Easy Ease.

Holds

A Hold keyframe prevents any change to a value until the next keyframe. Set it as follows:

- Context-click on the keyframe and choose Toggle Hold Keyframe.
- Use the shortcut **Ctrl+Alt+H** (**Cmd+Shift+H**).
- Choose the Hold button below the Graph Editor (the one with the graph lines all at right angles).

✔ Note

Hold keyframes solve problems any time you see unwanted in-between information creep into an animation; beware of this particularly with spatial animations, which can drift or even loop without holds.

In Layer Bar mode a hold is indicated by the square appearance on one or both sides of the keyframe. In the Graph Editor it appears as a flat horizontal line to the right of a keyframe.

To reposition a layer over time with no in-betweening whatsoever, begin by setting the first frame as a Hold keyframe; all keyframes that follow it in time will be Hold keyframes, signaled by their completely square appearance in layer bar mode or a series of right angles in the Graph Editor (**Figures 5.18a** and **b**). The result is that the property transitions instantly to the next held value, so for example, if you want to animate a layer's visibility on and off, set Opacity with Hold keyframes to 0% and 100%.

Spatial Data and Curves

When you are called upon to create a complex animation, the After Effects interface is up to it. I can't teach you to be a great animator, but I can focus on what you need to know to keyframe effectively and to avoid common pitfalls.

A closer look at the simple bouncing ball reveals a lot about animating spatial and temporal keyframes data (**Figures 5.19**

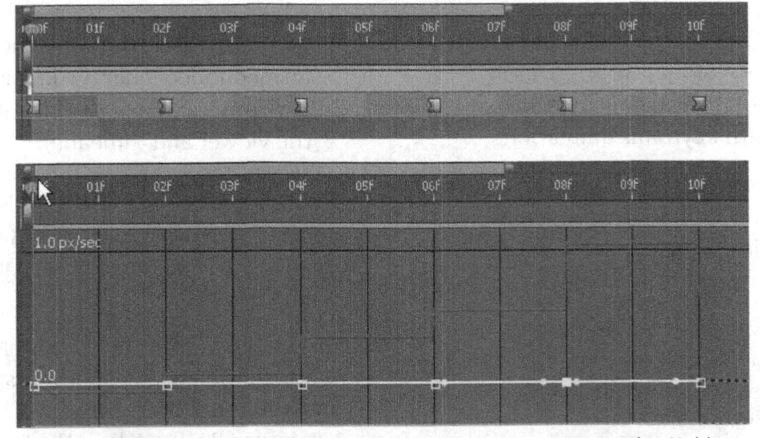

Figures 5.18a and b A series of Bézier keyframes have been converted to Hold keyframes, evident by the square shape at the right of each keyframe in the Layer Bar view (a) and right angles in the Graph Editor (b).

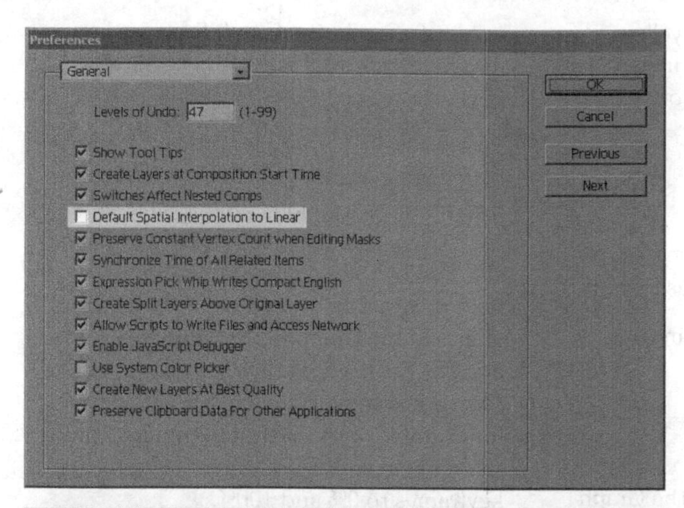

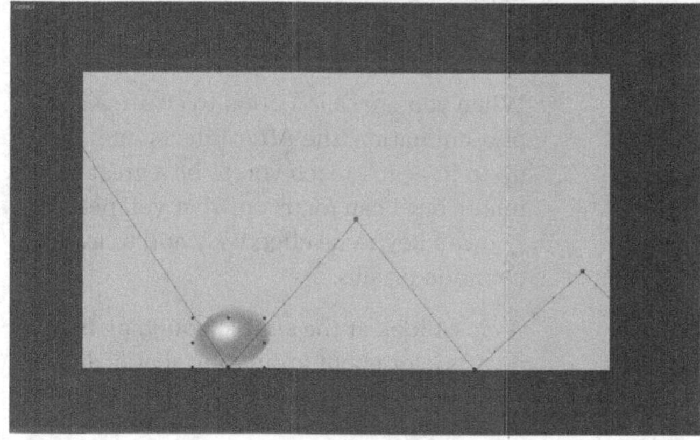

Figure 5.19a and b Under Preferences > General (**Ctrl+Alt+;** or **Cmd+Option+;**), Default Spatial Interpolation to Linear is off by default (a), producing this result (b) with three or more position keys.

to **5.22**). If this is new material and you are willing, try re-creating it yourself, as it reveals most of the fundamentals of expressing motion with keyframe animation.

In the (possibly likely) case that the need for a bouncing ball animation never comes up, what does this example show you? Let's recap:

- You can control a motion path in the Composition viewer, using Bézier tools and the Pen tool (described in detail in the next chapter).
- Realistic motion often requires that you shape the motion path Béziers and add temporal eases; the two actions are performed independently on any given keyframe, and in two different places (in the viewer and Timeline).

Animation can get a little trickier in 3D, but the same basic rules apply (see Chapter 15, "The Camera and Optics," for more).

Three preset keyframe transition types are available, each with a shortcut at the bottom of the Graph Editor: Hold, Linear, and Automatic Bezier. Adjust the handles or apply Easy Ease and the preset becomes a custom Bezier Shape.

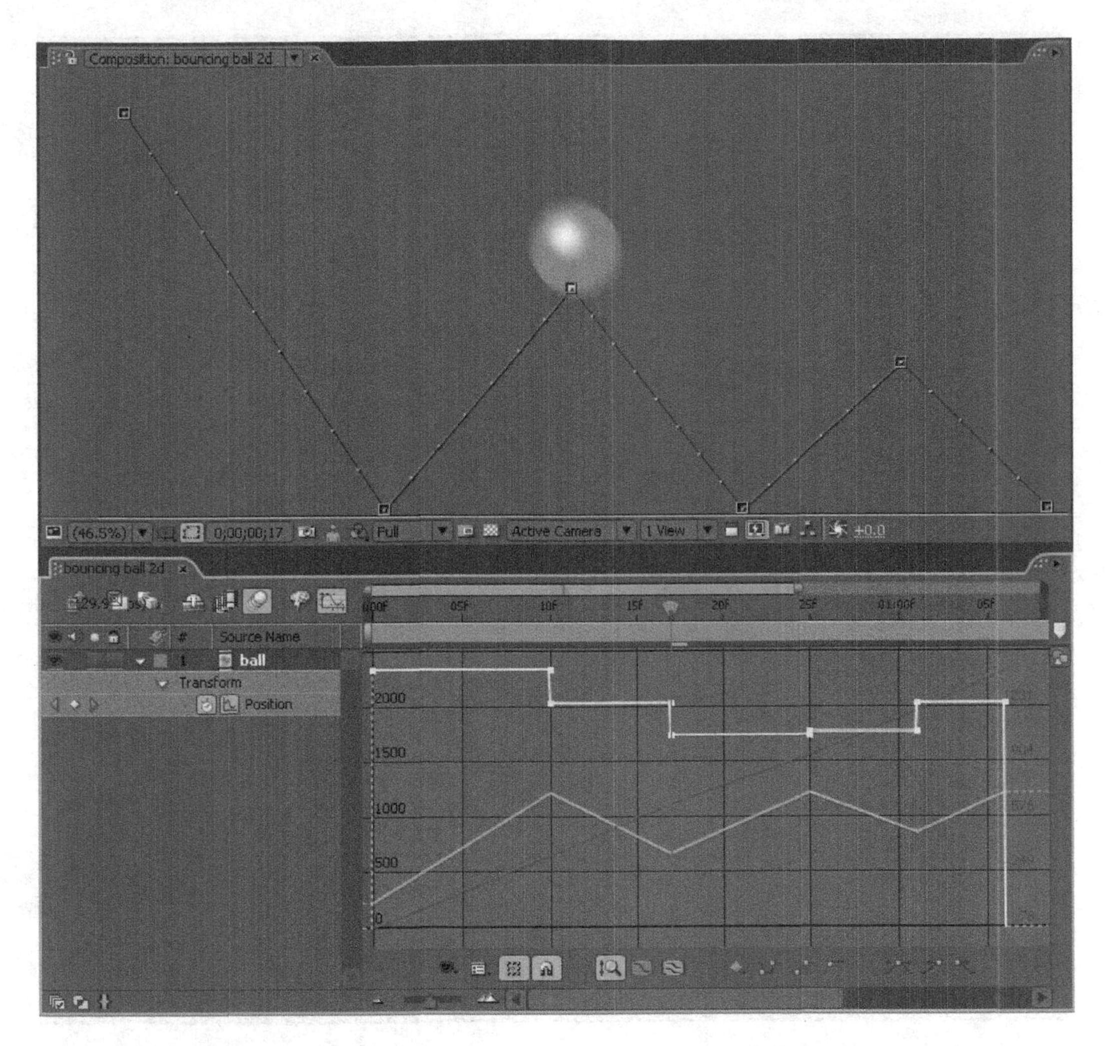

Figure 5.20 Click the check box for Default Spatial Interpolation to Linear, restart After Effects for the preference to take effect, and the result is three keyframes that are linear in both time and position.

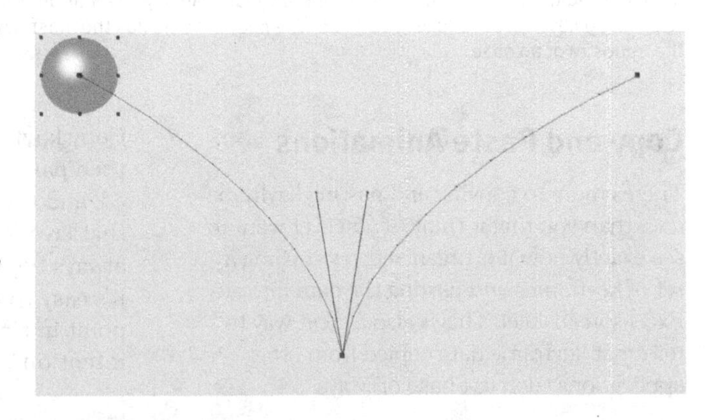

Figure 5.21 Hold down the Ctrl/Cmd key while clicking a spatial keyframe to activate its Bézier handles, then Ctrl/Cmd-click on one of the handles to "break" them. This enables you to form the V-shaped bounce shown here.

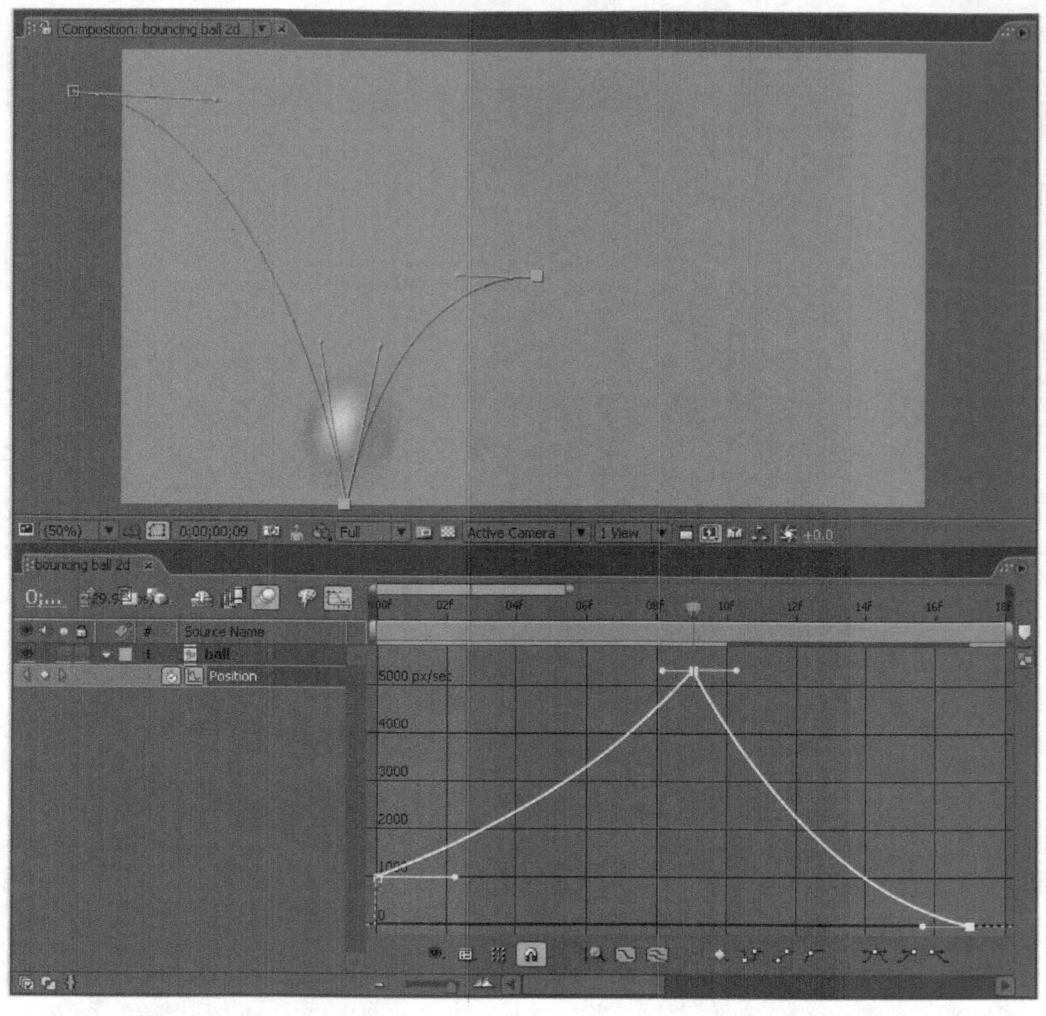

Figure 5.22 The Speed Curve below corresponds to the motion curve above, but it is showing completely different data and could have a very different shape without changing the motion. An ease has been applied to the final frame with the F9 key; eases reduce speed to 0. The middle frame has the most abrupt shift of motion, for the bounce—it's the opposite of an ease.

Copy and Paste Animations

There's more to copying and pasting keyframe data than you might think. If you ever want to see exactly how it is organized, try copying a set of keyframes and pasting the data into an Excel spreadsheet. This is also a great way to reformat keyframe data copied from other applications such as Shake or Maya.

Copy keyframes from a particular property, then paste them with another layer selected, and they are automatically pasted to that layer's corresponding property, but always beginning at the current time; thus it's easy to relocate keyframes to another point in time, whether or not that's your intention.

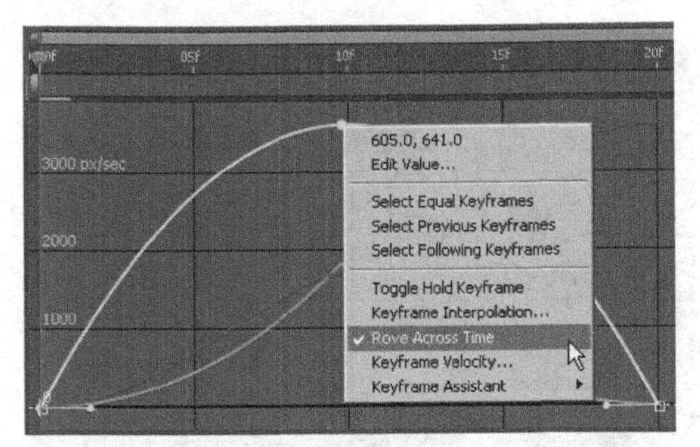

Figure 5.23 The middle keyframe is set to rove and thus is now positioned in between frames; the arc of its motion is now even in and out of the keyframe.

✔ Close-Up

Roving Keyframes Sometimes an animation must follow an exact path, hitting precise points, but progress steadily, with no variation in the rate of travel. This is the situation for which Roving keyframes were devised. Figure 5.23 shows a before and after view of the application of a roving keyframe to the animation in Figure 5.22; the path of the animation is identical, but the keyframes are now evenly spaced.

If that target property doesn't exist, because it's part of an effect applied only to the source layer, After Effects adds the effect as well as the keyframes, just as you might expect.

✔ Tip

- Enable a small lock icon that appears on the Effect Controls tab, and that effect remains visible even when you select a different layer.

Copy keyframes from a particular property and select a property with similar parameters; the animation data transfers to the new property, often very useful as long as you know it's happening. For example, apply a 2D Position keyframe to the Flare Center position of a Lens Flare effect by selecting the Flare Center property in the Timeline prior to pasting and the keyframes go to that property instead of Position.

That all means that you should pay attention to which item is currently selected when copying or pasting. **Figure 5.24** shows how easy it can be to miss that the Effect Controls panel is forward and has an effect highlighted, so that effect is copied, not the entire layer.

If the result of a copy and paste ever seems strange, just undo and try again, carefully selecting exactly the thing you want to copy.

✔ Tip

- Ctrl/Cmd-click on a keyframe to reset its Temporal Interpretation to linear. Alt+Ctrl+K/Opt+Cmd+K opens the Keyframe Interpolation dialog where you can choose any Temporal or Spatial interpolation, or set a keyframe to rove.

Layer vs. Graph

To summarize the distinction between Layer and Graph Editor views, in Layer view you can

- Block in keyframes with respect to the overall composition
- Establish broad timing (where Linear, Easy Ease, and Auto-Bezier keyframes are sufficient)

The Graph Editor is essential to

- Refine an individual animation curve
- Compare spatial and temporal data
- Scale animation data, especially around a specific pivot point
- Perform extremely specific timing (for example, a keyframe is needed between frames)

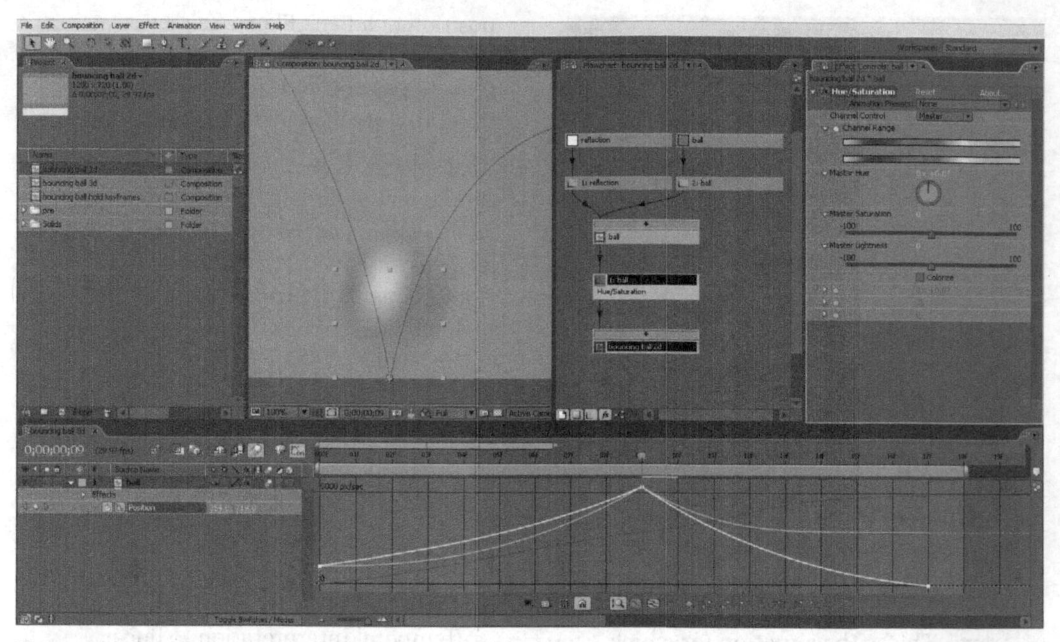

Figure 5.24 It's possible to have a different item selected in each panel, yet only one is the active item. If you were to press Delete in this case, the effect would be deleted because the Effect Controls panel is active.

- Adjust keyframe values not at the current time (difficult in the layer view)

With either view you can

- Edit expressions
- Change keyframe type (Linear, Hold, Ease in, and so on)
- Make editorial/compositing decisions regarding layers (start/stop/duration, split layers, order—possible in both, easier in Layer view)

By no means, then, does the Graph Editor obviate use of the Layer view, where the majority of compositing and simple animation is typically accomplished.

Über-duper

More than anything, knowing shortcuts makes you a rapid-fire animator. This section is not only about the überkey, which is among the most useful shortcuts in all of After Effects, but also about taking control of keyframe data in general.

✔ Note

The "überkey" plays of off Friedrich Nietzsche's übermensch—a man more powerful and important than others. It's one shortcut to rule them all.

The überkey is available in two delicious flavors: **U** and **UU**. In the same 02_graphEditor.aep project, highlight the ball layer, and press a single **U**. All properties with keyframes (Position and Scale in this case) are revealed. Press **U** again to toggle, and they are concealed. When arriving cold at an animation you've never seen, or returning to one of your own, this is how you immediately find out where the keyframes are.

✔ Tip

- To reveal only applied effects on a selected layer, use the E key. Or, if the überkey reveals effects and transforms and you want only the transforms, Shift+E toggles off revealed effects.

But wait, there's more. Now highlight the bg layer, which contains no keyframes whatsoever, and press **UU** (two Us in quick succession). All of the properties set to any value other than their default—including those with keyframes (none in this case)—are revealed.

The **U** shortcut is a quick way to find keyframes to edit or to locate a keyframe that you suspect is hiding somewhere. But **UU**—now *that* is a full-on problem-solving tool all to itself. It allows you to quickly investigate what has been edited on a given layer, is helpful when troubleshooting your own layer settings, and is nearly priceless when investigating an unfamiliar project. Highlight all of the layers in your comp, press **UU**, and you have before you all of the edits that have been made to all of the layer properties.

✓ Notes

- What, if anything, is beyond the reach of the UU shortcut when analyzing a comp?
- Contents of nested compositions, which must be opened (Alt/Option-double-click) and analyzed individually
- Locked layers
- Shy layers remain hidden if the Shy toggle is on
- Settings not related to properties, such as Blending Modes and Motion Blur

Dissect a Project

If you've been handed an unfamiliar project and need to make sense of it quickly, there are a couple of other tools to help you.

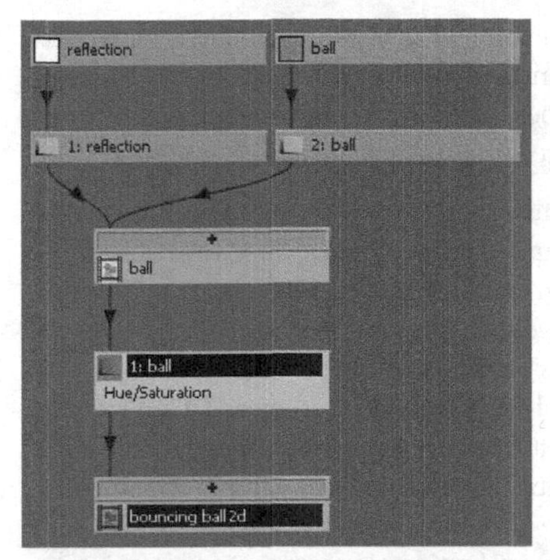

Figure 5.25 Although After Effects is a layer-based application, the underlying logic of compositing and the flow of images and effects is clearly displayed in Flowchart. Interaction here is limited—there is no way to change the pipeline order or add nodes directly.

The Flowchart view offers a broad overview of the project's structure; it is enabled with the right-most button along the bottom of the Composition panel, via Window > Flowchart or using **Ctrl+F11/Cmd+F11**. You have to see it to believe it: a nodal interface in After Effects (**Figure 5.25**), perhaps the least nodal of any of the major compositing applications.

This view shows how objects (layers, compositions, and effects) are used, and in what relationship to one another. The + button above a composition reveals its components; for the cleanest view, toggle layers and effects off at the lower left.

✓ Close-Up

Nerd-based Compositing How exactly is the node view in After Effects more limited than what you'd find in a node-based compositor? Essentially, you can't make creative decisions there; it's useful for project analysis only, offering some insight into the order in which items render. It's also less "atomic": Properties and effects are grouped directly with layers instead of being listed as their own nodes, because their render order cannot be freely reconfigured as it can with nodes.

To investigate a project, start with the end composition and work your way backward; open any comp by double-clicking it in the Flowchart. Turn off the Shy toggle at the top if it's on, highlight all of the layers (**Ctrl+A/Cmd+A**), and press **UU** to reveal all altered properties. Now preview the composition, stopping at any frame where you have questions and investigating which settings and animations apply to that point in time. If you find a nested composition, open it (Alt/Option-double-click) and investigate. With some patience, you can make sense of even the most complicated project, one step at a time.

✔ Note

In the panel menu you can choose your view; Left to Right fits well on a typical monitor. Whether you choose straight or curved connecting lines is up to you, but you can clean up the view by clicking this toggle holding the Alt/Option key.

Keyframe Navigation and Selection

Although no shortcut can hold a candle to the überkey, there are several other useful Timeline shortcuts:

- **J** and **K** keys navigate backward and forward, respectively, through all visible keyframes (and layer markers, and Work Area boundaries).

✔ Tip

- J and K hit all revealed keyframes, so to navigate one property only, click the arrows that appear under A/V Features (the Keys column). Or reveal only the keyframes in that channel; J and K will ignore the rest.

- To select all keyframes for a property, highlight that property's name in the Timeline. To delete any keyframes not visible in the Timeline (those occurring before or after the comp), select all, then Shift-drag a rectangular selection around the ones you want to keep (the visible ones). Now delete.
- Context-click on a keyframe to Select Previous Keyframes or Select Following Keyframes. There is even an option to Select Equal Keyframes (those with an identical value).
- **Alt/Option+Shift**+the shortcut corresponding to a transform property (**P, A, S, R,** or **T**) sets the first keyframe, no need to click anywhere.
- Any stopwatch in the Effect Controls sets the first keyframe for an effect property at the current frame. However, if keyframes are already set, clicking the stopwatch deletes them.
- To add a keyframe without changing any value, context-click on the stopwatch in Effect Controls and choose Add Keyframe.

✔ Note

Multi-selection works differently with keyframes in the Layer Bar view than anywhere else in the application. To add or subtract a single frame from a selected group, Shift-click. Ctrl/Cmd-clicking on keyframes converts them to Auto-Bezier mode. This is not the case in the Graph Editor view.

Read on; you are not a keyframe Jedi—yet.

Keyframe Offsets

To offset the values of multiple keyframes by the same amount in Layer view, select them all, *make certain that the Current Time Indicator is resting on a frame with one of the selected keyframes*, and drag text to offset. If instead, you edit one of these by typing in a new value, all keyframes will be set to that value—not, in most cases, what you want. The Graph Editor makes it easier to see what's happening.

Other tips for working with multiple keyframes include

- Nudge selected keyframes (one or many) forward or backward in time using **Alt+Right/Left Arrow (Option+ Right/Left Arrow)**, respectively.
- Deselect keyframes only using **Shift+F2**. Select all visible keyframes (without selecting their layers) using **Ctrl+Alt+A (Cmd+Option+A)**.

✔ **Tip**

- **Ctrl+Alt+A/Cmd+Option+A** selects all visible keyframes while leaving the source layers, making it easy to delete them when, say, duplicating a layer but changing its animation.

Spatial Offsets

The two most common ways to offset a transform animation—to edit its position, rotation, or scale from a point other than its center—are intuitive, easy to use, and well documented. In an individual layer, move the anchor point from the center to a specific point in the frame, typically using the Pan Behind tool (keyboard shortcut: **Y**). Details are in the "Anchor Point" section.

✔ **Tip**

- The transform box in the Graph Editor offers an easy method for scaling keyframes temporally, but in Layer view you can instead select a set of keyframes, Alt-drag (Option-drag) on a keyframe at either end of the set, and the entire set is scaled proportionally in time (with the opposite end of the selected set acting as the stationary anchor).

Alternatively, you can center several layers around the center point of a single layer by parenting them to that layer. The children take on all of the transforms of the parent layer (except Opacity, which, remember, isn't a real transform) plus whatever offsets they already have.

After Effects is generally designed to preserve the appearance of the composition when you are merely setting up animation, toggling 3D on, and so forth. Therefore editing an anchor point position with the Pan Behind tool triggers the inverse offset to the Position property. Parent a layer to another layer and the child layer maintains its position until you further animate either of them.

✔ **Tip**

- Edit anchor points or set up a parent-child relationship *before* animating, if at all possible, to avoid offsetting keyframes and messing up the whole animation.

That's all clear enough. But reset an offset anchor point in the middle of a Position animation, and the Position keyframe at that point in time changes. Or undo parenting at a frame other than the one where you set it, and its Position value changes so that it appears to remain in the same place. I have used this to my advantage for 3D setup; I start with the camera at or near its default, toggle the layer to 3D and parent it to the camera, move the camera to some crazy far-away position where the layer is to appear and un-parent the layer.

✔ **Tip**

- To adjust an anchor point or undo parenting without the automatic compensation

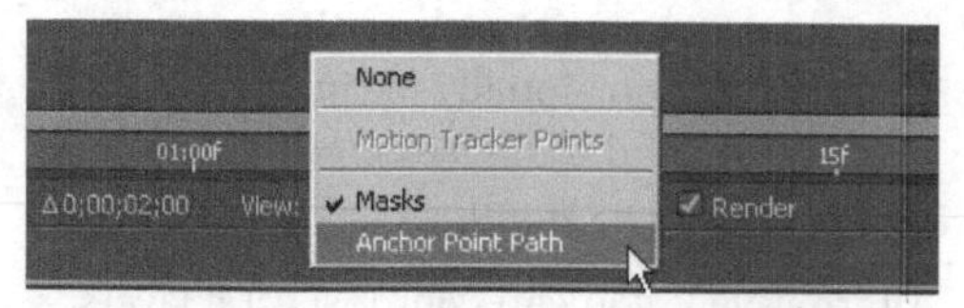

Figure 5.26 Masks, not Anchor Point Path, is the default Layer display mode. Change it as needed using this menu at the bottom of the Layer panel. Note that the bouncing ball examples included in 02_graphEditor.aep feature an offset (but not animated) anchor point, allowing squash and stretch animation to occur around the point of contact (at the base of the ball).

from the application, hold down the Alt (Option) key as you make the change.

Anchor Point

The most straightforward method to edit an anchor point in the Composition panel is to use the Pan Behind tool (**Y**); doing so offsets Position to maintain current appearance. For a similar result, you can edit anchor point values in the Timeline, but Position data is unaffected.

It can be difficult to edit animated anchor point data in the Composition viewer. Instead, activate the Layer viewer and change the View pull-down menu from Masks to Anchor Point Path (**Figure 5.26**).

✔ Note

The 02_graphEditor.aep project used for the bouncing ball animation earlier in this chapter includes an anchor point offset to the base of the ball; this allows the scaling involved for squash and stretch in the bounce to occur around the point of contact.

Parent Hierarchy

A parent-child relationship is set up by choosing the target parent layer from the child's pull-down menu in the Parent column of the Timeline, or by dragging the pickwhip adjacent to that menu to the target parent layer.

Parenting "sticks" even when you change layer order or duplicate or rename the parent. You can select all of the children of a parent layer by context-clicking it and choosing Select Children. To remove parenting from all selected layers, choose None from the pull-down menu of any one of them.

✔ Note

If you've ever worked with 3D animation, you are probably already aware how usefully parenting solves all kinds of animation puzzles, even just during setup. For example, you can array layers in a circle by parenting one layer, rotating the parent, parenting the next layer, rotating again, and so on.

To move layers relative to a point that is not represented in any current layer, you can add a null object (for the shortcut, go to Layer > New > Null Object). Null objects are actually 100 x 100 pixel layers that do not render. They possess all of the normal transform controls and can contain effects (and Masks for that matter, which are completely useless in null objects). Contained effects can be used by expressions as reference for other settings.

Motion Blur

Motion blur is essential to most realistic animated shots. If a layer and/or the camera is animated at a sufficiently high velocity, and the Motion Blur toggle is enabled at the Layer and Composition levels, then, for free, realistic blur is added to match the apparent motion of the scene, using settings you control.

Motion blur is the natural result of movement that occurs while a camera shutter is open, causing the image to smear. This can be the result of moving objects, or of movement of the camera itself. Far from something to avoid, however, motion blur not only can be aesthetically quite beautiful, it also helps create persistence of vision, the means by which the eye detects motion, and thus it is often more natural relaxing to the eye.

✔ Note

> You might not notice motion blur with your naked eye, but it does occur—watch a ceiling fan in motion, and then follow the individual blades with your eye; depending on how closely you can follow its movement, you will see more or less blur.

All of this helps explain why efforts to eliminate motion blur from a sampled image have tended to seem faddish and strange, although new cameras, from high-speed live-event HDTV to the Red camera, are capable of almost eliminating it. Who knows, along with grain, motion blur may become more of an arbitrary artistic choice as viewers adapt to 21st century electronic imaging.

After Effects offers control over how long and precisely when the camera shutter is open, via the Composition Settings dialog's Advanced tab (**Figure 5.27**). This latest version of After Effects offers major improvement to the quality and default effectiveness of motion blur.

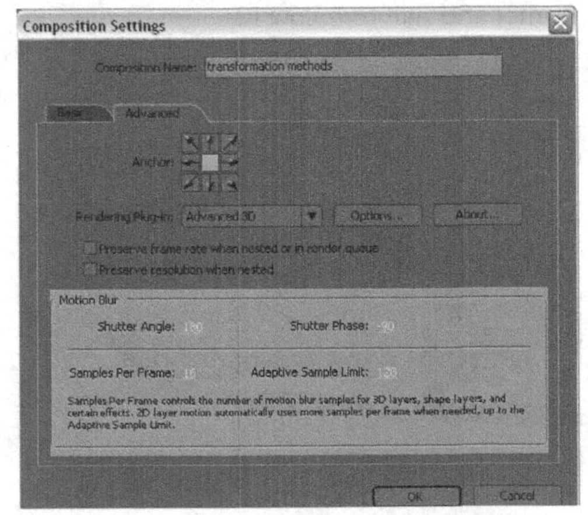

Figure 5.27 The Shutter Angle and Shutter Phase settings on the Advanced tab of the Composition Settings dialog control the appearance of motion blur.

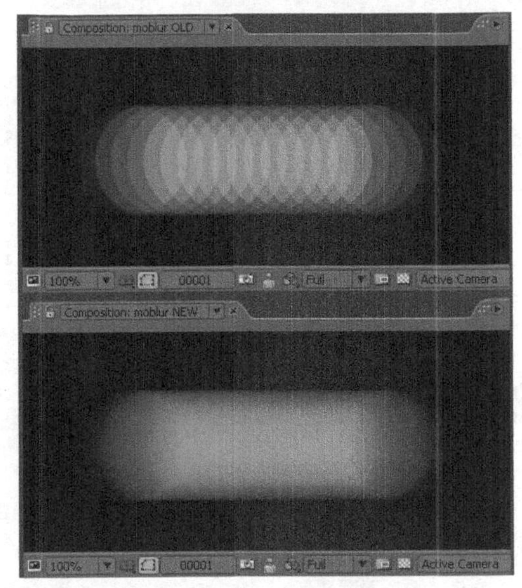

Figure 5.28 By raising Samples per Frame from the default shown in Figure 5.27, you can finally avoid steppy motion blur when creating fast motion in After Effects. This setting determines the minimum number of samples; Adaptive Sample Limit determines the maximum.

Shutter Angle controls how long the shutter is open; a higher number (up to a maximum of 720) means more blur. Shutter Phase controls at what point, during a given frame, the shutter opens. The new Samples Per Frame and Adaptive Sample Limit settings permit you to refine the look of the blur, to make it appear smoother and less "steppy" (at the expense of extra process cycles naturally), as in **Figure 5.28**.

What the Settings Mean

A physical film camera employs an angled mechanical shutter that opens in a circular motion anywhere between a few degrees and a full 360 degrees (an electronic shutter behaves differently, but never mind about that—it's the metaphor that's important here). Theoretically, 360 degrees provides the maximum open aperture, and thus the greatest amount of blur a shot would contain; After Effects doubles this ceiling for cases where you simply want more.

✔ Close-Up

The Virtual Camera Shutter Using a real, physical camera, the shutter setting (along with the aperture) determines the amount of light passed onto the film or video pickup. Low-lit scenes are blurrier because the shutter remains open longer, allowing it to gather more light. Other scenes will be deliberately taken with a slow shutter (and the aperture closed down) to produce, streaky, smeary blur, which, if taken with a high-quality video pickup or film, can look quite lovely.

Unlike an actual camera, After Effects is unconcerned with the need to gather light, and it does not produce (or even emulate) any other lens effects associated with a high or low shutter angle setting (nor the Aperture setting on a 3D camera, explored in Chapter 15). Therefore, by opening the aperture, you mimic only the desirable part—the blur itself.

A camera report can help determine this setting, although you can typically eyeball it by zooming in on an area where background and foreground elements should be blurred with the same motion and matching them (**Figures 5.29a** and **b**). If your camera report includes shutter speed, you can calculate the Shutter Angle setting using the following formula:

shutter speed = 1 / frame rate * (360 / shutter angle)

This isn't as gnarly as it looks, but if you dislike formulas, think of it like this: If your camera takes 24 frames per second, but Shutter Angle is set at 180 degrees, then the frame is exposed half the time (180/360 = $1/2$) or $1/48$ of a second. If the camera report shows a $1/96$ of a second exposure, Shutter Angle should be 90 degrees.

Shutter Phase determines when the shutter opens.

A setting of 0 opens the shutter and starts the blur at the beginning of the frame while the default –90 setting (with a 180° Shutter Angle setting) causes half the blur to start before the frame (blurring the layer in the frame) and half to follow it.

Figures 5.29a and b In 5.29a, the default Shutter Angle setting of 180 degrees appears too heavy for the white solid masked and tracked over the front hubcap. In 5.29b, Shutter Angle was cut down by 50% (to 90 degrees). In this case, blur has simply been eye-matched to that of the moving truck.

✔ **Notes**

180 Shutter Angle and –90 Phase are the default settings in After Effects CS3. However, the defaults change to whatever was set most recently, saved in Preferences.

Setting Shutter Phase to –50% of Shutter Angle is useful when motion tracking and should probably be the default. When motion blur is added to the tracked layer, the track stays centered, instead of appearing offset.

Manipulate Time

After Effects is quite flexible when working with time. You can retime footage or mix and match speeds and timing using a variety of methods, each of which is useful for a particular set of situations.

Absolute (Not Relative) Time

After Effects measures time in absolute (not relative) terms, using seconds (rather than frames, whose timing and number changes according to how many there are per second). If time were measured using the total number of frames, or frames per second, changing the frame rate would pose a problem. Instead, at the very deepest level, After Effects is entirely flexible about frame rate.

✔ **Close-Up**

Motion Blur without Motion You get motion blur for free with any layer animated in After Effects and toggled to generate it. However, there is no built-in provision to generate motion blur for footage that contains motion but insufficient blur—a 3D element, say, or footage shot with a high shutter speed. Directional Blur can help, until you deal with footage whose directionality isn't uniform (as is typical with natural motion). At that point, consider Reel Smart Motion Blur from RE:Vision Effects. This plug-in uses optical flow technology (for which the founders won a Technical Achievement Academy Award) to sample the motion in the scene and generate or enhance motion blur, with powerful controls to allow for transparency and sub-sampling. A demo is included on the book's disc.

So, you can change the frame rate of any comp on the fly, and the keyframes maintain their position in actual time. The timing of an animation won't change, only the number of frames per second used to display it (**Figure 5.30**).

Likewise, footage (or a nested composition) whose frame rate does not match th
t of the current composition displays in absolute time, even if the beginning of each frame matches up only at the one-second mark.

✔ **Note**

If time was measured as frames, or frames per second, a change to the frame rate would offset keyframes. Instead, After Effects consistently evaluates time in seconds; keyframes are allowed to fall between frames if necessary to keep the overall timing consistent.

This should make sense to musicians who know how to beat 3 against 4, or other polyrhythms, creating elaborate syncopations, against the steady beat of the metronome. In After Effects, one second is one beat of that metronome.

Time Stretch

Time Stretch lets you alter the duration (or speed) of a source clip; provided you don't need to animate the rate of

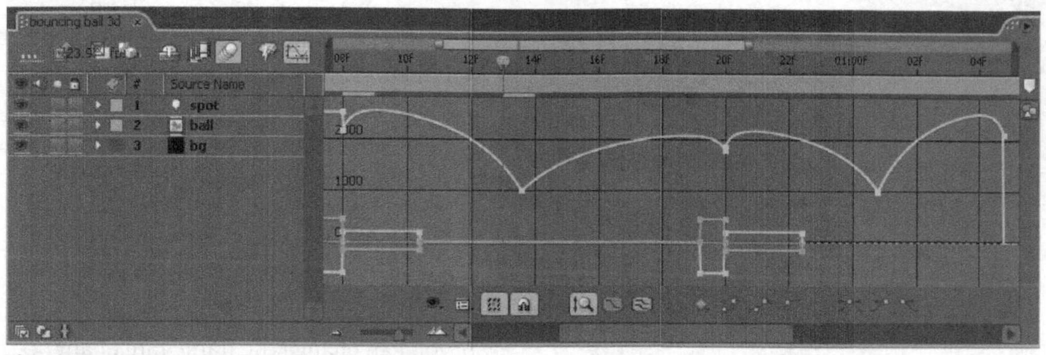

Figure 5.30 The composition's frame rate was altered from 29.97 fps to 24 fps after keyframes were set. All frames following the first one now fall in between the whole frames represented by the grid, but the timing of the animation itself, measured in seconds, is unchanged.

change (in which case only Time Remap will do).

The third of the three icons at the lower left of the Timeline reveals the In/Out/Duration/Stretch columns (**Figure 5.31**).

You can

- Edit the In or Out point: **Ctrl+Shift+comma (Cmd+Shift+comma)** stretches the In point to the current frame, **Ctrl+Alt+comma (Cmd+Option+comma)** stretches the Out point to the current time
- Change the duration of the layer
- Alter the stretch value from 100%

Alternatively, specify these settings in the Time Stretch dialog, activated by clicking the Duration or Stretch value, or choose Layer > Time > Time Stretch (**Figure 5.32**).

Figure 5.31 The highlighted icon reveals and conceals Time Stretch settings.

✔ Note

Stretching a layer does not "stretch" the timing of any applied keyframes; you can use the Graph Editor to stretch keyframes to match, or precompose the layer with its keyframes prior to Time Stretch to guarantee that the animation lines up.

Frame Blending

The noticeable side effect of lengthening or shortening a source clip is that motion becomes choppier as frames repeat (or skip).

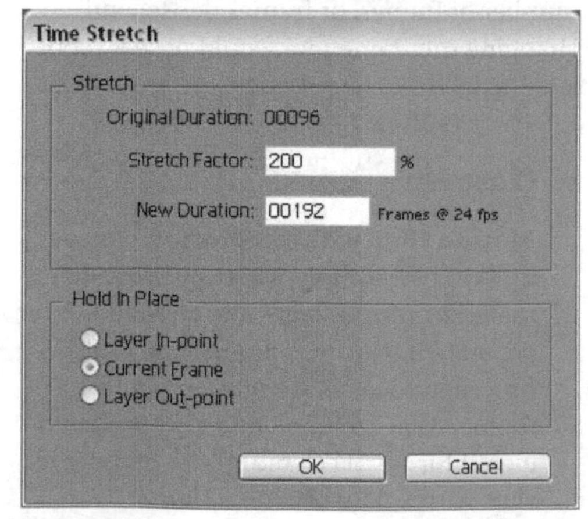

Figure 5.32 You can set an alternate Duration or Stretch Factor in the Time Stretch dialog. It's easy to miss that you can specify the pivot point: In point, Out point, or current time.

Unless the stretch value factors evenly into 100% (say, 50% or 200%), the repeating or skipping occurs in irregular increments, typically causing a distracting lurching motion.

Enable Frame Blending for the layer and the composition, and After Effects averages the adjacent frames together to create a new image on frames that fall in between the source frames.

✔ Tip

- Frame blending is available not only on layers with time stretching but with any footage that comes in at a frame rate other than that of the composition.

There are two basic modes for Frame Blending. Frame Mix mode overlays adjoining frames, essentially blurring them together. Pixel Motion mode uses optical flow techniques to track the motion of actual pixels from frame to frame, creating new frames that are something like a morph of the adjoining frames. Confusingly, the icons for these modes are the same as Draft and Best layer quality, respectively, yet there are cases where Frame Mix may be preferable.

✔ Note

The optical flow in Pixel Motion and the Timewarp effect was licensed from The Foundry. The same underlying technology is also used in Furnace plug-ins for Shake, Flame, and Nuke.

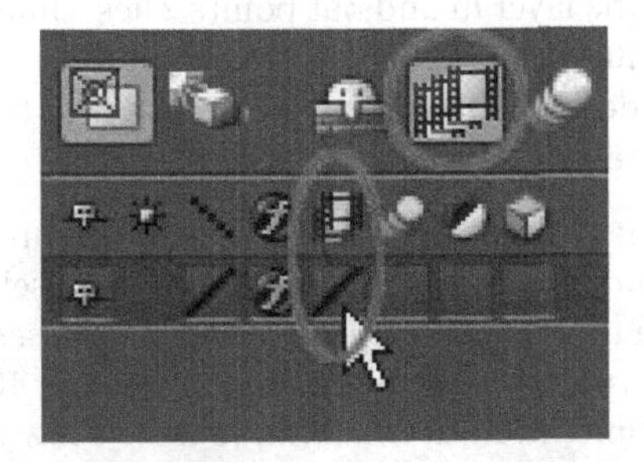

Figure 5.33 These toggles enable Frame Mix or Pixel Motion mode for a retimed layer.

Figure 5.33 shows where the mode is located. Whether the result is acceptable depends on a few predictable criteria. It may appear too blurry, too distorted, or contain too many noticeable frame artifacts, in which case either Frame Mix is preferable, or the Timewarp effect, because it offers control over how the frame blend happens, explained in detail below.

Time Reversal and Freeze Frame

A layer's timing can be reversed with a simple shortcut: Highlight the layer, and press **Ctrl+Alt+R** (**Cmd+Option+R**) or choose Layer > Time > Time-Reverse Layer to set the Stretch value to −100%. The layer's appearance alters to remind you that it is reversed (**Figure 5.34**).

The Layer > Time > Freeze Frame command applies the Time Remap effect and sets a Hold keyframe at the current time.

Time Stretch and Nested Compositions

If you apply Time Stretch (or Time Remap) to a nested composition, the nested comp behaves as if it now has the main composition's frame rate. Keyframe animations are resliced to fit the new rate instead of adhering to the old one.

You can instead force After Effects to use the frame rate of the embedded composition. On the Advanced tab of the

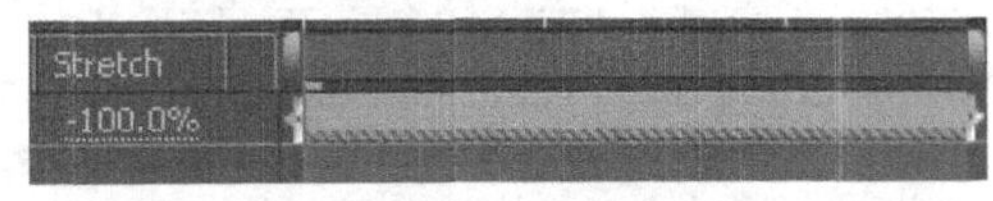

Figure 5.34 The candy striping along the bottom of the layer indicates that the Stretch value is negative and the footage will run in reverse.

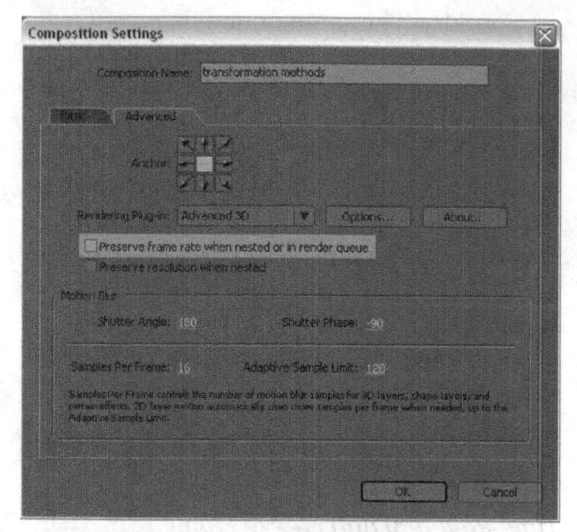

Figure 5.35 If you need a subcomposition to run at a different rate than the master composition, checking the highlighted box in the subcomp prevents After Effects from resampling keyframes at the master comp's rate.

Composition Settings panel of the *nested* comp, toggle Preserve Frame Rate When Nested or in Render Queue (**Figure 5.35**). This forces After Effects to use only whole frame increments in the underlying composition, just as if it were imported footage with that frame rate.

An alternative method to force a given layer to a particular frame rate, whether or not it is a nested composition, is to apply Effect > Time > Posterize Time, entering the desired rate (any value lower than the source rate).

Time Remap

However, once you're comfortable with Time Remap, you may find that you let go of the Time Stretch feature set altogether. The philosophy behind Time Remap is elusively simple: Time has a value, just like any other property, so you can keyframe it, ease in and out of it, loop and ping-pong it, and generally treat it like any other animation data.

✔ Tip

- The final Time Remap keyframe is one greater than the total timing of the layer (in most cases a nonexistent frame) to guarantee that the final source frame is reached, even when frame rates don't match.

Figures 5.36a, b, and **c** show sample timelines that contain typical uses for Time Remap. You needn't go completely nuts rolling footage back and forth, ramping the frame rate up and down, although you can of course do just that. From *The Matrix* to *300*, it's noticeable how accustomed audiences have become to fluid, stylized timing treatments over the past decade or so.

You can set Time Remap by selecting it under the Layer menu or using the shortcut **(Ctrl+Alt+T/Cmd+Option+T)**. This reveals two keyframes, at the beginning and one frame beyond the end of the layer. Time remapped layers have a theoretically infinite duration, so the final Time Remap frame effectively becomes a hold keyframe for the remaining layer duration.

✔ Tip

- Beware when applying Time Remap to a layer whose duration exceeds that of the composition; either default keyframe may be hidden beyond the Timeline boundaries. You can add keyframes at the layer in and out points, click Time Remap to highlight all keyframes, deselect the added ones, and delete the rest.

Time Remap can take a little while to understand in complex situations, but it is useful in a more daily way for retimes with eases, holds, time loops (discussed in Chapter 10), or time reversal. Once you've done a few of these, the more complicated stuff becomes easier.

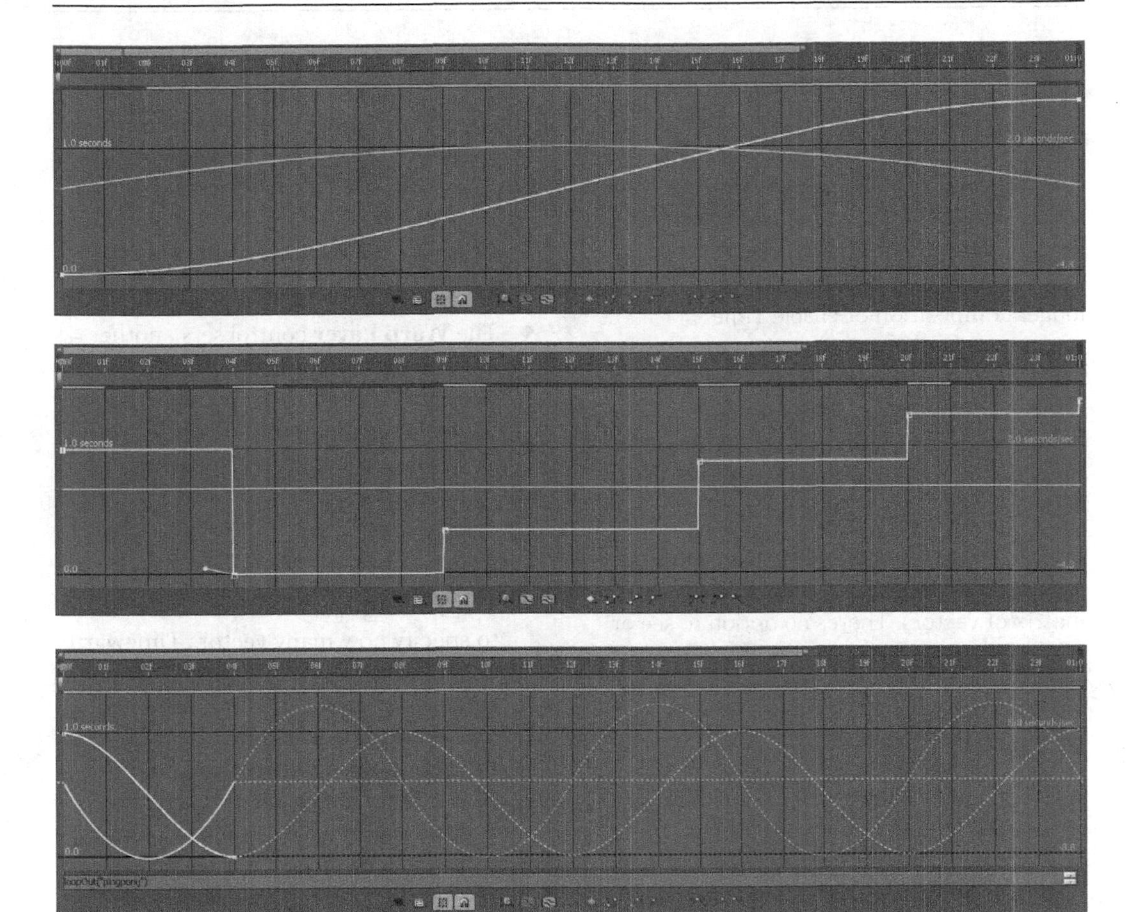

Figures 5.36a, b, and c Simple, everyday things you can do with Time Remap, shown with reference curves: speed up the source with eases (a), progress through a series of stills selected from the moving clip using Hold keyframes (b), and loop the source using a simple expression (c).

✔ Tip

- To reverse a clip via Time Remap, highlight all keyframes by clicking on the Time Remap property name. Next, context-click one of the highlighted keyframes, and select Keyframe Assistant > Time-Reverse Keyframes.

Timewarp

Although The Foundry's amazing Furnace plug-ins are not, at this writing, available for After Effects, Adobe did license one component of Furnace: Kronos, the retiming tool. It's the technology in Pixel Motion, and the Timewarp effect offers actual control over the way that Pixel Motion works with footage.

Timewarp can be used to speed up, slow down, or (like Time Remapping) dynamically animate the timing of a clip. When you speed up a clip with Timewarp, it can add the appropriate amount of motion blur (if so enabled under the Motion Blur settings of the effect).

Most of the time, however, Timewarp is used to slow footage down, creating new in-between frames, and to do this, a particular extra bit of setup is required. By default, Timewarp is set with a speed of 50.00, or 50% (half) of the original speed. Apply it directly to a footage layer and you'll find that the layer ends halfway through the retime operation. There's no way to extend the length of the original footage layer unless you either precompose it into a longer composition or enable Time Remapping. Leave the Time Remap keyframes at their defaults, as they are overridden by Timewarp's Speed or Source Frame property. You determine which of these two criteria to animate in Timewarp with the Adjust Time By setting.

Like Pixel Motion mode, Timewarp employs optical flow, tracking individual pixels via a matrix of vectors. There's no option to see or control those vectors directly, but you can influence how footage is analyzed as follows:

✔ Tip

- By default, Timewarp uses Pixel Motion as the Method setting, and it's hard to imagine changing this setting other than to temporarily compare what is happening with the source (Whole Frames) or a simple blend without optical flow (Frame Mix).

- The biggest improvement you can make to the result is to give Timewarp a mask specifying a given layer of movement. **Figure 5.37a** shows a typical case where this is helpful. Specify which portions of the footage are sampled using the **Matte Channel, Matte Layer**, and **Source Crops** options.
- The **Warp Layer** control sets another layer as a target for the Timewarp operation. This is vital when you are working footage that would be difficult for Timewarp to analyze without first adjusting its contrast or luminance, or keying it, but those adjustments don't belong in the final shot.

The **Tuning** section contains controls to specify how many vectors Timewarp uses (**Vector Detail**) and how much smoothing to add (**Global** and **Local Smoothing, Iterations**), as well as **Filtering, Error Threshold**, and **Block Size** settings. It's incorrect to assume that the best result will always come from raising Vector Detail, Smoothing, and Filtering, although in many cases it will help, even though it may slow image processing considerably.

Figures 5.37a and 5.37b In this shot, the camera viewpoint revolves around the subject (a), and Timewarp has no way of distinguishing foreground and background elements, so they tend to tear. You can help guarantee success by providing a traveling foreground matte (b).

Image tearing and pixel artifacts are the most common problems when using Timewarp. To solve these, specify a matte if at all possible. Next, you can increase Filtering from Normal to Extreme (although, even if Extreme helps, you may want to leave Filtering on Normal until it's time to render, as Extreme will slow things down considerably). You can even increase the amount of smoothing on the Global (all vectors) and Local (single vector) level.

✔ Tip

- Timewarp isn't the only optical flow option for After Effects users; before it ever existed, there was Twixtor from RE:Vision Effects, which may very well yield preferable results more easily. To explore whether this is the case with a given shot, try the demo version, available on this book's disc.

Increasing Error Threshold from the default of 1.00 results in fewer motion vectors and more blending, so it will also help with image tearing. However, a scene with heavy grain or other high-frequency detail will actually be improved by lowering this setting so that it is ignored.

Finally, you can increase Vector Details right up to the maximum setting of 100 and reduce Block Size from the default of 6.0, but this can be inadvisable when analyzing fast motion, where the vectors will not be spread across a wide enough matrix to track it.

Just like color keying successful retiming with optical flow requires that you learn to balance an interdependent set of adjustments, and to give the effect what it needs, source-wise, to maximize the possibility of success. And just as with keying, there is a third-party plug-in alternative that some users may prefer (see tip on this page).

In Conclusion

The elegance and logic of the After Effects Timeline is not always evident to the new user, but this chapter taught you that shortcuts and other workflow enhancements help streamline what might otherwise be tedious or exacting edits. The Timeline and Graph Editor, once mastered, give you the control you need over the timing and placement of elements.

If this chapter's information seems overwhelming on first read, keep coming back to it so that specific tips can sink in once you've encountered the right context to use them.

Layer Basics

Previous chapters laid the groundwork for the central activity of your After Effects work: manipulating a composition's layers. Over the next several chapters, you'll gradually increase your command over layers. This chapter focuses on the bare essentials, describing how to select, name, and label layers. You'll also learn how to control layer quality and how to choose whether to include layers in previews and renders. In addition, you'll see how to simplify working with layers by concealing ones you're not using and by locking ones you don't want to disturb. In the process, you'll become more familiar with your primary workspace, the Timeline panel.

Selecting Layers

As you would expect, you must select layers before you can adjust them. In the timeline, selected layers' names appear highlighted, as do their duration bars—the horizontal bar representing the layer under the time ruler. In the Composition panel, selected layers can appear with *transform handles* or simply, *handles*—six small boxes that demark each layer's boundaries and that you can use to transform the layer. However, you can specify whether you want these (or other layer controls) to appear in the Comp panel. See the sections "Viewing Spatial Controls in the Comp Panel" and "Properties and Keyframes," for more details.

To select layers in the Composition panel:

1. If you haven't already done so, cue the current frame of the composition so that the layer you want to select is visible in the Composition panel.
2. In the Composition panel, click the visible layer to select it (**Figure 5.38**).
   The selected layer's handles and anchor point appear, unless these options have been disabled (see "Viewing Spatial Controls in the Comp Panel").
3. To select more than one layer, Shift-click other visible layers in the Composition panel (**Figure 5.39**).

To select layers in the Timeline panel:

In the Timeline panel, *do any of the following:*

- Click anywhere in the horizontal track containing the layer.

Figure 5.38 You can select a layer by directly clicking it in the Composition panel. In this figure, the Comp panel is set to show selected layer handles.

Figure 5.39 Shift-click to select additional layers.

- To select a layer by its layer number, type the layer number on the numeric keypad (not the numbers on the main keyboard) (**Figure 5.40**).
- To select a range of layers, Shift-click other layers.
- To select a range of layers, drag a marquee around several layer names. (Take care not to drag a layer to a new position in the stacking order.)
  Selected layers appear highlighted in the Timeline panel. Selected layers are visible in the Comp panel only if the current time is cued to the layer.

To select all layers in a composition:

- Choose Edit > Select All, or press Command/Ctrl-A (**Figure 5.41**).

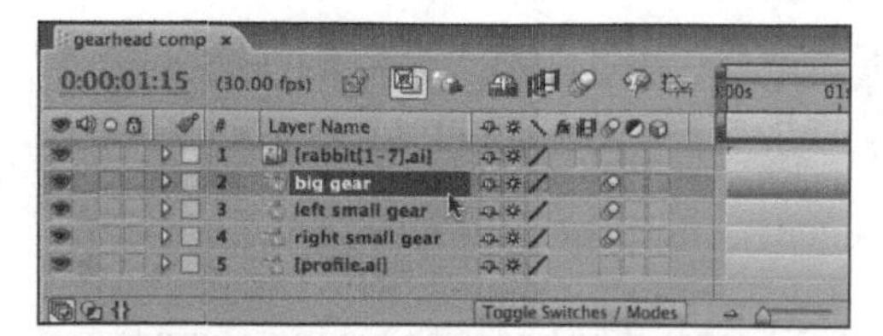

Figure 5.40 You can select layers by clicking them in the Timeline panel—or by entering the layer's number on the numeric keypad.

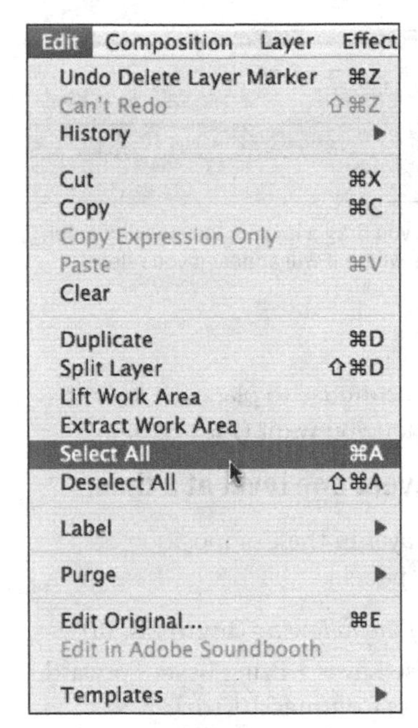

Figure 5.41 You can select all layers in the usual way—by choosing Edit > Select All (or using the keyboard shortcut).

All the layers in the composition are selected.

To deselect all layers in a composition:

Do one of the following:

- Click an empty area in the Timeline panel or the Composition panel.
- Choose Edit > Deselect All.

✔ Tips

- Press Command/Ctrl-Up Arrow to select the next layer up in the stacking order. See the next section, "Changing the Stacking Order."
- Press Command/Ctrl-Down Arrow to select the next layer down in the stacking order.

Changing the Stacking Order

In the Timeline panel, layers appear, well, *layered*. That is, each layer occupies a horizontal track that is stacked vertically with other layers. The horizontal position of a layer's duration bar determines its place in time; its vertical position shows its place in the *stacking order*. When layers occupy the same point in time, higher layers appear in front of lower layers when viewed in the Composition panel. You can change the relative positions of the layers in the stacking order to determine which elements appear in front and which appear behind (**Figures 5.42** and **5.43**).

A number directly to the left of a layer's name indicates a layer's position in the stacking order. The top layer is always layer 1, and the numbers increase as you go down the stack. Although layer numbers may not seem very informative, they can help you discern when layers are hidden temporarily (see "Making

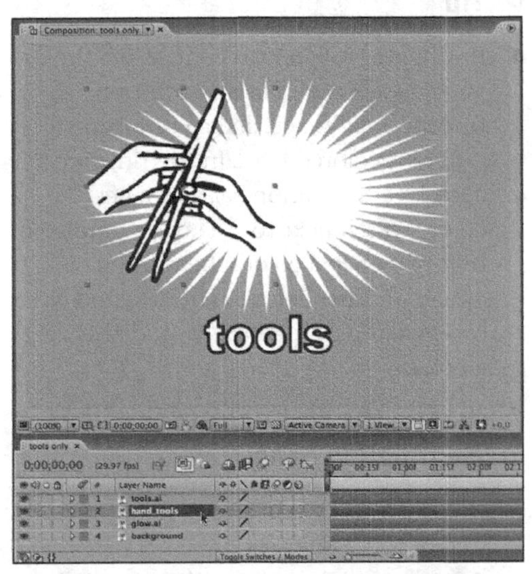

Figure 5.42 Layers higher in the stacking order appear in front of other layers in the Composition panel (provided they're positioned at the same point in time).

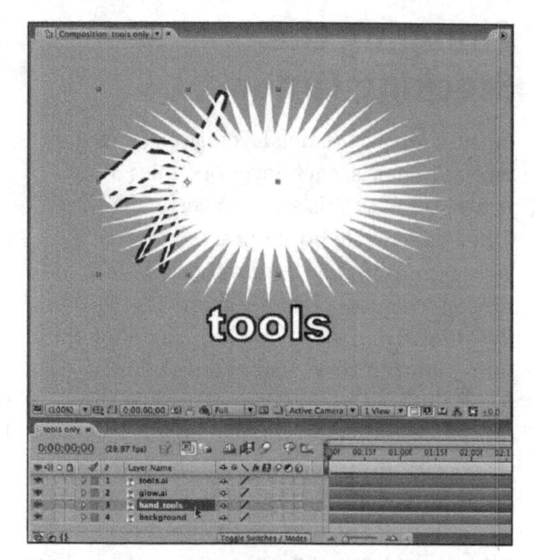

Figure 5.43 When a layer is moved to a lower position in the stacking order, it appears behind the higher layers in the Composition panel.

Layers Shy," later in this chapter) as well as provide a way for you to quickly select layers by number (see "Selecting Layers," earlier in this chapter).

✔ Tip

- In Chapter 4, you learned that the Project panel labels each file type (motion footage, still image, and so on) using a different colored label. In the timeline, each layer's duration bar and label (the color swatch next to the layer's number) reflect the label color scheme. You can assign another color to any selected layer by choosing Edit > Label > and selecting a color.

To change the stacking order of layers in the Timeline panel:

1. In the Timeline panel, drag a layer name to a new position.

   A horizontal line appears between other layers, indicating where the layer will appear in the stacking order (**Figure 5.44**).

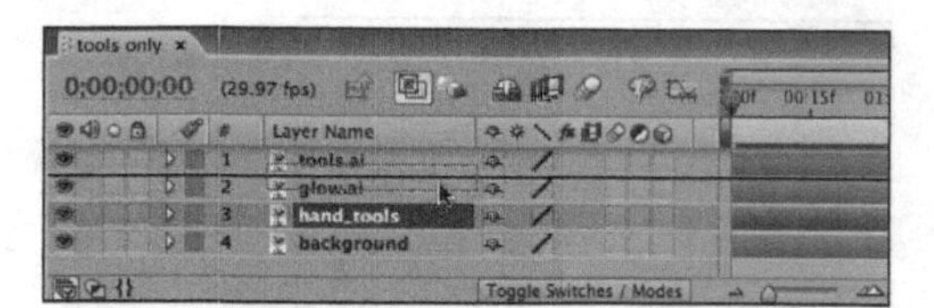

Figure 5.44 As you drag a layer in the stacking order, a line indicates where it will appear if you release the mouse.

2. Release the mouse to place the layer in the position you want (**Figure 5.45**).

To move layers one level at a time:

1. Select a layer in the Composition or Timeline panel.
2. *Do any of the following* (**Figure 5.46**):
   - ▲ Choose Layer > Bring Layer Forward, or press Command/Ctrl-].
   - ▲ Choose Layer > Send Layer Backward, or press Command/Ctrl-[.
   - ▲ Choose Layer > Bring Layer to Front or press Shift-Command-] (Mac) or Shift-Ctrl-] (Windows).
   - ▲ Choose Layer > Send Layer to Back or press Shift-Command-[(Mac) or Shift-Ctrl-[(Windows).

   The layer is repositioned in the stacking order according to the command you specified.

✔ Tip

- Just in case you missed it in the previous chapter, you aren't restricted to adding a layer to the top of the stacking order and

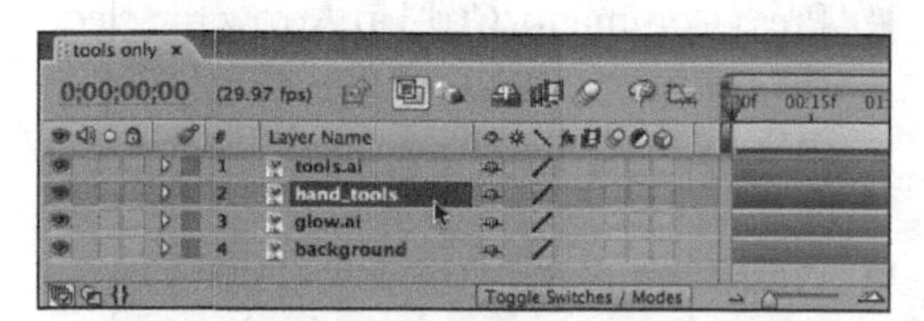

Figure 5.45 When you release the mouse, the layer appears in the new position.

Figure 5.46 To move the selected layer using menu commands, choose Layer > and the appropriate command.

then moving it down in a separate step (as in older versions of After Effects). After Effects lets you drag footage items directly to any level in the stacking order.

Naming Layers

Although you can rename comps and solids, you can't rename footage items in the Project panel (as explained in Chapter 4). However,

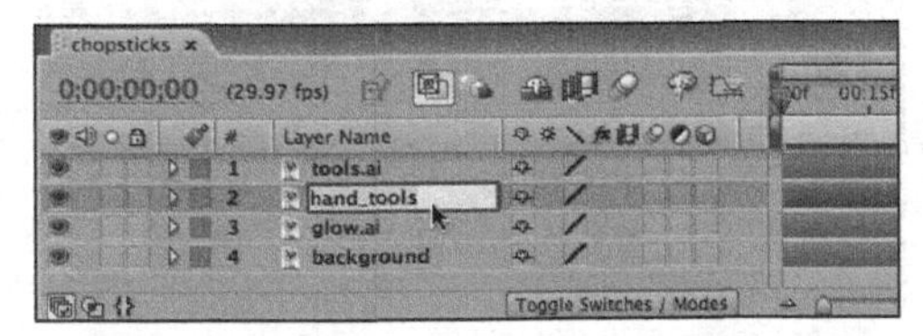

Figure 5.47 To change a layer's name, select the layer and press Return/Enter to edit the name.

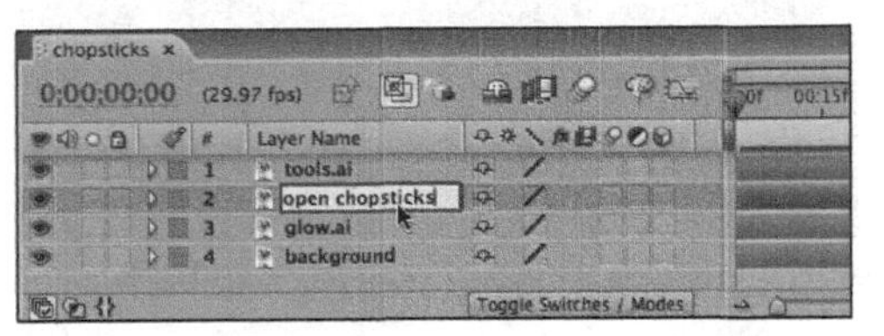

Figure 5.48 Enter a name for the layer, and press Return/Enter.

you can change the names of layers in a composition. (Typically, a footage item appears in the Project panel just once; however, it may make numerous appearances as layers in compositions.) In the Timeline panel, you can choose to view either the changeable layer name or the fixed source name.

To change the name of a layer:

1. In the Timeline panel, click a layer to select it.
2. Press Return/Enter.

   The layer name becomes highlighted (**Figure 5.47**).
3. Enter a new name for the layer, and press Return/Enter.

   The layer uses the name you specified; the source name can't be changed (**Figure 5.48**).

To toggle between layer name and source name:

- In the Timeline panel, click the Layer/Source Name button to toggle between

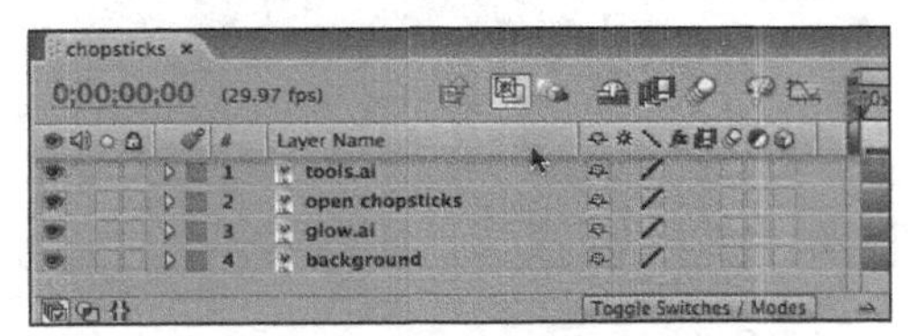

Figure 5.49 In the Timeline panel, click the Name panel heading to toggle between the layer name (which you can change) . . .

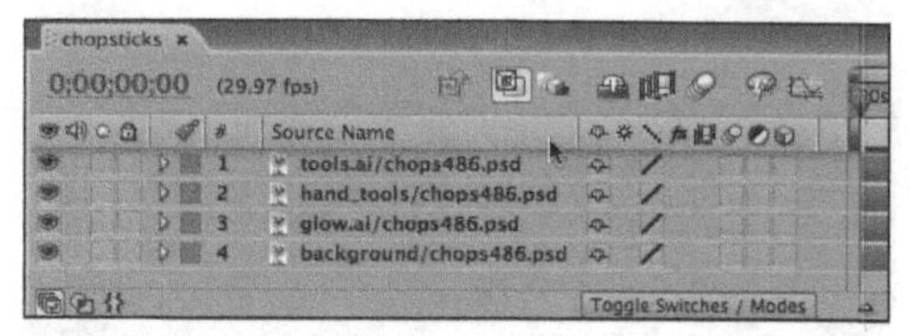

Figure 5.50 . . . and the source name (which is fixed).

the layer name and the source name for the layer. When the layer name and source name are the same, the layer name appears in brackets (**Figures 5.49** and **5.50**).

Switching Video and Audio On and Off

By default, the extreme left side of the Timeline panel displays the A/V Features panel (**Figure 5.51**). The first three columns of the A/V Features panel contain switches that control whether a layer's video and audio are included in previews or renders.

To show or hide the image for layers in the composition:

- Next to a layer in the Timeline panel, click the Video switch to toggle the Eye icon on and off.

  When the Eye icon is visible, the layer appears in the Composition panel (**Figure 5.52**); when the icon is hidden, the layer doesn't appear (**Figure 5.53**).

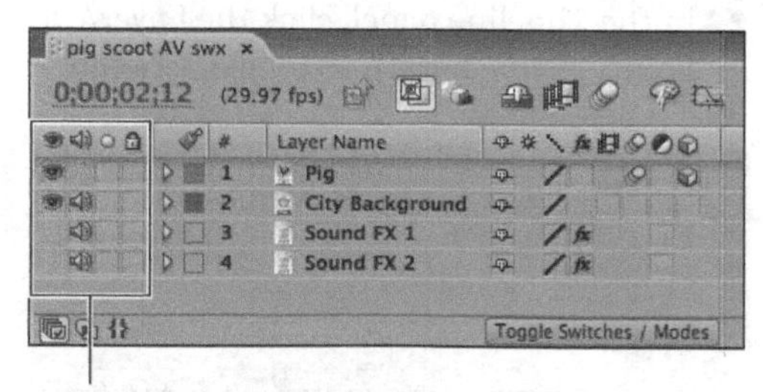

Figure 5.51 By default, the A/V Features panel appears to the extreme left in the Timeline panel. The panel contains three switches: Video, Audio, and Solo.

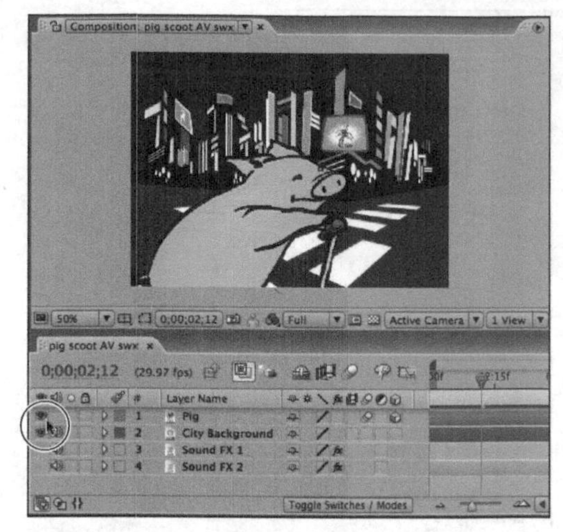

Figure 5.52 When the Video switch is on, the layer's image appears in the Composition panel.

To include a layer's audio track in the composition:

- Next to the layer in the Timeline panel, click the Audio switch to toggle the Speaker icon on and off.

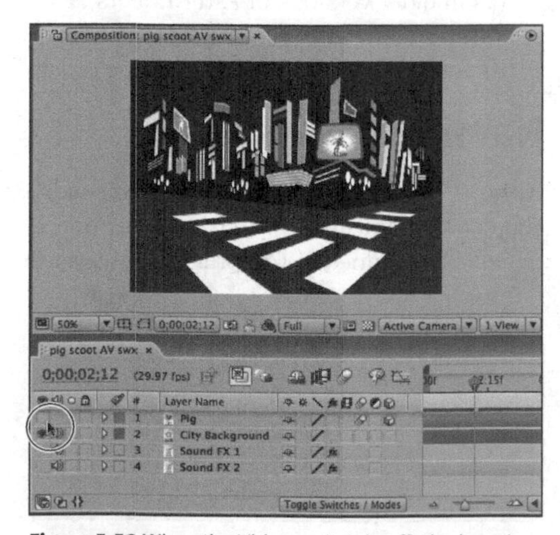

Figure 5.53 When the Video switch is off, the layer's image doesn't appear in the Composition panel, previews, or renders.

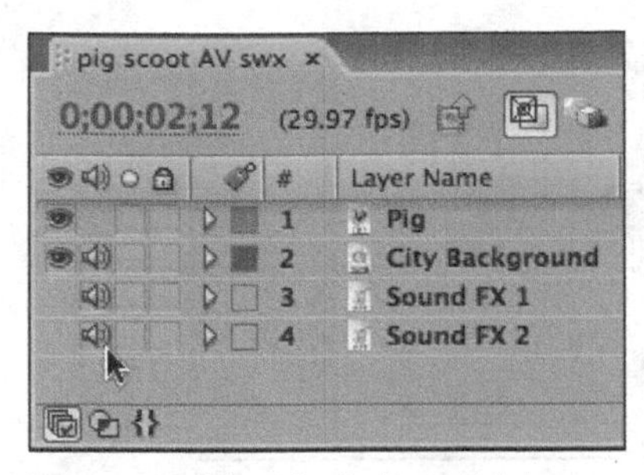

Figure 5.54 When the Audio switch is on, the layer's audio track is included in previews and renders.

When the Speaker icon is visible, the audio is included when you preview or render the composition (**Figure 5.54**); when the Speaker icon is hidden, the audio is excluded (**Figure 5.55**).

To solo a layer:

1. For the layer you want to solo:
   - ▲ Make sure the Eye icon is visible to solo the video.
   - ▲ Make sure the Speaker icon is visible to solo the audio.

   If the layer contains both video and audio, you can select either or both. If you select neither, the Solo button disappears, and you can't solo the layer.
2. Next to the layer you want to solo, click the Solo button (**Figure 5.56**).

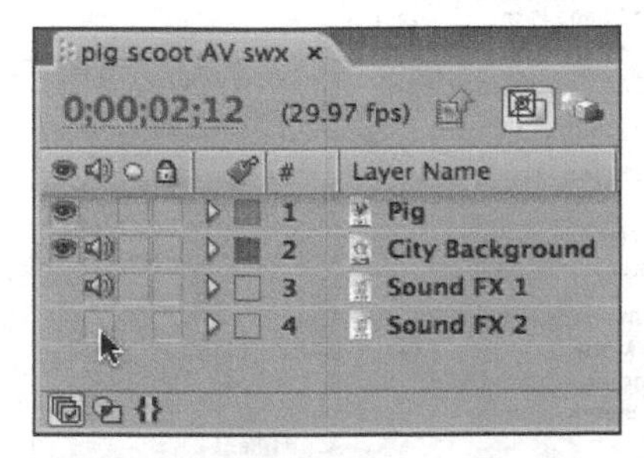

Figure 5.55 When the Audio switch is off, the layer's audio track isn't included in previews and renders.

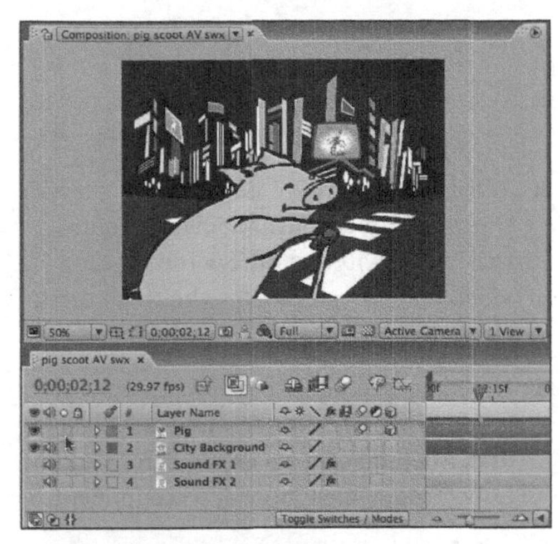

Figure 5.56 Make sure the Eye icon is visible to solo video and that the Speaker icon is visible to solo audio, and then click the Solo button.

If you solo the video, the Video switches for all other layers are deactivated; if you solo the audio, the Audio switches for all other layers are deactivated (**Figure 5.57**).

3. To stop soloing the layer and restore other A/V settings to their original states, click the Solo button again to deactivate it.

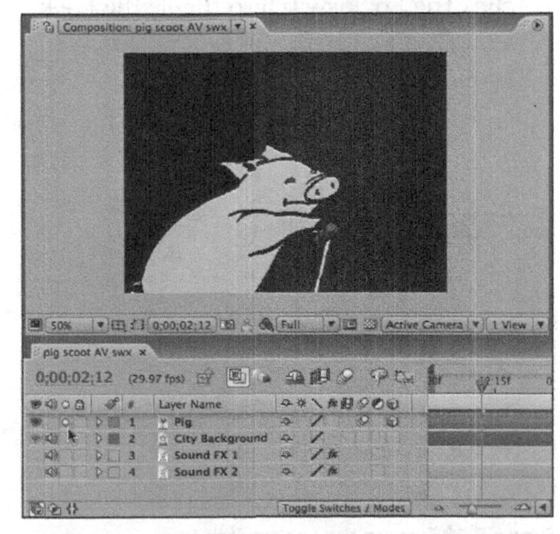

Figure 5.57 When you solo the layer's video and audio, A/V switches for other layers are deactivated.

✔ Tips

- When a transfer mode has been applied to a layer, the Eye icon looks like this: .
- When a track matte is applied to a layer, the video for the layer above it is automatically switched off. Switching the video back on eliminates the track matte effect.
- Not all layers are visible; adjustment layers, guide layers, lights, cameras, null objects, and, of course, layers created from audio-only footage have no video component.

Locking a Layer

The fourth column of the A/V Features panel contains the Lock switch, which you can use to lock layers so that they're protected against accidental changes. When you attempt to select a locked layer, its highlight blinks on and off to remind you that it's locked and thus can't be selected or altered. You must unlock the layer to make changes.

To lock or unlock a layer:

- Next to a layer in the Timeline panel, click the Lock switch to toggle the Lock icon on and off.

  When the Lock icon is visible, the layer can't be selected or modified (**Figure 5.58**); when the Lock icon is hidden, the layer is unlocked (**Figure 5.59**).

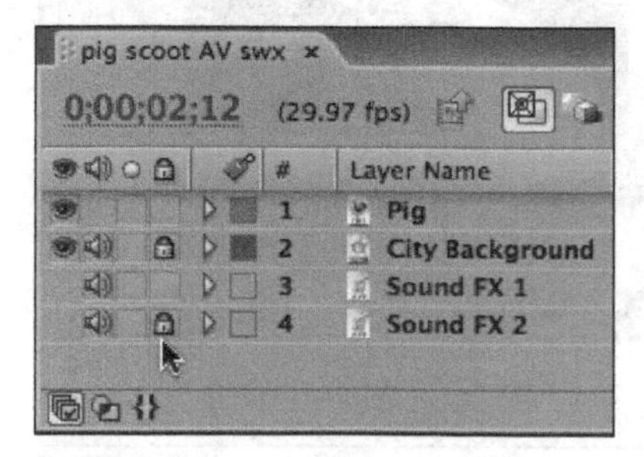

Figure 5.58 Turn on the Lock switch to protect the layer from inadvertent changes.

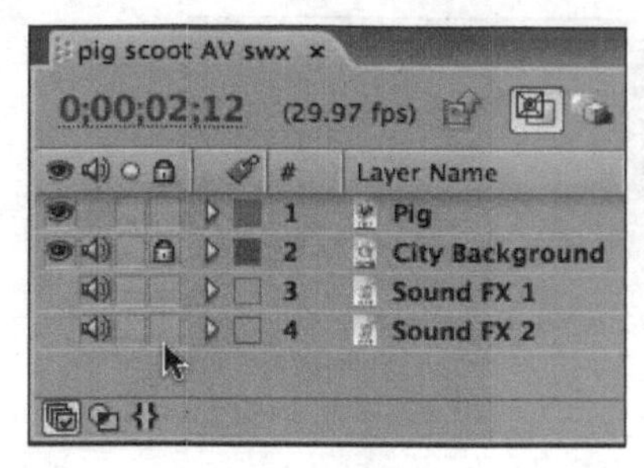

Figure 5.59 Turn off the Lock switch to unlock a layer.

To unlock all layers:

- Choose Layer > Switches > Unlock All Layers, or press Command/Ctrl-Shift-l (**Figure 5.60**).

✔ Tip

- Press Command/Ctrl-L to lock selected layers. You still have to click the Lock switch to unlock layers (you can't select locked layers).

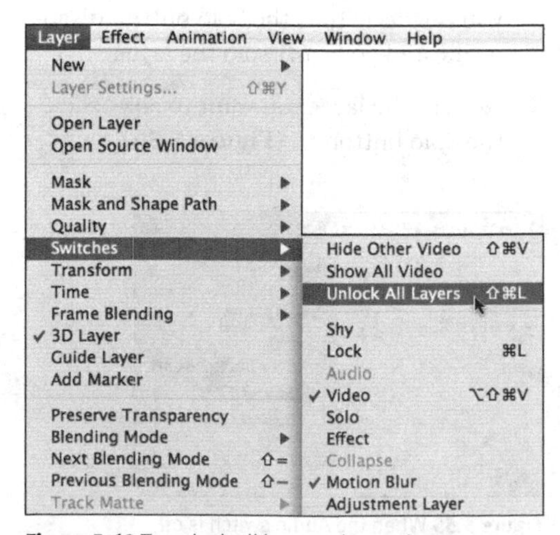

Figure 5.60 To unlock all layers, choose Layer > Switches > Unlock All Layers.

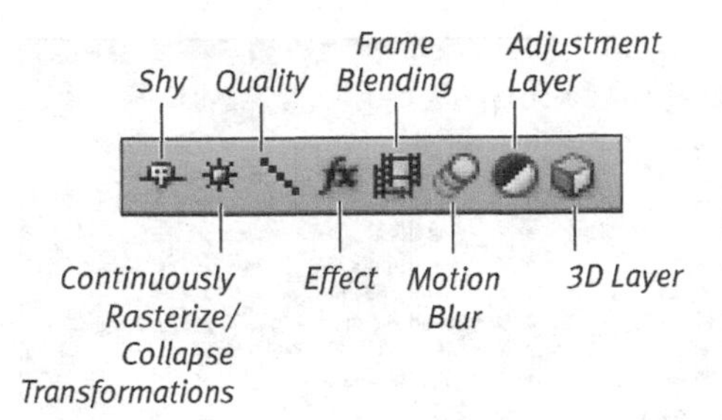

Figure 5.61 The Layer Switches panel contains eight switches.

Basic Layer Switches

By default, the Layer Switches column set appears to the right of the Name column in the Timeline panel.

The Layer Switches column consists of eight switches that control various features for each layer (**Figure 5.61**). This section covers the first three layer switches: Shy, Rasterize, and Quality. Other layer switches are covered later in the book.

Although you can control all of the layer switches via menu commands, the switches provide more direct access.

To show or hide the layer switches:

◆ In the Timeline panel, click the Expand / Collapse Layer Switches Pane button (**Figure 5.62**).

Clicking the button hides and shows the Switches pane (**Figure 5.63**).

✔ **Tip**

■ You can toggle between the Switches and the Transfer Modes controls by pressing the Toggle Switches / Modes button at the bottom of the Timeline panel.

Making Layers Shy

Because the Timeline panel contains so much information, you'll frequently find yourself scrolling through it or expanding it. Some users even use a secondary monitor

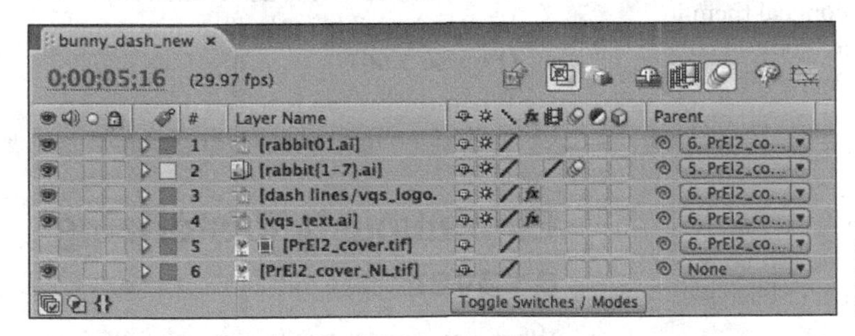

Figure 5.62 Clicking the Expand / Collapse Layer Switches Pane button . . .

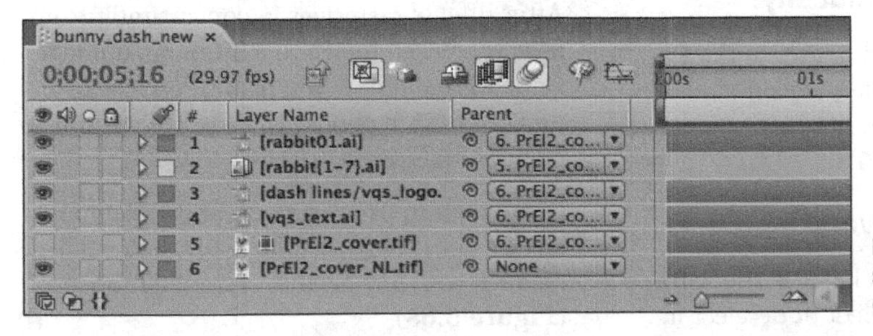

Figure 5.63 . . . toggles the switches controls open and closed (shown here).

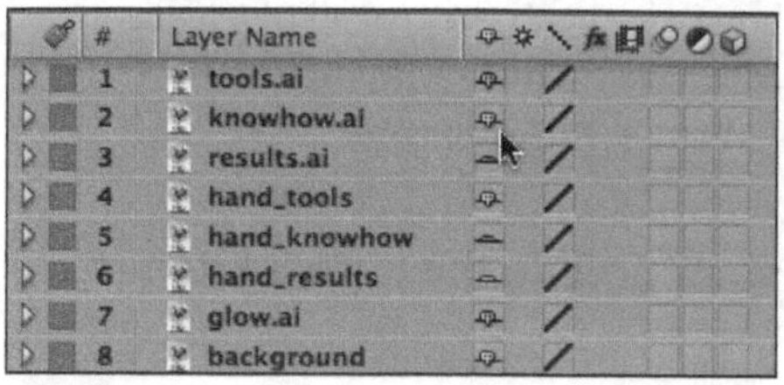

Figure 5.64 Click the Shy switch to toggle between Not Shy . . .

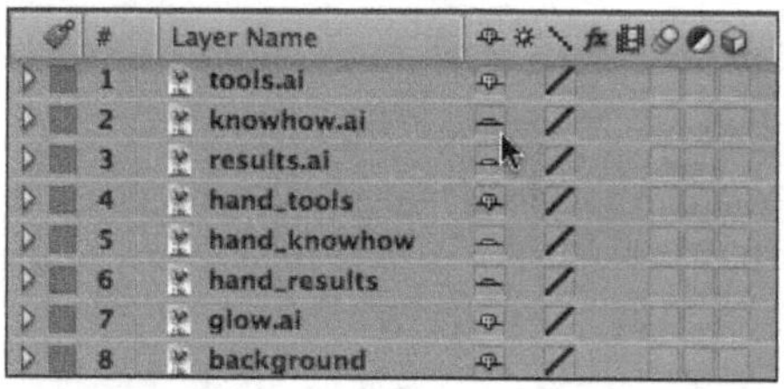

Figure 5.65 . . . and Shy.

just to accommodate a large Timeline panel. If you hate to scroll but are reluctant to buy another monitor, you may want to take advantage of the Shy Layers feature.

Marking layers you're not currently using as *shy* enables you to quickly conceal them in the Timeline panel. This way, you can concentrate on just the layers you're using and conserve precious screen space. Although shy layers may be hidden in the Timeline panel, they always appear in the Composition panel (provided they're visible and their corresponding video switch is on), and layer numbering remains unchanged.

To make a layer shy or not shy:

- Click the Shy switch for a layer in the Timeline panel to toggle the icon between Not Shy and Shy (**Figures 5.64** and **5.65**).

To hide or show shy layers:

- In the Timeline panel, click the Hide Shy Layers button to select or deselect it.

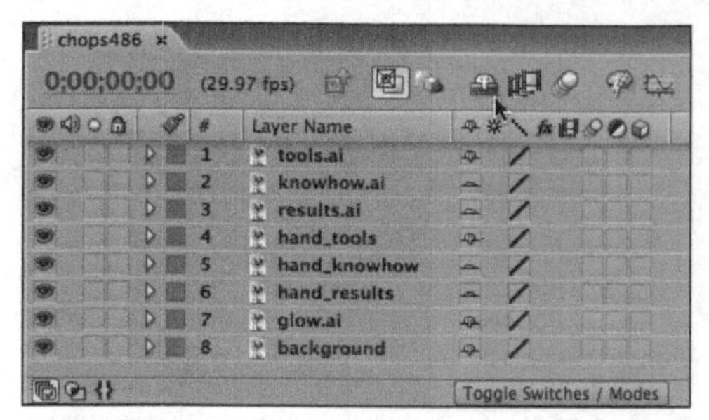

Figure 5.66 When the Hide Shy Layers button is deselected, shy layers appear in the Timeline panel.

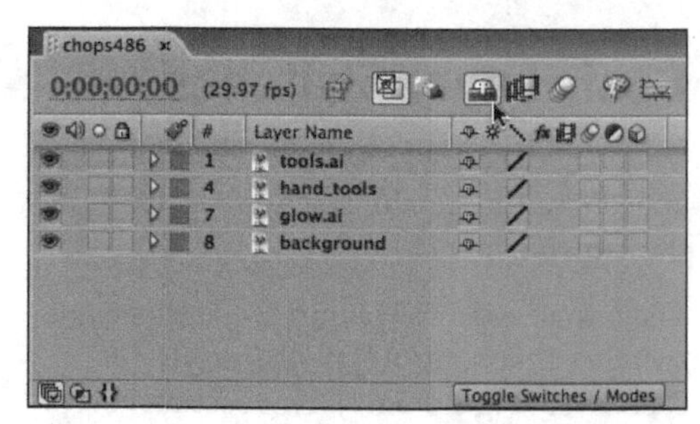

Figure 5.67 When the Hide Shy Layers button is selected, shy layers are concealed in the Timeline panel.

When the button is deselected, shy layers are visible in the Timeline panel (**Figure 5.66**).

When the button is selected, shy layers are hidden from view (**Figure 5.67**).

Continuously Rasterizing a Layer

When you import an Illustrator or EPS file, After Effects rasterizes it, converting it from a vector-based image to a bitmapped image. Depending on how you plan to use the image, you can choose to rasterize the image once or rasterize it continuously.

If you plan to use the image at its original size (After Effects' default setting) or smaller, you only need to rasterize it once (**Figure 5.68**).

Figure 5.68 By default, After Effects rasterizes the image at its original size.

Figure 5.69 Enlarging an image after it has been rasterized can make the pixels apparent.

Figure 5.70 When the Continuously Rasterize switch is on, the image is scaled before it's rasterized for each frame of the composition.

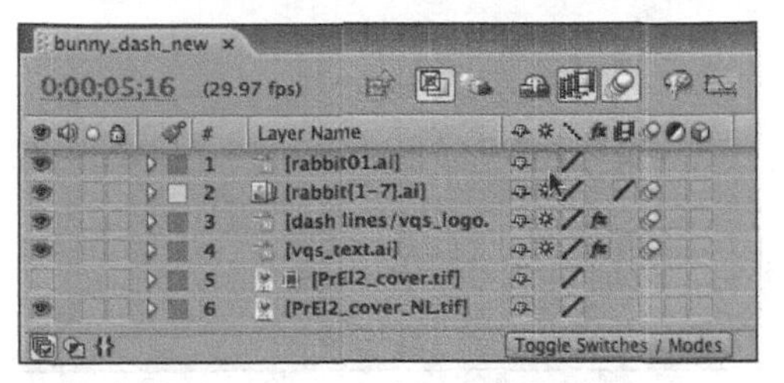

Figure 5.71 When the switch is off, the layer is rasterized once.

If you plan to scale the image more than 100 percent (or plan to change other geometric properties), you should choose to continuously rasterize the layer. Rasterizing the layer for each frame will ensure that image quality is maintained at any scale (**Figures 5.69** and **5.70**). Of course, these recalculations may also increase preview and rendering time. To save time, you may choose to turn off the Continuously Rasterize switch until you want to preview or render the composition at full quality.

When a composition is used as a layer, the Continuously Rasterize switch functions as the Collapse Transformations switch. Having this option selected can increase image quality while decreasing rendering time.

To change the rasterization method of a layer:

◆ In the Switches panel of the Timeline panel, click the Continuously Rasterize/Collapse Transformations switch for the layer.

  When the switch is set to Off (no icon), the image is rasterized once (**Figure 5.71**); when the switch is set to On , the image is continuously rasterized (**Figure 5.72**).

✔ Tips

■ Regardless of the Continuously Rasterize setting, setting the quality

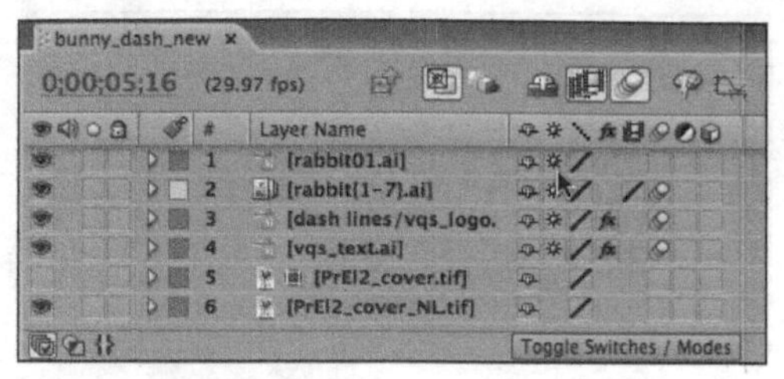

Figure 5.72 When the switch is on, the layer is continuously rasterized.

switch to Full smoothes (anti-aliases) the edges of the art.

- One way to avoid continuous rasterization and its slower rendering times is to steer clear of scaling the image beyond 100 percent. If possible, create the vector graphic at the largest dimensions it appears in the composition.
- In older versions of After Effects, you couldn't apply an effect to a layer that had the Continuously Rasterize switch on. This is no longer the case; you're free to apply effects to a continuously rasterized layer—and free to forget the workarounds you had to use in the past.

Quality Setting Switches

You can set the resolution of the composition to control its image quality and thereby the speed at which frames are rendered. Just as the resolution setting controls the overall image quality of the composition, a layer's Quality switch controls the quality of an individual layer in the composition.

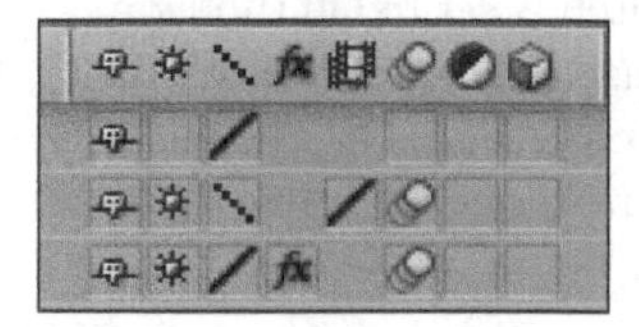

Figure 5.73 Set the switch to Draft Quality to display the layer at a lower quality in the Composition panel.

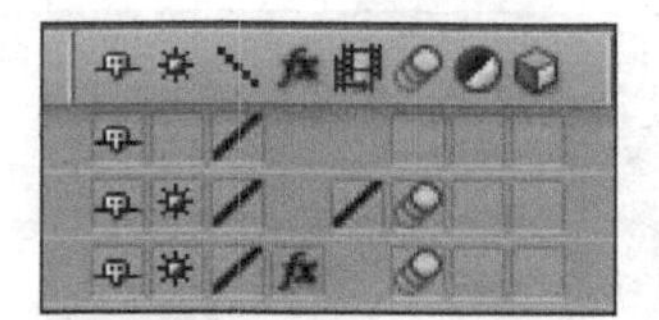

Figure 5.74 Set the switch to Full Quality to display the layer at the highest quality in the Composition panel.

To change the Quality setting of a layer:

- In the Timeline panel, click the Quality switch to set the quality for the layer:

  The Draft Quality icon indicates that the layer will preview and render at draft quality in the Composition panel (**Figure 5.73**).

  The Full Quality icon indicates that the layer will preview and render at full quality in the Composition panel (**Figure 5.74**).

  The Quality switch controls the quality of individual layers. To control your composition's image quality, use the Resolution controls.

Layer Editing

The term *editing*, in the sense that film and video makers use it, refers to the order and arrangement of images in time. Implicit in this definition, of course, is the term's broader meaning: to include some elements while excluding others to achieve a desired aesthetic effect. This chapter focuses on editing the layers of a composition—defining which segments to include and the order in which to present them.

You'll learn basic editing functions and terms such as *In point, Out point, duration,* and *trimming*. You'll also learn other techniques common to non-linear editing, such as setting markers and controlling the play-

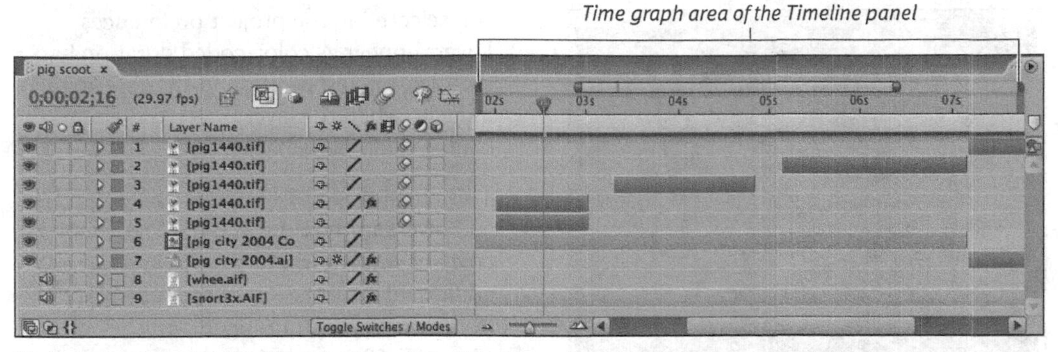

Figure 5.75 At the right side of the Timeline panel, all the layers of a composition are represented as bars in a time graph.

back speed and direction of layers. In the process, you'll get acquainted with the Layer panel and take a closer look at the time graph of the Timeline panel.

Viewing Layers in the Timeline and Layer Panels

When you arrange layers in time, you work in the Layer panel and the time graph area of the Timeline panel.

As you know, the Timeline panel lets you view all of a composition's elements as vertically stacked layers. On the right side of the Timeline panel, a *time graph* represents the layers in time (**Figure 5.75**). Each layer has a duration bar, and its horizontal position in the time graph indicates when it will start and end as you play back the composition.

You can view any layer in a composition in a Layer panel. As you'll remember from Chapter 4, the Layer panel closely resembles the Footage and Composition panels. Unlike its siblings, however, the Layer panel always includes a timeline and controls for setting the starting and ending points of the layer (**Figure 5.76**).

Both the Layer and Timeline panels depict layers as duration bars. However, each panel displays layers in a different context. In the time graph, the duration bar shows a layer in the context of the entire composition. In the Layer panel, the duration bar shows you the portion of the footage item that you chose to include in the composition.

Compare the Timeline (Figure 5.75), Layer (Figure 5.76), and Composition (**Figure 5.77**) panels to see how the same layer appears in

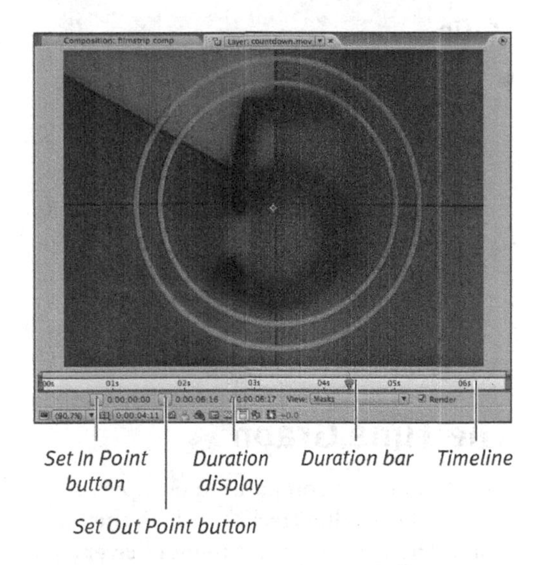

Figure 5.76 You can view a single layer of the composition in a Layer panel, which includes a timeline and controls for setting the layer's starting and ending points.

Figure 5.77 Compare the view of the layer in the Layer panel and Timeline panel to the same point in time in the Composition panel. In the Composition panel, you can see how the layer has been manipulated and composited with other layers.

each panel. (Note that the current time always matches in all the open panels of the same composition.) The distinctions between the time graph and the Layer panel are explained in greater detail in the sections to follow.

✔ Tip

- The Layer panel has a few other unique features not covered in detail here: the View pull-down menu and the Render check box. The section "The Layer Panel," later in this chapter, provides a brief explanation, but you'll learn more in later chapters. This chapter focuses on using the Layer panel's unique editing features—that is, on manipulating starting and ending points and on using layer markers.

The Time Graph

Each layer in the composition occupies a separate horizontal track, or cell, in the time graph. The vertical arrangement of layers indicates their position in the stacking order (covered in the previous chapter). Time is displayed horizontally, from left to right, and measured by a time ruler in the increments you selected in the project preferences. Layers appear as color-coded duration bars; their length and position in the time graph indicate when the layers start and end as the composition plays back.

This chapter focuses on how to view and edit layers in the time graph. Later chapters cover how to view and manipulate additional information in the time graph (for example, keyframing attributes). **Figure 5.78** summarizes the controls covered in the following sections.

Parts of the time graph

Time ruler—Measures time horizontally (according to the time units you selected in the project preferences).

Work area start—Marks the beginning of the work area bar, which determines the portion of the composition that will be rendered during previews (see Chapter 6, "Playback, Previews, and RAM").

Work area end—Marks the end of the work area bar, which determines the portion of the composition that will be rendered during previews (see Chapter 6).

Left Time View bracket—Changes the left edge of the part of the composition visible in the main time graph. (See "The navigator view," later in this chapter.)

Right Time View bracket—Changes the right edge of the part of the composition visible in the main time graph. (See "The navigator view," later in this chapter.)

Current time indicator (CTI)—Changes the current frame of the composition in the main time graph and in the navigator view. The current time is the same in all the views of the same composition.

Timeline panel menu button—Displays a menu of functions for controlling layers and

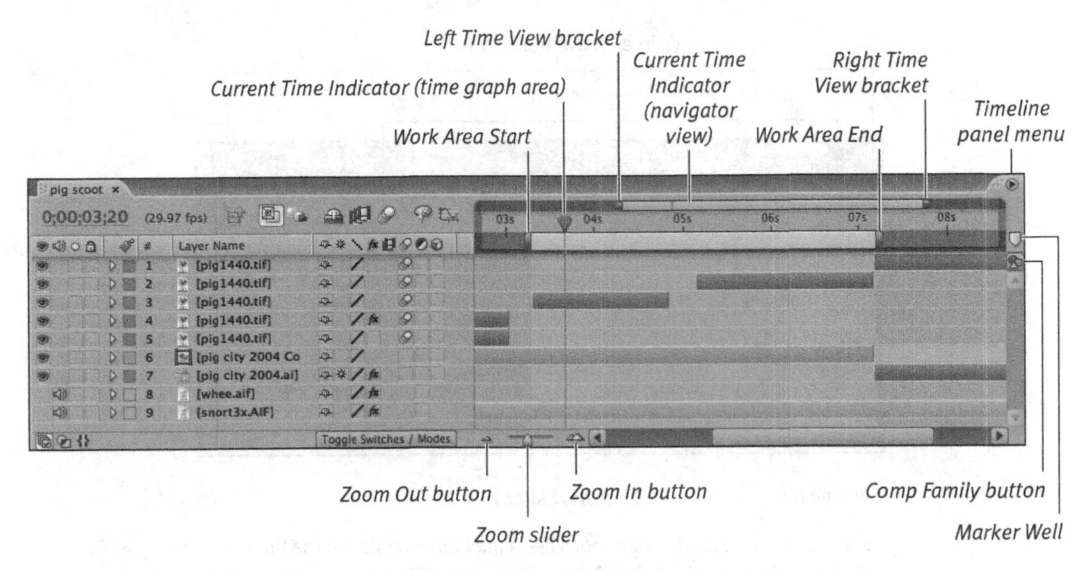

Figure 5.78 The following sections focus on the time graph area of the Timeline panel.

keyframes as well as accessing the Composition Settings dialog box.

Marker well—Adds markers to the time ruler. Drag a marker out of the well to add a marker or back into the well to remove it.

Comp Family button—Opens the Composition panel associated with the composition displayed in the Timeline panel.

Zoom slider—Displays the time graph in more or less detail.

Zoom In button—Displays a shorter part of the time graph in more detail.

Zoom Out button—Displays a greater part of the time graph in less detail.

Navigating the Time Graph

The Timeline panel allows you to view all or part of a composition. As you arrange the layers of a composition in time, you may need to zoom into the time graph for a detailed view or zoom out for a more expansive view.

The navigator view

After Effects' Timeline panel includes a *navigator view*, located at the top of the time graph (**Figure 5.79**). The navigator view looks like a tiny version of the time graph, including a small current time indicator and small work area markers. The navigator view always represents the entire duration of the composition; the white portion corresponds to the part of the composition you see in the larger main timeline. Thus, dragging the Time View brackets at either end of the white area changes the main view, and vice versa.

The navigator view helps you put the portion of the composition you see in the time graph in the context of its entire duration.

To view part of the time graph in more detail:

In the time graph area of the Timeline panel, *do any of the following* (**Figures 5.80** and **5.81**):

- Click the Zoom In button to view an incrementally more detailed area of the time graph.

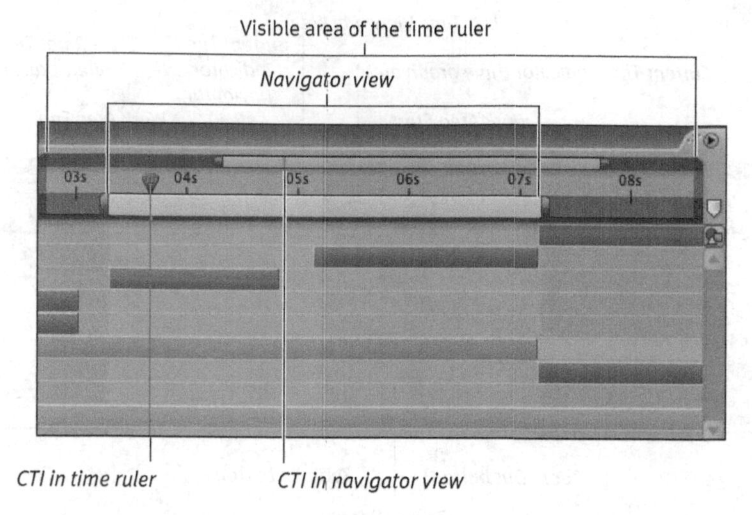

Figure 5.79 The navigator view looks like a miniature version of the time graph. By representing the entire duration of the composition, it helps you put the area visible in the main time graph in context.

- Drag the Zoom slider to the left.
- Drag the Left Time View bracket to the right.
- Drag the Right Time View bracket to the left.
- Press the equal sign (=) on your keyboard.

To view more of the composition in the time graph:

In the time graph area of the Timeline panel, *do any of the following:*

- Click the Zoom Out button to view an incrementally more detailed area of the time graph.

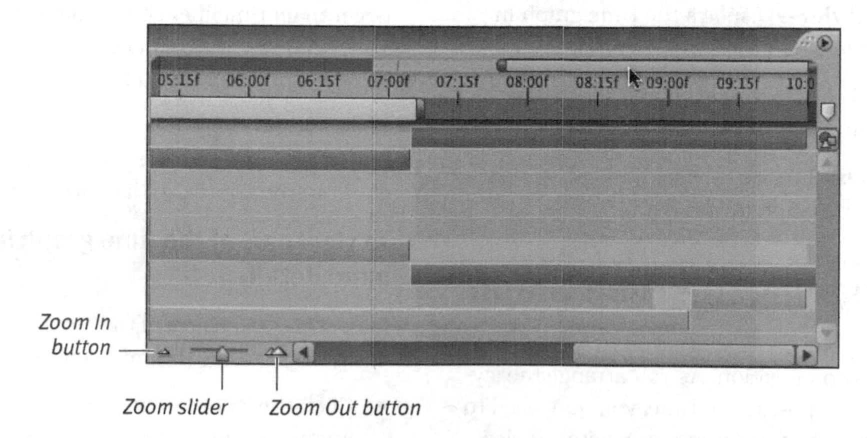

Figure 5.80 You can use the zoom controls at the bottom of the Timeline panel to control your view of the time graph.

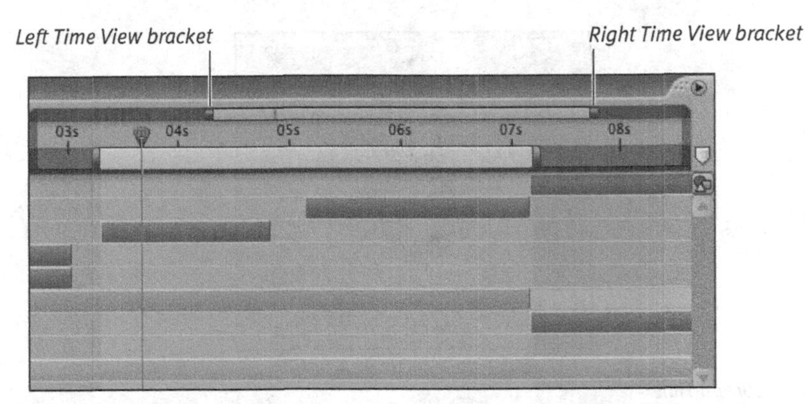

Figure 5.81 You can also drag the time brackets in the navigator view of the Timeline panel to change your view of the time graph.

- Drag the Zoom slider to the right to view more of the time graph gradually.
- Drag the Left Time View bracket to the left.
- Drag the Right Time View bracket to the right.
- Press the hyphen (-) on your keyboard.

✔ Tip

- Here's another good keyboard shortcut for zooming in and out of the time graph: Press the semicolon (;) to toggle between the frame view of the time graph and a view of the entire composition.

The Layer Panel

As you learned in Chapter 4, the Layer panel resembles the Composition and Footage panels. The following sections cover the Layer panel's unique editing features, including its timeline and controls for setting In and Out points (**Figure 5.82**). Chapters 5 and 7 cover the Layer panel's additional features, such as its View pull-down menu and Render check box, which help you to manipulate anchor points and masks.

A Layer panel timeline corresponds to the full, unedited duration of the source footage item. As you recall, the full durations of movie and audio footage are determined by the source; the full durations of still images are determined by the preferences you set (see Chapter 4).

Note that the Layer panel has its own version of the Timeline panel's navigator view, which works in much the same way as that one. See "The navigator view," earlier in this chapter.

Using the Layer panel's controls, you can set the portion of the full duration you want to use in the composition. Time displays show the exact In point, Out point, and duration you set, which are also reflected by a duration bar.

To open a Layer panel:

- In the Timeline panel, double-click a layer to open a Layer panel.

  Remember: Double-clicking an item in the Project panel opens a Footage panel, not a Layer panel.

Parts of the Layer panel

Layer panel time ruler—Matches the full, unedited duration of the source footage.

Current time indicator (CTI)—Corresponds to the current time of the composition and the framcorree of the layer displayed in the Layer panel.

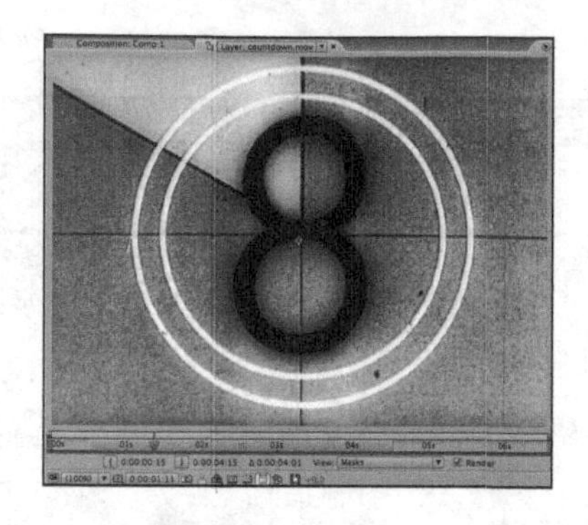

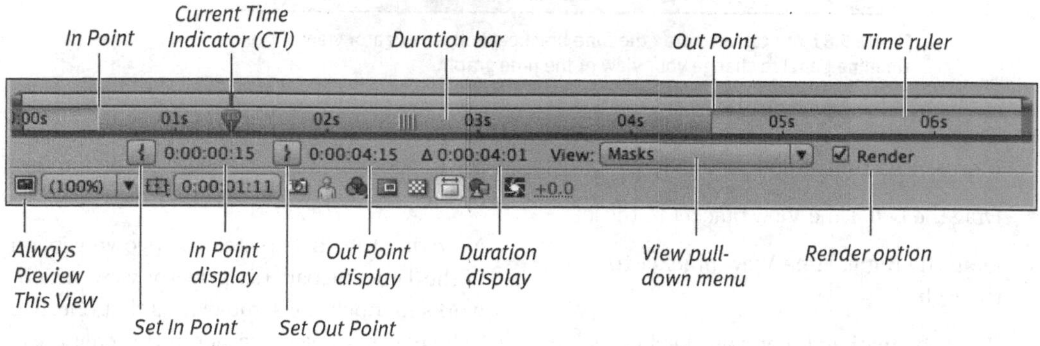

Figure 5.82 The Layer panel includes editing features not found in the Footage and Composition panels.

Duration bar—Corresponds to the portion of the source footage included in the composition.

Set In Point button—Marks the current frame of the layer as the first frame in the composition.

Set Out Point button—Marks the current frame of the layer as the last frame included in the composition.

Always Preview This View button—Designates the view as the default for previews (playback at or near the full frame rate) rather than whatever view is frontmost. (See Chapter 6 for more nformation.)

Region of Interest button—Limits the area of the image in the panel for previewing. (See Chapter 6 for more information.)

Transparency Grid button—Toggles transparent areas between a black background and a checkerboard pattern, or transparency grid.

Pixel Aspect Ratio Correction button—Corrects any distortion caused by differences in the layer's pixel aspect ratio (PAR) and the display's PAR.

View pull-down menu—Specifies whether to make additional information visible in the Layer panel, including motion-tracking points (Professional only), mask shapes, and anchor point paths. After Effects switches view options according to the task at hand. For example, selecting the Pen tool selects the layer's Mask view option automatically. (See Chapter 7 for more about masks.)

Comp Family button—Makes related composition and Timeline panels appear.

Render option—Specifies whether the window shows the layer's image only or the rendered result of any changes you make to it, such as masks and effects. (See Chapter 6 for more about previews.)

Trimming Layers

Changing a layer's In or Out point is known as *trimming*. Trimming a layer affects its duration; its timing in the composition depends on the trimming method you choose.

As you trim a layer in the Timeline panel, you also alter the time at which the layer starts or ends in the composition. This means you may have to shift the layer back to its original starting point after you trim it (**Figures 5.83** and **5.84**). Although the Timeline panel provides the most direct method of trimming, it can sometimes be difficult to use with precision.

When you trim a layer using controls in the Layer panel, the layer's duration changes accordingly but its starting point in the composition remains fixed (**Figure 5.85**). Thus, this method works best if you don't want to change the layer's start time in the composition.

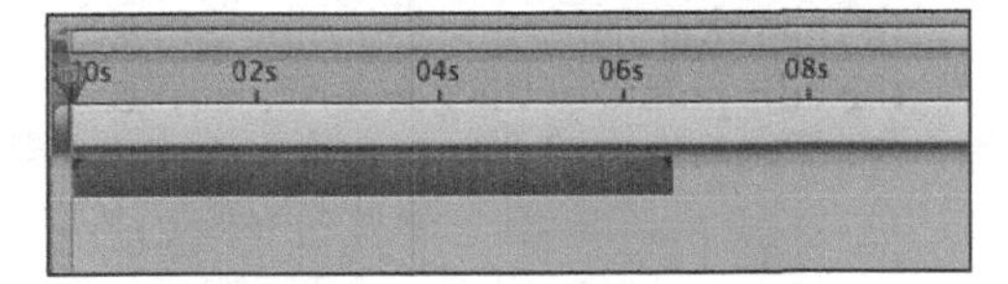

Figure 5.83 Note where the layer begins in the composition before trimming its In point.

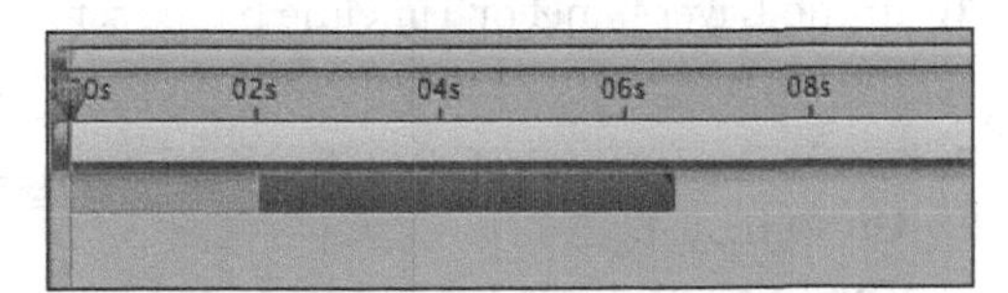

Figure 5.84 Trimming the layer's In point by dragging it in the time graph is direct and intuitive; naturally, it also moves the layer's starting point in the composition.

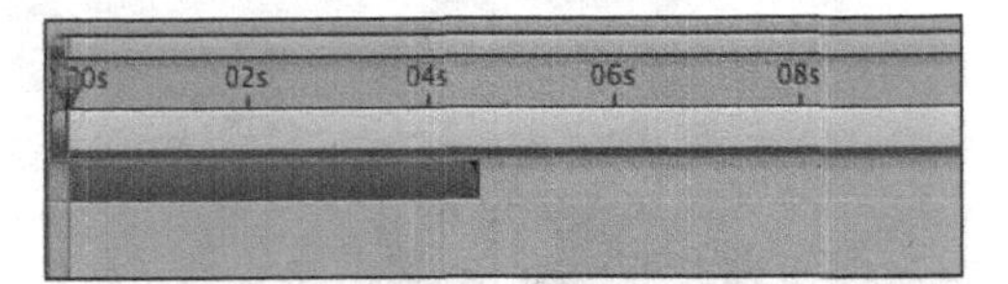

Figure 5.85 Trimming the In point using the Layer panel controls, on the other hand, doesn't affect the layer's starting point in the composition. It does, however, affect its duration.

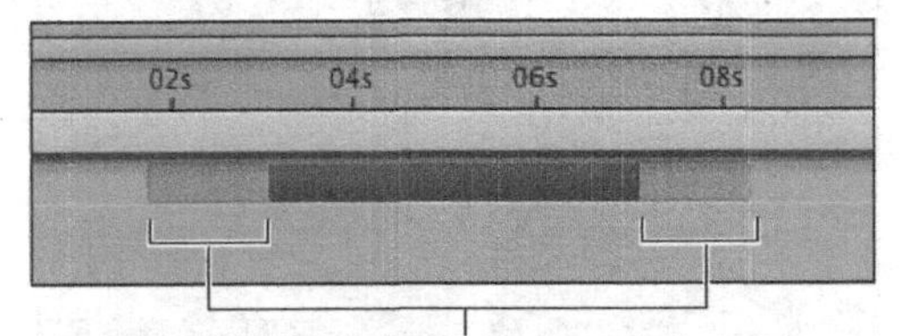

Figure 5.86 The trimmed frames of a layer appear as empty outlines extending from the layer's In and Out points. You can restore these frames at any time by extending the In or Out point again.

Whenever you *trim in* an edit point—making the layer shorter—the unused frames of the layer appear as empty outlines extending from the duration bar's In and Out points (**Figure 5.86**). You can always restore these frames by extending the In and Out points again.

✔ Tip

- You can also remove a range of frames by specifying the Work Area (covered in Chapter 6) and choosing Edit > Lift Work Area or Edit > Extract Work Area. Both commands remove all frames under the Work Area, splitting layers if necessary. Lifting leaves a gap in time, whereas Extract shifts subsequent frames back in time to prevent a gap. Extracting is also known as ripple deleting.

To set the In and Out points in the Layer panel:

1. Set the current time to the frame of the layer you want to trim (**Figure 5.87**).

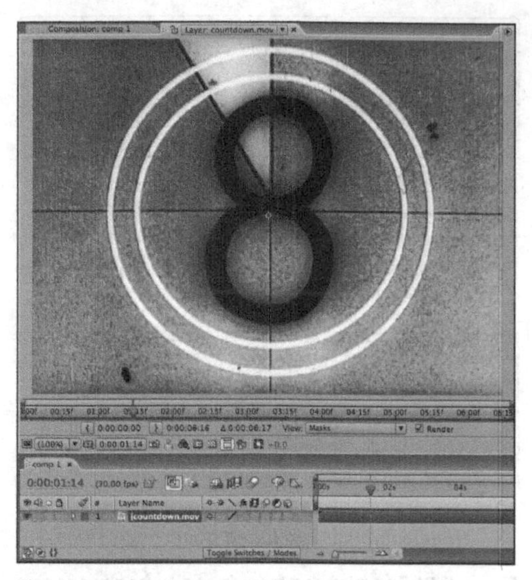

Figure 5.87 Set the current time to a frame of the layer you want to set as an edit point.

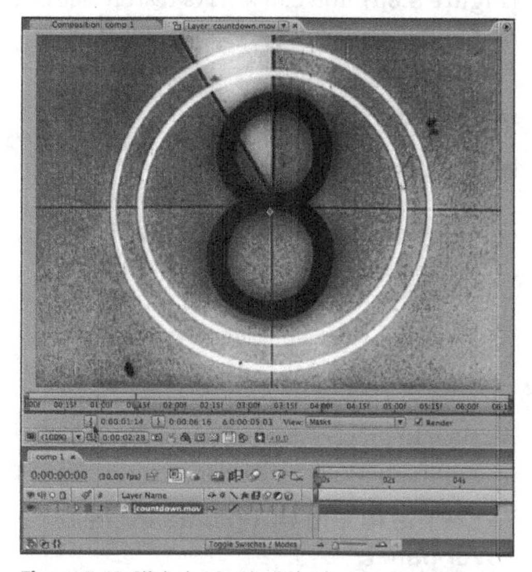

Figure 5.88 Click the Set In Point button in the Layer panel. In the Comp, the layer shifts back so the new In point starts at the same point in the comp time.

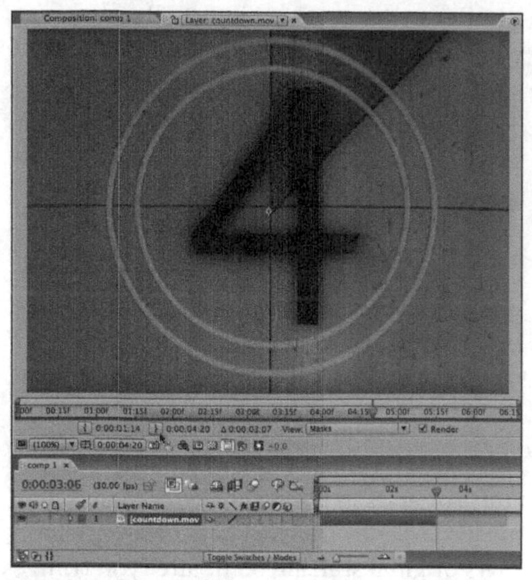

Figure 5.89 Click the Set Out Point button in the Layer panel to set the layer's Out point to the current time.

2. To set the In point, click the Set In Point button in the Layer panel (**Figure 5.88**).

   The current frame becomes the layer's In point, but the layer's starting time in the composition remains in place.

3. To set the Out point, click the Set Out Point button in the Layer panel (**Figure 5.89**).

   In the Layer panel and Timeline panel, the edit points of the Layer reflect the changes you made.

To set the In and Out points using keyboard shortcuts:

1. In the Layer panel or Timeline panel, set the current frame (**Figure 5.90**).

2. To set the In point of the layer, press Option/Alt-[.

   The In point of the layer is set to the current frame in the composition (**Figure 5.91**).

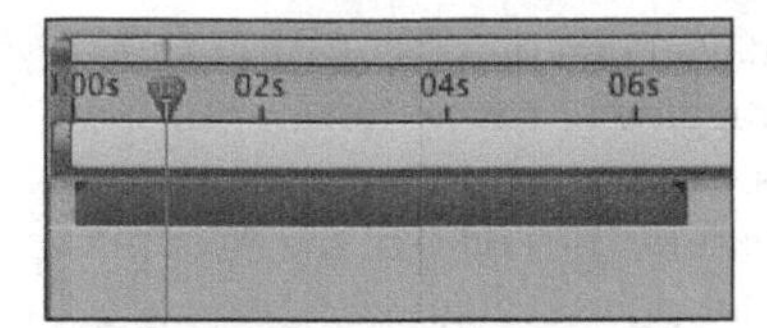

Figure 5.90 Set the current time to the frame of the layer you want to set as an edit point.

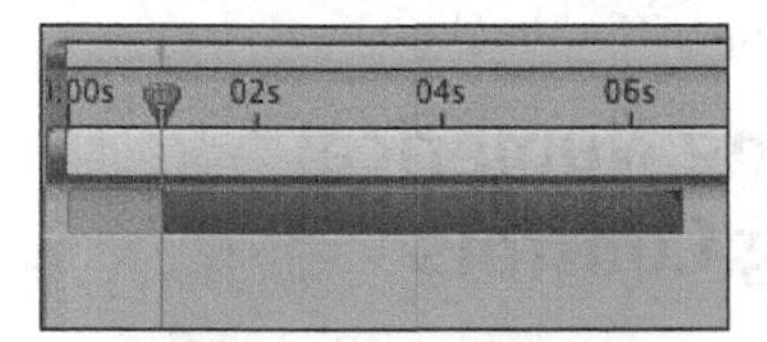

Figure 5.91 Press Option/Alt-[to set the In point of the selected layer to the current time.

3. To set the Out point of the layer, press Option/Alt-].

   In the Layer panel and Timeline panel, the edit points reflect the changes you made. The layer's frame at the current time becomes both the layer's In point and the layer's starting point in the comp. (See **Table 5.1** for more layer editing shortcuts.)

To set the In and Out points by dragging:

In the time graph panel of the Timeline panel, *do either of the following*:

- To set the In point, drag the In point of a layer's duration bar (the handle at the left end of the duration bar) (**Figure 5.92**).

Table 5.1

Layer Editing Shortcuts	
EDIT	SHORTCUT
Move layer's In point to CTI	[(open bracket)
Move layer's Out point to CTI	] (close bracket)
Trim layer's In point to CTI	Opt/Alt-[
Trim layer's Out point to CTI	Opt/Alt-]
Nudge layer one frame forward	Opt/Alt-Page Up
Nudge layer one frame back	Opt/Alt-Page Down

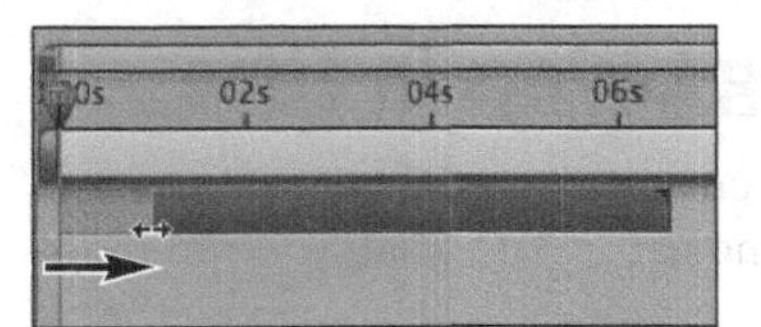

Figure 5.92 Drag the In point handle of a layer's duration bar to change both its In point and where it starts in the composition.

- To set the Out point, drag the Out point of a layer's duration bar (the handle at the right end of the duration bar) (**Figure 5.93**).

  Make sure you drag the ends of the layer's duration bar, not the bar itself. Otherwise, you could change the layer's position in time rather than its In or Out point.

✔ Tips

- Pressing Shift after you begin to drag causes the In or Out point to *snap to edges*. That is, the layer's edit point behaves as though it's magnetized and aligns with the edit points of other layers, the current time indicator, and the layer and composition markers.
- You can see the exact position of an edit point in time by looking at the Info panel's time display as you drag.
- If you reach a point where you're unable to further increase a layer's duration, it means you've run out of source footage.

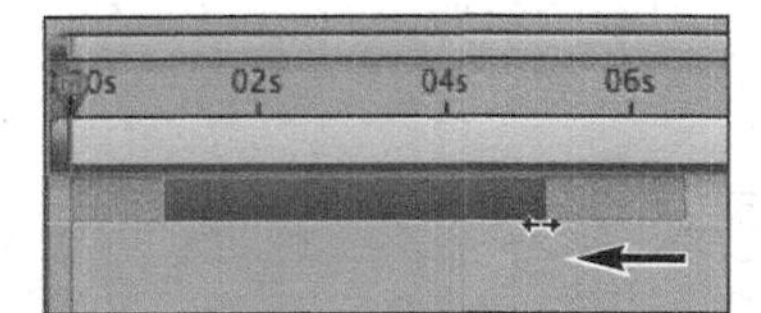

Figure 5.93 Drag the Out point handle of a layer's duration bar to change both its Out point and where it ends in the composition.

Moving Layers in Time

When you create a layer, it begins at the current time indicator. After that, you can move its position in time either by dragging the layer's duration bar or by using the controls in the In/Out panel of the Timeline panel.

To move a layer in time by dragging:

- In the time graph area of the Timeline panel, drag a layer to a new position in time (**Figures 5.94** and **5.95**).
- Dragging a layer to the left causes the layer to begin earlier in the composition.
- Dragging a layer to the right causes the layer to begin later in the composition.

  Make sure you drag from the middle section of the layer's duration bar; dragging either end changes the duration of the layer.

✔ Tips

- A layer's In point can occur before the beginning of the composition, just as its Out point can occur after the end of the composition. As you would expect, any frames beyond the beginning or end of the comp won't be included in previews or output.

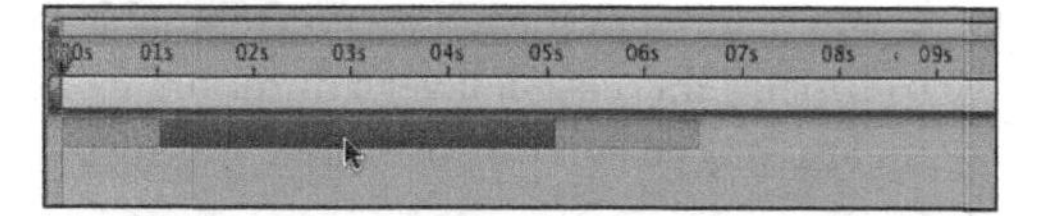

Figure 5.94 Drag a layer from the center portion of its duration bar . . .

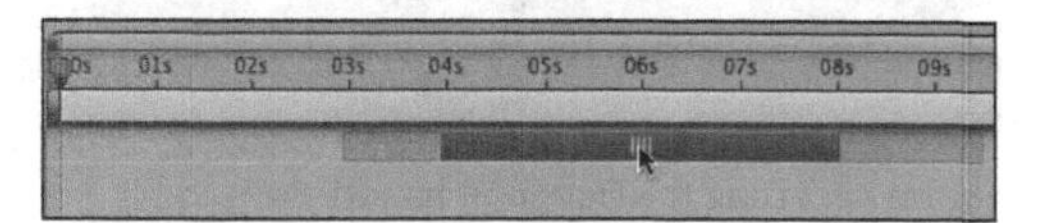

Figure 5.95 . . . to shift its position in time (without changing its duration). Press Shift after you begin dragging to activate the Snap to Edges feature.

- As usual, you can press Shift after you begin dragging to cause the layer to snap to edges. When you activate the Snap to Edges feature, the edges of the layer (its In and Out points) align with the edges of other layers as well as with the current time indicator as you drag them near each other. The layer also snaps to layer and composition markers.

Showing Numerical Editing Controls

You can view and control the timing of each layer in the timeline by revealing four columns of information:

In—The layer's starting time in the comp. Enter a value to change the layer's starting point in the comp (*not* the layer's first frame).

Out—The layer's ending time in the comp. Enter a value to set the layer's ending time in the comp (*not* the layer's last frame).

Duration—The length of the layer, expressed as a corollary of *speed*. Entering a value changes the layer's playback speed and, indirectly, its Out point.

Stretch—The layer's playback frame rate expressed as a percentage of the layer's native playback rate. Entering a value changes the layer's playback rate and, indirectly, its duration and Out point. See the next section, "Changing a Layer's Speed."

The timeline lets you expand all four columns as a set or each one individually.

Because this book covers several other, more convenient ways to move and trim layers, using the In and Out panels won't be covered in detail. However, turn to the next section to find out how to use the Duration and Stretch columns.

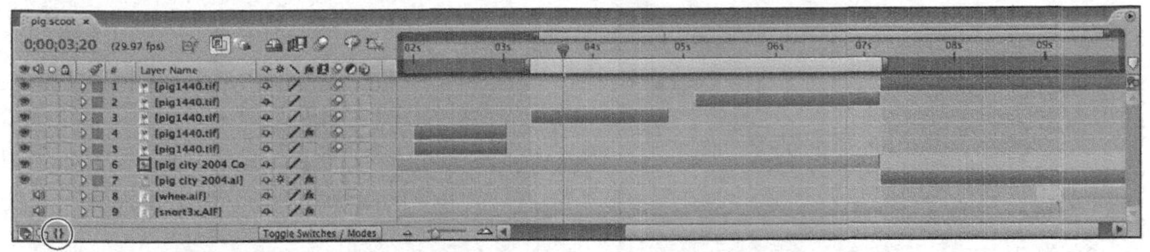

Figure 5.96 Click the In/Out/Duration/Stretch button to change the In/Out/Duration/Stretch panel from hidden . . .

To show and hide the In, Out, Duration, and Stretch columns:

- *Do either of the following:*
  - In the Timeline panel, click the In/Out/Duration/Stretch button {} to reveal the In/Out/Duration/Stretch panel; click the button again to hide the panel (**Figures 5.96** and **5.97**).
  - Control-click/right-click any panel of the Timeline panel, and choose the panel you want to view from the context menu (**Figure 5.98**).

Changing a Layer's Speed

Changing a layer's playback speed is yet another feature After Effects shares with typical non-linear editing programs. However, you should note a crucial difference between how you set the values in those programs and in After Effects. In many non-linear editing programs, you enter a *speed*: A value greater than 100 percent *increases* the speed, and a value less than 100 percent decreases the speed. In After Effects, you can enter a *stretch factor* value: A stretch factor greater than 100 percent *decreases* the speed of a layer (stretching, or increasing, its duration), and a stretch factor less than 100 percent *increases* the speed of a layer.

Entering a negative value reverses the playback direction of the layer—and also reverses the order of its property keyframes. (For more about properties and keyframes, see Chapter 7.) To reverse a layer's speed without also reversing its keyframes, you can use the Time Remapping feature, explained in Chapter 14, "More Layer Techniques." (Time remapping also lets you adjust the playback speed of a layer over time or create a freeze-frame effect.)

✔ Tips

- You can also perform a slip edit by dragging the layer's "hidden" trimmed frames (you can see their outlines extending beyond the layer's In and Out handles).
- To review how to perform insert and overlay edits, see Chapter 4, "Compositions."

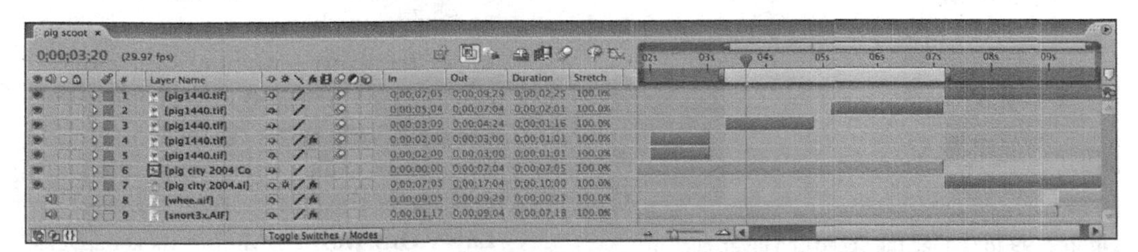

Figure 5.97 . . . to visible. Click the button again to hide the panel.

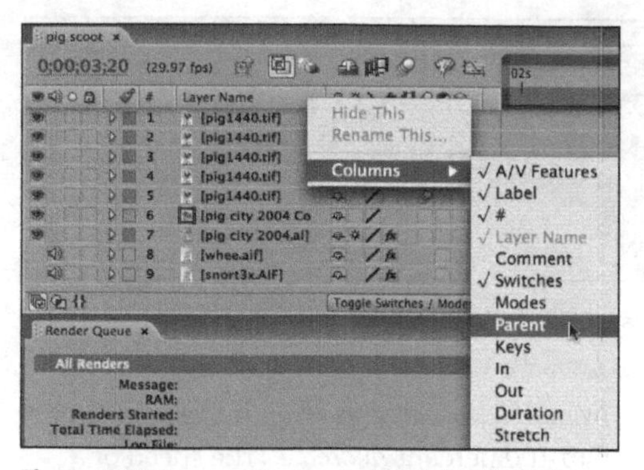

Figure 5.98 You can also Control-click/right-click any panel to access a context menu that allows you to show or hide a panel in the Timeline panel.

■ Those who use non-linear editing software know that the counterpart to the slip edit is the *slide edit.* Because each layer in After Effects occupies a separate track, slide editing is an inherent feature: Simply drag the layer to a new position in the time ruler.

To change the playback speed of a layer:

1. *Do one of the following:*
   - ▲ In the Timeline panel, click the Duration display or Stretch display for a layer (**Figure 5.99**).
   - ▲ In the Timeline panel, select a layer and choose Layer > Time Stretch.

   The Time Stretch dialog box opens (**Figure 5.100**).

2. In the Stretch section, *do either of the following:*

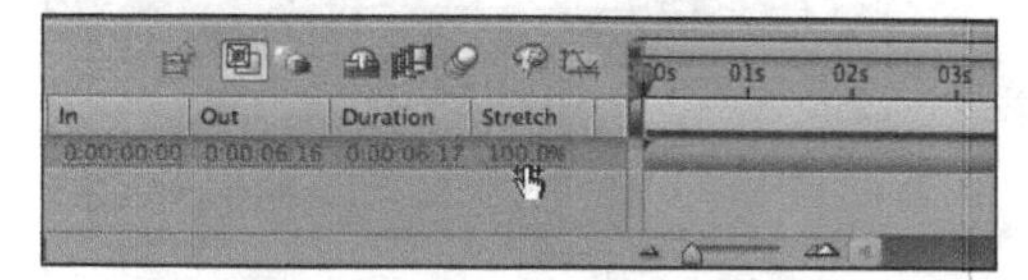

Figure 5.99 To change the speed of a layer, click its Duration or Stretch display.

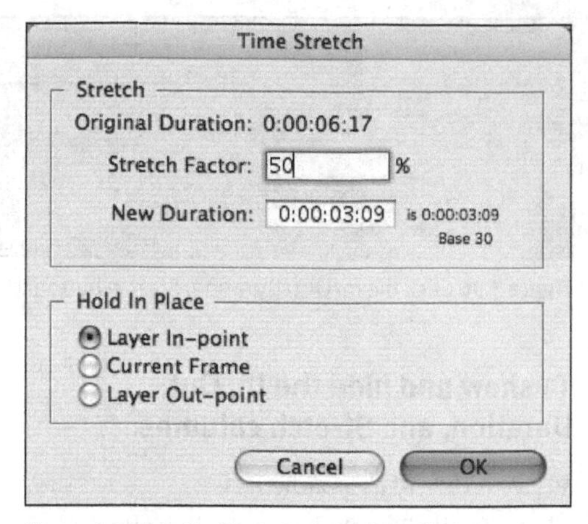

Figure 5.100 In the Time Stretch dialog box, enter a new duration or stretch factor to change the speed of the layer. In the Hold In Place section, choose which frame of the layer will maintain its position in the time graph.

   - ▲ For New Duration, enter a new duration for the layer.
   - ▲ For Stretch Factor, enter the percentage change of the layer's duration.

   To slow playback speed, enter a duration greater than that of the original or a stretch factor greater than 100 percent. To increase playback speed, enter a duration less than that of the original or a stretch factor less than 100 percent. Enter a negative value to reverse a layer's playback direction.

3. In the Hold In Place section of the Time Stretch dialog box, *select one of the following* options to determine the position of the layer when its speed and duration change:

   Layer In-point—Maintains the layer's starting point position in the composition

   Current Frame—Moves the layer's In and Out points while maintaining the frame's position at the current time indicator

   Layer Out-point—Maintains the layer's ending point position in the composition

4. Click OK to close the Time Stretch dialog box.

   The selected layer's speed, duration, and placement in time reflect your changes. However, the range of footage frames you specified to include—the layer's In and Out points—remain the same.

✔ Tips

- To quickly reverse a layer's playback (a stretch factor of –100 percent), select the layer and press Command-Option-R (Mac) or Ctrl-Alt-R (Windows).
- You can freeze-frame the current frame of the selected layer by choosing Layer > Time > Freeze Frame. This command automatically applies the appropriate time remapping settings.

Performing a Slip Edit

After Effects includes another editing feature common to non-linear editing programs: *slip edits.*

When you're working with layers created from motion footage, you'll find that you often need to change a portion of video without altering its position or duration in the time ruler. Although you can do this by reopening the Layer panel and setting new In and Out points, you must be careful to set edit points that result in the same duration. By using a slip edit, however, you can achieve the same result in a single step.

To slip a layer:

1. In the Tools panel, select the Pan Behind tool (**Figure 5.101**).
2. Position the mouse over a layer created from motion footage.

   The mouse pointer becomes a Slip Edit icon (**Figure 5.102**).

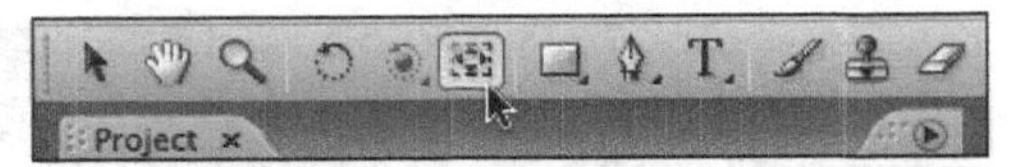

Figure 5.101 Select the Pan Behind tool.

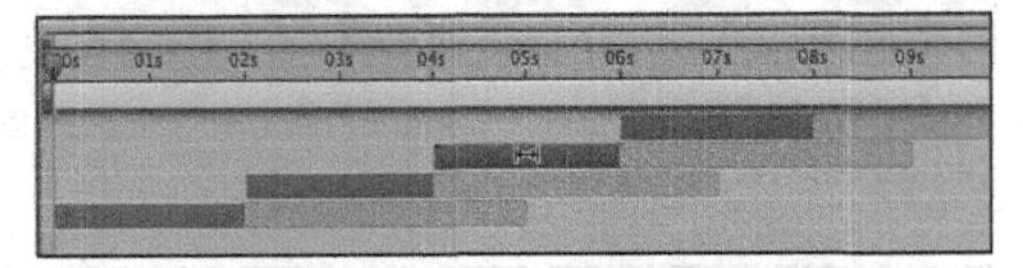

Figure 5.102 When you position the mouse over a layer created from motion footage, the mouse pointer becomes a Slip Edit tool.

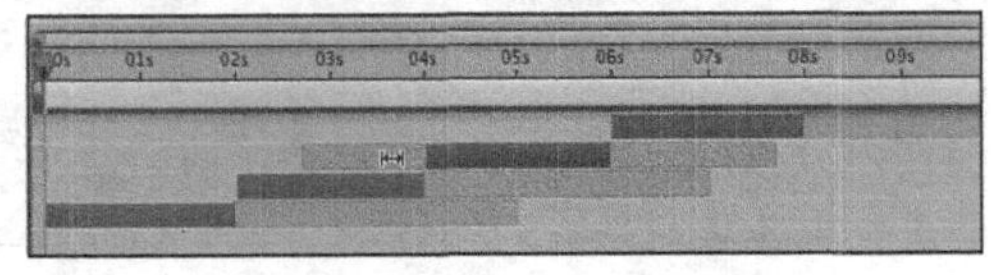

Figure 5.103 Dragging with the Slip Edit tool changes the portion of the motion footage used without changing its duration or position in the time ruler.

3. *Do either of the following:*
   - ▲ **Drag left** to slip the footage left, using frames that come later in the footage.
   - ▲ **Drag right** to slip the footage right, using frames that come earlier in the footage.

   The In and Out points of the source footage change by the same amount, which means the layer maintains its duration and position in the time ruler. As you drag, you can see the "hidden" footage extending from beyond the layer's In and Out points (**Figure 5.103**).

Sequencing and Overlapping Layers

Although you might not choose After Effects for editing, per se, you may find yourself starting many projects by creating a simple sequence. Fortunately, After Effects

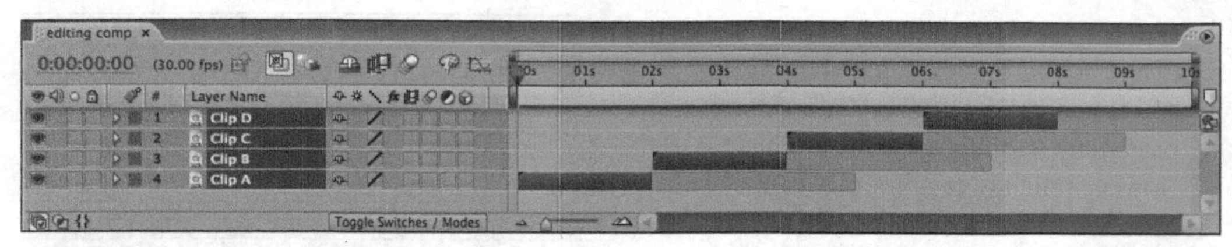

Figure 5.104 The Sequence command places selected layers one after another in the time graph in an uninterrupted sequence.

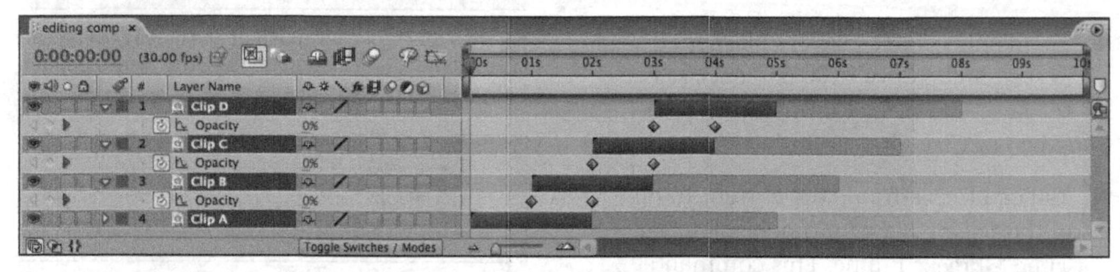

Figure 5.105 The Overlap option places the selected layers in a sequence that overlaps by a specified amount of time. It can automatically set keyframes for simple cross-fades between the layers.

automates this common request with its Sequence and Overlap features.

The Sequence command quickly places selected layers one after another in the time graph, seamlessly aligning their Out and In points so that the layers play back in an uninterrupted sequence (**Figure 5.104**).

The Overlap option also places the selected layers one after another in the time graph—but in this case, they overlap by a specified amount of time (**Figure 5.105**). Using the Overlap option prepares layers for transition effects; it can even automatically create cross-fades between layers.

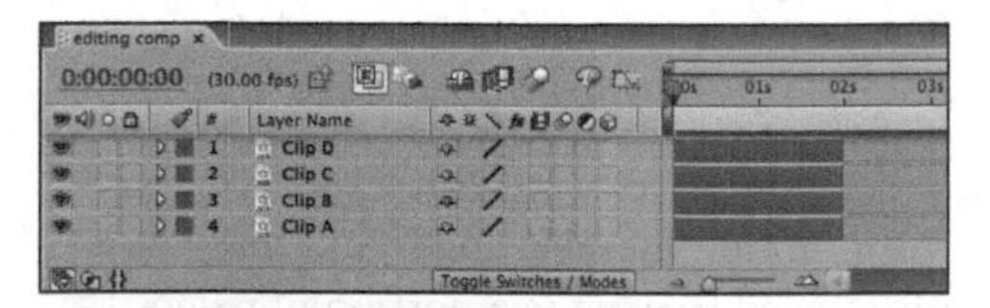

Figure 5.106 Select the layers you want to sequence.

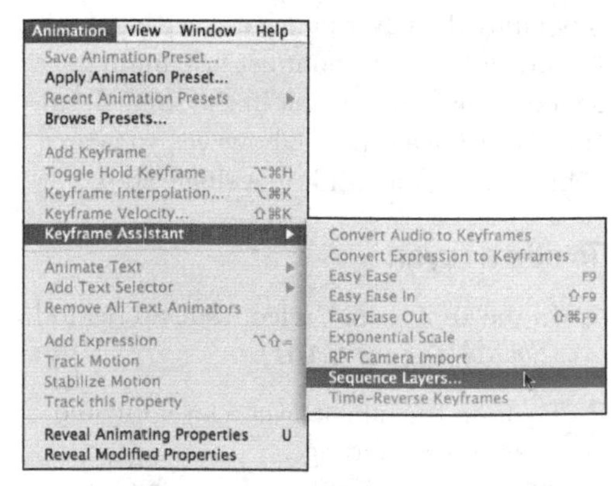

Figure 5.107 Choose Animation > Keyframe Assistant > Sequence Layers.

To arrange layers in a sequence:

1. In the Timeline panel, select the layers you want to sequence (**Figure 5.106**).
2. Choose Animation > Keyframe Assistant > Sequence Layers (**Figure 5.107**).

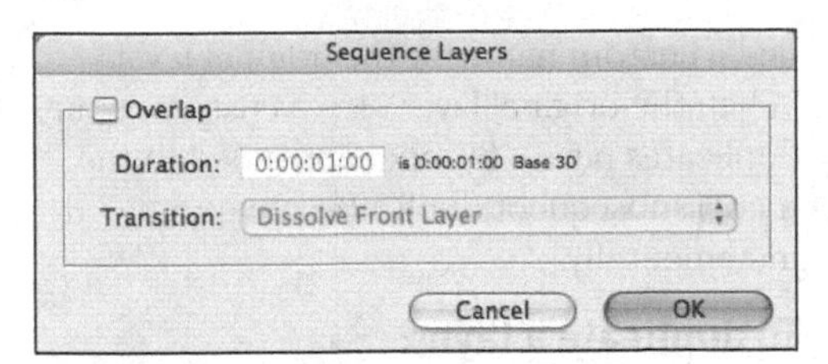

Figure 5.108 In the Sequence Layers dialog box, make sure Overlap is unchecked . . .

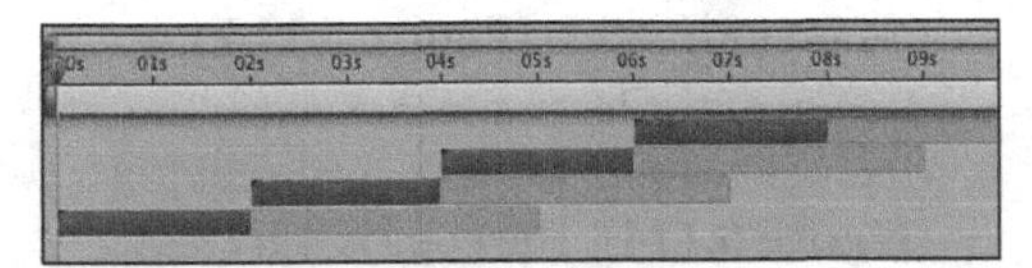

Figure 5.109 . . . to arrange the selected layers into a simple sequence.

The Sequence Layers dialog box opens (**Figure 5.108**).

3. Make sure Overlap is unchecked.
4. Click OK to close the dialog box.

   The selected layers are arranged in sequence, top layer first (**Figure 5.109**).

To arrange layers in an overlapping sequence:

1. In the Timeline panel, select the layers you want to arrange in an overlapping sequence.
2. Choose Animation > Keyframe Assistant > Sequence Layers.

   The Sequence Layers dialog box opens.
3. Check Overlap (**Figure 5.110**).
4. In the Duration field, enter the amount of time that the layers should overlap.
5. *Choose one of the following* cross-fade options from the Transition pull-down menu (**Figure 5.111**):
   - **Off**—For no cross-fade
   - **Dissolve Front Layer**—To automatically fade out the end of each preceding layer
   - **Cross Dissolve Front and Back Layers**—To fade out the end of each preceding layer automatically, and to fade up the beginning of each succeeding layer
6. Click OK to close the dialog box.

   The selected layers are arranged in an overlapping sequence (top layer first) and use the cross-fade option you specified (**Figure 5.112**).

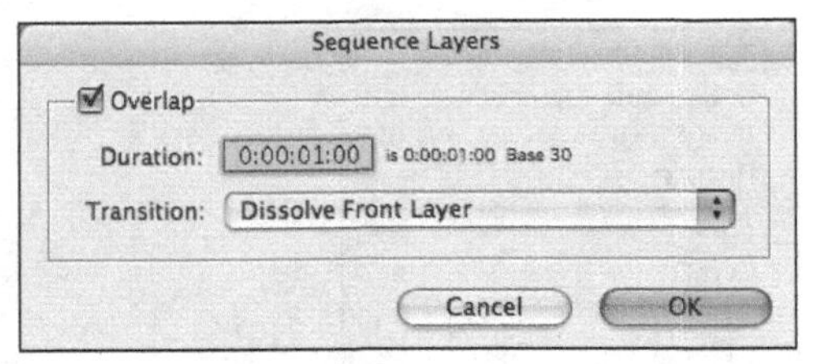

Figure 5.110 To overlap the layers of a sequence, check Overlap in the Sequence Layers dialog box. For Duration, enter the amount of time you want the layers to overlap.

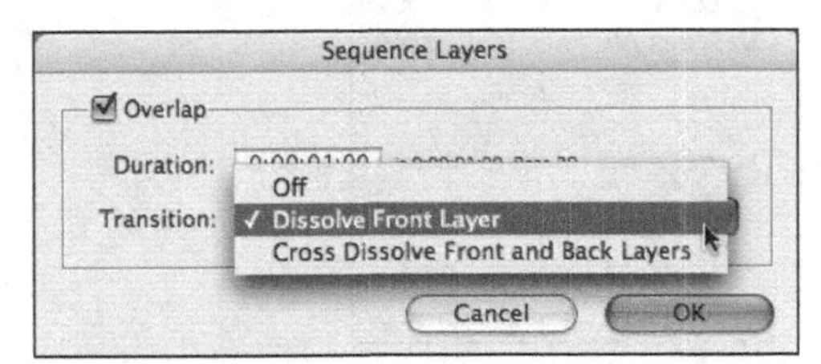

Figure 5.111 In the Transition pull-down menu, choose the appropriate option.

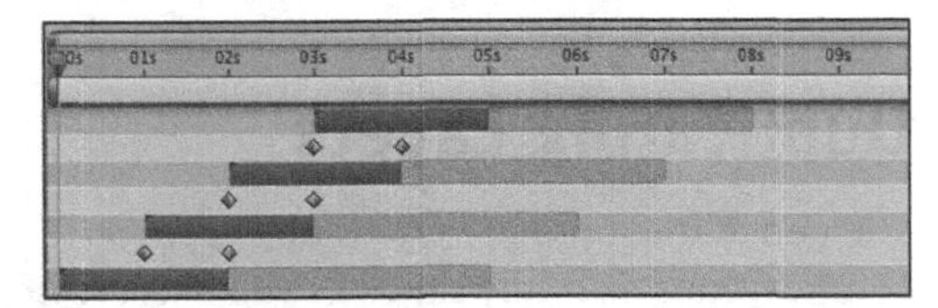

Figure 5.112 The selected layers are arranged in an overlapping sequence.

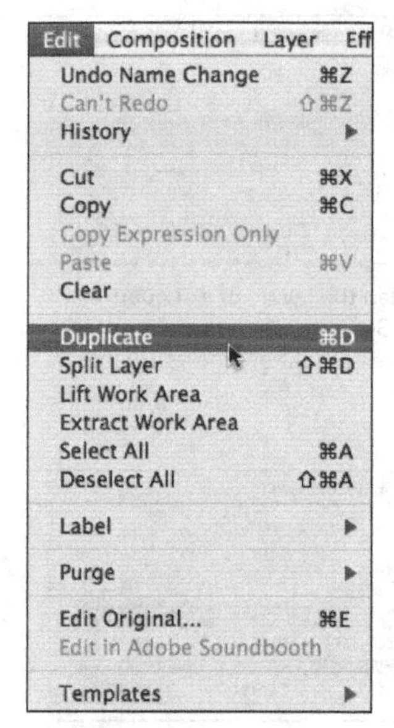

Figure5.113 To duplicate a layer, select the layer and choose Edit › Duplicate, or press Command/Ctrl-D.

Duplicating Layers

You can add a footage item to one or more compositions as many times as you like, creating a new layer each time. However, it's often easier to duplicate a layer that's already in a composition, particularly when you want to use its edit points or other properties (such as masks, transformations, effects, and layer modes). When you create a duplicate, it appears just above the original layer in the stacking order. The duplicate uses the same name as the original, unless you specified a custom name for the original layer. When the original layer uses a custom name, duplicates have a number appended to the name; subsequent duplicates are numbered incrementally.

To duplicate a layer:

1. In the Timeline panel, select a layer.
2. Choose Edit > Duplicate, or press Command/Ctrl-D (**Figure 5.113**).

   A copy of the layer appears above the original layer in the stacking order (**Figure 5.114**). The copy is selected; you may want to rename the new layer.

Splitting Layers

You can set a preference to determine which layer—the layer before the split point or the layer after the split point—is higher in the stacking order.

To split a layer:

1. In the Timeline panel, select a layer.
2. Set the current time to the frame at which you want to split the layer (**Figure 5.115**).
3. Choose Edit > Split Layer, or press Shift-Command-D (Mac) or Shift-Ctrl-D (Windows) (**Figure 5.116**).

   The layer splits in two, creating one layer that ends at the current time indicator and another that begins at the current time indicator (**Figure 5.117**). The layer

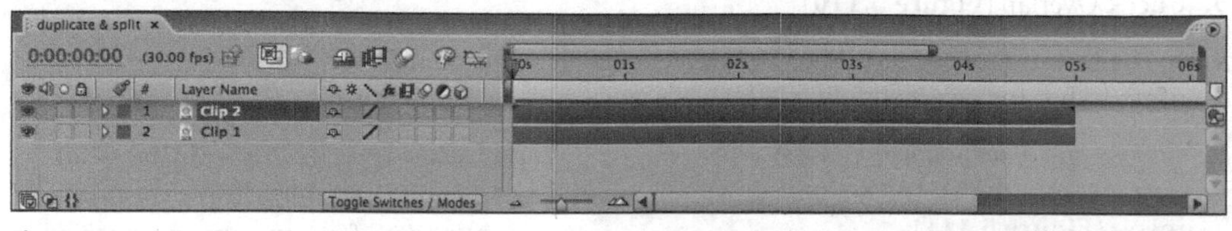

Figure 5.114 A duplicate layer appears in the composition, distinguished by an incrementally higher number (in this case, "2") after its name.

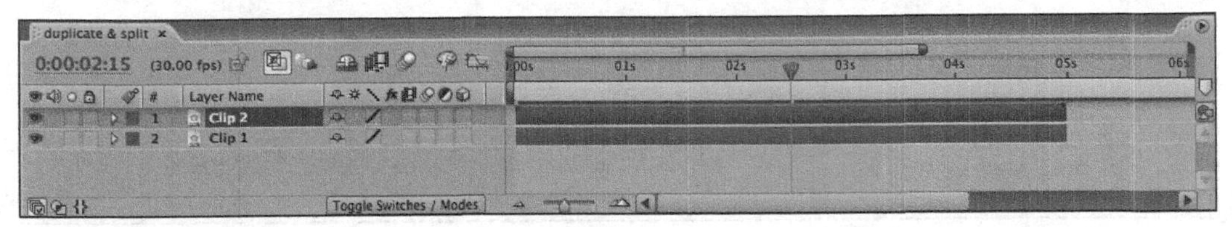

Figure 5.115 Set the current time to the frame at which you want to split the selected layer.

that becomes higher in the stacking order depends on the preference you specify in the General Preferences dialog box.

Using Markers

Like most non-linear editing programs, After Effects enables you to mark important points in time with a visible stamp. *Markers* allow you to identify music beats visually and to synchronize visual effects with sound effects. They can also help you quickly move the current time to particular points in the composition. You can add as many as ten numbered markers to the time graph. And in individual layers, you can add any number of markers, which can include text comments to help you identify them. Because markers are for personal reference, they only appear in the time ruler and layer duration bars; they don't appear in the Composition panel or in previews or renders.

In addition to text comments, layer markers can also contain Web or chapter links. These links are retained when you export to certain Web- or DVD-friendly formats. When a marker containing a link is reached during playback, a Web link automatically opens as a Web page in your browser; a chapter link cues a QuickTime movie or DVD to a specified chapter. Check the After Effects Help system for more detailed information on these specialized features.

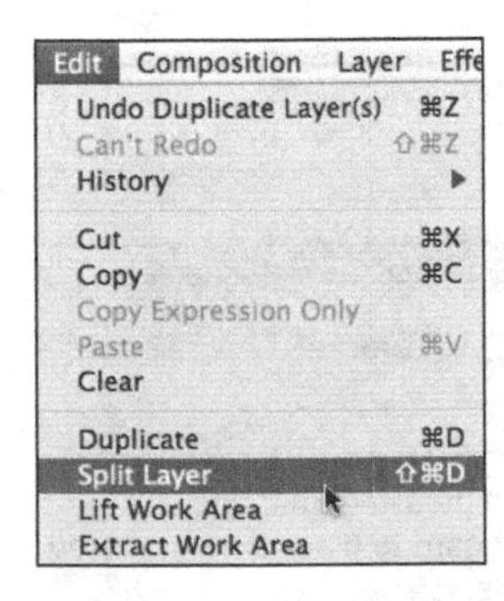

Figure 5.116 Choose Edit › Split Layer.

To add a composition marker by dragging:

- In the Timeline panel, drag a composition time marker from the marker well to the desired point in the time graph (**Figure 5.118**).

  A marker appears in the time ruler of the Timeline panel (**Figure 5.119**).

To add a composition marker at the current time indicator:

1. Move the current time indicator to the frame you want to mark in the composition (**Figure 5.120**).
2. Press Shift and a number on the main keyboard (not the numeric keypad).

   A marker with the number you pressed appears in the time ruler of the Timeline panel (**Figure 5.121**).

To move a composition marker:

- Drag a composition marker to a new position in the time ruler of the Timeline panel (**Figure 5.122**).

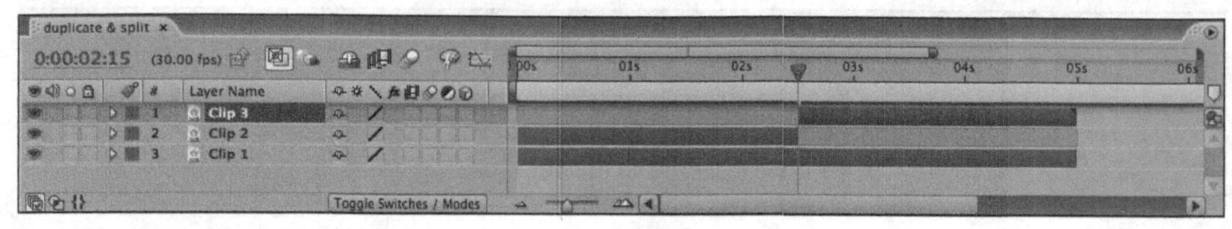

Figure 5.117 The selected layer splits into two layers at the current time.

To move the current time indicator to a composition marker:

- Press the number of a composition marker on the main keyboard (not the numeric keypad).

  The current time indicator moves to the composition marker with the number you pressed.

To remove a composition marker:

- Drag a composition marker to the right until the marker well is highlighted and the marker disappears from the time ruler (**Figure 5.123**).

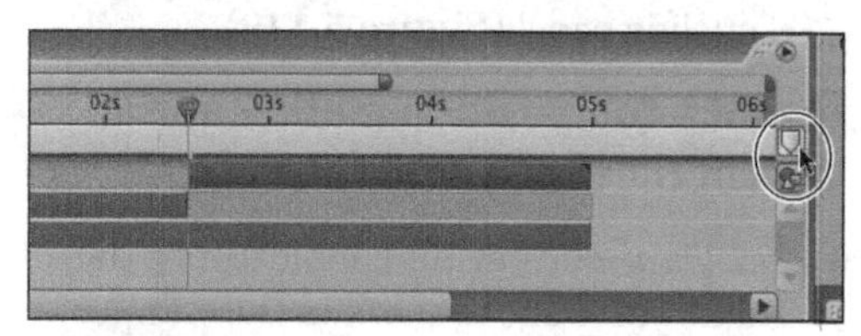

Figure 5.118 To add a composition marker, drag a marker from the marker well . . .

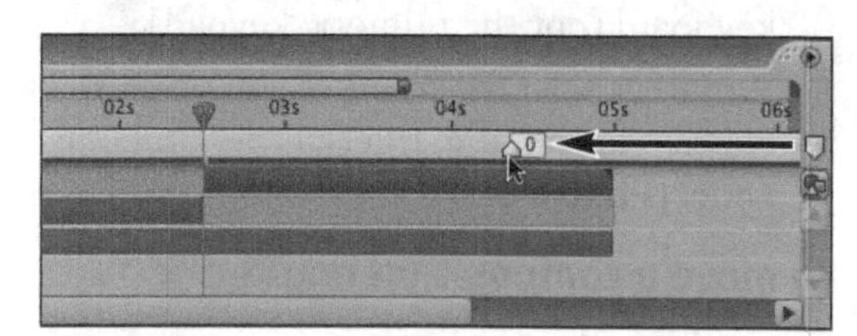

Figure 5.119 . . . and drop the marker at the frame you want to mark in the time ruler. Watch the current time display of the Timeline panel to help accurately place the marker.

To add a layer marker:

1. Select the layer to which you want to add a marker.
2. Set the current time to the frame to which you want to add a marker (**Figure 5.124**).
3. *Do one of the following:*
   - Choose Layer > Add Marker (**Figure 5.125**).
   - Press the asterisk (*) on the numeric keypad (not the main keyboard).

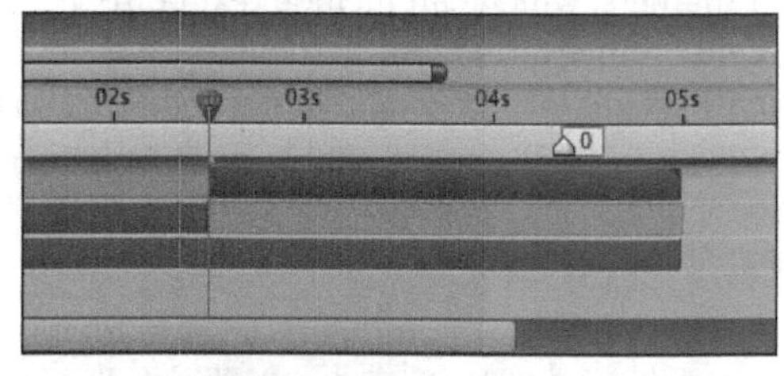

Figure 5.120 You can also place a composition marker by setting the current time . . .

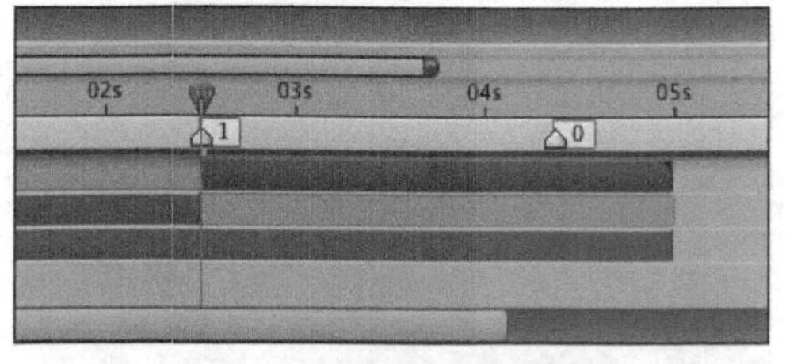

Figure 5.121 . . . and then pressing Shift and a number on the main keyboard to place the numbered marker at the current time.

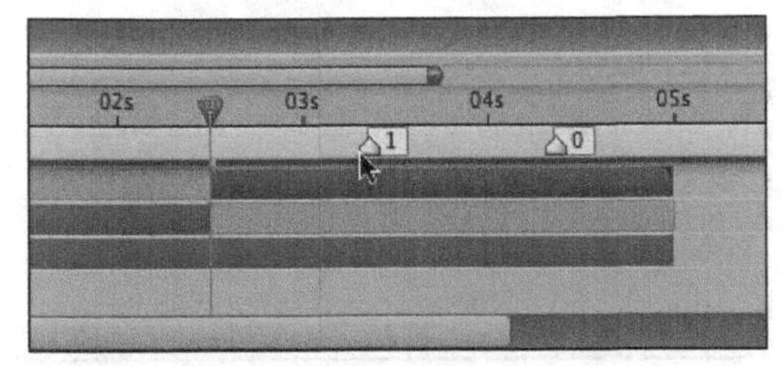

Figure 5.122 You can drag a composition marker to a new position in the time ruler.

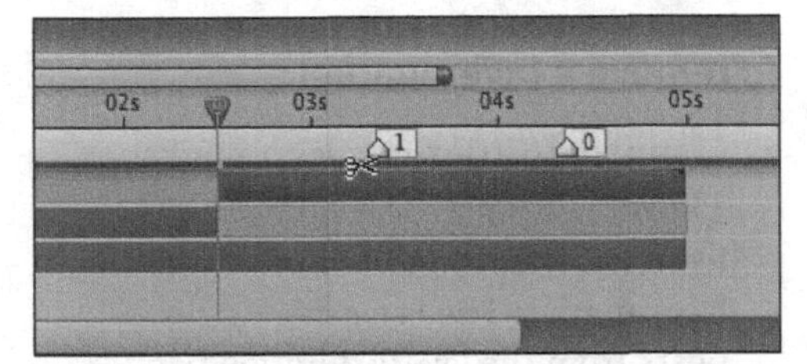

Figure 5.123 To remove a composition marker, drag it to the extreme right, until the marker well is highlighted and the marker disappears.

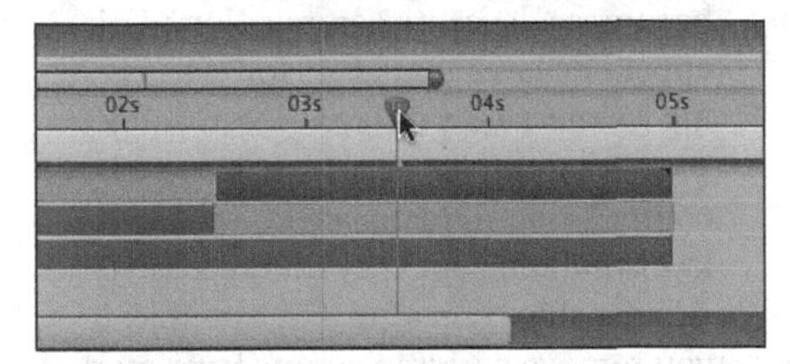

Figure 5.124 To add a layer marker, select a layer and set the current time to the frame you want to mark.

Figure 5.125 Choose Layer › Add Marker, or press the asterisk on the numeric keypad.

A marker appears on the layer's duration bar at the current time indicator (**Figure 5.126**).

To add a layer marker comment:

1. Double-click a layer marker in a layer's duration bar (**Figure 5.127**).

   A Marker dialog box opens. If a Layer panel opens, you must have double-clicked the layer's duration bar or marker name rather than the marker itself.

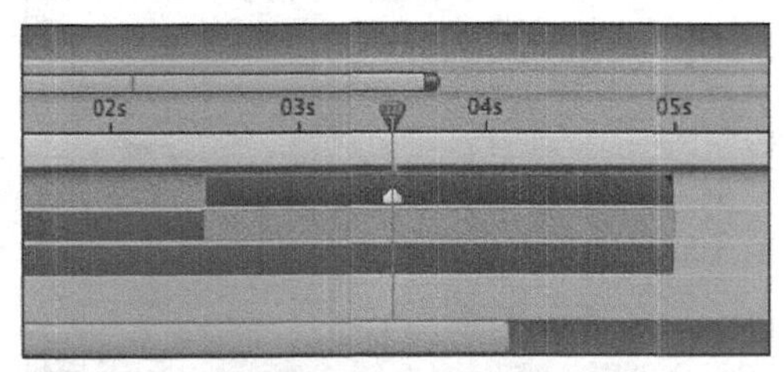

Figure 5.126 The marker appears in the duration bar of the selected layer at the current time indicator.

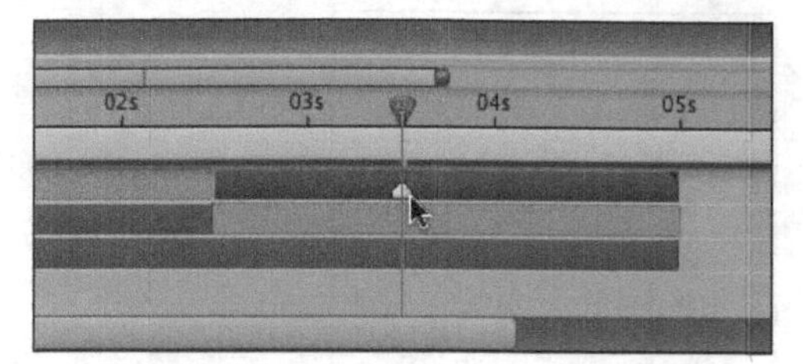

Figure 5.127 Double-click a layer marker to add a name to the marker. Make sure to double-click the marker, not the layer (or the marker name, if it already has one).

2. In the Marker dialog box, enter a comment for the marker in the Comment field (**Figure 5.128**).

   You can also add chapter links or Web links if your output format supports these features.

3. Click OK to close the dialog box.

   The comment you specified appears next to the layer marker (**Figure 5.129**).

To move a layer marker:

- Drag a layer marker to a new position in the layer's duration bar (**Figure 5.130**).

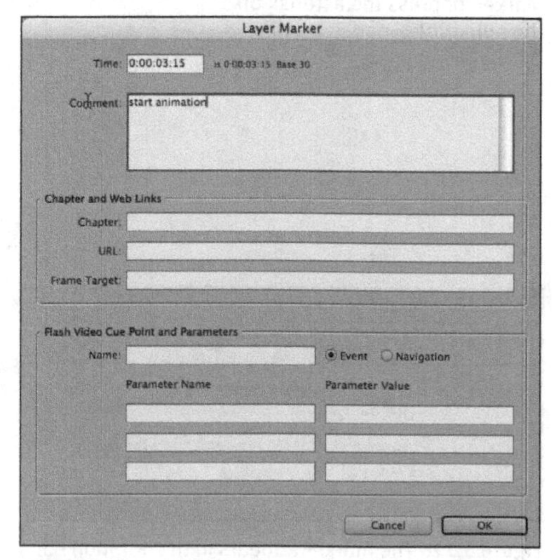

Figure 5.128 In the Marker dialog box, enter a comment for the marker.

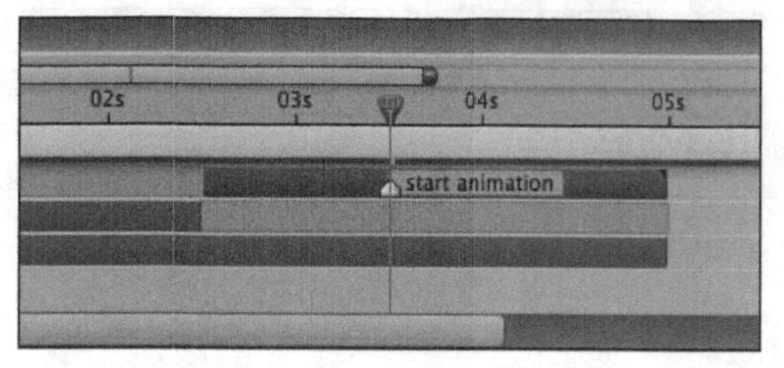

Figure 5.129 The comment you specified appears next to the marker.

To remove a layer marker:

- Command/Ctrl-click a layer marker.

  The mouse pointer becomes a Scissors icon ✂ when you position it over the layer marker. The layer marker disappears from the layer's duration bar.

✔ Tips

- When a composition is nested and becomes a layer, its composition markers appear as layer markers. However, changing its markers as a layer doesn't affect its markers as a comp. In other words, composition markers are converted into layer markers, but they don't retain a relationship thereafter. For example, if you remove a nested comp's layer marker, the corresponding marker in the original comp remains.
- You can add layer markers on the fly as you preview audio. This makes it especially easy to mark the beats of music or

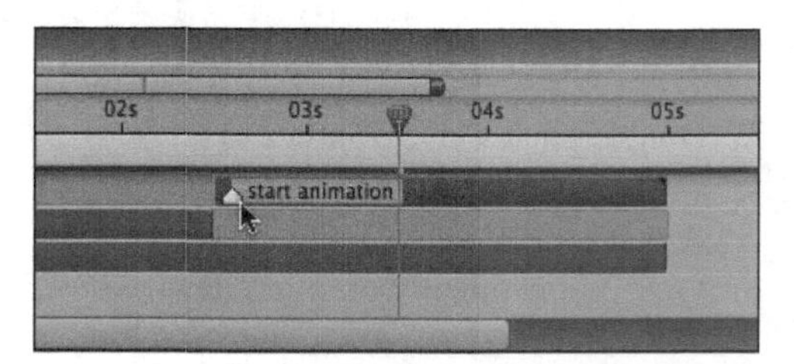

Figure 5.130 Drag a layer marker to a new frame in the layer. Make sure to grab the marker, not its name or the layer's duration bar.

other audio. Press the decimal point (.) on the numeric keypad to preview audio only. As the audio previews, press the asterisk (*) key on the numeric keypad. (Adobe Premiere Pro users should recognize this technique.)

Properties and Keyframes

Once they see what After Effects can do, most folks can't wait to take a closer look at the program that produces such artful results. Upon closer inspection, however, it's easy to recoil from the cryptic array of controls that look more like the tools of a scientist than those of an artist.

But don't let a few numbers and graphs intimidate you! This chapter fearlessly unveils layer properties and demystifies animation. Once you understand how to define properties, you can extend a few simple techniques to control practically any property of any layer in a composition. Having conquered that paper tiger, you'll be ready to animate those properties using something called *keyframes*.

As any scientist or artist can tell you, it's important to have full control over the variables, but some of the best innovations are arrived at randomly. By generating random variations on specified properties, After Effects' new Brainstorm feature lets you freely experiment and achieve results you might not have otherwise—in a manner not unlike a plant breeder or a Jackson Pollack. You'll find that the techniques you learn in this chapter are fundamental, and you'll be able to apply them to the features covered in subsequent chapters, from masks to effects to 3D layers. But first, you'll want to see the animation in action, using techniques covered in Chapter 6, "Playback, Previews, and RAM." You'll realize that animating in After Effects isn't rocket science, after all. But mastering it is still an art.

Layer Property Types

A *property* refers to any of a layer's visual or audio characteristics to which you can assign different values over time. Properties fall into these main categories: masks, effects, and transform (**Figure 5.131**). In addition, layers that contain audio include an Audio property, and 3D layers include a Material Options property.

The order in which these categories are listed reflects the order in which After Effects renders each layer's masks, effects, transform, and audio properties. Although you don't need to concern yourself with rendering order now, it does become important as your animations grow in complexity.

Masks

Like the acetate layers used in traditional compositing, masks let you include some portions of an image and exclude others. They also make it possible for you to apply effects to selected portions of layers.

You can apply one or several masks to each layer in a composition and then define the way those masks interact. Not only can you control the shape and feather of a mask, you can also animate these attributes over time.

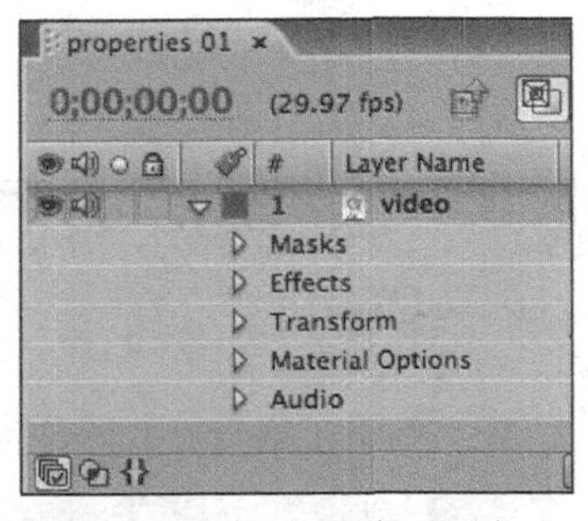

Figure 5.131 There are three major categories of visual properties: masks, effects, and transform. Layers with an audio track contain an Audio property; layers you designate as 3D have a Material Options property.

Chapter 7, "Mask Essentials," describes using masks in more detail.

Effects

Effects include a wide range of options for modifying sound and images. You can use them to make simple adjustments—such as correcting color or filtering audio—or to make more dramatic changes, such as distorting and stylizing. *Keying effects* help to composite images, and *transition effects* blend one layer into another. You can even use effects to generate visual elements such as text, light, and particles.

You can add to your effects repertoire by using After Effects Pro or by downloading third-party plug-ins.

Transform properties

Although you may not choose to apply any masks or effects to the layers of your compositions, you must still define their basic properties, including position, scale, rotation, and opacity—known as *transform properties.* This chapter focuses on these essential layer properties as they relate to 2D layers.

Audio properties

Layers that contain audio display an Audio property in the layer outline. Because only images can have masks or transform properties, audio-only layers contain only the Effects and Audio property categories. The Audio category includes a Levels property to control audio volume as well as a waveform display. Along with transform properties, this chapter explains how to set audio levels.

Viewing Properties

You can view any combination of layer properties in the Timeline panel in what's called a *layer outline* (**Figure 5.132**). That is, each layer works like the heading of an outline: Expanding the layer reveals property headings, which in turn can be expanded to reveal individual properties. (The property headings that are revealed depend on the layer; a layer without masks or audio won't include those headings in the outline.) Using keyboard shortcuts, you can reveal properties selectively and prevent the outline from becoming long and unwieldy.

Revealing a property also displays its current value and its *property track*, an area under the time ruler that shows the property's keyframes. Keyframes, as you'll learn, indicate points at which you define a property's values in order to make them change over time. In other words, the property track is where you can view and control animation.

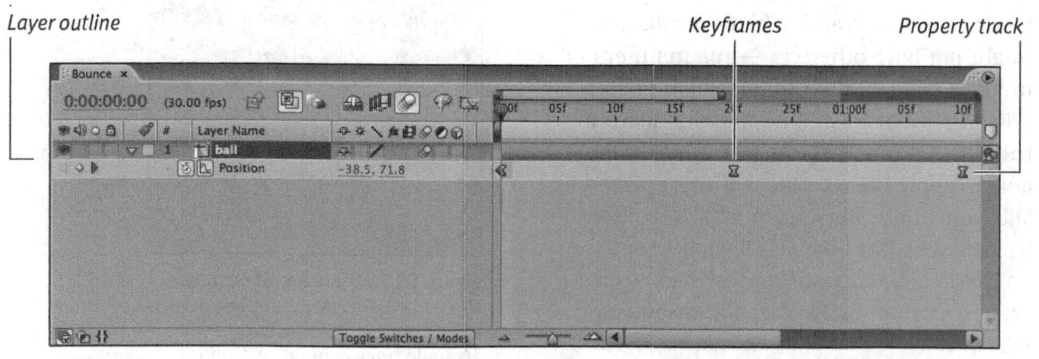

Figure 5.132 Expanding a layer reveals its properties in outline form, or layer outline. Appearing next to the property's name are its current value (under the layer switches) and keyframes (under the time ruler).

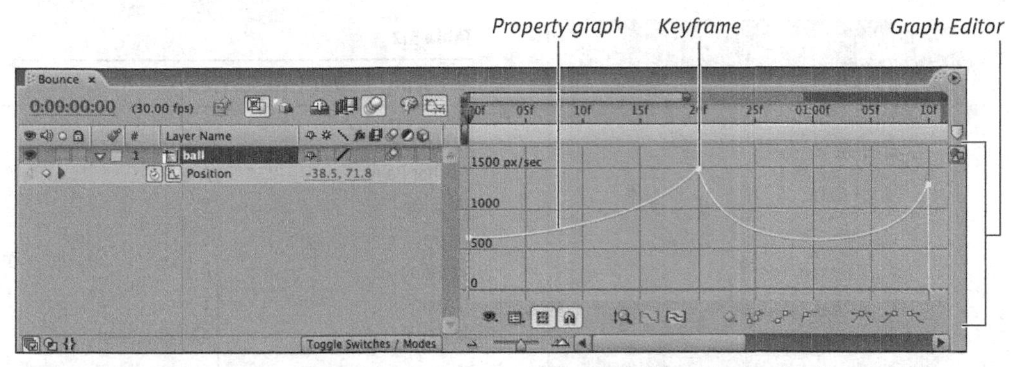

Figure 5.133 You can toggle the area under the time ruler to the Graph Editor. The Graph Editor depicts property values in graph form, allowing you to adjust both keyframed values and the manner in which After Effects calculates values between keyframes.

To fine-tune an animation—particularly between the keyframes—you can go in for an even more detailed view using the Graph Editor (**Figure 5.133**). As its name suggests, the Graph Editor lets you see selected property values as a graph. You can manipulate the graph directly, manually changing not only the keyframes, but also how the values change between keyframes (the interpolated values).

But don't let yourself get overwhelmed by unfamiliar terminology or seemingly complex choices. For the moment, rest assured that the Timeline panel allows you to reveal the properties you want at the level of detail you need. This chapter covers setting property values and basic keyframing.

To expand or collapse a layer outline by clicking:

- In the Timeline panel, *do any of the following:*
  - To expand the first level of property headings, click the triangle to the left of a layer (**Figure 5.134**).

    The triangle spins clockwise to point down, revealing the first level of the layer outline.
  - To further expand the outline, click the triangle to the left of a property heading (**Figure 5.135**).

    The triangle spins clockwise to point down, revealing the next level of the outline.
  - To collapse an expanded layer outline heading, click the triangle again.

  The triangle spins counterclockwise, hiding that level of the layer outline.

✔ Tips

- You can expand the outline for multiple layers simultaneously by selecting more than one layer before expanding the outline. Expanding the outline for one

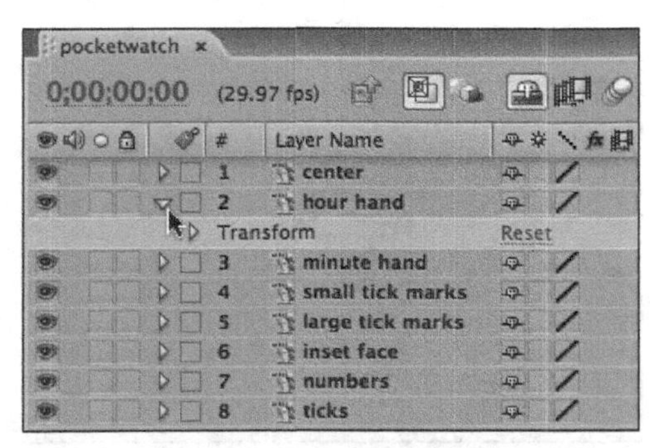

Figure 5.134 Click the triangle to the left of a layer to reveal the first level of properties.

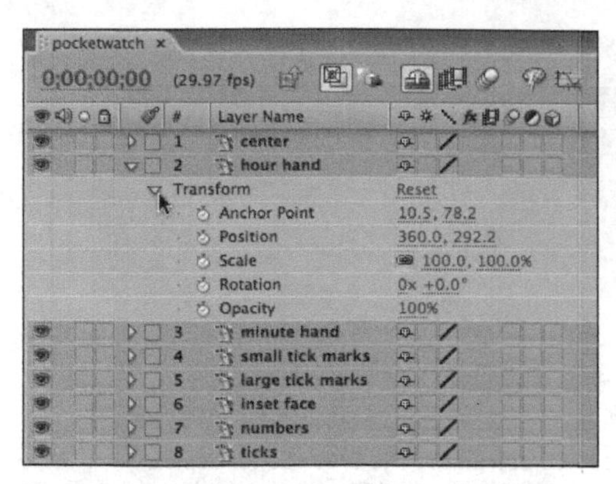

Figure 5.135 Continue to expand the outline by clicking the triangles. Click the triangles again to collapse the outline.

selected layer expands all selected layers (**Figure 5.136**).

- There are several ways to expand and collapse a layer outline. Although clicking the Timeline panel may be the most intuitive method, doing so often reveals more than you need. Keyboard shortcuts let you expand layer properties selectively.

To view layer properties using keyboard shortcuts

- To expand the layer outline by using keyboard shortcuts, select one or more layers, and use the appropriate keyboard shortcut (see **Table 5.2**).

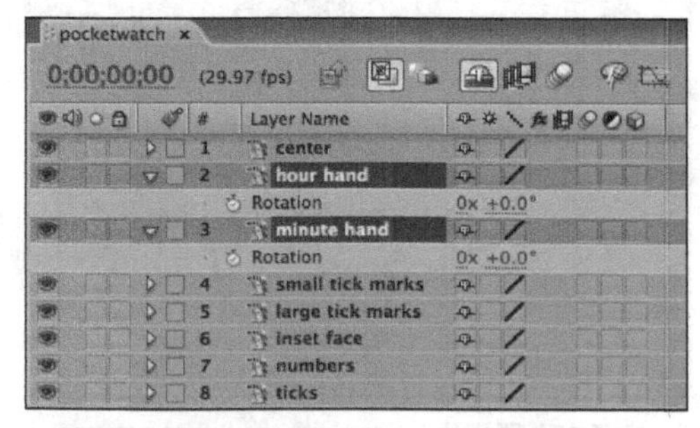

Figure 5.136 Select multiple layers to expand the outline for all of them at once.

Table 5.2

Viewing Layer Properties

To expand/collapse	Press this shortcut
Transform	
Anchor Point	A
Position	P
Scale	S
Rotation	R
Opacity	T
Material Options	AA (3D layers)
Mask	
Mask Shape	M
Mask Feather	F
Mask Opacity	TT
Mask Properties	MM
Effects	
Effects	E
Paint Effects	EE
Audio	
Audio Levels	L
Audio Waveform	LL
Headings	
Add/remove from outline	Shift-property shortcut
All animated	U (keyframed values)
All modified	UU

✔ Tip

- Some shortcuts work differently for light and camera layers. Because lights aren't visible (only their effects are), pressing T reveals a light layer's Intensity property. For both lights and cameras, A reveals the Point of Interest property, and R reveals the Orientation property.

Setting Global vs. Animated Property Values

Now that you know how to view layer properties, you can set their values. The following sections describe how to set property values globally—that is, how to set a single value

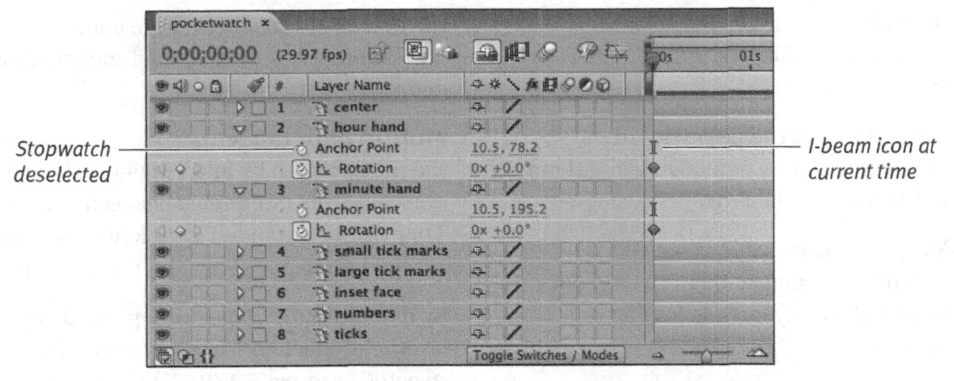

Figure 5.137 A deselected Stopwatch icon and an I-beam icon in the selected property track identify a static property.

for the duration of the layer. Then, you'll animate properties by setting different values at different points in time. But before we continue, it may be helpful to understand a few basic differences between global and animated properties.

As you proceed, you'll notice that a property that has a *global*, or unchanging, value has an I-beam icon at its current time in the time graph, and the Stopwatch icon next to the property's name appears deselected (**Figure 5.137**).

An animated property, in contrast, displays keyframes, which designate values at specific points in time, and an activated Stopwatch icon (**Figure 5.138**). You can set global properties without regard to the current time, but you must always specify the current frame before setting an animated property. Although global and animated properties look different in the timeline, you always reveal and use property controls the same way.

Viewing Spatial Controls in the Comp Panel

As you know, the Composition panel lets you view how layers will appear in your final

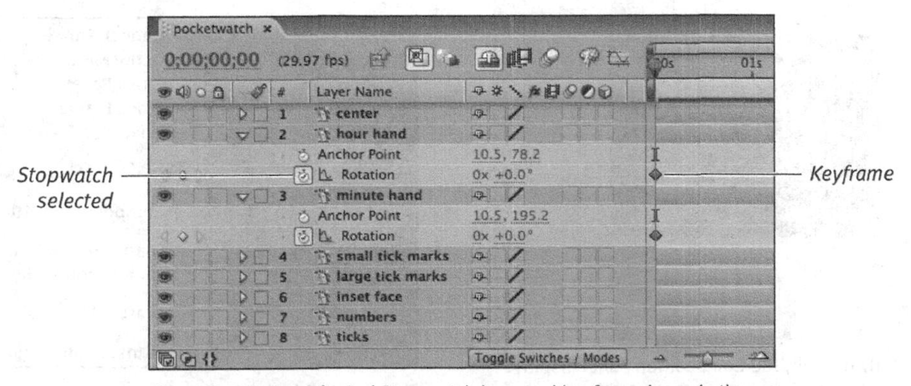

Figure 5.138 An activated Stopwatch icon and keyframe icons in the property track identify an animated property.

output. It also provides controls for the spatial properties of layers, including the following:

Handles appear at the perimeter of the layer, at each compass point. Dragging them affects the scale of the layer.

Masks appear as editable, color-coded mask paths. You can use them to crop out some parts of the layer while leaving other parts visible.

Effect controls show the spatial controls of many effects, such as the end points of path text.

Keyframes show the position keyframes you set as marks in the motion path. You can move and add keyframes directly in the motion path.

Motion paths show a layer's position as it changes over time as a dotted line. You can't change the path directly, but you can change the keyframes that define the ends of the line segments, as well as the tangents that define the line.

Motion path tangents control the curve of the motion path by affecting how the position values are interpreted between keyframes. They can be extended from keyframes and dragged directly to alter the motion path.

By default, the Composition panel displays layer and effect controls whenever a layer is selected (**Figure 5.139**). You can also toggle these view options on and off in the View Options dialog box or, in some instances, by using buttons in the Composition panel. You'll appreciate each control more fully as you employ corresponding techniques explained later in this and future chapters.

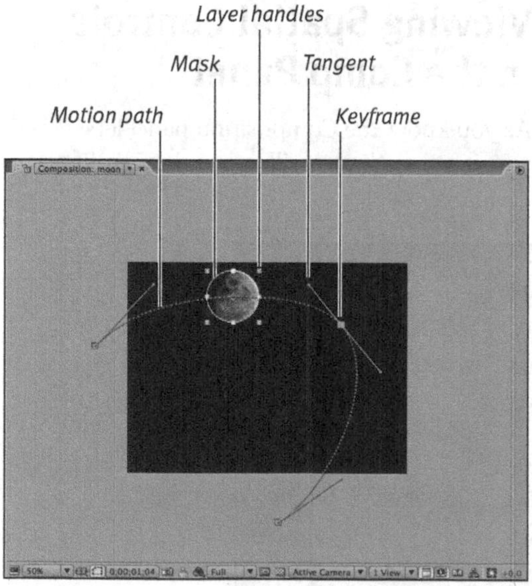

Layer handles
Mask
Tangent
Motion path
Keyframe

Figure 5.139 By default, the Composition panel displays spatial information and controls for selected layers, such as layer handles, keyframes, and the motion path.

To view layer and effect controls in the Composition panel:

1. In the Composition panel's pull-down menu, choose View Options (**Figure 5.140**).

   The View Options dialog box appears.
2. Select Layer Controls, and then specify the layer controls you want to make visible in the Composition panel.

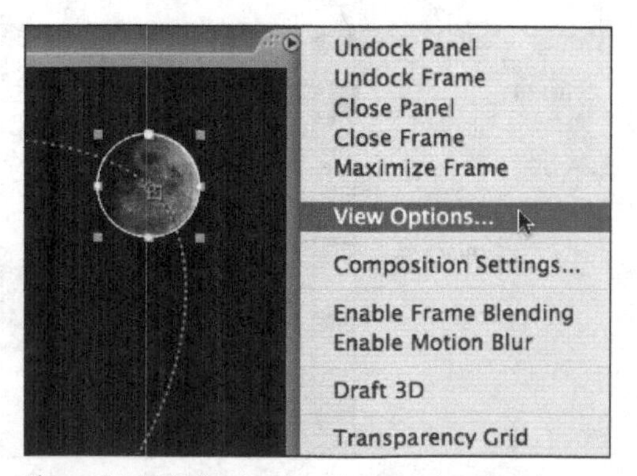

Figure 5.140 In the Composition panel menu, choose View Options.

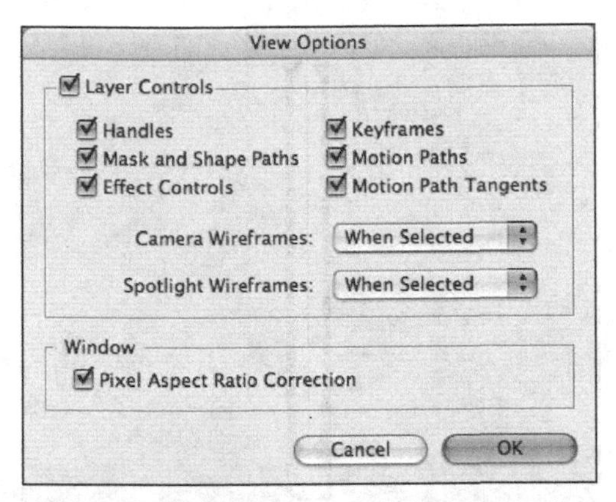

Figure 5.141 In the View Options dialog box, specify the layer controls you want to be visible in the Composition panel.

A check indicates that the controls are visible in the Composition panel when a layer is selected; no check indicates that the controls are hidden (**Figure 5.141**).

✔ Tips

- You can specify whether the motion path is visible and how many keyframes it shows at once in the Display pane of the Preferences dialog box.
- Instead of selecting Masks in the View Options dialog box, you can use the Toggle View Mask button at the bottom of the Composition panel.

Transform Properties

Although a layer may not use masks or effects, its transform properties—the nchor point, position, scale, rotation, and opacity—are fundamental (**Figure 5.142**). When you create a layer, you actively set its position, either by dragging to the timeline or to the Composition icon to center it, or by dragging to the Composition panel to place it manually. The other transform properties all have default initial values.

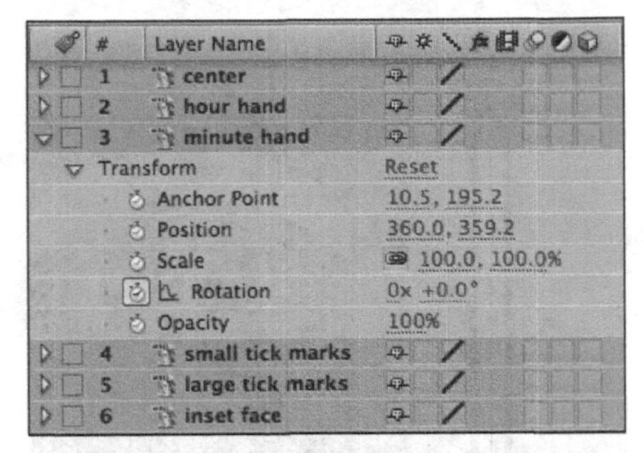

Figure 5.142 Although a layer may not use masks or effects, each of its transform properties has a value—either by default or as you choose to set them.

The following sections describe each transform property and how to change its values.

Keep in mind that even though the following sections focus on transform properties, you employ similar techniques to set values for all types of layer properties.

Anchor point

After Effects calculates the position, scale, and rotation of a layer by its anchor point. The anchor point defines the position of a layer, the point around which a layer is scaled, and the pivot point of the layer's rotation. The placement of the anchor point relative to the layer image can mean the difference between animating, say, a propeller or a pendulum.

By default, a layer's anchor point is positioned in the center of the layer (**Figure 5.143**). You can move the anchor point by using controls in the Layer panel or by using the Pan Behind tool in the Composition panel.

When you change the anchor point in the Layer panel, it may appear that you've also changed the layer's position in the Composition panel. Actually, the layer's Position property remains the same; you simply

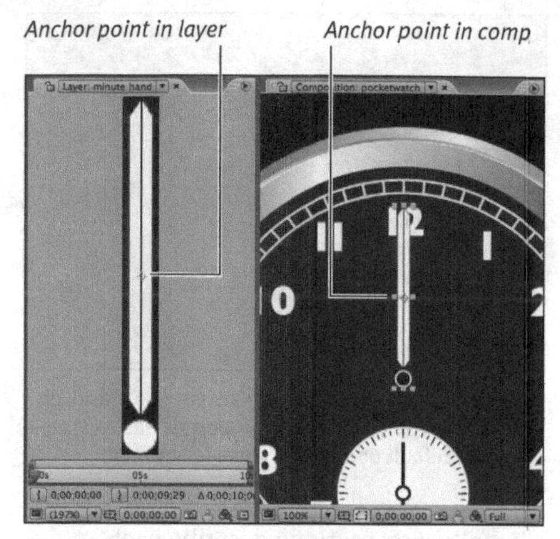

Figure 5.143 Typically, the anchor point is located at the center of a layer. After Effects uses the anchor point to calculate position, rotation, and scale.

changed the spot in the layer that determines its position in the composition.

Use the Layer panel to change the anchor point if you haven't already positioned the layer relative to other layers, or if you prefer to manipulate the layer in its own panel.

If you want to change a layer's anchor point without disturbing the layer's position in the composition, use the Pan Behind tool. Using the Pan Behind tool to drag the anchor point in the Composition panel recalculates the layer's position value to compensate for the new anchor point value. This way, the layer maintains its relative position in the composition.

To change the anchor point in the Layer panel:

1. In the Timeline panel or Composition panel, double-click a layer.

   A Layer panel appears.

2. In the Layer panel's View menu, choose Anchor Point Path (**Figure 5.144**).

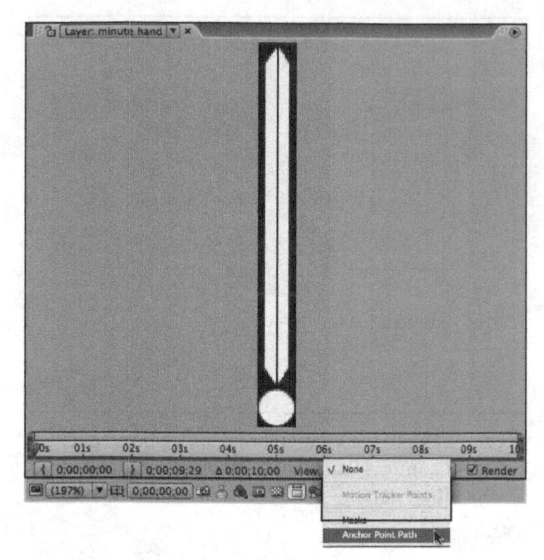

Figure 5.144 In the Layer panel's View menu, choose Anchor Point Path.

   The layer's anchor point icon appears at its current position. When the anchor point's position is animated, a dotted line represents its motion path.

3. In the image area of the Layer panel, drag the anchor point to the position you want (**Figure 5.145**).

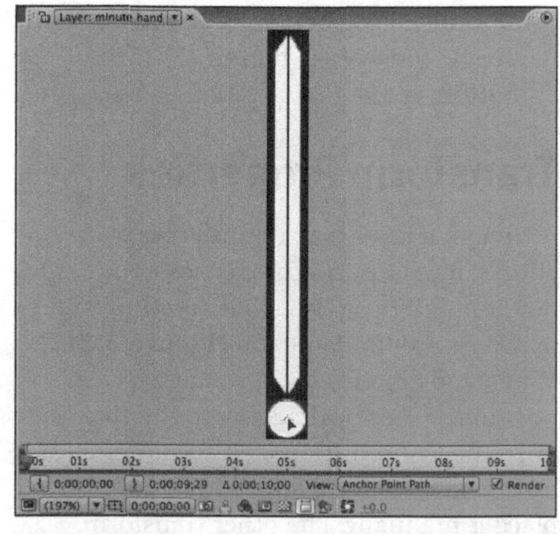

Figure 5.145 When you move an anchor point in a Layer panel . . .

Figure 5.146 . . . the anchor point maintains its position in the comp. Here, the minute hand moves up as the anchor point is moved down to its proper point in the layer.

Because the anchor point maintains its position in the Composition panel, the image in the Comp panel moves relative to the anchor point in the Layer panel (**Figure 5.146**).

To change the anchor point without moving the layer in the composition:

1. Select a layer in the composition.
2. If the selected layer's anchor point isn't visible in the Composition panel, choose View Options in the Composition panel menu and select Handles.
3. In the Tools panel, select the Pan Behind tool (**Figure 5.147**).
4. In the Composition panel, drag the anchor point to a new position (**Figure 5.148**). (Make sure to drag the anchor point, not the layer itself.)

Figure 5.147 To move the anchor point without disturbing the arrangement of the layers, select the Pan Behind tool.

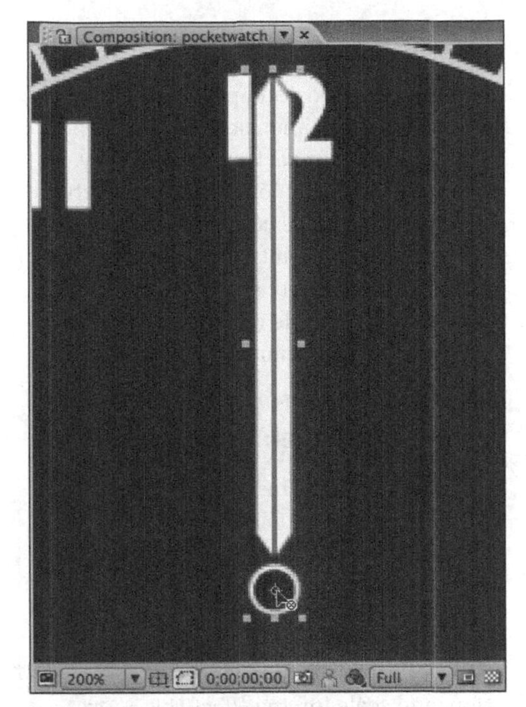

Figure 5.148 Using the Pan Behind tool recalculates the layer's position as you move the anchor point in the Composition panel. This moves the anchor point without disturbing the layer's placement.

The anchor point and position values for the layer change, so the layer maintains its relative position in the Composition panel.

✔ Tips

- When importing a layered file as a composition, you can opt to import layers at each layer's size or at the document's size. The choice you make helps determine the anchor point's initial position relative to the layer's image. See Chapter 4, for more information.
- You can use the Pan Behind tool to change a layer's position relative to its mask. See Chapter 7 for more information.

Position

Setting a layer's position places its anchor point in the two-dimensional space of the composition. The exact position of a layer is expressed in (X, Y) coordinates, where the top-left corner of the composition is (0, 0). (Moving the zero point of the rulers doesn't change the coordinate system.) You can position a layer inside or outside the visible area of the composition.

To change a layer's position in the Composition panel:

1. Select a layer in the Composition or Timeline panel.

> **Subpixel Positioning**
>
> When you set a layer to Draft quality, After Effects calculates the position, rotation, and scale (or any effect that moves the pixels of an image) by using whole pixels. When layers are set to Best quality, however, these values are calculated to the thousandth of a pixel, or on a *subpixel* basis. The more you zoom in to the Composition panel, the greater the precision with which you can move a layer.
>
> Because subpixel positioning allows layers to move with a precision greater than the resolution of the composition, movement appears much smoother than when you're not using subpixel positioning. You can see the difference by contrasting the movement of layers set to Draft quality with the same movement set to Best quality.
>
> Subpixel positioning also requires more precise calculations, which means it takes After Effects longer to render images. Thus, you may want to do much of your work in Draft quality and then switch to Best quality when you're ready to fine-tune.

Figure 5.149 You can drag selected layers to new positions.

2. In the Composition panel, drag the layer to the position you want (**Figure 5.149**).

   To move a layer offscreen, drag it to the pasteboard, or workspace, outside the visible area of the Composition panel.

   The layer is placed at the position you chose. If the Stopwatch icon hasn't been activated for the layer, the layer will remain at this position for its entire duration. If the Stopwatch is active, a position keyframe is created at this frame.

✔ Tips

- Dragging a footage item to the Timeline panel or a Composition icon into the Project panel centers the layer automatically.
- Use the Info panel to view the exact X and Y coordinates of the layer as you move it. If you set a custom zero point for the rulers, look at the X1 and Y1 display to see the coordinates in terms of the rulers you set.

Scale

By default, a layer is set to 100 percent of its original size, or scale. You scale a layer around its anchor point. In other words, the

Figure 5.150 A selected layer's handles can be dragged to scale it . . .

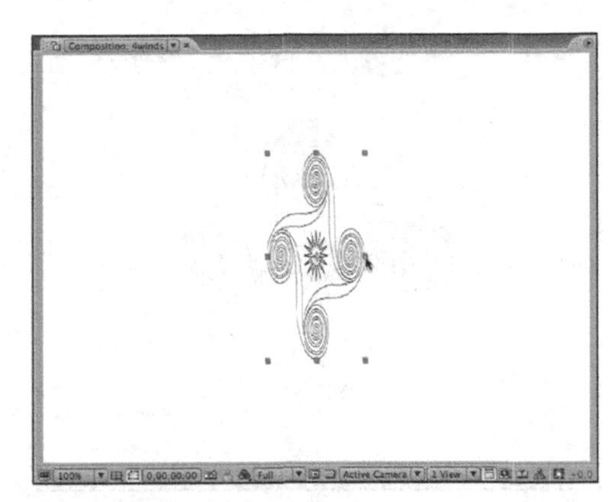

Figure 5.151 . . . horizontally . . .

anchor point serves as the mathematical center of a change in size. When you scale a layer by dragging, you'll notice how the handles of the layer seem to stretch from the anchor point.

Remember that bitmapped images look blocky and pixelated when scaled much beyond 100 percent. When you scale path-based images beyond 100 percent, you can use the Continuously Rasterize switch to help maintain image quality. Review Chapter 4 if you need more information about image size and rasterization.

To scale a layer by dragging:

1. Select a layer, and make sure its layer handles are visible in the Composition panel (see "Viewing Spatial Controls in the Comp Panel," earlier in this chapter) (**Figure 5.150**).
2. In the Composition panel, *do any of the following:*
   - ▲ To scale the layer horizontally only, drag the center-left or center-right handle (**Figure 5.151**).
   - ▲ To scale the layer vertically only, drag the center-bottom or the center-top handle (**Figure 5.152**).
   - ▲ To scale the layer horizontally and vertically, drag a corner handle.
   - ▲ To scale the layer while maintaining its proportions, press Shift as you drag a corner handle (**Figure 5.153**).
   - ▲ To flip a layer, drag one side of the layer's bounding box past the other side (**Figure 5.154**).
3. Release the mouse.

   In the Composition panel, the layer appears with the scale you set. If the Stopwatch icon hasn't been activated for the layer, the layer will retain this scale for its duration. If the Stopwatch is

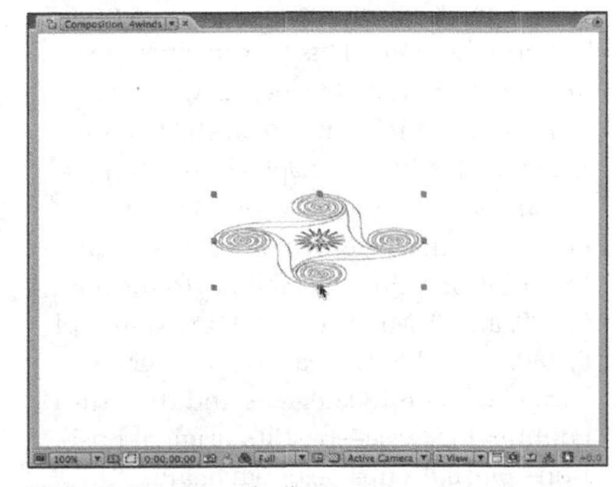

Figure 5.152 . . . vertically . . .

Figure 5.153 . . . or by both aspects. Shift-drag a corner handle to scale the layer while maintaining its proportions.

active, a scale keyframe is created at this frame.

✔ Tip

■ You can quickly reset the scale of a layer to 100 percent by selecting the layer and double-clicking the Selection tool.

Rotational Values

Rotation is expressed as an absolute, not relative, value. You might even think of it as a rotational position. A layer's default rotation is 0 degrees; setting its rotation to 0 degrees always restores it to its original upright angle. This is true when you keyframe rotational values as well (see "Viewing Spatial Controls in the Comp Panel" earlier in this chapter). For example, if you want to rotate a layer 180 degrees clockwise (upside down) and back again, the rotation values at each keyframe are 0, 180, and 0. Mistakenly setting values of 0, 180, and –180 will cause the layer to turn clockwise 180 degrees and then turn counterclockwise—past its original position—until it's upside down again.

Figure 5.154 You can flip a layer by dragging one side past the other. Note how the spirals in this logo face the opposite direction.

Rotation

When you rotate a 2D layer, it rotates in two-dimensional space, using the anchor point as its pivot point.

To rotate a layer by dragging:

1. Select a layer.
2. In the Tools panel, choose the Rotate tool (**Figure 5.155**).
3. In the Composition panel, drag a layer to rotate it around its anchor point.

   As you drag, a bounding box represents the layer's new rotation position (**Figure 5.156**).
4. Release the mouse to set the rotation.

   In the Composition panel, the layer appears with the rotation you set. If the Stopwatch icon isn't active for the layer, this is the rotation of the layer for its entire duration. If the Stopwatch icon is

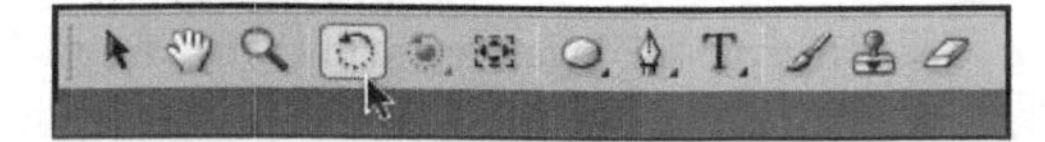

Figure 5.155 Choose the Rotate tool.

Figure 5.156 In the Composition panel, drag the layer to rotate it around its pivot point.

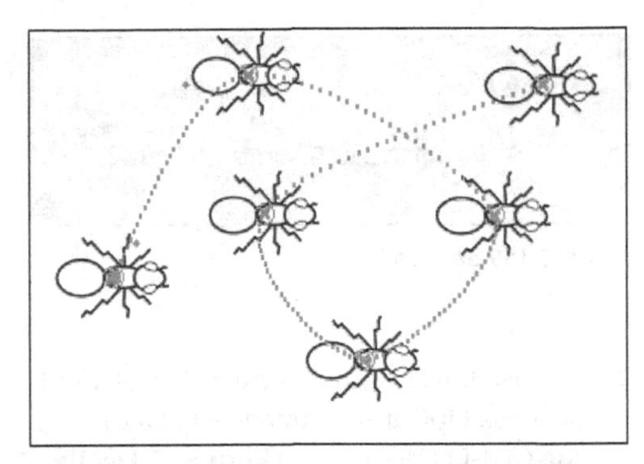

Figure 5.157 Without auto-orient rotation, objects remain upright as they follow the motion path (unless you add rotation). Notice that the ant remains horizontal regardless of the direction of motion.

active, a rotation keyframe is created at this frame.

✔ Tips

- To quickly reset a selected layer's rotation to 0 degrees, double-click the Rotate tool.
- If you want an object to turn (rotate) in the direction of its motion path (animated position), you can avoid the pain of setting a lot of rotational keyframes by using the Auto-Orient Rotation command instead.

Orienting Rotation to a Motion Path Automatically

As a layer follows a motion path, its rotation remains unaffected. The layer maintains its upright position as it follows the path: Picture, for example, someone riding up an escalator, or the cabins on a Ferris wheel; they remain upright although they follow a sloped or curved path (**Figure 5.157**). Frequently, you want the object to orient its rotation to remain perpendicular to the motion path: Now picture a roller coaster climbing a hill (**Figure 5.158**).

Fortunately, you don't have to painstakingly keyframe a layer's Rotation property to ensure that it remains oriented to the motion path; After Effects' Auto-Orient Rotation command does that for you. Technically, auto-orient rotation isn't a type of spatial interpolation; however, like an interpolation method, it dictates the behavior of a layer along a motion path—and in so doing saves you a lot of keyframing work.

To auto-orient rotation to the motion path:

1. Select a layer (**Figure 5.159**).

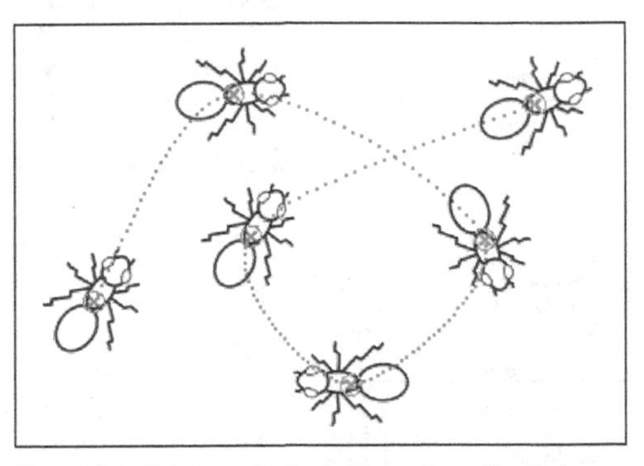

Figure 5.158 Auto-orient rotation automatically keeps a layer perpendicular to the motion path. Here, the ant faces the direction of motion.

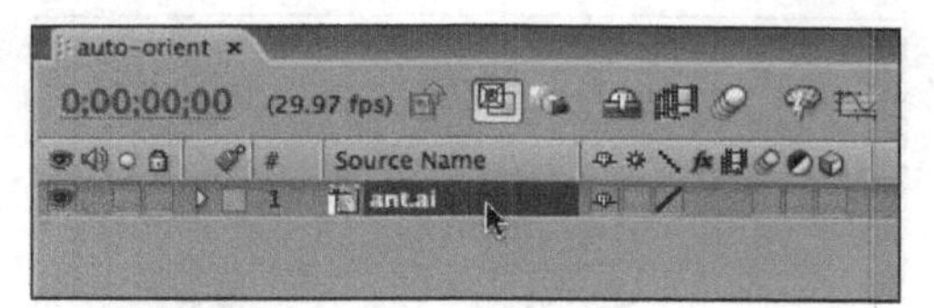

Figure 5.159 Select a layer.

2. Choose Layer > Transform > Auto-Orient, or press Option-Command-O (Mac) or Alt-Ctrl-O (Windows) (**Figure 5.160**).
   The Auto-Orientation dialog box appears.
3. *Choose either of the following:*
   - **Off**—Controls the layer's rotation manually
   - **Orient Along Path**—Makes the layer automatically orient its *X*-axis tangent to the motion path

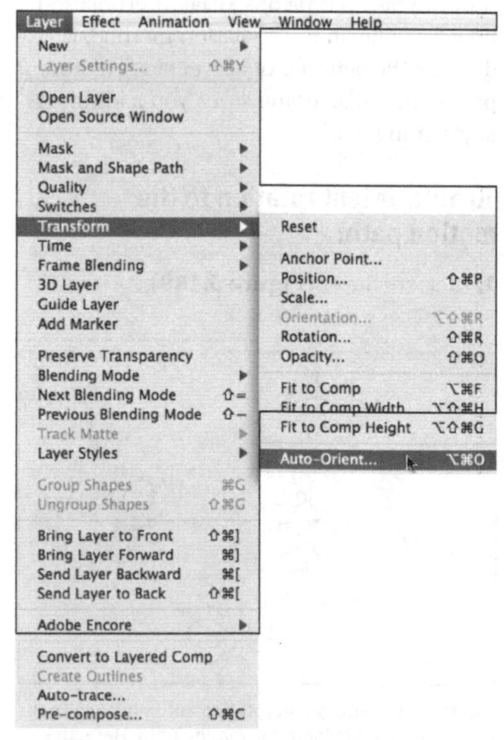

Figure 5.160 Choose Layer › Transform › Auto-Orient.

4. Click OK to close the Auto-Orientation dialog box.

✔ Tip

- You can use the Path Text effect to make text follow a path while automatically remaining perpendicular to it. Text you create using the text-creation tools can also follow a path you specify.

Opacity

At any point in time, a layer can be anywhere from 0 percent opaque (completely transparent, and thus invisible) to 100 percent opaque (with absolutely no transparency).

Bear in mind that the Opacity property merely controls the layer's overall opacity. There are plenty of other ways to define areas of transparency and opacity, including transfer modes, track mattes, keying effects, and masking techniques.

Because opacity is the only transform property you can't "grab onto" in the Comp panel, you must alter it by using numerical controls.

To change the opacity of a layer:

1. Select a layer in the Timeline panel or Composition panel.
2. Press T to display the Opacity property for the selected layer.
   The layer's Opacity property appears in the layer outline, and the current value for opacity appears across from the property under the Switches column (**Figure 5.161**).
3. Under the Switches column across from the layer's Opacity property, *do any of the following:*
   - To decrease the current opacity value, drag the opacity value left (**Figure 5.162**).
   - To increase the current opacity value, drag the value right.

Figure 5.161 Press T to reveal the Opacity property value.

▲ To set the value in a dialog box, Control-click/right-click the opacity value, and select Edit Value in the context menu.

As you change the opacity value, the layer's opacity changes in the Composition panel. If the Stopwatch icon isn't active for the layer, the layer retains this opacity for its duration. If the Stopwatch icon is active, an opacity keyframe is created at this frame.

✔ Tip

- The keyboard shortcuts that display most transform properties are often the first letter of the name of the property: P for position, S for scale, and so on. However, you reveal the Opacity property by pressing T.

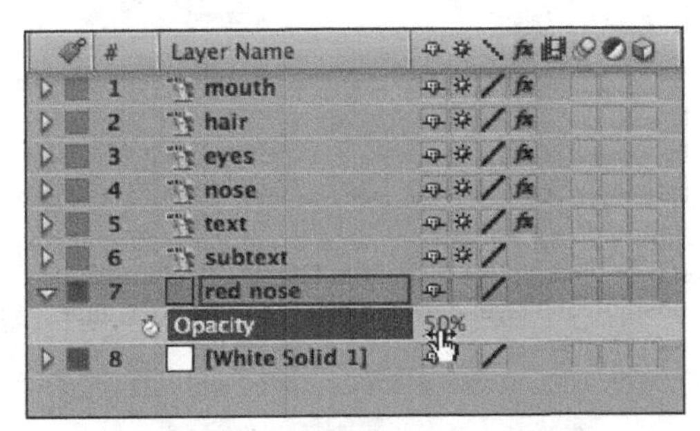

Figure 5.162 To change the value, drag right to increase the value or left to decrease it (as shown here).

Specifying Property Values

As in most other Adobe programs, numeric values in After Effects appear colored and underlined, indicating that the values are *scrubbable*. This means you can alter a property's current value by dragging, or *scrubbing*, the value display. Clicking the value highlights it so you can enter a numeric value. Pressing Return/Enter verifies the value; pressing Tab highlights the next value display. Because these controls are familiar to most users, they won't be covered here.

Alternatively, you can open a dialog box to enter property values (**Table 5.3**). Although a dialog box may not offer the convenience of scrubbing or entering the value directly, it does allow you to enter decimal values or to employ different units of measurement for the property value.

You can also use keyboard shortcuts to slightly change, or *nudge*, the position, rotation, or scale of a layer. When you nudge a layer, After Effects counts pixels at the current magnification of the Composition panel, not the layer's actual size. Therefore, nudging a layer's position moves it one pixel when viewed at 100 percent magnification, two pixels when viewed at 50 percent, four pixels at 25 percent, and so on. When layer quality is set to Best, you can nudge layers

Table 5.3

Property Dialog Box Shortcuts

To show this dialog box	Press this
Anchor Point dialog box	Command-Option-Shift-A (Mac) or Ctrl-Alt-Shift-A (Windows)
Opacity dialog box	Command-Shift-O (Mac) or Ctrl-Shift-O (Windows)
Other dialog boxes (works with P, R, F, and M)	Command-Shift-property shortcut (Mac) or Ctrl-Shift-property shortcut (Windows)

Table 5.4

Nudging Layer Properties	
To nudge this value	Do this
Nudge position one pixel	Press arrow keys (up, down, right, left)
Nudge rotation 1 degree	Press plus (+) on numeric keypad
Nudge rotation –1 degree	Press minus (-) on numeric keypad
Nudge scale 1%	Press Option-plus (+) (Mac) or Alt-plus (+) (Windows) on numeric keypad
Nudge scale –1%	Press Option-minus (-) (Mac) or Alt-minus (-) (Windows) on numeric keypad
Nudge x10	Press Shift-keyboard shortcut for nudge

on a subpixel basis (see the sidebar "Subpixel Positioning," earlier in this chapter). Therefore, a layer set to Best quality can be nudged .5 pixel when viewed at 200 percent, .25 pixel when viewed at 400 percent, and so on. **Table 5.4** lists the keyboard shortcuts for nudging properties.

Animating Layer Properties with Keyframes

To produce animation, you change a layer's properties over time—for example, achieving motion by changing a layer's position over time. In After Effects (as with other programs), you use keyframes to define and control these changes.

A *keyframe* defines a property's value at a specific point in time. When you create at least two keyframes with different values, After Effects interpolates the value for each frame in between. After Effects calculates how to create a smooth transition from one keyframe to another—how to get from point A to point B (**Figure 5.163**).

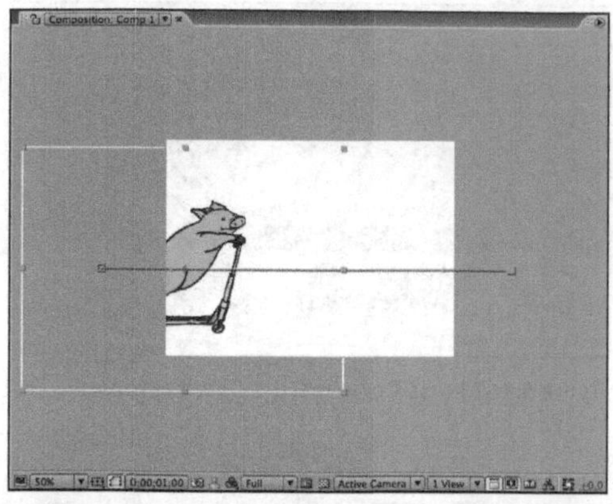

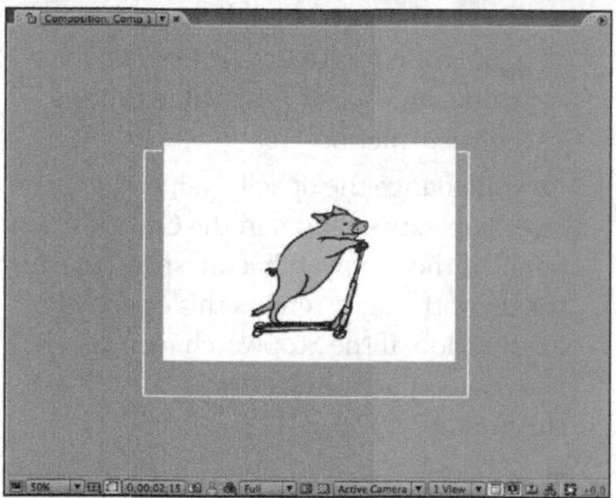

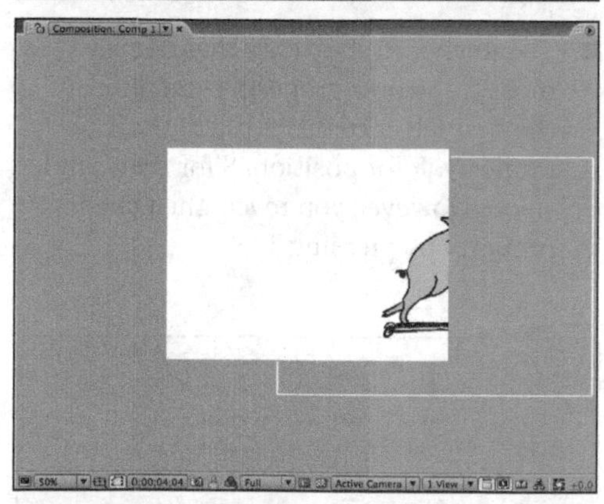

Figure 5.163 You can keyframe any property to animate it over time. In this case, After Effects calculates the position of a layer between two keyframes to create movement.

Basic keyframing

Essentially, keyframing is nothing more than repeating a two-step process: setting the current frame, and setting the property value for that frame. The specific steps are outlined in this section.

If you're new to animating with keyframes, you may want to start with one of the transform properties such as Scale.

To set keyframes for a property:

1. In the Timeline panel, view the property of the layer (or layers) you want to keyframe.
   You may view the same property for more than one layer but not different properties.
2. Set the current time to the frame at which you want to set a keyframe.
   It's possible to set a keyframe beyond the duration of a layer.
3. Click the Stopwatch icon next to the layer property you want to keyframe to activate the icon (and the keyframe process) (**Figure 5.164**).
   The Stopwatch icon appears selected. In the property tracks of the selected layers, an initial keyframe appears; in the keyframe navigator, a check appears.
4. If the property isn't set to the value you want, set the value (as explained earlier in this chapter).
   As long as the current time is set to the keyframe, any new value is applied to the keyframe.
5. Set the current time to another frame.
6. To create additional keyframes, *do one of the following:*
   ▲ To create a keyframe with a new value, change the value of the property (**Figure 5.165**).
   ▲ To create a keyframe without changing the current property value, select the diamond in the keyframe navigator (**Figure 5.166**).
   A new keyframe appears at the current time, and the diamond at the center of the keyframe navigator is highlighted.
7. To create additional keyframes, repeat steps 5 and 6.
8. To see your changes play in the Composition panel, use the playback controls or create a preview (see Chapter 6).

✔ Tips

- The Motion Sketch plug-in panel provides another quick and easy way to create position keyframes: You can draw them in the Composition panel.
- The Motion Tracker included in After Effects Pro helps you generate keyframes

Keyframes

Keyframe is a term borrowed from traditional animation. In a traditional animation studio, a senior animator might draw only the keyframes—what the character looks like at key moments in the animation. The junior animators would then draw the rest of the frames, or *in-betweens* (a process sometimes known as *tweening*). The same principle applies to After Effects animations: If you supply the keyframes for a property, the program calculates the values in between. And you can keyframe any property, not just movement.

With After Effects, you're always the senior animator, so you should only supply the keyframes—just enough to define the animation. Setting too many keyframes defeats the purpose of this division of labor.

Figure 5.164 Activate the Stopwatch icon to set the first keyframe for the property at the current time indicator.

Figure 5.165 To set a keyframe with a new value, set the current time to a new frame and change the property value.

Figure 5.166 To set a keyframe without manually changing the value, select the diamond icon in the keyframe navigator.

by detecting an object's movement within an image.

- People often use After Effects to pan and scale large images, emulating the motion-control camera work frequently seen in documentaries. In such cases, you create pans by animating the anchor point, not the position. This technique achieves the panning you want while keeping the anchor point in the viewing area. Because the anchor point is also used to calculate scale, you'll get more predictable results when you zoom in to and out of the image.

Keyframe icons

A property's keyframes appear in its property track of the time graph. When a property heading is collapsed, the keyframes of the properties in that category appear as circles. When an individual property is visible, its keyframes appear as icons by default (**Figure 5.167**). (By checking Use Keyframe Indices in the Timeline panel's pull-down menu, you can make keyframes appear as numbered boxes instead of icons.)

Keyframe icons vary according to the interpolation method used by the keyframe. The diamond-shaped icons shown here reflect linear interpolation. Regardless of its interpolation method, shading indicates that the property value either before or after the keyframe hasn't been interpolated (**Figure 5.168**). This occurs for the first and last keyframes as well as for keyframes that follow hold keyframes, which are used to prevent interpolation.

Cueing the Current Time to Keyframes

You can only set or change a keyframe's values at the current time indicator—one reason you need a quick and convenient way to cue the time marker to keyframes. You may also want to jump to keyframes to step through your animation or to create keyframes in other layers or properties that align with existing keyframes. The *keyframe navigator* provides the solution (**Figure 5.169**).

And as you saw in the section, "Basic Keyframing," the diamond at the center of the keyframe navigator serves as the Add/Delete Keyframe button. Because it's highlighted only when the current time is cued to a keyframe, it also provides a visual confirmation, particularly if you want to

Setting a New Keyframe with the Keyframe Navigator

As you learned in the section "Basic Keyframing," you can set a new keyframe by selecting the keyframe navigator's Add/Delete Keyframe button—the diamond icon ◇. Instead of using a value you actively specify, a keyframe created this way uses the value already calculated for that frame.

Usually, you use the check box to create keyframes when you want to modify an animation—or, when no animation exists yet, to repeat a value. Initially, the new keyframe doesn't alter the animation; it hasn't changed the property's value at that time. The new keyframe can serve as a good starting point for changing the animation by changing the keyframe's value or interpolation method.

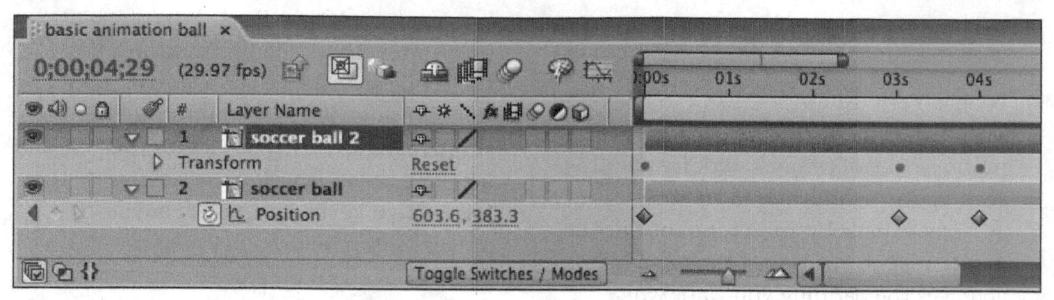

Figure 5.167 When the property heading is collapsed (as they are in the top layer), keyframes appear as small dots. When the property track is visible (as in the bottom layer) keyframes appear as icons.

confirm that keyframes in different properties are perfectly aligned.

To cue the current time to keyframes:

1. Make sure the property with the keyframes you want to see is visible in the layer outline.
2. In the Timeline panel, *do any of the following:*
   - ▲ Shift-drag the current time indicator until it snaps to a visible keyframe.
   - ▲ In the keyframe navigator for the property, click the left arrow to cue the current time to the previous keyframe.
   - ▲ In the keyframe navigator for the property, click the right arrow to cue the current time to the next keyframe (**Figure 5.170**).

   The current time cues to the adjacent keyframe (**Figure 5.171**). If no keyframe exists beyond the current keyframe, the appropriate arrow in the keyframe navigator appears dimmed.

Selecting and Deleting Keyframes

Select keyframes when you want to move them to a different position in time, delete them, or copy and paste them to other properties or layers.

To select keyframes:

◆ *Do any of the following:*
   - ▲ To select a keyframe, click it in the property track.
   - ▲ To add keyframes to or subtract them from your selection, press Shift as you click additional keyframes (**Figure 5.172**).
   - ▲ To select multiple keyframes, drag a marquee around the keyframes in the property track (**Figure 5.173**).
   - ▲ To select all the keyframes for a property, click the name of the property in the layer outline (**Figure 5.174**).

   Selected keyframes appear highlighted.

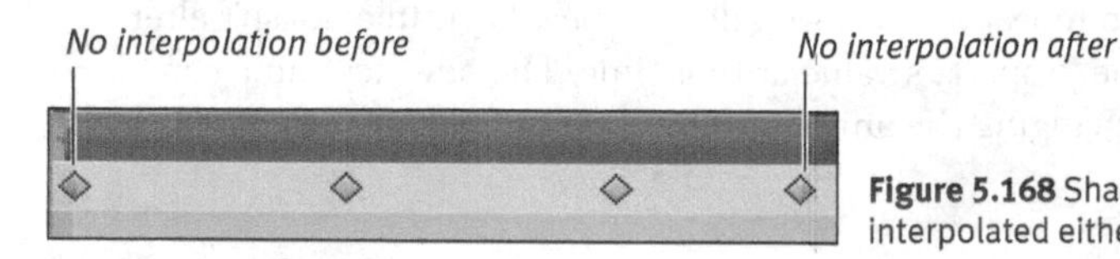

Figure 5.168 Shading indicates that the property value isn't interpolated either before or after the keyframe.

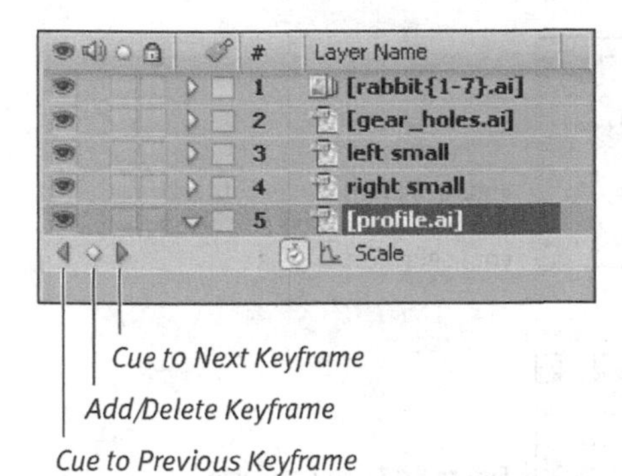

Figure 5.169 Use the keyframe navigator to cue the current time indicator to the previous or next keyframe. The diamond icon (aka Add/Delete Keyframe button) is highlighted only when the current time is exactly on a keyframe.

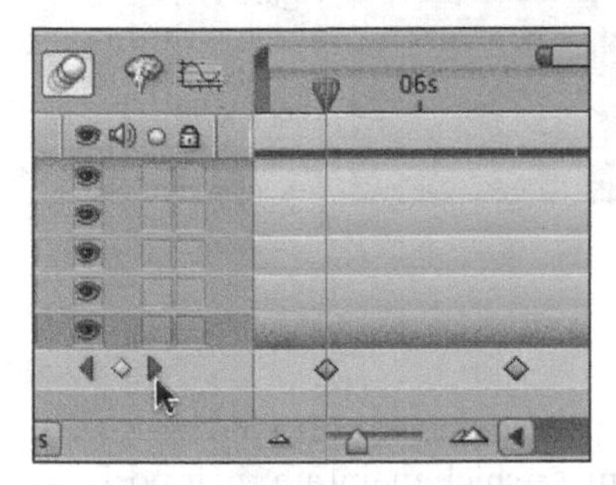

Figure 5.170 Clicking an arrow in the keyframe navigator (in this case, the right arrow) . . .

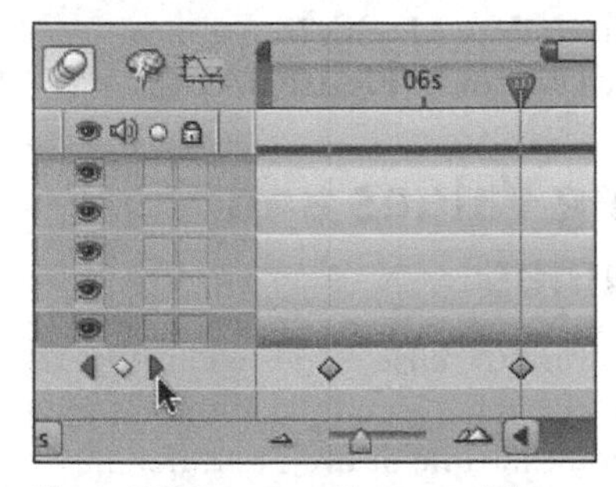

Figure 5.171 . . . cues the current time indicator to the property's adjacent keyframe (here, the next keyframe). (Note that the A/V features panel has been moved closer to the time graph for the purpose of illustration.)

To deselect keyframes:

- *Do either of the following:*
  - To deselect all keyframes, click in an empty area of the Timeline panel.
  - To deselect certain keyframes, Shift-click an already selected keyframe.

  Deselected keyframes no longer appear highlighted.

✔ Tip

- Selecting a keyframe allows you to move it in time, delete it, or copy it. It doesn't let you edit the values of that keyframe. You can only change the value of a property at the current time.

To delete keyframes:

1. Select one or more keyframes, as explained in the previous section.
2. *Do any of the following:*
   - Press Delete.
   - Choose Edit > Clear.
   - With the current time cued to the keyframe, click the keyframe navigator's Add/Delete Keyframe button.

   The keyframe disappears, and the property's interpolated values are recalculated based on the existing keyframes.

To delete all the keyframes for a property:

- Deactivate the Stopwatch icon for the property (**Figure 5.175**).

  All keyframes disappear. You can't restore the keyframes by reactivating the Stopwatch (doing so only starts a new keyframe process).

✔ Tip

- If you mistakenly remove keyframes by deselecting the Stopwatch icon, choose Edit > Undo to undo previous

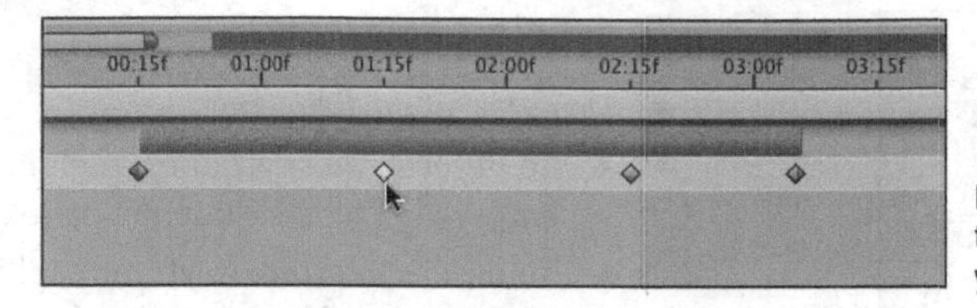

Figure 5.172 Click a keyframe to select it; Shift-click to add to your selection.

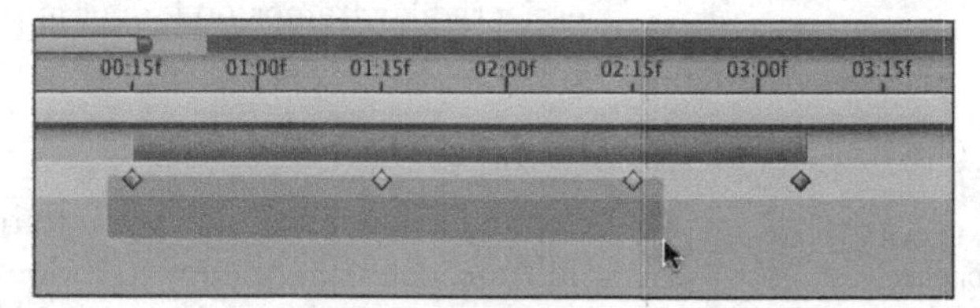

Figure 5.173 You can also select multiple keyframes by dragging a marquee around them.

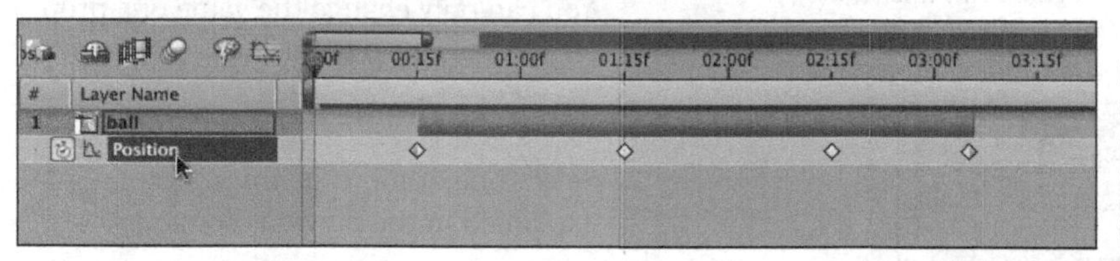

Figure 5.174 Select all the keyframes for a property by clicking the property's name in the layer outline.

commands, or choose File > Revert to return to the last saved version of your project.

Moving Keyframes

You can move one or more keyframes of one or more properties to a different point in time.

To move keyframes:

1. Select one or more keyframes (as explained earlier in this chapter) (**Figure 5.176**).
2. Drag the selected keyframes to a new position in the time graph (**Figure 5.177**).

   To activate the Snap to Edges feature, press Shift after you begin dragging.
3. Release the mouse when the keyframes are at the position in time you want.

✔ Tip

- Moving a layer in time also moves its keyframes, which maintain their positions relative to the layer. Trimming a layer, on the other hand, doesn't affect the keyframes. In fact, you can set a keyframe before a layer's In point or after its Out point (**Figure 5.178**).

Copying Values and Keyframes

When you want to reuse values you set for a property, you can copy and paste them to a different point in time or even to different layers. Not only can you paste keyframes to the same property (such as from one position to another), you can also paste them to different properties that use the same kind of values (such as from a position to an anchor point).

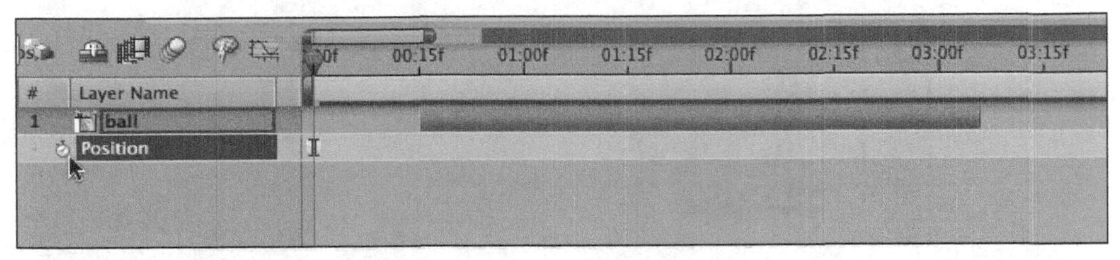

Figure 5.175 Deselecting the property's Stopwatch icon removes all keyframes. The property uses the value at the current time.

Pasted keyframes appear in the property track of the destination in the order and spacing of the original, starting at the current time.

After Effects permits you to copy and paste keyframes one layer at a time. You can copy and paste keyframes of more than one property at a time, as long as you paste them into the same properties. If you want to copy and paste to different properties, however, you must do so one property at a time.

To copy and paste keyframes:

1. Select one or more keyframes (as explained earlier in this chapter) (**Figure 5.179**).
2. Choose Edit > Copy, or press Command/Ctrl-C (**Figure 5.180**).
3. Set the current time to the frame where you want the pasted keyframe(s) to begin.
4. To select the destination, *do one of the following:*
   - ▲ To paste keyframes to the same property, select the destination layer.
   - ▲ To paste keyframes to a different property, select the destination property by clicking it in the layer outline.
5. Choose Edit > Paste, or press Command/Ctrl-V (**Figure 5.181**).

   The keyframes are pasted in the appropriate property in the destination layer (**Figure 5.182**).

✔ Tips

- You can also copy and paste a global (nonkeyframed) value using the same process. Selecting the property highlights the I-beam icon in the property track rather than the keyframes.

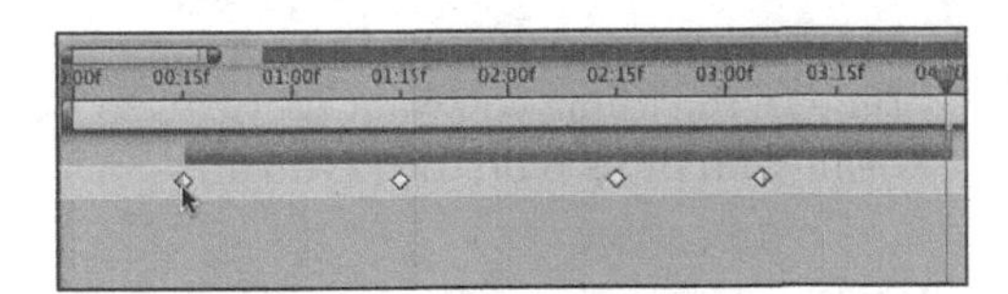

Figure 5.176 Select the keyframes you want to move . . .

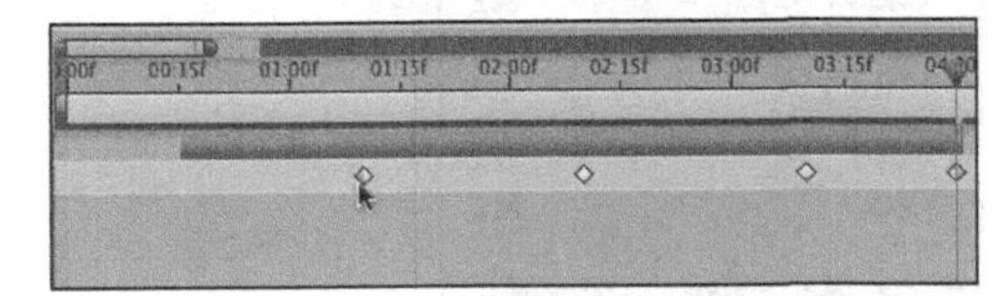

Figure 5.177 . . . and drag them to a new position in the timeline. Shift-drag to activate the Snap to Edges feature.

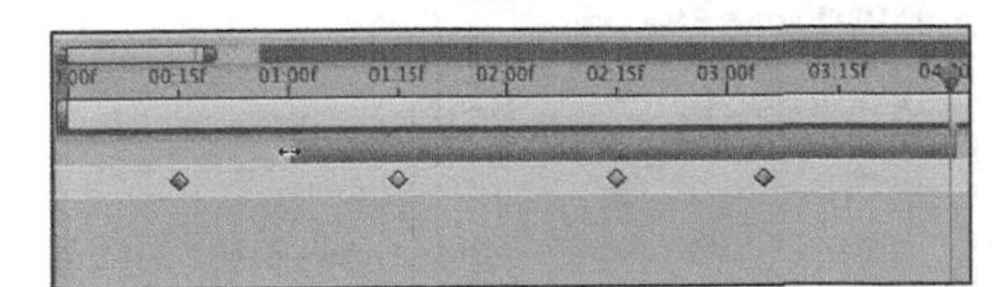

Figure 5.178 Although dragging a layer also moves its keyframes, trimming a layer doesn't trim off its keyframes, which still affect property values.

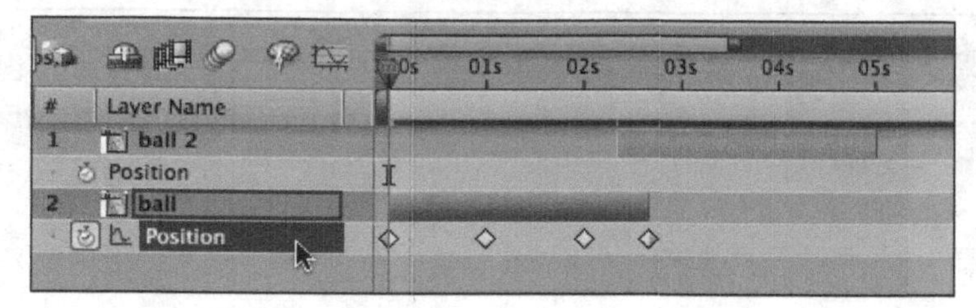

Figure 5.179 Select the keyframes you want to copy.

- To reuse an animation, you can save it as an animation preset. After Effects ships with numerous useful presets.
- Certain types of animations are best accomplished by using an expression instead of numerous keyframes.

Generating Property Values with the Brainstorm Feature

At times, having full control over a multitude of property values is more of a curse than a blessing. Trying out even a handful of the countless combinations can be a time-consuming and potentially fruitless endeavor. The aptly named Brainstorm feature generates variations of any combination of properties automatically, and lets you preview them before committing to your favorite.

To set the frames to preview for Brainstorming:

1. In the Timeline panel, set the current time to the frame you want previews to begin and press B on the keyboard.

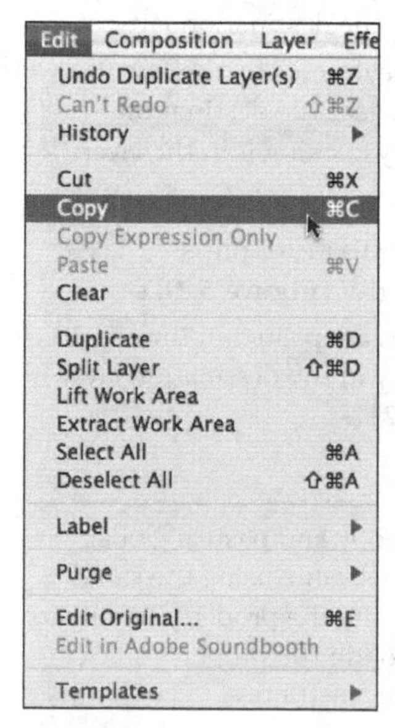

Figure 5.180 Choose Edit › Copy, or press Command/Ctrl-C.

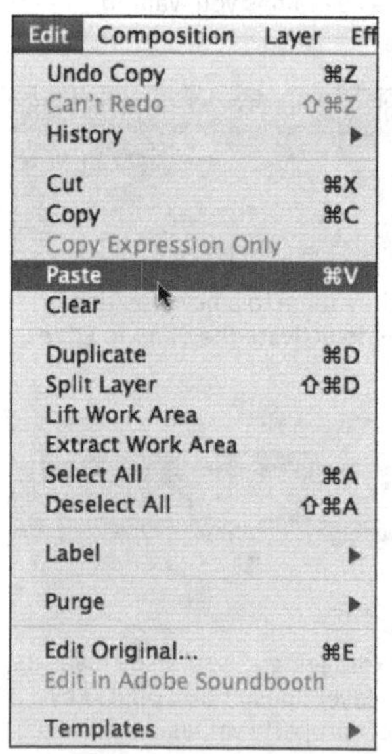

Figure 5.181 Set the current time, select the destination layer or property, and choose Edit › Paste.

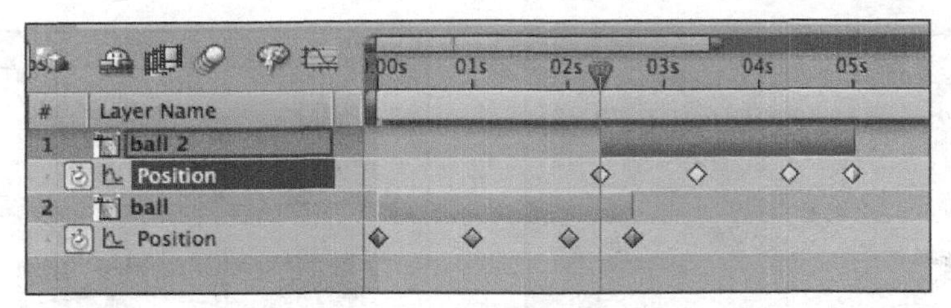

Figure 5.182 The selected keyframes appear in the destination property track, beginning at the current time.

The beginning of the Work Area Bar aligns with the current time indicator (**Figure 5.183**).

2. In the Timeline panel, set the current time to the frame you want previews to end and press N on the keyboard.

 The ending of the Work Area Bar aligns with the current time indicator (**Figure 5.184**).

To specify the properties for Brainstorming:

1. In the Timeline panel, select any combination of global properties or keyframed property values.
2. At the top of the Timeline panel, click the Brainstorm button (**Figure 5.185**).

 The Brainstorm panel appears. It displays nine preview images, each using a different random variant of the property values you specified in step (**Figure 5.186**).

To generate new variants:

1. To specify the magnitude of variations in the Brainstorm panel, *do either of the following:*
   - ▲ For multidimensional properties, specify a value for Randomness (**Figure 5.187**).
   - ▲ For single-dimensional properties, specify a value for Spread.

 Specifying a relatively high value results in greater variations of the initial selected values.

2. Click the Brainstorm button.

 The Brainstorm panel displays a new generation of variants, using the value you specified (**Figure 5.188**).

3. To keep a variant in the next Brainstorm, hover the mouse pointer over the variant

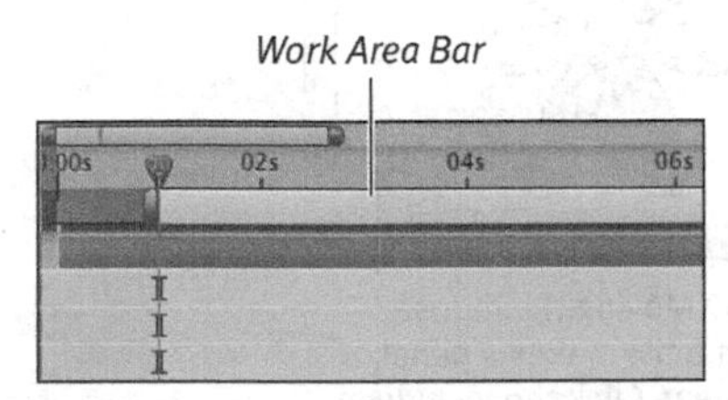

Figure 5.183 Type B to set the beginning of the Work Area Bar . . .

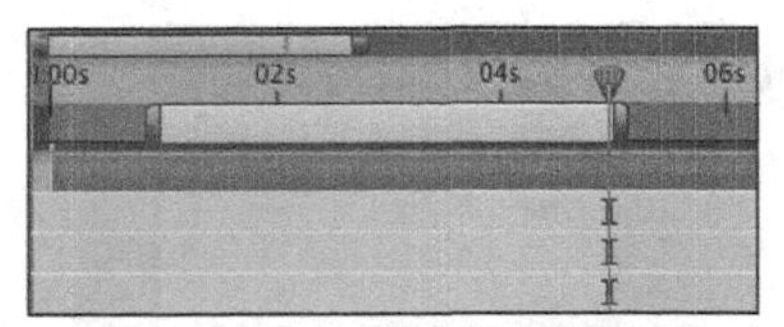

Figure 5.184 . . . and type N to set the ending of the Work Area Bar. It defines the range of frames to preview—in this case, Brainstormed property values.

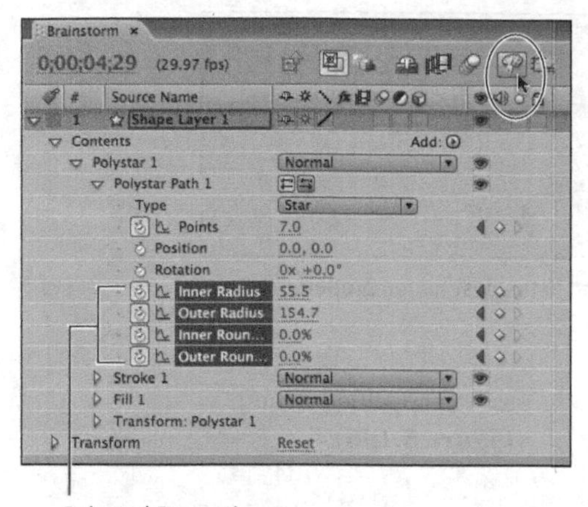

Figure 5.185 Select any combination of properties and keyframes for which you want to generate values and click the Brainstorm button.

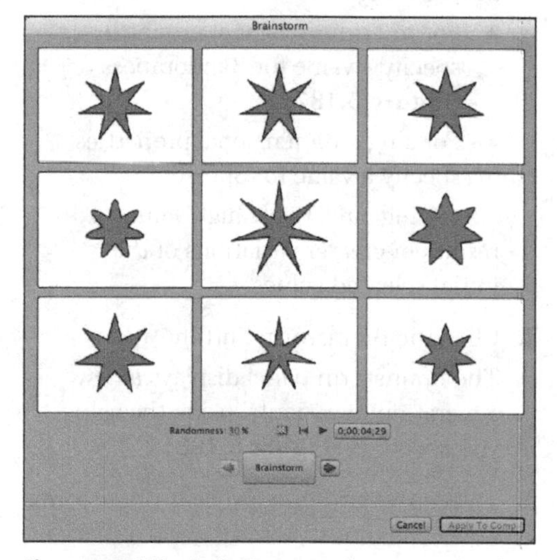

Figure 5.186 The Brainstorm panel appears, showing nine variations of the selected properties.

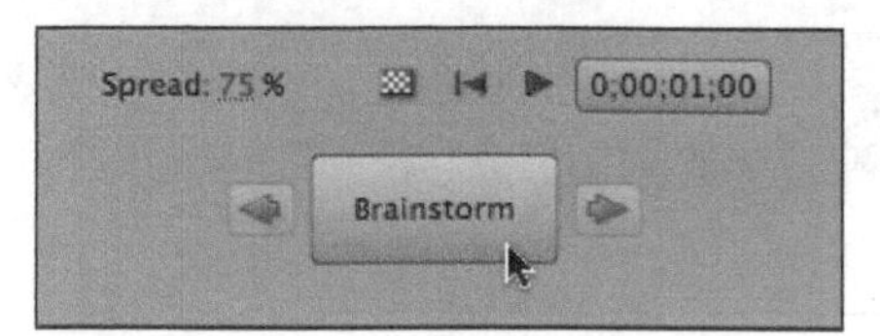

Figure 5.187 Specifying a value for Randomness or Spread (depending on the selected property type) and clicking the Brainstorm button . . .

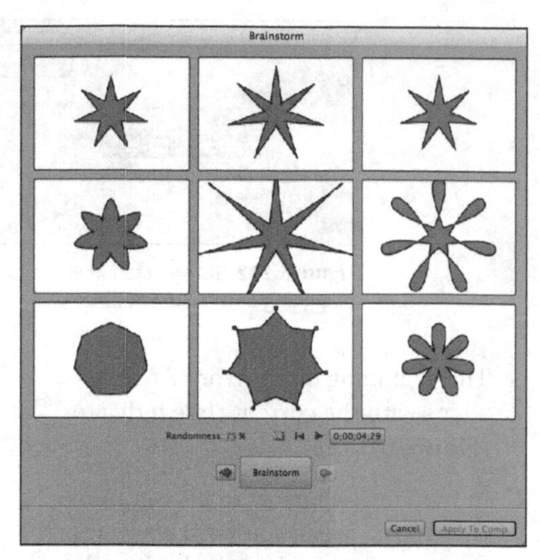

Figure 5.188 . . . generates a new set of Brainstormed values.

and click the Include in Next Brainstorm button (**Figure 5.189**).

4. Repeat steps 1 through 3, as needed.

To preview variants in the Brainstorm panel:

1. In the Brainstorm panel, *do any of the following* (**Figure 5.190**):

▲ To toggle transparent areas between the background color and transparency grid, click the Toggle Transparency Grid button.

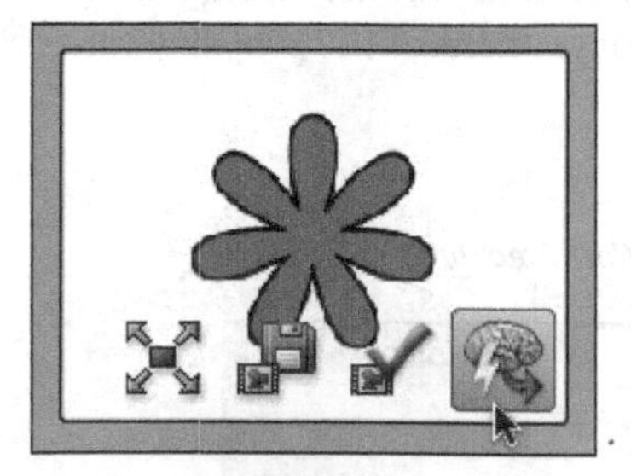

Figure 5.189 Moving the mouse pointer over a tile makes a panel of buttons appear. Click the Include in Next Brainstorm button to retain that variant when you repeat the process.

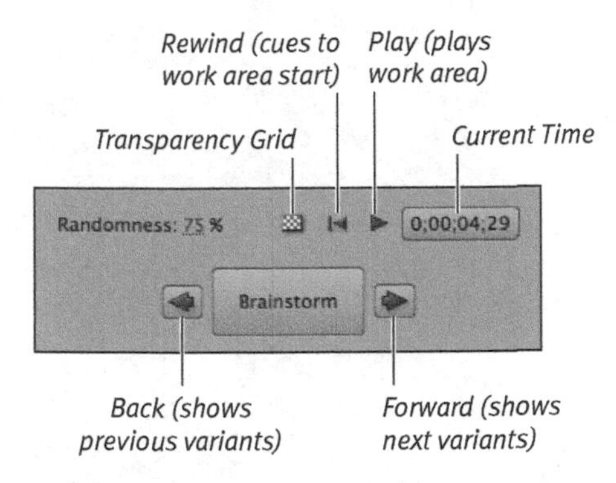

Figure 5.190 The Brainstorm panel's buttons help you preview the variants it generates.

- ▲ To preview the visible variants for the Work Area you specified, click the Play button.
- ▲ To rewind playback to the beginning of the Work Area you specified, click the Rewind button.
- ▲ To view the previous generation of variants, press the Back button.
- ▲ To view the next generation of variants, press the Forward button.

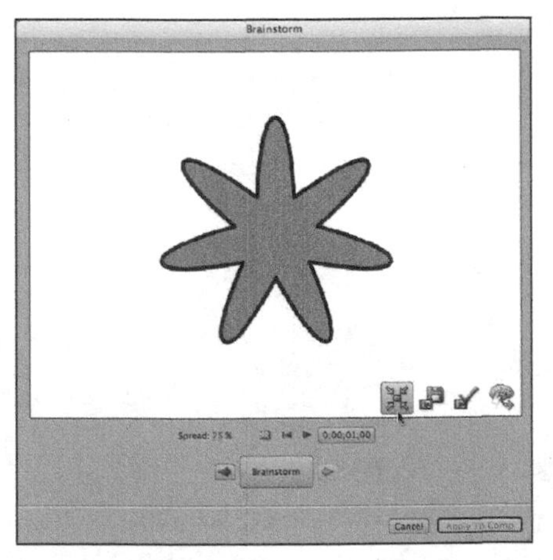

Figure 5.191 Click the Maximize Tile button to enlarge that variant. Click the button again to view all nine variants again.

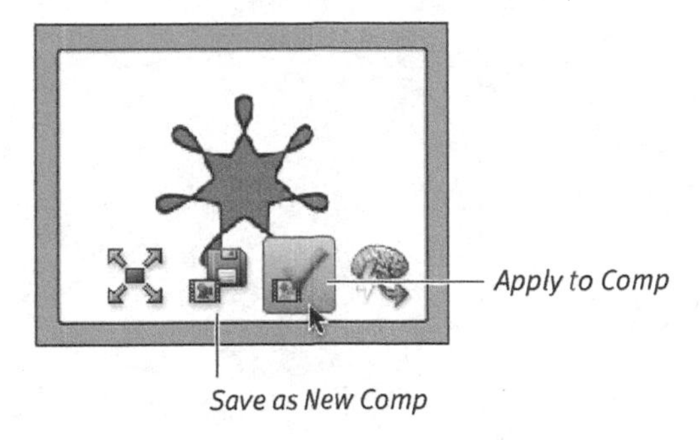

Figure 5.192 Clicking the Save as New Composition button creates a new comp containing a layer with the variant's values; clicking Apply to Composition (selected here) applies the variant's property values to the selected layer in the current comp.

To magnify a variant:

1. Move the mouse pointer over the variant you want to view so that a panel of buttons appears, and then click the Maximize Tile button (**Figure 5.191**).
2. To restore the Brainstorm panel to nine tiles, click the button again.

To apply a variant:

1. In the Brainstorm panel, move the mouse pointer over the variant you want. A panel of four buttons appears over the tile.
2. *Do any of the following* (**Figure 5.192**):
   - ▲ To create a new comp containing a copy of the layer using the selected variant, click Save as New Composition.
   - ▲ To apply the variant's property values to the selected layer in the current comp, click Apply to Composition.

   The variant either appears in a new composition or its values are applied to the selected layer in the comp, according to your choice.

To magnify a variant

To apply a variant

6

Playback, Previews, and RAM

You've already used some of the standard playback methods for each panel in After Effects. This chapter expands your repertoire and provides a more in-depth explanation of how After Effects renders frames for viewing.

You'll focus on using the Time Controls panel, which can serve as a master playback control for any selected panel. It also includes a button to render a specified range of frames (or *work area*) as a *RAM preview*. And you'll learn about other options, such as viewing your work on a video monitor, how to view changes you make to a layer interactively, and how to preview audio.

Whether you're using standard playback controls, rendering a RAM preview, or adjusting layers, After Effects utilizes RAM to store and more readily display frames. Consequently, the more RAM you have, the more rendered frames you can store (or *cache*) at once. After Effects makes the most of your RAM supply by retaining rendered frames as long as possible, a feature called *intelligent caching*. But you can also control the demand side of the rendering equation. Specifying RAM preview options to skip frames or reduce the resolution can lighten the rendering load—or eliminate the image altogether (along with the associated rendering delays) by previewing a bare-bones *wireframe* version of an animation. In addition, you can limit the area of the image to render by specifying a region of interest. After Effects can also reduce processing demands automatically, as needed, by employing *adaptive resolution*. Adaptive resolution reduces image resolution in exchange for increased rendering speed.

But rendering speed isn't necessarily attained at the expense of resolution; you can also utilize a compatible *OpenGL* graphics card. Because software-based processing usually can't match hardware dedicated to the same task, utilizing your OpenGL card's hardware-based graphics processing capabilities renders frames quickly, smoothly, and often without sacrificing resolution.

Rendering and RAM

Before proceeding to the tasks, you should familiarize yourself with how After Effects utilizes RAM. This section contrasts two basic methods used to display frames.

Cache flow

Adobe likes to describe the way After Effects uses RAM as "interactive" and "intelligent." Here's why.

Unless you specify otherwise, After Effects renders frames interactively. Whenever the current time is set to a previously unrendered frame, After Effects renders it and stores, or *caches*, it into RAM—which, as you're probably aware, is the memory your computer can access most quickly. Although it can take time to render a frame, once cached, the frame plays back more readily. The Timeline panel indicates cached frames with a green line at the corresponding point under the time ruler (**Figure 6.1**).

When a change (such as an adjustment to a layer property) makes a rendered frame obsolete, After Effects removes the frame from the cache. However, it intelligently retains the unaffected frames. In other words, After Effects doesn't stupidly discard the entire cache when you make changes that affect only some of the frames. When the cache becomes full, the oldest frames are purged from RAM as new frames are added. You can also purge the cache yourself using a menu command.

Playback and previews

Although the terms *playback* and *preview* are often used interchangeably, this book uses them to refer to two rendering methods that differ in a few important respects. Standard playback caches frames at the current time: sequentially when you click Play

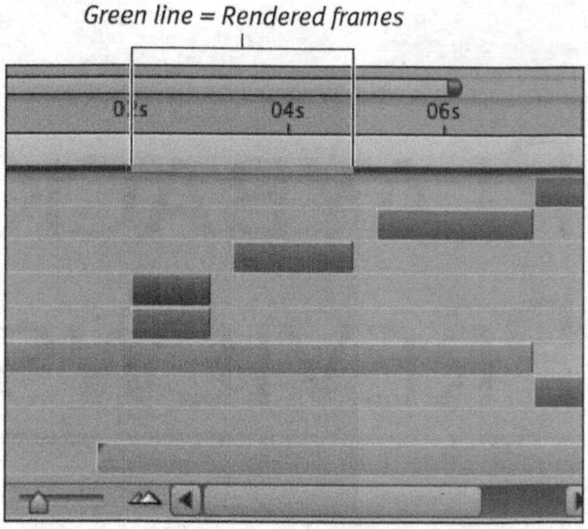

Green line = Rendered frames

Figure 6.1 Cached frames are signified by a green line in the time ruler.

Figure 6.2 Options help you balance quality and rendering speed. The Comp panel's Fast Previews button gives you access to several standard playback options...

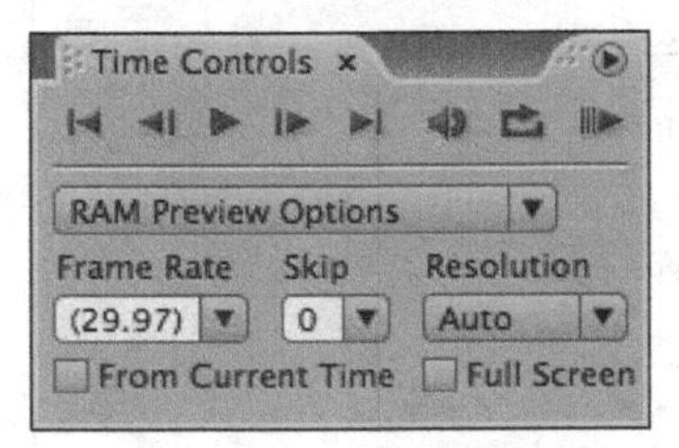

Figure 6.3 ...whereas expanding the Time Controls panel allows you to set options for RAM previews.

✔ Tips

- The playback performance of Footage panels doesn't benefit from the same RAM-caching mechanism as the Layer and Composition panels. Until footage becomes a layer in a composition, it depends on the movie-player software installed on your system.
- In the Display pane of the Preferences dialog box, you can enable an option to show rendering in progress in the Info panel and the Flowchart panel.

or nonsequentially as you cue the current time. A RAM preview, in contrast, loads a specified range of frames into RAM *before* playing them back.

Both the standard playback mechanism and RAM previews utilize RAM in a similar way, caching frames and retaining them intelligently (see the previous section, "Cache flow"). But whereas standard playback respects the resolution you specified for the panel you're viewing, a RAM preview specifies resolution independent of the panel's current setting. Each method includes different options to help you balance image quality and rendering speed. In addition to the current layer quality and comp resolution settings, standard playback abides by options you set in the Comp panel's Fast Previews button (**Figure 6.2**); you set RAM preview options in the expanded Time Controls panel (**Figure 6.3**). Finally, standard playback options govern how After Effects depicts a frame while you make adjustments—or, in After Effects' parlance, during *interactions*. A RAM preview, on the other hand, only displays a range of frames at or near their full frame rate and doesn't influence the quality or speed of interactions.

No matter what method you use to view frames, processing demands are always related to the footage's native image size (and/or its audio quality) as well as any modifications you make to it as a layer in a composition: masks, transformations, effects, and so on. Note that because the Comp panel's magnification setting (not to be confused with scaling a layer) doesn't change the number or quality of pixels to be rendered, it has little influence on rendering times.

Previewing to a Video Device

If your system includes a video output device (such as an IEEE-1394/FireWire/iLink connection), you can view your project on a video monitor—which is crucial for evaluating images destined for video output.

Even though you can preview full screen on your computer monitor (as explained later in this chapter), a computer monitor differs from a television monitor in several important respects. (Refer to this book's sections on interlaced video fields, pixel aspect ratio, safe zones, and NTSC video standards.)

To set video preferences:

1. Choose After Effects > Preferences > Video Preview (Mac) or Edit > Preferences > Video Preview (Windows) (**Figure 6.4**).

   The Video Preview pane of the Preferences dialog box appears (**Figure 6.5**).

2. In the Preferences dialog box, choose an option from the Output Device pull-down menu (**Figure 6.6**).

   Your choices will depend on your particular setup.

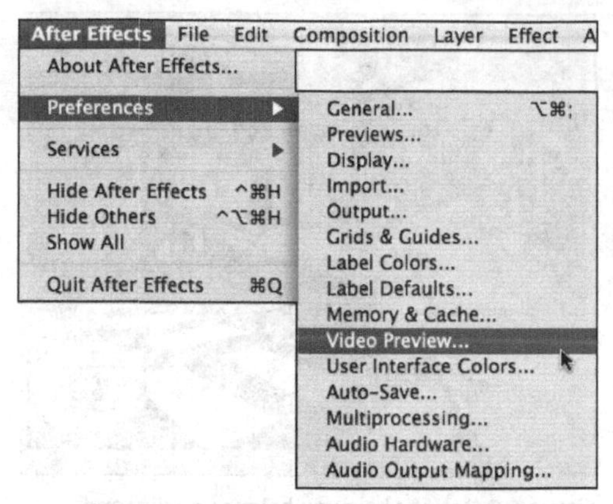

Figure 6.4 Choose Edit › Preferences › Video Preview.

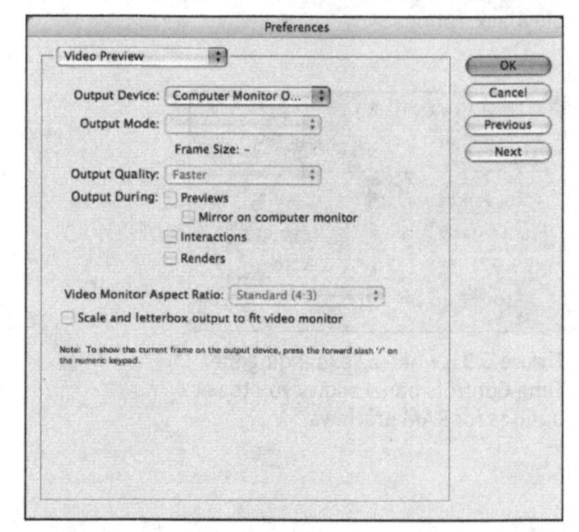

Figure 6.5 The Video Preview pane of the Preferences dialog box appears.

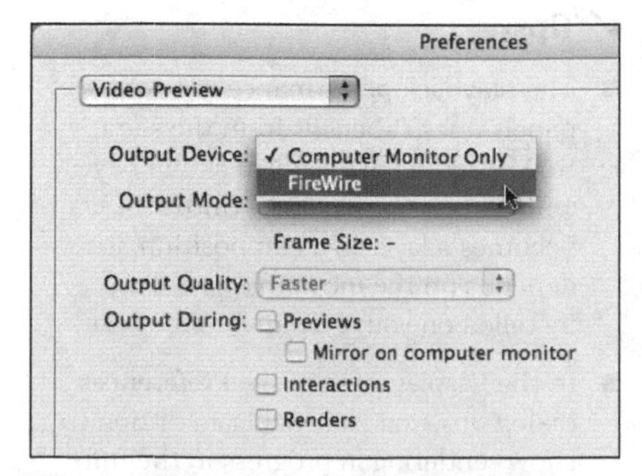

Figure 6.6 Choose an option in the Output Device pull-down menu.

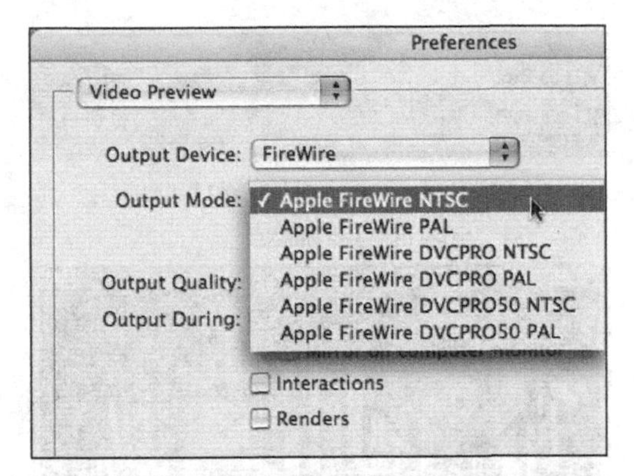

Figure 6.7 Choose an option in the Output Mode pull-down menu.

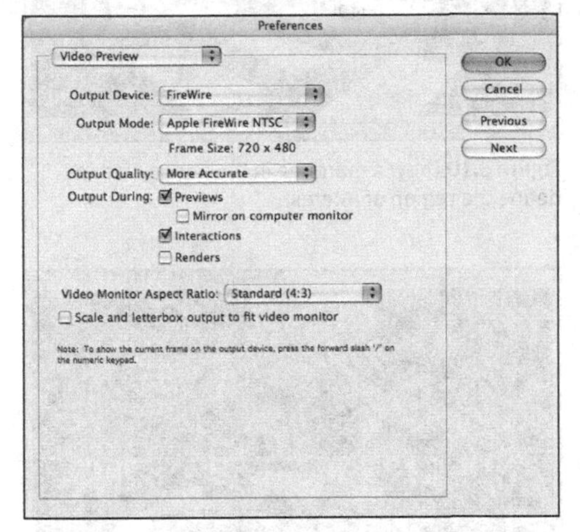

Figure 6.8 Choose an Output Quality and select other options.

3. Choose an option from the Output Mode pull-down menu (**Figure 6.7**).

   Typically, you should choose an option that's equivalent to full-screen video for your output device.

4. For Output Quality, choose whether it's more important to output the video using a Faster or More Accurate method.

5. For Output During, *choose any of the following* (**Figure 6.8**):

   ▲ **Previews**—Displays RAM previews on the NTSC monitor

   ▲ **Interactions**—Displays all window updates (such as while making adjustments to a layer's properties) on the NTSC monitor

   ▲ **Renders**—Displays rendered frames on the NTSC monitor

6. If you selected Previews in step 5, select "Mirror on computer monitor" to display previews on your computer's monitor in addition to the video device.

   To output previews to your video device only, leave this option unchecked.

7. For Video Monitor Aspect Ratio, choose the option that matches your video monitor:

   Standard (4:3)

   Widescreen (16:9)

8. If you wish, select "Scale and letterbox output to fit video monitor."

9. Click OK to close the Preferences dialog box.

   Previews appear on the connected NTSC monitor according to the preferences you set.

Setting the Region of Interest

You can limit the portion of an image to be included in playback or previews by setting a *region of interest*. By restricting the image area to render, you decrease each frame's RAM requirements and increase both the rendering speed and the number of frames you can render.

To set the region of interest:

1. In a Comp, Layer, or Footage panel, click the Region of Interest button (**Figure 6.9**).
2. Draw a marquee in the image area to define the region of interest (**Figure 6.10**).

   The area of the image included in playback and previews will be limited to the area within the region of interest (**Figure 6.11**).
3. To resize the region of interest, drag any of its corner handles.

To toggle between the region of interest and the full image:

◆ In the Comp, Layer, or Footage panel, click the Region of Interest button.

  When the button is selected, the panel shows the region of interest; when the button is deselected, the panel displays the full image.

✔ Tips

- To redraw the region of interest from the full image, make sure the Region of Interest button is deselected; then, Option/Alt-click the Region of Interest button.
- As always, you can reduce rendering times by reducing your composition's resolution or by setting layers to Draft quality.

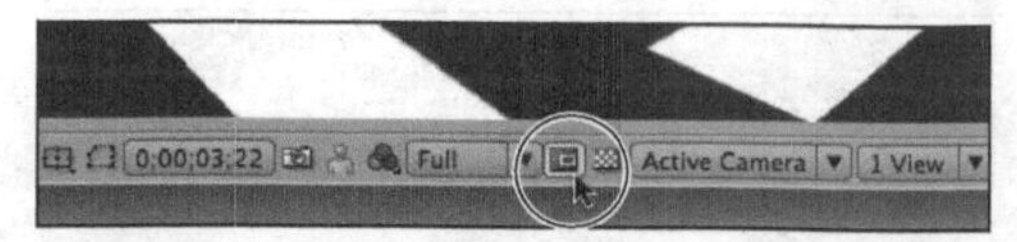

Figure 6.9 Click the Region of Interest button.

Figure 6.10 Draw a marquee in the image area to define the region of interest.

Figure 6.11 The region of interest limits the image included in playback and previews. Click the Region of Interest button to toggle between the region you specified and the full composition image.

Using the Time Controls

Although the Footage, Layer, Composition, and Timeline panels all have their own playback controls, you can use the Time Controls panel to set the current frame in any selected panel. By default, the times of related panels are synchronized. For example, changing the current frame in a Layer panel also changes the current time in its related Timeline and Composition panels. You can change this setting in the General pane of the Preferences dialog box.

You'll recognize most of the following buttons from the Time Controls panel (**Figure 6.12**); however, a few of these aren't on your home VCR:

First Frame cues the current time to the first frame in the window.

Frame Back cues the current time one frame back.

Play/Pause plays when clicked once and stops when clicked again. Playback performance depends on After Effects' ability to render the frames for viewing. During playback, the Time Controls panel displays two frame rates side by side: the frame rate your system is currently able to achieve and the frame rate you set for the composition.

Frame Forward cues the current time one frame forward.

Last Frame cues the current time to the last frame in the panel.

Audio lets you hear audio tracks when you preview a composition. Deselect it to suppress audio playback during previews. (Standard playback doesn't include audio.)

Loop comprises three states: Loop, Play Once, and Palindrome (which plays the specified area forward and backward). The frames affected by the loop setting depend on the panel selected. In a Footage panel, the entire duration of the footage loops. In a Layer panel, the layer loops from In point to Out point. In a composition—as viewed in the Composition and Timeline panels—frames loop from the beginning to the end of the work area (see "Previewing the Work Area," later in this chapter).

RAM Preview creates a RAM preview by rendering a specified range of frames, as defined by the Timeline's work area (explained later in this chapter).

The **Time Controls panel menu** opens a menu to show or hide RAM Preview and Shift-RAM Preview settings in the Time Controls panel (see the sections on RAM previews later in this chapter).

Collapse/Expand collapses the window to hide all controls or expands it to include RAM Preview Options or show the standard controls.

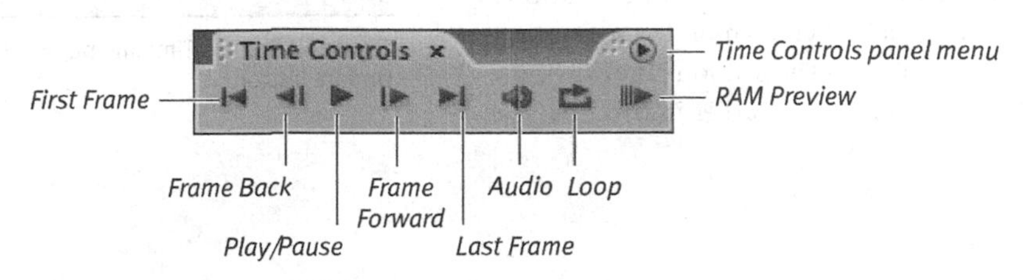

Figure 6.12 The Time Controls panel can control the playback of any selected window.

Using the Live Update Option

The Live Update option lets you specify how the Comp panel depicts changes during *interactions*, or while you make changes to a layer property. With Live Update enabled, you can see the layer change dynamically *while* you adjust the property. When Live update is off, the Comp panel doesn't update until *after* you alter the property (**Figures 6.13** and **6.14**).

Live Update works with the current Fast Previews setting (explained in "Specifying a Fast Previews Option," later in this chapter). With adaptive resolution enabled (either the standard option or with OpenGL), After Effects temporarily degrades the image quality during interactions until it can process and display the layer at the specified quality and resolution (see "Using Adaptive Resolution," later in this chapter).

You should choose the combination of settings most appropriate to the task at hand, the processing demands of the frame, and your system's processing capability.

To toggle Live Update on and off:

- In the Timeline panel, click the Live Update button (**Figure 6.15**).

✔ Tip

- You specify whether to view interactions on an attached video monitor separately, as explained in the section "Previewing to a Video Device," earlier in this chapter.

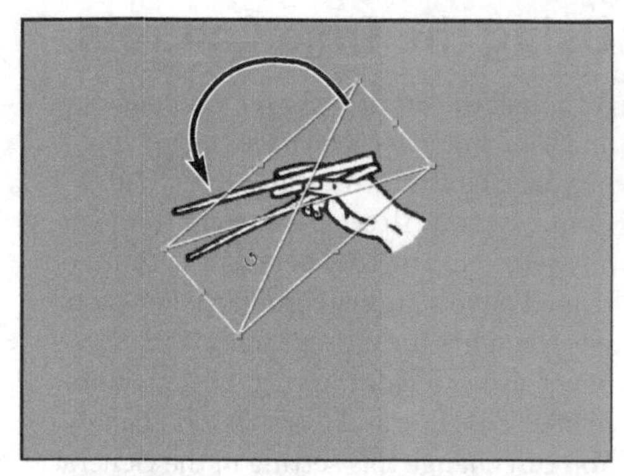

Figure 6.13 With Live Update off, the image doesn't update as you make an adjustment. Here, only the bounding box indicates the layer is being rotated...

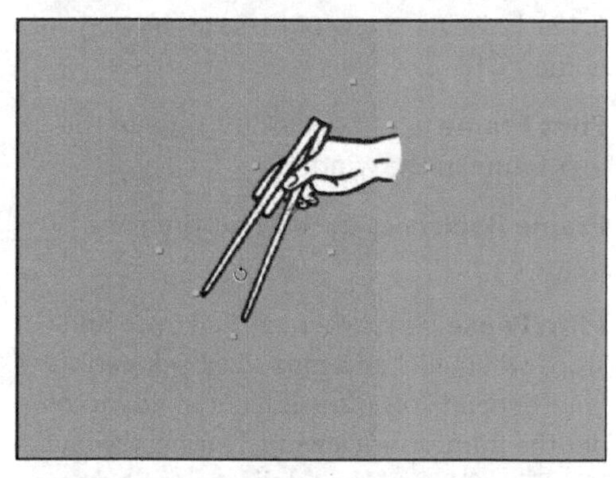

Figure 6.14 ...and the layer doesn't reflect the change until you release the mouse.

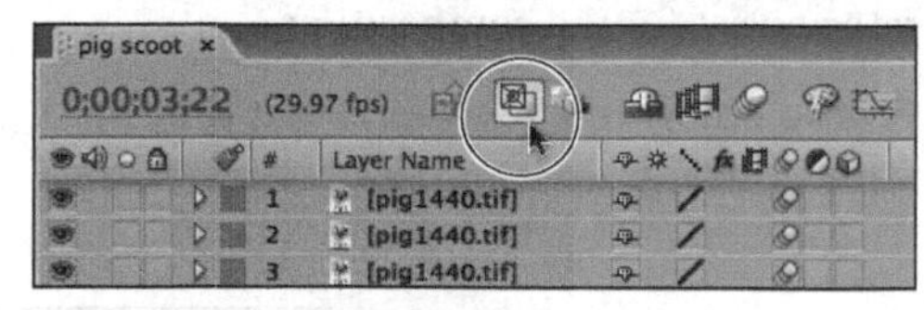

Figure 6.15 In the Timeline panel, click the Live Update button.

Specifying a Fast Previews Option

As you learned in earlier chapters, the standard playback method (pressing Play or cuing the current time) is influenced by a comp's resolution as well as the quality settings of the layers it contains. (Everything else being equal, lowering quality and resolution results in shorter rendering times.) You can specify several other options to view frames as quickly as possible by using the Comp panel's Fast Previews button.

This section covers how to specify the option you want to use and summarizes each choice. Some choices (Adaptive Resolution and OpenGL options) include additional settings, which are explained fully in later sections.

To enable a Fast Previews option:

1. In a Composition panel, choose an option from the Fast Previews button's pull-down menu (**Figure 6.16**):

   Off deactivates the Fast Previews option. Standard playback quality is governed by the comp resolution setting and layer quality settings.

   Wireframe displays layer outlines only, allowing you to quickly evaluate aspects of an animation such as movement and timing by sacrificing image content.

   Adaptive Resolution temporarily reduces the image resolution to a specified minimum setting in order to display changes to layers interactively or to maximize the frame rate.

   OpenGL—Interactive utilizes a compatible OpenGL graphics card to process every frame requested, such as when you scrub to preview. When active, the Comp panel's Fast Previews icon appears lit.

   OpenGL—Always On utilizes a compatible OpenGL graphics card for all previews. The notice *OpenGL* in the upper-left corner of the Comp panel indicates this mode is active.

   OpenGL options are available only if you have a compatible OpenGL graphics card installed in your system and you've enabled OpenGL options in the Previews pane of the Preferences dialog box.

2. To use a compatible OpenGL graphics card to process the image of motion footage layers by using a still frame, choose Freeze Layer Contents in the Fast Previews pull-down menu.

   Using a still image as a proxy for motion footage reduces rendering requirements. This option is available only when you choose an OpenGL option in step 1.

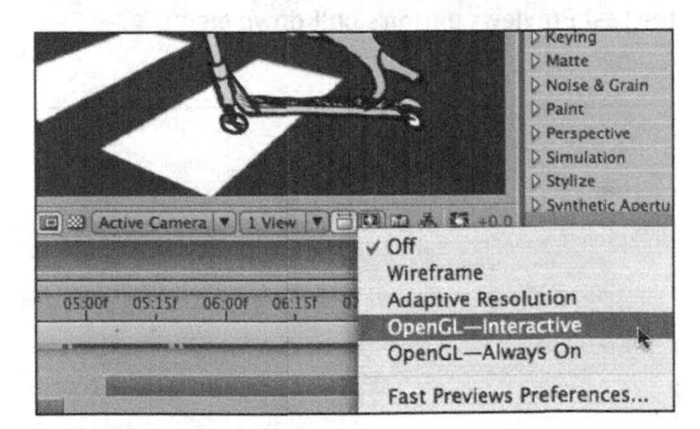

Figure 6.16 Choose an option from the Fast Previews button's pull-down menu.

Using Adaptive Resolution

If your system is slow to update the Comp panel's image, After Effects can reduce the image's resolution automatically—a feature called *adaptive resolution* (**Figures 6.17** and **6.18**). This way, you can get visual feedback even when your system can't keep up at the resolution you previously specified for the panel. You set the maximum amount by which adaptive resolution degrades images in the Previews pane of the Preferences dialog box.

Figure 6.17 With adaptive resolution enabled, the image degrades to keep pace with your adjustments...

Figure 6.18 ...and then assumes the comp's resolution when you stop transforming the layer.

To set Adaptive Resolution settings:

1. In a Comp panel, click the Fast Previews button, and choose Fast Previews Preferences from the pull-down menu (**Figure 6.19**).

   The Previews pane of the Preferences dialog box appears.

2. *Select one of the following* options from the Adaptive Resolution Limit pull-down menu (**Figure 6.20**):

   ▲ **1/2**—After Effects temporarily displays the image at no less than one-half resolution while updating the comp preview.

   ▲ **1/4**—After Effects temporarily displays the image at one-quarter resolution while updating the comp preview.

   ▲ **1/8**—After Effects temporarily displays the image at one-eighth resolution while updating the comp preview.

3. Click OK to close the Preferences dialog box.

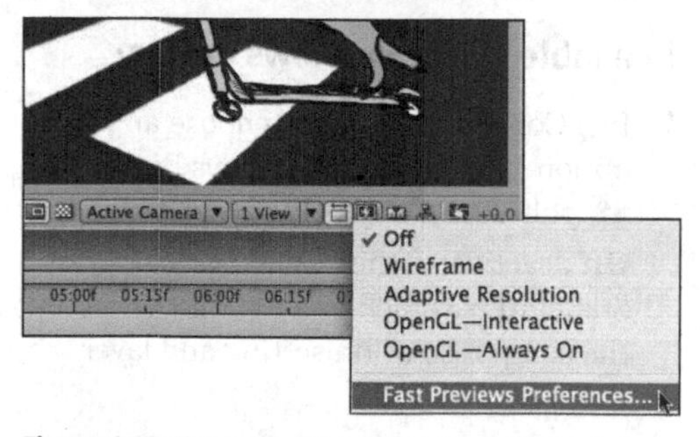

Figure 6.19 Choose Fast Previews Preferences from the Fast Previews button's pull-down menu.

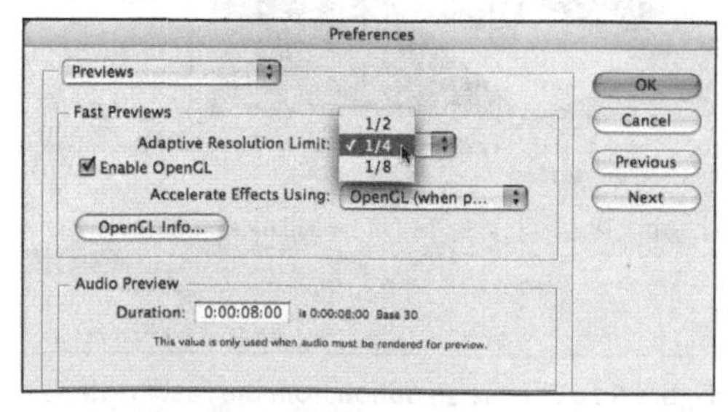

Figure 6.20 Limit the amount of degradation by choosing an option in the Adaptive Resolution Limit pull-down menu.

Using OpenGL

Generally speaking, software processing can't match hardware dedicated to the same task. After Effects takes advantage of this fact by utilizing the graphics processing power of (After Effects-certified) OpenGL graphics cards.

After Effects detects whether your system has an OpenGL graphics card automatically and, if so, activates it as the default preview option.

When OpenGL is in effect, the Fast Previews button turns green. By default, OpenGL kicks in whenever you drag layers in a comp, scrub a motion-related property, or scrub a comp's current time. However, it doesn't provide a rendering boost to nonmotion related effect properties. To view effects-intensive frames, you may opt to switch to another Fast Previews method.

Overall, OpenGL provides faster, smoother screen updates than you would get otherwise, and it does so without degrading the image. But as the following task explains, you can set OpenGL to switch to adaptive resolution as you adjust effect property values (see "Using Adaptive Resolution," earlier in this chapter). This way, you can take advantage of OpenGL for most interactions, and adaptive resolution when you're adjusting effects.

You already know how to specify your OpenGL card as the Fast Previews option (see "Specifying a Fast Previews Option" earlier in this chapter). This section explains how to set several options specific to OpenGL.

OpenGL Graphics Cards

OpenGL is a technology utilized by many advanced video graphics cards that helps to enhance graphics processing, particularly for 3D objects and subtleties like shading, lights, and shadows. When a program is designed to recognize OpenGL, the increase in graphics performance can be substantial.

Usually, a high-end graphics card isn't a standard component in an average system configuration; instead, it's an often-expensive option. However, PC gamers and graphics professionals value graphics performance and are eager to upgrade to a more advanced graphics card.

Features and processing power vary from card to card. Whether your card supports features like lights and shadows in After Effects depends on the particular card.

Before you upgrade your graphics card, check Adobe's Web site to ensure the card has been certified to work with After Effects. This is another quick way to see which features the card supports. And in addition to the card itself, make sure you install the latest software drivers, which should be available for download from the manufacturer's Web site.

To set OpenGL preferences:

1. In a Comp panel, click the Fast Previews button and choose Fast Previews Preferences from the pull-down menu (**Figure 6.21**).

   The Previews pane of the Preferences dialog box appears.
2. Select Enable OpenGL.
3. For Accelerate Effects Using, choose an option (**Figure 6.22**):

   Adaptive Resolution

   OpenGL (when possible)
4. Click OK to close the dialog box.

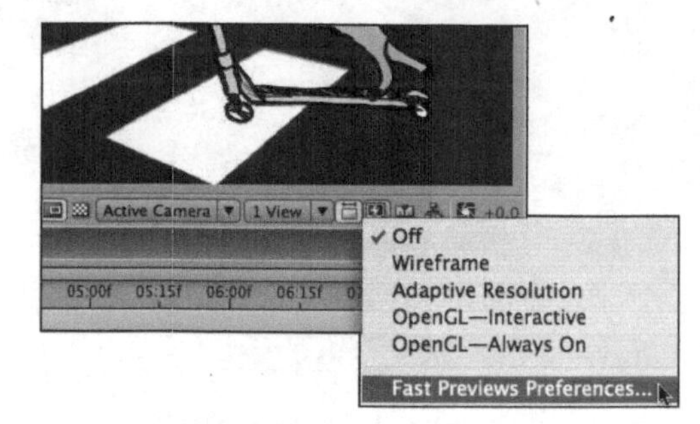

Figure 6.21 Choose Fast Previews Preferences from the Fast Previews button's pull-down menu.

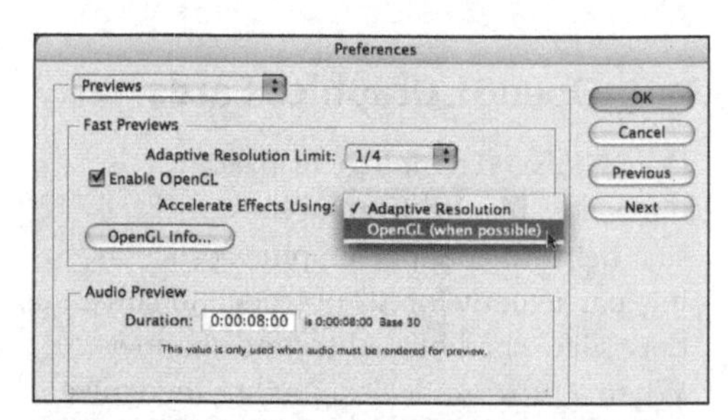

Figure 6.22 Select the OpenGL options you want.

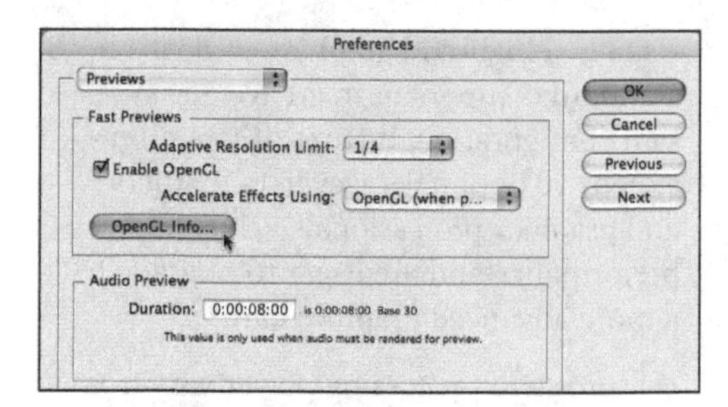

Figure 6.23 Click OpenGL Info to access more options.

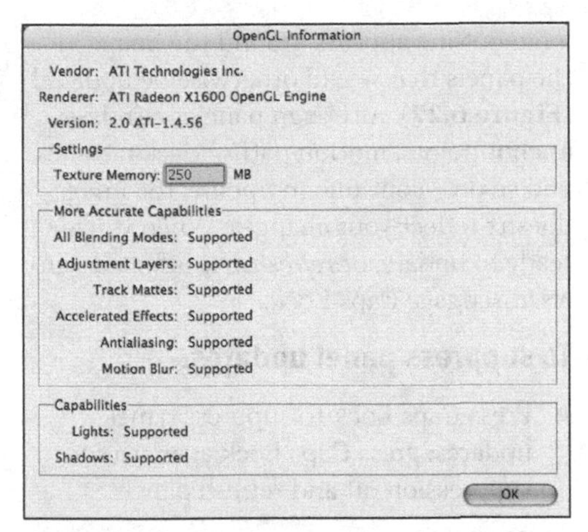

Figure 6.24 In the OpenGL Information dialog box, specify an amount for Texture Memory.

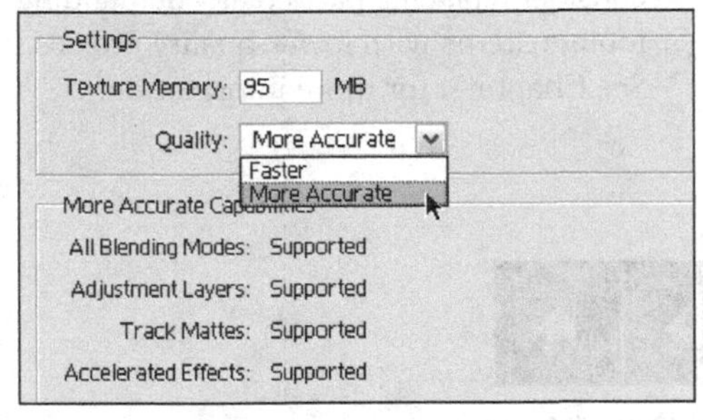

Figure 6.25 If available, choose an option from the Quality pull-down menu.

To specify other OpenGL options:

1. In the Previews pane of the Preferences dialog box, click OpenGL Info (**Figure 6.23**).

   An OpenGL Information dialog box appears.

2. Specify the amount for Texture Memory, in megabytes (MB) (**Figure 6.24**).

   Adobe recommends allocating no more than 80 percent of the video RAM (VRAM) on your display card when using Windows; on a Mac, After Effects determines the ideal value automatically.

3. Specify an option in the Quality pull-down menu (**Figure 6.25**):

   Faster—Processes more quickly, at the expense of the quality of lighting, shading, and blending, and by excluding blending modes

   More Accurate—Includes blending modes, and improves the quality of lighting, shading, and blending

4. Click OK to close the OpenGL Information dialog box, and click OK to close the Preferences dialog box.

Suppressing Panel Updates

If frames are difficult to render, it can take time to update an image. You may have already noticed how the Selection tool cycles between black and white as a particularly difficult frame renders (**Figure 6.26**). The lower-right corner of the Composition panel also includes a small activity bar (provided the window is sized wide enough for you to see it). When previewing gets in the way of your progress, you can prevent the Footage, Layer, and Composition panels from updating by activating your keyboard's Caps Lock key.

When you suppress updates, panels continue to display the current frame, even after you make changes. When you alter the image in the current frame or move to a new frame, a red outline appears around the image in the panels that would otherwise be updated (**Figure 6.27**). Although panel controls—anchor points, motion paths, mask outlines, and so on—continue to update, the image doesn't reflect your changes. When you're ready to update, or *refresh*, the affected panels, disengage Caps Lock.

To suppress panel updates:

◆ Press Caps Lock to suppress panel updates; press Caps Lock again to turn suppression off and refresh panels.

✔ Tip

■ If slow updates are a problem, you should consider replacing particularly demanding footage items with lower-quality proxies. See Chapter 4 for more information.

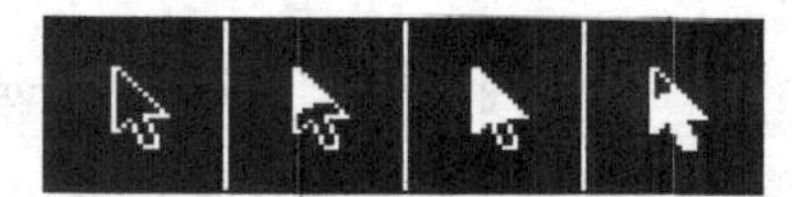

Figure 6.26 The Selection tool cycles between black and white as the program pauses to render frames.

Figure 6.27 When Caps Lock is active, a red outline appears around the image in the windows that would otherwise be updated. The window also displays a friendly reminder.

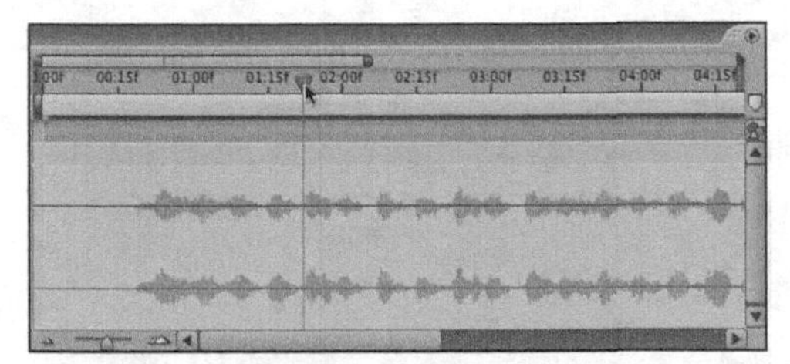

Figure 6.28 Scrubbing the audio provides an alternative (or an enhancement) to expanding the Audio Waveform property to cue the current time to a particular sound.

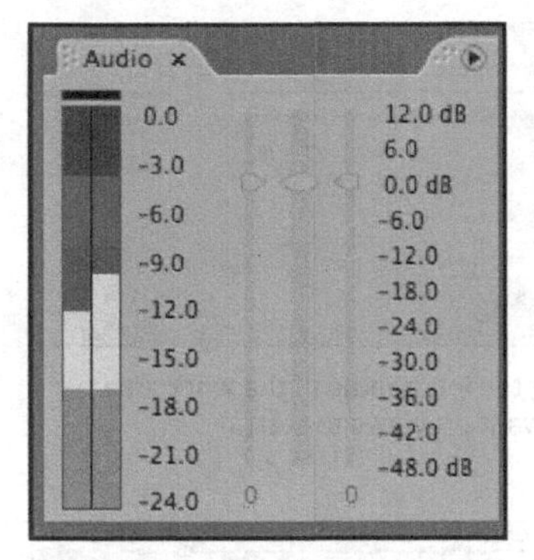

Figure 6.29 As usual, use the VU meter of the Audio panel to see audio levels as they play.

✔ Tip

- To hear every syllable and beat, there's no substitute for scrubbing. Once you find the sound you're looking for, don't forget that you can mark the frame in the layer or the composition (see Chapter 5). You can also set markers on the fly during audio previews by pressing the asterisk (*) key on the numeric keypad.

Scrubbing Audio

In After Effects, finding a particular frame based on the image is easy. Finding a particular moment based on the sound is a different matter. An audio preview plays your audio layers, but it doesn't make it easy to cue to a particular sound. When you halt an audio preview (see the next section), the current time indicator goes back to the starting point—the current time indicator doesn't remain at the moment you stop it. Viewing the audio waveform usually doesn't help you pinpoint a sound, either; individual sounds are difficult to discern in a waveform display (**Figure 6.28**). (See Chapter 5).

Fortunately, After Effects allows you to *scrub* the audio—that is, play it back slowly as you drag the current time indicator. The term *scrubbing* refers to the back back-and-forth motion of tape over an audio head. This feature has always been taken for granted in the analog world, but it's long been considered a luxury for digital tools. (High-end equipment is still required to approximate old-fashioned tape scrubbing.)

Remember, you can always see audio levels—even while you scrub—in the Volume Units (VU) meter of the Audio panel (**Figure 6.29**).

To scrub audio:

◆ In the time ruler of the Timeline panel, Command/Ctrl-drag the current time indicator.

  The audio plays back as you drag.

Previewing the Work Area

Until now, this chapter has focused on playback options and methods you can use to control the way the Composition panel updates when you transform layer properties. The following sections discuss previewing a specified area of the composition, a span defined by the *work area*.

The *work area bar* is an adjustable bar located above the time ruler in the Timeline menu (**Figure 6.30**). To make it easier to identify the part of the composition that's included, the entire area under the work area bar is highlighted; it appears a little brighter than the area outside the work area.

As you learned in Chapter 5, the navigator view of the Timeline panel includes a miniature version of the work area bar; however, it's for your reference only.

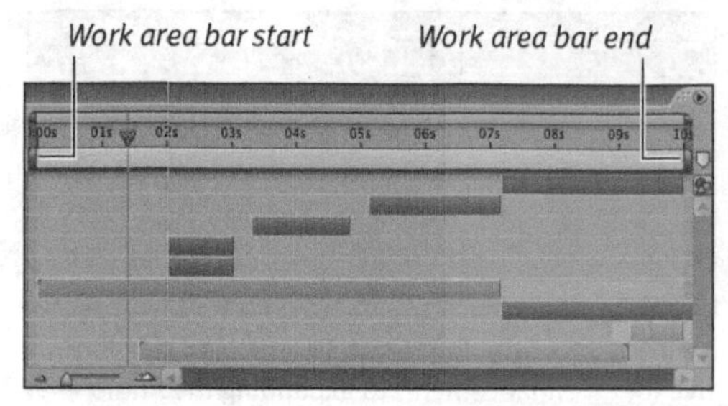

Figure 6.30 The work area bar defines the range of frames in the composition for previews.

To set the work area by dragging:

In the Timeline panel, *do any of the following:*

- Drag the left handle of the work area bar to the time you want previews to start (**Figure 6.31**).
- Drag the right handle of the work area bar to the time you want previews to end (**Figure 6.32**).
- Drag the center of the work area bar to move the work area without changing its duration (**Figure 6.33**).

  Make sure to grab the center of the bar, where vertical lines imply a textured grip. Otherwise, you'll cue the current time indicator instead.

  Press Shift as you drag to snap the edges of the work area bar to the edges of layers, keyframes, markers, or the time indicator.

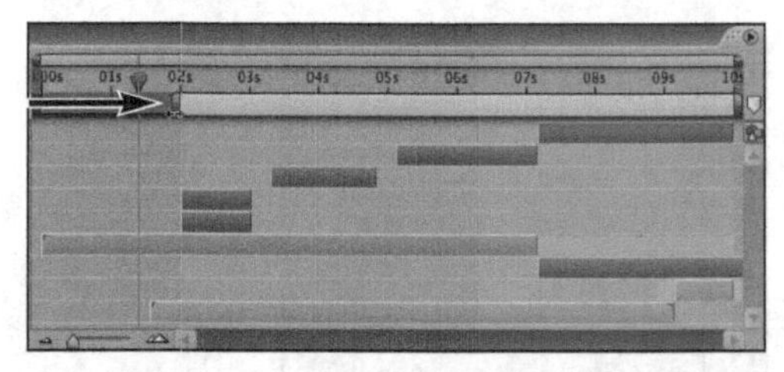
Figure 6.31 Drag the left handle of the work area bar to the time you want previews to start.

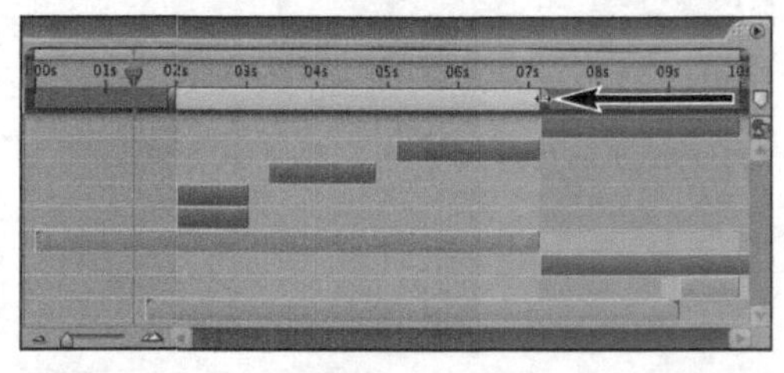
Figure 6.32 Drag the right handle of the work area bar to the time you want previews to end.

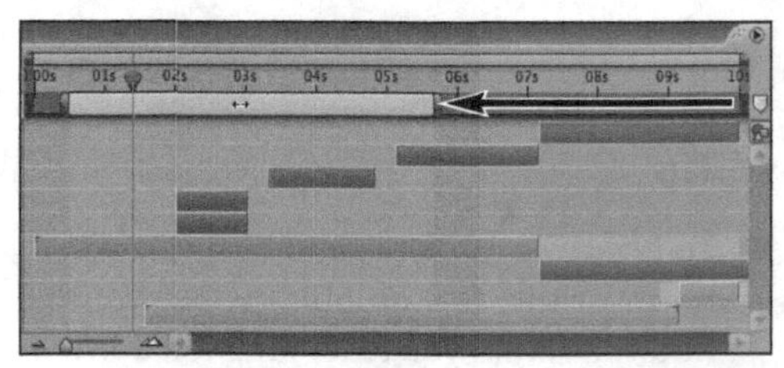
Figure 6.33 Drag the center of the work area bar to move the work area without changing its duration.

To set the work area using keyboard shortcuts:

1. In the Timeline panel, set the current time to the frame at which you want the work area to begin or end.
2. *Do one of the following:*
   - ▲ Press B to set the beginning of the work area to the current time.
   - ▲ Press N to set the end of the work area to the current time.

✔ Tips

- ■ You can't set the beginning of the work area bar after the end, or vice versa. If you can't move the end of the work area where you want, you probably have to move the other end first.
- ■ Using an extended keyboard, you can cue the time to the beginning of the work area by pressing Shift-Home or to the end of the work area by pressing Shift-End.
- ■ In principle, After Effects' work area bar is equivalent to the one in Premiere Pro. In practice, however, there are a few differences. For example, you can't use the same keyboard shortcuts for setting the work area (unless you create a custom shortcut in Premiere Pro).

Previewing Audio Only

If you only need to hear the audio tracks of your composition, you don't have to wait for a time-consuming video preview.

To preview audio only under the work area:

1. Set the work area over the range of frames you want to preview (**Figure 6.34**).

   See the previous section, "Previewing the Work Area."

2. Choose Composition > Preview > Audio Preview (Work Area) (**Figure 6.35**).

   The audio under the work area plays.

To preview audio only from the current time:

◆ In the Composition or Timeline panel, cue the current time to the frame at which you want to begin your audio preview and then press the decimal point (.) on the numeric keypad (not the period on the main keyboard).

The audio plays back from the current frame for the duration you set in the Preferences.

✔ Tips

- You can set the quality of audio previews (and thereby the rendering times) in the Previews pane of the Preferences dialog box.
- When you preview audio from the current time, it plays for the duration you set in the General pane of the Preferences dialog box.

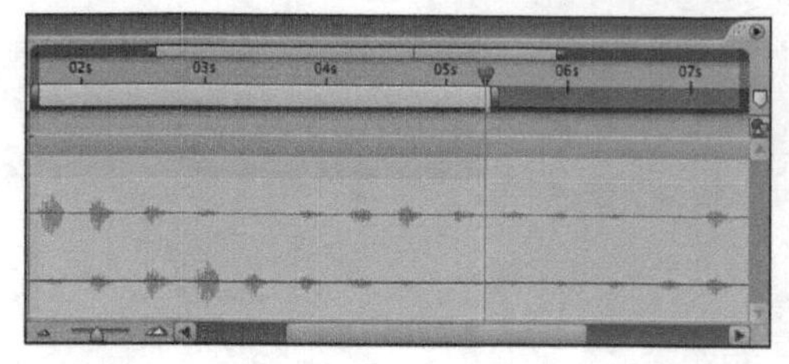

Figure 6.34 Set the work area bar over the range you want to preview.

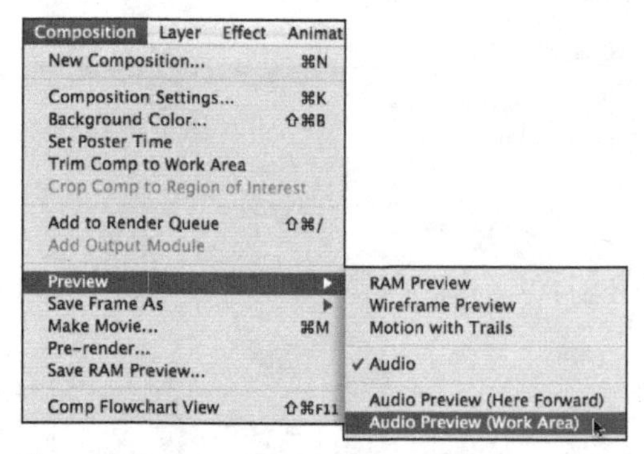

Figure 6.35 Choose Composition › Preview › Audio Preview (Work Area).

Figure 6.36 A full preview shows everything in detail but requires both more RAM and more processing time.

Figure 6.37 A wireframe preview represents the layer as an empty outline. It renders much faster but still shows you the motion of one or more layers.

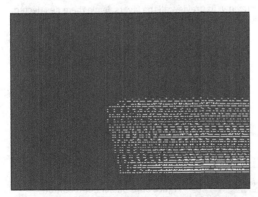

Figure 6.38 You can also preview motion with trails, in which case the wireframes at each frame remain visible as the preview progresses.

Previewing Wireframes

When you want to see just the motion of an animation—changes in position, scale, and rotation—you don't have to waste precious time by rendering a full-fledged preview of the work area. Instead, use a wireframe preview for selected layers.

A *wireframe preview* represents the motion of one or more layers as an empty outline, or wireframe. A wireframe preview gives you a clear sense of motion without consuming much of your RAM or your time (**Figures 6.36** and **8.37**). To get a sense of the sweep of the layer's complete motion, the wireframe can include a trail, which leaves the previous frames visible as the preview progresses (**Figure 6.38**). Because wireframe previews don't render frames fully, no images are stored in the cache, and no green line indicator appears below the work area bar.

To create a wireframe preview:

1. In the Timeline panel, *do one of the following:*
   - ▲ Select the layers you want to preview.
   - ▲ Deselect all layers to preview all of them.
2. Set the work area over the range of frames you want to preview (as explained in the section "Previewing the Work Area") (**Figure 6.39**).
3. *Do one of the following:*
   - ▲ Choose Composition > Preview > Wireframe Preview (**Figure 6.40**).
   - ▲ Choose Composition > Preview > Motion with Trails.
4. Press the spacebar to stop the preview.

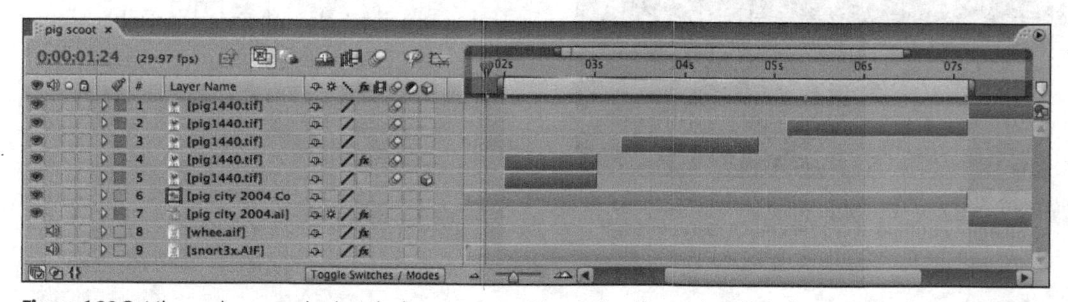

Figure 6.39 Set the work area and select the layers you want to preview. To preview all the layers, leave them deselected.

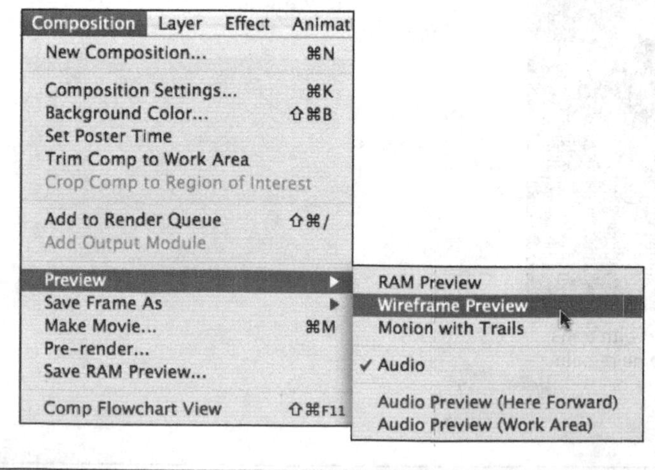

Figure 6.40 Select Composition › Preview › Wireframe Preview to view a wireframe preview, or choose Composition › Preview › Motion with Trails to view a wireframe preview with trails.

Table 6.2

Keyboard Shortcuts for Playback and Preview

To do this	Press this
Start/pause	Spacebar
Frame advance	Page Down
Frame reverse	Page Up
First frame	Home
Last frame	End
Scrub video	Option/Alt-drag (Windows) the current time indicator
Scrub audio	Command/Ctrl-drag the current time indicator
Stop window updates	Caps Lock
Preview audio from the current time	Decimal point (.) on the numeric keypad
RAM preview	Zero on the numeric keypad
Shift+RAM preview	Shift-zero on the numeric keypad
Save RAM preview	Command/Ctrl-zero on the numeric keypad
Wireframe preview	Option/Alt-zero on the numeric keypad
Wireframe preview using a rectangular layer outline	Command-Option-zero (Mac) or Ctrl-Alt-zero (Windows) on the numeric keypad
Show layers as background during wireframe previews	Add Shift to the wireframe preview shortcut: Shift-Option-zero (Mac) or Shift-Alt-zero (Windows) on the numeric keypad

Rendering RAM Previews

To see a comp at (or near) its full frame rate, you typically render a RAM preview. In contrast to using standard playback controls, a RAM preview renders frames first and then plays them back. By default, a RAM preview renders frames in the work area only; but you can set an option to render frames beginning at the current time (similar to standard playback). RAM previews include several options to balance rendering speed with image quality and frame rate.

You can set separate options for two kinds of RAM previews: a standard RAM preview and a Shift-RAM preview. You can customize each type according to your project's demands, choosing the best RAM preview option for the task at hand. For example, you could set the standard RAM preview to render a relatively smooth, high-resolution image, and set the Shift-RAM preview to render more quickly, at the expense of smooth motion and image quality.

By default, rendering a RAM preview (including a Shift-RAM preview) renders the active panel. But you can specify a particular panel to preview, even if it isn't the currently active panel. Doing so can streamline your workflow by freeing you from finding a particular panel to preview (especially in complex projects). For example, by designating your final comp as the panel to always preview, you can work in other panels and then quickly view your changes in the final comp.

For an overview of keyboard shortcuts for rendering a RAM preview and other playback options, see **Table 6.2**.

To show and hide RAM preview options:

- In the Time Controls panel's menu, *select an option* (**Figure 6.41**):
  - **RAM Preview Options**—Expands the panel to reveal the RAM preview options
  - **Shift+RAM Preview Options**—Expands the panel to reveal the Shift-RAM preview options

  The Time Controls panel expands to reveal the options you selected (**Figure 6.42**). Reselect an option to hide the RAM preview options.

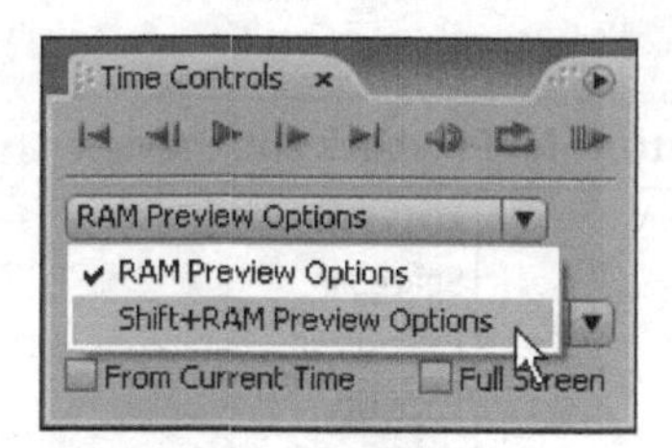

Figure 6.41 In the pull-down menu, choose the RAM preview options you want to show.

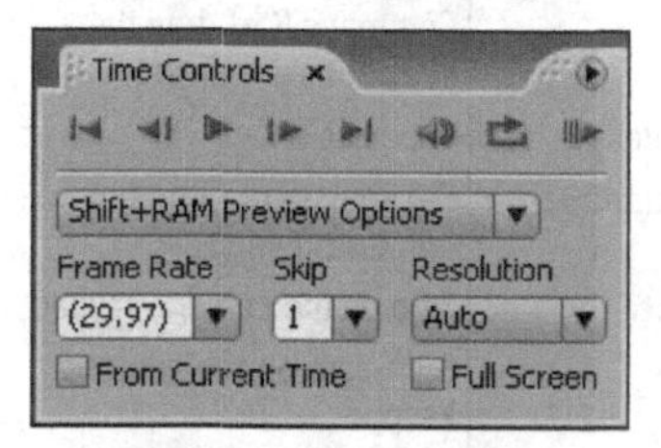

Figure 6.42 The Time Controls panel expands to reveal the options you selected.

✔ Tip

- Remember, you can repeatedly click the Time Controls panel to cycle through different views: to show the panel tab only, to add the playback controls, or to add the selected RAM or Shift-RAM preview options.

To set RAM preview options:

1. In the Time Controls panel, reveal either the RAM preview or Shift-RAM preview options, as explained in the previous task.
2. In the RAM Preview Options or Shift+RAM Preview Options area of the Time Controls panel, *enter the following*:

   Frame Rate—Enter the frame rate for the preview, or choose one from the pull-down menu (**Figure 6.43**).

   Lower frame rates render more quickly but at the expense of smooth motion.

   Skip—Enter the frequency with which frames are skipped and left unrendered.

   Skipping frames speeds rendering but results in choppier motion.

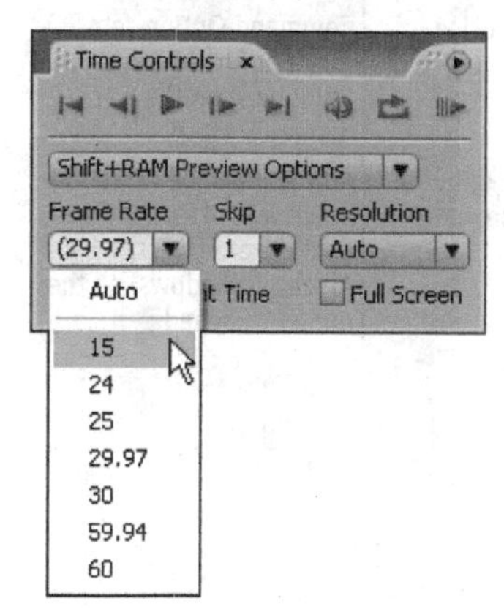

Figure 6.43 Enter a frame rate used by the preview, or choose one from the pull-down menu. Also enter the frequency at which frames are skipped.

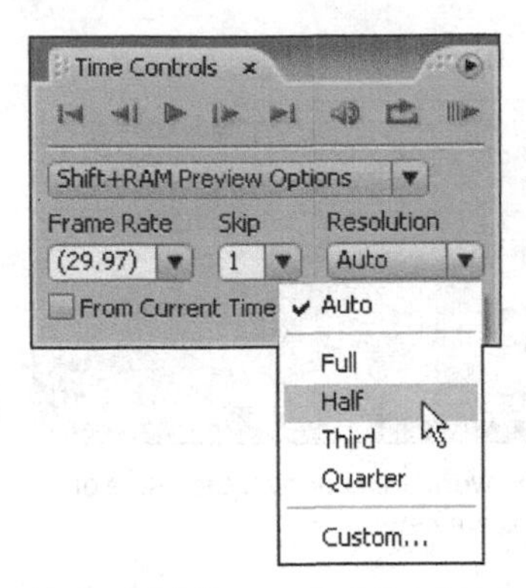

Figure 6.44 Choose an option from the Resolution pull-down menu. Select the other options you want.

Resolution—*Choose one of the following* options from the pull-down menu (**Figure 6.44**):

- **Auto**—Previews use the Composition panel's current resolution setting.
- **Full**—After Effects renders and displays every pixel of the composition, resulting in the highest image quality and the longest rendering time.
- **Half**—After Effects renders every other pixel, or one-quarter of the pixels of the full-resolution image in one-quarter of the time.
- **Third**—After Effects renders every third pixel, or one-ninth of the pixels in the full-resolution image in one-ninth of the time.
- **Quarter**—After Effects renders every fourth pixel, or one-sixteenth of the pixels in the full-resolution image in one-sixteenth of the time.
- **Custom**—After Effects renders whatever fraction of pixels you specify.

3. *Select either of the following* options:
   - **From Current Time**—After Effects renders previews from the current time (instead of the frames defined by the work area).
   - **Full Screen**—After Effects displays previews on a blank screen (with no windows visible).

To create a RAM preview:

1. In the Timeline panel, set the work area bar to the range of frames you want to preview (**Figure 6.45**).
2. To preview audio as well as video, click the Audio button in the Time Controls panel (**Figure 6.46**).
3. Select an option by clicking the Loop button in the Time Controls panel (**Figure 6.47**).

   Loop —loops playback beginning to end.

   Ping Pong —loops playback from beginning to end, then end to beginning.

   Play Once —plays once.

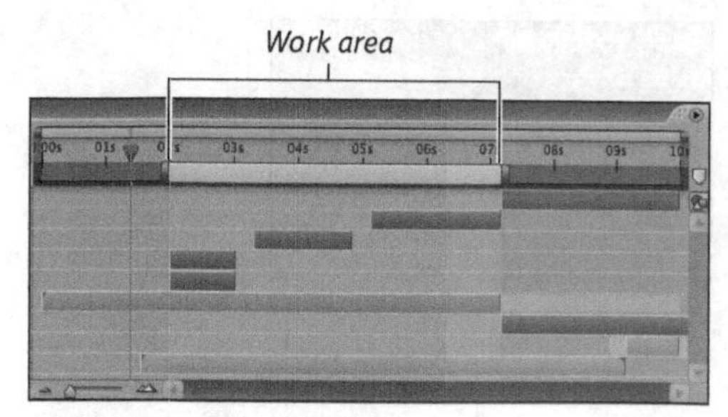

Figure 6.45 Set the work area bar over the range of frames you want to preview.

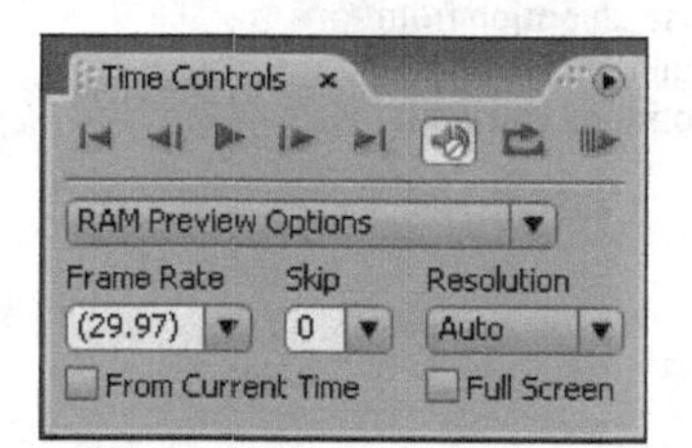

Figure 6.46 To preview audio in addition to video, click the Audio button in the Time Controls panel.

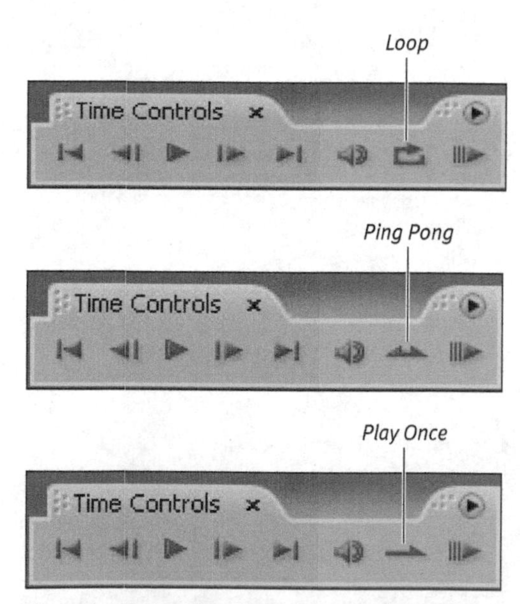

Figure 6.47 In the Time Controls panel, click the Loop button repeatedly so the icon corresponds to the option you want.

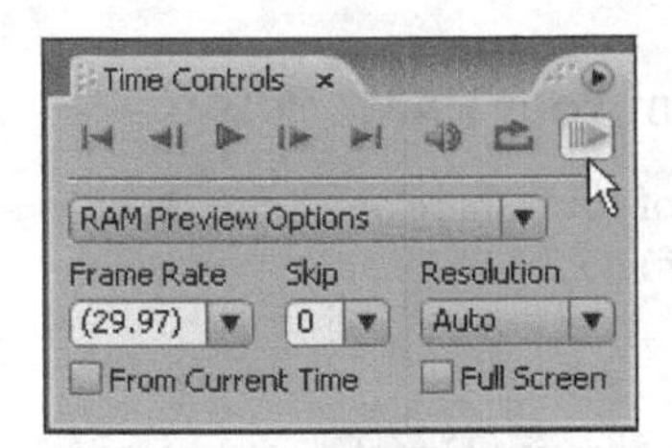

Figure 6.48 Click the RAM Preview button in the Time Controls panel, or press 0 in the numeric keypad.

Figure 6.49 In the lower-left corner of the window you want to designate, click the Always Preview This View button.

- The Memory & Cache pane of the Preferences dialog box allows you to specify the size and location of a disk cache. When the RAM cache is full, After Effects can move rendered frames to the location you specify. For best performance, the disk that stores source footage and the disk cache disk should use different drive controllers.

4. To use the standard RAM preview settings, *do any of the following:*
   - ▲ Choose Composition > Preview > RAM Preview.
   - ▲ Click the RAM Preview button in the Time Controls panel (**Figure 6.48**).
   - ▲ Press 0 on the numeric keypad.
5. To use the Shift-RAM preview settings, *do either of the following:*
   - ▲ Shift-click the RAM Preview button in the Time Controls panel.
   - ▲ Hold Shift as you press 0 on the numeric keypad.

   In the Timeline panel, a green line appears over the frames that are rendered to RAM. When all the frames in the work area have been rendered, or when the amount of available RAM runs out, the frames play back in the Composition panel.

To specify a panel to always preview:

- ◆ Click the Always Preview This View button in the panel you want to designate for previews (**Figure 6.49**).

  RAM previews (including Shift-RAM previews) always render the panel you specified, which becomes active for you to view.

✔ Tips

- Choosing Composition > Save RAM preview lets you save a RAM preview as a movie file that you can use, for example, as a draft version for your own reference or for sharing with clients.
- After Effects discards cached frames as they become obsolete or as new frames are added to a full cache. But you can empty the cache manually by choosing Edit > Purge and selecting the type of cache.

RAMming Speed: Getting the Most Out of Your RAM

In addition to using a computer with a fast processor and loads of RAM, here are some other things you can do to use RAM effectively and improve RAM playback.

Optimize Your Display

- Use a high-quality display card. Better yet, choose an Adobe-approved OpenGL graphics card, which can take over much of the processing.
- Use the latest drivers for your video display. Check with the manufacturer's Web site to make sure you're using the latest and greatest version.

Optimize Your RAM

- Reduce the number of undoable actions in General Preferences.
- Purge the image cache to free up RAM.

Reduce Memory Requirements for Compositions

- Set the composition to a low resolution (half, third, and so on) to achieve higher frame rates in previews.
- Match the composition's resolution and magnification factor. RAM previews work faster this way. For example, preview half-resolution compositions at 50 percent magnification.
- Use proxies when possible.
- Avoid footage items that use temporal compression (MPEG footage, for example). The frame differencing utilized by the compression scheme requires intensive processing.
- Prerender nested compositions when possible.
- Collapse transformations when possible.

Selections and Mask Essentials

I'm fixing a hole where the rain gets in
And stops my mind from wandering
Where it will go.

–John Lennon and Paul McCartney

Selections: The Key to Compositing

A particle physicist works with atoms, bakers and bankers each work with their own types of dough, and compositors work with selections—many different types of selections, potentially thousands, each derived uniquely.

If compositing were simply a question of taking pristine, perfect foreground source A and overlaying it onto perfectly matching background plate B, there would be no compositor in the effects process; an editor could accomplish the job before lunchtime.

Instead, compositors break sequences of images apart and reassemble them, sometimes painstakingly, first as a still frame and then in motion. Often, it is one element, one frame, or one area of a shot that needs special attention. By the clever use of selections, a compositor can save the shot by taking control of it. This chapter focuses on how a layer merges with those behind it.

Many Ways to Create Selections

After Effects offers a number of ways to create selections. Here are the most common.

Pull a Matte

Not only keying out the blue or green from an effects film shoot (**Figure 7.1**), but also high-contrast, or *hi-con, mattes,* are created by maximizing the contrast of a particular channel or area of the image. Other types of mattes exist as well, such as the elusive *difference matte.*

Figure 7.1 This split-screen image shows a bluescreen shoot (left) and the resulting matte. (All baseball images courtesy of Tim Fink Productions.)

Import with Alpha Channel

Alpha and transparency channels are accurate selections that are included for free with computer-generated footage (typically 3D animations, **Figure 7.2**). They make life easier until you run into problems with alpha channel interpretation, described in Chapter 4. At that point, the fact that After Effects is not explicit about alpha interpretation can actually make life more difficult.

This is something to watch for not only when you interpret alpha on import but also

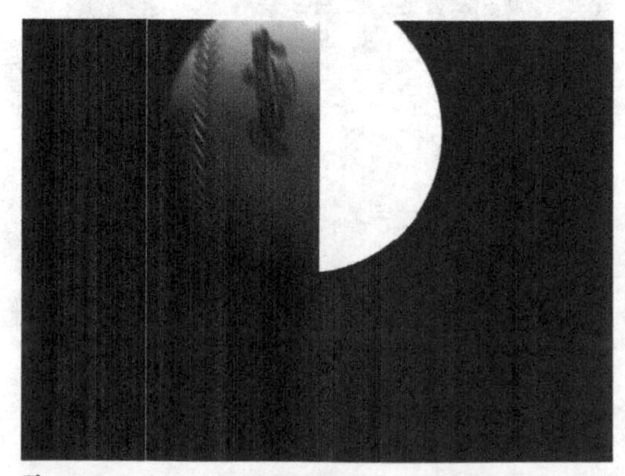

Figure 7.2 A computer-generated baseball's color and alpha channels.

Figure 7.3 This split-screen view shows the garbage matte mask that was added to remove areas of the stage not covered by the blue screen.

when applying effects to layers with an alpha. The "Alpha Channels and Premultiplication" section later in this chapter offers the lowdown on how to deal with edge multiplication.

Mask

A mask is a vector shape that determines the opaque and transparent areas of an image (**Figure 7.3**). This chapter introduces the fundamentals of creating and combining masks.

Masks are generally created by hand, one vertex at a time, or beginning with a simple primitive shape such as an ellipse. After Effects can also generate them automatically by examining the raster data of an image, using Layer > Auto-trace.

Auto-trace creates detailed and accurate outlines using the contrast of the image, overall or on individual color channels. With all but the very simplest shots, lots of overlapping outlines are created—dozens, typically—too many for effective rotoscoping (**Figure 7.4**).

Blending Modes

Blending modes (e.g. Add, Multiply, Screen) combine color channels mathematically, pixel by pixel, in ways that mimic real-world optics (**Figure 7.5**). Inexperienced compositors will sometimes use selections where blending modes are preferable; expert compositors are good at combining both.

Figure 7.4 The result of Auto-trace on a complex image is interesting but with these settings would likely have only abstract artistic applications.

You can also use selections combined with blending modes to get the best of both worlds.

This chapter focuses in-depth on the modes most relevant to effects compositing and

Figure 7.5 Blending modes are the preferred way to composite elements that are composed predominantly of light rather than matter, such as fire.

gets into the nitty-gritty of what they are actually doing as they combine pixel data.

Effects

Several effects create or refine transparency selections. Effects such as Levels and Curves include control of the transparency (alpha) channel, and effects in the Channel submenu work with the alpha channel directly.

Combine Techniques

Even an ordinary effects shot will typically combine more than one of the above techniques; for example, you will often apply a garbage matte prior to a color key, or enhance the effect of a blending mode by adding a hi-con matte.

The art is in knowing which approach to apply for a given situation, how to apply it, and when to try something else. No single technique is as sophisticated as the result of combining and refining them together, sometimes in clever and unexpected ways.

Compositing: Science and Nature

What exactly is happening in a simple A over B composite? Is it just like placing one object on top of another, like laying a drawing on your desk? A over B makes intuitive sense, but to master compositing, it helps to know what is going on—not only in the virtual world of software but the physical or "real" world, and beyond that, the equally real physical world of optics.

These three worlds do not always operate according to the same rules, and while it might seem like the digital artist re-creates, as faithfully as possible, what is happening in the natural world, it is the world of optics, the way that the camera sees the world, that a compositor is actually trying to emulate. And edge detail between objects, in particular, distinguishes these worlds rather sharply.

Bitmap Alpha

A *bitmap selection channel* is one in which each pixel is either fully opaque or fully transparent. This is the type of selection generated by the Magic Wand tool in Photoshop. You can feature or blur the resulting edge, but the initial selection contains no semitransparent pixels.

✔ Note

The Color Key and Luma Key effects also generate bitmap selections, making them tools largely to be avoided.

This type of selection may have an occasional use, but it belongs to the world of computers, not nature (or optics). An edge made up of pixels which are either fully opaque or invisible cannot describe a curve or angle smoothly, and even a straight line looks unnatural in a natural image if it completely lacks edge thresholding (**Figure 7.6**).

Feathered Alpha

Although it's easy enough to see that a bitmap edge does not occur in nature, it's hard to imagine that hard objects should

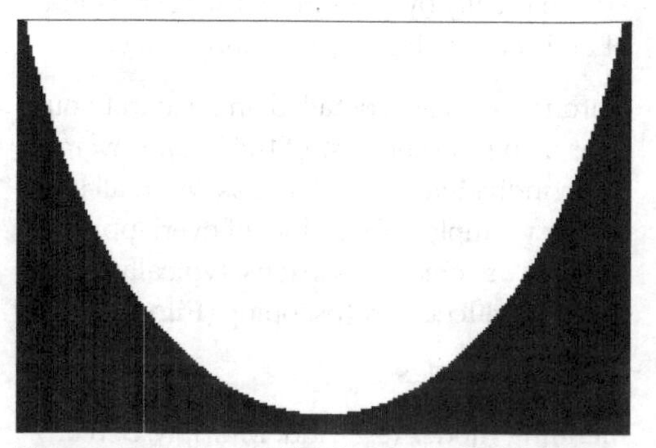

Figure 7.6 400% magnification shows the flaws of a curved or angled shape described by only bitmap pixels, those that are either fully transparent or opaque.

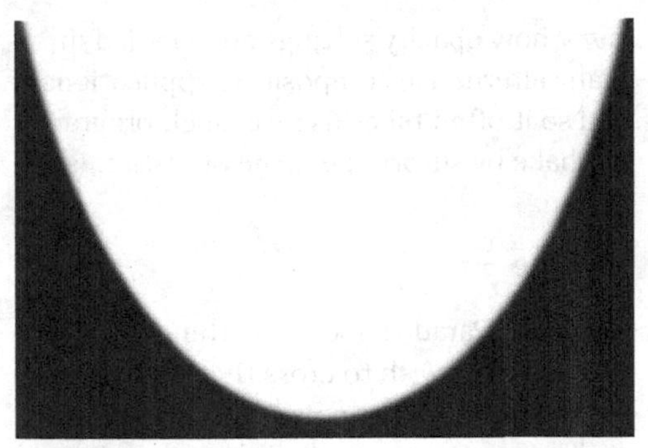

Figure 7.7 Ah—better. Even at 400%, a feathered and anti-aliased edge more properly describes a smooth, soft curve.

have transparent, feathered edges. Examine the edge of this book. Do you see a soft, semitransparent edge? Of course not.

But now study an image of the same thing, and you'll find it isn't razor sharp in its hardness, either. It so happens that semitransparent edge pixels are the digital approximation for overlapping edges in optics because they solve two problems in translating the world of objects to the world of pixels:

- They come closer to describing organic curves (**Figure 7.7**).
- They mimic optics behavior, the way light and objects interact when viewed through a lens.

The first point is intuitive enough once you've gained some experience working with *raster images*, digital images made up of pixels. The second point is easier to miss.

Study a digital photo with no compositing whatsoever close-up (**Figures 7.8a and b**). In the digital image, areas at the edge of objects become a fine wash of color combining the foreground and background. This is what happens to light as it travels around objects in the physical world and then through the lens of the camera.

Opacity

The real world also informs After Effects' handling of opacity, which can seem illogical, as in the following quiz.

✔ Close-Up

Geek Alert: The Compositing Formula So, what *does* happen when you layer a raster image with semitransparent alpha over an opaque background image? The foreground pixel values are multiplied by the percentage of transparency, which, if not fully opaque, reduces their value. The background pixels are multiplied by the percentage of opacity (the inverse of opacity), and the two values are added together to produce the composite. Expressed as a formula, it looks like

(Fg * A) + ((1–A)*Bg) = Comp

With real RGB pixel data of R: 185, G: 144, B: 207 in the foreground and R: 80, G: 94, B: 47 in the background, calculating one edge pixel only might look like

[(185, 144, 207) 3.6] + [.43 (80, 94, 47)] = (143, 124, 143)

The result is a weighted blend between the brightness of the foreground and the darker background.

Other effects compositing programs, such as Shake, do not take this operation for granted the way that After Effects and Photoshop do. You can't simply drag one image over another in a layer stack—you must apply an Over function to create this interaction. Is there a difference? Not until you add to the discussion the operations that go along with an Over, in particular premultiplication, which is detailed later in this chapter.

Figures 7.8a and b This image (a) has no compositing. Natural softness is apparent along hard edges (b) despite that they are in focus.

Take two identical layers, no alpha/transparency information for either layer. Set each layer to 50% Opacity, and the result does not add up to 100%. Here's why.

A lead developer on the After Effects team once described the program's opacity calculations as follows: Imagine you have a light which is 1, and place a 50% transparent filter (say, a sheet of vellum) in front of it. Half the total light is permitted through the vellum (0.5 * 1 = 0.5). Put another 50% transparent sheet of vellum on top of that. Now half of half the light shows through (0.5 * 0.5 = 0.25). You can theoretically repeat ad infinitum without reaching 0% light transmission, at least in a pure digital environment.

Hence, and in some tangential relationship to Zeno's Paradox, After Effects mimics how transparency behaves in the real world. This is *not* how opacity settings are handled in many alternative compositing applications, and so it often takes users of such programs as Shake by surprise, but the operation is by design.

✔ Note

Zeno's Paradox goes something like this: Suppose I wish to cross the room. First, of course, I must cover half the distance. Then, I must cover half the remaining distance. Then, I must cover half the remaining distance. Then I must cover half the remaining distance, and so on forever. The consequence is that I can never get to the other side of the room.

Alpha Channels and Premultiplication

One major source of confusion and even occasional derision with After Effects has to do with its handling of alpha channels and premultiplication. After Effects has a persistent concept of the alpha channel as part of every image, and this channel is expected always to be un-multiplied within After Effects, whether it originated that way or not. Thus premultiplication is set on import, in the Interpret Footage dialog, and you are more or less expected not to consider edge multiplications until it's time to render.

This works surprisingly well given the correct import settings, but it doesn't free you from the need to understand premultiplication and how problems with edges may be related to it.

Premultiplication Illustrated

Premultiplication exists for one reason only: so that rendered images look nice, with realistic, anti-aliased edges against a neutral background, *before they are composited.*

All premultiplication does is composite the foreground against the background, so that the edges and transparency blend as well into that solid color (typically black) as they would against the final background.

When you ask After Effects to "guess" how to interpret the footage (on import, by choosing Guess in the Interpret Footage dialog, or pressing **Ctrl+F/Cmd+F**), it looks for repeated pixels indicating a solid color background and the difference between that background color and the foreground in the edge pixels.

What does it mean to have the background multiplied into the edge pixels? Revisit "Geek Alert: The Compositing Formula," and imagine the background value to be 0,0,0; edge pixels are multiplied by 0 (they turn pure black) and are added to the source, weighted by the percentage of transparency as determined by the corresponding alpha channel pixel. The overall effect is to darken semitransparent edge pixels if the background is black, to lighten them if it's white, and to really wreak havoc with them if it's any other color.

The close-ups in **Figures 7.9a** and **b** show a section of the same foreground image with the alpha interpreted properly and with it misinterpreted. A misinterpreted alpha either fails to remove the background color from the edge pixels, or removes color that should actually be present.

Figures 7.9a and b Motion blur and a white background clearly reveal improper edge multiplication, especially when compared with the correct version (a). There is dark matting all around the edges, including areas of the canopy meant to be translucent, and around the blur of the propeller (b).

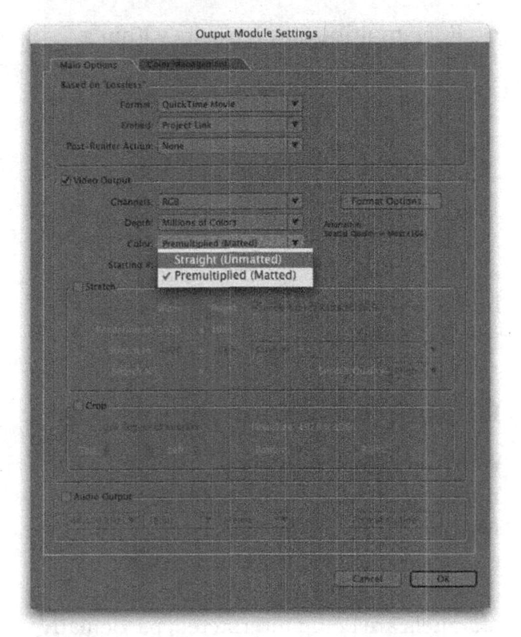

Figure 7.10 Although premultiplied alpha is typically the default setting, the Color pull-down menu in Output Settings can be used to generate straight alphas.

You may find these artifacts presenting themselves although you've carefully managed alpha channel interpretation on import; nonetheless, elements have black fringing. Your job depends on getting to the bottom of this. There are two basic ways this can occur:

✔ Note

Most computer-generated images are premultiplied, unless specific steps are taken to counteract the process. The Video Output section of the Output Module Settings for items in the Render Queue includes a pulldown to specify whether you render with Straight or Premultiplied alpha; by default, it is set to Premultiplied (**Figure 7.10**).

- An alpha channel is misinterpreted in Interpret Footage (see "Getting It Right on Import")

- Edge multiplication occurs within a composition, probably unintentionally, by applying a matte and adding a background (see "Solving the Problem Internally")

Unfortunately, artists who misunderstand the underlying problem will resort to all sorts of strange machinations to fix the black edge, ruining what may be a perfectly accurate edge matte.

Getting It Right on Import

A preference in Preferences > Import determines what happens when footage is imported with an alpha channel; if this is set to anything other than Ask User (the default), you may not know how alpha channels are being interpreted, particularly with the Guess option enabled (**Figure 7.11**).

Guess can be wrong if the factors it expects in a premultiplied alpha are there in a straight image or vice versa. Thus it is preferable not to trust to automation.

✔ Tip

- To see any alpha channel displayed in straight alpha mode (all pixels with any transparency displaying as pure white), choose RGB Straight from the Show Channel pull-down menu, below the Composition and Layer panels **(Alt+Shift+4/Option+Shift+4)**.

✔ Note

With a premultiplied image, After Effects attempts to guess not only the setting but also the color of the background; generally this will be black or white, but watch out for situations where a 3D artist has become creative and rendered against canary yellow or powder blue. For that reason, there is an eyedropper adjacent to the Matted with Color setting (Figure 7.11).

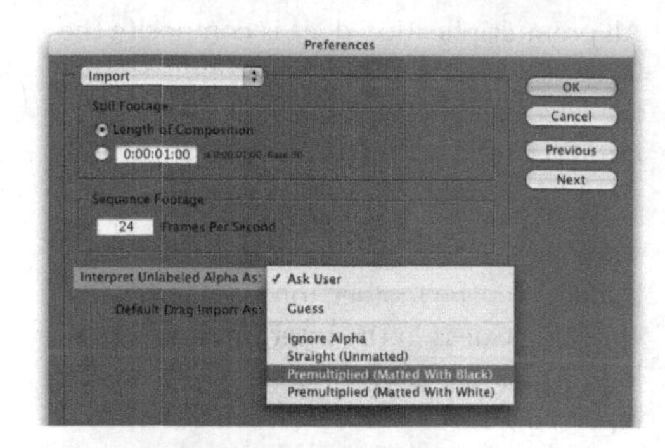

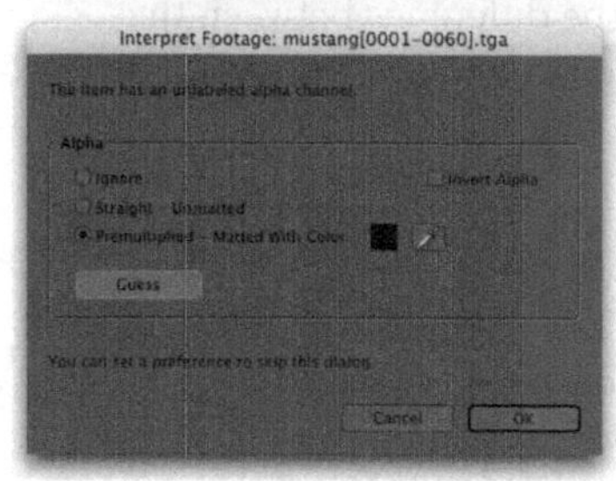

Figures 7.11a and 7.11b Import preferences default to Ask User about alpha channel interpretation (a); this presents the Interpret Footage dialog (b) which includes a button marked Guess that will typically get the setting right, or generate a beep in cases of uncertainty.

When in doubt, examine your footage without the alpha applied: If you see a solid background that is neither pure black nor white and After Effects isn't detecting it, use the eyedropper.

Fundamentally, though, as an effects compositor you need to be able to examine your images and spot the symptoms of a misinterpreted alpha: dark or bright fringing in the semi-opaque edges of your foreground.

Solving the Problem Internally

The really gnarly fact is that premultiplication errors can be introduced within a com-

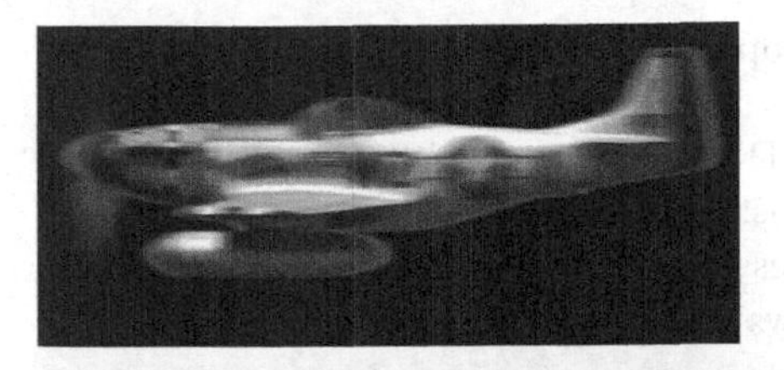

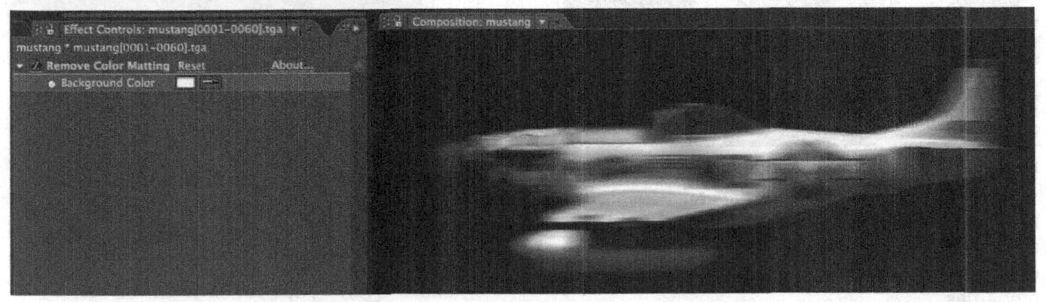

Figures 7.12a and b The plane was matted against a white background, but transparency has been applied via a track matte (the equivalent of a straight alpha), so white fringing appears against black (a). Remove Color Matting with Color set to pure white corrects the problem (b), but only when applied to a precomp of the image and matte.

position, typically by applying a matte to footage that is already somehow blended—multiplied—with a background.

✔ **Tip**

- Remove Color Matting will not work properly on a layer with a track matte; be sure to precompose the layer and its track matte prior to applying Channel > Remove Color Matting.

If you see fringing in your edges, you can try the Remove Color Matting effect (**Figures 7.12a** and **b**). This effect has one setting only, for background color, because all it does is apply the unpremultiply calculation (the antidote to premultiplication) in the same manner that it would be applied in Interpret Footage.

✔ **Tip**

- UnMult, originally created by John Knoll and available free from Red Giant Software, is useful in tricky situations in which Remove Color Matting won't do the job because there is no alpha channel. It uses the black areas of the images to create transparency and remove premultiplied black from the resulting transparent pixels.

Masks

Although hand-created and animated for the most part, masks open up all kinds of possibilities in After Effects. Masks are the principal method for defining transparency regions in a clip without regard to actual pixels because they are vector shapes. This section lays down the basics for smart use of masks.

Typical Mask Workflow

Masks are the principal non-procedural method to define transparency in a layer, using vector shapes. There are five basic automated shapes and the Pen tool (**G**) for drawing free-form. The **Q** key activates and then cycles through the basic mask shapes.

Figure 7.13 If an image is selected in the Timeline, selecting a shape tool in the toolbar and dragging in the viewer creates a mask (and so there are five basic mask shapes where previously there were two); otherwise, a new Shape layer is added with its own properties.

✔ Tip

- Shape layers are a new addition to After Effects CS3. These are directly related to masks; they are drawn with the same tools (**Figure 7.13**). Generally, if a selected layer can receive a mask, then After Effects draws a mask by default; otherwise, it creates a new Shape layer, generally to serve as a design element in a motion graphics project, rather than to define transparency, although it can be used as a track matte. More about Shape layers is found below.

A mask can be drawn in either the Composition or Layer viewer. Layer makes it easier to draw while continuing to look at the source; you can toggle Render with Masks Selected in the pull-down menu to disable all mask selections (**Figure 7.14**).

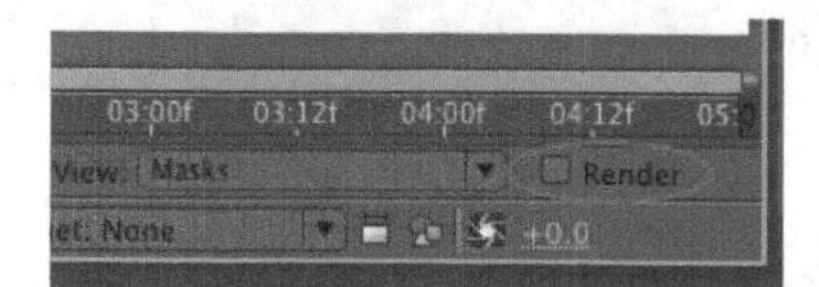

Figure 7.14 Use this toggle in the Layer viewer to disable a mask; as long as it's selected, it's still visible.

Composition allows you to see the layer in context, but if a layer is, for example, rotated in 3D space, it can be difficult to draw or adjust a mask; an ideal compromise in such cases is to open the Layer and Composition views side-by-side.

When drawing with a mask tool

- Double-click the Mask tool (in the Tools palette) to set the boundaries of the mask shape to match those of the layer.
- Use **Shift** to constrain the shape; **Ctrl/Cmd** draws the shape from the center.
- The Mask Shape dialog is useful in rare cases where your mask requires exact dimensions. Access it by clicking the underlined word "Shape" under Mask options (**M** with the layer highlighted).

✔ Tip

- Even if your mask can't be completed with one of the five preset shapes, it can be helpful to use them as a starter and then edit with the Pen tool if they are anything like what you're trying to draw.
- Double-click the shape itself to activate Free Transform mode, which enables you to offset, rotate, or scale the entire mask shape (**Figure 7.15**). As always, hold down Shift to keep the scale proportional, snap the rotation to 45-degree increments, or constrain movement to one axis.
- Highlighting a layer with a mask and pressing **MM** (the **M** key twice in rapid succession) reveals the full Mask options for that layer.
- Feather is applied to the entire mask, and is always centered around the mask path (half the amount of feather is applied inside and outside the mask). Big, soft masks are useful for all kinds of lighting, smoke, and glow effects, detailed throughout this book (**Figure 7.16**).

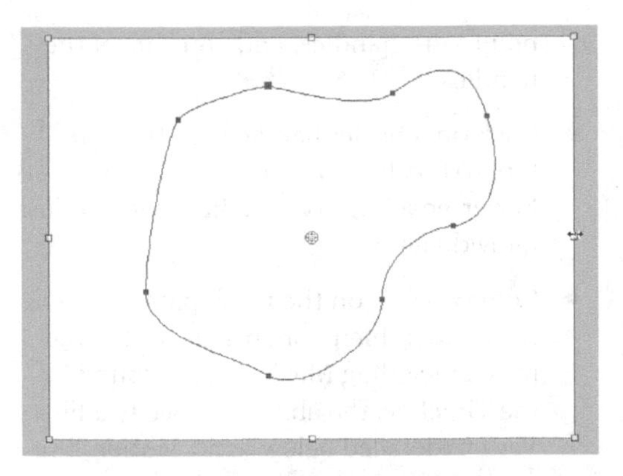

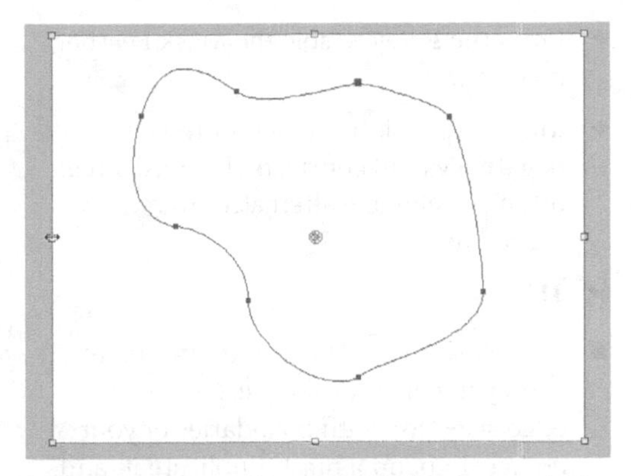

Figure 7.15 How do you flip a mask symmetrically in After Effects? Enable View > Show Grid and View Snap to Grid, then double-click the Rectangular Mask tool to create a second mask that is the exact size of the layer. Select both masks, then double-click a point to set the Free Transform tool. Now drag the handles at the image boundaries to the opposite sides, deleting the layer-sized mask when you're done.

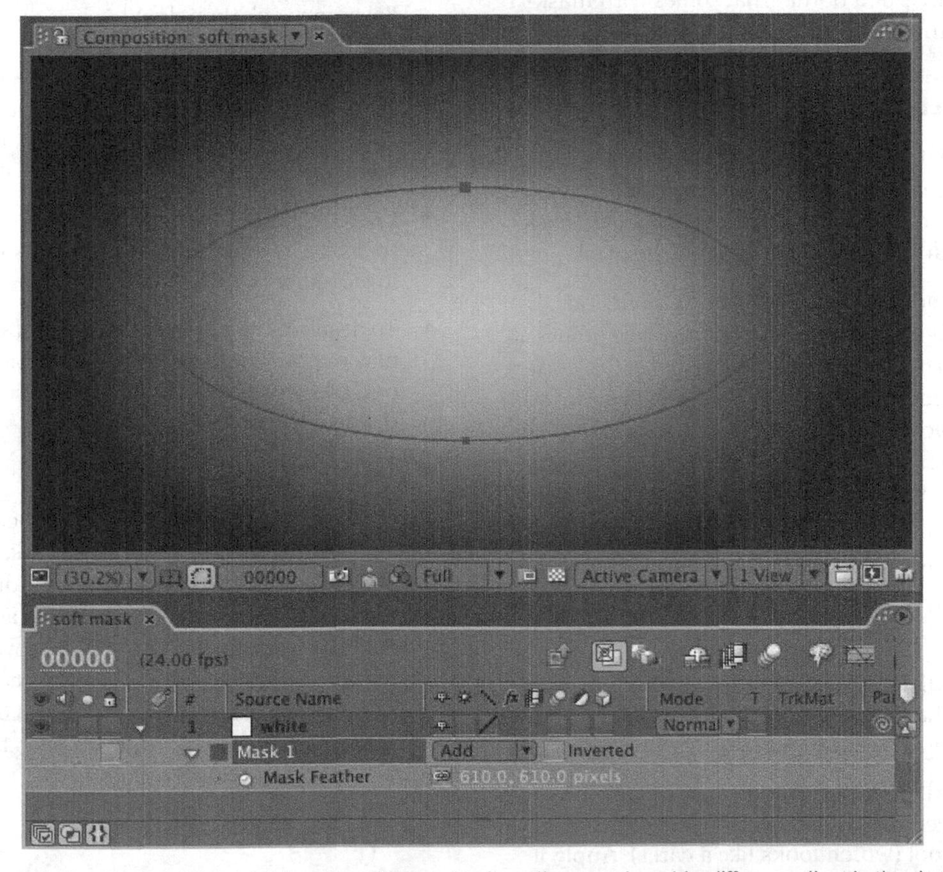

Figure 7.16 The Feather of this mask is set roughly equal to its radius, creating a big, diffuse gradient in the shape of the mask (in this case, elliptical), useful for many types of lighting effects.

- Press the **F** key to solo the Mask Feather property.
- Mask Expansion expands or (given a negative value) contracts the mask area, often a preferable alternative to redrawing a mask.

✔ Tip

- The Mask Expansion feature has many uses; you can, for example, create an edge selection with boundaries of your choice. Expand a mask, duplicate it, and set the duplicate to Subtract with a negative Mask Expansion value.

Keyboard shortcuts help eliminate a lot of the fuss and bother that comes with masking in After Effects.

Bézier Masks

By default, the Pen tool creates Bézier shapes; learn the keyboard shortcuts and you can fully edit a mask without ever clicking anywhere except right on the mask.

I sometimes draw a Bézier mask first as straight lines only, clicking to place points at key transitions and corners. Once I've completed the basic shape, with the Pen tool still active, I can go back point-by-point and edit the shape, because I have instant access to all of the mask shortcuts shown in the Pen Tool pulldown:

- Click on a point with the Pen tool active to delete it (look for the minus "-" sign in the cursor).
- Click on a segment between points with the Pen tool active to add a point (a plus sign in the cursor).
- Alt/Option-click on a point with the Pen tool to enable the Convert Vertex tool (which looks like a caret): Apply it to a point with no handles, and you can drag out to create handles. Apply it to a point with handles, and you cancel the handles.
- Click on a Bézier handle with the Pen tool to break the center point of the Bézier, enabling you to adjust the handles individually.
- Context-click on the mask path to enable the context menu of options for that mask, including Mask settings found in the Timeline, the ability to specify a First Vertex (detailed below), and Motion Blur settings for the mask, which can be toggled on or off separate from the layer itself.
- Hold down **Ctrl/Cmd** to enable the Selection tool, then double-click the shape to activate free transform. Alternatively, you can always switch to the Selection tool by pressing **V**. The **G** and **V** keys enable the Pen and Selection tools, respectively, at any time.
- Click on a point with the Pen tool active to delete it (look for the minus "=" sign in the cursor).
- To deselect the current mask and start a new one without switching tools, use **F2** or **Ctrl+Shift+A** (**Cmd+Shift+A**) to deselect the active mask.

✔ Tip

- Standard in all Adobe mask tools, including After Effects: as you draw a mask, to move a vertex into exact place after drawing it, keep the mouse button down and hold the spacebar; you can freely move the vertex until you release the spacebar, and if the mouse is still held you can drag out tangent handles. Toggle between the two modes as often as necessary.

Shape Layers

Because the focus of this book is realistic visual effects more than abstract motion graphics, the Shape tools don't get as much attention here as they might in a book that assumed you to be a visual designer rather than an effects artist. Like the Type tools, Shape isn't essential to effects work, where masks are the bread and butter.

However, if you fully understand what makes a Shape layer unique from a masked solid, it may help you discover creative uses for it (and in any case, most of us actually fall somewhere on the spectrum between pure realism and abstraction in our work). Try creating some shapes, then create a solid and with it selected, try selecting the same shapes as masks for that solid. Here's what you discover:

- There are five basic shapes, equally available as Shape layers or mask paths, with a key difference: when you create a Star, Polygon, or Rounded Rectangle as a mask its vertices can be edited as normal Béziers. A shape's points cannot themselves be edited; instead, you edit the entire shape either by adjusting existing properties in the Timeline or by adding new ones—some of which, such as Pucker & Bloat, Twist, or Zig Zag, will deform the entire shape.
- Shapes all have two basic characteristics: Fill and Stroke, each optional and editable. With a Shape active, Alt/Option-click on Fill and Stroke in the toolbar to cycle through the options (also available in the Timeline).
- Shapes can be instanced and repeated in 2D space.

The last point may be the most significant: Consider shapes when you need a repeatable pattern of some type, such as the film sprockets in **Figure 7.17**. You could create something like this using masks as well, but a Shape layer has the advantage of letting you edit a single set of parameters and apply it to the entire pattern. There is no 3D

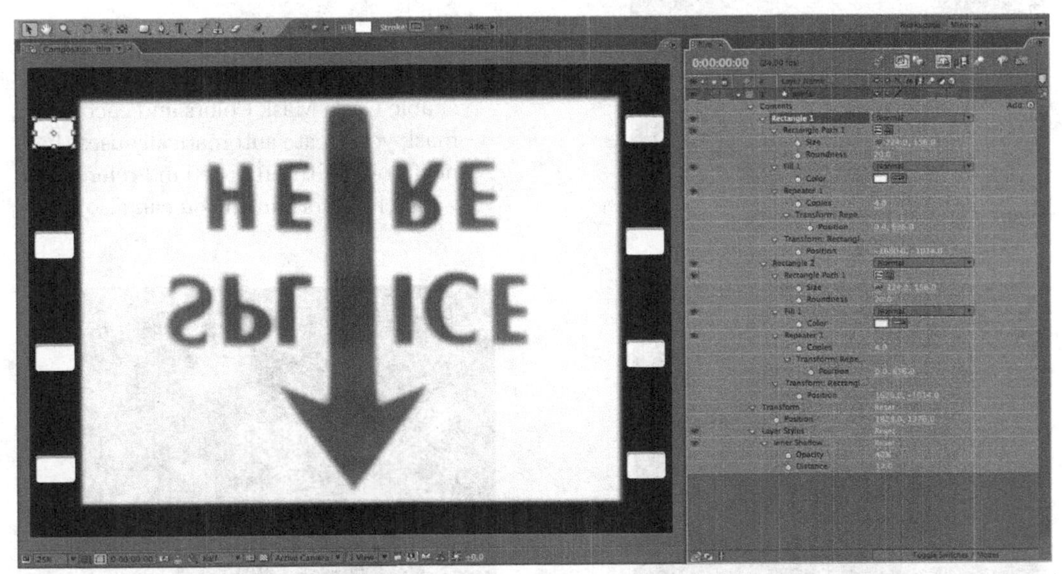

Figure 7.17 It's easy to create a repeatable pattern such as these film sprocket holes using a shape and the Repeater property, although it results in a lot of editable properties that can appear confusing. Here I've even added an Inner Shadow Layer Style to give a little feeling of depth and dimension.

repeat option—that will have to wait for a future version of the software.

Combining Multiple Masks

By default, all masks are drawn in Add mode, meaning that the contents of the mask are added to the layer selection, and the area outside all of the masks is excluded. There are other options for combining them, however; the five primary mask modes are

- **Add:** The default mode; adds the opacity values to the image as a whole, including masks higher in the stack (**Figure 7.18**).
- **Subtract:** Subtracts opacity values from areas which overlap with masks higher in the stack or from the image as a whole if no other masks precede it (**Figure 7.19**).

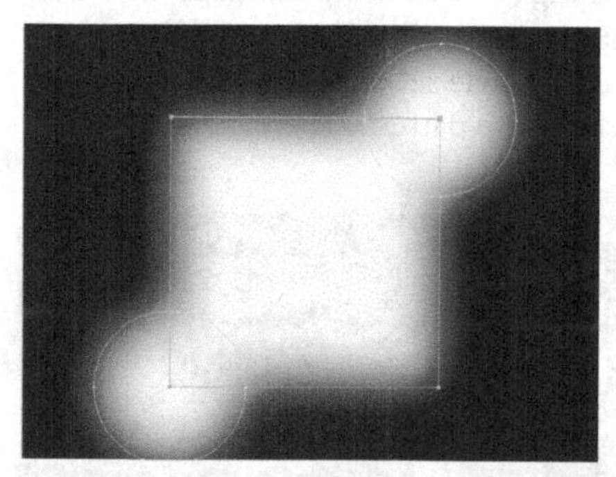

Figure 7.18 Add mode combines the luminance values of overlapping masks.

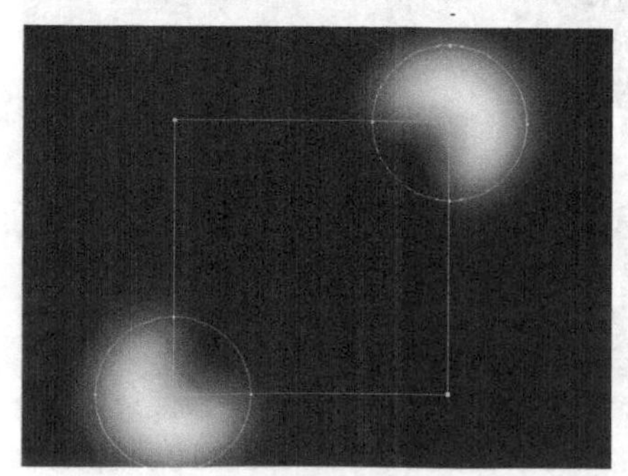

Figure 7.19 Subtract mode is the inverse of Add mode.

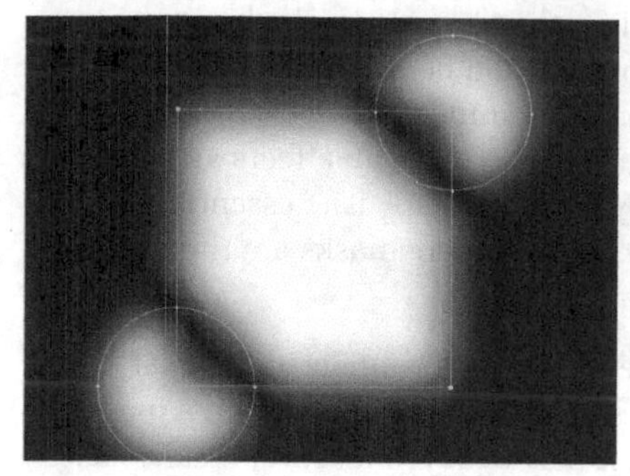

Figure 7.20 Intersect mode adds only the overlapping areas of opacity.

- **Intersect:** Combines only the areas of opacity that overlap (intersect), with masks higher in the stack (**Figure 7.20**).
- **Difference:** Subtracts overlapping areas (**Figure 7.21**).
- **None:** Has no effect on the image whatsoever; this is like turning off or disabling the mask. It can be useful as a placeholder or for effects that use masks (**Figure 7.22**).

✔ Tip

- In Preferences > User Interface Colors, enable Cycle Mask Colors and each new mask you create automatically uses the next color of the 16 listed in Preferences > Label Colors (which you can also cus-

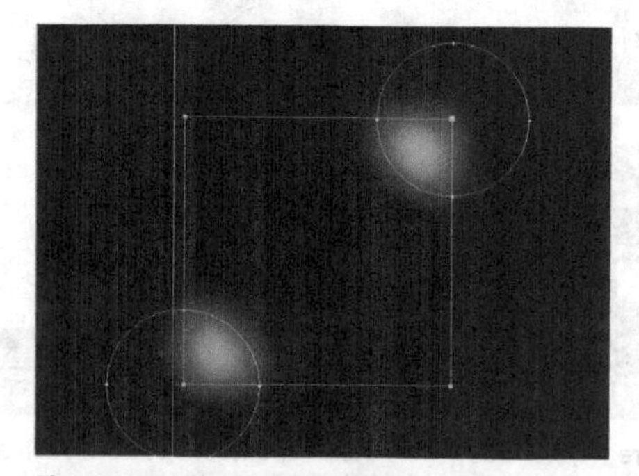

Figure 7.21 The inverse of Intersect, Difference mode subtracts overlapping areas.

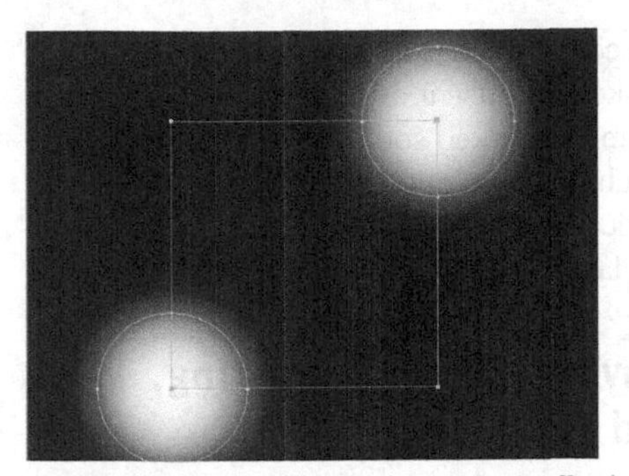

Figure 7.22 With None mode, the mask is effectively deactivated.

tomize). It's much easier to work with several masks on one layer when they're not all yellow.

Two variables change the above mask interactions in somewhat mind-bending ways. A toggle labeled Inverted sits adjacent to the mask mode pull-down menu. Inverting an Add mask is straightforward enough; all of the areas outside the mask are selected, instead of those inside. The Mask Opacity property (revealed by twirling open the mask) lets you dial back the strength of a mask; setting any mask other than the first one to 0% is like disabling it.

The behavior of Mask Opacity works a little differently for the first mask. A single Add mask set to 0% Mask Opacity causes the entire layer to disappear. That's logical, because otherwise setting that mask to, say, 50% would have to cause 50% of the area outside the mask to reappear. However, if the first mask is set to Subtract, setting Mask Opacity to 50% does just that—instead of the area inside the mask reappearing, the rest of the scene becomes 50% transparent. I call this a bug, and the development team has acknowledged that it only stays this way for backward compatibility; the workaround is to start with a full-frame mask set to Add mode, then add a Subtract mask. Generally speaking, it's easier to understand masks if the first mask is set to Add, whether it is inverted or not.

✔ Tip

- When rotoscoping it is wise to employ multiple masks, as attempting to animate a complex shape that does not move in a single direction can become cumbersome, or even impossible.

Overlapping Transparency

"Density" is traditionally a film term describing how dark (opaque) the frame of film is at a given area of the image. It is therefore the inversion of opacity or alpha values; the higher the density, the less light is transmitted. In the digital world we sometimes speak of masks and alpha channels as having "density," and overlapping semitransparent areas must be managed to avoid having the densities build up in undesirable ways.

✔ Tip

- Trouble keeping multiple masks organized? Name them in the Timeline (Return key, then type), change the color if it could be more visible, and lock masks you're not using. You can even context-click on the mask you're editing and choose Mask > Lock Other Masks, and if overlapping masks are still too much in your way, Mask > Hide Locked Masks.

When combining masks that have semitransparent areas, either because the opacity of the masks is less than 100% or, as in the examples shown here, because the edges are heavily feathered, two overlapping pixels each with 50% transparency would become fully opaque, not usually the desired behavior. That's when Lighten and Darken modes come into play.

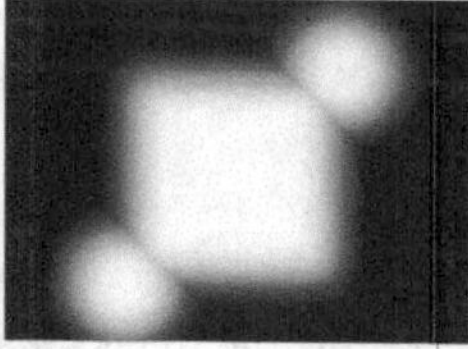

Figures 7.23a and b A Darken (a) or Lighten (b) mask uses only the darker (lower) or lighter (higher) value, respectively, for overlapping pixels.

Figures 7.23a and **b** show the result of using each of these modes; they prevent mask densities from building up the way that they do with the other modes. No pixel within the combined masks will have a value greater or lesser than the same pixel in the overlapping masks; either the lighter or the darker of the two will be represented.

Remember that masks render from top to bottom, so each mask's mode applies to its relationship with the layers above it. Thus applying these modes to the top mask in the stack has no effect.

Masks in Motion

Here are the basics to put a mask in motion.

Interpolation Basics

You can set a temporal ease on a mask keyframe (and adjust it in the Graph Editor), but there is no corresponding spatial curve to adjust, as there is with Position keyframes. Each point will travel in a linear fashion to its next keyframed position. Thus in order to precisely mask an object traveling in an arc, you must set many more keyframes than for an object traveling in a single direction.

Despite that After Effects now lets you apply expressions to a mask, there's no way to get at the translation data of the mask points directly, and thus you can't translate a group of mask keyframes together. As soon as you move, rotate, or scale it, your selection snaps to the current keyframe only.

You can instead duplicate the layer being masked and use it as an alpha track matte for an unmasked source of the same layer, in which case you're free to transform (or even motion track) the duplicate using the normal layer transforms.

Moving, Copying, Pasting, and Masks

You can freely copy a mask path from one source (a different mask, a different keyframe in the same mask animation, or even another Adobe application that uses mask paths such as Illustrator, or Photoshop) and paste it into an existing Mask Path channel, but beware of the following situational rules:

- **With no Mask Path keyframes in the source or target:** Copying the mask and pasting it to another layer automatically either creates a new mask, or applies it to any mask that is selected.
- **Source mask contains Mask Path keyframes, target has none:** Highlighting the mask (not the specific keyframes) and pasting creates a new mask as if pasting from time 0. Highlighting any or all Mask Path keyframes pastes a new mask with keyframes starting at the current time.
- **Target layer contains masks (with or without keyframes):** To paste Mask Path keyframes into a particular mask at a particular time, highlight the target mask before pasting. Highlighting the target Mask Path property highlights any keyframes and replaces them, effectively deleting the previous shape.

✔ **Note**

If the target layer has different dimensions than the source, a mask stretches to maintain its relationship to the boundaries of

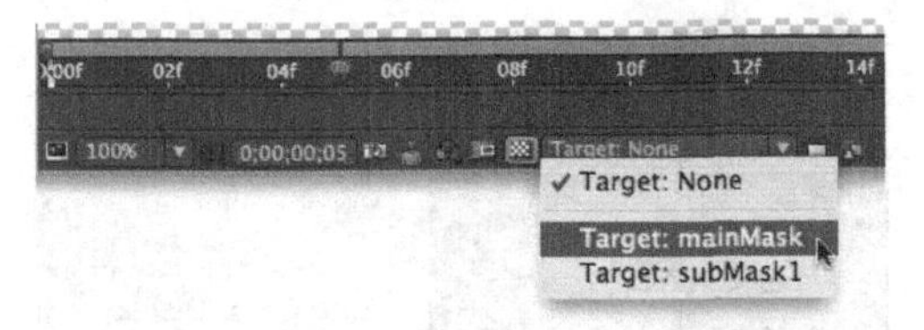

Figure 7.24 This pull-down menu along the bottom of the Layer panel makes it easy to create a new mask path that replaces the shape in the target mask. If the target mask has keyframes, After Effects creates a new keyframe wherever the new shape is drawn.

that layer when copied and pasted. This is an advantage when the target is different sized but identically proportioned.

When you need to replace a specific mask path at a specific keyframe, there is a somewhat hidden feature in the Layer panel to make it less of a blind operation than the final option above. The Target pulldown along the bottom of the window lets you choose an existing mask as the target; you can start drawing a new mask anywhere in the frame and it replaces the shape in the target mask layer (**Figure 7.24**).

✔ Note

Smart Mask Interpolation (available via a panel in the Window menu) is designed to help you transition between two radically different shapes. It's not too essential to normal masking and rotoscoping, but if you're ever out of luck with normal mask vertex interpolation, you could check it out, with the help of the online documentation.

First Vertex

When pasting in shapes or radically changing the existing mask by adding and deleting points, you may run into difficulty lining up the points. Hidden away in the Layer > Mask (or Mask context) menu, and available *only with a single vertex of the mask selected*, is the Set First Vertex command. If your mask points twist around to the wrong point during an interpolation, setting the First Vertex to two points that definitely correspond should help straighten things out. This also can be imperative for effects that rely on mask shapes, such as the Reshape tool.

Blending Modes: Compositing Beyond Selections

After Effects includes 34 blending modes, each created with a specific purpose (**Figure 7.25**)—although no one is quite sure in what context Dancing Dissolve was

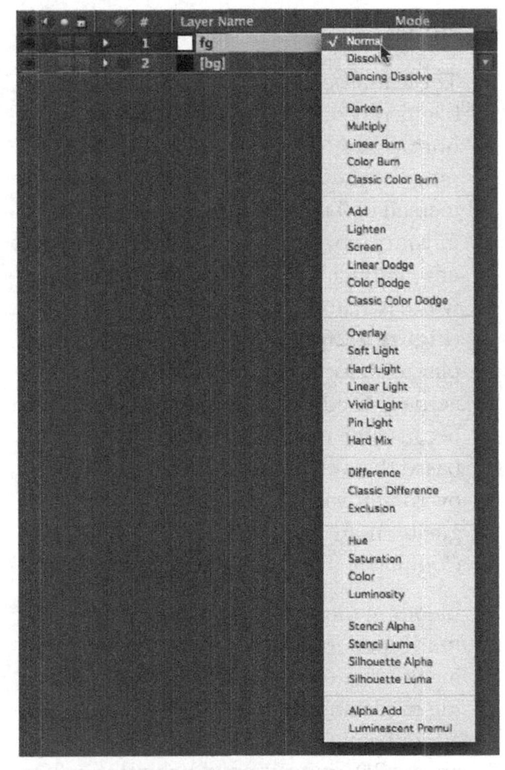

Figure 7.25 With 34 blending modes to choose from, it's virtually guaranteed that less experienced users will be easily overwhelmed and compelled to play hunt and peck. You will likely use a small subset of these 90% of the time.

ever useful (and I'm only half joking). For effects work, moreover, the majority of them are not particularly recommended.

✔ Note

Traditional optical compositing—covering all movies made prior to the 1990s—was capable of bi-packing (multiplying) and double-exposing (adding) two source frames (layers). Many sophisticated effects films were completed using only these two "blending modes."

So how do you tell which are the useful ones? Once you understand how your options work, you can make informed compositing decisions instead of relying on trial and error.

✔ Notes

These mathematical descriptions of blended pixel values use a color range normalized to 1; in other words, the full range of pixel values is described as 0 to 1 instead of 0 to 255, as it typically appears in your color controls. A medium gray on any channel is 0.5 instead of 128, pure white is 1, and pure black is 0 (**Figure 7.26**). This makes it much simpler to show the calculations that are actually used to create the blended pixels, because the internal math typically is based this way. For information about overbright values, which have a value greater than 1, see Chapter 16, "32 Bit HDR Compositing and Color Management."

Blending modes are all based on mathematical operations for combining pixels in the layer containing the given blending mode and the pixels behind it—either below it in the stack, if all the layers are 2D, or positioned behind it in 3D space, if all the layers are 3D.

To help you understand what the various blending modes are doing, **Figures 7.27** through 7.33 blend a grayscale gradient over a fully saturated background. Contextual examples using these blending modes follow in the next section.

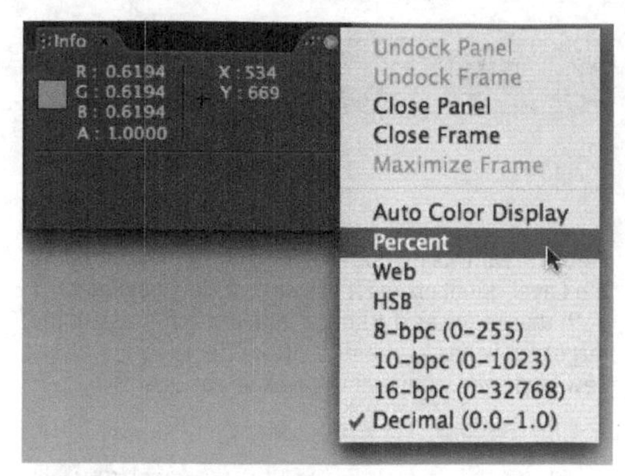

Figure 7.26 The Info panel can display pixel values in several optional modes (accessed via the panel menu). Shown here are decimal values with the cursor on medium gray. Visible decimal values are "normalized" to the range of 0.0 to 1.0, which makes calculations more straightforward than 0 to 255, the standard 8-bit range (or the even more obtuse 0 to 32768 for 16-bit). Select a color mode for the Info palette via its wing menu; whatever mode you select is thereafter also used by the Adobe Color Picker.

Add and Screen

Add and Screen modes both brighten the foreground image while making darker pixels transparent. Screen yields a subtler blend than Add in normal video color space, but

Figure 7.27 Blending in this figure is set to Normal for purposes of comparison with those that follow.

Figures 7.28a, b, c and d Add mode (a) takes the source foreground element, the fire shot against a black background (b), and adds its pixel values channel by channel to the background (c), causing the pure black pixels to disappear completely (d).

does not work correctly with linear color (details in Chapter 16).

Add mode is every bit as simple as it sounds; the formula is

$$\text{newPixel} = A + B$$

where A is a pixel from the foreground layer and B is a background pixel. The result is clipped at 1 for 8- and 16-bit pixels.

Add is incredibly useful with what After Effects calls a Linearized Working Space, where it perfectly re-creates the optical effect of combining light values from two images. It is useful for laying fire and explosion elements shot in negative space (against black) into a scene, adding noise or grain to an element, or any other element that is made up of light and texture (**Figures 7.28a, b, c**, and **d**).

✔ **Note**

Linear Dodge and Add are identical blending modes; the former is merely Photoshop's term for the latter.

Screen mode has an influence similar to Add mode's, but via a slightly different formula. The pixel values are inverted, multiplied together, and the result is inverted:

✔ **Note**

In Screen mode, fully white pixels stay white, fully black pixels stay black, but a midrange pixel (0.5) takes on a brighter value (0.75), just not as bright as would be with Add (1).

$$\text{newPixel} = 1-((1-A) * (1-B))$$

Once you discover the truth about working linearized with a 1.0 gamma, you understand that Screen is a workaround, a compromise for how colors blend in normal video space. Screen is most useful in situations where Add would blow out the highlights too much—glints, flares, glow passes, and so on (**Figure 7.29**).

Multiply

Multiply is another mode whose math is as elementary as it sounds; it uses the formula

Figure 7.29 The difference between Screen and Add (Figure 3.28) may be subtle in printed figures until you look closely; notice there's less brightness in the "hottest" areas of the fire.

✔ **Note**

To fully comprehend the difference between Add and Screen requires an understanding of a linearized working space, which is offered in Chapter 16.

newPixel = A * B

Keep in mind that this formula uses color values between 0 and 1 to correspond to the colors on your monitor. Multiplying two images together, therefore, actually has the effect of reducing midrange pixels and darkening an image overall, although pixels that are full white in both images remain full white.

Multiply or Add has the inverse effect of Screen mode, darkening the midrange values of one image with another. It emphasizes dark tones in the foreground without replacing the lighter tones in the background, useful to create for texture, shadow, or dark fog (**Figure 7.30**).

Overlay and the Light Modes

✔ **Note**

Overlay and the various Light modes do not work properly with values above 1.0, as can occur in 32 bpc linearized working spaces (see Chapter 16).

Overlay uses Screen or Multiply, depending on the background pixel value. Above a threshold of 50% gray (or .5 in normalized terms), Screen occurs, and below the threshold, Multiply. Hard Light operates similarly, instead using the top layer to determine whether to screen or multiply, so the two are inverse effects.

✔ **Note**

Reversing layer order and swapping Overlay for Hard Light yields an identical result.

Figure 7.30 Dark smoke (actually a grayscale fractal noise pattern) is multiplied over the background, darkening the areas that are dark in either the foreground or background further.

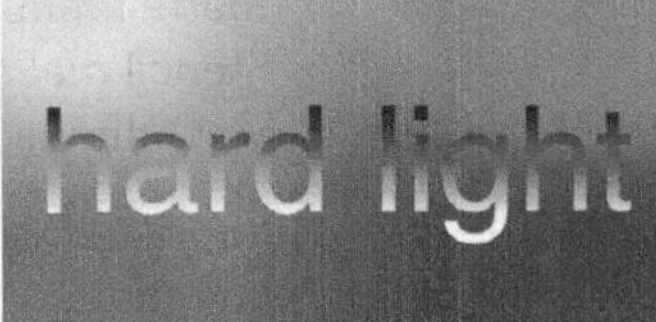

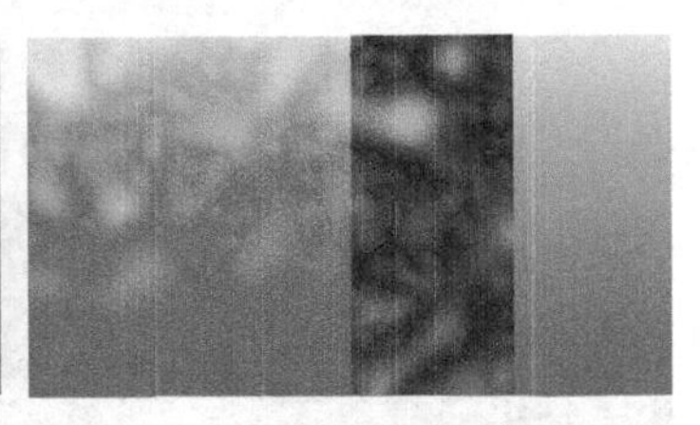

Figure 7.31 Overlay and its inverse, Hard Light, are useful for combining color and texture. Here, an instant lava lamp texture was created using the components shown at the right: a solid with Fractal Noise applied set to Overlay mode on top of a red-to-yellow gradient.

These modes, along with Linear and Vivid Light, can be most useful for combining a layer that is predominantly color with another layer that is predominantly luminance, or contrast detail (**Figure 7.31**). Much of the lava texturing in the Level 4 sequence of *Spy Kids* 3-D was created by using Hard Light to combine a hand-painted color heat map with moving fractal noise patterns.

Difference

Difference inverts a background pixel in proportion to the foreground pixel. It can help you line up two identical layers, which is helpful while working even if you rarely use it for final output (**Figure 7.32**).

HSB and Color Modes

The Hue, Saturation, and Brightness modes each combine one of these values (H, S, or B) from the foreground layer with the other two from the background layer. Color takes both the hue and saturation from the top layer, using only the luminance (or brightness of) from the underlying background (**Figure 7.33**).

These modes are often useful at an Opacity setting below 100%, to combine source HSB values with ones that you choose.

✔ **Note**

Stencil Alpha and Silhouette Alpha are useful to create custom edge mattes as

Figure 7.32 The selection area in the foreground is identical to the background; when they are perfectly aligned, all pixels cancel out to black.

Figure 7.33 Setting a deep-blue-colored solid to Color mode and overlaying it on the plate footage has the effect of tinting the colors in the image blue. Artistic uses of this mode are explored in Chapter 17, "Light."

well as a light wrap effect, demonstrated in Chapter 17.

Stencil, Silhouette, Preserve Transparency

Commonly overlooked, Stencil and Silhouette blending modes operate only on the alpha channel of the composition. The layer's alpha or luminance values become a matte for all layers below it in the stack. Stencil makes the brightest pixels opaque, and Silhouette the darkest.

Suppose instead you have a foreground layer that is meant to be opaque only where the underlying layers are opaque, as in **Figure 7.34**. The small highlighted checkbox, labeled Preserve Underlying Transparency, makes this happen, much to the amazement of many who've wished for this feature and not realized it was already there.

Alpha Add and Luminescent Premultiply

Alpha Add and Luminescent Premultiply are blending modes that affect semitransparent edge pixels only.

Just as two overlapping layers with 50% opacity are not fully opaque when layered together (see "Opacity"), the same behavior applies to semitransparent pixels. Just as

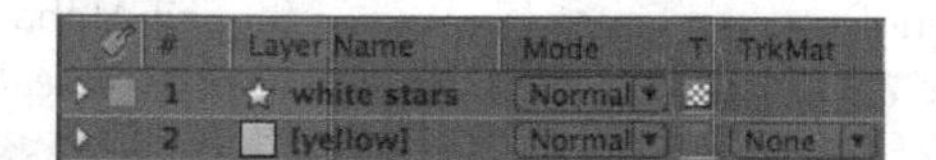

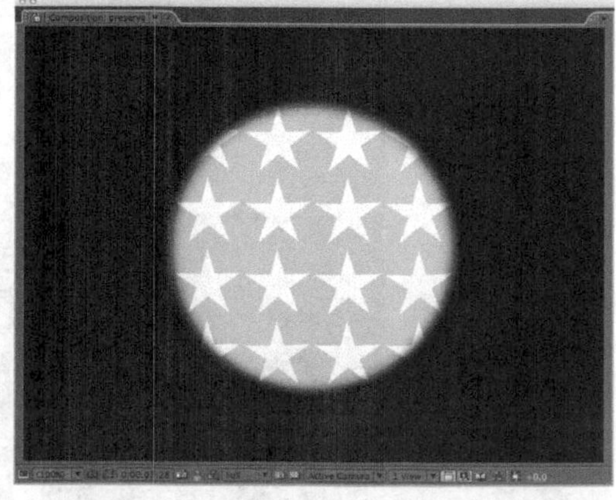

Figure 7.34 Among the hardest-to-find and most-easily-forgotten features in the Timeline is the Preserve Underlying Transparency toggle, highlighted. This recreates behavior familiar to Photoshop users, where a layer's own transparency only applies where it intersects with that of the underlying layer, one more way to avoid track mattes or precomping.

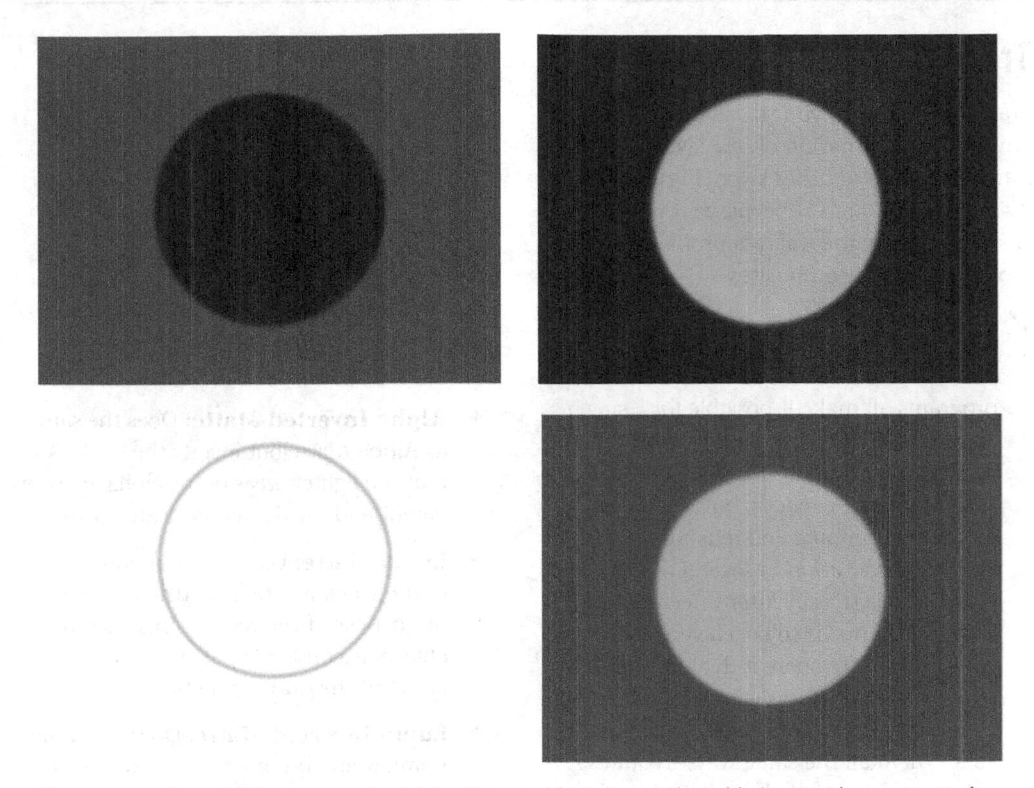

Figures 7.35a through d It seems as though matting an object over another with the exact inverse matte (a, b) would result in a fully opaque image. Instead, edge pixels form a semitransparent halo (c). Alpha Add does just what the title implies, adding the alpha values together so that inverse pixels add up to 100% transparency throughout the image (d).

the name implies, Alpha Add directly adds transparency pixels, so, for example, two 50% opaque pixels combine to become 100% opaque (**Figures 7.35a** through **d**).

✔ Tip

- Alpha Add is useful when recombining two layers that have been matted from a single object.

Why would you combine a layer with itself, inverting the alpha? You probably wouldn't. But you might combine two layers with overlapping transparency that would require this method—for example, two parts of the same layer.

Luminescent Premultiply is one method to remove premultiplication on the fly from source footage, retaining bright values in edge pixels that are otherwise clipped. Premultiplication over black causes all semitransparent pixels to become darker; removing it can cause them to appear dimmer than they should.

✔ Tip

- Luminescent premultiply can be useful in cases where an element with transparency has been created against a black background within After Effects, bypassing the opportunity to remove premultiplication on import.

Track Mattes

Track mattes allow you to use the alpha or luminance information of one layer as the transparency of another layer (**Figure 7.36**). It's a simple enough concept, yet one that is absolutely fundamental as a problem-solving tool for complex composites.

✔ Close-Up

Share a Matte Node-based compositing programs all make it possible for a single node to provide transparency to as many others as is needed. After Effects also has a one-to-many capacity, but it generally means precomping and reusing the nested composition in several places. The point here is that in After Effects, each track matte needs to be a layer in the composition. To share it dynamically among several layers—allowing you to change the matte and have the change affect them all the same way—requires either that the matte be precomposed and all the changes made in the precomp, or that you use expressions to link essential properties together (this being the more complicated and limited approach, but one that avoids precomping).

The perceptual difference between an alpha channel and a track matte isn't, for the most part, too difficult to grasp. In both cases, you have pixels with a value (in 8-bit color space) between 0 and 255, whether a grayscale alpha channel or three channels of color. With color, the three channels are simply averaged together to make up a single grayscale alpha. With 16 and even 32 bpc, it's finer increments in the same range.

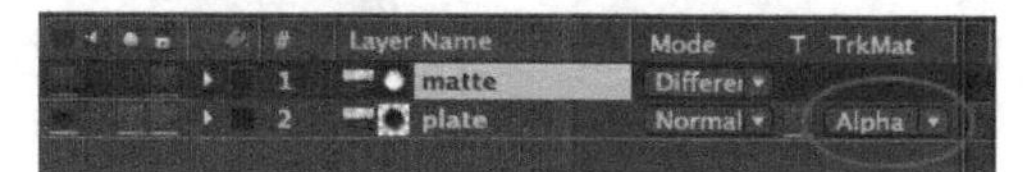

Figure 7.36 The alpha of layer 1 is set as the alpha of layer 2 via the highlighted pull-down menu. The small icons to the left indicate which is the image and which is the matte.

To set a track matte, place the layer that contains the transparency data directly above its target layer in the Timeline and choose one of the four options from the Track Matte pull-down menu:

- **Alpha Matte:** Uses the alpha channel of the track matte layer as if it were the alpha of the underlying target layer
- **Alpha Inverted Matte:** Does the same as Alpha Matte but inverts the result, so that the lighter areas of the alpha are transparent and the darker areas are opaque
- **Luma Matte:** Uses the luminance data of the track matte layer (the relative brightness of the red, green, and blue channels combined) as if it were the alpha of the underlying target layer
- **Luma Inverted Matte:** Does the same as Luma Matte but inverts the result, so that the lighter areas of the alpha are transparent and the darker areas are opaque

By default, visibility of the track matte layer is disabled when you activate it from the layer below by choosing one of these four modes, which is generally desirable. Some clever uses of track mattes leave them on; for example, by matting out the bright areas of the image and turning on the matte, setting it to Add mode, you could naturally brighten those areas even more.

Track mattes solve a lot of compositing problems. They also help overcome limitations of After Effects. For example, it's not possible to track a mask in After Effects. But it is possible to apply the mask to a track matte instead, and then to track that layer (instead of the mask itself). Any procedural matte that you create can be applied as a track matte rather than directly on a layer; this allows you, for example, to create a matte with Keylight without having it change the color of the matted layer.

Gotchas

Even an advanced user has to pay attention when working in a composition with track mattes. They are exceptional in certain ways that can bite you. Unlike parented layers, track mattes do not stay connected with their target if moved around; instead, if you move a layer that has a track matte set to it without moving the matte along with it, the layer will use whatever layer is above it. Move it to the top of the composition and it will use no track matte until you add another image above it, but at that point you may have forgotten all about having applied the track matte in the first place.

After Effects does at least help you in certain ways. Duplicate a layer (**Ctrl+D/Cmd+D**) with a track matte activated and it moves up two layers, above the track matte layer. Include the track matte when you duplicate and it also moves up two layers, so layer order is preserved (**Figure 7.37**).

✔ Note

If the layer to which the track matte is applied already has an alpha channel, then the new selection area created by the track matte is opaque only in the areas that intersect.

Render Order

Render order when using track mattes can be tricky. In most cases, adjustments and effects that you apply to the matte layer are calculated prior to creating the target matte, but in other cases you must first precompose for applied effects and adjustments to activate prior to application of the track matte.

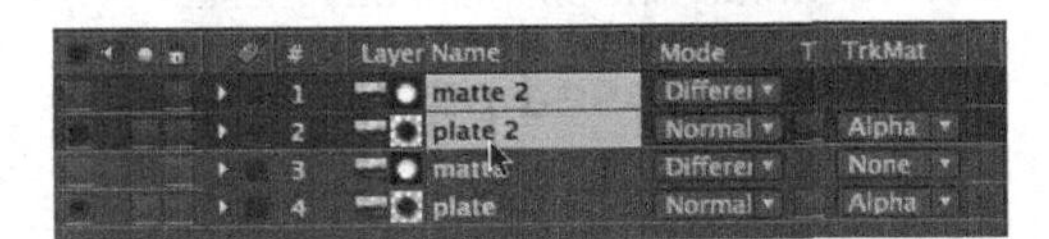

Figure 7.37 Select and duplicate the layers from Figure 3.41, and the two new layers leapfrog above to maintain the proper image/matte relationship.

✔ Note

If there seems to be some doubt as to whether edits you are applying to the track matte are properly affecting the target, be scientific about it. First crank up the effect applied to the track matte, so it's obvious whether it is applied or not. If it's not, you must precompose the track matte layer; this forces it to render prior to track matting.

And what happens when you apply a track matte to another track matte? Generally speaking, this will not work and the practice should be avoided. It will work in some cases, however, and the user interface does not prohibit doing so. A better idea is certainly to precompose the first instance of track matting and apply the second track matte to that nested composition.

The next chapter looks in depth at solving issues related to render order such as these; you'll begin to see how to use the Timeline as a visual problem-solving tool for such situations.

Mask Essentials

A *mask* is a shape, or path, that you create in a layer. You can draw a mask manually with a tool, define it numerically using the Mask Shape dialog box, or copy it from Adobe Illustrator or Photoshop. A mask can be a closed shape (such as a circle) or an open path (such as a curved line). Masks are essential to compositing images and to creating a number of other effects.

A *closed mask* modifies or creates an alpha channel—which, as you recall, defines the opaque and transparent areas of an image. The image within the masked area remains visible; the area outside the mask reveals the layers below. An open path, in contrast, consists of a curve, or path, with two endpoints. By itself, an open path can't define areas of opacity, but it can be used to achieve a variety of other effects. For example, you can use the Stroke effect to trace a mask with a color. Or, you can paste a mask path into the Comp panel to use it as a motion path. A mask can also define a curved baseline for path text. You can apply these techniques to both open and closed masks, but you can imagine how an open mask is sometimes the more appropriate choice.

The rest of this chapter is devoted to the fundamentals of mask making. You can apply what you learn in other chapters to animate mask properties, apply effects to masks, and combine masks with other techniques, such as layer modes. Later, you'll discover that the same tools that apply masks to layers can also be used to define a new type of layer, graphical objects called *shape layers*.

Understanding Masks

Masks are shapes you can apply to a layer to define areas of opacity or to specify a path on which to base other effects. For example, you can have text follow a mask path or apply effects to masks to generate graphical elements.

After Effects includes a number of tools for creating masks, which can be closed shapes or open paths. You can control the contour of mask paths manually using Bézier curves or allow After Effects to calculate curves automatically with RotoBézier curves.

Remember that you always apply a mask to a layer. You can use many of the same tools and techniques to create a new layer, called a shape layer. For creating certain graphical elements, shape layers have some advantages over using masks.

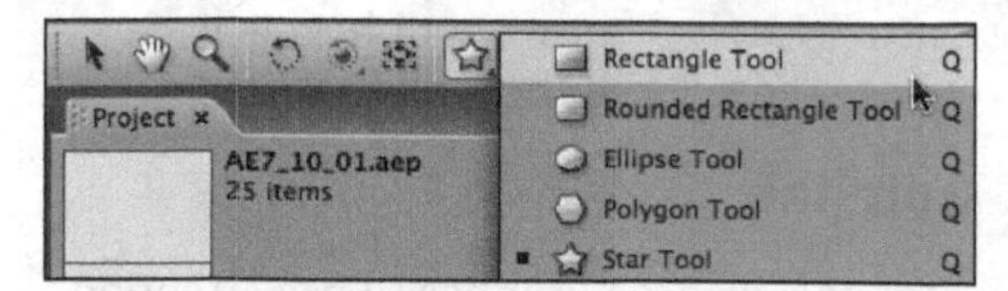

Figure 7.38 Press and hold on the current Shape tool to reveal an extended panel of Shape tools...

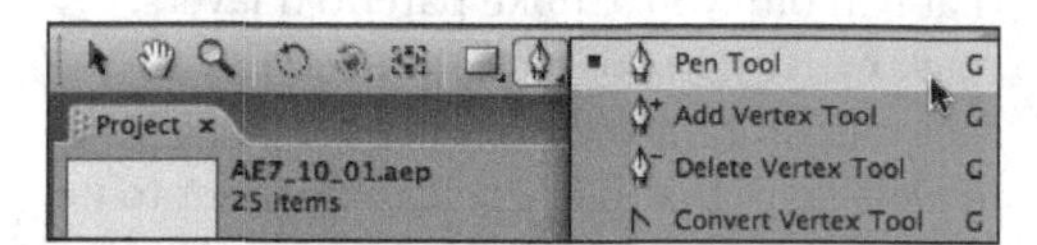

Figure 7.39 ...or the current Pen tool to show various Pen tools.

Mask creation tools

The Tools panel contains several tools for creating and modifying masks, but they fall into two main categories: Shape tools and Pen tools.

Shape tools allow you to draw some common geometric shapes with just a single drag of the mouse (**Figure 7.38**). Pressing certain keyboard modifiers as you drag lets you customize the shape. For example, you can constrain an ellipse's dimensions to a perfect circle or specify the number of points in a star.

Pen tools let you create custom shapes defined by Bézier curves used by many drawing programs, such as Illustrator. To create custom shapes using a simpler procedure, you can enable the RotoBézier option (**Figure 7.39**). You can also use the Pen tools to modify the shape of any mask.

Open and closed paths

Masks can be closed shapes or open paths.

Closed masks—Strictly speaking, the term *mask* refers to a closed shape that defines areas of opacity. You can draw closed paths

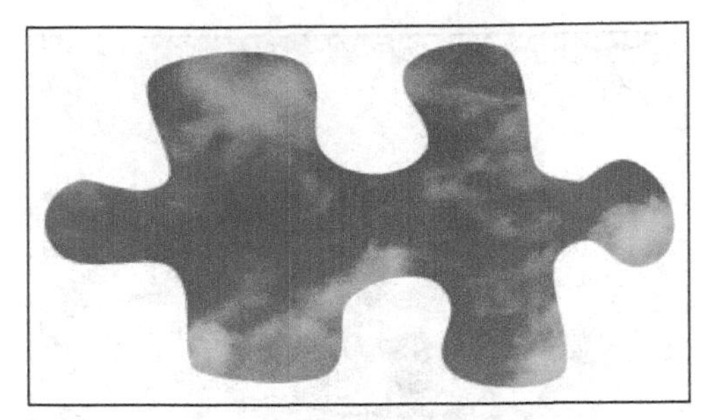

Figure 7.40 A closed path creates a typical mask, which defines the opaque areas of the layer image.

with any of the drawing tools (**Figure 7.40**). By default, the interior of a closed mask shape defines the opaque area of a layer; the exterior defines transparency. However, you can manipulate the transparency numerous ways.

Open masks—You can create open paths with the Pen tool, or you can open a closed path by using a menu command. Open paths aren't used as masks per se, but they can serve as the basis for path text and path-based effects (**Figure 7.41**). For example, they can serve as the baseline for text or be pasted into a motion path.

Bezier and RotoBézier curves

It can be useful to describe the contour of a mask as a path. When creating a path, you

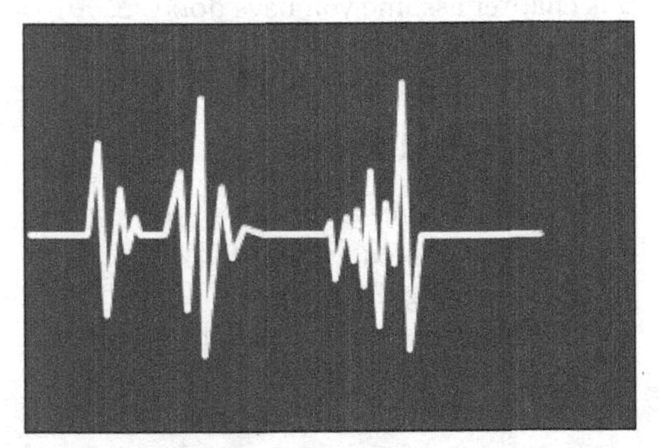

Figure 7.41 An open path doesn't create a mask per se, but it can be used for other effects, such as creating stroked lines. Open paths can also be used to create motion paths.

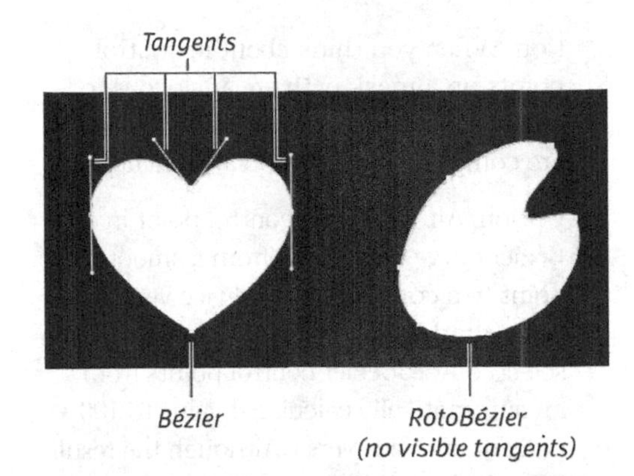

Figure 7.42 It's easier to create shapes like the palette using the RotoBézier option, but manually adjusting tangents in a Bézier shape lets you create cusps like the ones at the top and bottom of the heart.

specify the position of control points (aka vertices), which are connected by line segments automatically. You can always control the position of each vertex, but the amount of control you have over the connecting segments depends on whether you're using Bézier or RotoBézier curves (**Figure 7.42**).

Bézier curves—In a standard mask, each line segment is a Bézier curve that you control manually. In a Bézier curve, each vertex can have direction lines, or tangents. The length and angle of the direction line at each end of a segment determines the shape of the curve.

RotoBézier curves—When you create a mask using the RotoBézier option, you set vertices only, not direction lines. After Effects calculates the curves automatically; however, you can change the relative amount of each curve by adjusting each point's *tension*. It's often easier to create masks using the RotoBézier option, but you can't create certain types of shapes, such as cusps.

✔ Tips

- Bézier curves should be a familiar concept by now; the same math used to calculate curves also applies to keyframe interpolation. When you think about it, control points on a mask path are analogous to keyframes, and line segments on a mask are comparable to interpolated values.

- Option/Alt-clicking a control point in a Bézier curve converts it from a smooth point to a corner point and vice versa; the same shortcut changes the tension of selected RotoBezier control points from an automatically calculated value to 100 percent and vice versa. Although the result is equivalent, this action doesn't convert the mask from one type to another.

Viewing Masks in the Layer and Comp Panels

Although you mask a layer, you can create and work with masks not only in the Layer panel but in the Composition panel as well. The panel you use will depend on the task at hand as well as your personal preference. A Layer panel shows masks in the context of a single layer, letting you view the image outside the masked areas (**Figure 7.43**). In addition, the Layer panel shows you the layer before any property changes (Scale, Rotation, and so on) are applied. In contrast, the Composition panel shows only the masked portions of a layer and places them in the context of all the layers that are visible at the current time (**Figure 7.44**). By the time you're able to view a layer in the Comp panel, Mask, Effect, Transform, and 3D properties have all been applied.

Figure 7.43 The Layer panel shows masks in the context of the layer; it also lets you see the image outside the mask.

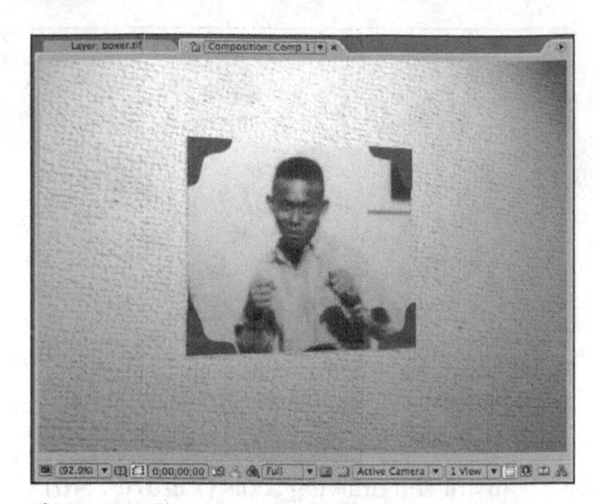

Figure 7.44 The Comp panel shows the layer after masks and other property changes have taken effect.

When you want to create or modify a mask in the Comp panel, you must select the layer that contains the mask. Tasks throughout this chapter assume you have done so.

Viewing Masks in the Layer Outline

Each mask you create appears in the layer outline of the Timeline panel under the Mask property heading. The Target pull-down menu of the Layer panel also lists the layer's masks. The most recent mask appears at the top of the stacking order (**Figure 7.45**).

When you expand the Mask property heading, it reveals four properties: Mask Shape, Mask Feather, Mask Opacity, and Mask

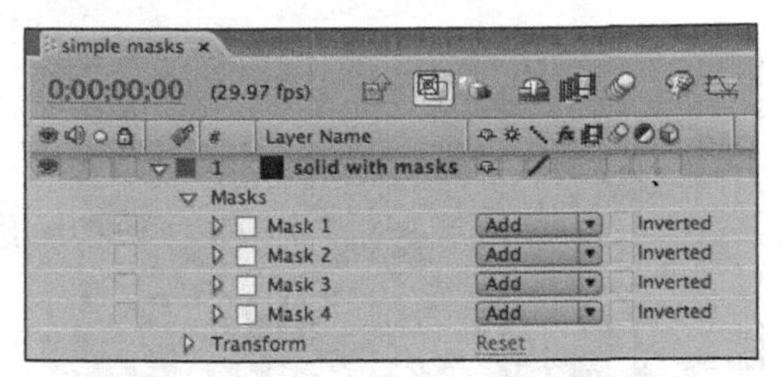

Figure 7.45 Masks appear in the layer outline in the order they were created. Expanding a mask reveals several properties: Shape, Feather, Opacity, and Expansion.

Expansion. The following sections deal with these properties as well as other ways to control layer masks.

Because you can rename, reorder, and lock masks just like layers, that information won't be covered here (**Figure 7.46**). (See Chapter 5, to learn the analogous procedures for layers).

You can also hide and apply motion blur to masks much as you can with a layer as a whole. But instead of clicking a button in the Timeline panel, you access these commands in the Layer > Mask menu (**Figure 7.47**). For example, masks don't have a video switch, but you can hide locked masks via the Layer > Mask > Hide Locked Masks command. Again, these commands won't be covered in detail here.

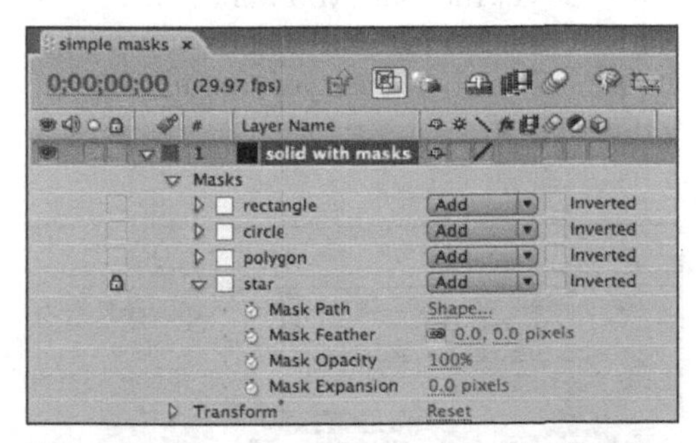

Figure 7.46 You can rename, reorder, and lock masks just like layers. Here, the default names have been replaced with more descriptive names, and the "star" mask has been locked.

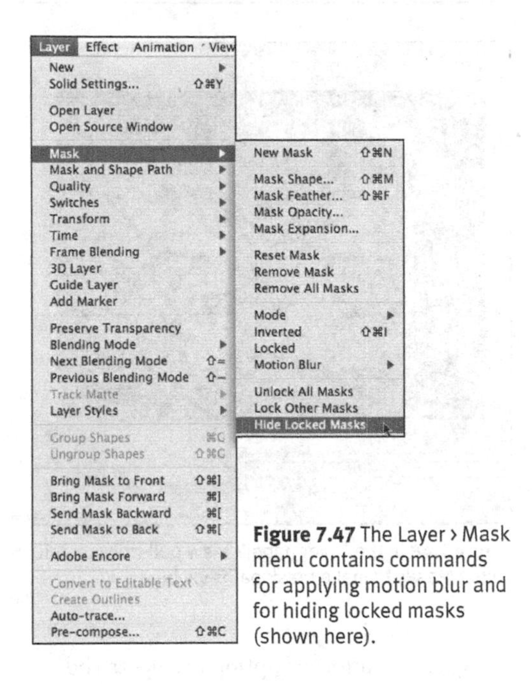

Figure 7.47 The Layer › Mask menu contains commands for applying motion blur and for hiding locked masks (shown here).

✔ Tip

- Although locked and hidden masks are invisible in the Layer panel, their masking effect can still be seen in the Comp panel's image.

Hiding and Showing Mask Paths

Because the Layer and Comp panels serve several purposes, sometimes you'll want to hide the mask paths from view. When you want to work with the layer masks, you can make them visible again. Creating a new mask reveals the masks for the selected layer automatically.

To view and hide masks in the Layer panel:

1. View a layer in a Layer panel.
2. In the Layer panel's View pull-down menu, select Masks to make mask paths visible (**Figure 7.48**).

Figure 7.48 In the Layer panel's View pull-down menu, select Masks to make mask paths visible.

Selecting another option deselects the Masks option.

To view and hide masks in the Composition panel:

◆ In the Comp panel, click the View Masks button (**Figure 7.49**).

Mask paths for selected layers can be viewed and edited in the Composition panel (**Figure 7.50**). Deselect the View Masks button to hide mask paths.

✔ Tips

- You can hide locked masks only by choosing Layer > Mask > Hide Locked Masks. Although invisible in the Layer panel, locked and hidden masks still function in the Comp panel.

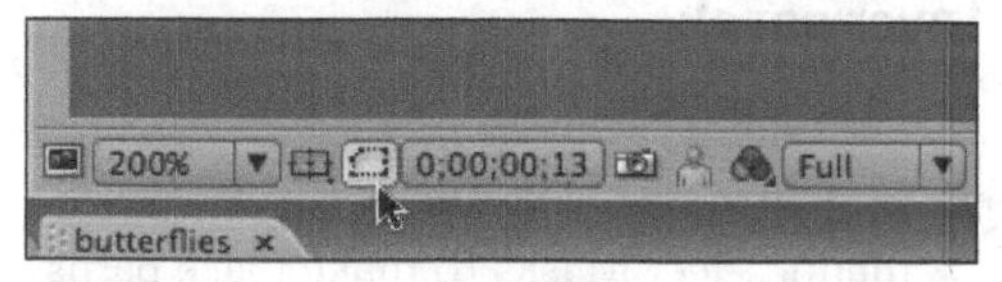

Figure 7.49 In the Comp panel, click the View Masks button...

Figure 7.50 ...to reveal the selected layer's masks.

- By default, mask paths appear yellow. By double-clicking a mask's color swatch in the timeline, you can assign a unique color to help distinguish one mask from another.
- You can even have After Effects assign each subsequent mask a different color automatically by selecting the Cycle Mask Colors option in the User Interface Colors pane of the Preferences dialog box.

Targeting Masks

You can create as many as 127 masks for each layer. The Target pull-down menu at the bottom of the Layer panel provides one way to select the mask you want to use. Note that the Target pull-down menu appears only when the layer contains one or more masks.

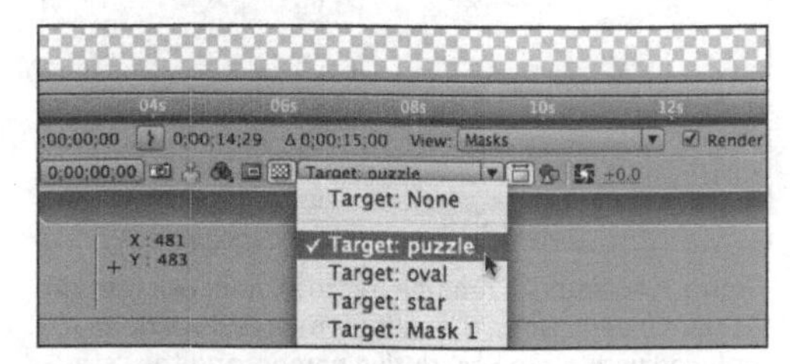

Figure 7.51 In the Target menu, choose a mask you want to select, or target, for changes.

Figure 7.52 The targeted mask appears selected, with solid square vertices. If you create a new mask shape, it replaces the targeted mask.

To choose the target mask:

1. View a layer containing one or more masks in a Layer panel.
2. At the bottom of the Layer panel, choose a mask from the Target pull-down menu (**Figure 7.51**):
   - ▲ Choose None to create a new mask without changing an existing mask.
   - ▲ Choose the name of an existing mask to target that mask for changes.

   The mask you choose appears selected (**Figure 7.52**).

✔ Tip

- Don't forget: To create an additional mask in the same Layer panel, make sure the Target pull-down menu is set to None. Otherwise, the new mask *replaces* the target mask.

Creating Masks Using Shape Tools

You can create simple mask shapes quickly with the Shape tools. On the other hand, a simple rectangle or ellipse can serve as the starting point of a more complex shape. As you'll see in later sections, you can easily alter any mask's shape. In addition, you can

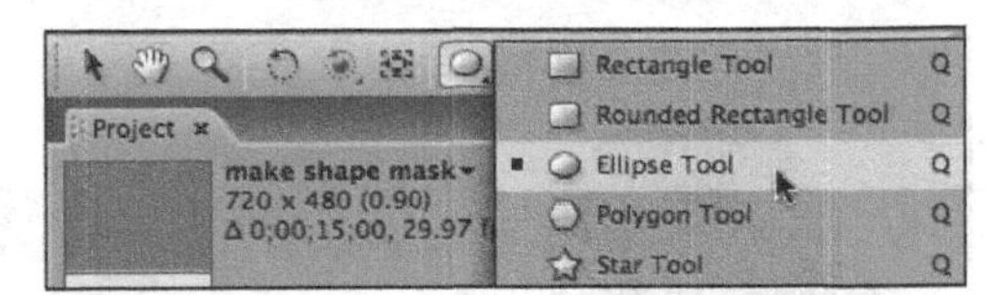

Figure 7.53 In the Tools panel, choose a Shape tool.

effectively combine masks using mask modes.

To draw a shape mask:

1. View the layer you want to mask in a Layer panel, or select it in the Composition panel.

   Dragging a Shape tool in the Comp panel when a layer is not selected results in a new shape layer, not a mask.
2. In the Tools panel, select a Shape tool (**Figure 7.53**).
3. In the Layer or Comp panel, drag to define the position and size of the mask on the layer.
4. To modify the shape as you drag, press the appropriate keyboard modifier (**Figures 7.54–7.56**).

   For a list of modifiers and their results, see **Table 7.1**.

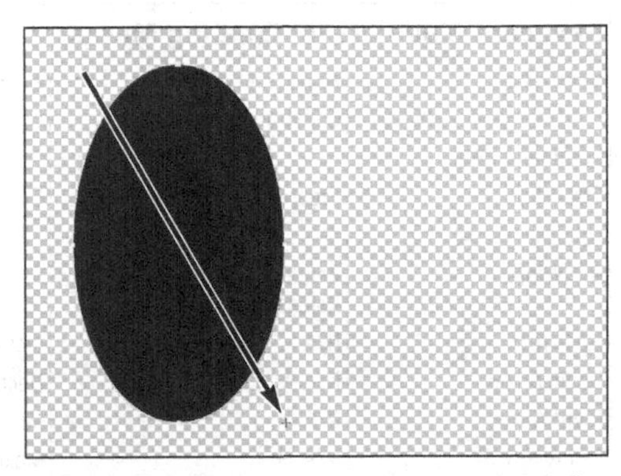

Figure 7.54 In the Layer or Comp panel, drag to define the shape from one corner of the shape to its opposite corner.

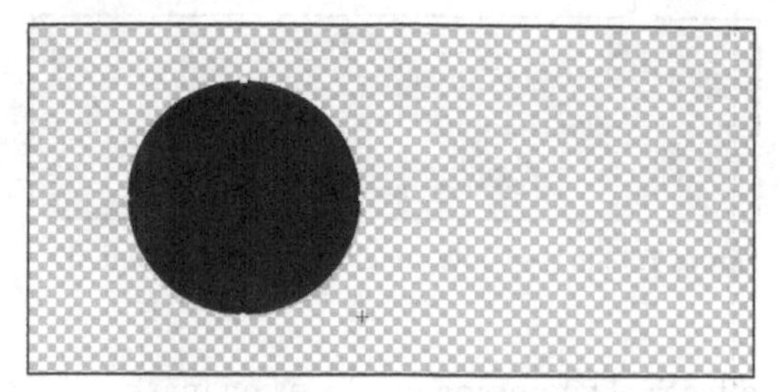

Figure 7.55 Shift-drag to constrain the shape to equal proportions so that you can create a square or circle.

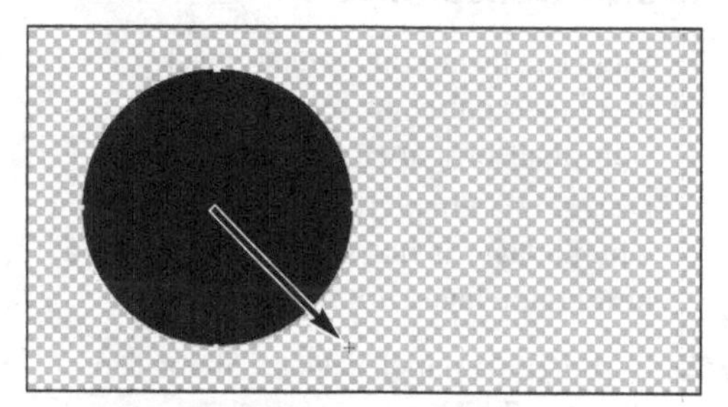

Figure 7.56 Command-drag (Mac) or Ctrl-drag (Windows) to create a mask shape that extends from the center instead of the corner.

5. Release the mouse when you've finished creating the mask.

   In the Layer and Comp panels, the mask appears as a path with selected control points (as long as you set the window to display masks; see "Hiding and Showing Mask Paths," earlier in this chapter). In the Composition panel, the areas of the layer outside the mask are concealed, whereas the areas inside the mask are visible. In the timeline, the layer's outline includes a Mask property.

✔ **Tip**

- To create a mask that fills the layer, double-click the Shape tool.

Building a Standard Mask with the Pen

The following steps explain how to create a path using the Pen tool and Bézier curves. You'll probably want to start by creating simple straight segments. Then, as you become comfortable, you can try using smooth points to create curves and then corner points to create even more complex shapes. Once you're fluent in using the keyboard modifiers listed in **Table 7.2**, you've mastered making mask paths.

Table 7.1

Keyboard Modifiers for Creating Masks

Modifier	Ellipses/Rectangles	Rounded Rectangle	Polygon/Star
Shift	Constrain Proportions	Constrain Proportions	Constrain Rotation
Command (Mac) Ctrl (Win)	Create from Center	Create from Center	Maintain Inner Radius
Opt (Mac) Alt (Win)	Render Mask After Releasing Mouse		
Up Arrow	N/A	Increase Corner Roundness	Increase Sides/Points
Down Arrow	N/A	Decrease Corner Roundness	Decrease Sides/Points
Right Arrow	N/A	Minimum Corner Roundness	Increase Star Outer Roundness
Left Arrow	N/A	Maximum Corner Roundness	Decrease Star Outer Roundness
Page Up	N/A	N/A	Increase Star Inner Roundness
Page Down	N/A	N/A	Decrease Star Inner Roundness

Table 7.2

Keyboard Modifiers for Mask Paths

To do this	Press this
Constrain new segment to 45 degrees	Shift
Temporarily switch to the Vertex tool	Option (Mac) Convert or Alt (Windows)
Temporarily switch to the Selection tool	Command (Mac) or Ctrl (Windows)

In later sections, you'll use the RotoBezier option to create curved segments without using direction lines.

To build a path:

1. *Do either of the following:*
   - ▲ Open a Layer panel for the layer for which you want to create a mask.
   - ▲ Select a layer in the Composition panel.
2. In the Tools panel, select the Pen tool (**Figure 7.57**).
3. In the Layer or Comp panel, *do one of the following:*
   - ▲ To create an anchor point, click (**Figure 7.58**).
   - ▲ To create a smooth point, drag (**Figure 7.59**).
   - ▲ To create a corner point, drag to create a smooth point, select one of the smooth point's direction handles, and then drag again (**Figure 7.60**).
4. Repeat step 3 to create straight and curved segments between points.

   Don't click an existing segment unless you want to add a control point to the path. Don't click an existing direction handle unless you want to convert it.
5. To leave the path open, stop clicking in the Layer panel (**Figure 7.61**).
6. To close the path, *do one of the following:*
   - ▲ Double-click in the Layer panel to create the final control point and connect it to the first control point.
   - ▲ Position the Pen tool over the first control point until a circle icon appears, and then click (**Figure 7.62**).
   - ▲ Choose Layer > Mask > Closed.

   If the first control point is smooth, the path is closed with a smooth point.

Figure 7.57 In the Tools panel, select the Pen tool.

Figure 7.58 Click to create an anchor point with no direction lines.

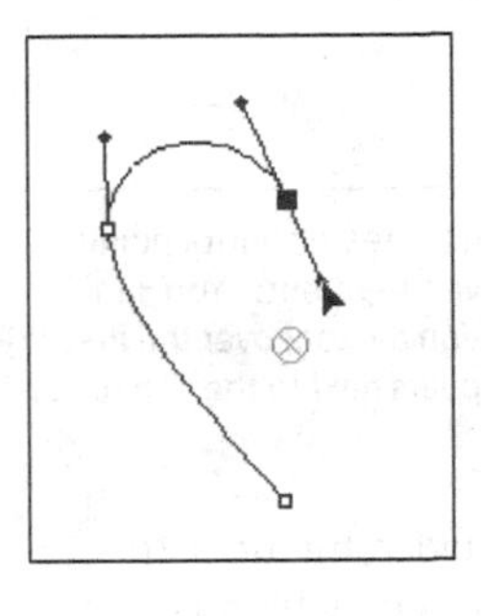
Figure 7.59 Click and drag to create a smooth point with two continuous direction lines.

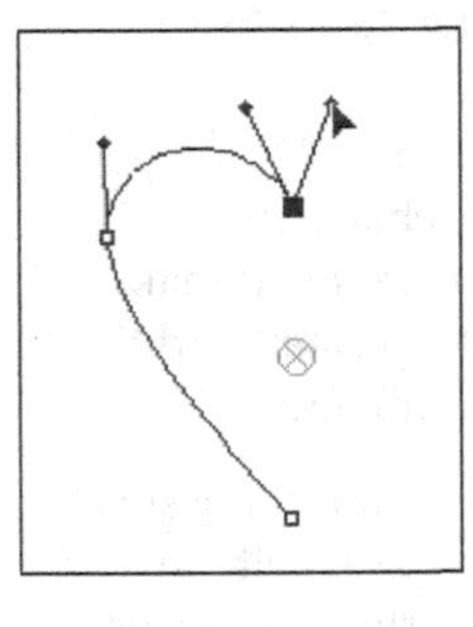
Figure 7.60 Drag a direction handle to break the relationship between the two handles, converting the point into a corner point.

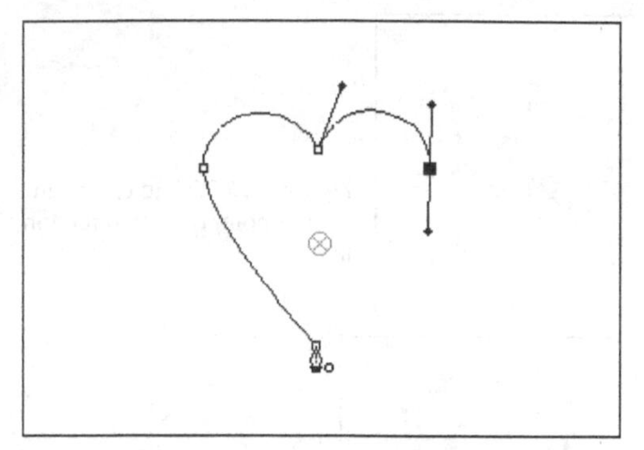

Figure 7.61 Continue clicking to create control points that define straight and curved segments. You can leave the path open, or position the tool over the first point so that a circle icon appears next to the Pen tool...

When you are finished, remember to choose the Selection tool, which is required for most other tasks.

✔ Tips

- In most cases, you'll achieve the smoothest-looking curve if you make each direction line about one-third the length of the curve it influences.
- Typically, using the minimum possible number of control points results in a curve that's both smoother and easier to control.
- Combining several simple masks can be faster and more effective than drawing a single complex path. Similarly, you can start with a simple shape and then modify it using techniques explained in the section "Changing the Shape of a Mask," later in this chapter.

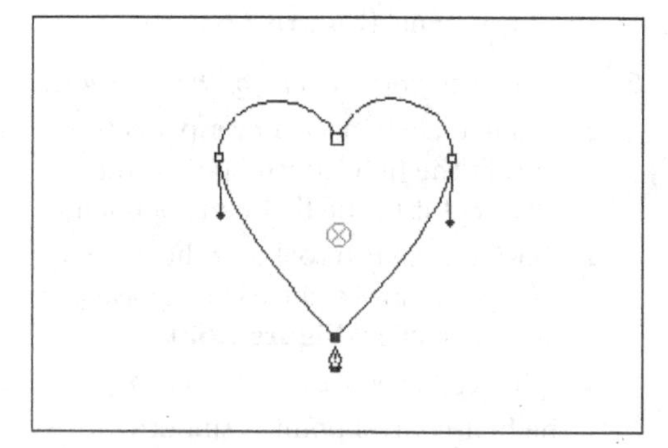

Figure 7.62 ...and click to close the path.

- The Pen tool changes into the Add Vertex tool when positioned over a path; it changes into the Convert Vertex tool when positioned over a direction handle.

Creating a RotoBezier Mask

Even if you're a master of Bézier curves, you can often create a mask more quickly and easily using a *RotoBezier mask*. The Pen tool's RotoBezier option lets you define a curved path by clicking to create control points; After Effects calculates curved segments automatically. You avoid using direction lines, which can take time to adjust properly.

To create a RotoBezier mask:

1. In the Tools panel, select the Pen tool and then select the RotoBezier option (**Figure 7.63**).
2. In the Layer or Composition panel, click with the Pen tool to create the vertices of the mask shape.
3. Repeat step 2 to create additional control points connected by curved segments (**Figure 7.64**).

   Don't click an existing segment unless you want to add a control point to the path.

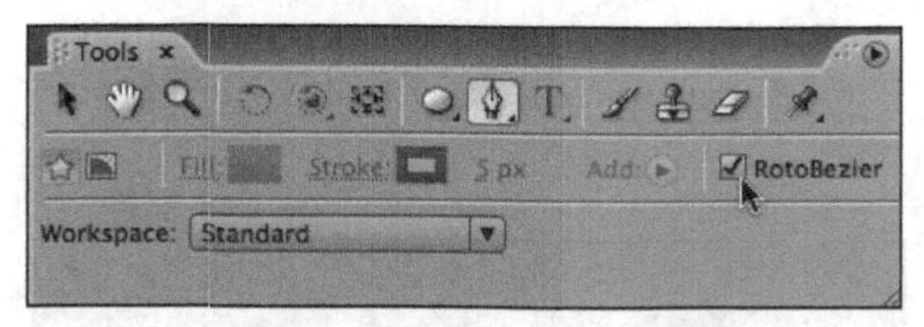

Figure 7.63 Select the Pen tool, and select the RotoBezier option.

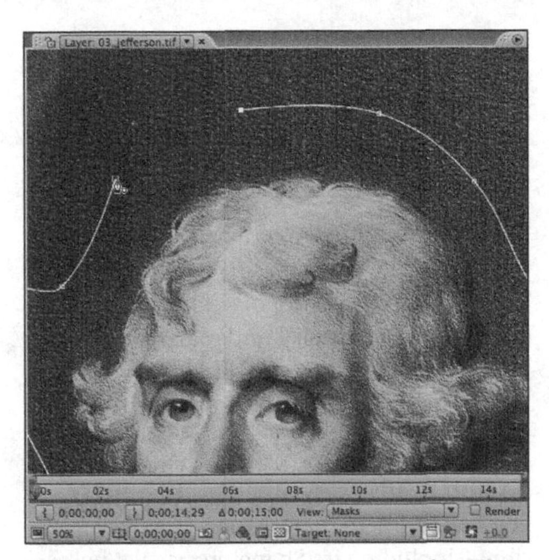

Figure 7.64 Click to create control points. After Effects calculates the curved segments automatically.

Figure 7.65 Position the Pen tool over the first control point so that a small circle appears next to the tool and click to close the shape. Otherwise, you can leave the mask open and choose another tool.

4. To close the path, *do one of the following*:
   - ▲ Double-click in the Layer panel to create the final control point and connect it to the first control point.
   - ▲ Position the Pen tool over the first control point until a circle icon appears, and then click.
   - ▲ Choose Layer > Mask > Closed.

   The mask path closes (**Figure 7.65**).
5. To leave the path open, stop clicking in the Layer panel.

   You may want to choose a new tool, such as the Selection tool.

✔ Tips

- You can convert a RotoBézier to a Bézier mask and vice versa by selecting the mask and choosing Layer > Mask > RotoBézier.
- Although RotoBézier curves are calculated automatically, you can adjust the relative amount of curves, or *tension*. Select the points you want to affect and then drag one with the Convert Vertex tool. Dragging right increases the tension until adjacent segments are flat, making sharp corners. Dragging left makes adjacent segments more curved (**Figure 7.66**).
- The way curves adjust to changes depends on whether the mask consists of Bézier or RotoBezier curves. As you learned in the earlier section, "Understanding Masks," Bézier curves use direction lines you specify manually, whereas RotoBezier curves are

Figure 7.66 The two figures started as identical RotoBezier masks. However, selecting control points and then dragging with the Convert Vertex tool changes *tension* at the selected vertices.

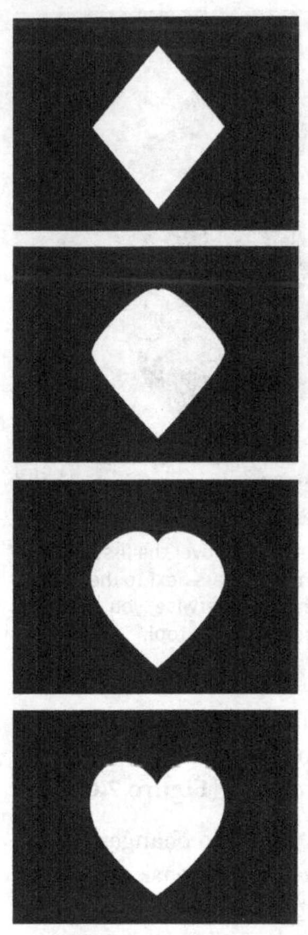

Figure 7.67 You can animate mask properties—including a mask's shape (shown here).

calculated automatically. Each mask type's characteristic behavior continues to operate when you edit it.

Changing the Shape of a Mask

You can modify the shape of a mask at any time by applying the same Pen tool techniques covered in the task, "Building a Standard Mask with the Pen," earlier in this chapter. Because you use essentially the same techniques to add, remove, and convert vertices on masks as you do in a motion path (or for that matter in other graphics programs, like Photoshop and Illustrator) those techniques aren't repeated here.

Later sections cover techniques that affect the entire mask (such as using the Free Transform command), mask properties (mask feather, opacity, and expansion), and mask modes. These tasks don't vary according to the type of mask, and the results are identical.

As with nearly every other layer property, you can animate mask properties over time—including its Shape property. There's no need to reiterate those methods in this chapter, but it's worth remembering that an animated mask can serve many uses—from adapting a garbage mask in conjunction with a keying effect, to transforming graphical elements (**Figure 7.67**).

✔ Tip

- This chapter covers the essentials of After Effects' powerful mask and path making features. When you're ready, you can explore the Create Outlines and Auto-Trace commands, and how Smart Mask Interpolation can aid in animating mask shape.

Selecting Masks and Points

To alter all or part of a mask, you must first select its control points—usually accomplished via (what else?) the Selection tool. Select one or more control points to change the shape of a mask. Select all the points to move the mask. You can use the same methods to select masks and control points in both standard and RotoBezier masks. As usual, selected vertices appear as solid squares; deselected vertices appear as hollow squares.

Figure 7.68 In the Tools panel, choose the Selection tool.

To move, scale, or rotate the entire mask, use the transform technique described in the section "Scaling and Rotating Masks," later in this chapter.

To select masks or points in a Layer or Comp panel:

1. In the Tools panel, choose the Selection tool (if you haven't done so already) (**Figure 7.68**).
2. Make sure the Layer or Comp panel is set to show masks.
   See the sections on viewing masks, earlier in this chapter.
3. To select mask points in the Comp panel, select the layer containing the mask.
4. To select mask points in either the Layer panel or the Comp panel, *do any of the following*:
   - ▲ To select a control point, click the control point on a mask.
   - ▲ To add to or subtract from your selection, press Shift as you click or drag a marquee around control points.
   - ▲ To select points at both ends of a segment, click the segment.

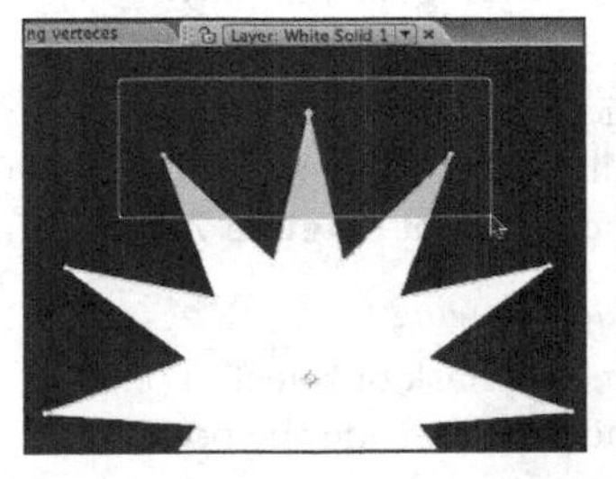

Figure 7.69 In the Layer panel, you can select several mask vertices simultaneously by dragging a marquee around them.

Figure 7.70 Selected points appear as solid squares; deselected points appear as hollow squares.

   - ▲ To select an entire mask with the mouse, Option/Alt-click the mask.
5. To select mask points in the Layer panel only, *do any of the following*:
   - ▲ To select any or all control points, drag a marquee around the points you want to select (**Figure 7.69**).
   - ▲ To select all mask points, press Command/Ctrl-A.
   - ▲ To select an entire mask by name, choose the mask from the Target pull-down menu in the Layer panel.

   In the Layer or Comp panel, selected control points appear solid; other control points appear as hollow outlines (**Figure 7.70**). Segments associated with the selected points also display direction lines. When no control points of a mask are selected, only the path is visible in the Layer or Comp panel.

Opening and Closing Paths

You can use menu commands to close an open path or open a closed one.

To close an open path:

1. In a Layer panel, choose the control points at each end of an open path (**Figure 7.71**).
2. Choose Layer > Mask > Closed (**Figure 7.72**).
   The control points are connected to close the path (**Figure 7.73**).

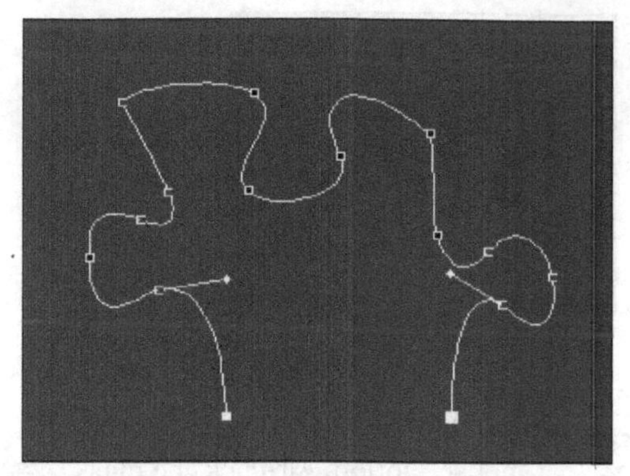

Figure 7.71 Choose the control points at each end of an open path.

To open a closed path:

1. In a Layer panel, choose two adjacent control points in a closed path.
2. Choose Layer > Mask > Closed.

   The Closed option is deselected, and the segment between the control points disappears.

Scaling and Rotating Masks

Using the Free Transform Points command, you can scale and rotate all or part of one or more masks. Masks are rotated and scaled around their own anchor points, separate from the anchor point of the layer that contains them. As the word *free* suggests, these adjustments are controlled manually, not

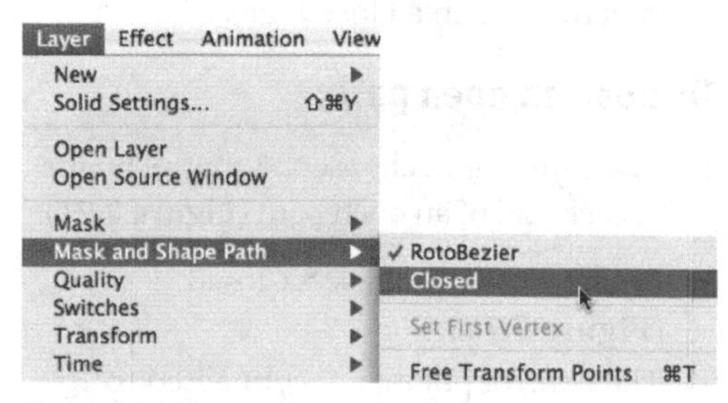

Figure 7.72 Choose Layer › Mask › Closed.

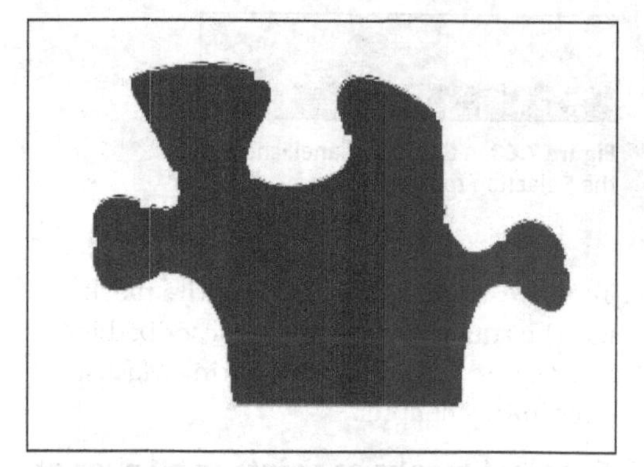

Figure 7.73 The open path becomes closed. You can use the same method to open a closed path.

numerically, and they can't be keyframed to animate over time. Of course, you can still keyframe the rotation and scale of the layer containing the masks.

To move, scale, or rotate all or part of a mask:

1. Open a Layer panel for the layer that contains the mask you want to transform, or select the layer in the Comp panel.
2. *Do one of the following:*
   - Select the mask or mask points you want to transform, and Choose Layer > Mask > Free Transform Points.
   - Double-click a mask to transform it completely.

   A bounding box and mask anchor point appear (**Figure 7.74**).
3. To reposition the anchor point for the mask's bounding box, drag the anchor.

   The Selection tool turns into a Move Anchor Point icon when you position it over the anchor point (**Figure 7.75**).
4. *Do any of the following:*
   - To move the mask or selected points, place the cursor inside the bounding

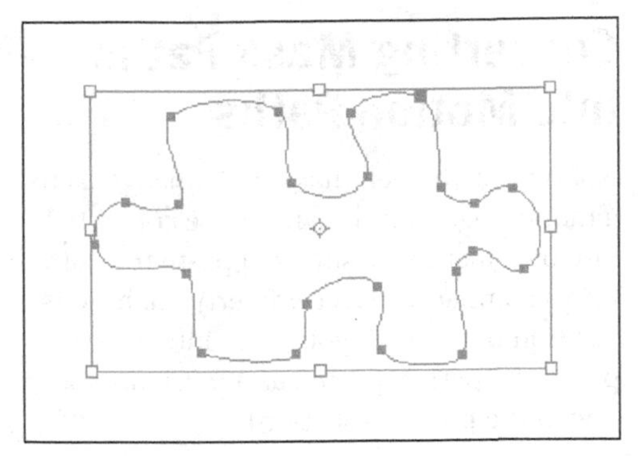

Figure 7.74 A bounding box and mask anchor point appear.

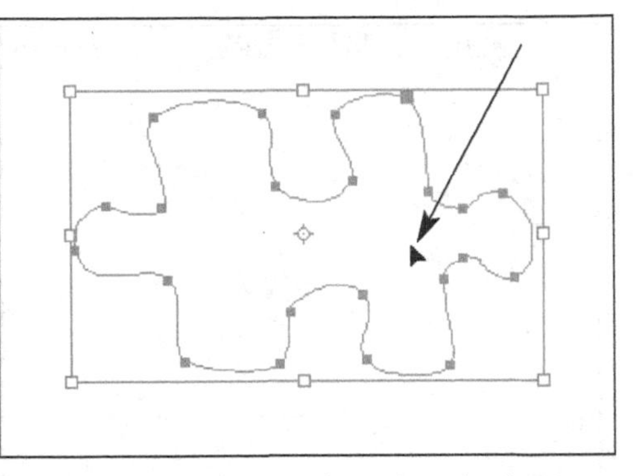

Figure 7.76 To move the mask or selected points, place the cursor inside the bounding box and drag to a new position.

box and drag to a new position (**Figure 7.76**).

- To scale the mask or selected points, place the cursor on one of the handles of the bounding box until it becomes a Scale icon, and then drag (**Figure 7.77**).
- To rotate the mask or selected points, place the pointer slightly outside the bounding box until it becomes a Rotation icon, and then drag (**Figure 7.78**).

5. To exit Free Transform Points mode, double-click anywhere in the Layer or Comp panel, or press Return/Enter.

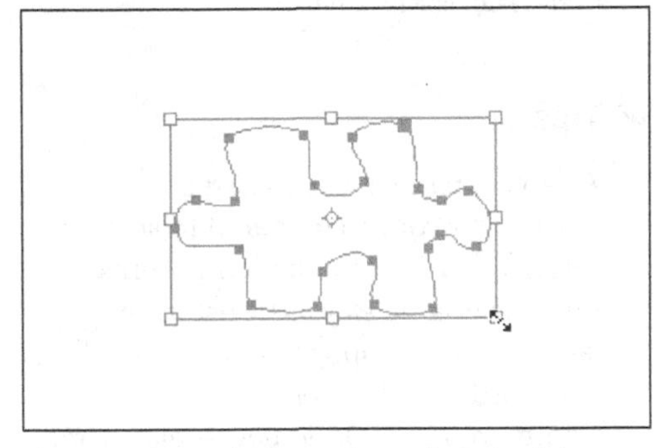

Figure 7.77 To scale the mask or selected points, place the cursor on one of the handles of the bounding box until it becomes a Scale icon, and then drag.

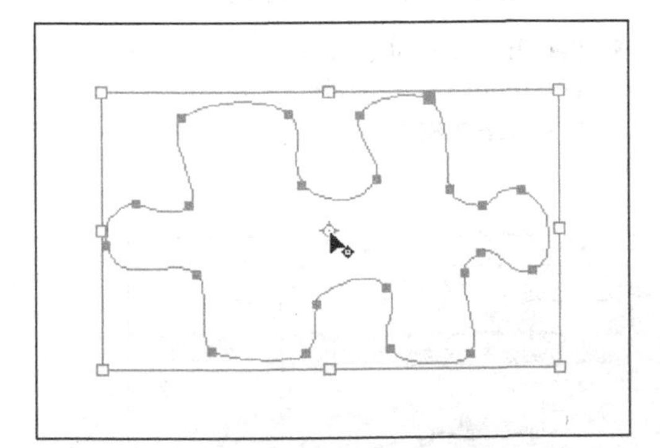

Figure 7.75 If you drag the mask's anchor point, the Selection tool becomes a Move Anchor Point icon.

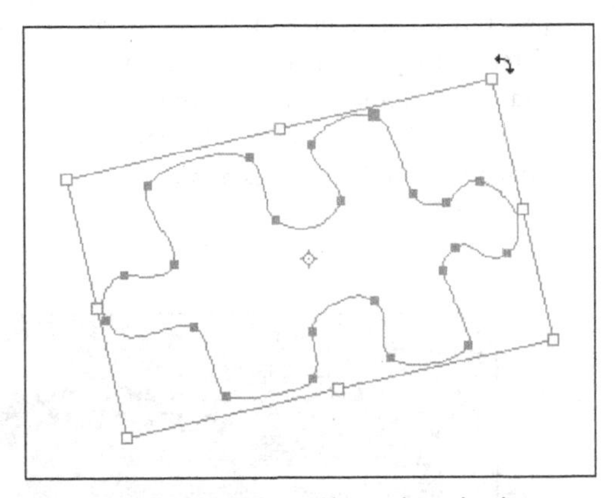

Figure 7.78 To rotate the mask or selected points, place the pointer slightly outside the bounding box until it becomes a Rotation icon, and then drag.

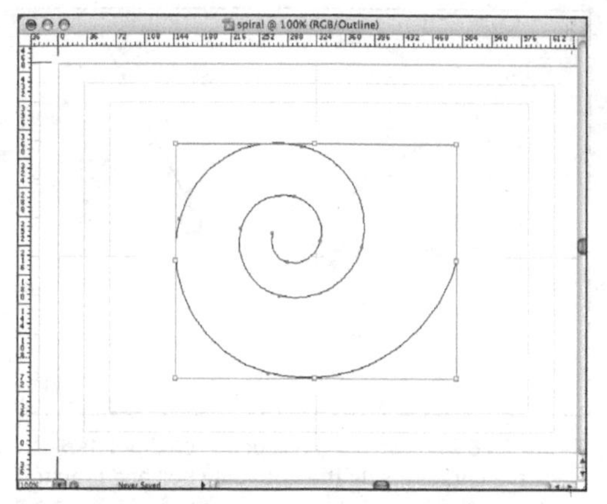

Figure 7.79 Select an open mask path in a layer in After Effects, or in Photoshop or Illustrator (shown here). Press Command/Ctrl-C.

✔ Tips

- As you can see, using the Free Transform Points command to scale and rotate a mask or mask points works much the same way as transforming a layer. You'll be happy to know that all the keyboard modifications—Shift, Command/Ctrl, Option/Alt—also work the same.
- You can copy paths from Adobe Photoshop or Illustrator and paste them as a layer mask in After Effects. By pasting a path as a layer mask, you can take advantage of After Effects' ability to animate its Shape, Feather, Opacity, and Expansion properties.

Converting Mask Paths into Motion Paths

Not only is an open mask path analogous to a motion path, but it can also be converted into one. Just make sure you paste the path into a compatible layer property, such as its Position property. If you paste into a Layer panel, the path is pasted as a mask (as you saw in the previous section).

To paste a mask path as a motion path:

1. *Do either of the following:*
   - ▲ Select an open mask path in a layer in After Effects.
   - ▲ Select an open mask path in Photoshop or Illustrator.
2. Choose Edit > Copy, or press Command/Ctrl-C (**Figure 7.79**).
3. In the Timeline panel, expand the layer outline to reveal the spatial property you want to paste the path into.
   You can use the Position, Effect Point, or Anchor Point property.
4. Select the property name.
   The property's keyframes are highlighted. If the property has no keyframes, the I-beam icon is highlighted.
5. Set the current time to the frame where you want the pasted keyframes to start (**Figure 7.80**).

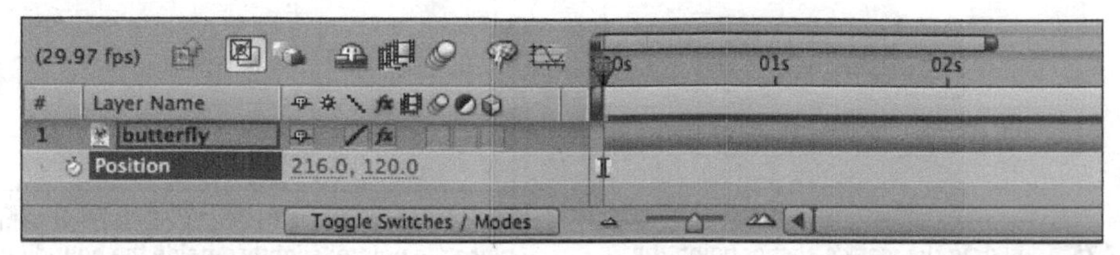

Figure 7.80 In After Effects, select a layer property, and set the current time to the frame you want the pasted motion to start.

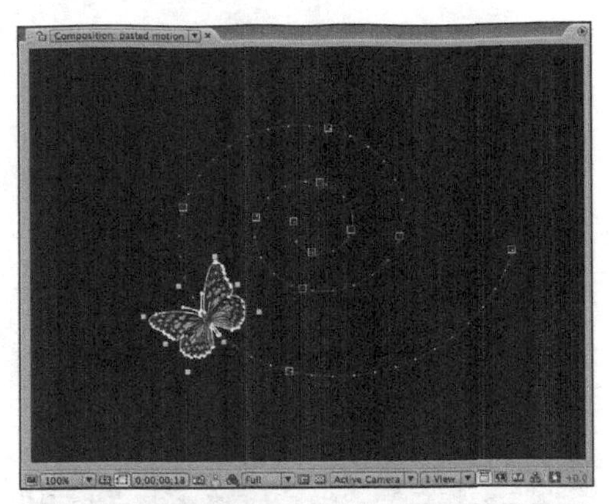

Figure 7.81 Pressing Command/Ctrl-V pastes the path in the composition as a motion path...

6. Choose Edit > Paste, or press Command/Ctrl-V.

   The path appears in the Comp panel as a motion path (**Figure 7.81**). In the property's track, keyframes begin at the current time and end two seconds later (**Figure 7.82**). The first and last keyframes are standard keyframes; the rest are roving keyframes (see Chapter 5).

7. Edit the motion path as you would any other.

Moving Masks Relative to the Layer Image

You can move a mask to reveal a different part of a layer in two ways: in a Layer panel or in a Composition panel.

When you move a mask in a Layer panel, its relative position in the Composition panel also changes (**Figures 7.81** and **7.82**). This approach works well if you want to change both the part of the image revealed by the mask and the mask's position in the composition. The mask moves, but the layer's position remains the same. Think of an iris effect at the end of a cartoon, in which the circular mask closes in on the character for a final good-bye.

Alternatively, you can use the Pan Behind tool in the Composition panel. Panning the layer behind the mask reveals a different part of the image without moving the mask's relative position in the composition. When you look back at the Layer panel, you can see that the mask has moved. However, After Effects recalculates the layer's position to compensate for this movement, maintaining the layer's position in the composition (**Figures 7.83** and **7.84**). Imagine a scene from a pirate movie, in which a spyglass scans the horizon. The circle doesn't move, but the horizon pans through the viewfinder to reveal an island.

To move a mask in the Layer panel:

1. Select an entire mask in the Layer panel.

2. Drag one of the control points to move the entire mask to a new position.

   Make sure to drag a control point, not a path segment. The mask changes position in both the Layer panel and the composition.

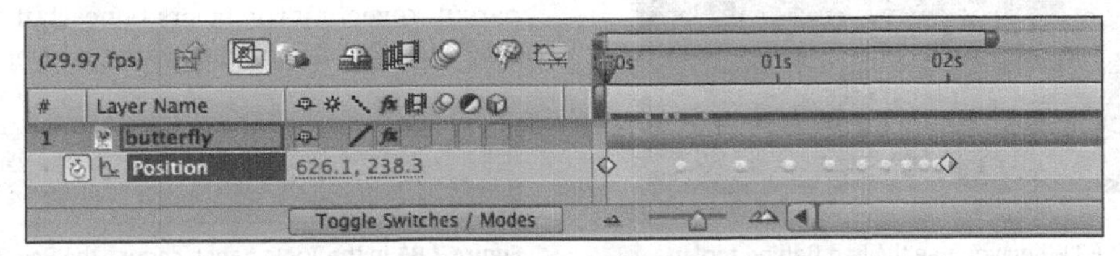

Figure 7.82 ...and in the property's track as keyframes starting at the current time.

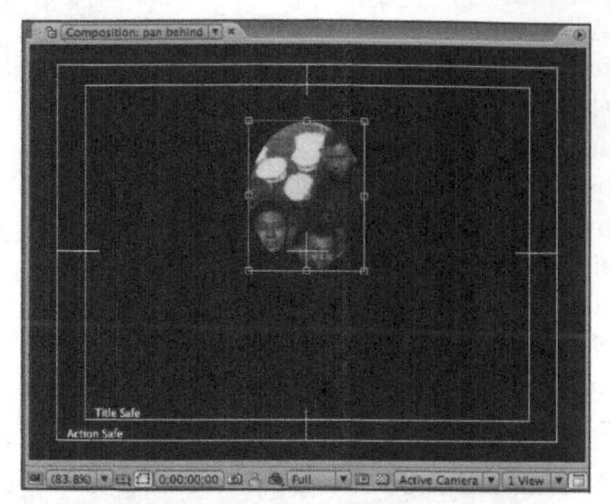

Figure 7.81 When you move a mask in a Layer or Comp panel...

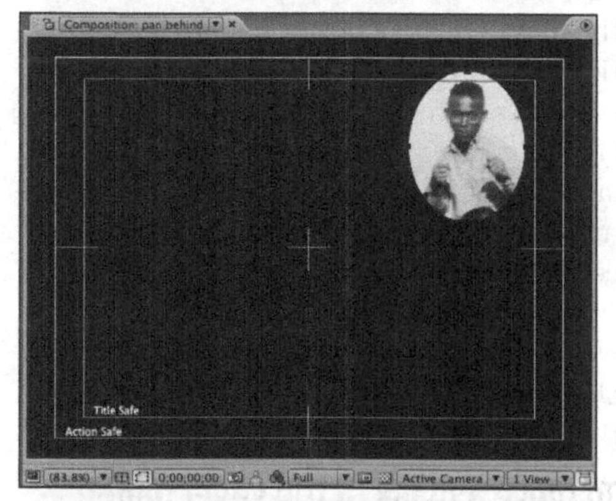

Figure 7.82 ...the mask's position changes in both the Layer and the Comp panel. The position value of the layer containing the mask doesn't change.

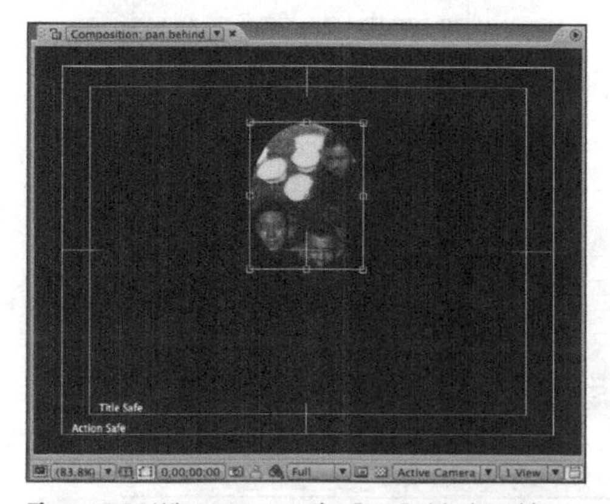

Figure 7.83 When you use the Pan Behind tool in the Composition panel...

Figure 7.84 ...the mask changes its position in the layer while maintaining its position in the composition. After Effects recalculates the layer's position value automatically. You can see the anchor point's new position in the Comp panel.

To pan a layer behind its mask:

1. In the Tools panel, select the Pan Behind tool (**Figure 7.85**).
2. In the Composition panel, position the Pan Behind tool inside the masked area of the layer, and then drag (**Figure 7.86**).

   In the Composition panel, the mouse pointer becomes the Pan Behind icon, and the layer pans behind the masked area. After Effects calculates the layer's position in the composition and the mask's placement in the Layer panel.

Inverting a Mask

Ordinarily, the area within a closed layer mask defines the opaque parts of the layer's image; the area outside the mask is transparent, revealing the layers beneath it. However, just as you can invert a layer's

Figure 7.85 In the Tools panel, choose the Pan Behind tool.

Figure 7.86 In the Comp panel, place the Pan Behind tool inside the masked area and drag.

alpha channel, you can invert a layer mask to reverse the opaque and transparent areas.

To invert a mask created in After Effects:

1. In the Layer, Comp, or Timeline panel, select the mask you want to invert.
2. *Do one of the following:*
   - ▲ In the Timeline panel, click Inverted for the selected mask (**Figure 7.87**).
   - ▲ Choose Layer > Mask > Invert.
   - ▲ Press Shift-Command-I (Mac) or Shift-Ctrl-I (Windows).

   Viewed in the Composition panel, the mask is inverted (**Figures 7.88** and **7.89**).

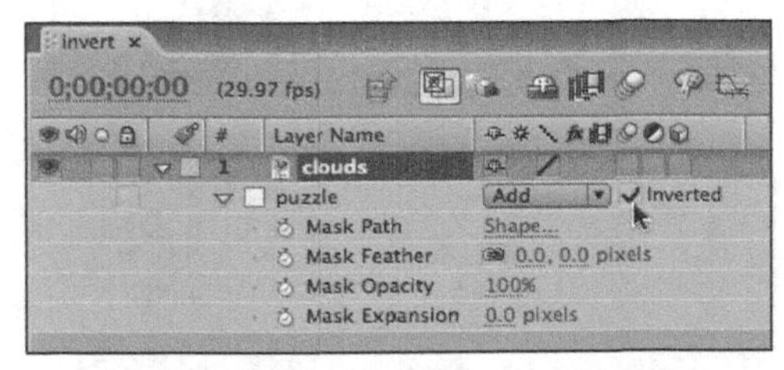

Figure 7.87 Click Inverted for the mask in the layer outline of the Timeline panel, or use the equivalent menu command or keyboard shortcut.

Figure 7.88 Ordinarily, the area within the mask defines the opaque parts of the layer's image.

Mask Modes

When you add multiple masks to the same layer, you can determine how the masks interact by selecting a mask *mode*. Although modes don't create true compound paths (as do the Boolean functions in Illustrator), you can use them to achieve similar effects (**Figures 7.90**).

None eliminates the effects of the mask on the layer's alpha channel. However, you can still apply effects (such as strokes or fills) to the mask.

Add includes the mask with the masks above it to display all masked areas. Areas

Figure 7.89 Inverting the mask reverses the opaque and transparent areas of the layer.

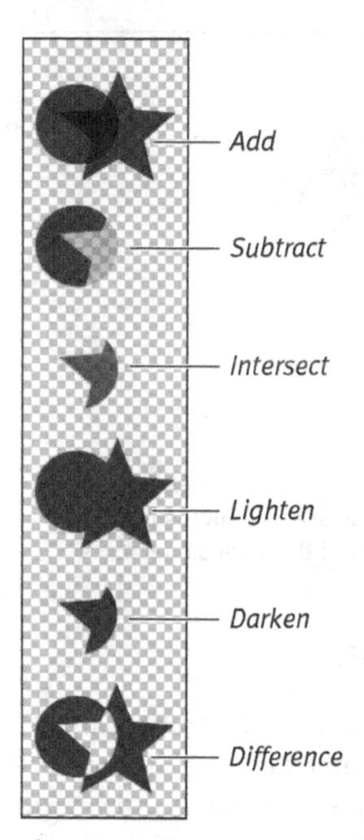

Figure 7.90 Here, both masks are applied to a black solid and are set to 75 percent opacity. The upper mask (left) is set to Add. Changing the lower mask's mode changes how it interacts with the one above it.

where the mask overlaps with the masks above it use their combined opacity values.

Subtract cuts, or subtracts, areas where the mask overlaps with the mask above it.

Intersect adds the mask to all the masks above it so that only the areas where the mask overlaps with higher masks display in the composition.

Lighten adds the mask to the masks above it to display all masked areas. Areas where the mask overlaps with the masks above it use the highest opacity value, not the combined values.

Darken adds the mask to the masks above it to display only the areas where the masks overlap. Areas where multiple masks overlap use the highest opacity value, not the combined values.

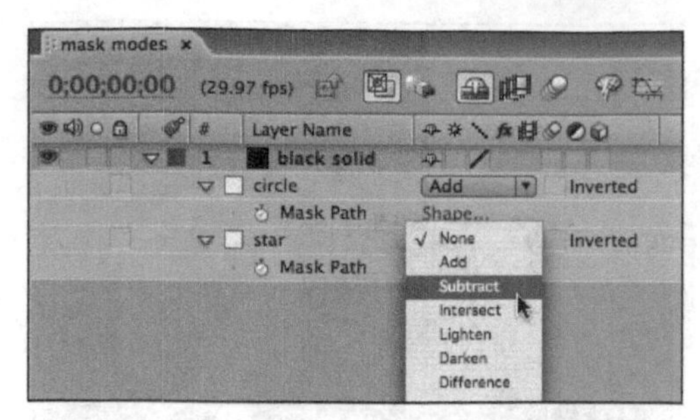

Figure 7.91 To the right of the mask in the Timeline panel, choose a mask mode from the pull-down menu.

Difference adds the mask to the masks above it to display only the areas where the masks don't overlap.

To set the mask mode:

1. Select the mask for which you want to set the mode.
2. *Do one of the following:*
   - ▲ In the Timeline panel, choose a mode from the pull-down menu across from the mask (in the Switches/Modes panel) (**Figure 7.91**).
   - ▲ Choose Layer > Mask > Mode > and select a mode from the submenu.

   The mode you choose affects how the mask interacts with the masks above it in the layer outline (for that layer only).

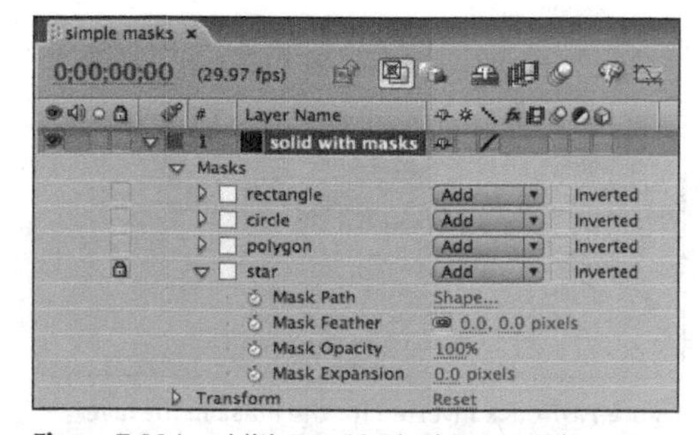

Figure 7.92 In addition to Mask Shape, mask properties include Feather, Opacity, and Expansion.

Figure 7.93 These masks are identical except for their Mask Feather values.

Figure 7.95 This figure shows three masks with identical shapes and feather values. However, each mask's Expansion value is different.

Adjusting Other Mask Properties

In addition to Mask Shape, mask properties include Feather, Opacity, and Expansion (**Figure 7.92**). Along with Mask Shape, you can view, adjust, and animate them as you would any layer property.

Feather controls the softness of a mask's edge; the Mask Feather value determines the width of the edge's transition from opacity to transparency. The feathered width always extends equally from each side of the mask edge—that is, a Feather value of 30 extends 15 pixels both outside and inside the mask edge (**Figure 7.93**).

Opacity controls the mask's overall opacity—that is, how solid the masked area of the layer appears. Mask opacity works in conjunction with the layer's Opacity setting. If the layer is 100 percent opaque and a mask is 50 percent opaque, the masked area of the layer appears 50 percent opaque. Each mask's opacity also influences the net effect of mask modes, which are explained in the previous section, "Mask Modes." (**Figure 7.94**).

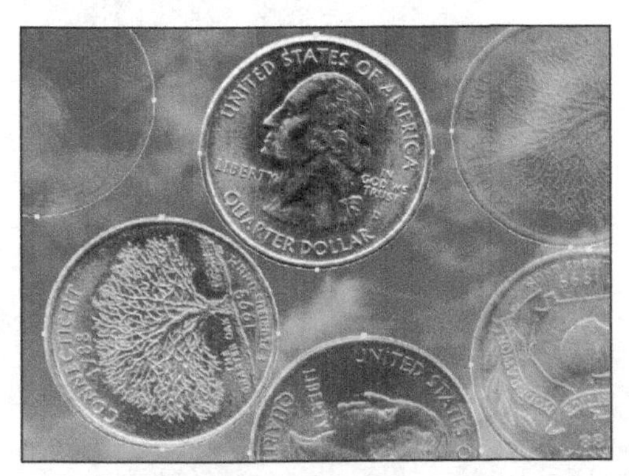

Figure 7.94 In this figure, several masks in the same layer use different opacity values.

Expansion lets you expand or contract a mask's edges and is particularly useful for fine-tuning the feathered edge of a mask (**Figure 7.95**).

✔ Tip

- If you set the feather to extend beyond the perimeter of the layer containing the mask, the feather will appear cut off and the edges of the layer will be apparent. Make the mask or feather small enough to fit within the confines of the layer. If the layer is a solid or nested composition, you can also increase the size of the layer.

Adjusting Other Mask Properties

THE WORKFLOW

8

THE MILLENNIUM

We can all fondly look back to 1999 and remember the excitement surrounding the "historical" moment when the clock struck twelve midnight, bringing us into the year 2000. The months leading into the millennium left most people in the world questioning their computers' Y2K compliance. If that wasn't enough, the media heightened our awareness of terrorist plots and national safety and reminded us how much our lives depend on computers.

Although some people simply shrugged off the warnings and continued as normal, others took them seriously and stocked up on bottled water, flashlights, batteries, and franks 'n' beans. I am sure we can all remember exactly what went through our minds during those times. I will always remember exactly where I was during the days leading into the new century—staring at a computer screen wondering how I was going to get all my work finished.

The dawn of the new millennium didn't bring most of the world much of anything; however, it did provide me with some absolutely beautiful O.T. checks.

Ready, Set, Go!

In my opinion, there are two types of news: *expected* news and *unexpected* news. As you probably already figured out, *expected* news is an event like a football game. Unexpected news, on the other hand, is what the news industry thrives on. When something incredible catches the world off guard, they report it and rake in the ratings.

The millennium was a little bit of both though, because the unexpected eerily loomed over Y2K's head. We saw it coming; we all knew it was on December 31, 1999. You would think we would start making the graphics months in advance. Yeah, you would think that, wouldn't you?

The reality of life, work, and the world, however, held much more in store for me. Yes, anyone could see that the big day was getting closer and closer, but there was plenty of other work I needed to finish before I could start creating the graphics for the project. By the time I finished all my work and was ready to start the graphics for the millennium, I had three weeks until the big day.

Right around the time I was getting geared up to create the Millennium animation for MSNBC, NBC News was finishing up their title animation. I needed to see what they had produced before I could start creating the animation for MSNBC, because the two had to appear to be part of the same package.

The Creative Director, Sam Mandragona; the Assistant Creative Director, Joe Dettmore; and I examined what the graphics department for NBC News (New York) had cooked up for their look (see **Figure 8.1**). We needed to incorporate into our animation the logo design that had been created at NBC News.

After looking at the logo, Joe, Sam, and I brainstormed ideas for the animation. What we came up with was, in a nutshell, clocks and globes.

Figure 8.1 The design NBC News used for the Millennium.

I created more than thirty animations of the earth spinning, illustrating the individual time zones. Each time zone was highlighted with texture maps and volumetric beams. These took a great deal of organization, attention to detail, and time. When I finished the time zone animations, I moved on to creating the open.

Creating the Animation

When it finally came time to concentrate on creating the title animation for MSNBC millennium coverage, I had about a week and a half to complete it. While I was generating visual ideas and blocking out basic objects, Joe Dettmore was in Sound Design with Gordon Miller, creating the score for the animation.

Joe had the very basic principals of the animation in his head. He wanted clocks, globes, and a strong NBC identity. The animation was designed to have particles expanding outwardly, like the universe, during the beginning of the animation. When the animation was complete, the particles would be brought together to form the "Millennium" type, bringing the whole concept together as well.

Joe and I decided that the animation should be broken up into four sections. Those four sections are described below. You can view realwld1\millennium.avi to see the completed animation.

Shot I: The Clocks

The establishing shot of the animation contains three different colored clocks with rapidly changing faces (see **Figure 8.2**). The purpose of this shot is to engage the viewers by introducing them to the time and space theme, which will play throughout the animation. This section concludes with a veil of particles.

Figure 8.2 A frame of the clocks from the final animation.

This shot was the simplest shot for me, personally, to complete. Although it appears first, it was the third shot (of the four) that I completed for this animation. Joe completed most of the pre-production. Anna Kostyrko, a staff designer, captured the clock face images into the Quantel Paintbox Express (a proprietary video image processing tool). Joe loaded the still clock face images from the Paintbox into the Quantel Hal Express (a proprietary video compositing tool), color corrected them, and assembled the images into an animated sequence.

Joe then manipulated the resulting clock face animation to create three separate clock face animations: one red, one blue, and one gold. These animations were recorded to my DDR (Digital Disk Recorder) and were imported onto my hard drive as individual Targa files.

Once the three colored clock face images sequences were on my hard drive, I began to build some test scenes to illustrate some of the different ways the rendered output could appear. The first sample I created, RW2\jclck01.avi (see **Figure 8.3**), has all three clocks self-intersecting, which created a thick, layered and almost chaotic appearance.

The second sample, RW2\jclck02.avi (shown in **Figure 8.4**) shows the three clocks layered and parallel to each other. When they were fully rendered, I called Sam and Joe to examine these thumbnails and offer their creative criticism. We agreed that the first one was little too confusing for an establishing shot, so we decided we should use something closer to the second one.

Someone offered up the suggestion to put glass over the clock faces to give them more punch. The glass over the clock faces would not only create extra highlights and dimension, but also refract the clock faces beneath them, adding more depth.

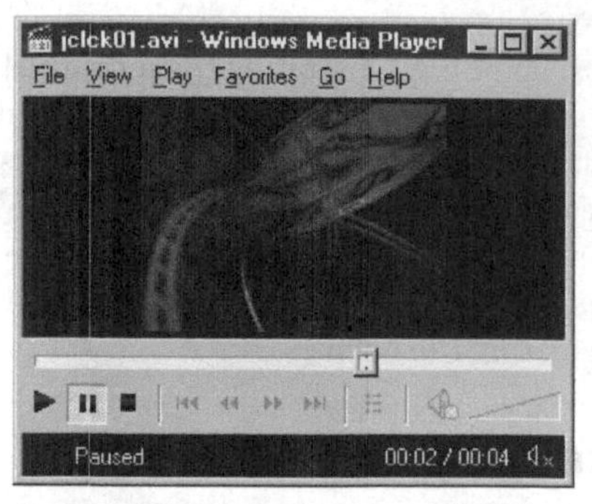

Figure 8.3 The first test I created for the first shot, jclck01.avi.

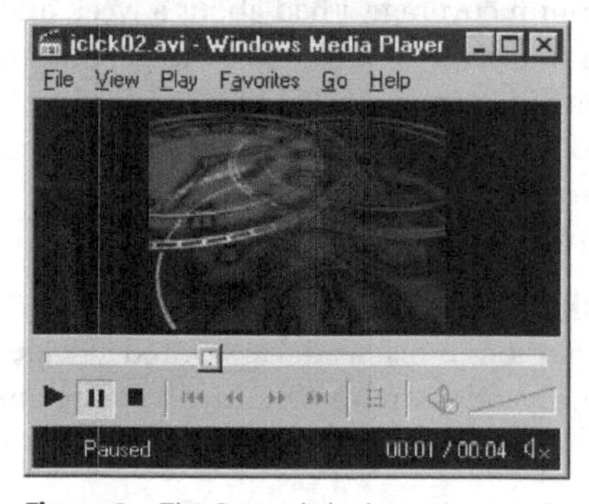

Figure 8.4 The Second clock test I created, jclck02.avi.

In the next few sections, I quickly step you through how the clocks were created. To fully understand the process, you will want to load **RW2\scenes\clock01.max** from the accompanying CD (see **Figure 8.5**). Four objects are visible in the scene: the circular framework of the clock (Clock-In01 and Clock-Out01), the glass lens (Clock-Glass0l), and the billboard for the clock face images (Clock-Map0l).

You will notice four objects in the scene: a square, two tube primitives, and a squashed hemisphere. We will concentrate our attention on how to create the clock face map and the refractive clock lens. To do so, we will examine each object individually.

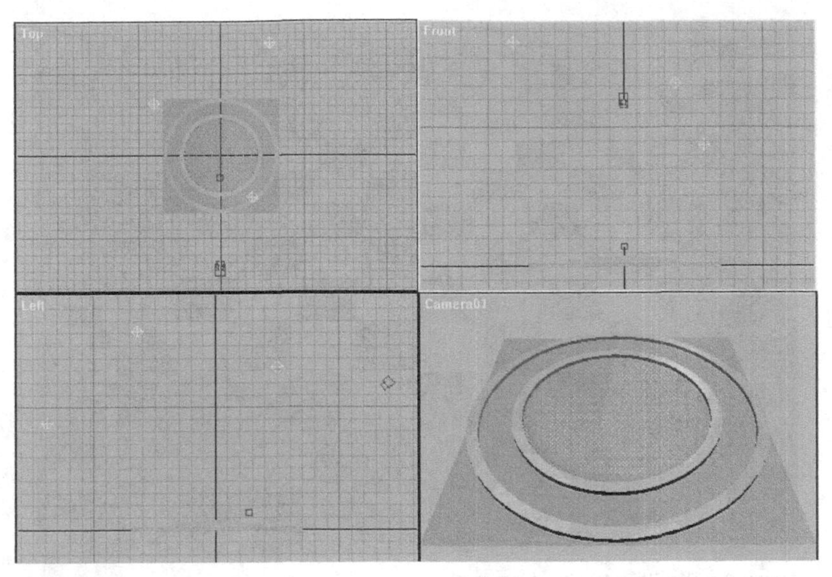

Figure 8.5 Clock01.max.

The Clock-Map01 Object

This object is the billboard in which the clock face texture map was applied. For this example, I substituted the clock face map with a checkerboard texture (see **Figures 8.6** and **8.7**).

If you examine the Clock01.max file, you will notice that the Clock-Map01 object is simply a square shape with a Mesh Select and UVW Map modifier applied. How, then, does this rectangle render as a circle? The answer to this question is easily discovered in the Material Editor (see **Figure 8.8**).

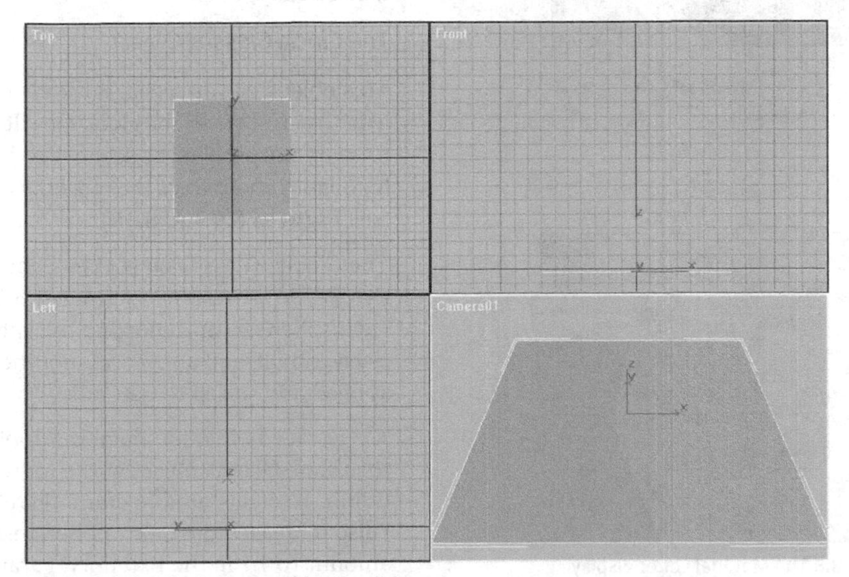

Figure 8.6 The Clock-Map01 Object in all four views.

Figure 8.7 The Clock-Map01 object rendered.

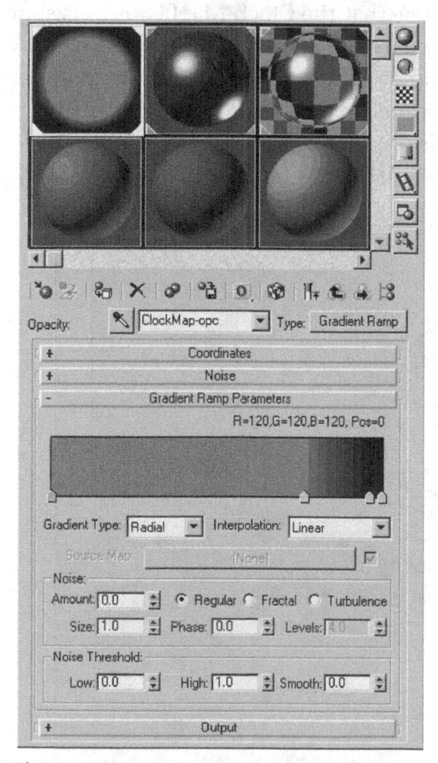

Figure 8.8 The Material Editor displaying Clock-Map01's opacity map.

The Clock-Map01 object's material has a Gradient Ramp map in its Opacity slot. The Gradient Type is set to Radial, which creates the circular gradient that is visible in the material preview slot. Because of this radial gradient, the square Clock-Map0l object renders as a soft circle.

The Clock-Glass01 Object

This object, as you recall, is the clear glass lens that rests over the clock face. Its primary purpose in the scene is to catch highlights and refract the objects below it (see **Figures 8.9** and **8.10**).

The Clocks-Glass01 object is a Sphere primitive with a Hemisphere setting of 5. The Hemisphere setting chopped the sphere precisely in half, and an XForm modifier was applied and scaled to flatten it.

A Raytrace Refraction map was applied to the Clock-Glass0l object in the Material Editor. To create a more dramatic refraction, I also increased the Index of Refraction amount to 1.7 in the Extended Parameters rollout of the material.

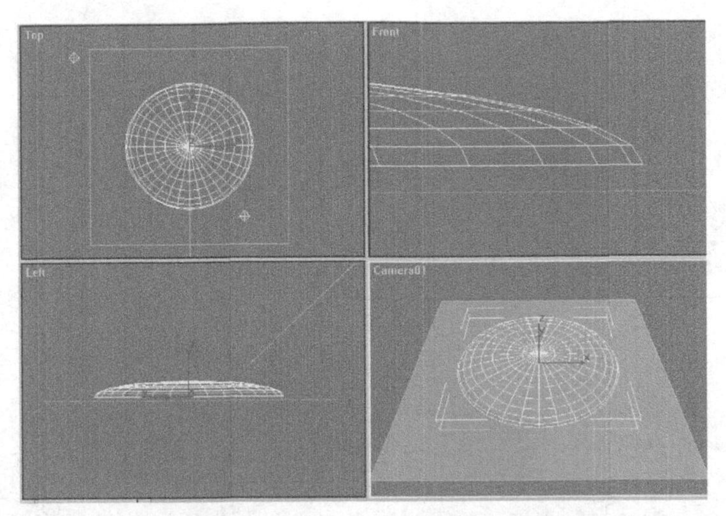

Figure 8.9 The Clock-Glass01 object resting above the Clock-Map01 object.

Figure 8.10 The rendered scene with both the Clock01-Glass01 and the Clock-Map01 object.

The Clock-In01 object was intended to appear as though it were supporting the Clock-Glass01 object (see **Figure 8.11**). This makes the clock seem to be a more solid and realistic fixture. In **Figure 8.12**, you can see two of these clocks overlapping one another and how the lower clock is refracted in the higher clock.

In Clock01.max, both clocks are included in the file; however, you need to unhide the second one.

These clocks perfectly demonstrate how a little ingenuity can build a simple scene with dramatic results. As mentioned above, the clock scene was the easiest

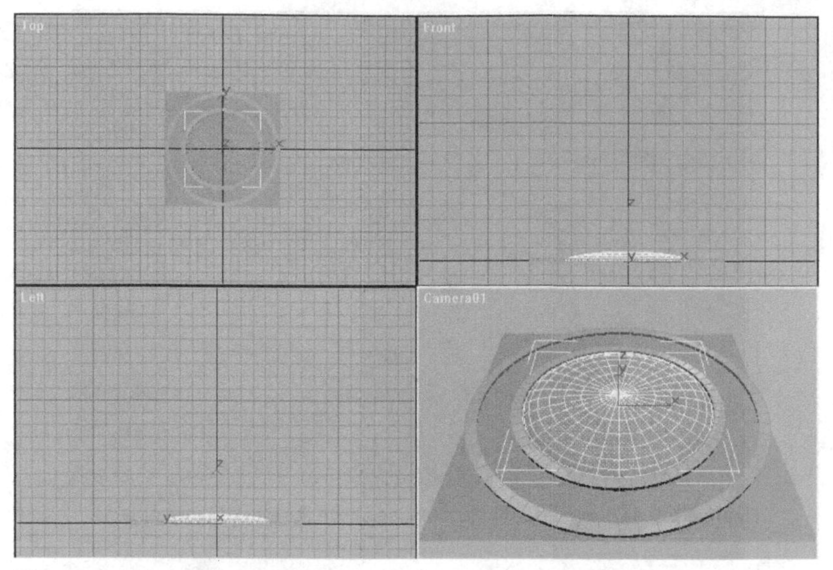

Figure 8.11 All four objects of the clock.

Figure 8.12 Two overlapping clock objects rendered to illustrate refraction.

of the scenes I created. Even though it was easy to complete, however, the actual rendered look is sophisticated. This animation (Shot 1) was created, rendered, and approved with no re-renders, all in one day.

Shot 2: The NBC Peacock

The shot of the NBC peacock inside the globe (shown in **Figure 8.13**) is probably my favorite of the four shots in the animation. Although it wasn't the first section I created,

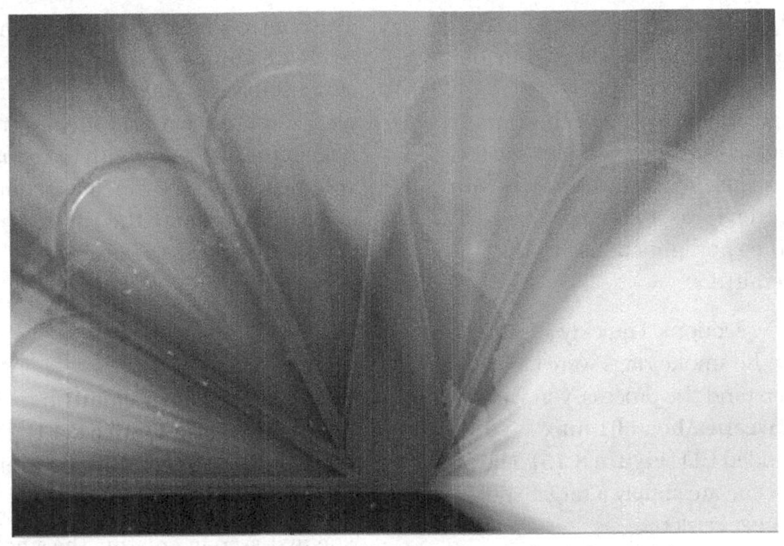

Figure 8.13 A frame from the NBC peacock scene of the Millennium animation.

it was the one that ultimately excited me about working on this project. This shot was actually the first shot completed and approved. It set the pace for the rest of the scenes.

Joe and I started by discussing ideas for new things we could do with the NBC peacock. During our discussion, I remembered that I had always wanted to build or the volumetric peacock I had created for CNBC's *Upfront Tonight.* I told Joe that I had an idea, and I asked him to give me a few hours to put something together.

I wanted to make smoke rings that traveled along the length of the volumetric beams of the peacock as they swept into position. The file RW2\peakbeam.avi (shown in **Figure 8.14**) shows my first complete test rendering of the volumetric peacock with smoke rings. When it finished rendering, I called Sam and Joe in to take a look at it so I could get their input. Thankfully, they loved it as much as I did. So I went to work creating the completed shot.

First, I created the volumetric light beams that would ultimately become the feathers of the NBC peacock. To make the colorful streaks of light in each beam, I applied a Gradient Ramp map in each light's Projector slot. You will examine that process shortly, when you look at how the smoke beams were created.

Figure 8.14 My first test of the volumetric peacock.

When the light beams were created in position and a test had been rendered, I made each light a child to its own personal Dummy helper. The rotation of the Dummy helper is what causes the beams to sweep through the scene. When I was happy with the way the scene was animated, I created clone of all the spotlights to use as the smoke ring emitters.

In the next few sections, I quickly step you through how the smoke rings were created. To fully understand the process, you will want to load **RW2\scenes\beam01.max** from the included CD (**Figure 8.15**). The contents of the scene are simply a target spot light and a target camera.

Volumetric lights are commonly used in 3D animations because of their simplicity. Used correctly, volume lights add subtle accents that heighten the overall aesthetics of an image. However, in some cases, a bold, bright volume light adds the brazen punch the animation needs.

The controls 3ds max provides make it easy to create animated volume lights. Going into this animation, I decided to build on a simple technique that was already in my arsenal: animating the length (attenuation) of a volume tight. The principle behind this effect is to animate the Far Attenuation of the light, making the beam of light appear to grow.

The Cross-Section

Load **RW2\scenes\beam01.max** from the included CD (see **Figure 8.15**). The contents of the scene are simply a target spotlight and a target camera.

The first step in creating the smoke ring effect was to animate the Attenuation of the light. As I mentioned previously, animating the Far Attenuation of the spotlight animates the length of the beam (or where the beam ends). To make the light appear to be blowing smoke rings, the Near Attenuation of the light must also be animated in sync

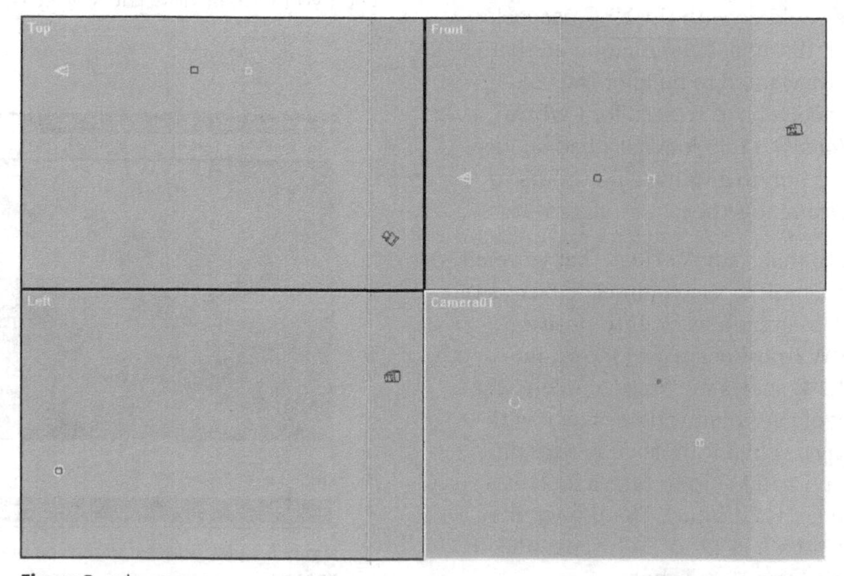

Figure 8.15 beam01.max.

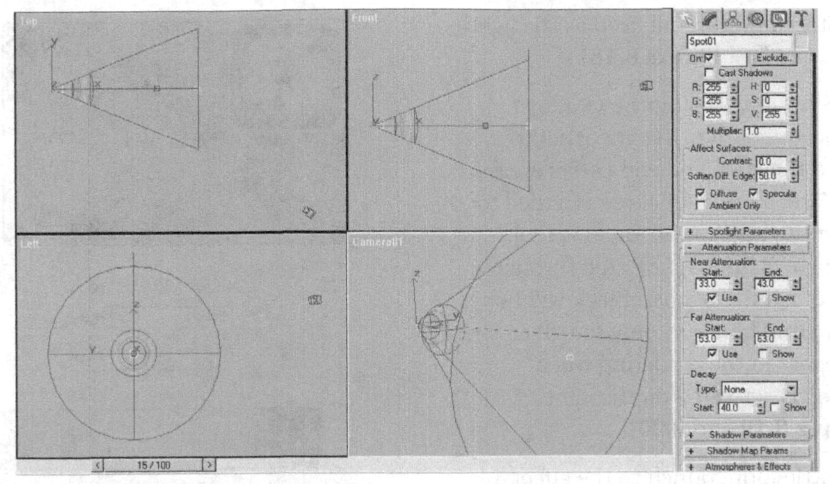

Figure 8.16 At frame 15, the Near Attenuation and Far Attenuation are near the source of light.

with the Far Attenuation. This will create a thin cross-section of light emanating from the light. If you were to select the Spot01 object in the Beam01.max scene and play the animation, you would notice that the Near Attenuation and Far Attenuation are slightly apart but move together (see **Figures 8.16** and **8.17**).

This animated cross-section creates the motion of the smoke ring the volume light will create.

The Ring of Light

This effect is intended is look like a smoke ring, except it uses light instead of smoke. To that end, a special map had to be created

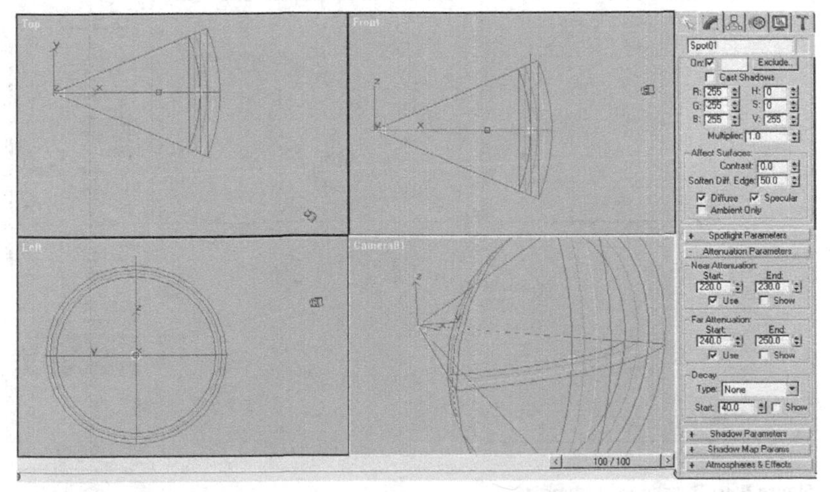

Figure 8.17 At frame 100, the Near Attenuation and Far Attenuation are animate further away from the light source.

in the Material Editor and used as the light's Projector Map (see **Figure 8.18**).

The Projector map is simply a Gradient Ramp procedural map. Its type is set to Radial, and the start and end colors are set to black. Also, a touch of Noise is added to the gradient to add a more organic look. This Gradient Ramp is projected through the beam of light. The color black will not emit any light. Therefore, only the green circle will appear in the rendering when Volume Fog is activated on the light (see **Figures 8.19** and **8.20**).

To add a little more punch to the effect, I animated the phase of the Noise on the Radial Gradient Ramp. This created an undulating smoke/light effect that's visible in the rendered animation. beam0l.avi. When applied to the growing beams of light that formed the peacock, this added the necessary punch to make the effect new and fresh.

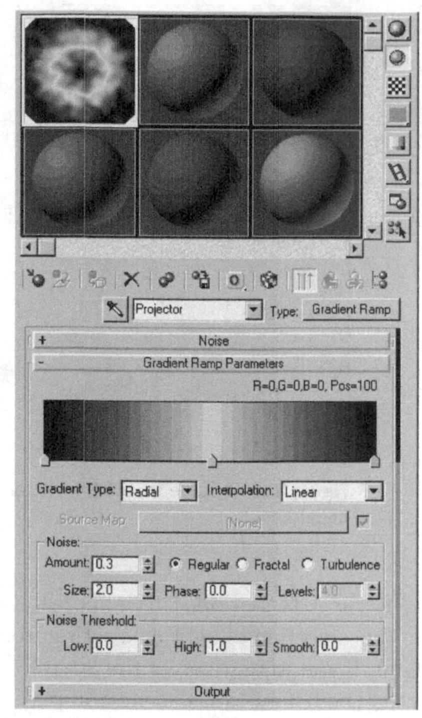

Figure 8.18 The Material Editor with the spotlight's Projector Map active.

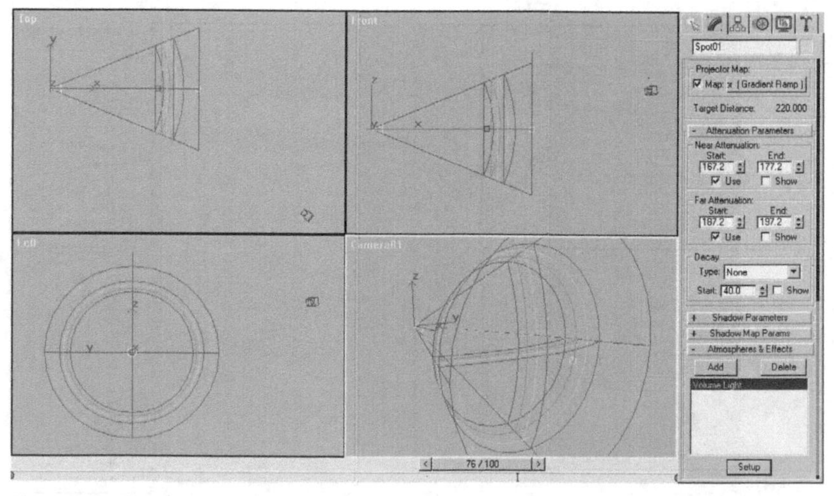

Figure 8.19 The scene at frame 76.

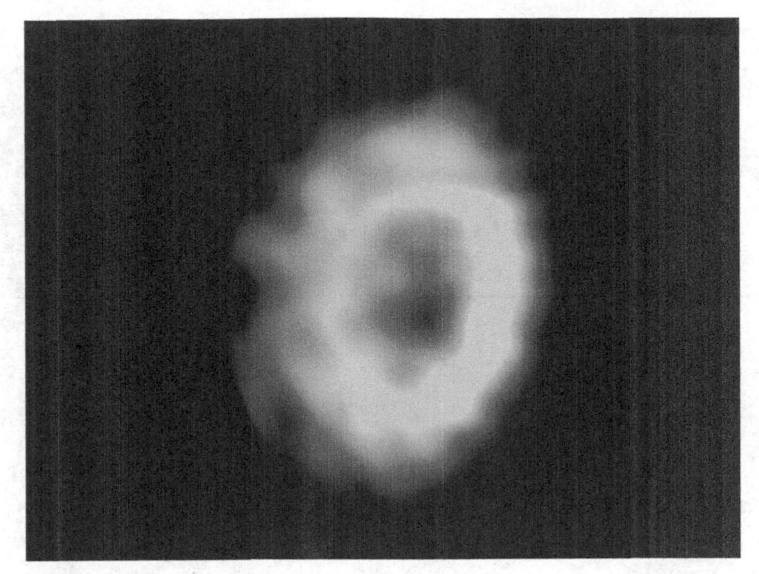

Figure 8.20 The rendered smoke ring effect.

The Peacock Feathers

I created the six feathers of the NBC peacock with twelve volume lights. Six of the volume lights grew from the center and created the solid beams; the other six were the "smoke ring" volume lights you just learned about. I framed this volumetric peacock with a rounded framework of the peacock (see **Figure 8.21**).

The peacock was placed inside a model of the earth's continents. The camera was animated to orbit from right to

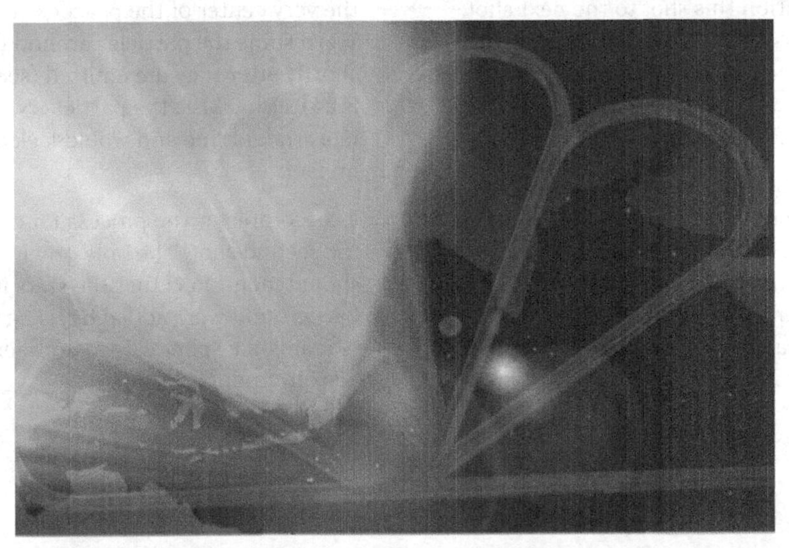

Figure 8.21 A frame from the final animation from the right side of the image clearly shows the rounded frame-work of the peacock.

Figure 8.22 The four views of the rendered frame shown in Figure 8.20.

left through the inside of the globe (see **Figure 8.22**).

One final volume light was placed in the rear of the scene to backlight the peacock as the shot reaches the end. This volume light helps transition this shot to the next shot, which shows the exterior of the globe with the clocks surrounding it.

The Peacock Particle Effect

As the peacock resolves, particles emit from the framework of the peacock. A Particle Array with a copy of the peacock shape as the Object-Based Emitter created this effect. Since the Particle Array cannot use shapes as an Object-Based Emitter, I simply applied a Mesh Select Modifier to the shape, which turns the shape into a mesh. If you load RW2/scenes/peakpart.max, you will see the elements used for the particle effects from the original scene (shown in **Figure 8.23**).

You will also notice a Motor Space Warp in the very center of the peacock. This Space Warp spins the particles around the peacock shortly after they are emitted (see **Figure 8.24**). Otherwise, the particles would travel in a straight line and would lack dramatic impact.

This completes the process for creating the second shot. The only other thing I should mention is that the stars in the background were added by using a bitmap of stars on a spherical environment background.

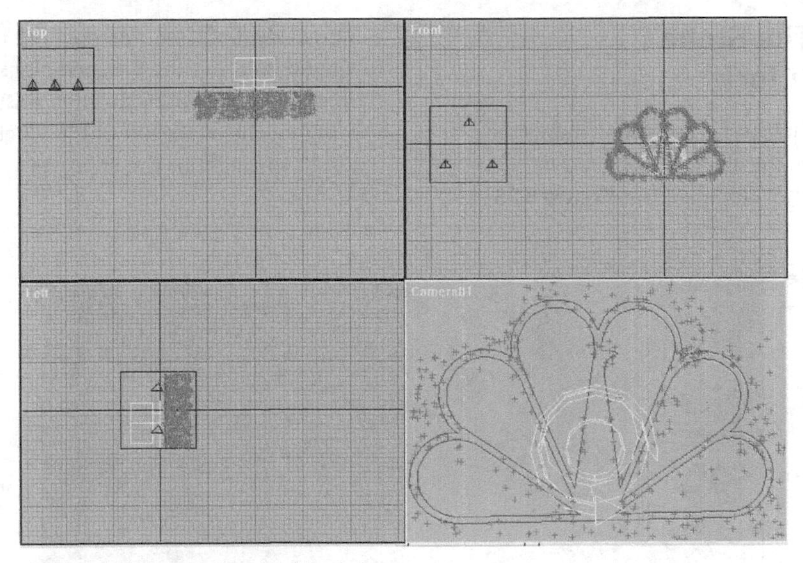

Figure 8.23 Frame 90 from Peakpart.max.

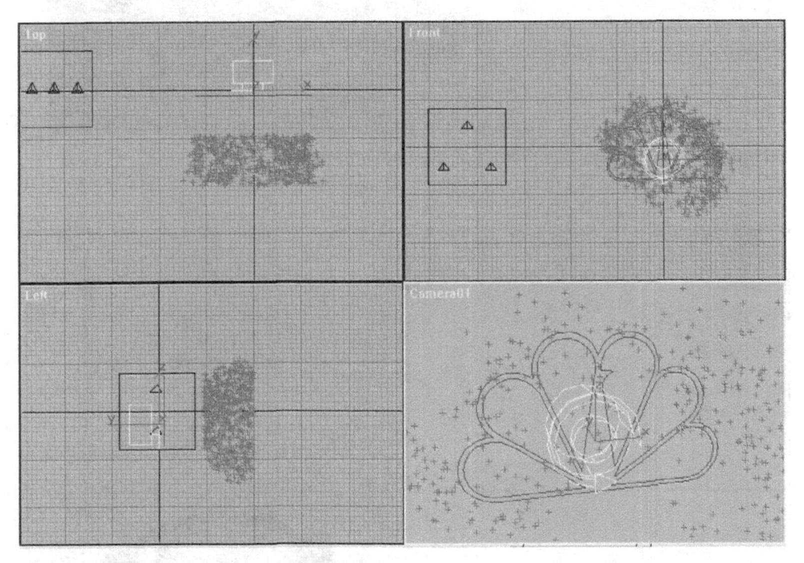

Figure 8.24 Frame 117 from peakpart.max.

Shot 3: The Globe and the Clock

The third shot in this animation marks the first time you see the globe exterior and the clock apparatus surrounding it (see **Figure 8.25**).

A great deal of time was put into designing and creating the finished clock Object. **Figures 8.26** through **8.28** illustrate the evolution of the clock design throughout the creative process.

Figure 8.25 An image from Shot 3 of the final animation.

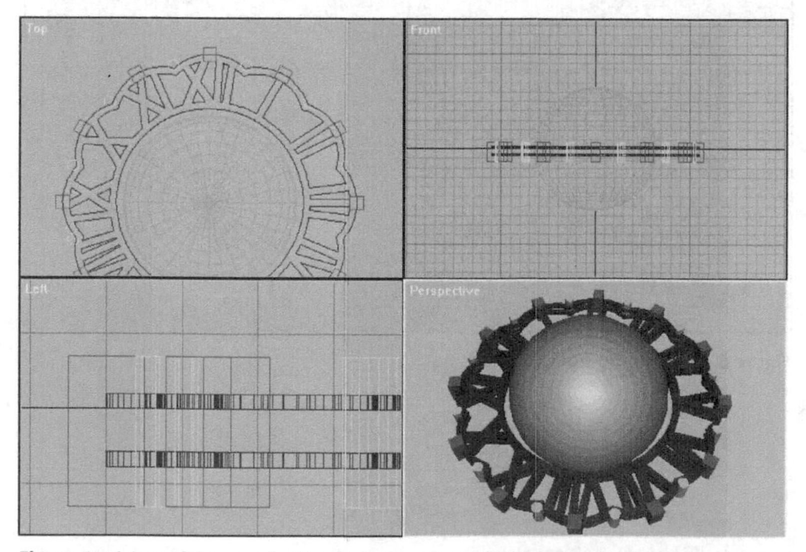

Figure 8.26 One of the very first basic designs for a clock created for the Millennium project. Notice how this clock makes the earth (sphere) to be more of a toy than the real earth.

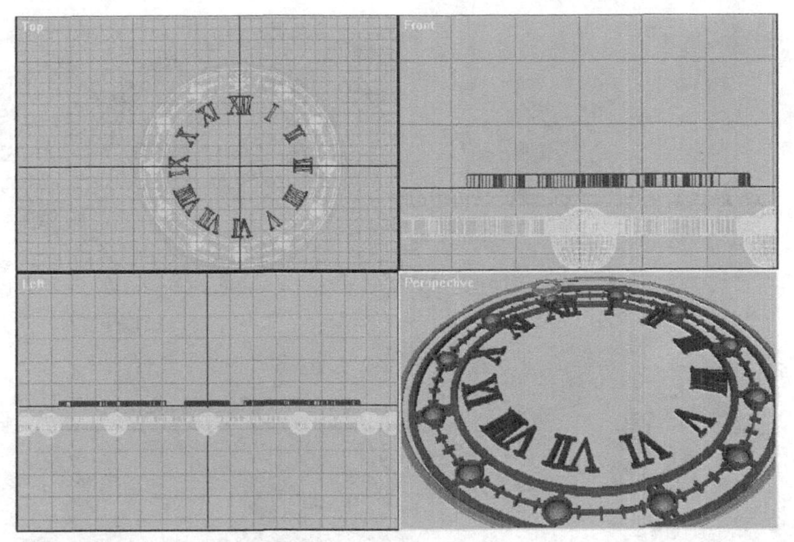

Figure 8.27 A more refined and polished version of the clock. However, it was not used because it was too visually complicated.

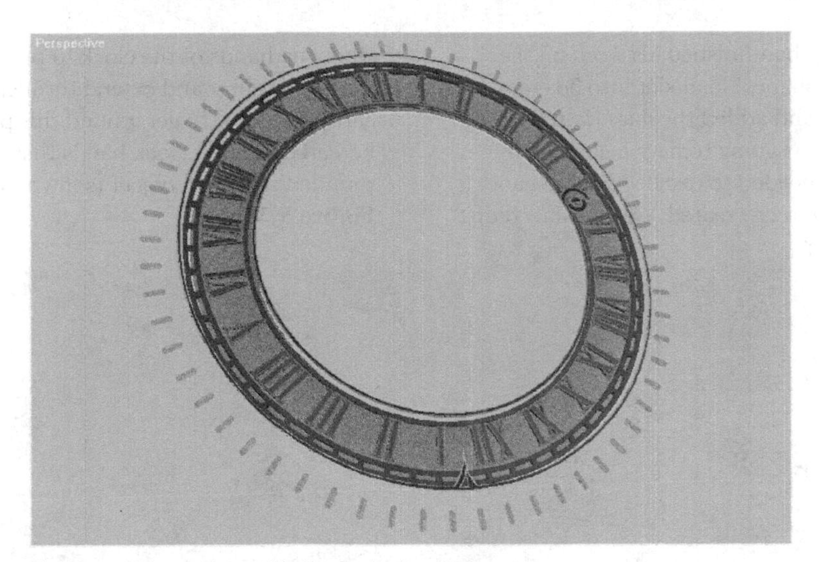

Figure 8.28 The clock, used in the final animation.

The Clock Face

Joe Dettmore and I agreed that we should create a clock with twenty-four hours on it. In the final design, the clock has the Roman numerals for one through twelve repeated on its face twice. After we decided on the design for the clock, I handed it off to Jonathan Burleson to create the spline of the clock face. Along with being a unique clock face, this clock appealed to me because of how huge it appears to be. By this I mean that when it wraps around the earth, the earth makes the clock look huge (see **Figure 8.29**) as opposed to the clock making the earth look like a toy.

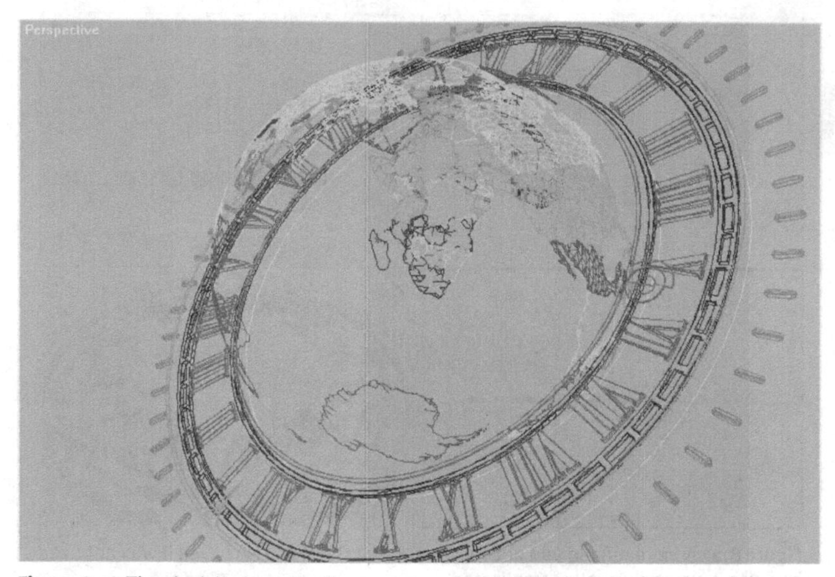

Figure 8.29 The clock looks natural wrapping around the earth.

When Jonathan finished his work on the clock face shape, I loaded it into 3ds max, beveled it, and added the materials. Because the clock was going to have a globe in the center, we needed to decide how the hands were going to be created. We certainly didn't want the hands of the clock to project from the center and extend through the earth's surface. To get around this problem, I created circular clock hands that surrounded the earth object (shown in **Figure 8.30**).

Figure 8.30 A close-up wireframe detail of the hands of the Millennium clock.

The model of the globe was purchased from a popular 3D stock object company. The globe was then imported and transformed to occupy its designated place within the clock.

The Globe's Volumetric Beams

A Free Spot light, with a falloff of 85 degrees, created the volumetric light beams that emanate from the center of the globe. The Free Spot light was assigned a Look At Motion Controller with the Camera designated as its Target. The Look At controller kept the Free Spot light pointed directly at the camera, keeping the effect uniformly round no matter where the camera moved. I used a Free Spot instead of an Omni light because the Omni threw too many beams (in all directions). The Free Spot creates the illusion that light is shooting 360 degrees, but it is not so overwhelming. This is clearly illustrated in the example file RW2\scenes\vollight.max on the CD (shown in **Figure 8.31**). **Figure 8.32** shows a rendered frame from this scene. Both lights use the same attenuation and volume light settings; however, because the Free Spot (right) emits an 85-degree cone of light, its effect is subtler.

The Camera

With the geometry and effects of the scene created, I added a camera and animated the scene. The camera was very close to the clock object in the beginning of the animation and considerably further away at the end. To animate the camera's position smoothly, I roughly animated it until I was happy with where the camera was located at each position key during the animation.

Because of the Bézier interpolation of the keys, the camera moved undesirably. To fix it, I entered the Motion panel, went to the Trajectories rollout, and clicked Convert To

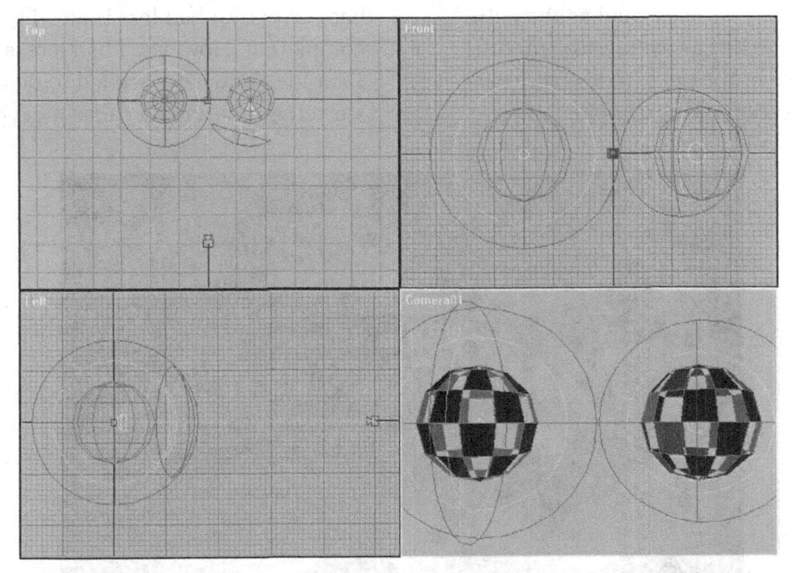

Figure 8.31 Vollight.max illustrates the difference between using an Omni light and a Free Spot light to generate the volume light effect.

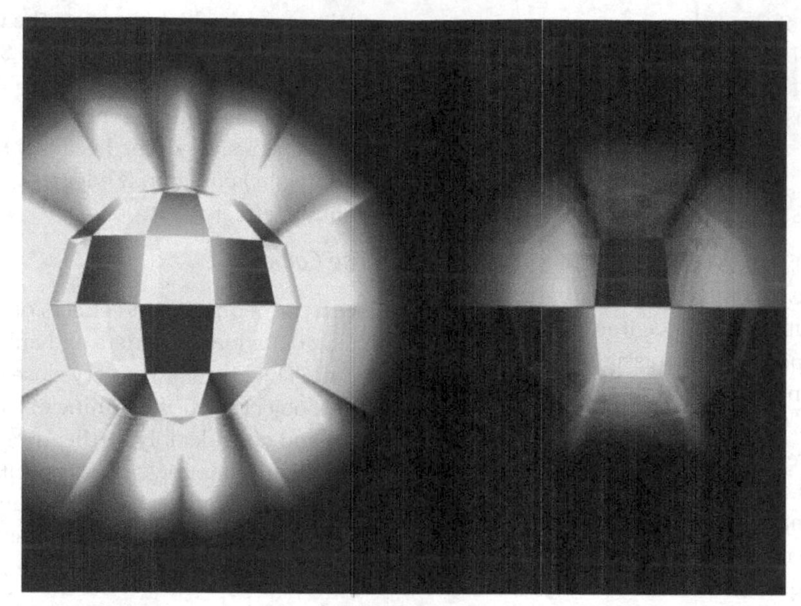

Figure 8.32 A rendered frame from vollight.max.

in the Spline Conversion group. This converted the camera's trajectory into an editable spline. A Path controller was then assigned to the camera, and the converted trajectory shape was assigned as the path. I then used the Beziér handles to smooth out the shape of the path to desirably animate the position of the camera.

Shot 4: The Millennium Logo

Figure 8.33 shows the final shot I put together for the animation, and if I remember correctly, I had less than 24 hours to complete it. However, I had a reasonably clear idea of what I needed to do before I started animating. Because most of the

Figure 8.33 A frame from the fourth shot of the Millennium animation.

background (the clock and globe) was already done, all I really needed to do was build the text, and then I was ready to start animating.

Joe and I had discussed this shot from the very beginning of production. We knew the general effects we wanted to see, such as the particles traveling backwards to create the Millennium type. Just to make sure Joe and I were on the same base, Joe quickly drew up storyboards on sticky notes; those storyboards are shown in **Figures 8.34** through **8.37**.

Frame One (**Figure 8.34**) shows the camera looking straight down on the globe and surrounding clock. Frame Two of the story-board (**Figure 8.35**) illustrates the desired angle of clock/globe relationship. Notice the NBC peacock out of the frame above. Frame Three (**Figure 8.36**) demonstrates the desired animation of the logo's elements. The trapezoid to the right is the Millennium type, and an arrow indicates its rotation into place. The arrow on the left specifies that the MSNBC type is to write on from the left. And once again the peacock is shown flying in from the top of the frame. Frame Four (**Figure 8.37**) depicts all the elements in their final positions, completing the animation.

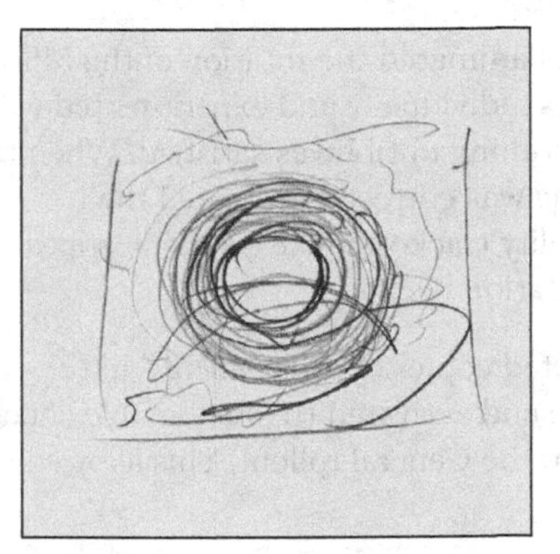

Figure 8.34 Frame One of the Sticky note storyboard.

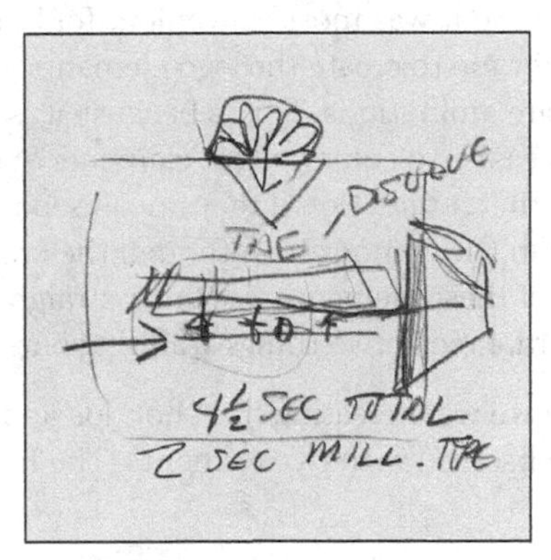

Figure 8.36 Frame Three.

Figure 8.35 Frame Two.

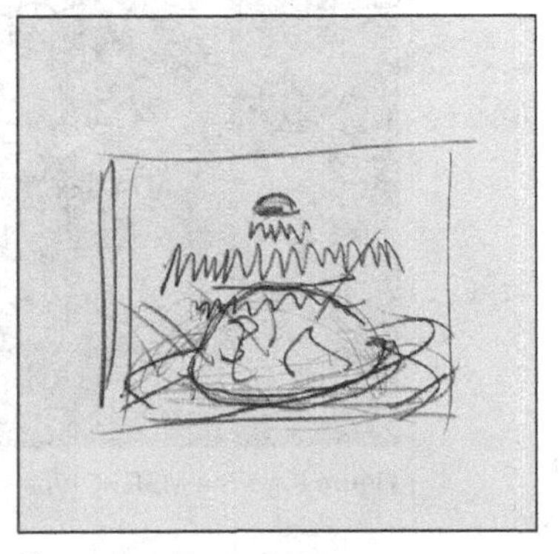

Figure 8.37 Frame Four.

Although primitive, a storyboard such as the one above is an easy way to verify that all the minds working on a project are on the same track. In an ideal world, I would certainly have preferred to work with a beautifully illustrated storyboard. However, time usually doesn't afford us that luxury.

Building the Logo

Because I was able to recycle the clock and globe element from shot to shot, creating the background was simple. All I really had to do was animate the camera. When the motion of the globe and clock element was satisfactory, I sent it off to the render farm to render away.

Joe was compositing most of my elements in the Hal, so it was most convenient for both of us for me to create the logo elements as separate animations. This is because it is much easier to color-correct elements and offset their animation if they are all separate layers in the composite. Although the creation of these elements was fairly straightforward, I recall two things standing out.

When we were creating this shot, Joe and I were obsessed with two elements. The first was that we wanted to do something we had never done before with the MSNBC type, and the second related to the Millennium text particles. In the following sections, you will examine how each scene was created.

The MSNBC Type

View the file RW2\msnbc.avi and the corresponding Max file RW2\scenes\mlmsnbc.max. The MSNBC type rotates unto the screen, letter by letter, in a flurry of fairy dust and lens flares (see **Figure 8.38**). This scene could be broken down into four elements: the MSNBC objects, the particles, the MSNBC outline objects, and the lens flares. Even though the action passes very quickly, a lot happens.

First, I animated the rotation of the MSNBC letters individually and experimented with their timing until I was satisfied. When their timing was correct, I animated their Visibility track to make each one appear as its rotation begins.

I created copies of each MSNBC letter shape and activated the Renderable check box in the General rollout. This allowed me

Figure 8.38 The MSNBC type element.

to create the outlines of the MSNBC letters that emanate after they finish rotating into place. The Visibility tracks of the MSNBC outline objects were animated to make them appear and disappear.

One thing about the Visibility tracks in this scene is particularly noteworthy. For the MSNBC and the MSNBC outline objects, different animation Controllers are assigned to the tracks (see **Figure 8.39**). The MSNBC, (solid) objects have a simple On/Off controller, indicated by the blue line, which provides a simple on or off control. However, the MSNBC outline objects have a Linear Float controller that allows for the effect of being dissolved on and off.

The fairy dust effect is created with multiple Particle Cloud emitters, each of which generates particles for only seven frames. The lens flares are added In Video Post; you can see their settings by accessing their individual dialogs.

The Millennium Particles

Joe had approached me early during this project and asked "Can we make particles go backward?" I thought to myself, "Even it they were going backward, they would have to be traveling forward." I answered, "Yes." Confused? I was too. Luckily it wasn't as hard as it seemed at first. Joe simply wanted the screen to be filled with random particles that were suddenly sucked back in space to spell the word "Millennium."

The easiest way to create the effect was to create the particles traveling forward and have Joe reverse the animation in the Hal. You can view RW2\milparts.avi to see the particle animation I sent to Joe to reverse (see **Figure 8.40**). Load RW2\scenes\millprts.max as well to see the file that created this animation.

If you look at the RW2\scenes\millprts.max scene, you may be overwhelmed by all the Space Warps that make up the scene (see **Figure 8.41**). When it's broken down, it becomes quite simple.

The particles are emitted from a Particle Array particle system using the Millennium type as an Object-Based Emitter. The first Gravity Space Warp uses Spherical Force

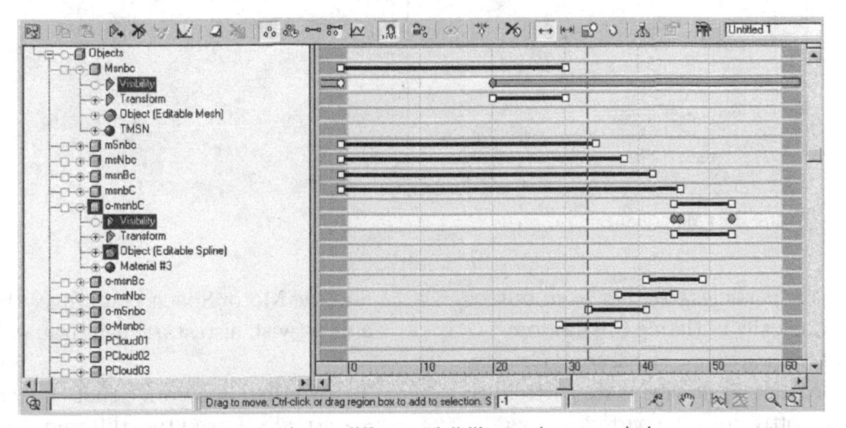

Figure 8.39 The Track View with two different Visibility tracks expanded.

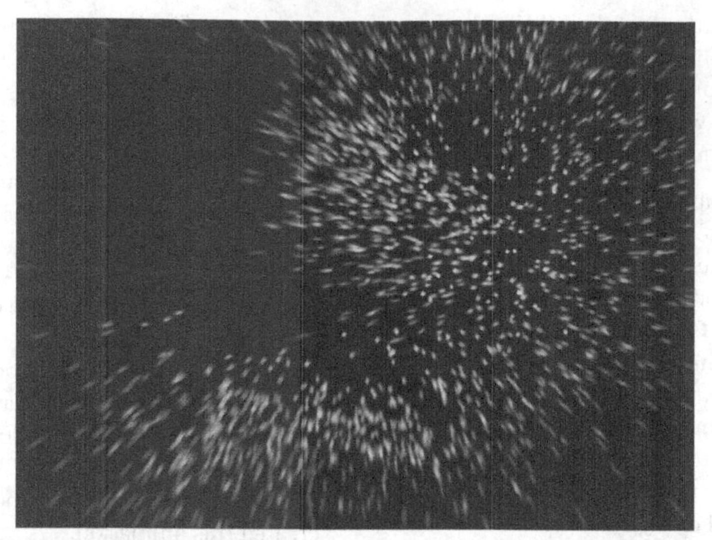

Figure 8.40 The Millennium particles.

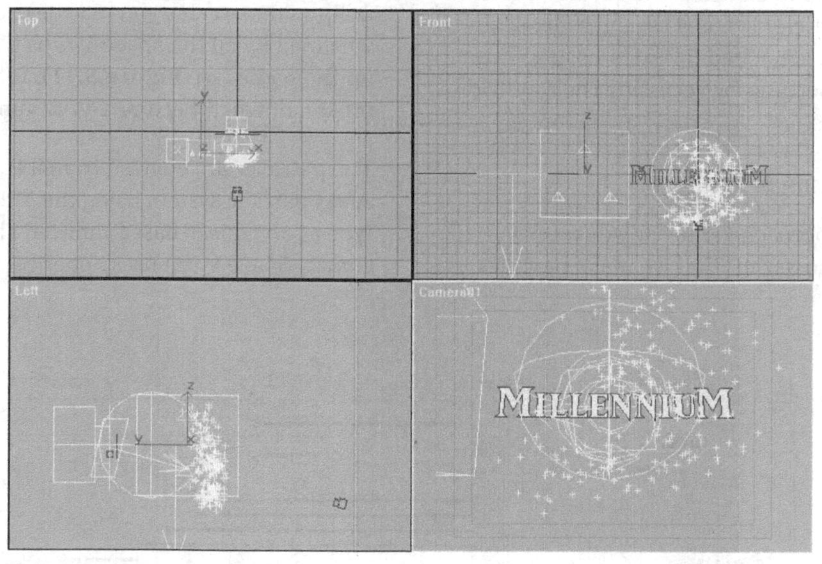

Figure 8.41 Millprts.max.

and pulls the particles together from frames 150–220, basically initiating the random motion of the particles. The second Gravity Space Warp acts as gravity as we earthlings know it: It softly pulls the particles downward. The Wind Space Warp blows the particles toward the camera, starting at frame 200, and the Motor Space Warp gives the particles a nice twist, also starting at frame 200.

To give the appearance that the particles are streaks, I used two different types of Motion Blur on them. I used Object Motion Blur with a Duration of 1 frame, 16 Samples,

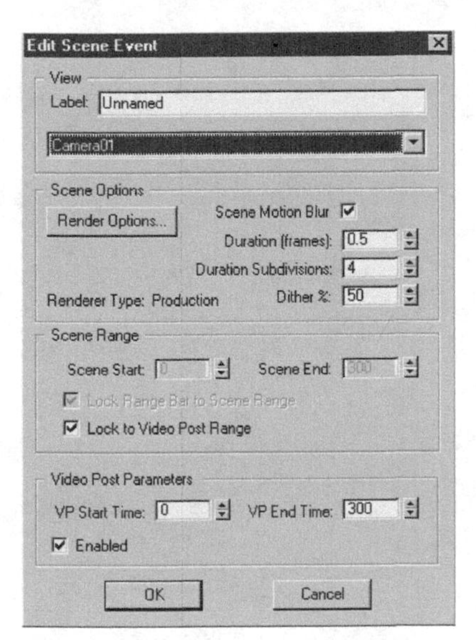

Figure 8.42 The Edit Scene Event dialog with Scene Motion Blur activated.

and 16 Duration Subdivisions. The second motion blur I used is available only in Video Post; It's called Scene Motion Blur, and it's shown in **Figure 8.42**.

Scene Motion Blur renders each frame multiple times, as indicated in the Duration Subdivisions field and then it dithers all the renderings for the frame together. So the combination of the Object and Scene Motion Blur created a very nice streaking effect.

Rendering the Final Composite

Joe color-corrected and composited the individual layers I had created and rendered. When each individual shot was finished, Joe created all the transitions from shot to shot. The final piece is right on the money—exactly what Joe and I had anticipated. Everyone was happy with the final product, and no changes were required, which was good because it was finished only hours before it was scheduled to air.

9

Project 1: Part 1

In Project 1, the focus now turns to the 3d environment and how to utilize 3ds Max to generate graphic content. In the Project 1, you will create a television news opening. The skills learned by completing this project will emphasize the power of 3ds Max for generating media content.

Creating the Globe Environment

You head over to John's workstation and look at the storyboards (see **Figure 9.1**). John then begins to explain that he would like to see a real world, with wireframe latitude/longitude lines and solid metal continents.

"This is just the concept for the animation," John adds. "It's up to you to really stylize it."

You nod and then inquire about his intent for the logo's manifestation: "Do you see the camera traveling through those blue Venetian blinds as a transition to the logo?" John confirms your hunch, informing you that the project is basically two animations: the globe environment and the logo. The transition element will be the blue Venetian blinds that remain behind the logo.

You turn to John and add, "Thanks John, I'll do the best I can to bring this to life," and you turn to head back to work.

By examining the storyboards and talking with John, you've learned you will need to make two scenes in order to create the animation. To see a JPG image of the storyboard, just open **Project1\images\news-board.jpg**. The first scene will be the globe environment, illustrated by the first three storyboard panels, and that is what you will create in this chapter. You'll animate the scene in the next chapter.

In this chapter, you're going to learn the following:

- Deciding whether to use Wire materials or Circle shapes
- Creating renderable splines
- Creating an Include list to illuminate particular isolated objects
- Effectively using Opacity Maps
- Working with Raytrace reflection maps and materials
- Using a Specular Level map

Creating the Objects

In this chapter you will be building and adding lights to the globe scene. When you examine the storyboard, you see that the objects are all basic primitive objects, mostly a sphere and tube primitives. Using these primitive shapes, however, it is up to you to develop their materials and bring them to life.

Setting Up the Wireframe-Like Object

Talking with John, you learned that the globe needs to appear as though there are

Figure 9.1 John's storyboard for the TV 3 News opening.

solid metal continents on a wireframe frame. You will build this framework first so you can place the metal continents over it.

At first you think, "I can just create another sphere and assign a Wire material to it." Then you remember the pitfalls of Wire materials (see **Figure 9.2**). To create this Wire material, all you had to do was check Wire in the material's Shader Basic Parameters rollout (shown in **Figure 9.3**). Checking that box instructs the renderer to render the object in a wireframe representation. The thickness of this wireframe representation is adjusted in the Wire group of the Extended Parameters rollout. Using Pixels instructs the renderer to render all the lines the same thickness, regardless of their distance from the camera. Using Units instructs the renderer to render the lines in varying thickness, as determined by their distance from the camera.

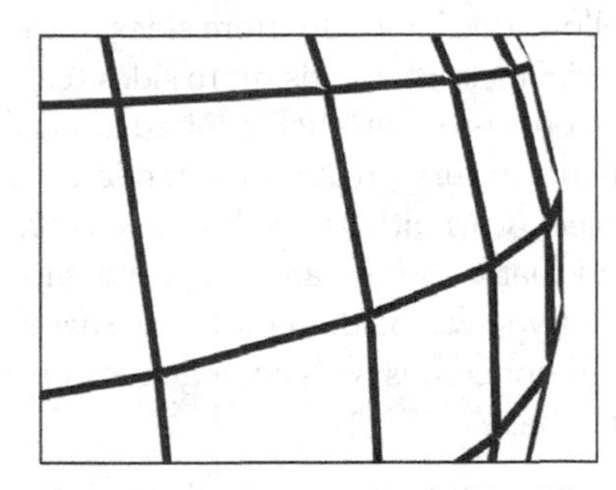

Figure 9.2 A sphere rendered with a Wire material.

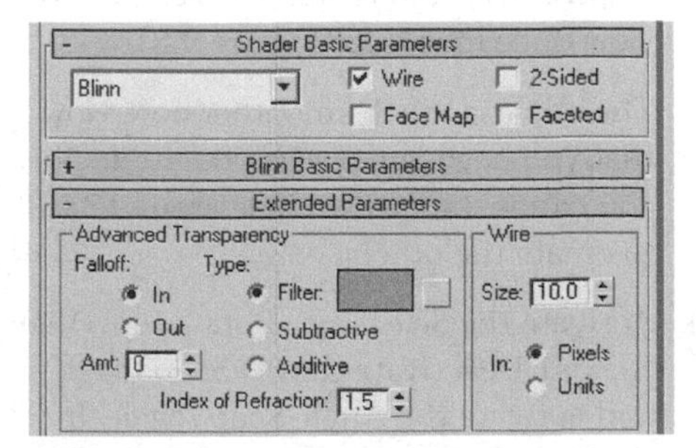

Figure 9.3 You can check Wire in the Shader Basic Parameters rollout to create a wireframe material.

The pitfalls of using Wire to generate a wireframe effect in your renders is obvious in **Figure 9.2**. When the renderer creates the polygons on the wireframe to be rendered, it often leaves gaps and undesired triangular artifacts. A Wire material works if you are in a pinch; however, you will need to create the wireframe globe frame a different way.

Exercise 9.1 Using Circle Shapes to Create the Illusion of a Wireframe Object

To create the frame, you will build longitudinal and latitudinal lines using renderable circle shapes.

1. Choose File > Reset 3DS Max and activate the 3D Snap toggle. Open the Create > Shapes panel, click the Circle button, and in the Front view, create a Circle Shape at XYZ: **0, 0, 0** with a Radius of **60** (as shown in **Figure 9.4**). Leave the name **Circle01**.

   This circle is the first of the globe's longitude lines. Right now, if you rendered any of the views, nothing would render. 3ds max, however, allows you to make shapes renderable with precise control. Make those adjustments now.

   ✔ Note

   In my scene I have colored the shape blue by clicking the color swatch next to its name. This helps me to visually organize my scene because I know I will be adding a blue material to it later.

2. With Circle01 still selected, open the Modify panel and expand the Rendering rollout. Check Renderable (as shown in **Figure 9.5**) and Render the Perspective view (shown in **Figure 9.6**).

   That was easy—making the Circle01 shape render that is—however the shape is stepping far too much. By saying,

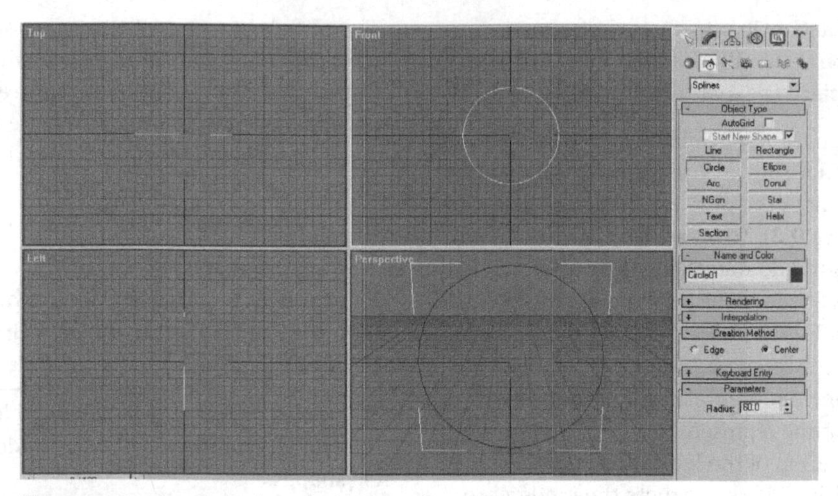

Figure 9.4 Create a circle shape in the Front view at XYZ: 0, 0, 0.

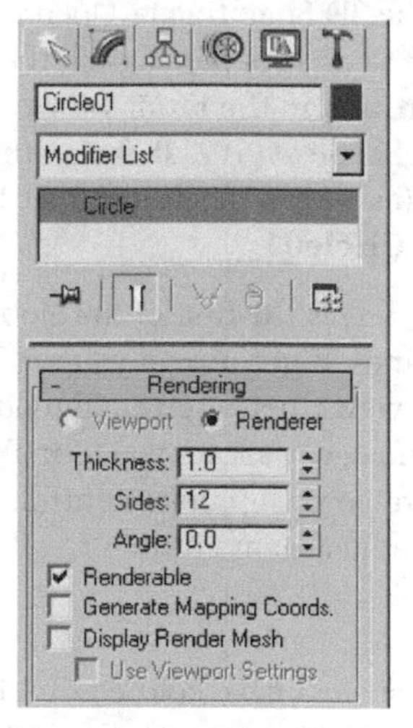

Figure 9.5 Check Renderable to make the shape render.

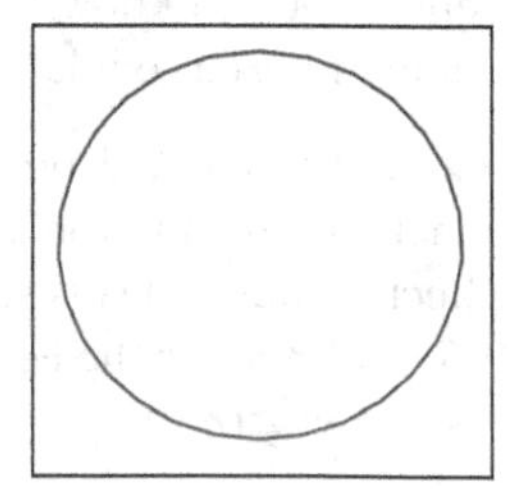

Figure 9.6 The rendered Circle01 shape (the background is changed to white for figure clarity).

"stepping," I mean there aren't enough polygons to create the illusion of roundness. You need to add more steps to the shape. The Sides value in the Rendering rollout does not add more sides to the circle; instead it adds more sides to the cross-section that is lofted along the shape, in turn creating the rendered object. Currently, the Sides value is 12, and that is more than enough sides for what you will be doing with the shape; your concern is with adding more steps to the shape.

3. Open the Interpolation rollout, change the Steps value to **20** (as shown in **Figure 9.7**), and render the Perspective view once more (see **Figure 9.8**).

   The circle is much smoother now. Now that you have one perfect longitude line, you can instance the circle around itself to create the others.

4. Activate the Select and Rotate tool (View Z-axis). Deactivate the 3D Snap toggle and activate the Angle Snap toggle. In the Top view, Shift+drag the circle to rotate it Z: **–30** degrees. In the Clone Options dialog, choose Instance and

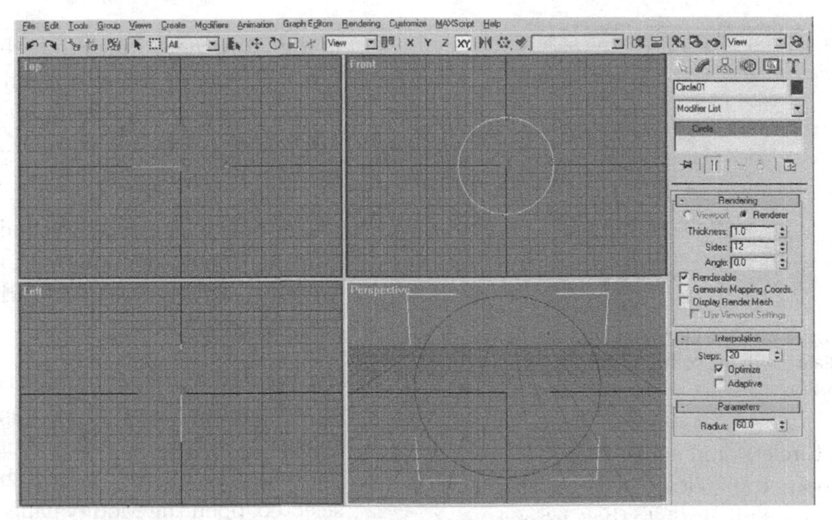

Figure 9.7 The Steps value in the Interpolation is increased to 20, making a smoother circle shape.

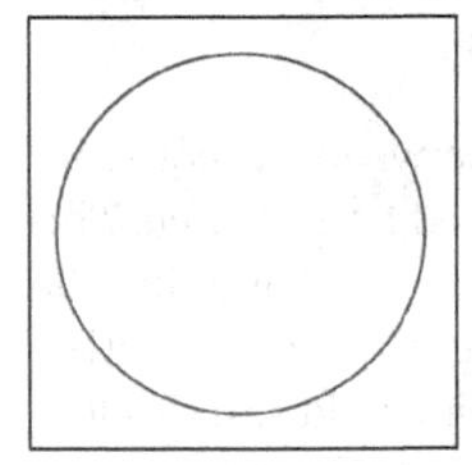

Figure 9.8 The rendered circle shape with a Steps value of 20 (the background is changed to white for figure clarity).

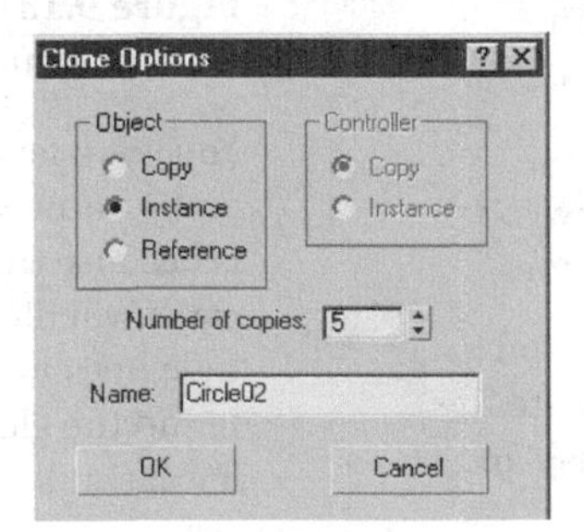

Figure 9.9 The Clone Options dialog with the correct settings to create the remaining longitude lines.

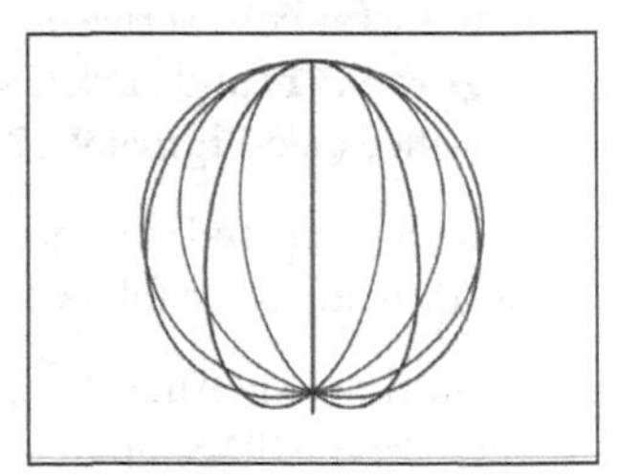

Figure 9.10 The rendered longitude lines from the Perspective view.

change the Number of Copies to **5** (as shown in **Figure 9.9**). Click OK to create the instances. Then render the Perspective view (see **Figure 9.10**).

You chose to create 5 instances because you rotated the circle 30 degrees. 180 degrees is half a full rotation, and 180 (degrees) divided by 30 (degrees) is 6 (circles). Subtracting the initial circle, you need 5 instances.

The rendered circles are too thick for my taste. You need to thin them.

5. In the Rendering rollout of the Modify Panel, with any Circle shape selected, change the Thickness value to **.5** and render the Perspective view again.

The longitude lines are perfect now. Now you can start to lay out the latitude lines. For the equator, you can simply instance a circle that we already created. For the others, you will have to copy a circle shape, move it into position, and size it accordingly.

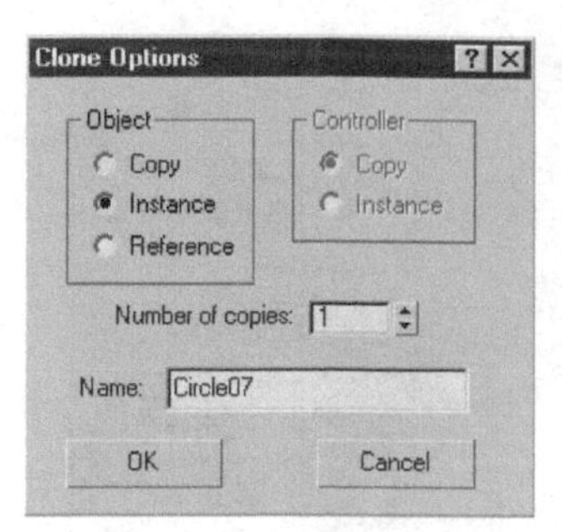

Figure 9.11 The Clone Options dialog with the correct Instance settings.

6. Select Circle04 and activate the Select and Rotate tool (View Z-axis). In the Front view, Shift+rotate the Circle04 shape Z: **–90** degrees to create the equator. In the Clone Options dialog, make sure Instance is active (as shown in **Figure 9.11**) and click OK to create the instance (see **Figure 9.12**).

   You have created the equator, now you need to create its fellow latitude lines.

7. Deactivate the Angle Snap toggle and activate the 3D Snap toggle. Activate the Select and Move tool (View Y-axis), and in the Front view, Shift+drag the Circle07 (equator) shape upward Y: **30**. In the Clone Options dialog, choose Copy in the Object area and click OK to create the copy.

   The circle shape is too large and doesn't fit on the longitude framework snugly. You can easily fix this by adjusting the circle shape's Radius.

8. Use the Pan and Zoom tools to view the upper-right quadrant of the frame. Right-click the Front view label and uncheck Show Grid. With the Circle08 shape selected, open the Modify panel and lower the Radius value until the circle touches the latitude lines (as shown in **Figure 9.13**). In my scene, I came up with a Radius of 51.95.

   You left a large gap between the equator and your newly created latitude line. This is because the gold rings surrounding the earth will fill in that gap. Any extra latitude lines in that area would simply clutter up the globe's design. Having just a few latitude lines will be enough to hold

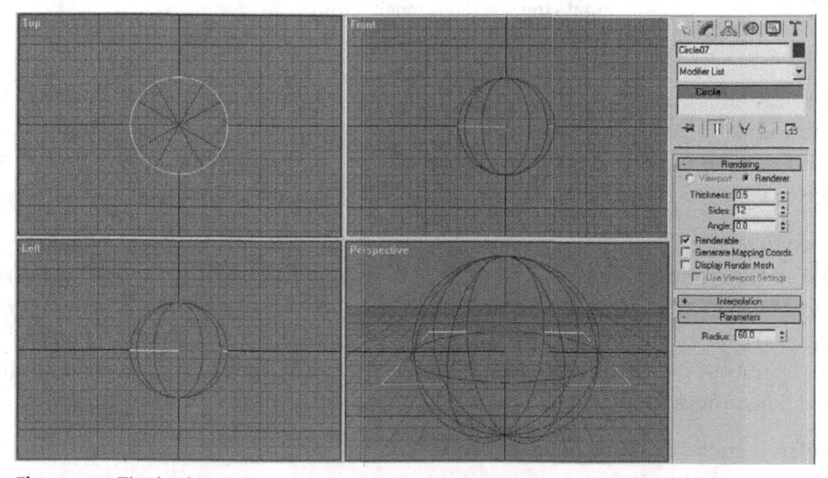

Figure 9.12 The horizontal equator has been added to the vertical longitude lines.

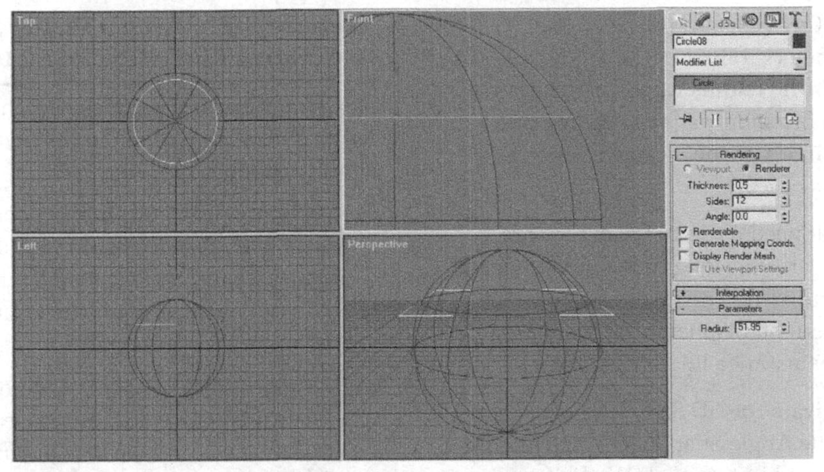

Figure 9.13 The second latitude line is in its correct location and is also sized correctly.

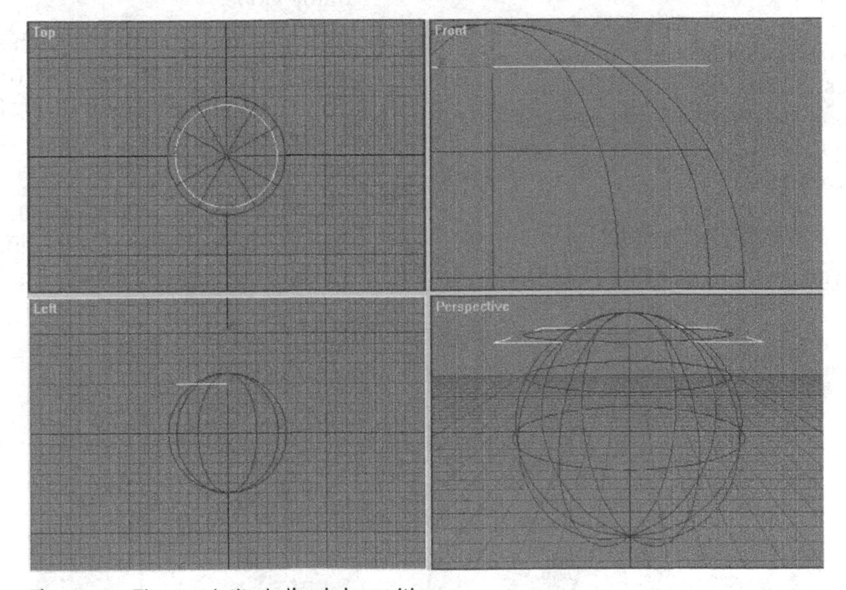

Figure 9.14 The new latitude line is in position.

it together visually, yet that will not detract from the more important aspects in the scene. To finish the northern hemisphere, you will create one more latitude line.

9. With the Select and Move tool (View Y-axis) active, Shift+move the Circle08 shape up Y: **20** in the Left view. In the Clone Options dialog, make sure Copy is active and click OK to create the copy (see **Figure 9.14**).

Now, just as you did for the previous latitude line, you need to size the Radius to fit snugly on the longitude lines.

10. With Circle09 selected, open the Parameters rollout of the Modify panel. Adjust the Radius value until the circle shape fits snugly against the longitude lines. In my scene, I came up with a Radius of 33.1.

All you need to do to finish the wire-frame latitude/longitude frame is create the southern hemisphere. Because the northern hemisphere is finished, you can simply instance it.

11. Deactivate the 3D Snap toggle and activate the Angle Snap toggle. Activate the Select and Rotate tool (World Y-axis—Use Transform Coordinate Center). Select the two latitude lines of the northern hemisphere (Circle08 and Circle09) and Shift+rotate the two circle shapes Y: **180** degrees. In the Clone Options dialog, choose Instance and click OK to create the instances (see **Figure 9.15**).

The framework of the globe is complete.

12. Save your work as **09TV01.max**.

Exercise 9.2 Using a Phong Shader to Create a Blue Metallic Material

Next you'll apply the material to the wire-frame globe so you don't have to worry about that later.

1. Make sure **09TV01.max** is open, select all 11 of the Circle shapes, and open the Material Editor. Make sure the first material preview slot is active and name the material **wireframe**.

Because the storyboard does not depict the desired globe, you must use your own artistic sense and creative judgment. You know that the globe must be blue metal; so put a shiny blue material on the wire-frame globe.

2. Click the Ambient color swatch and enter RGB: **105**, **105**, **250** into the Color Selection: Ambient Color dialog (shown in **Figure 9.16**). Click Close to close the color selector.

Now you need to make the material shinier. To create the metallic effect, you will use a Phong shader. The Phong

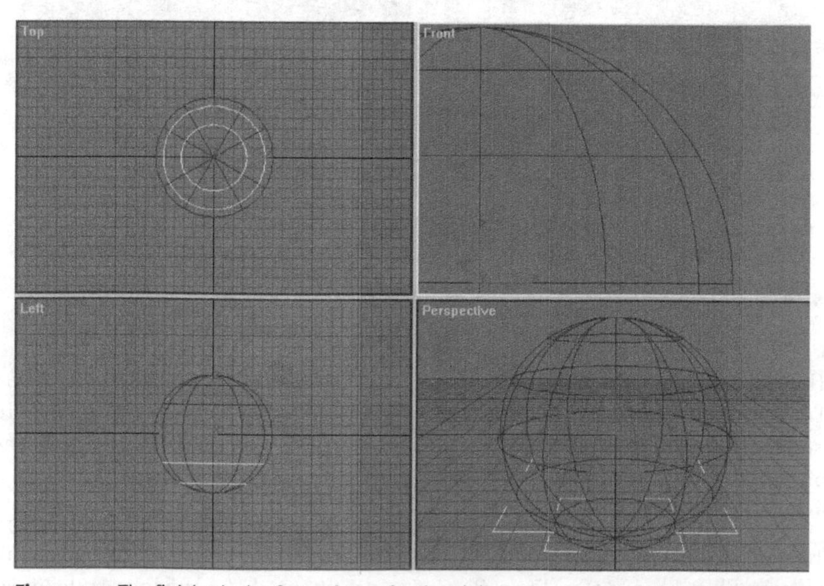

Figure 9.15 The finished wire-frame frame for the globe.

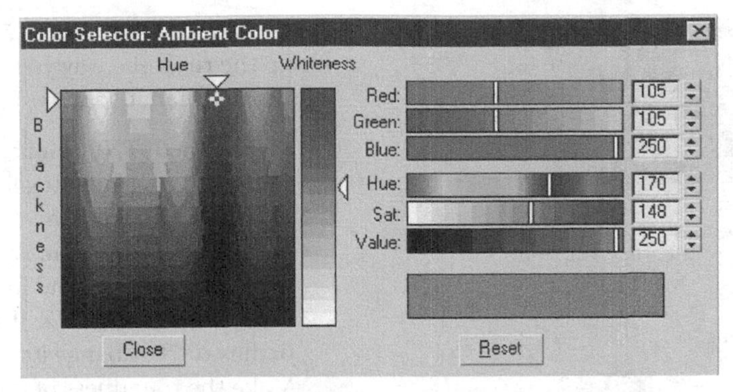

Figure 9.16 The correct shade of blue is selected in the Color Selector.

shader is ideal for creating plastic materials. However, you can also use it to create a metallic material. The metal shader, although also good for creating metallic materials, is not as versatile as the phong shader because it does not allow the user to change the specular color.

3. In the Shader Basic Parameters rollout, change the shader from Blinn to Phong. In the Phong Basic Parameters rollout, change the Specular Level to **88** and Glossiness to **17** (as shown in **Figure 9.17**).

4. With all 11 circle shapes selected, click the Assign Material to Selection button. Then render the Perspective view (see **Figure 9.18**).

   That looks good, however you need to add a little Self-Illumination to it to brighten the color in the darker areas.

5. In the Phong Basic Parameters rollout, change the Self-Illumination value to **50**

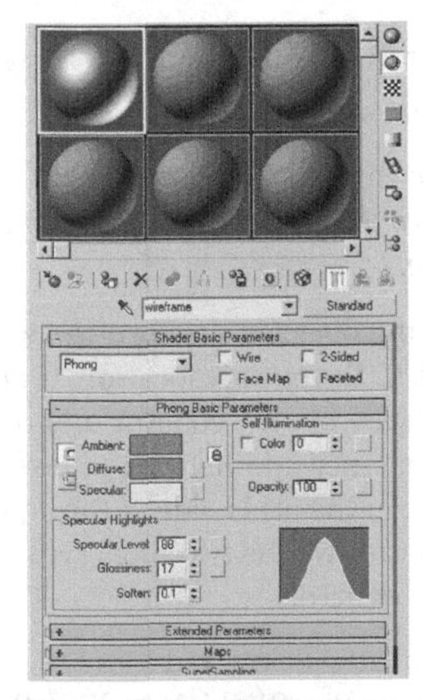

Figure 9.17 The wireframe material with the correct settings so far.

Figure 9.18 The rendered wireframe material in the Perspective view.

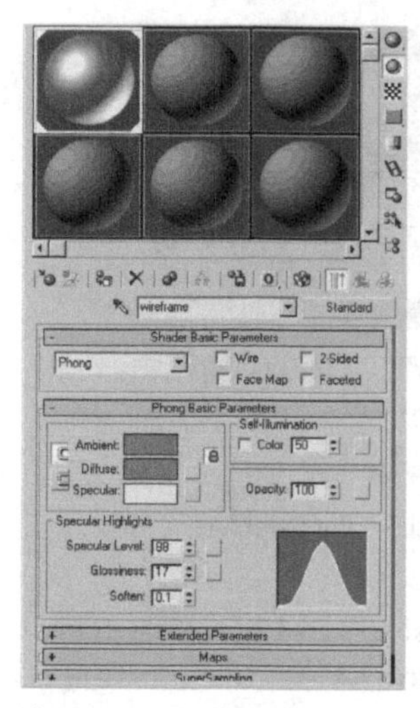

Figure 9.19 The finished wireframe material in the Material Editor.

(see **Figure 9.19**). Render the Perspective view again.

In the rendered Perspective view, you will notice the Self-Illumination brightening up some of the dark areas of the wireframe objects. The material is perfect now.

6. Save your work as **09TV02.max** and close the Material Editor.

Adding the Globe and Its Rings

Now that you've created the internal wireframe structure of the globe, you can place the continents on top of it. You will not be placing the continents directly on the surface; instead you will opacity map the continents above the wireframe structure on a sphere, thereby creating depth and interest. Then you will create the rings that wrap around the globe.

Exercise 9.3 Working with the Sphere and Tube Shapes and the Mirror Tool

In one step, you can create the globe. Then it's on to using Tube, the Use Transform Coordinate Center option, the World Coordinate system, and the Mirror tool to set up the rings the way you want them. It's a lot easier than it sounds.

1. Make sure **09TV02.max** is open, deactivate the Angle Snap toggle if it is still active, and activate the 3D Snap toggle. Open the Create > Geometry panel, click the Sphere button, and in the Top view, create a sphere at XYZ: **0, 0, 0** with a Radius of **70**. Change its name to **Globe**. Make the roundness of the globe smoother by changing the Segments value to **64** (see **Figure 9.20**).

   The globe object is finished; you will create the continents by using maps in the material. But before you apply the material to the globe, you should add the rings.

2. In the Create > Geometry panel, click the Tube button and in the Top view, create a tube with these settings:

   Radius 1: **85**

   Radius 2: **70**

   Height: **1**

   Height Segments: **1**

   Sides: **64**

   Name this object **Ring01** (as shown in **Figure 9.21**). Deactivate the 3D Snap toggle.

   The ring object is the correct size, but it is not in the correct location. It needs to be offset from the equator, and then you will instance another ring to be equally offset on the other side of the equator. The result will be two rings symmetrical to the equator.

3. Activate the Select and Move tool and move the Ring01 object to XYZ: **0, 0, −12**. With Ring01 selected, activate the Select and Move tool (World XY-axis—Use

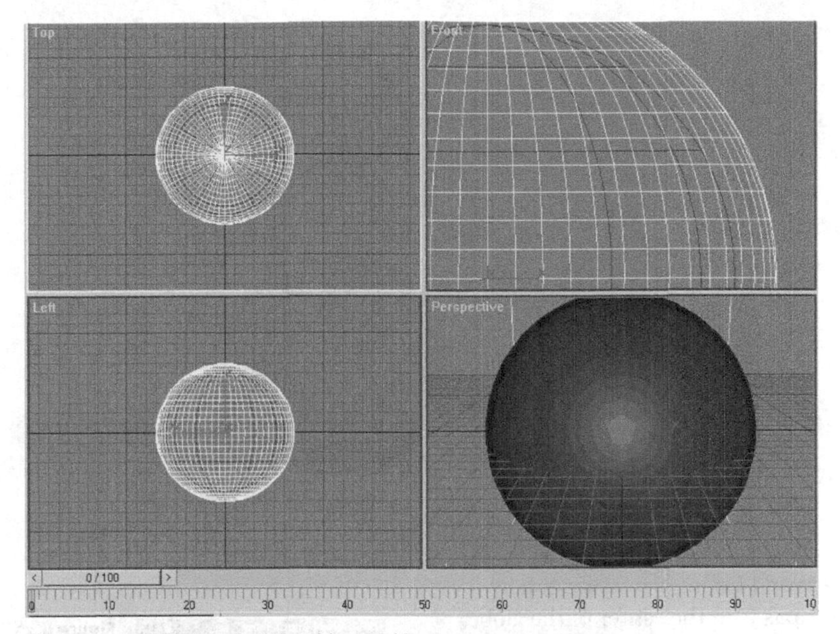

Figure 9.20 The finished Globe object and its correct parameters.

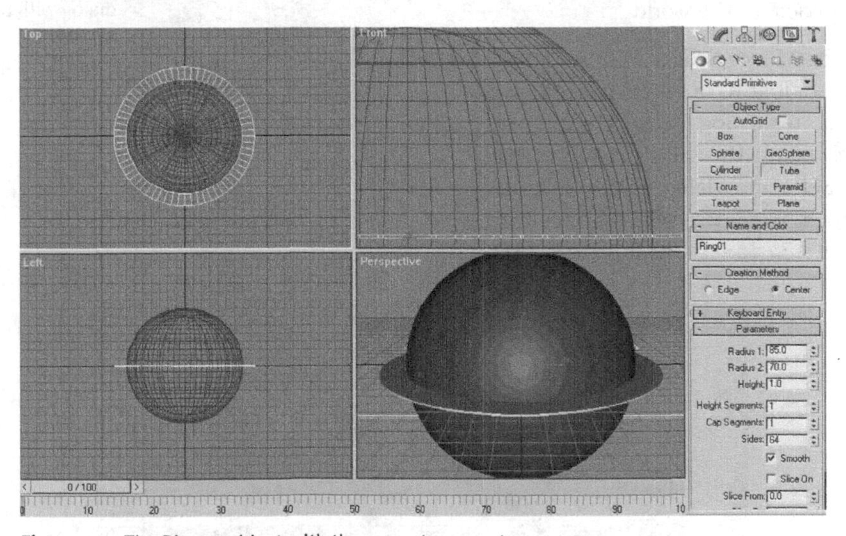

Figure 9.21 The Ring01 object with the correct parameters.

Transform Coordinate Center), as shown in **Figure 9.22**.

When Use Transform Coordinate Center is active on the World Coordinate system, the transform axis moves to the center of the world (XYZ: 0, 0, 0). The Mirror tool will use the axis as it is currently being used. Therefore, if you use the Local Coordinate system, the object would mirror, but it would mirror on its local axis and therefore would not be positioned the way you want it. If you

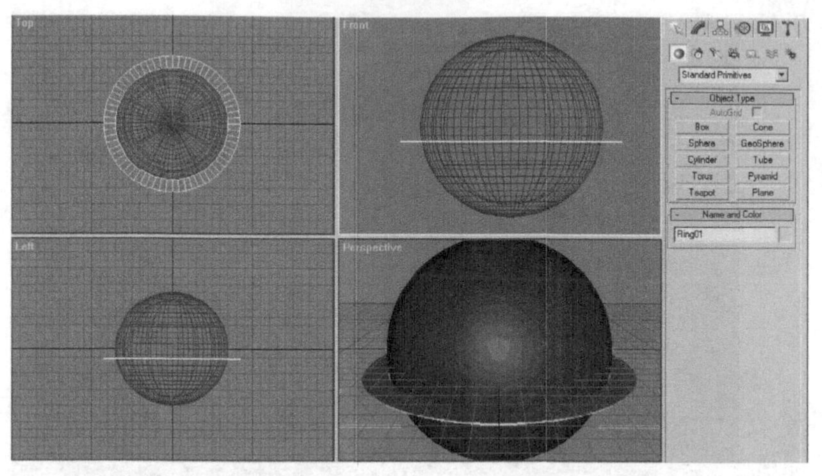

Figure 9.22 Ring01 is selected with the Select and Move tool set to Use Transform Coordinate Center.

use the World Coordinate system, however, the axis is in the center of the globe (XYZ: 0, 0, 0), and the object will mirror symmetrical to the world.

4. Click the Mirror Selected Objects button on the toolbar to open the Mirror: World Coordinates dialog. In the Mirror Axis group, change the axis to **Z** and in the Clone Selection dialog, choose Instance (as shown in **Figure 9.23**). Click OK to create the instance (see **Figure 9.24**).

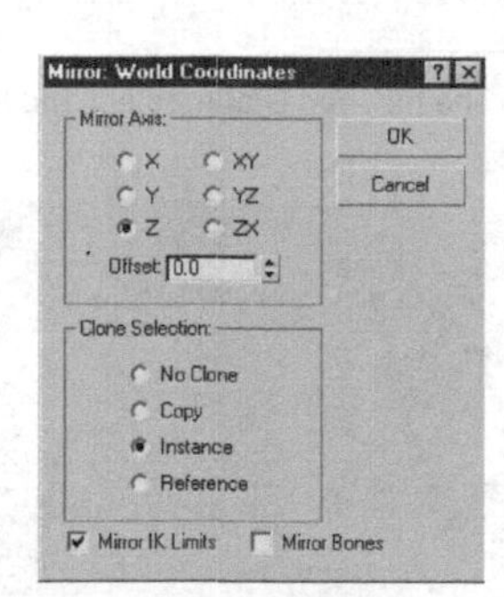

Figure 9.23 The Mirror: World Coordinates dialog with the correct settings.

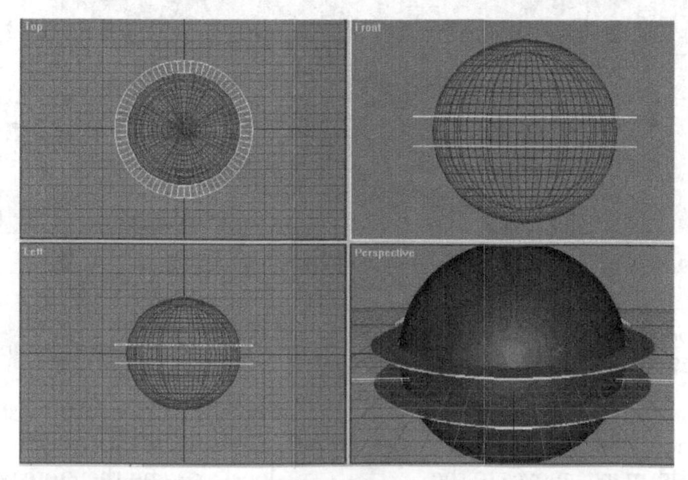

Figure 9.24 By mirroring the Ring01 object on the World Coordinate Center, you have created the Ring02 object.

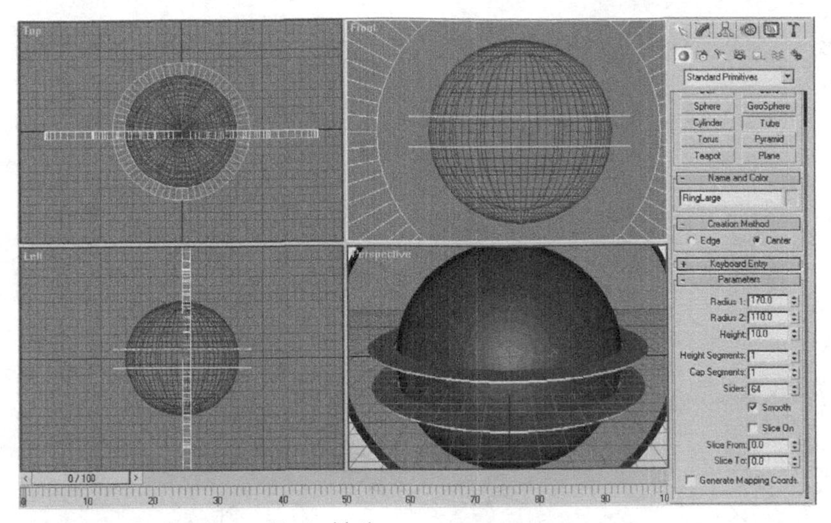

Figure 9.25 The RingLarge object with the correct parameters.

There is one final ring that orbits the globe. It is larger than the symmetrical rings you just created, so you can't simply instance one that is already in the scene. You will simply create a new, larger tube and place it in the correct location.

5. Activate the 3D Snap toggle and in the Create > Geometry panel, click the Tube button. In the Front view create a Tube with these settings:

   XYZ: **0, 0, 0**

   Radius 1: **170**

   Radius 2: **110**

   Height: **10**

   Name this object **RingLarge** (see **Figure 9.25**).

   The RingLarge object is centered to the world when viewed through the Front view. However, it is not centered to the world when you peer down on it from the Top view. You will need to center the RingLarge's local pivot to its height and then center the object to the world.

6. With RingLarge selected, open the Hierarchy panel. Activate the Affect Object Only button and click the Center to Pivot button so that the RingLarge object is centered to pivot and to the world (as shown in **Figure 9.26**). Deactivate the Affect Object Only button.

   All three ring objects are now properly created and oriented in the scene.

7. Save your work as **09TV03.max**.

Shedding Light on the Scene

As a general rule of thumb, I place the main light of my scene to the front-right of the objects. This light is "key light" in our scene. Another rule of thumb I have is to always start with a luminance of 180 units emitting from any light. That way you are creating your materials for optimal viewing for that amount of light. However, if more light is needed, you can increase the value up to 255. If the 255 value still isn't enough light, you can increase the Multiplier value of the light. However, I change the multiplier only

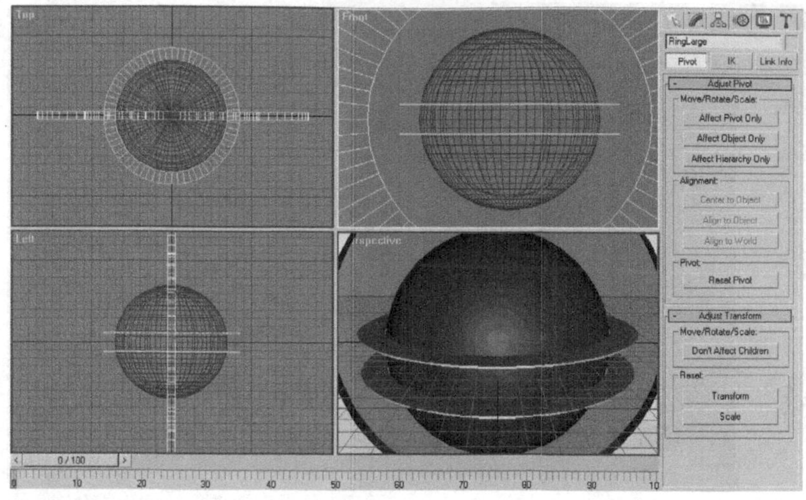

Figure 9.26 The Ring Large object is centered to the world.

in extreme cases in which I need additional light or negative light (which removes light from the scene).

You should also add a backlight to "pop" the objects off the background. You may need to add "special" lights to illuminate certain areas of particular objects. To do so, you can create lights with Include lists. The Include list allows the light to illuminate designated objects.

Exercise 9.4 Using Lighting to Aid in the Creation of Materials and to Create a Dramatic Effect

The globe object and the rings are now ready to have materials applied to them. Before you go ahead and start placing materials on the objects, add a few lights to the scene. This will allow you to more accurately view our materials.

1. With **09TV03.max** open, open the Create > Lights panel. Click the Omni button and click in the Top view to create an Omni light. Activate the Select and Move tool and move the Omni to XYZ: **235,−140, 15**. You will need to use the Zoom All tool to see the Omni light (see **Figure 9.27**).

   Adjust the light so its value is only 180 units.

2. In the Modify panel, with the Omni01 light selected, change its color to RGB: **180, 180, 180**. Also, rename the light **Omni-Key** (as shown in **Figure 9.28**).

   The key light is finished in the scene. You should also add a back light to the scene to illuminate the upper-right area of the globe object. This back light will help to "pop" the globe off the background.

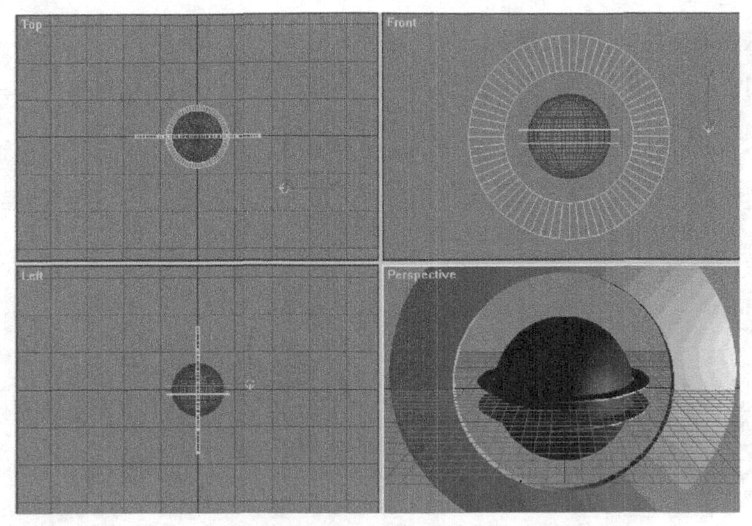

Figure 9.27 Create the Omni light and move it to XYZ: 235, –140, 15.

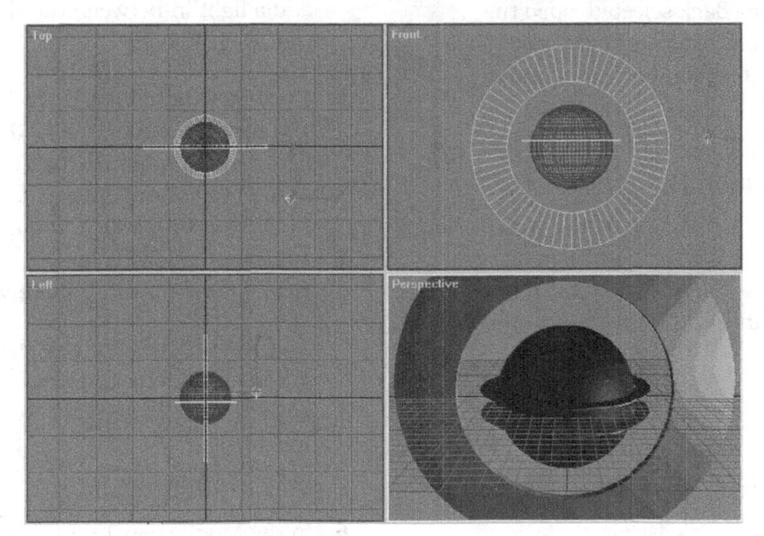

Figure 9.28 The Omni-Key light with correct settings.

3. In the Create > Lights panel, click the Omni button and create an Omni light in the top view. Move it to XYZ: **630, 350, 380** and name it **Omni-Back**. You will need to use the Zoom All tool to see it (see **Figure 9.29**).

   Because the back light should be more subtle, you need to lower its intensity to be less than the key light's, which currently is 180. Also, to create a dramatic effect you will also add a little color to the back light.

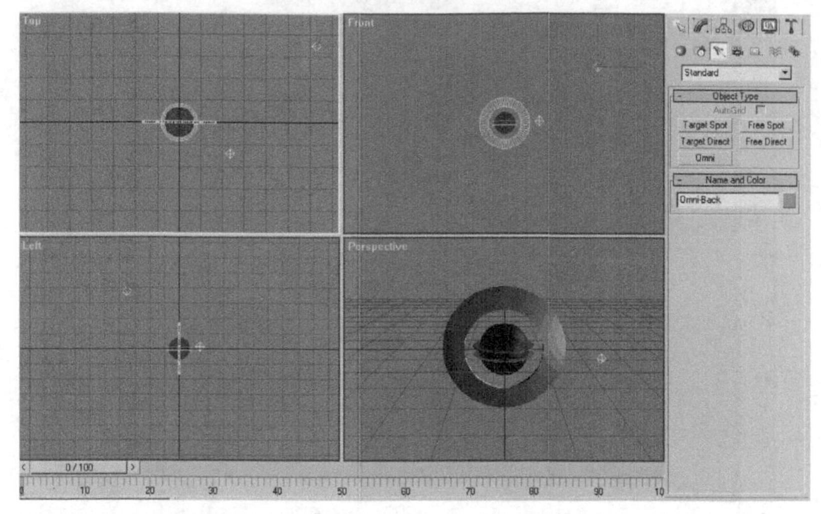

Figure 9.29 The Omni-Back light is named and in position.

4. With Omni-Back selected, open the Modify panel. Change its color to RGB: **100**, **100**, **150** (as shown in **Figure 9.30**).

   The back light now has a bluish hue that will add a little drama to the scene.

   Looking at John's storyboard, you can see that the sides of the rings that face one another are brightly lit, especially in the second panel of the storyboard. You will add a light in-between the rings orbiting the globe object.

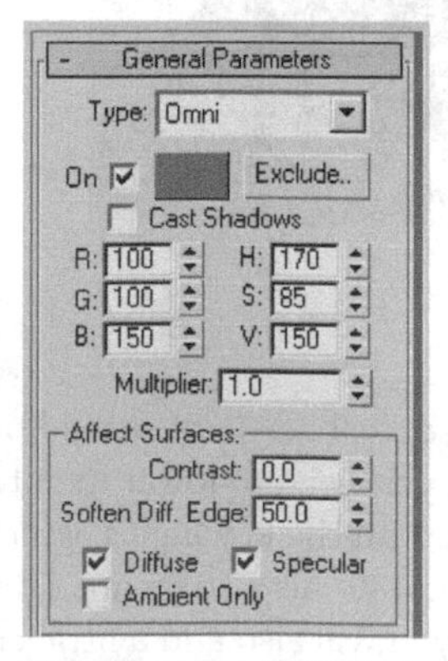

Figure 9.30 The Omni-Back light has the correct parameters.

5. Create an Omni light in the Top view and move it to XYZ: **78**, **0**, **0**. Name the light **Omni-SpecialRing01**. Open the Modify panel and change its color to RGB: **180**, **180**, **180**. You might need to adjust your view to see the Omni light clearly (as shown in **Figure 9.31**).

   This light should not cast light on any objects except for the Ring01 and Ring02 objects. Luckily, you can create an Include list, which enables you to accomplish that very task.

6. In the Modify panel, with Omni-SpecialRing01 light selected, click the Exclude button in the General Parameters rollout. In the Exclude/Include dialog, choose Include, select Ring01 and Ring02, and click the arrow pointing to the right (see **Figure 9.32**). Click OK to create the Include list.

   Since you created the Include list, the Omni-SpecialRing01 light will illuminate

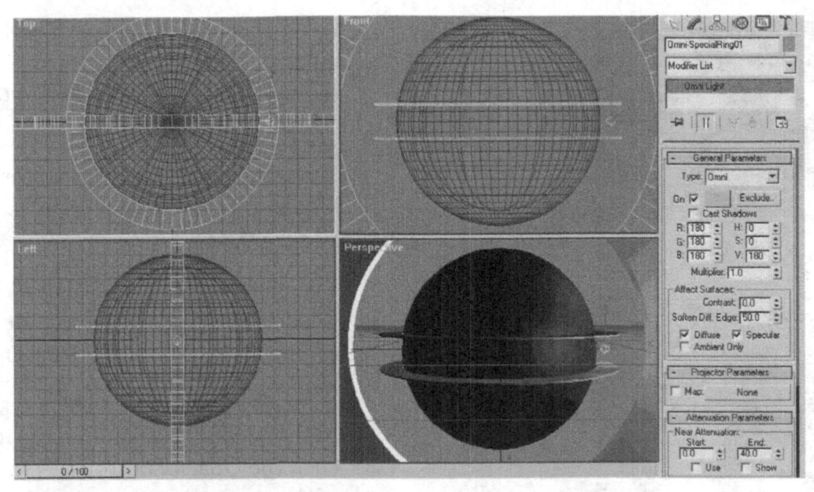

Figure 9.31 The Omni SpecialRing01 light is in the correct position with the correct parameters.

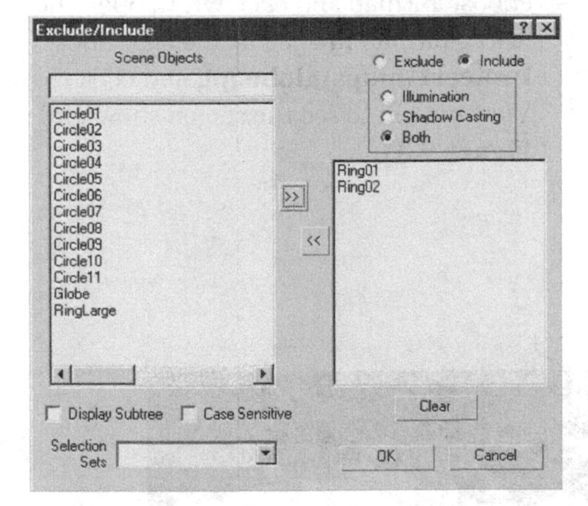

Figure 9.32 The Include list includes the Ring01 and Ring02 objects.

only the Ring01 and Ring02 objects. Save your work before adding the materials.

7. Save your work as **09TV04.max**.

Applying a Material to the Globe Object

You now have the groundwork for the scene laid out correctly, lights and all. That said, you could begin to apply the materials to the objects. You will start by creating the material for the globe object.

Exercise 9.5 Using an Opacity Map to Create the Illusion of Oceans

Earlier when you spoke with John, he told you that he envisioned the globe having metallic blue continents floating off the wireframe latitude/longitude lines. You will create that effect by using an opacity map to make the oceans of the globe invisible, allowing the wireframe to show through. Go ahead and get started.

1. With **09TV04.max** open, select the Globe object and open the Material Editor. Activate the second material preview slot of the top row and name it **Globe**. Click the Assign Material to Selection button to apply the material to the Globe object.

   Now make the material appear to have a polished blue metallic appearance.

2. In the Shader Basic Parameters rollout, change the shader from Blinn to Metal. Click the Ambient color swatch and change its color to RGB: **80, 80, 240**. Because the Ambient and Diffuse colors are locked (the buttons next to their

titles appear to be pressed in), both colors change simultaneously. Change the Specular Level to **100** and Glossiness to **60**.

A reasonably good metal material, a dark blue polished metallic, appears (see **Figure 9.33**).

The globe material is still solid. You need to add the Opacity map in order for the oceans to disappear. Add the Opacity map now.

3. In the Metal Basic Parameters rollout, click the Opacity button (it's to the right of the spinner) to open the Material/Map Browser. In the Material/Map Browser, choose Bitmap and click OK to open the Select Bitmap Image File dialog. Choose **Project1\maps\globe.jpg** and click the View button to see the screen shown in **Figure 9.34**.

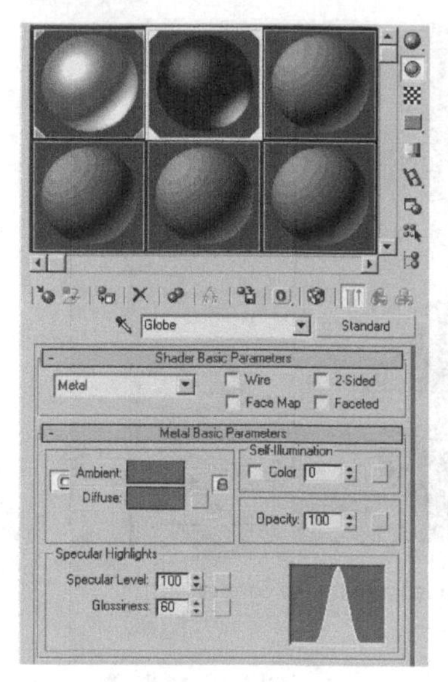

Figure 9.33 The Globe material has a dark blue polished metallic appearance.

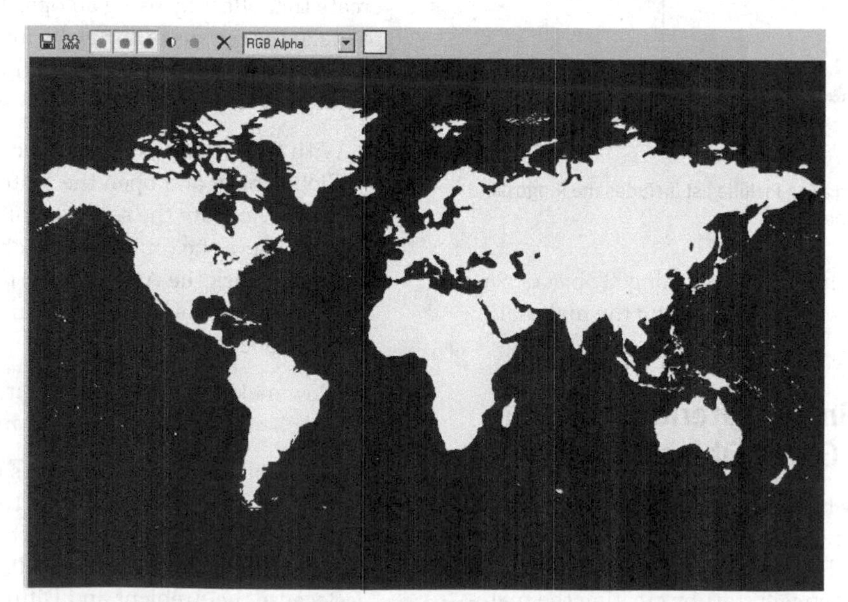

Figure 9.34 The Globe.jpg dialog opens after you click View in the Select Bitmap Image File dialog.

The "(1:2)" that appears after "globe.jpg" in the title bar indicates that you are currently viewing the image at one-half its actual size, which means the bitmap has a pretty large resolution. One of the most valued images a media animator could possess is a good texture of the earth to map on spheres. Let's face it, everybody and their brother wants a spinning globe in their logo somewhere, especially when it comes to news. The resolution needs to be large in case you need to view a particular location of the globe and still want the edges of the continents to appear crisp. This globe image may not be 100 percent geologically correct, but it is a fantastic representation.

4. Close the globe.jpg (1:2) image and click Open to load globe.jpg as the Opacity map. Change the name to **Globe-opc** (as shown in **Figure 9.35**).

   Notice in the material preview slot that the oceans have sort of been removed from the material. The reality is that only the diffuse and ambient colors of the globe are transparent. The black pixels of the image result with a transparent ambient and diffuse channels, and the white pixels of the image result with opaque ambient and diffuse channels. For any gray pixels would apply partial opacity, the brighter the pixel, the more opaque it is.

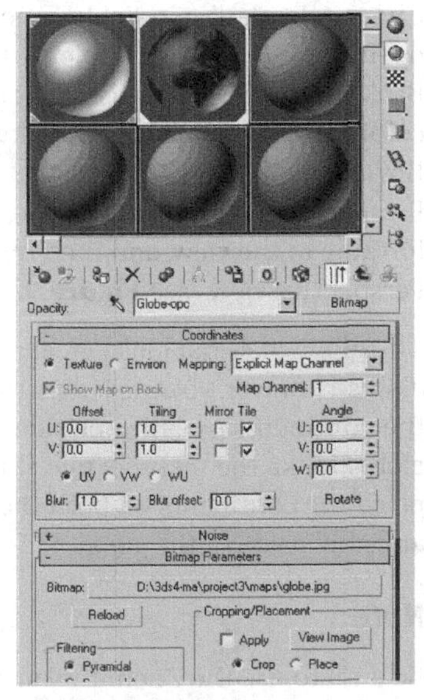

Figure 9.35 The Globe-opc opacity map is loaded.

   The specular highlight remains. There are two ways to mask the specular highlight: by applying a map to the Specular Level, or by applying a map to the Glossiness level. Both are effective, but they yield slightly different results. Putting the opacity map on the Specular Level channel gets rid of the specular color; putting it on the Glossiness channel changes the sharpness of the specular highlights.

   In this exercise, you will choose to map the glossiness because that creates a sparkling artifact on the shoreline where the oceans meet the land. This effect will become evident when you apply the map.

5. Click Return to Root to return to the root of the Globe material. In the Metal Basic Parameters dialog, drag the Opacity map button to the Glossiness map button and release the mouse. In the Copy (Instance) Map dialog, choose Copy and click OK to copy the map (see **Figure 9.36**).

   Hmm, very interesting. It seems as though the exact reverse of what you wanted to happen happened. The specular highlight is showing up on the oceans instead of the continents. If you invert the output of the globe.jpg in the Glossiness map channel, it will create the desired effect.

6. Click the Glossiness map button to open its parameters. Change its name to

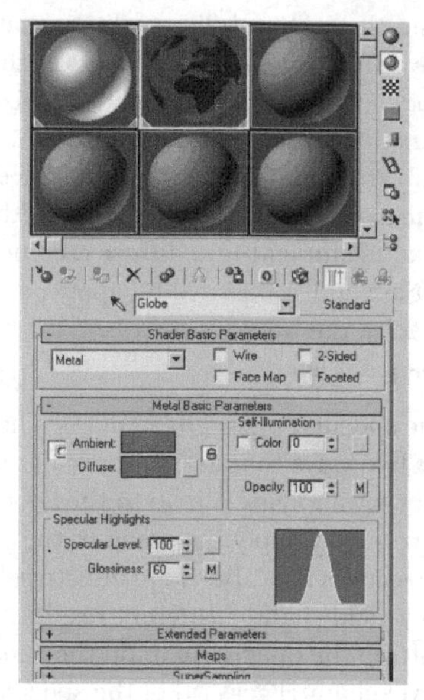

Figure 9.36 The Globe material with the Opacity map copied to the Glossiness map button.

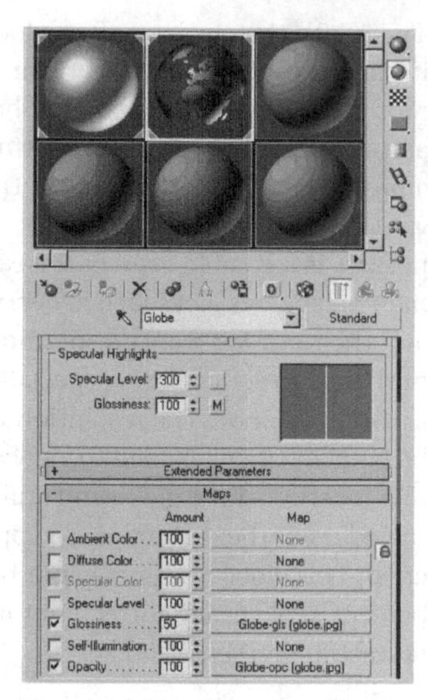

Figure 9.37 The Globe material with correct Glossiness and Specular Level settings.

Globe-gls and open the Output rollout. Check Invert. The effect is faint, but correct. Click Go to Parent to return to the root of the Globe material.

The Glossiness map is now doing its job, it's just not doing it very well. You can tweak the material's settings to improve the effect.

7. In the Specular Highlights group of the Metal Basic Parameters dialog, change the Glossiness value to **100**. Open the Maps rollout and change the Glossiness map amount to **50**. The effect improves, but you can strengthen it by dramatically increasing the Specular Level value. In the Specular Highlights group of the Metal Basic Parameters dialog, change the Specular Level value to **300** (see **Figure 9.37**).

By making a few adjustments to the Glossiness and Specular Level values, you have created the perfect blue metallic globe material. Render a frame to see the results. Before you do though, change the background color.

8. Choose Rendering > Environment to open the Environment dialog. Click the Background Color swatch and change its color to RGB: **150, 150, 150**. Close the Environment dialog. Adjust the Perspective view until the globe fits comfortably in the view, and then render the Perspective view (see **Figure 9.38**).

The globe material looks great on the globe. However, you are currently seeing the continents on only one side of the globe. Make the material two sided to place the continents on both the outside and the inside of the globe.

✔ Note

Be sure to use the Zoom tool and not the FOV tool to adjust the view. Using the Zoom tool to adjust the view allows you

Figure 9.38 The globe rendered through the Perspective view.

to correctly view environment later in the chapter.

9. With the Globe material selected in the Material Editor, check 2-Sided in the Shader Basic Parameters rollout. Render the Perspective view again (see **Figure 9.39**).

   The globe now has continents on both the outside and inside. When you checked 2-Sided in the material's parameters, the material was applied to both sides of the polygons creating the globe. Because the same material is on both the inside and outside, it might become difficult at times to discriminate what is the front and what is the back. To take care of this issue, you will apply an entirely different and much darker material to the inside of the globe. You will do so by changing the Globe material into a double-sided material.

10. In the Shader Basic Parameters dialog, uncheck 2-Sided to return the globe material to its original setting. Click the Standard button to open the Material Map Browser. Choose Double Sided and click OK to create the new material. In the Replace Material dialog, leave Keep Old Material As Sub-Material? selected and click OK.

    Now the original Globe material is in the Facing Material sub-material slot. The default gray material is in the Back Material sub-material slot. If you were to render the Perspective view again, you would see that the front of the globe looks fine. However, the inside is now a solid gray material (as shown in **Figure 9.40**).

    You now need to add a globe material to the Back Material sub-material slot as well in order to put the continents on the

Figure 9.39 The globe material is now two sided.

Figure 9.40 The new double sided material rendered in the Perspective view.

inside again. The continents on the inside will be solid black. To create the back material, you will simply copy the facing material and adjust its settings.

11. In the Material Editor, drag the Facing Material button over the Back Material button and release the mouse. In the Instance (Copy) Material dialog, choose Copy and click OK to copy the material.

    The facing globe material is now copied into the back material slot. You can now open the material and adjust its parameters.

12. Click the Back Material button to open its parameters, and then change its name to **Globe-Back**. Because the material is going to be black, you no longer need any Specular Highlights. In the Metal Basic Parameters rollout, drag the Specular Level button (to the right of its spinner) over the Glossiness map button. The map is removed from the Glossiness channel. Change both the Specular Level and Glossiness values to **0** (as shown in **Figure 9.41**).

    The specular highlight has been removed from the Globe-Back sub-material. To finish this sub-material, you need to change its color to black.

13. Click the Ambient swatch and change its color to RGB: **0**, **0**, **0**. Render the Perspective view again (see **Figure 9.42**).

    The globe material, as a whole, looks great. Add a raytraced reflection map to the facing sub-material to add a little Hollywood to it.

14. In the Material Editor, click the Go Forward to Sibling button to access the facing sub-material settings. Expand the Maps rollout and click the Reflection button to open the Material/Map

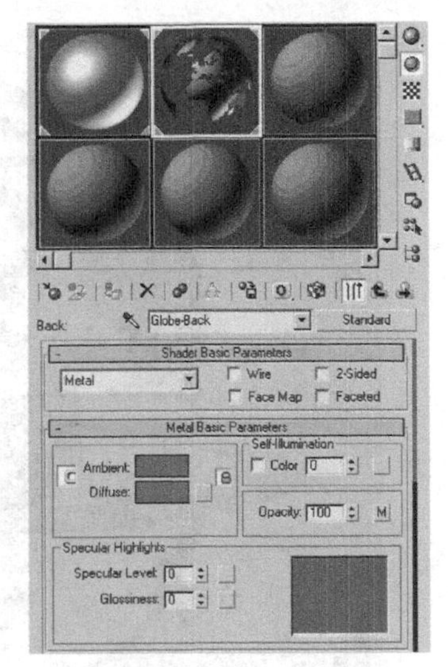

Figure 9.41 The Globe-Back back sub-material.

Browser. Choose Raytrace and click OK to load the map.

You have just crossed the line from "relatively quick renders" to the world of "unbelievably long renders." Raytraced reflections are the most realistic reflections you can create in 3ds max. It uses complex algorithms to trace rays of light as they bounce through the scene until they reach the camera. All of this calculation takes a great deal of time.

By default, no antialiasing is applied in the raytrace calculations. Therefore, the reflection may seem pixilated and not smooth. If you are working on a machine with a fast processor, you can turn Antialiasing on by clicking the Options button in the Raytracer Parameters rollout; in the Global column check Antialiasing (see **Figure 9.43**). This will result in a cleaner effect.

However, in this scene, you will leave Antialiasing deactivated. You will only be applying a subtle reflection, so you

Figure 9.42 The Rendered double-sided globe material.

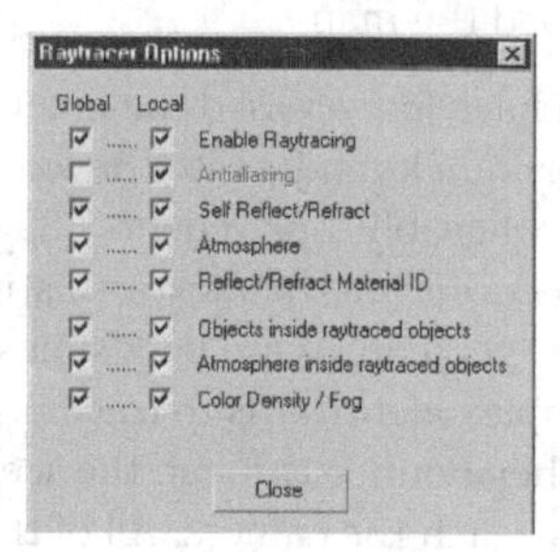

Figure 9.43 By default, Global Antialiasing is deactivated; for better quality, you can check Global Antialiasing.

might be able to get away with not using antialiasing.

15. Name this map **Globe-rfl** and click the Go to Parent button to return to the root of the Globe facing sub-material. In the Maps rollout, change the Reflection Amount to **50** and render the Perspective view again (see **Figure 9.44**).

You can now see the rings reflected on the globe. Pretty cool, isn't it? Since you

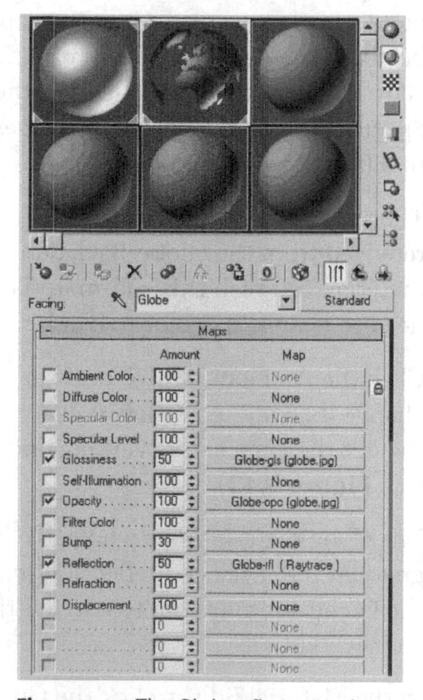

Figure 9.44 The Globe-rfl amount has been changed to 50 to reduce the overall appearance of the reflection.

didn't mask the reflection, the reflection is applied to the entire globe, not just the continents. For this particular scene, this will work well. Right now your background color is a bright gray. But when the scene is finished, the background will be almost black, so the reflection on the globe will not be as bright.

16. Save your work as **09TV05.max**.

Applying a Material to the Ring Objects

You just finished the globe material, complete with a raytrace reflection map. You also want the ring objects to have raytraced reflections. Instead of using the raytrace reflection map, however, you will use the raytrace material to create the reflective gold material for the ring objects.

3ds max has both a raytrace map and a raytrace material. Each has its own strengths and weaknesses. The major difference is that the Raytrace map has more extensive attenuation controls than the Raytrace material does. If you are having problems creating a certain effect using the Raytrace map, you might want to try to create it using the Raytrace material. Often you can achieve much different results experimenting with both.

Exercise 9.6 Creating a Reflective Gold Material

You will be adding a reflective Raytrace material to the ring objects. The reflective effect should be very similar to what you accomplished with the Globe material.

1. Make sure **09TV05.max** is open, and select all three ring objects (Ring01, Ring02, and RingLarge). In the Material Editor, select the third material preview slot in the top row and name it **GoldRing**. Click the Standard button and in the Material/Map Browser, choose Raytrace and click OK to load the material.

   The material type has been changed from Standard to Raytrace. You can now adjust its parameters to create a gold reflective material.

2. In the Raytrace Basic Parameters rollout, change the Ambient color to RGB: **240, 100, 60** and change the Diffuse color to RGB: **255, 150, 40**. Deselect Reflect and enter a value of **15**. Click the Assign Material to Selection button and render the Perspective view (see **Figure 9.45**).

   The gold ring material is starting to take shape. The reason you deselected Reflect was to access its numeric value. If you were to leave Reflect checked, and then you changed the color in the swatch, the reflection would appear but would be tinted to that color. In this scene, however, you want the colors to reflect as realistically as possible. Therefore, you will use the value spinner.

   The material would look better with a more pronounced gold-colored specular highlight. Make the necessary adjustments now.

3. In the Specular Highlight group, change the Specular Color to RGB: **255, 195, 80**. Change the Specular Level value to **143** and the Glossiness to **27** (as shown in **Figure 9.46**).

   If you were to render the Perspective view again, you would notice that the specular highlights on the rings are larger and more gold colored. Creating this material is a testament to how quickly you can create complex and attractive materials in 3ds max.

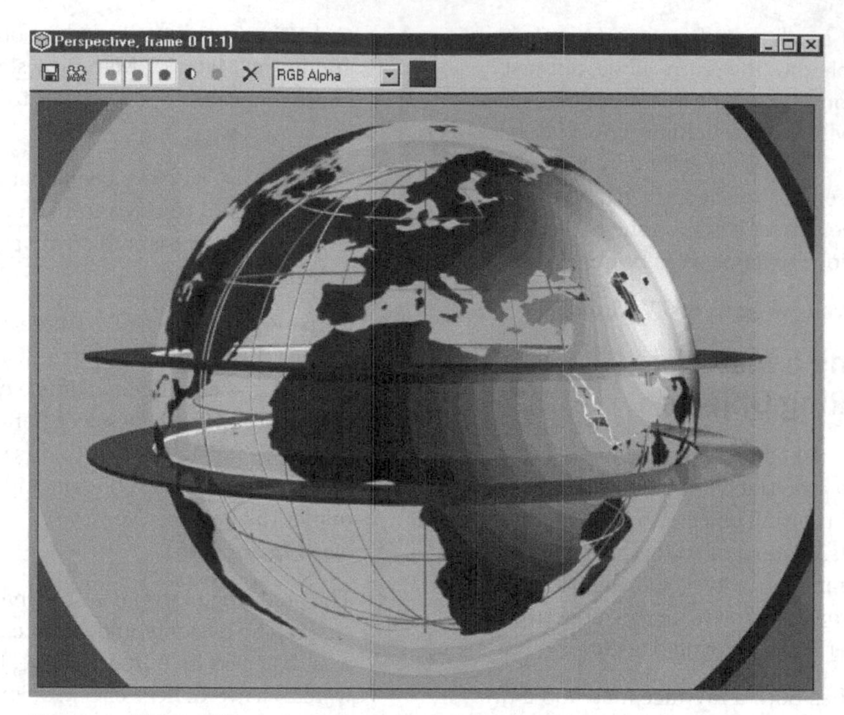

Figure 9.45 The GoldRing material is rendered on the ring objects.

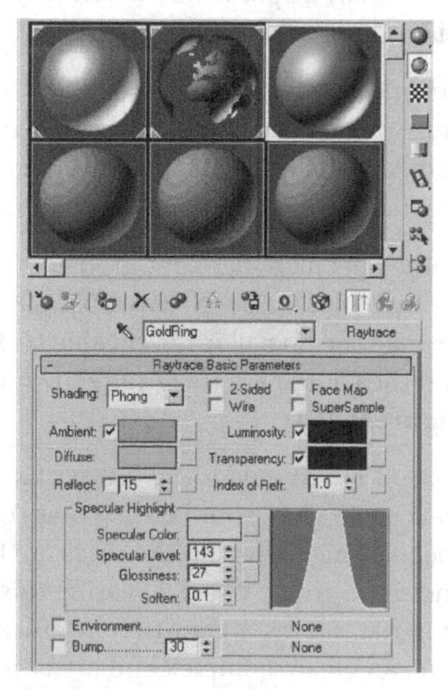

Figure 9.46 The parameters of the finished GoldRing material.

✔ **Note**

You can significantly speed up renderings by reducing the (Rendering) Sides of the circles. Reducing the number of sides from 12 to 4 can almost cut the rendering time in half.

Adding the Environment

You are really starting to fine-tune the materials and the rendered appearance of the scene, so get rid of that drab gray background and add the environment map. Looking at John's storyboard, you can see that the environment background appears to be blue Venetian blinds. To accomplish that effect, you will load a blue-striped image into the environment map channel.

Exercise 9.7 Offsetting an Image Map to Improve Its Position

Adding the Environment map will be a breeze. You will load a JPG image and map it on Spherical Environment Mapping. After you have accomplished that, you will use the offset values to position the image so it renders in the correct location.

1. Choose Rendering > Environment to open the Environment dialog. In the Background group, click the Environment Map button to open the Material/Map Browser, choose Bitmap, and click OK to open the Select Bitmap Image File dialog. Choose **Project1\maps\streakblue.jpg** and click View to view a sample of the image.

   The image is a square image that is mostly black. In the center of the image is a hi-tech circle shape that is created by dark blue horizontal lines of varying thickness. This image was created in Photoshop by basically creating a blurred circle image, applying a pixelate > color halftone filter to it, and applying some horizontal motion blur and contrast (see **Figure 9.47**).

2. Close the preview image and in the Select Bitmap Image File dialog, click Open to open the streakblue.jpg (as shown in **Figure 9.48**).

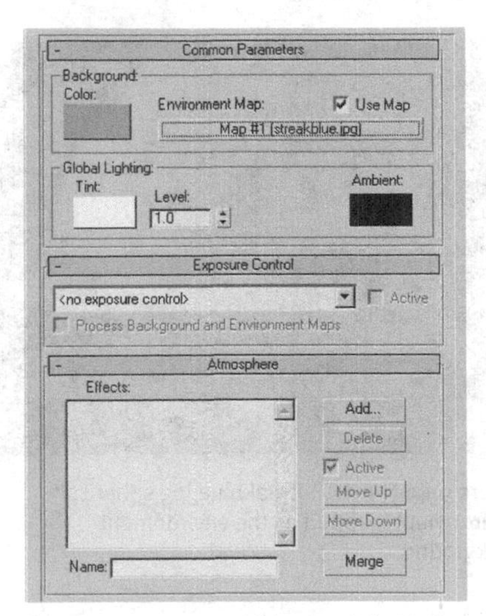

Figure 9.48 The streakblue.jpg is loaded into the environment map slot.

By default, the environment map is mapped using screen mapping, meaning the image is resized to fit perfectly in the view, no matter where the camera is pointed. You want the environment to interact with the camera, so you will need to change its mapping type to spherical.

3. Drag the Environment Map button from the Environment dialog to the first material preview slot of the second row in the Material Editor. In the Instance (Copy)

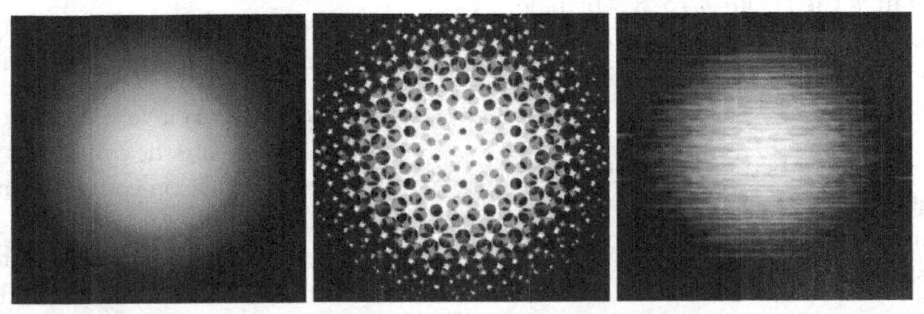

Figure 9.47 The three basic steps to creating the streakblue.jpg image: blurred circle, color halftone, motion blur.

Figure 9.49 The new streakblue.jpg spherical environment mapped as the environment background.

Figure 9.50 The rendered perspective view with the blue streaks offset correctly.

Map dialog, choose Instance and click OK to instance the map into the Material Editor. Close the Environment dialog. Name this map **Env** and in the Coordinates rollout, change the Mapping from Screen to Spherical Environment. The streakblue.jpg is now mapped on an imaginary sphere surrounding the scene. Render the Perspective view (see **Figure 9.49**).

Hmm, the blue streaks don't seem to be behind the globe. That's because they are in front of the globe. In fact, you can see them reflected on the continents. You need to offset the map in order to position the blue streaks behind the globe.

4. In the Coordinates rollout of the Env map, change the U Offset to **.5**. The blue streaks disappear from the preview slot. Render the Perspective view again (see **Figure 9.50**).

   That looks much better. The scene is really starting to shape up. Save your work and continue adding the remaining objects.

5. Save your work as **09TV06.max** and close the Material Editor.

Adding the Type Elements

You need to create only two more objects to finish this scene: the large type that orbits the globe and the small type that is on the lower ring object (you can see it on the first and second panels of the storyboard).

Exercise 9.8 Using an Opacity Map to Create Type

You will add the large GlobalNews type to the scene first. To do so, you will opacity map the text on a cylinder, in much the same way as you opacity mapped the continents on the globe.

1. With **09TV06.max** open, open the Create > Shapes panel. Activate the 3D Snap toggle, click the Circle button, and in the Top view, create a circle at XYZ: 0, 0, 0 with a radius of **75**. Name the circle **GlobalNews** (as shown in **Figure 9.51**).

   You now have a circle shape that you will extrude to create the cylinder to map the type on. The reason you are creating the cylinder by creating a circle and extruding it (as opposed to creating a cylinder primitive object) is that when you extrude it, you can turn off Start and End capping so the cylinder will have no top or bottom.

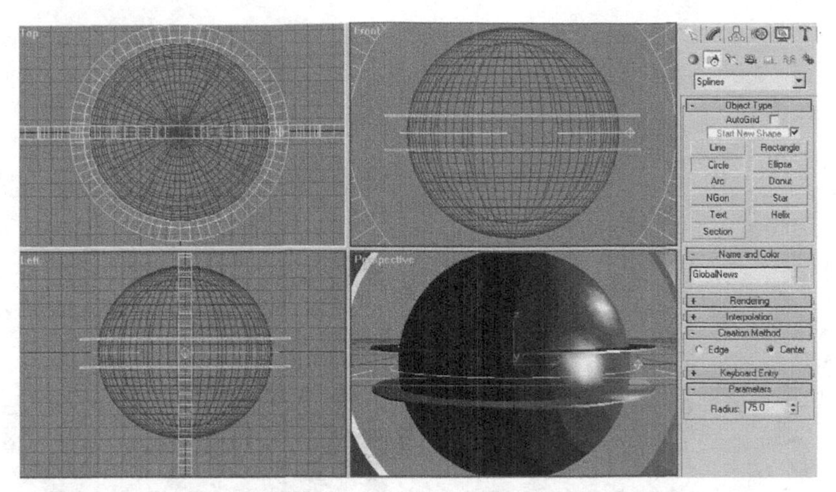

Figure 9.51 Create the GlobalNews circle shape at XYZ: 0, 0, 0.

You don't need the top or bottom; you only need the curved side to map the type on.

2. With GlobalNews selected, open the Modify panel and apply an Extrude modifier. Enter an Amount of **8** and deselect Cap Start and Cap End (as shown in **Figure 9.52**).

   With The GlobalNews object finished, move it into position and apply its material.

3. Activate the Select and Move tool and move the GlobalNews object down to XYZ: **0, 0, −4** (see **Figure 9.53**).

   The material for the GlobalNews object is going to be simple. It will consist of a 100 percent self-illuminated white material with no specular highlight. The type will be "cut out" with an opacity map.

4. Open the Material Editor and select the second material preview slot in the

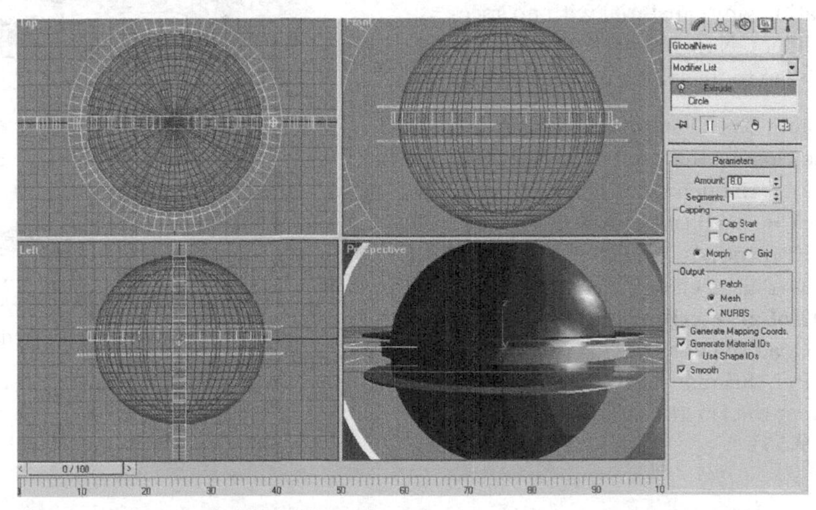

Figure 9.52 The extruded GlobalNews shape.

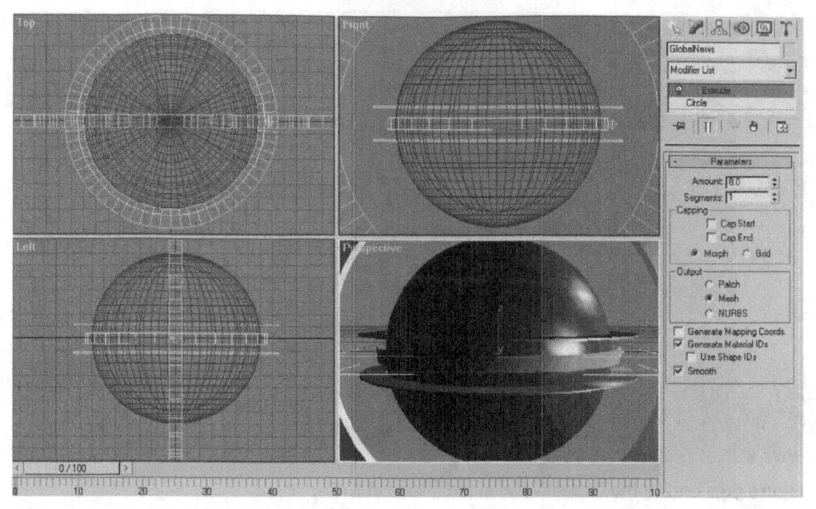

Figure 9.53 The GlobalNews object is moved into position.

second row. Name this material **GlobalNews** and assign it to the GlobalNews object. Change the Diffuse color to RGB: **255, 255, 255** and change the Self-Illumination value to **100** (see **Figure 9.54**).

As of now, you have a 100 percent self-illuminating white material with no specular highlight. Now you need to apply the opacity map to finish this material.

5. In the Blinn Basic Parameters rollout, click the Opacity button (to the right of the spinner) to open the Material/Map Browser. Choose Bitmap and click OK to close the browser. In the Select Bitmap Image File dialog, choose **Project1\maps\GlobalNewsBlur.jpg** and click Open to load the image as an opacity map. Name this map **GlobalNews-opc** and render the Perspective view (see **Figure 9.55**)

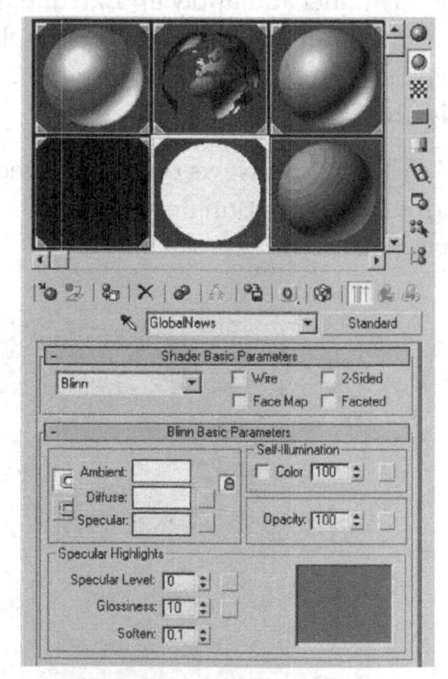

Figure 9.54 The GlobalNews material to this point.

Figure 9.55 The GlobalNews material is applied to the GlobalNews object.

Dang, that looks good. It is a bit stretched though. Let's change its U Tiling amount to thin the letters a tad.

6. In the Coordinates rollout of the GlobalNews-opc map, change the U Tiling to **1.5** (as shown in **Figure 9.56**), and then render the Perspective view again (see **Figure 9.57**).

   The strand of type now appears 1 and a half times around the GlobalNews object. You don't want to see the extra half on the ring, so you will deselect Tile to ensure it only appears once on the ring.

7. To view the map in the shaded Perspective view, click the Show Map in Viewport button. To get rid of the extra tiled map, deselect U Tile in the Coordinates rollout. The extra type caused by the tile disappears in the shaded view (see **Figure 9.58**).

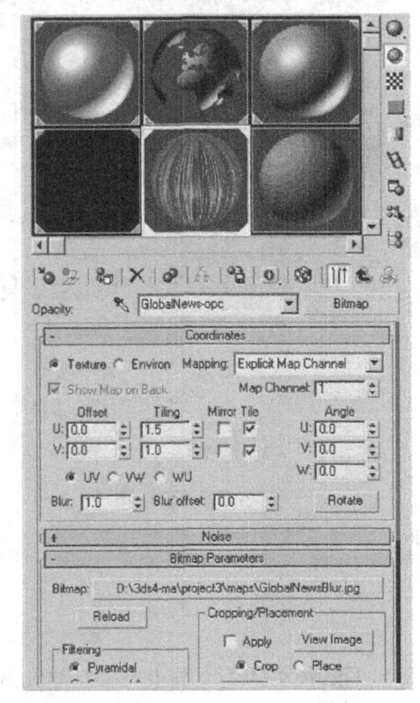

Figure 9.56 The GlobalNews-opc map thus far.

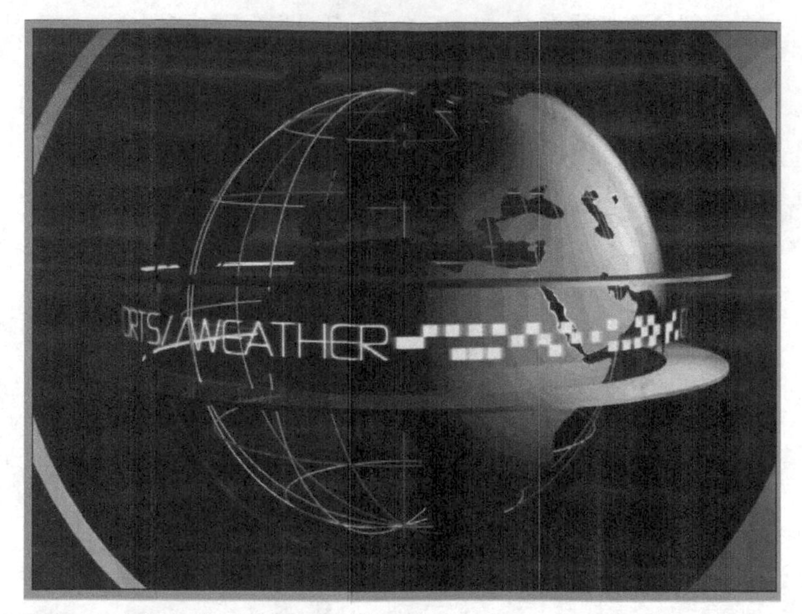

Figure 9.57 The rendered Perspective view.

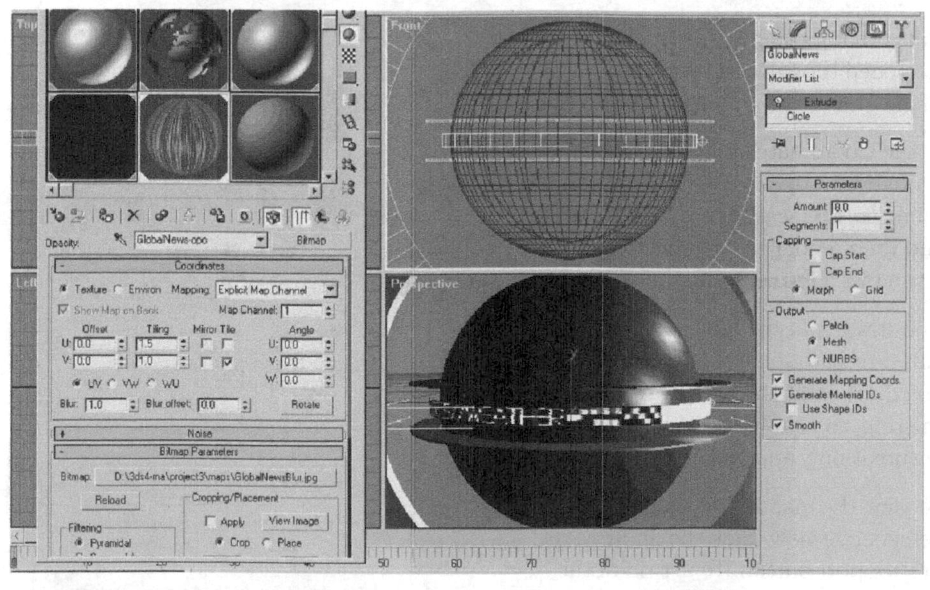

Figure 9.58 The GlobalNewsBlur.jpg type appears only once on the GlobalNews object.

Figure 9.59 The GlobalNews-opc map no longer tiles.

If you render the Perspective view again, you will see that the map no longer tiles (see **Figure 9.59**).

The Global News object and material are finished. Save your work.

8. Save your work as **09TV07.max** and close the Material Editor.

Exercise 9.9 Opacity Mapping Text from Glossy Material

You must tend to one last embellishment before you can say you are finished creating all the objects in your scene. That object is the type on the edge of the bottom ring. To create that effect, you will approach it very similarly to the way you created the GlobalNews type object. You will extrude a circle shape and add the texture.

1. Make sure **09TV07.max** is open and make sure the 3D Snap toggle is active. Open the Create > Shapes panel and click the Circle button. In the Top view, create a circle shape with a Radius of **86** at XYZ: 0, 0, 0. Name the shape **RingType**. Because the rings have 64 faces around their perimeter, you should have 64 faces around the perimeter of your circle shape as well. Because 4 vertices create the circle shape, each segment should have 16 steps in order to create 64 segments (16 × 4 = 64). Expand the Interpolation rollout and change the Steps value to **16** (as shown in **Figure 9.60**).

The radius of the circle is 86—one unit larger than the rings. You want to place the RingType object so that it will be rendered over the side of the ring objects.

Figure 9.60 The correct parameters for the RingType circle shape.

Extrude the circle and move it into position.

2. With RingType selected, open the Modify panel and apply an Extrude Modifier with an Amount of 1. Make sure Cap Start and Cap End are not checked. Activate the Select and Move tool and move the RingType object to XYZ: 0, 0, −12 (see **Figure 9.61**).

   Because the object is so small in the view, you should adjust the Perspective view to observe a more realistic image.

3. Use the Zoom and Pan tools to adjust the Perspective view to roughly match **Figure 9.62**. What is important is to see the RingType object more closely.

   Instead of using an opacity map to map out the opacity of the material, you will make the material completely transparent. You will map the shininess of the material to create the text.

4. Open the Material Editor and select the third material preview slot of the second row. Name the material **RingType** and

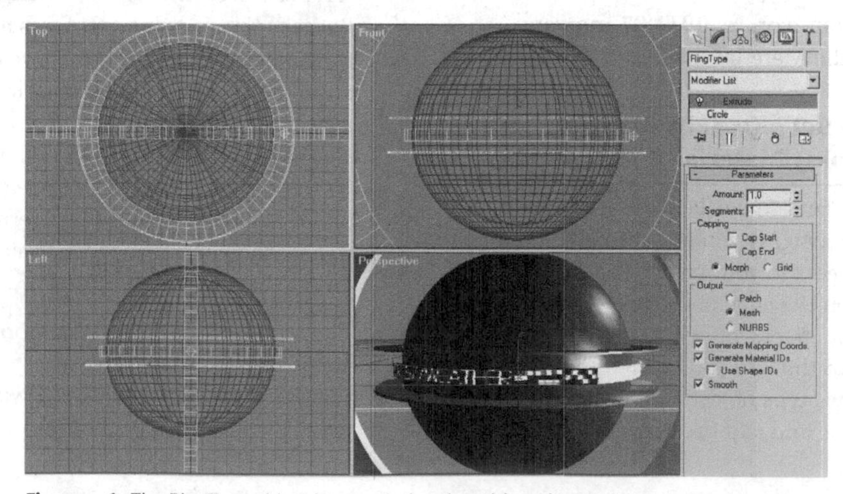

Figure 9.61 The RingType object is extruded and positioned correctly.

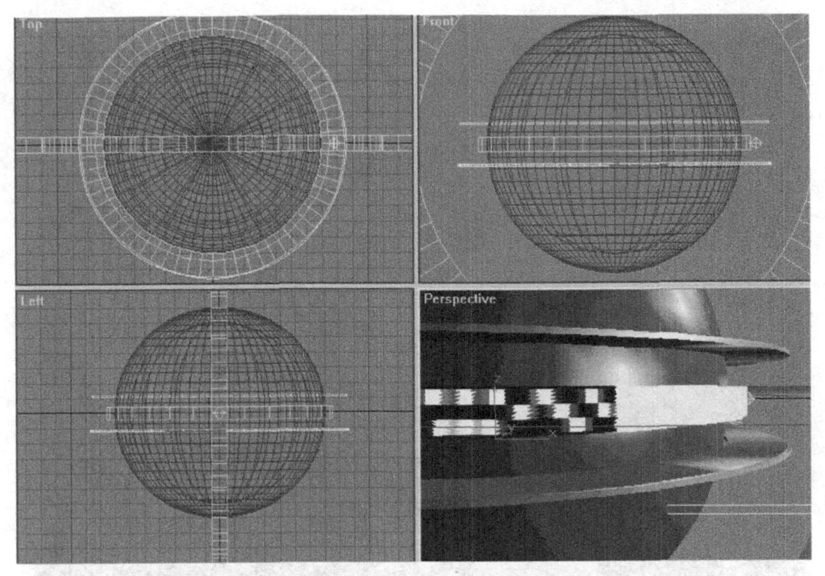

Figure 9.62 Adjust the Perspective view to observe the RingType object more closely.

apply it to the RingType object. In the Blinn Basic Parameters rollout, change the Opacity value to **0**. The RingType object disappears in the shaded Perspective view.

Now you will map the Specular level of the material to make the type appear.

5. In the Specular Highlights group of the Blinn Basic Parameters rollout, click the Specular Level map button (to the right of the spinner) to open the Material/Map Browser. Choose Bitmap and click OK to open the Select Bitmap Image File dialog. Choose **Project1\maps\type-ring.jpg** and click View to view the image (see **Figure 9.63**). This is the type you will be mapping around the RingType object. Notice the amount of blank space before the word "Business," and note how close "Entertainment" is to the edge of the bitmap. This map was created to tile seamlessly. Therefore, you can increase Tile value (in whole numbers), and the map will seamlessly create an endless wrap of text around the object. Close the type-ring.jpg preview window and click Open to load the map into the Specular map slot. Name this map **RingType-spc**,

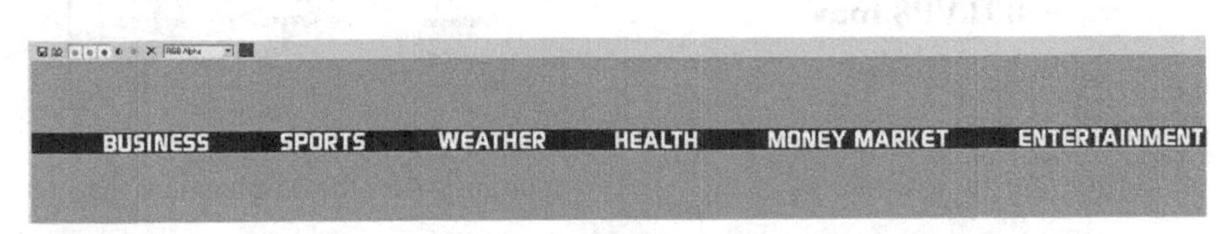

Figure 9.63 The type-ring.jpg image is ready to be tiled along its U-axis.

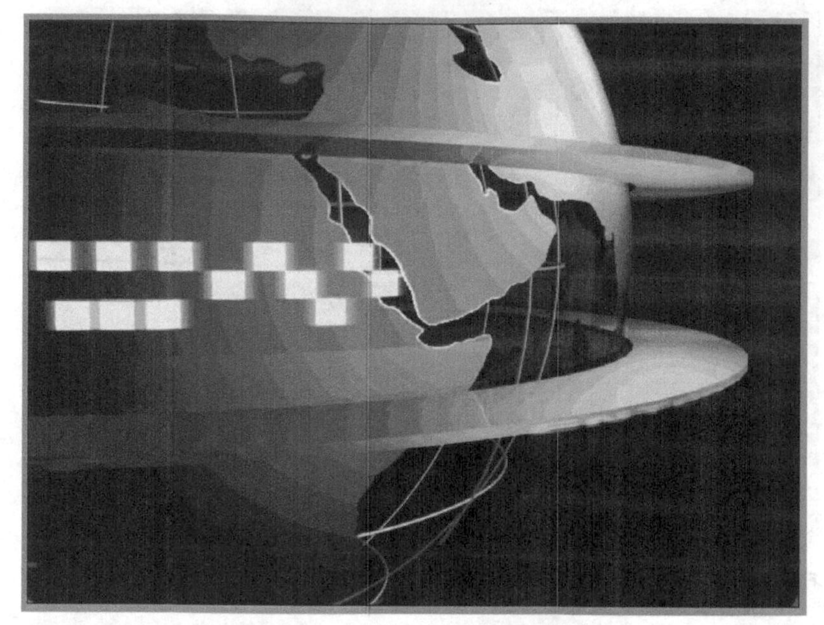

Figure 9.64 Stretched type appears around the lower ring object.

click Show Map in Viewport, and render the Perspective view (see **Figure 9.64**).

The effect looks good. However, you need to tile the RingType-spc map along its U-axis in order to make the type more legible.

6. In the Coordinates rollout of the RingType-spc map, change the U Tiling to **5** (as shown in **Figure 9.65**), and then render the Perspective view again (see **Figure 9.66**).

   The material looks great. The text looks like a hologram floating in front of the ring objects. Neat! Let's save our work and get ready to animate this scene.

7. Save your work as **09TV08.max**.

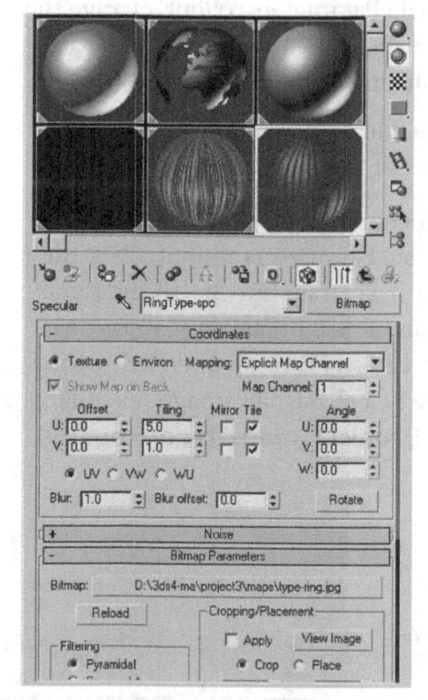

Figure 9.65 The correct Tiling coordinates for the RingType-spc map.

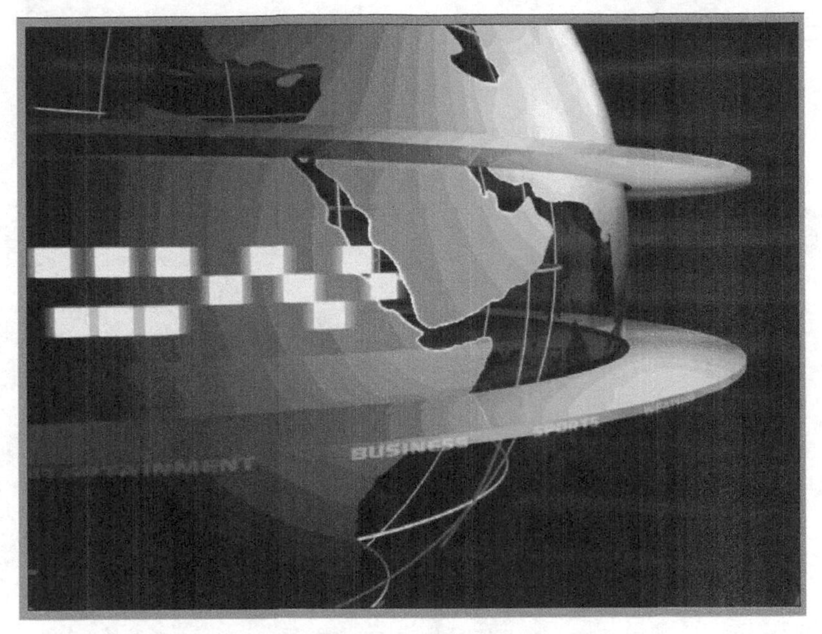

Figure 9.66 The type looks much better now that it's tiled five times.

In Conclusion

You are finished creating the objects and applying the appropriate materials, and you have added lights in the scene to illuminate the objects in a dramatic and artistic manner. By examining test images you've rendered through the Perspective view, you know that your scene matches the mood of John's storyboard.

In the next section, you will key the animation, add any necessary special effects, and render the first scene.

10

Project 1: Part 2

In the previous chapter, you built and added materials to all the objects you will need to create the first half of the TV 3 news animation. Now you will add the music, animate the scene, and render it. This rendering will be used as the screen mapped environment background for the second half of the animation.

In this chapter, you gain experience in the following areas:

- Animating to Audio
- Grouping objects
- Applying the Video Post Lens Flare Filter
- Adding Inferno to a Lens Flare effect

Adding Sound to the Scene

Gordon provided you with a piece of audio to sync your animation to. Because you have already had the experience of adding sound in the previous projects, it'll be easy this time. Add it to the scene, and then listen to what you have.

Exercise 10.1 Adding the Soundtrack

While you are adding the soundtrack to the scene, you need to be aware that you will need pre-roll and pad for this animation.

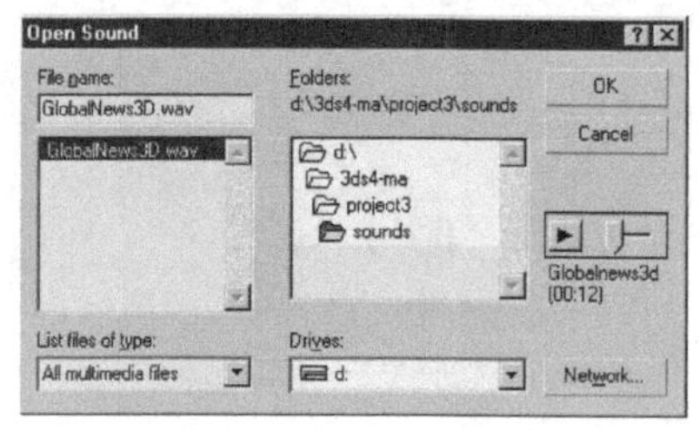

Figure 10.1 The Open Sound dialog with GlobalNews3D.wav selected.

Keeping this in mind, you should examine the audio to see if you need to offset the time the music starts to add pre-roll.

1. With **09TV08.max** open, open the Track View. Select the Sound track title, right-click it, and choose Properties from the resulting list to open the Sound Options dialog. Click the Choose Sound button and choose **Project1\sounds\GlobalNews3D.wav**. Notice that this wav file is 12 seconds long (see **Figure 10.1**). Click the Play button to preview the audio. That certainly sounds like news music to me! Click OK to open the sound, and then click OK again to close the Sound Options dialog.

   The music does not have pre-roll included, so you need to add pre-roll to this animation. To do so, you will offset the sound's starting point by 30 frames.

2. In the Track View, expand the Sound track. Use the Zoom tool to view time in 10 frame intervals. Using the Move Keys tool, move the track forward 30 frames (as shown in **Figure 10.2**). Close the Track View.

   The music doesn't start until after frame 30, which gives you plenty of pre-roll. However, your scene is still 100 frames long. If the music is 12 seconds (360 frames) and you add 1 second

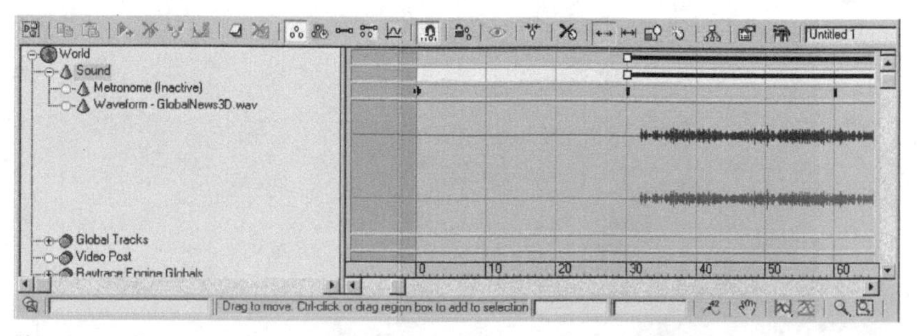

Figure 10.2 The sound track is offset forward 30 frames in the Track View.

(30 frames) of pre-roll, the animation will be 13 seconds or 390 frames long. However, this scene is only half the animation. Therefore, you need to figure out where the transition will occur so you know how long to make this scene.

✔ Note

You should not hear anything during the first 30 frames. However, because the music loops, you can hear the faint ending of the music during the first 30 frames before the music states to play. 3ds max allows you to work with audio for choreographic purposes, not to add a music track in the final product. Usually when you finish an animation, you will take it into a composite software such as Combustion or After Effects and color correct, add extra effects, and add the final audio track.

3. Click the Time Configuration button to open the Time Configuration dialog. In the Animation group, change the Length to **390** (see **Figure 10.3**). Click OK to exit the dialog. Then play the animation to hear the music again.

   The music is in 4/4 time, meaning there are four beats to a measure. Examining the storyboard and listening to the music, it seems logical that the globe animation will encompass the first two measures, or eight beats. By the ninth beat (the first beat of the third measure), you will see the Venetian blinds (from the second scene's animation) moving in over the globe animation. The globe animation should be completely gone by the first beat of the fourth measure (around frame 180), but you should add an extra second, just in case you need it. That means the length of the animation should be 210 frames long, and that will be more than you'll need to complete the animation.

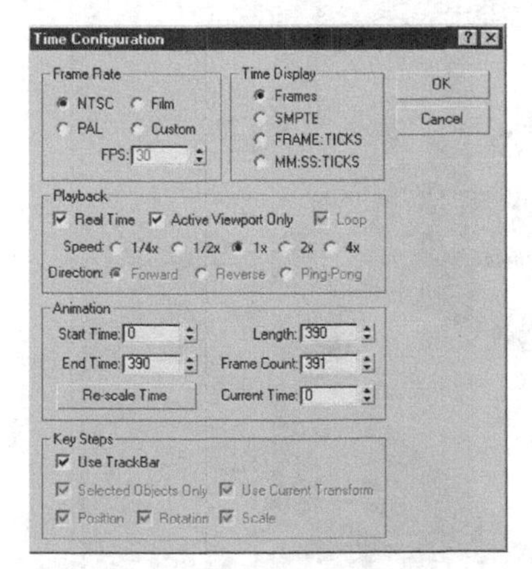

Figure 10.3 The animation is now 390 frames long.

4. Click the Time Configuration button again and change the Length to 210. Click OK to close the dialog. Save your work as **10TV01.max**.

Animating the Camera

The animation of this scene is relatively simple. The most complicated aspect of this scene is the camera move. This is because the camera will start close to the objects and move to examine them, and then it will quickly accelerate to pull away from the globe. You need to create the camera and its animation before you do anything else in the scene.

Exercise 10.2 Animating a Free Camera

Take a good look at the storyboard. The camera's path seems simple enough, so create the animation without the use of Dummy helpers (that technique we have all grown to love).

1. Make sure **10TV01.max** is open. Select Create > Cameras, and then click the Free button. Click in the Front view to create a Free camera. In the Stock Lenses group, click 35mm to use a standard

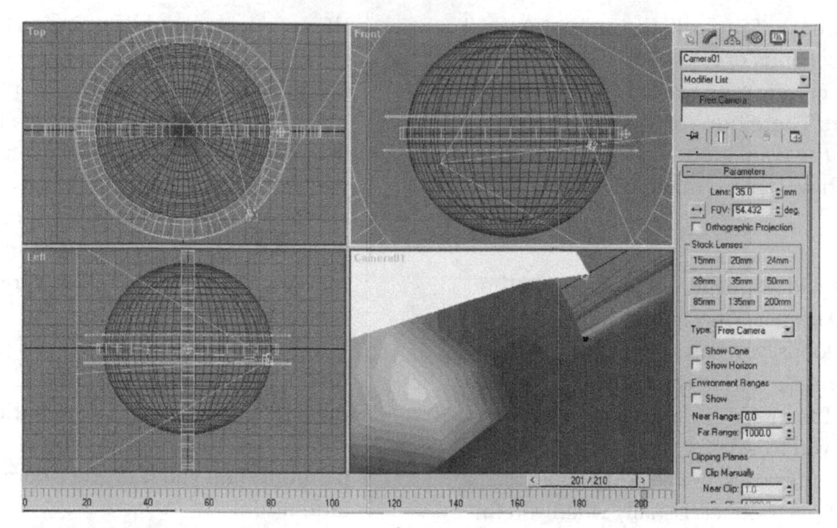

Figure 10.4 Camera01 is in the correct position and orientation.

35mm lens. Move the camera to XYZ: **55, −68, −8** and rotate the camera to XYZ: **90, 30, 0**. Activate the Perspective view and press the C key to change it to the Camera01 view (shown in **Figure 10.4**).

The camera's view is very similar to the first storyboard panel. Basically all you need to do now is dolly the camera backward to get a wider view of the globe.

You should, however, keep the camera close to the globe for a few beats so the viewers can enjoy the close-up and can familiarize themselves with what is going on in the animation.

2. Advance to frame 60 and activate the Auto Key button. With Camera01 still selected, move it to XYZ: **52, −77, 1** (see **Figure 10.5**).

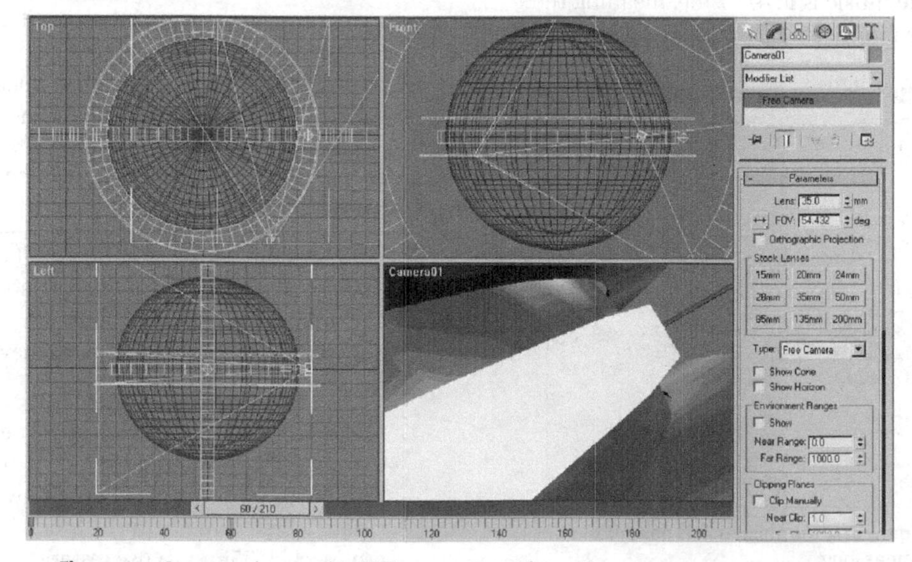

Figure 10.5 Camera01 is moved to XYZ: 52, −77, 1 at frame 60.

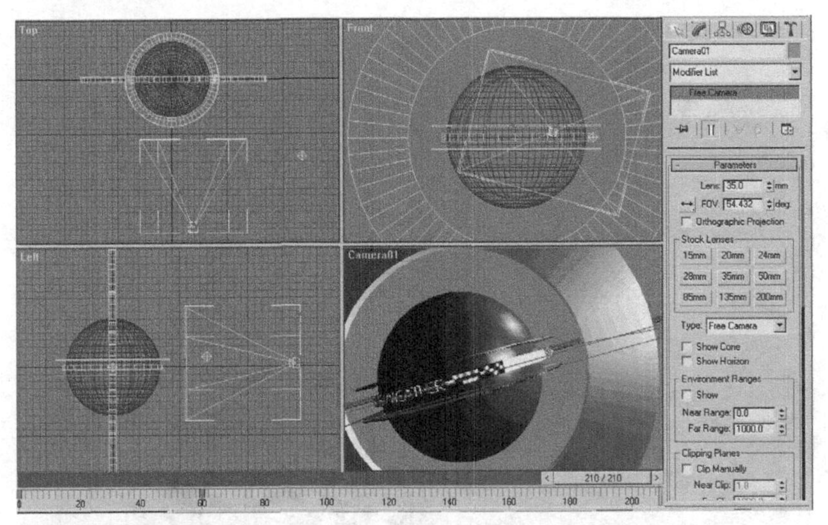

Figure 10.6 Camera01 is in the correct position and orientation at frame 210.

To complete the animation, you need to dolly it back further and rotate a slight counterclockwise turn to the camera.

3. Advance to frame 210, and with the Auto Key button still active, move Camera01 to XYZ: **38**, **−270**, **5**. Rotate Camera01 to XYZ: **90**, **15**, **0** (as shown in **Figure 10.6**). Then deactivate the Auto Key button.

The animation for the camera is complete. Feel free to play the animation and view the results. The camera should linger on a close-up of the globe and then slowly dolly backward to a wider shot.

Bringing the Scene to Life

Now that you know what the camera move is, you can animate the globe exactly the way you want it to rotate. You should keep in mind that the earth rotates counterclockwise (if you were looking down on the North Pole). You don't want to play god and change the ways of nature, so you better rotate the continents in that direction. The wireframe, on the other hand, will rotate in the opposite direction, adding visual interest to the scene.

Exercise 10.3 Animating the Objects

Before you can animate the rotation of the continents, you need to see them in the shaded Camera01 view.

1. Open the Material Editor and select the Globe material. Navigate to the Facing Material: Globe material and open its Opacity map's parameters. Click Show Map in Viewport. Close the Material Editor. The continents are visible in the shaded Camera01 view now (as shown in **Figure 10.7**).

Because you are in the United States, you want to focus on North America. If you want to view any other continent during your animation, feel free to do so.

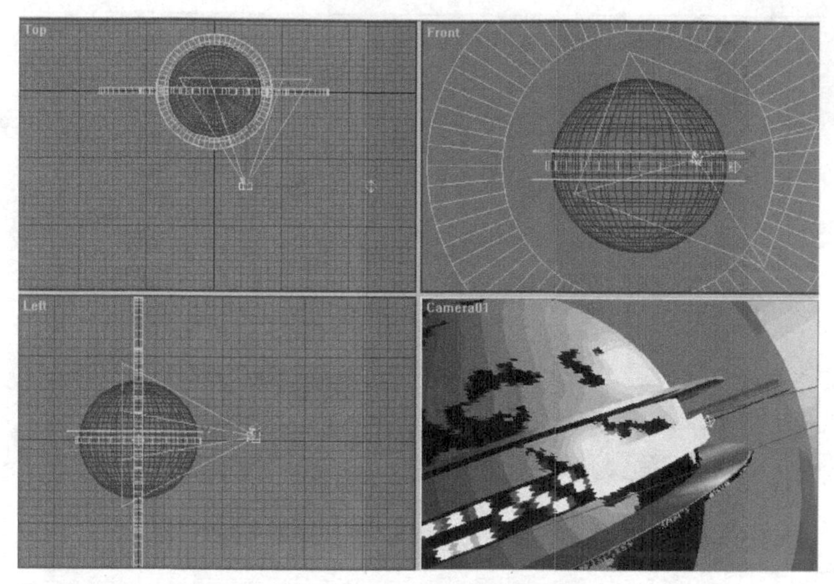

Figure 10.7 The continents are visible in the shaded Camera01 view.

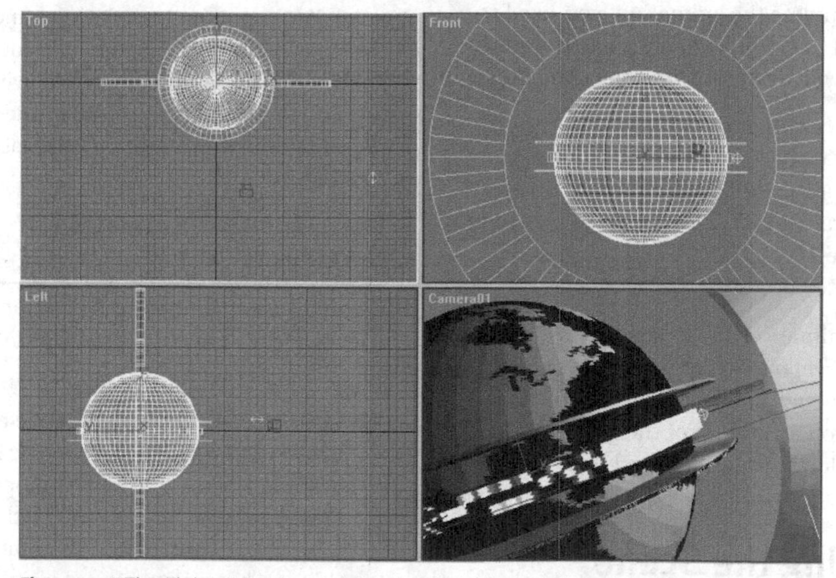

Figure 10.8 The Globe object is rotated to the desired start orientation.

2. Advance to frame 150 for a clear view of the globe. Deactivate the 3D Snap toggle if it is still active, activate the Select and Rotate tool (View Z-axis), and in the Top view, rotate the Globe object to its starting orientation (see **Figure 10.8**). Remember it is going to rotate (in the camera view) from the left to the right.

You're ready to animate the rotation now.

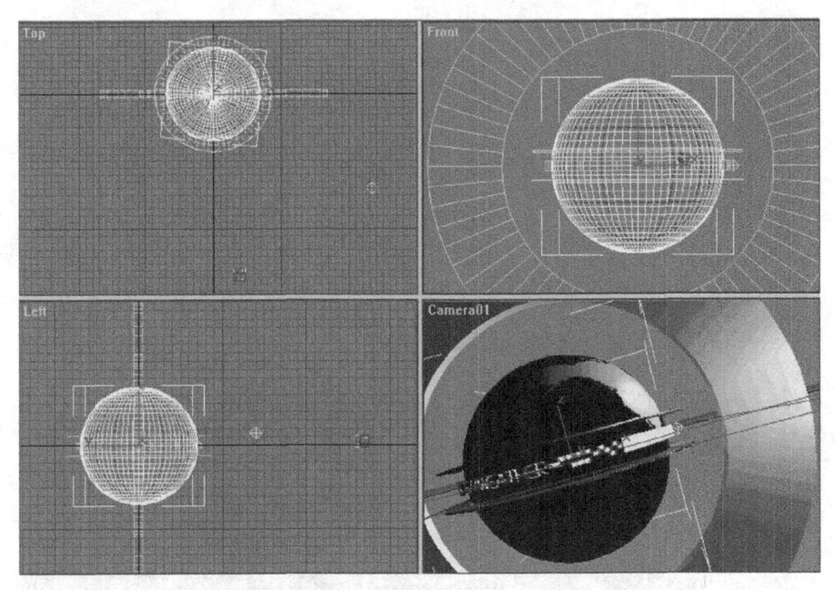

Figure 10.9 The Globe object is rotated approximately 60 degrees.

3. Advance to frame 210 and activate the Auto Key button. Using the Select and Rotate tool (View Z-axis) in the Top view, rotate the Globe object approximately 60 degrees (see **Figure 10.9**). Deactivate the Auto Key button.

   It's time to animate the rotation of the wireframe frame of the globe. However, the frame is made of several circle shapes, and you don't want to have to animate each one separately. So group them into one unit.

4. Press the H key to open the Select from Scene dialog. Select all the Circle shapes and click Select to select them in the scene.

5. Choose Group > Group from the toolbar. In the Group dialog, enter the Group name: **wireframe** and click OK to group all the circle shapes together.

   Because the circle shapes are now grouped together, they will act as one object. Now you can animate the whole wireframe group.

6. Advance to frame 210 and activate the Auto Key button. Activate the Select and Rotate tool (View Z axis) and in the Top view rotate the wireframe group Z: −120 degrees (**Figure 10.10**). Deactivate the Auto Key button. The globe and the wireframe are animated correctly.

7. Save your work as **10TV02.max**.

   Looking at John's storyboard, you can clearly see the squares to the left of the global news type first, and then the type rotates around the globe from the right to the left. Taking that into account, orient the object into its start position.

8. Advance to Frame 120 for a good look at the globe. Select the GlobalNews object and activate the Select and Rotate tool (Local Z-axis). Rotate the GlobalNews object Z: **−80** degrees. You should just barely see the black of the image rounding

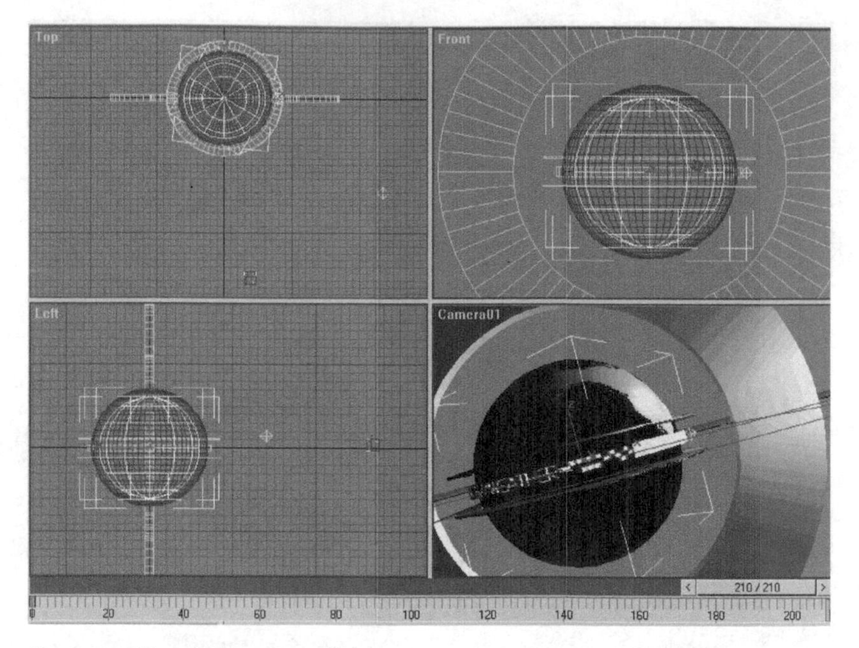

Figure 10.10 The wireframe group has been rotated –120 degrees in the Top view.

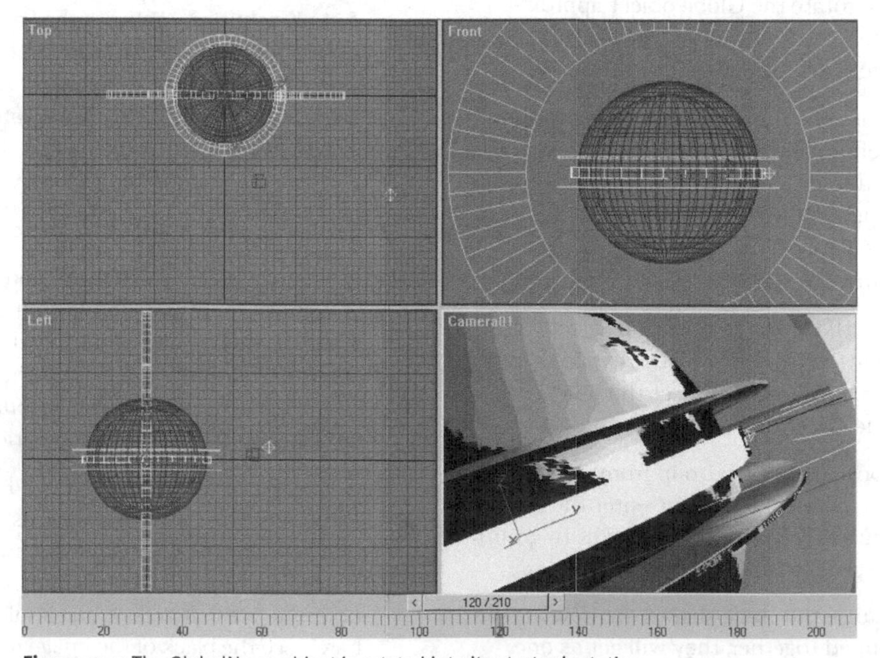

Figure 10.11 The GlobalNews object is rotated into its start orientation.

the right side in the distance (as shown in **Figure 10.11**).

Now you can animate the rotation of the GlobalNews object. You don't necessarily want to read all the type on the ring. The most important type is the "Global News" type; everything else is filler.

9. Advance to frame 210 and activate the Auto Key button. Using the Select and Rotate tool (Local Z-axis), rotate the GlobalNews object Z: **−180** degrees (as shown in **Figure 10.12**). Deactivate the Auto Key button.

If you play the animation, you should see the Global News type rotate around the globe from the right to the left.

There is only one object left to animate: the RingLarge object. Its animation is just as simple as the others. It will sweep through the scene to add a little interest to the background. After you animate the RingLarge object, you will tweak the settings of the lights and perfect the rendered appearance of the scene.

10. Activate the Select and Rotate tool (View Z-axis), and in the Top view, rotate the RingLarge object Z: **60** degrees into its start orientation (see **Figure 10.13**). Now you can animate the rotation of the RingLarge object into its end orientation.

11. Advance to frame 210 and activate the Auto Key button. Using the Select and Rotate tool (View Z-axis) in the Top view, rotate the RingLarge object Z: **−110** degrees to its end orientation (shown in **Figure 10.14**). Then deactivate the Auto Key button.

The animation for the objects in the scene is complete. Now you can turn your attention to making sure the scene is lit correctly.

12. Save your work as **10TV03.max**.

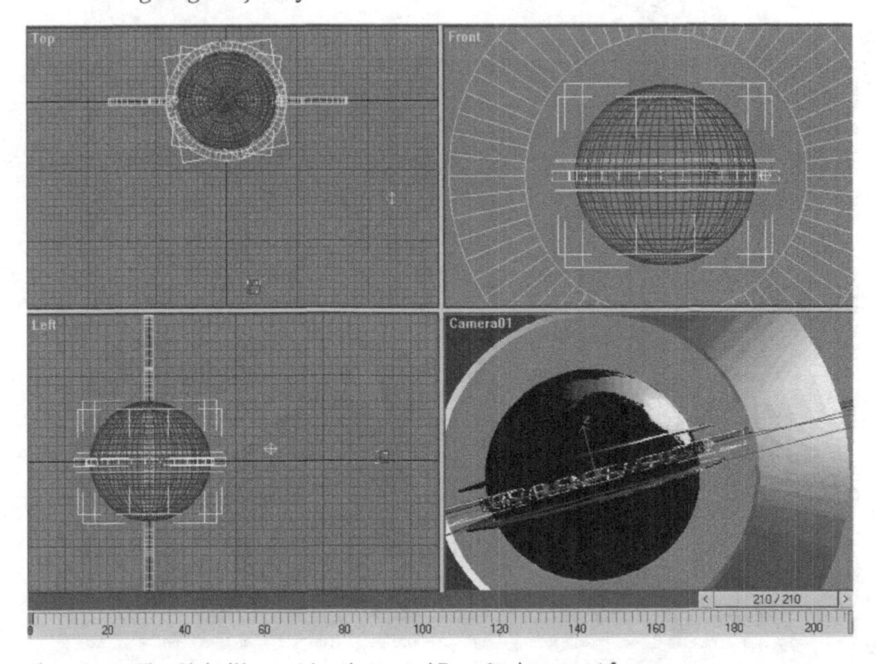

Figure 10.12 The GlobalNews object is rotated Z: −180 degrees at frame 210.

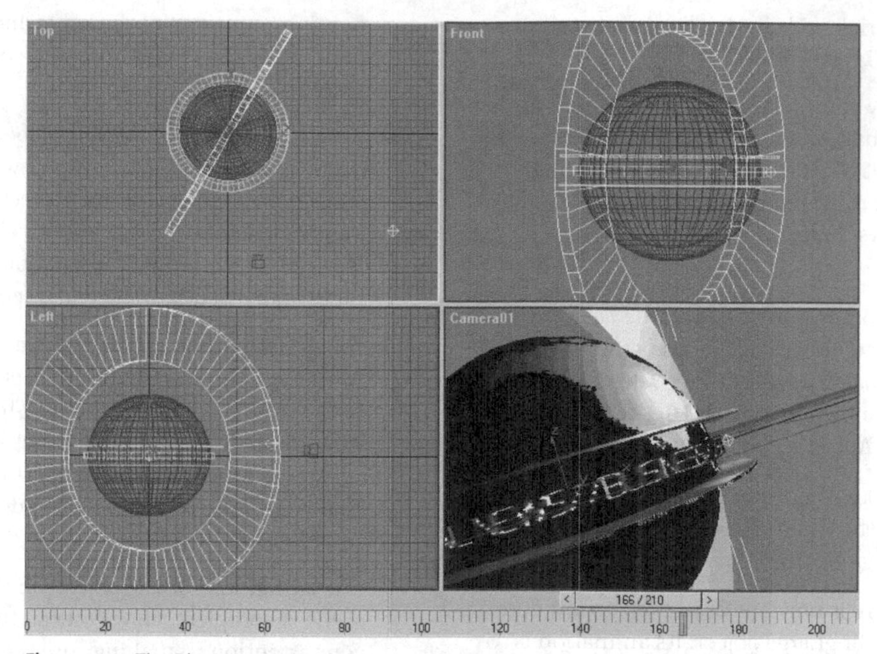

Figure 10.13 The RingLarge object is in its start orientation.

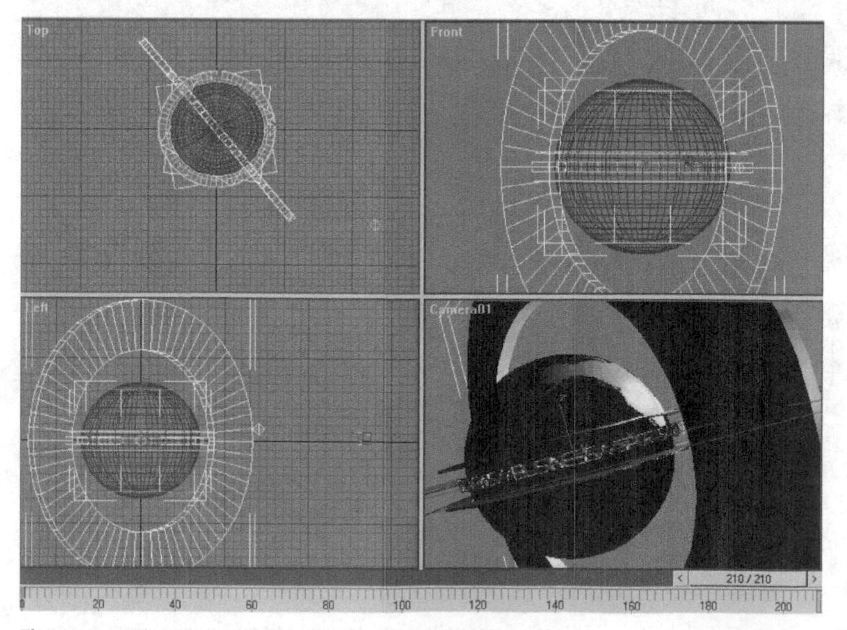

Figure 10.14 The RingLarge object in its end orientation.

Checking the Lighting in the Scene

You are thrilled with the animation of the objects and the camera in your scene. However, you haven't really been rendering too many test frames to ensure the beauty of the rendered animation. Now that everything is in place, you can focus on checking the lights in your scene, and you can decide where you should add more.

Exercise 10.4 Tweaking the Lights in a Scene

Roll up your sleeves, render a test frame, and begin to artistically tweak the scene.

1. With **10TV03.max** open, advance to frame 180 and render it through the Camera01 view (as shown in **Figure 10.15**).

   The rendering looks good, but the RingLarge object is nearly in complete darkness. You should shed some light on it.

2. Create an Omni light in the Top view with the color RGB: **150, 150, 150** and move it to XYZ: **−700, −400, 100**. Name this light **OmniRingLFront** and click the Exclude button to open the Exclude/Include dialog. In the Exclude/Include dialog, choose Include, select RightLarge, and click the arrow pointing to the right (see **Figure 10.16**). Click OK to create the Include list.

   As you can see in **Figure 10.17**, the light is now correctly adjusted. The OmniRingLFront light casts its light on only the RingLarge object.

3. Render frame 180 again through the Camera01 view (as shown in **Figure 10.18**).

Figure 10.15 The Camera01 view rendered at frame 180.

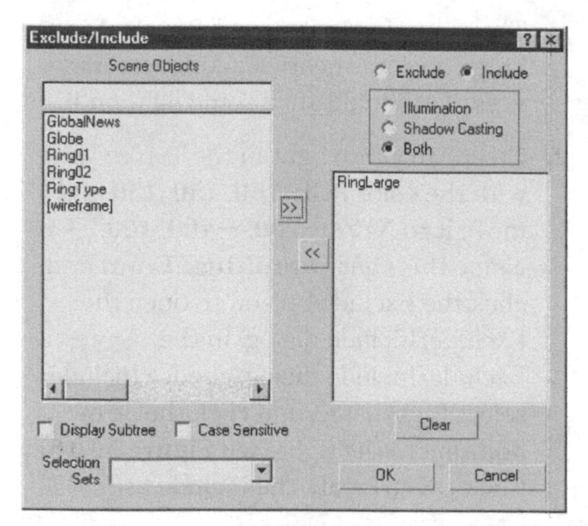

Figure 10.16 The correctly configured Include list for the OmniRingLFront light.

Plenty of light is now cast on the RingLarge object throughout the animation.

Exercise 10.5 Adding More Special Ring Lights

There is only one more area I think could be improved with more light: in-between the rings. There is only one light there currently, and the rest of the ring looks dull and boring. If you add two more lights inside the ring, you can animate them to travel within the rings, adding even more interest to the rendered animation.

If you select the Omni-SpecialRing01 light and move its pivot to XYZ: **0, 0, 0**, you can then instance the light twice along that pivot. After creating the instances, you can animate them along the pivot as well.

1. Select the Omni-SpecialRing01 light and open the Hierarchy panel. Activate the Affect Pivot Only button, and using the Select and Move tool, move the pivot to XYZ: **0, 0, 0** (see **Figure 10.19**). Deactivate the Affect Pivot Only button.

   The Omni-SpecialRing01's pivot is at the center of the globe. You can now create the two instances of the light.

2. With Omni-SpecialRing01 selected, activate the Select and Rotate tool (View Z-axis). In the Top view, Shift+rotate the

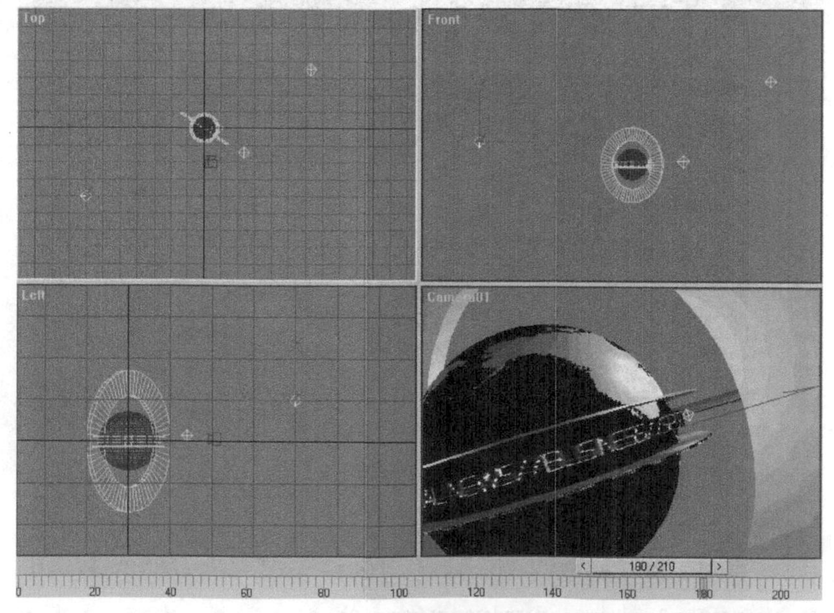

Figure 10.17 The OmniRingLFront light is in the correct position with the correct parameters.

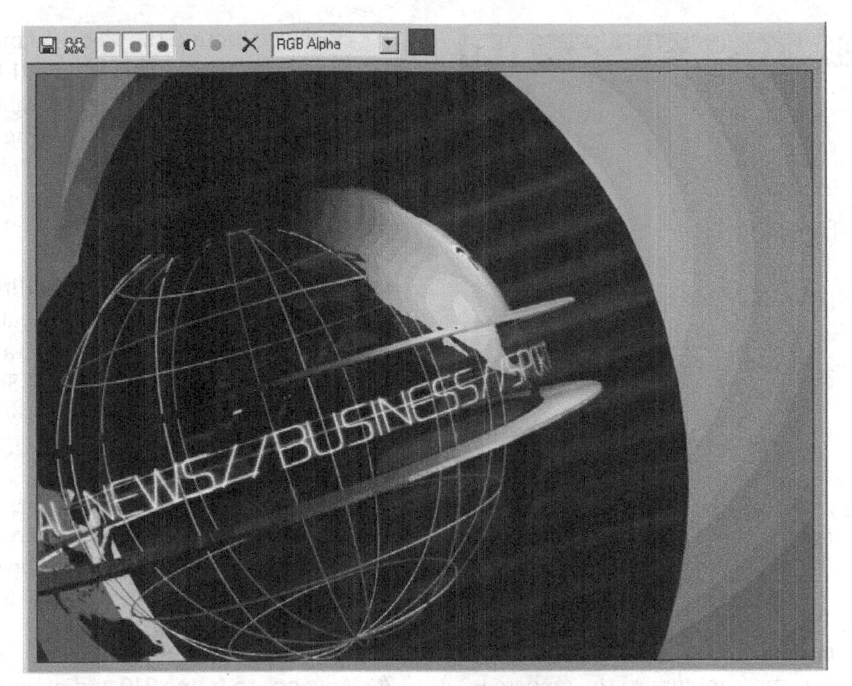

Figure 10.18 The RingLarge object now has ample light on it at frame 180.

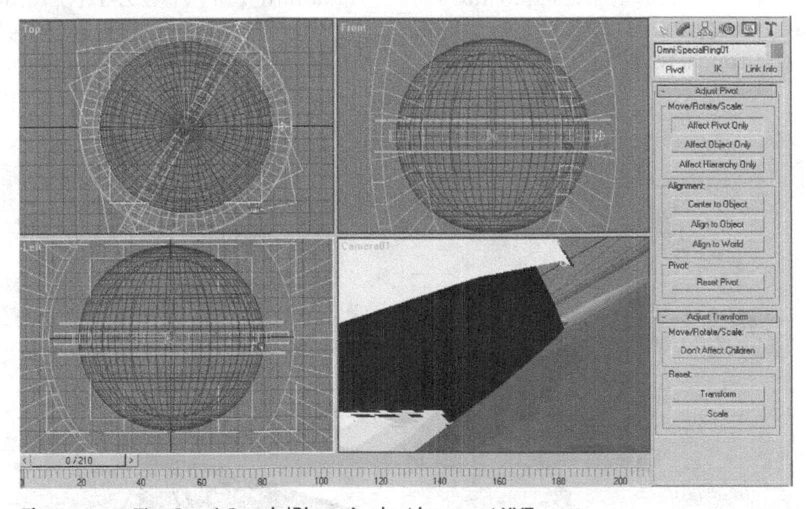

Figure 10.19 The Omni-SpecialRing01's pivot is now at XYZ; 0,0,0

Omni light Z: **120** degrees, and then release the mouse button. In the Clone Options dialog, choose Instance and change the Number of Copies to 2 (as shown in **Figure 10.20**). Click OK to create the two instances (see **Figure 10.21**).

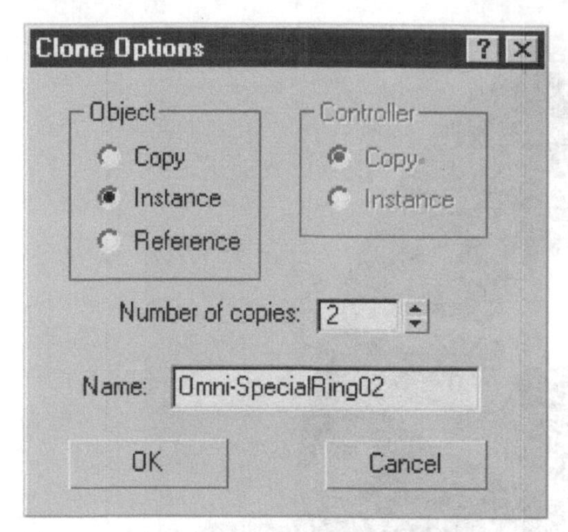

Figure 10.20 The Clone Options dialog with the correct settings.

You can now animate the three lights to add a little more interest to the rendered animation. Before you can animate though, you need to rotate the lights into their start orientations. Looking down through the Top view, the lights will rotate clockwise around the globe. To make sure the original Omni-SpecialRing01 light illuminates the most important right side of the globe's rings in the beginning of the animation, you will rotate the lights counterclockwise a few degrees before animating them forward.

3. Select the three Omni-SpecialRing Omni lights (01, 02, and 03) and activate the Select and Rotate tool (View Z-axis—Use Selection Center). Activate the Selection Lock toggle, and in the Top view, rotate the three selected lights Z: **30** degrees (see **Figure 10.22**).

   The Omni-SpecialRing lights are in the optimal start orientation for the scene now. You can advance to frame 210 and animate their rotation.

4. Advance to frame 210 and activate the Auto Key button. Using the Select and Rotate tool (View Z-axis), rotate the three Omni-SpecialRing lights Z: **−160** degrees in the Top view (as shown in

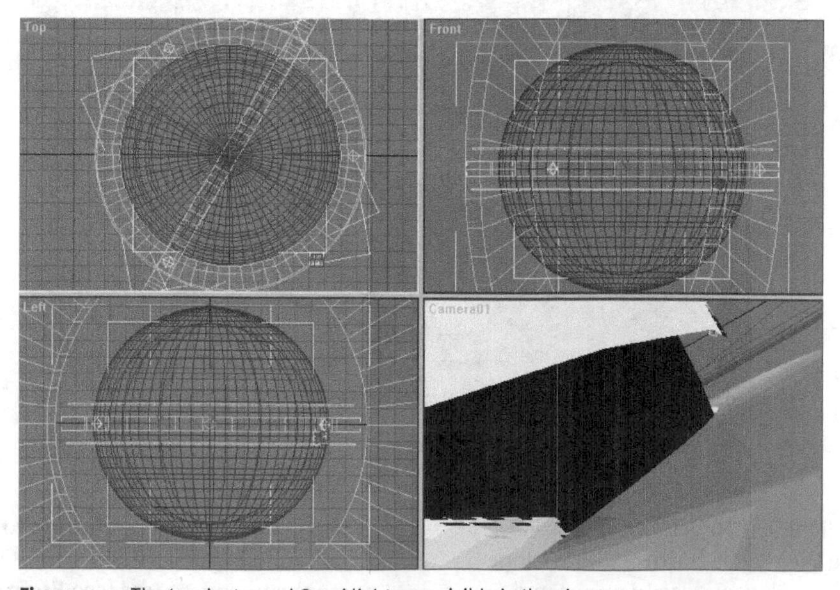

Figure 10.21 The two instanced Omni lights are visible in the views.

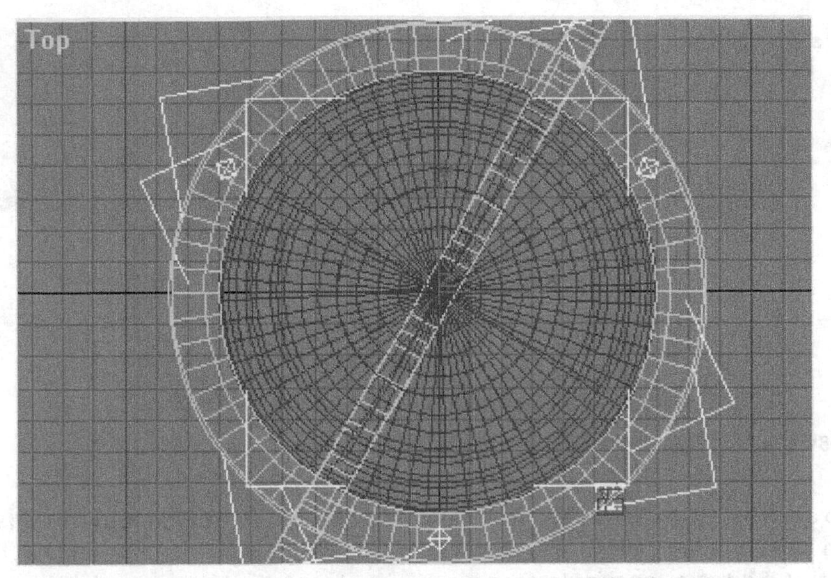

Figure 10.22 The Omni-SpecialRing lights are rotated Z:30 degrees in the Top view.

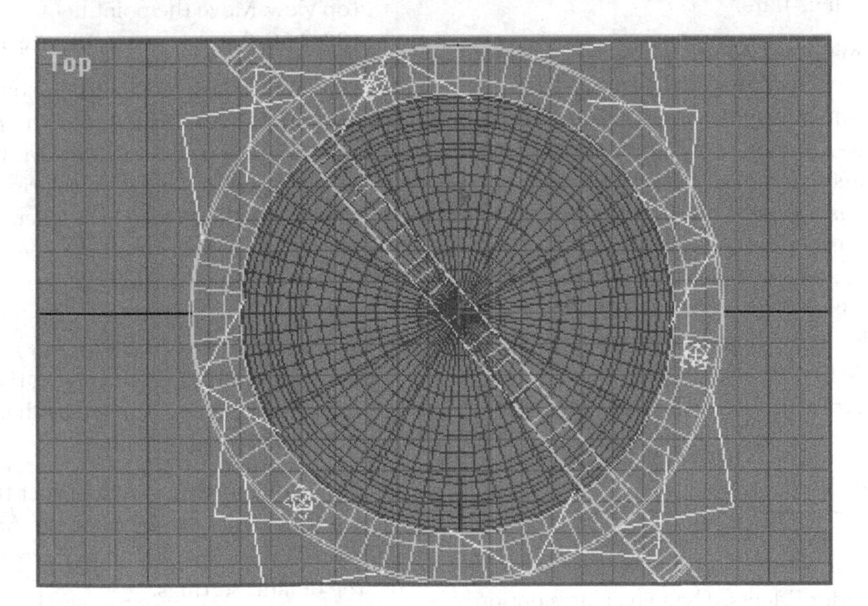

Figure 10.23 The three Omni lights have been rotated Z: −160 degrees.

Figure 10.23). Deactivate the Auto Key button and Selection Lock toggle.

5. The lights are all perfect now. Save your work as **10TV04.max**. If you play the animation, you will see the effect of the lights traveling between the rings.

Adding the Lens Flare

It is not hard to notice the lens flares on John's storyboard (see **Figure 10.24**). The truth is that lens flares are a great graphic device that easily adds visual interest and

Figure 10.24 John's storyboard for TV 3 News.

realism to an image. If you have ever watched a news program on TV, you probably know that not too many minutes go by without a lens flare.

This animation is no exception. You will be adding two lens flares to the complete animation: one during the first section and one during the second section to punctuate the logo. John's storyboard clearly illustrates a flare that is centered between the two rings and that gets brighter as the scene progresses. You will actually use the flare as a transition device to help bring on the second scene smoothly. As the flare of the first shot brightens, the Venetian blinds will reveal themselves, completing the transition.

Exercise 10.6 Adding Lens Effects in Video Post

There are two ways to create lens flares in 3ds max: by using a Video Post filter or by using Render Effects. The Lens Flares option in Render Effects is good for creating less-complicated flares; the Video Post filter allows you to visually build lens flares quickly. The one thing both flares have in common is that both need a source. In this scene, you will create a point helper to be the source of the flare.

1. Make sure **10tv04.max** is open and select Create > Helpers. Click the Point button and create a point helper in the Top view. Move the point helper to XYZ: **130**, **166**, **0** (as shown in **Figure 10.25**).

   The Point01 helper will be the source of the lens flare in this scene. If you play the animation, you will see it always stays relatively snug in between the rings. You have to create a Video Post Queue in order to create the lens flare effect. You will need to create three basic events: the scene input event (the camera), the image filter event (the lens flare), and the image output event (saving the rendered image). It's as simple as that. Now start creating the queue.

2. Choose Rendering > Video Post to open the Video Post dialog. Click the Add Scene Event button. Click OK to accept the default settings.

   The Camera01 event is now in the queue (see **Figure 10.26**).

   Now add the flare event.

3. Click the Add Image Filter Event button. In the Add Image Filter Event dialog,

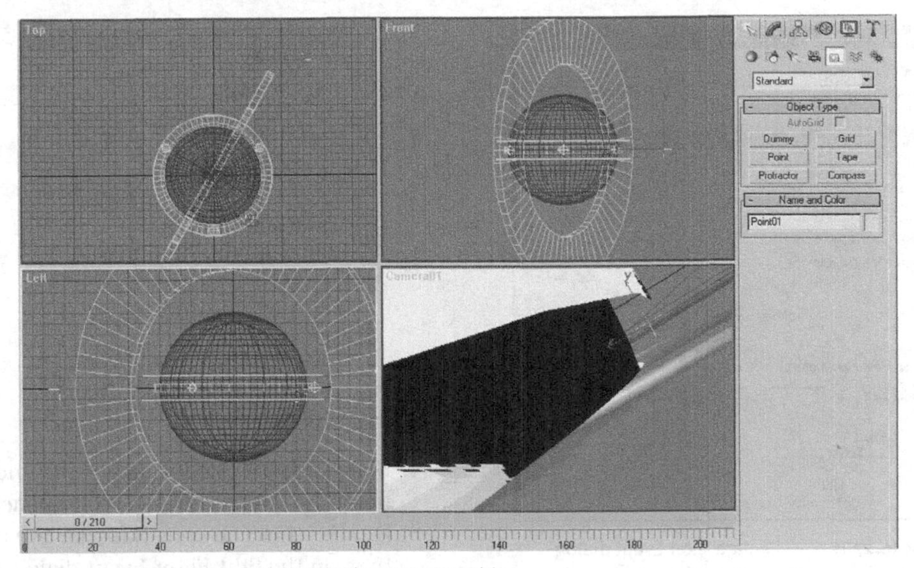

Figure 10.25 The Point01 helper is in the correct position.

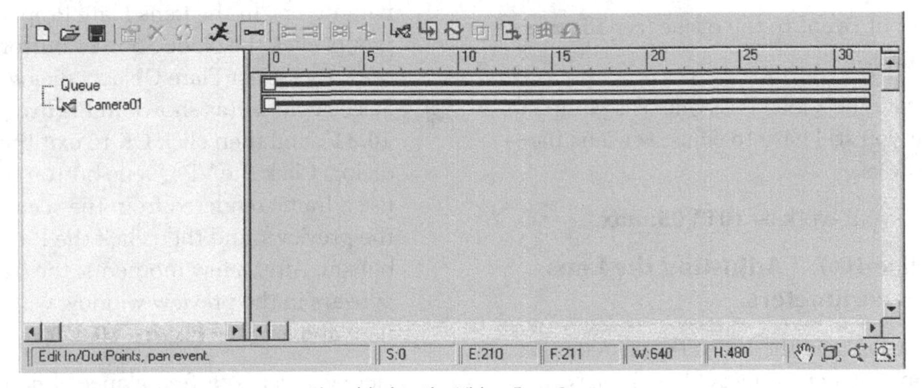

Figure 10.26 The Camera01 event is added to the Video Post Queue.

change Adobe Photoshop Filter to Lens Effects Flare (see **Figure 10.27**), and then click OK to close the dialog.

The Lens Effects Flare event is added to the queue (see **Figure 10.28**). To complete the queue, you will add the Image Output Event.

4. Click the Image Output Event button. In the Image Output Event dialog, click the Files button. In the Select Image File for Video Post Output folder, enter the desired filename. In my scene, I entered Project1\images\shota.avi, and in the Video Compression setup, I chose Full Frames (Uncompressed) (as shown in **Figure 10.29**). Full Frames will allow me to save a playable avi file without sacrificing image quality. When I composite it into the second scene, the quality will be perfect (as compared to a compressed format). Click OK to add the Image

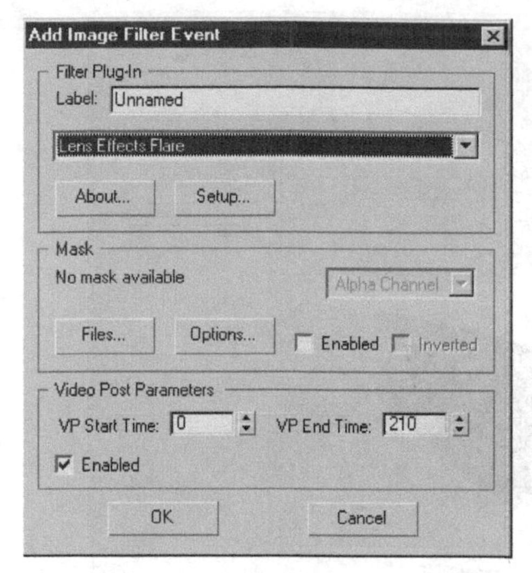

Figure 10.27 The Add Image Filter Event dialog with Lens Effects Flare selected.

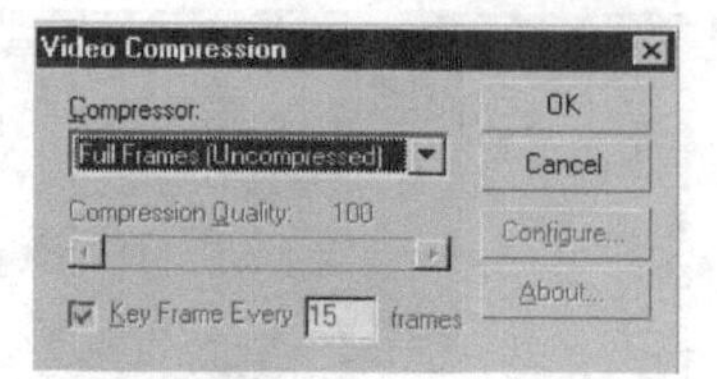

Figure 10.29 The Video Compression dialog with Full Frames (Uncompressed) selected.

Output Event to the queue (see **Figure 10.30**).

Great! The Video Post Queue is complete. But you still have to adjust the lens flare's settings.

5. Save your work as **10TV05.max**.

Exercise 10.7 Adjusting the Lens Flare's Parameters

You just finished the Video Post Queue that contains the Lens Effects Flare filter. Now you need to open the Lens Effect Flare's parameters and adjust them to design the desired flare effect.

1. Make sure **10TV05.max** is open and at frame 0. Open the Video Post Queue. Double-click the Lens Effects Flare event to open the Edit Filter Event dialog. Click the Setup button to open the lens flare's parameters. In the Lens Flare Properties group, click the Node Sources button to open the Select Flare Objects dialog. Select Point01 (as shown in **Figure 10.31**), and then click OK to exit the dialog. Click the VP Queue button (to use a frame rendered from the scene in the preview), and then click the Preview button. After a few moments, the frame appears in the preview window with the flare applied (see **Figure 10.32**).

   Here you get your first glance at how the default lens flare looks on your objects.

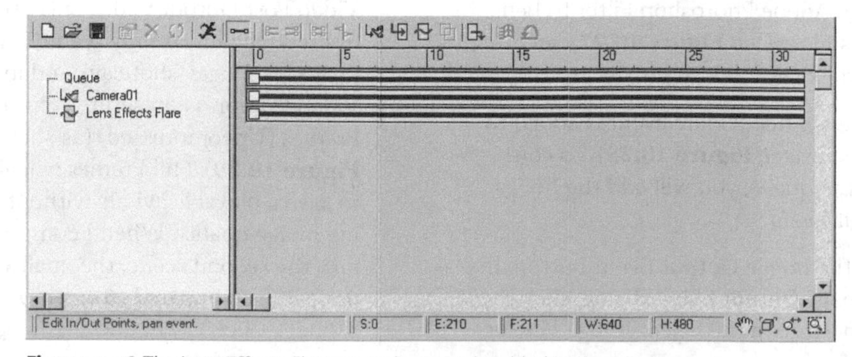

Figure 10.28 The Lens Effects Flare event is properly added to the queue.

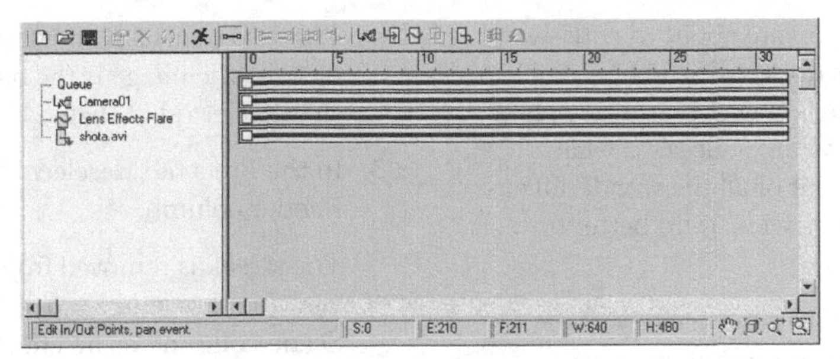

Figure 10.30 The finished Video Post Queue.

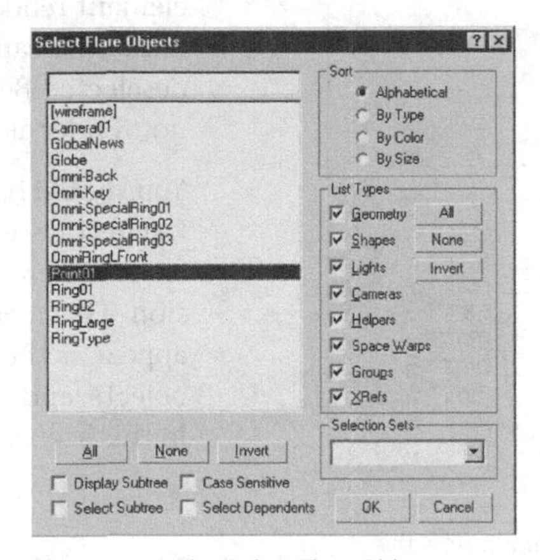

Figure 10.31 The Select Flare Objects dialog with Point01 selected.

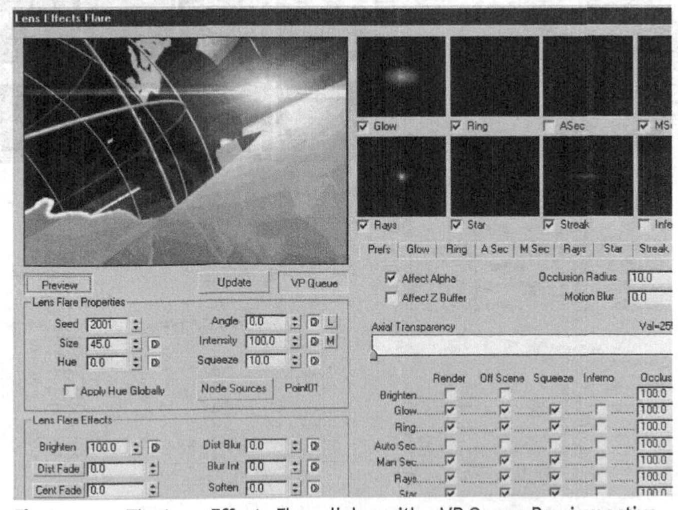

Figure 10.32 The Lens Effects Flare dialog with a VP Queue Preview active.

It looks like you are about to enter warp speed! That's not good. The first problem with the flare is that Squeeze is applied to all its elements. Squeeze is what makes ovals out of all the wonderful circle flare secondaries. You'd better turn off Squeeze.

2. In the Prefs tab, remove every check mark in the Squeeze column (see **Figure 10.33**).

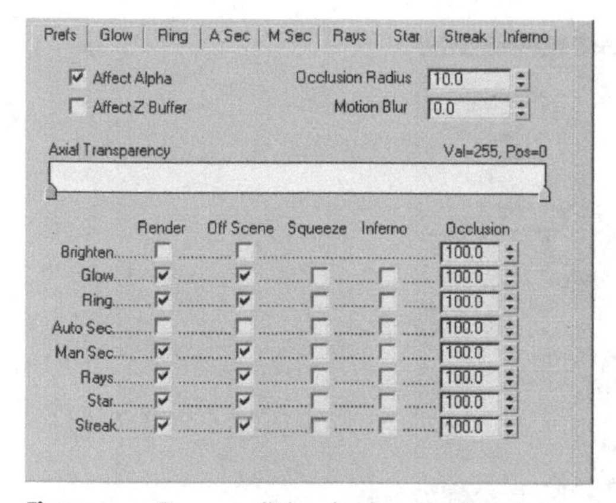

Figure 10.33 Remove all the check marks from the Lens Effects Flare dialog's Squeeze column.

The next aspect of the flare that doesn't fit in to the image is the blue warp speed streak. Get rid of that.

3. In the Prefs tab, deselect Streak from the Render column.

The streak is removed from the flare preview (as shown in **Figure 10.34**). The Off Scene column has no effect on the flare if the element isn't checked in the Render column. If Off Scene is checked, the flare element renders even when the source is out of the camera view. Because you deselected Render for the Streak, it will not render at all.

You should be concerned with the Occlusion value as well. Currently all the elements are set to 100 percent occlusion. This means that the elements disappear as the source passes behind objects, and you don't want that to occur in this scene.

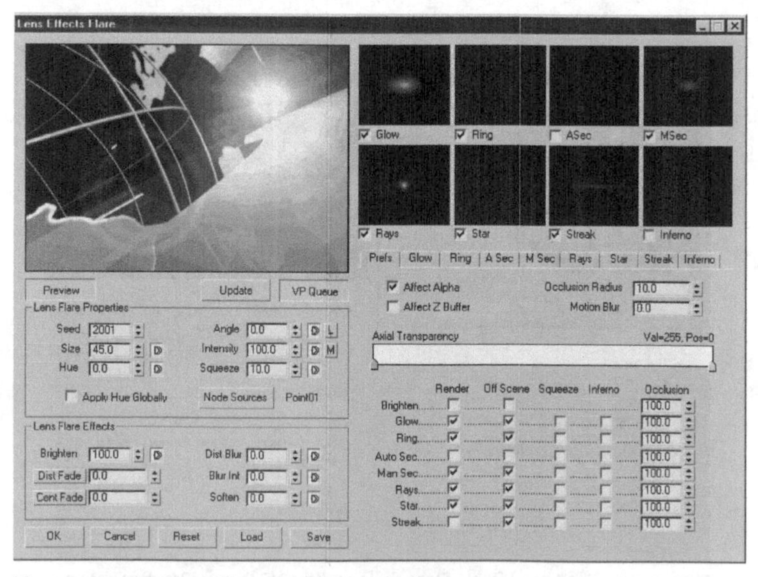

Figure 10.34 The Streak is removed from the flare.

4. Lower all the Occlusion values to **0**.

   You don't need the Star either, so you can get rid of it as well.

5. Deselect Star in the Render column (see **Figure 10.35**). John's storyboard shows the flare as more of an orange color, but right now it looks bluish. Adjust the Glow element's color gradient to add much more gold to the glow. Before you do that though, advance to a frame that will allow you to view the flare over the background.

6. Advance to frame 120 and click the Update button in the Lens Effects Flare dialog so that the image renders again and you can see the scene at frame 120. Then click the Glow tab (see **Figure 10.36**).

   If you look at the Radial Color gradient, you can see why the glow is so bluish. Make it more gold.

7. Double-click the first gradient flag (the first one on the left) and change its color to RGB: **210, 150, 0**. Double-click the middle flag and change its color to RGB: **120, 0, 0**. Right-click the middle flag and choose Copy. Right-click the last flag and choose Paste. The result should be a gradient from orange to red. Also, check Hide Behind Geometry.

   The Radial Color gradient is now good. When you clicked the Hide Behind Geometry option, the glow effect was applied only to the background environment; therefore, the glow effect hides behind the geometry. This creates a great backlit effect. However, the flare isn't as intense as it could be. By adjusting the Radial Transparency gradient, you can increase the intensity of the glow.

8. Click the pointer on the whitest pixels of the Radial Transparency gradient and drag right to create a new flag at Pos=60 (as shown in **Figure 10.37**). The flare looks about perfect.

9. Save your work as **10TV06.max**.

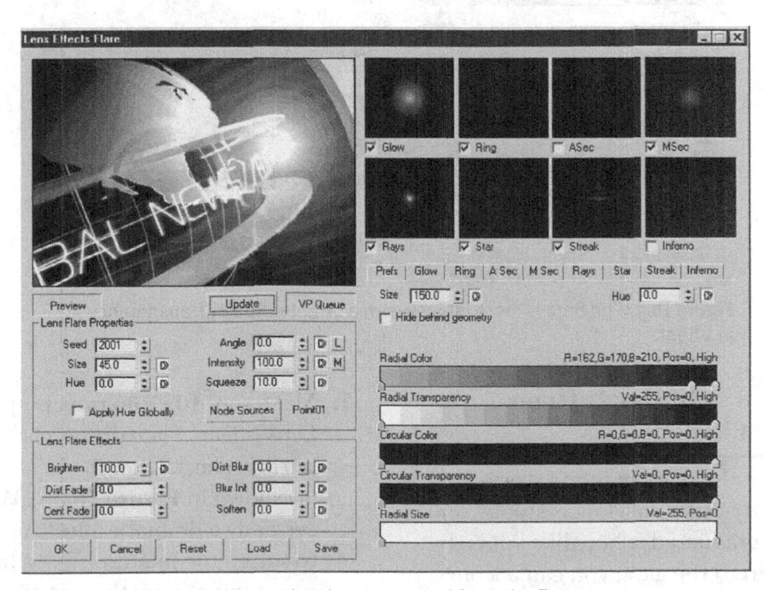

Figure 10.35 The Star element has been removed from the flare.

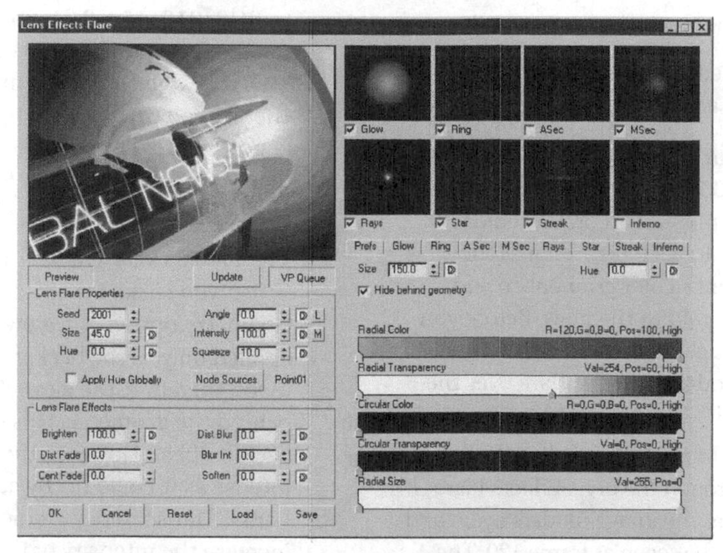

Figure 10.36 The Glow tab is open in the Lens Effects Flare dialog.

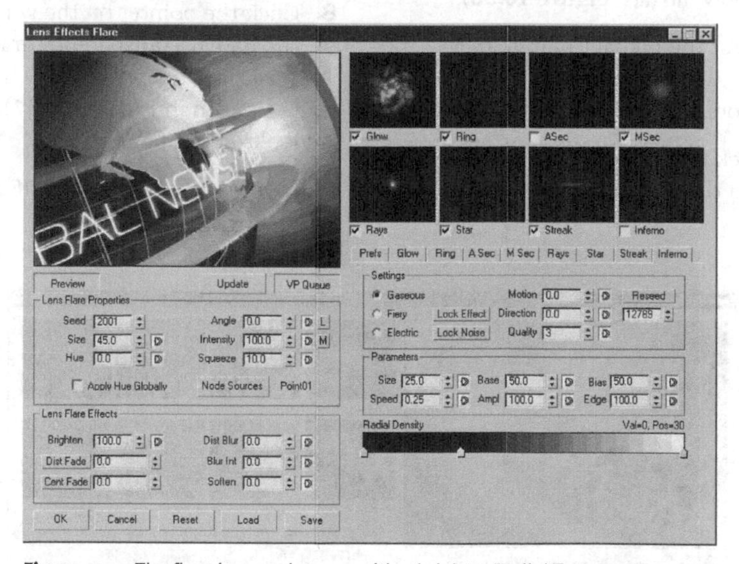

Figure 10.37 The flare is more intense with a brighter Radial Transparency gradient.

Exercise 10.8 Adding Inferno to the Glow Element

If you examine the flare on John's storyboard, you will notice the glow is smoky, and not a perfect graduated sphere like yours. By adding Inferno to the glow, you can accomplish this smoky effect.

1. Make sure **10TV06.max** is open. In the Lens Effects Flare dialog, click the Prefs tab and check Glow in the Inferno column (as shown in **Figure 10.38**). Well, that is certainly a dramatic effect! You will need to soften the Inferno effect a bit before you can stamp it with the seal of approval.

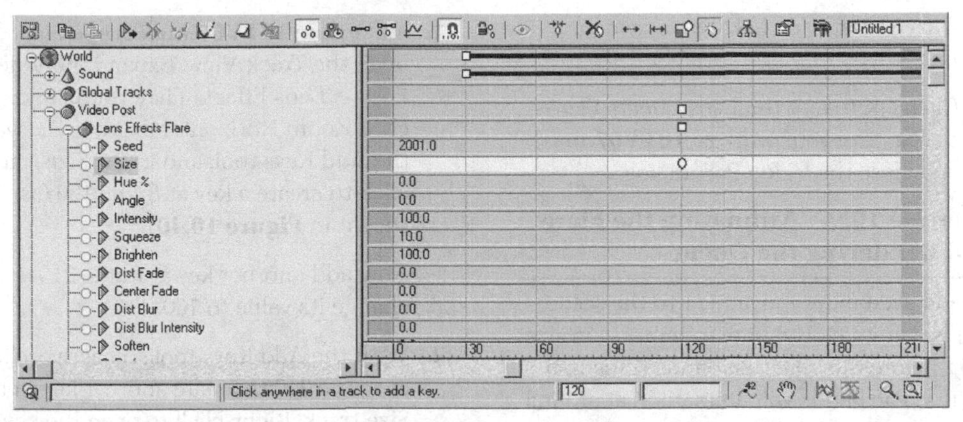

Figure 10.38 Glow is checked in the Inferno column.

2. Click the Inferno tab. In the Settings group, change the Motion value to **0**. You change the Motion value to **0** because Motion pans the noise effect through the scene, as if the wind were blowing. The Direction value assigns the direction the "wind" blows (0 being 12 o'clock, and the direction changing clockwise as the value increases). The value of 360 returns the direction to 12 o'clock). You do not want any "wind" in this scene.

3. In the Parameters group, change the Size to **25** and the Speed to **.25**. You are increasing the size of the effect to create larger, more realistic clouds. You are changing the Speed value to .25 (from 1) to slow down the undulation of the clouds. This will create a slow billowing cloud time-lapse effect. The Inferno effect allows for large gaps to form between the clouds. You always want the center of the glow effect to be a solid glow, which you can accomplish by adjusting the Radial Density gradient.

4. In the Inferno tab, double-click the left flag of the Radial Density gradient and change its color to black RGB: **0, 0, 0** to make the glow more solid toward the source. Then make it even a little more solid. Click the pointer over a black pixel in the gradient and drag to create a flag at Pos=30 (see **Figure 10.39**).

   The flare is perfect now. Save it so you can use it over the second shot in the animation as well.

✔ Note

If the Inferno effect does not appear in the Glow sample slot, turn the check box for the Glow sample slot off and then back on to update it.

5. In the Lens Effects Flare dialog, click the Save button. In the Save Filter Settings dialog, choose a folder to save the flare to (**Project1**), enter the filename

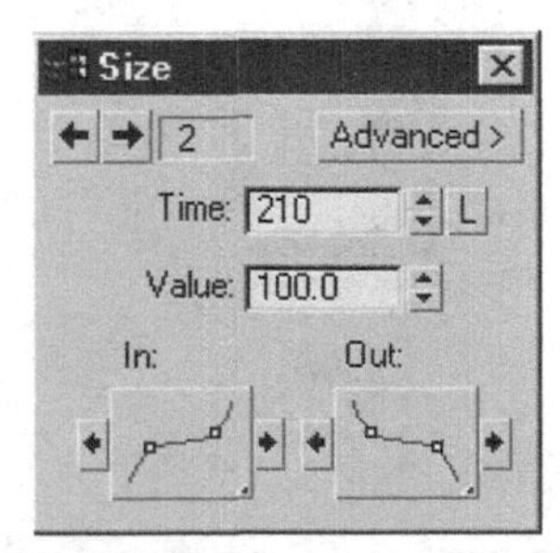

Figure 10.39 The finished Inferno effect.

flare01.lzf, and click OK to save the flare effect.

6. Click OK to exit the Lens Effects Flare dialog, save your work as **10TV07.max**, and close the Video Post dialog.

Exercise 10.9 Animating the Flare and Rendering the Queue

To add even more movement to the scene, you will animate the flare to increase in size right before the Venetian blinds transition occurs. The blinds will animate in at around the start of the third measure of music, roughly frame 130. So you will precede that by starting growth of the flare at frame 120.

1. Make sure **10TV07.max** is open and open the Track View. Expand the Video Post > Lens Effects Flare tracks and click Zoom Horizontal Extents. Activate the Add Keys tool, and in the Size track, click to create a key at frame 120 (as shown in **Figure 10.40**).

   Now add another key at frame 210 and change its value to 100.

2. With the Add Keys tool still active, click at frame 210 to create another key in the Size track. Right-click to open the key's Size dialog and change the Value to **100** (see **Figure 10.41**). Close the Size dialog.

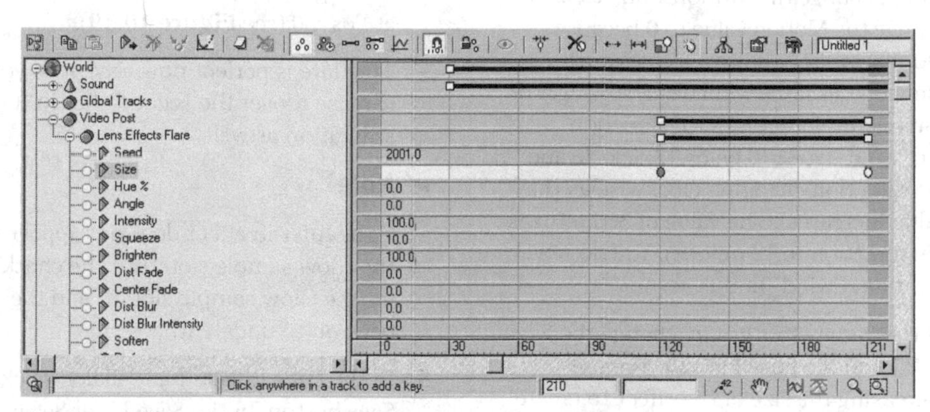

Figure 10.40 The Track View with a key at frame 120 in the Size track.

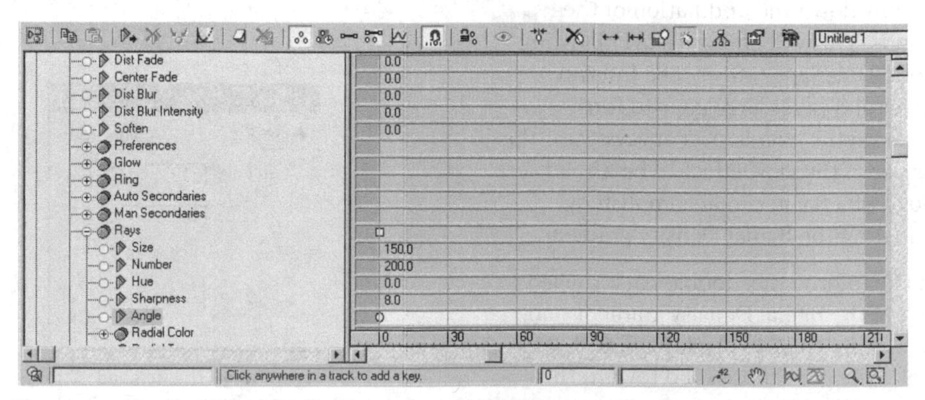

Figure 10.41 The Size dialog shows a Value of 100 at frame 210.

The two keys in the Size track will animate the overall size of the flare from 45 (the default value) to 100 between frames 120 and 210 (see **Figure 10.42**).

While you are in the Track View and editing the Lens Effects Flare settings, go ahead and add a little rotation to the rays of the flare.

3. Expand the Rays track of the Lens Effects Flare in the Track View. Activate the Add Keys tool—if it's not already active—and click on the Angle track at frame 0 to create a key (see **Figure 10.43**).

   You can add a key to frame 210 and change its value to add rotation to the rays.

4. Create a second key at frame 210 on the Angle track and right-click it to open its Angle dialog. Change the Value to **−90** (as shown in **Figure 10.44**), and then close the dialog. The Angle track is finished (see **Figure 10.45**). Close the Track View.

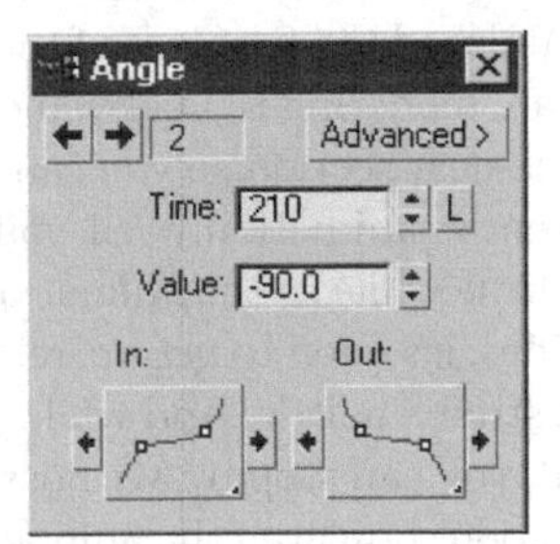

Figure 10.42 In the Track View, you see the Size track's keys at frames 120 and 210.

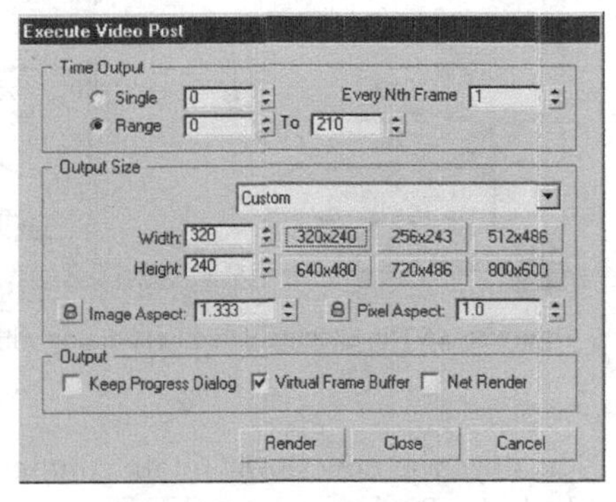

Figure 10.44 The Angle dialog shows a Value of −90 at frame 210.

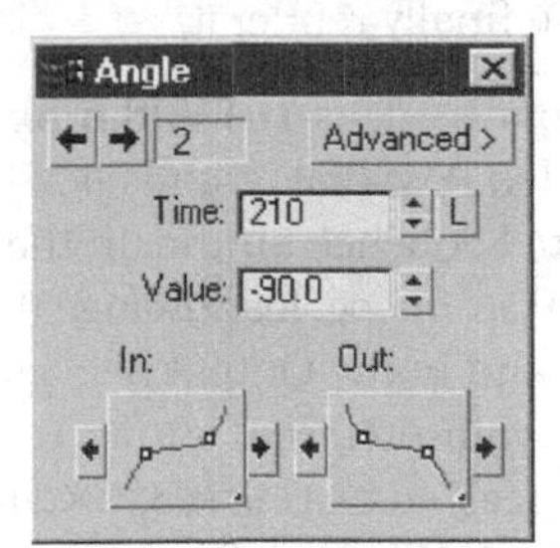

Figure 10.45 The Angle track has keys at frames 0 and 210.

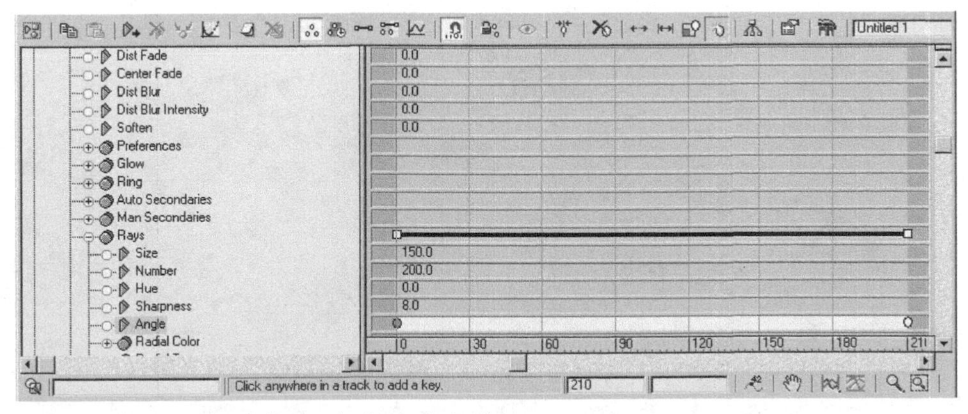

Figure 10.43 Create a key at frame 0 in the Angle track.

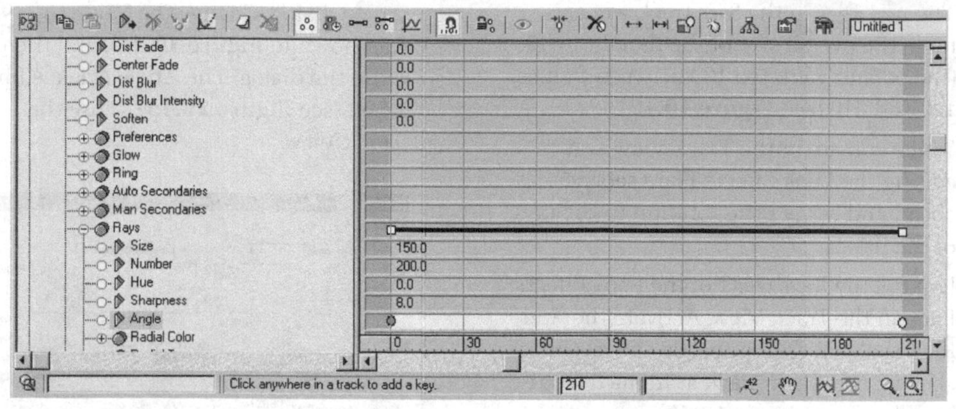

Figure 10.46 The Execute Video Post dialog with the suggested settings.

The Rays will now slowly rotate counterclockwise 90 degrees over the course of the animation. The first scene is finished. You can finally render it.

5. Save your work as **10TV08.max**, open the Video Post dialog, and click the Execute Sequence button. In the Execute Video Post dialog, leave Range 0 To 210 active, and in the Output Size group, choose your preferred output resolution. The suggested setting is 320×240 (see **Figure 10.46**). Click Render to render the queue.

   The queue will render frames 0 to 210.

In Conclusion

The animation looks great. You have successfully finished the first half of the animation and are rendering it. I bet you can't wait to start the next section so you can complete the entire animation. Well, you'll need to wait a little while as the animation renders. Besides, it's good to get up, relax your eyes, and stretch a little. And while you're up and about, you can stop by Mr. Boss's office and brag about how well the animation is turning out!

11

Project 1: Part 3

You now have the first half of the animation "in the bag," so to speak. The globe scene is rendered and looks great. To finish the TV 3 news opening, you need to create the second half of the animation: the TV 3 logo and the Venetian blinds.

Figure 11.1 John's storyboard for the TV3 news opening.

Looking at John's storyboard (shown in **Figure 11.1**), you think re-creating the animation will be fairly simple.

In this section, you gain experience in the following areas:

- Using the Refine tool to adjust long and narrow shapes for beveling
- Using the Place Highlight tool to accurately position lights
- Using an XForm modifier to perform sub-object animations
- Using multiple mapping coordinates in one material
- Creating complex animated gradient maps
- Using Color Map to adjust an image's output
- Creating a key using the Motion panel
- Tracing the logo with a flare using Path Constraints

Creating the TV 3 Logo Scene

Basically, you need to create the TV 3 logo, the Venetian blinds, a bar of text, and a lens flare. The camera motion is going to be a very linear dolly backward, revealing the objects as it passes by them. The finish line is in sight; keep up the stride.

Exercise 11.1 Adding the Sound and Background to a Scene

You will be choreographing the animation to Gordon's music in this scene, so you need to load the audio and offset it 30 frames. You will adjust your scene length to 390 frames (13 seconds) so you can hear the entire cut of audio.

1. Choose File > Reset. Open the Track View, select and right-click the Sound track, and choose Properties to open the Sound Options dialog. Click the Choose Sound button, choose **Project1\sounds\GlobalNews3D.wav**, and click OK twice to load the audio into the Track View. Use the Zoom tool until the time is shown in 10 frame intervals. Drag the Sound track to move its start to frame 30 (see **Figure 11.2**). Close the Track View.

   The animation's length is currently 100 frames; you need to change it to **390** frames to match the length of the audio.

2. Click the Time Configuration button to open the Time Configuration dialog.

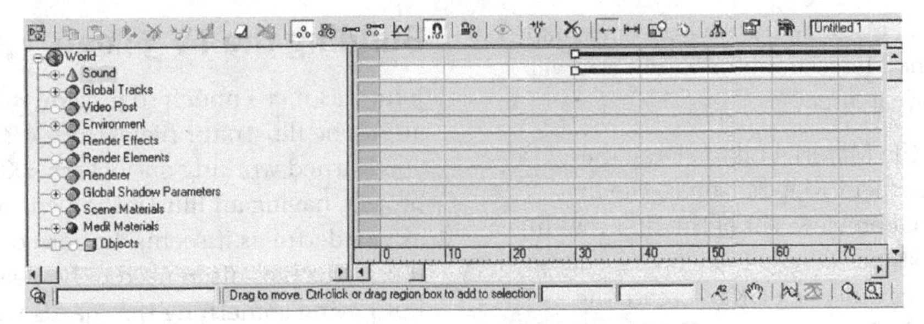

Figure 11.2 The sound track is loaded and offset to start at frame 30.

Change the End Time to **390** (as shown in **Figure 11.3**) and click OK to close the dialog.

If you were to play the animation, you would hear the music play in its entirety. The audio is correctly placed in the scene, and the scene is the right length. Now load the first half of the animation as the environment background image.

3. Choose Rendering > Environment to open the Environment dialog. Click the Environment Map button to open the Material/Map Browser, choose Bitmap, and click OK to open the Select Bitmap Image File for Import dialog. Locate the file you rendered in the last chapter and open it into the Environment dialog; in this case, the file is **Project1\images\shota.avi** (see **Figure 11.4**).

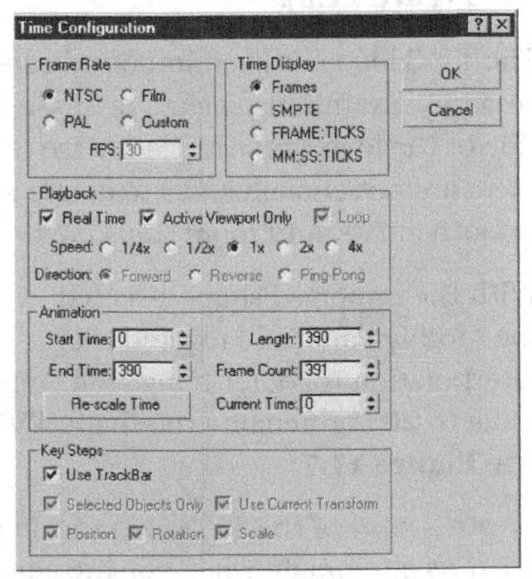

Figure 11.3 The Time Configuration dialog with an End Time of 390.

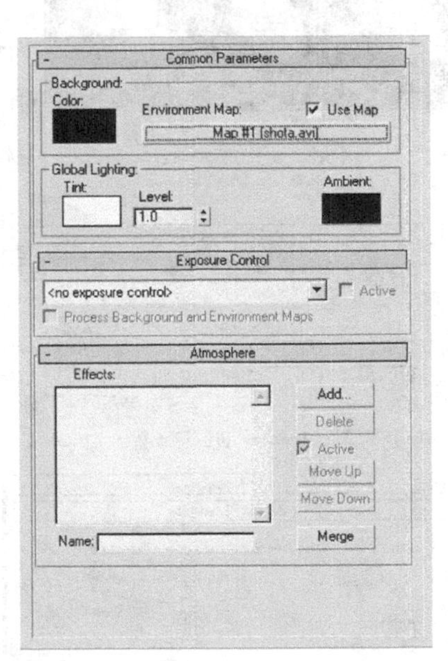

Figure 11.4 The Environment dialog with the rendered animation from the previous chapter loaded.

You will instance the environment map into the Material Editor, where you will animate it later.

4. Open the Material Editor. Drag the Environment Map button to the first material preview slot of the first row. In the Instance (Copy) Map dialog, choose Instance and click OK to create the instance. Name the map **Env** (as shown in **Figure 11.5**). Close the Environment dialog and the Material Editor.

   The scene is ready; now you can do your magic.

5. Save your work as **11TV01.max**.

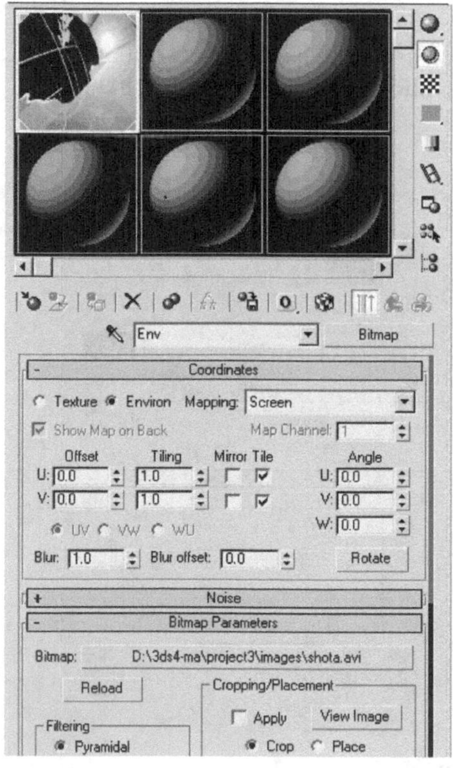

Figure 11.5 The Environment Map is instanced into the Material Editor.

Building the TV 3 Logo

John was nice enough to provide you with an Adobe Illustrator file of the TV 3 logo. As you learned working on Victor's 2002 Vote project, having an Illustrator file is often not as wonderful as it seems. Imported Illustrator files often need to be cleaned up. But having something that needs work is usually better than having to start from scratch.

Exercise 11.2 Importing and Editing the Logo Shape

You will import John's TV 3 logo file and copy it so you can use it as a template.

1. With **11TV01.max** open, choose File > Import to open the Select File to Import dialog. Change Files of Type to Adobe Illustrator (*.AI), choose **Project1\ai\tv3_logo.ai**, and click Open to open the AI Import dialog. Leave Merge Objects with Current Scene active, and click OK to open the Shape Import dialog. Choose Single Object and click OK to import the shape. Maximize the Top view and turn off the view's grid (see **Figure 11.6**).

   The TV 3 logo has been imported successfully. Examining the curve on the left side of the logo, you can plainly see that there are not enough steps to create a smooth curve. Add more steps now.

2. With the imported shape selected, open the Modify Panel and expand the Interpolation rollout. Change the Steps value to **20** and rename the shape **TV3** (see **Figure 11.7**).

   Create a copy of the TV 3 logo so you can use it as a template when you are editing the imported shape.

Figure 11.6 The TV 3 logo is imported from an Adobe Illustrator file.

Figure 11.7 The TV 3 logo has enough steps to smoothly curve.

3. With TV3 selected, choose Edit > Clone to open the Clone Options dialog. In the Object group, leave Copy selected, change the name to **TV3-template** (see **Figure 11.8**), and click OK to create the clone. Use the Select Objects dialog to re-select the TV3 shape.

4. Work on the outline of the TV 3 logo using **Figure 11.9** as a guide. (It shows

the preferred layout for vertices and the adjustments of their tangent handles.)

If you completed the billboard in the first project and the vote machine in the second project, cleaning up an outline is old hat. If not, you'll want to use these tips:

- ▲ Beware of two or more vertices occupying the same space. To determine how many vertices are in a specific area, drag a rectangular selection around the area in question and check the Modify panel for the vertex count.
- ▲ If you need to change the vertex type, right-click the vertex and choose a different type from the quad menu.
- ▲ Use Shift+drag when you want to adjust one Bézier handle separately from its partner.

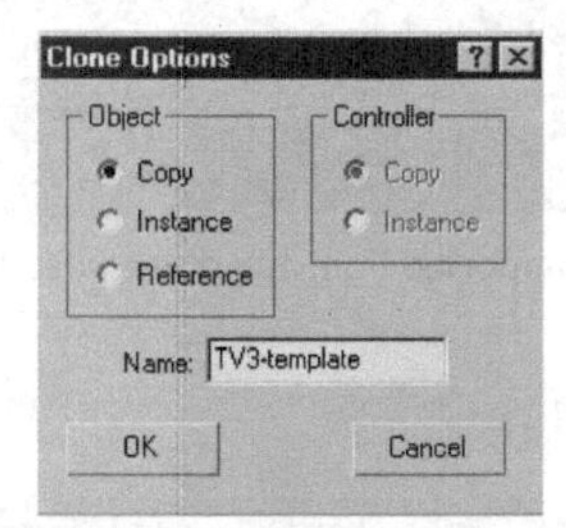

Figure 11.8 The clone Options dialog with the correct settings.

Figure 11.9 The correct configuration of vertices to optimally create the TV 3 logo.

- Be sure to change the vertex back to Bézier type in order to ensure a smooth uniform texture when you bevel the shape.

5. When you are happy with the TV 3 logo shape, exit sub-object mode, delete the TV3-template object, and save your work as **11TV02.max**.

Exercise 11.3 Beveling a shape

You now have a clean logo shape to work with. But before you bevel it, you should apply an XForm modifier to the shape and increase the scale to better accommodate the bevel. After the shape is scaled correctly, you will collapse it back to an editable shape.

1. With **11TV02.max** open, minimize the Top view. Add an XForm modifier to the TV3 shape. Using the Select and Uniform Scale tool, scale the XForm gizmo 3000 percent. Click Zoom Extents All Selected (see **Figure 11.10**).

   Even though the shape looks the same, you know that a bevel will more easily be applied to this larger shape (you learned *that* while working on the vote machine). Collapse the stack.

2. With the TV3 shape selected, right-click the TV3 shape and choose Convert To > Convert to Editable Spline.

   Now you can apply the bevel to the shape.

3. In the Modify stack, apply a Bevel modifier to the TV3 shape and enter these settings:

   Start Outline: **0**

   Level 1: Height: **1** Outline: **1**

   Level 2: Height: **8** Outline: **0**

   Level 3: Height: **1** Outline: **−1**

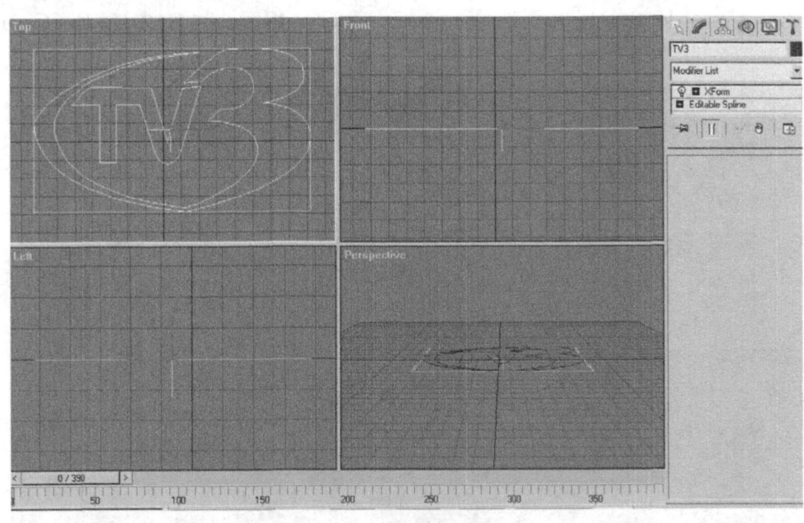

Figure 11.10 The shape has been scaled 3000 percent.

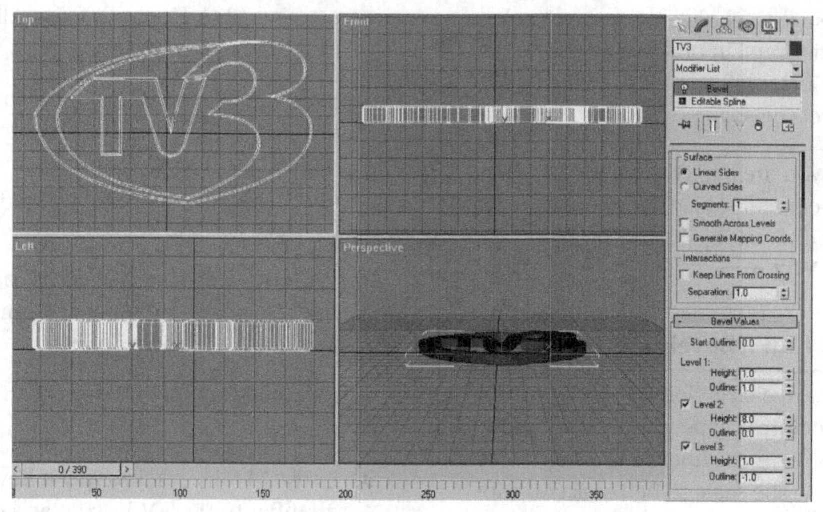

Figure 11.11 The correct bevel on the TV 3 logo.

As you can see in **Figure 11.11**, the TV 3 logo is now beveled.

The bevel looks good on the logo, but one thing distresses you. The top point of the left crescent is pointing through the number 3 now. Since the point of the shape is so long and narrow, the bevel needs to be extended into the number 3 in order for the bevel's outline to remain uniform. You can use the Refine tool to add more vertices to the point to smooth it out, rounding the point.

4. Maximize the Top view and return to the Editable Spline in the Modify stack. Zoom into the point of the left crescent and activate Vertex sub-object mode (see **Figure 11.12**). In the Geometry

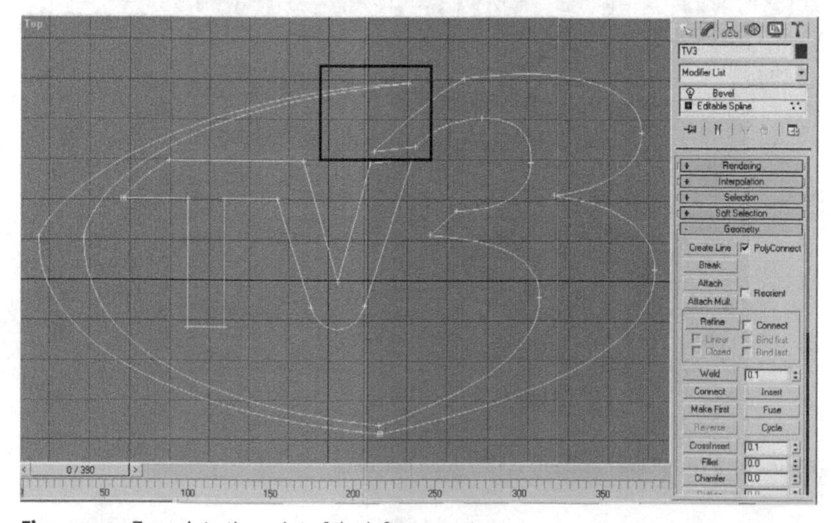

Figure 11.12 Zoom into the point of the left crescent.

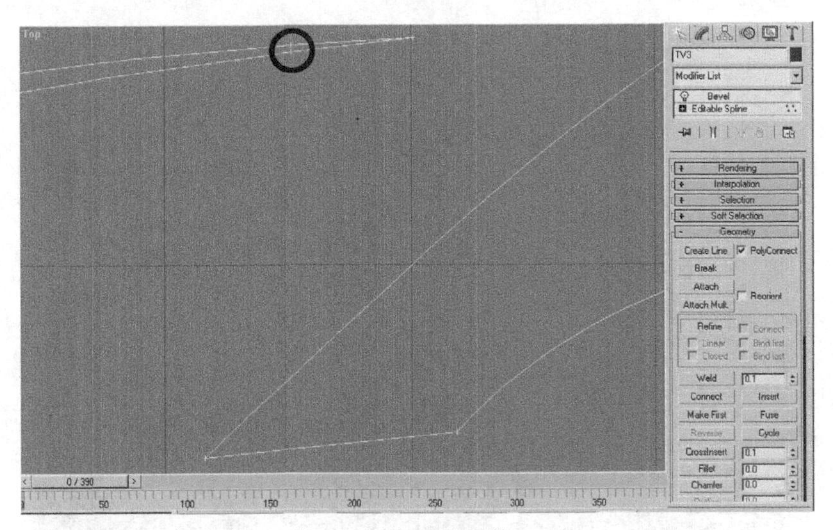

Figure 11.13 Use the Refine tool to create two new vertices.

rollout, activate the Refine button and click on the point to create two new vertices (see **Figure 11.13**).

5. Deactivate the Refine tool, select the vertex at the very point of the crescent, and delete it (see **Figure 11.14**).

That should fix the problem you were having with the bevel. Take a look and see.

6. Minimize the Top view and click Zoom Extents All. Return to the root of the TV3 shape and activate the Bevel modifier in the stack.

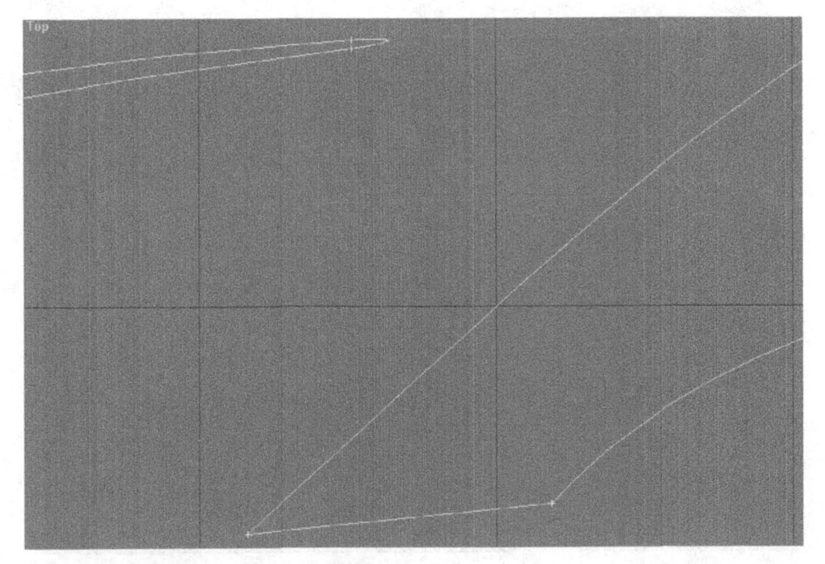

Figure 11.14 The point vertex is deleted.

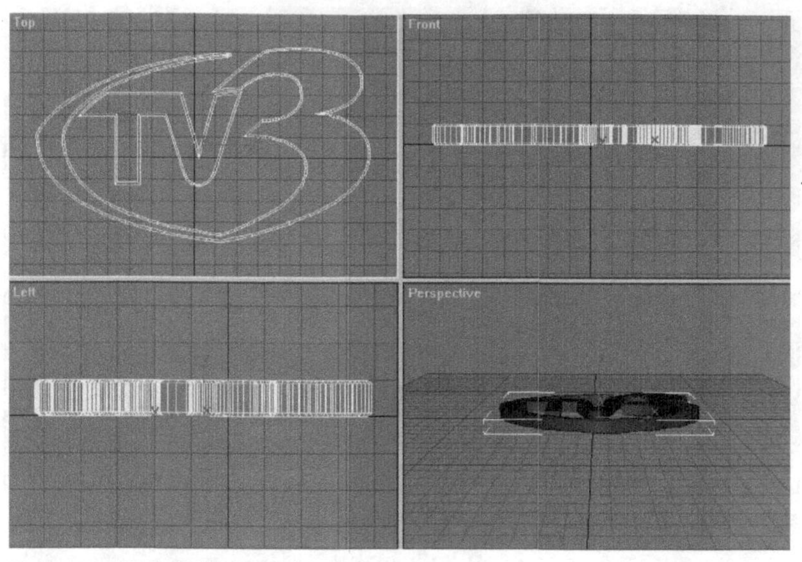

Figure 11.15 The bevel of the TV 3 logo is complete.

Ahh, much better (see **Figure 11.15**)

Once the TV 3 logo is built, you can move it into its correct orientation.

7. Open the Hierarchy panel and activate the Affect Pivot Only button. Click the Center to Object button and deactivate the Affect Pivot Only button.

The TV 3 logo's pivot is centered to the object.

8. Activate the Select and Move tool and move the TV3 object to XYZ: **0, 0, 0**. Activate the Select and Rotate tool (Local X-axis) and rotate the TV3 object X: **90** degrees (as shown in **Figure 11.16**).

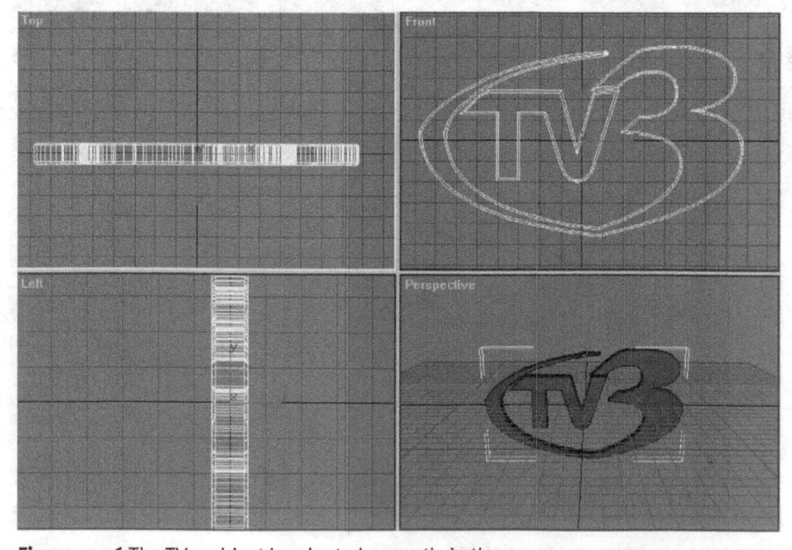

Figure 11.16 The TV 3 object is oriented correctly in the scene.

The TV 3 logo is ready for its material.

9. Save your work as **11TV03.max**.

Exercise 11.4 Adding a Camera and a Light

Before you create the gold material for the TV 3 logo, you need to add a camera and a light to the scene. For this scene, you will use only one light, which will illuminate the face of the TV 3 logo and will create a very dramatic effect as the logo turns into position during the animation.

1. Make sure **11TV03.max** is open and open the Create > Cameras panel. Click the Free button and create a camera with a 35mm lens in the Front view. Move the camera to XYZ: **0, −210, −3**. Change the Perspective view to the Camera01 view and click Zoom Extents All. Turn off the grid in the Camera01 view and activate Show Safe Frames (**Figure 11.17**).

   This is where the logo will reside at the end of the animation. Now add an Omni light to the scene to illuminate the TV 3 logo.

2. Open the Create > Lights panel, click the Omni button, and create an Omni light in the Top view with a color of RGB: **180, 180, 180** (see **Figure 11.18**). Position the light as closely as possible to the position in **Figure 11.18**.

   In the following step, you will use the Place Highlight tool that will position the highlight on the surface but keep the light the same distance from the surface. If the light is positioned closer or further than the light in **Figure 11.18**, the rest of the objects in the scene might be lit undesirably.

   Now position the light to create a highlight where the letter "T" meets the letter "V".

3. Activate the Place Highlight tool (on the toolbar from the Align flyout). In the Camera01 view, drag the mouse in the area where the T meets the V so that the light will move, and then create a highlight in that precise area. Release

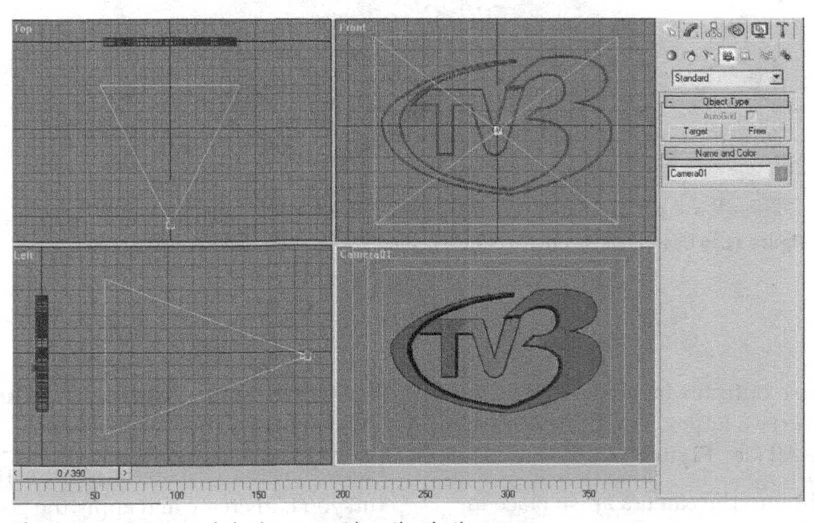

Figure 11.17 Camera01 is in the correct location in the scene.

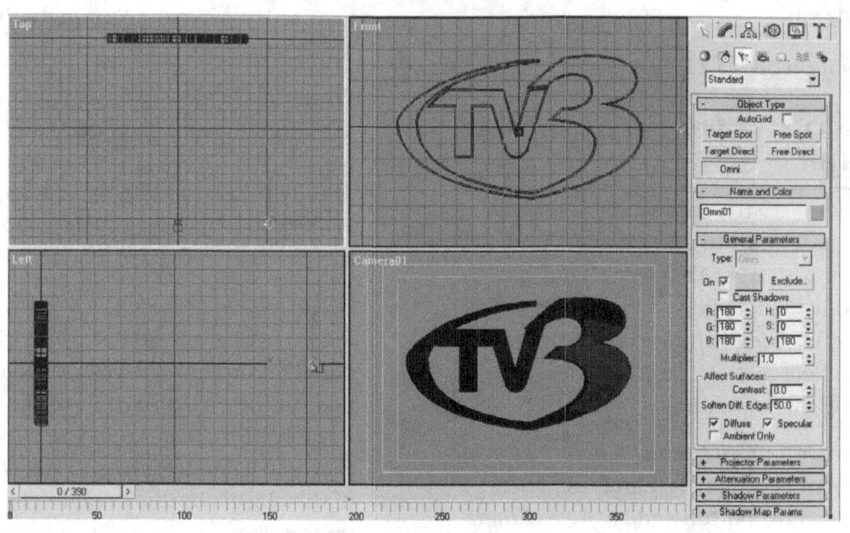

Figure 11.18 The Omni01 light is created in the Top view with a color of RGB: 180, 180, 180.

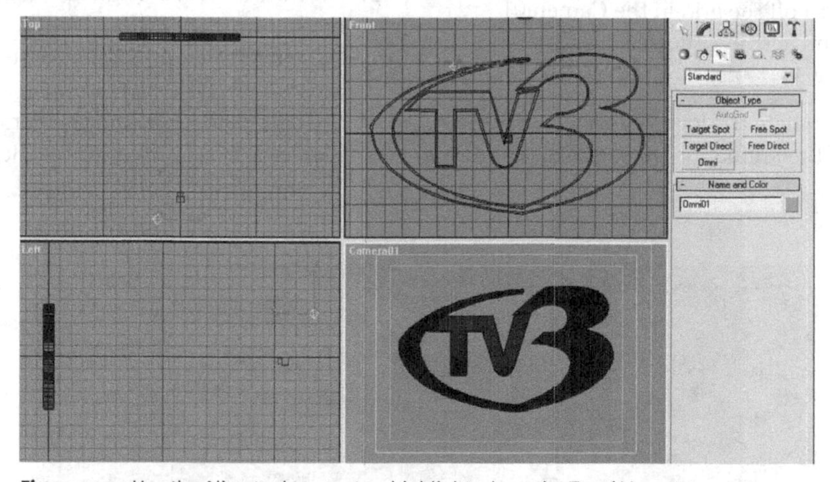

Figure 11.19 Use the Align tool to create a highlight where the T and V meet.

the mouse button when the highlight is where the two letters join. Click Zoom Extents All (see **Figure 11.19**).

The light and the camera are in place for the scene.

Exercise 11.5 Adding the Gold Material to the TV3 Object

Now that the TV3 object is correctly lit, you can create and apply the gold material.

1. Select the TV 3 logo and open the Material Editor. Select the second preview slot of the first row. Name the material **Gold** and assign it to the TV3 object.

   In the Shader Basic Parameters rollout, change the shader from Blinn to Metal. In the Metal Basic Parameters rollout, click the Ambient swatch and change the color to RGB: **137**, **71**, **0**. To create a polished metal highlight, change the Specular Level to **200** and the Glossiness to **70** (as shown in **Figure 11.20**).

   The gold material looks great, but what is a polished metal material without a reflection map? Just add one now.

2. Expand the Maps rollout and click the Reflection button to open the Material/Map Browser. In the Material/Map Browser, choose Bitmap and click OK to open the Select Bitmap Image File dialog. Choose **Project1\maps\gold-ref.jpg** (a gold version of the reflection map we used on the vote machine) and click Open to load the image. Name the map **Gold-rfl** and in the Coordinates rollout, change the Blur offset to **.01** to soften the image (see **Figure 11.21**).

   The reflection is a little too intense; decrease its amount slightly.

3. Click Go to Parent to return to the root of the Gold material. In the Maps rollout, change the Reflection Amount to **60** (as shown in **Figure 11.22**).

   The Gold material is finished.

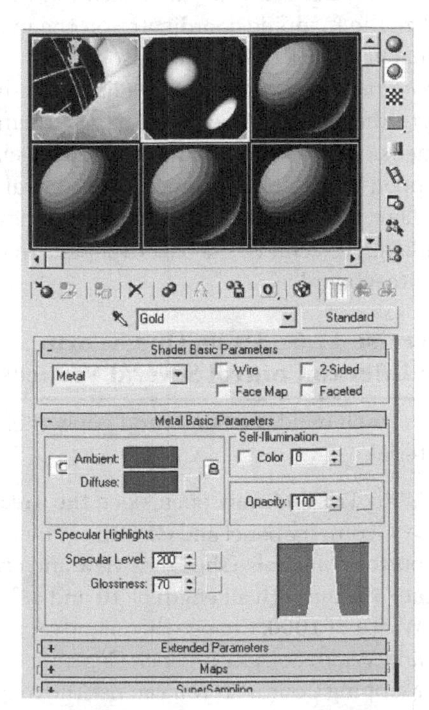

Figure 11.20 The Gold material with the correct settings so far.

Figure 11.21 The finished reflection map for the gold material.

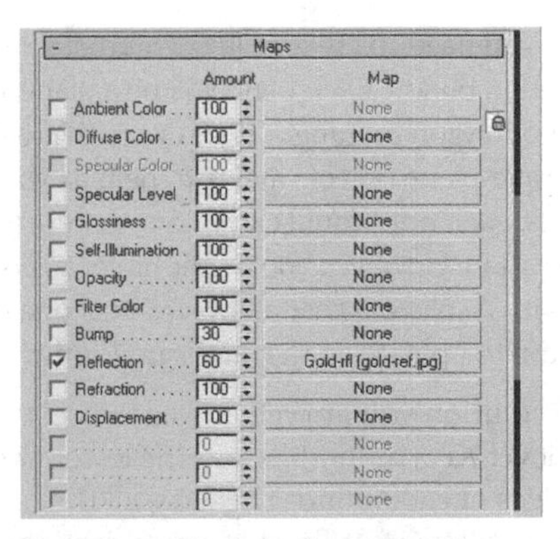

Figure 11.22 The Reflection amount is lowered to 60 to create a less-intense reflection.

Figure 11.23 The rendered TV 3 logo with the new Gold material.

4. Render the Camera01 view to see the gold material on the TV3 object (see **Figure 11.23**).

   The TV 3 logo looks great. It's a keeper.

5. Save your work as **11TV04.max** and close the Material Editor.

Creating Animatable Venetian Blinds

Now you need to create a set of animatable Venetian blinds. Each blind will be a plane, or a two-polygon rectangle. If you were to create multiple-plane objects and use them as your blinds, each one would carry its own keys for animation. However, you might prefer to come up with a solution that allows for only one set of keys to operate all the blinds uniformly.

The solution you arrived at was to use a vertex level XForm modifier on the lower two vertices of each blind. This way, all the blinds will be contained in one object and controlled by one XForm modifier, acting on selected vertices.

The blind material you will be creating will utilize the mapping coordinates on the individual blind objects and will also utilize screen mapping. You will add a linear gradient to the length of the blinds to give them dimension and separation from each other. Mapped in the color channels of the linear gradient, you will place screen mapped radial gradients to achieve the blue oval pattern on the storyboard.

Exercise 11.6 Using One XForm Modifier to Control Several Vertices

First, you'll build the blinds and apply their material.

1. With **11TV04.max** open, open the Create > Geometry panel and click the Plane button. Maximize the Front view and create a plane with a Length of **10** and a Width of **1000**. Change the Length Segs and Width Segs to **1**. Check Generate Mapping Coords so you can use the mapping coordinates when applying the blind texture to the object. Move the plane

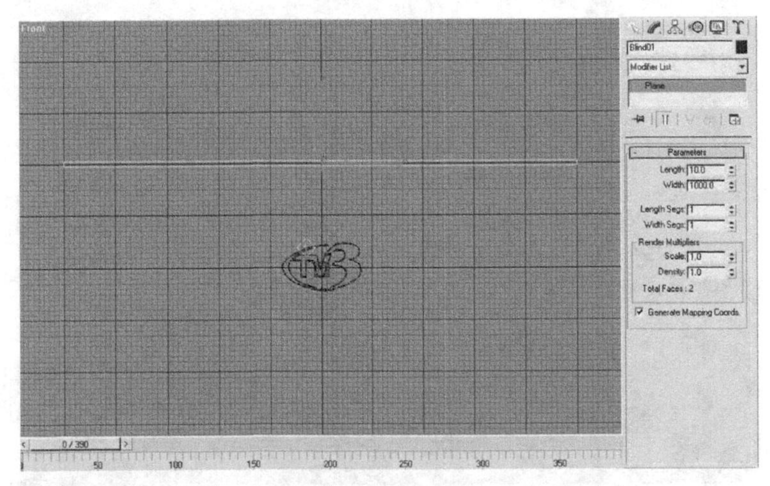

Figure 11.24 The Blind01 object in the correct location in the Front view.

object to XYZ: **0, 150, 200** and name the plane object **Blind01**. Click Zoom Extents All (see **Figure 11.24**).

You will copy the Blind01 object to create the remaining blinds. However, before you do that, collapse it into an Editable Poly and select the two bottom vertices.

2. Right-click the Blind01 object and choose Convert To > Convert to Editable Poly. Activate Vertex sub-object mode and drag a rectangular selection around the bottom two vertices to select them (as shown in **Figure 11.25**).

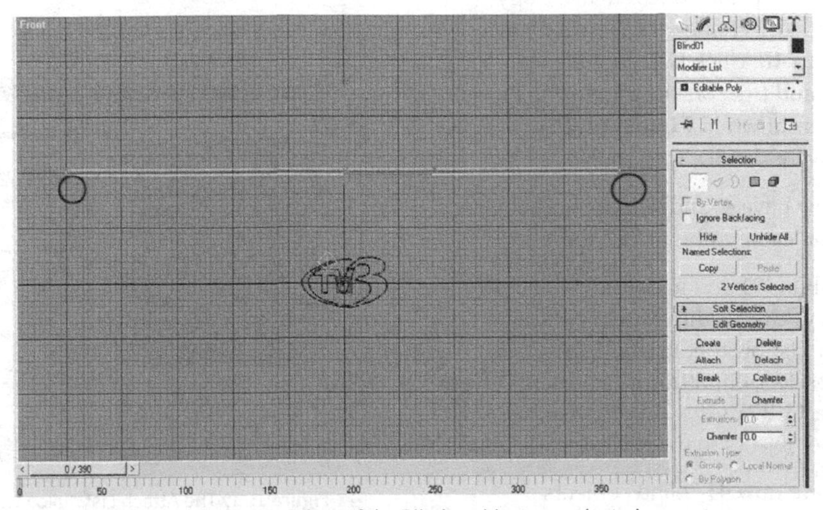

Figure 11.25 The two bottom vertices of the Blind01 object are selected.

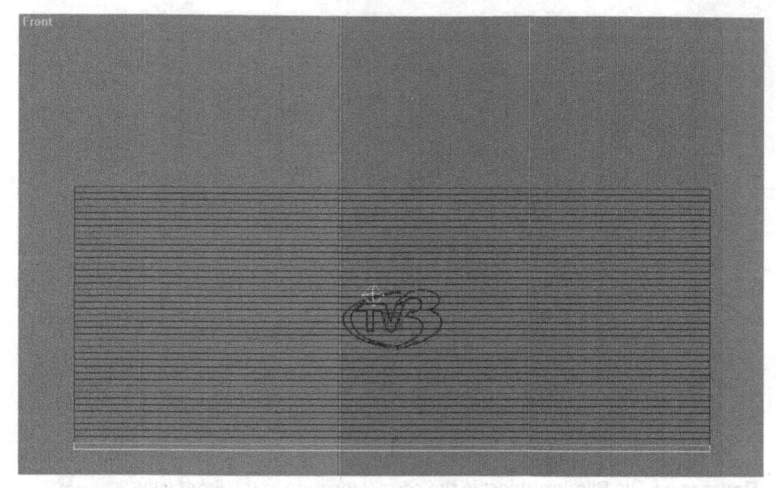

Figure 11.26 Create 40 copies of the Blind01 object in the Front view.

Now when you create copies of the Blind01 object, all of them will have the bottom two vertices selected in sub-object mode.

3. Deactivate Vertex sub-object mode and activate the 3D Snap toggle. Activate the Select and Move tool (View XY-axis), and then Shift+drag the Blind01 object down one grid line and release the mouse. In the Clone Options dialog, leave Copy selected and change the Number of copies to **40**. Click OK to create the copies and turn off the grid in the Front view (as shown in **Figure 11.26**). Deactivate the 3D Snap toggle.

   You now have 41 individual blind objects that you can combine into one.

4. Select Blind01 and in the Edit Geometry rollout of the Modify panel, click the Attach List button. In the Attach List dialog, select Blind02 through Blind41 (see **Figure 11.27**). Click Attach to attach the 40 blind objects to the original.

   There are now 41 "blind" objects attached together into one object.

   Because you selected the bottom two vertices of the first blind object before you copied it, the two bottom vertices of all the blind objects are selected.

5. Enter Vertex sub-object mode.

   It appears that only the two very bottom vertices are selected and no others. Rest assured, all the bottom vertices are selected; the Selection rollout informs

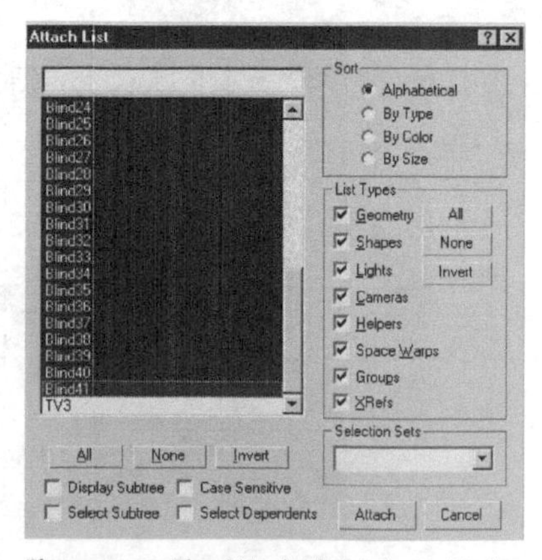

Figure 11.27 The Attach List dialog with the 40 copied Blind objects selected.

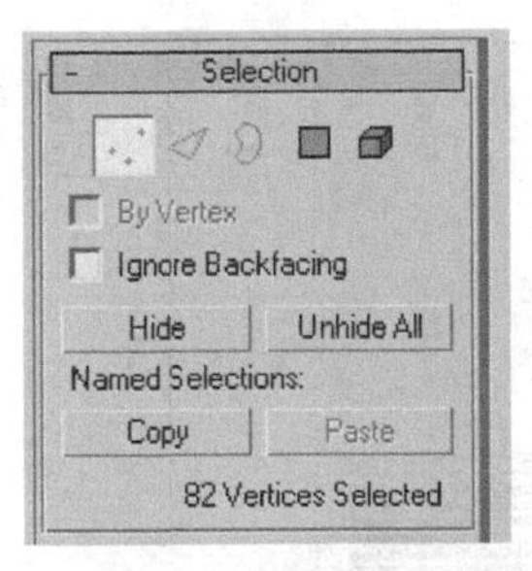

Figure 11.28 It appears that only the bottom two vertices are selected; however, the Selection rollout tells the truth.

upi that 82 vertices are selected (see **Figure 11.28**).

You will now apply an XForm modifier to the selected vertices. Then, by animating the XForm gizmo, you will be able to animate the blinds uniformly with only one animation track.

6. With Vertex sub-object still active, apply an XForm modifier. Minimize the Front view and click Zoom Extents All. With the XForm gizmo still active, activate the Select and Move tool and move the gizmo to XYZ: **0**, **140**, **5** (as shown in **Figure 11.29**).

   You now have the blinds all ready to animate.

7. Advance to frame 390 and activate the Auto Key button. Using the Select and Move tool, move the XForm gizmo to XYZ: **0**, **140**, **−5** (as shown in **Figure 11.30**). Deactivate the Auto Key button and return to the top level of the XForm modifier.

   If you play the animation, you will see the blinds slowly close over the course of the animation. Because you won't even see the blinds until roughly 130, you should move the start key to frame 140 to get the most of the animation.

8. With the Blind01 object selected, drag the key from frame 0 to frame 140 on the track bar.

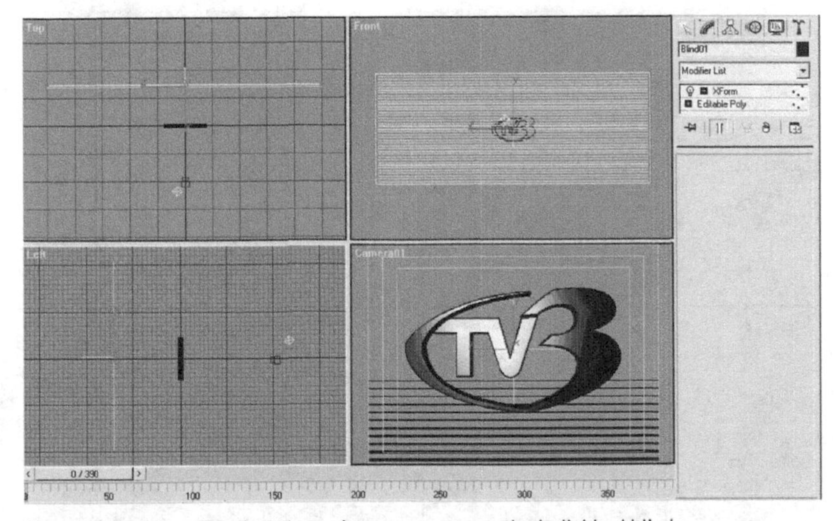

Figure 11.29 By moving the XForm gizmo, you can see the individual blinds.

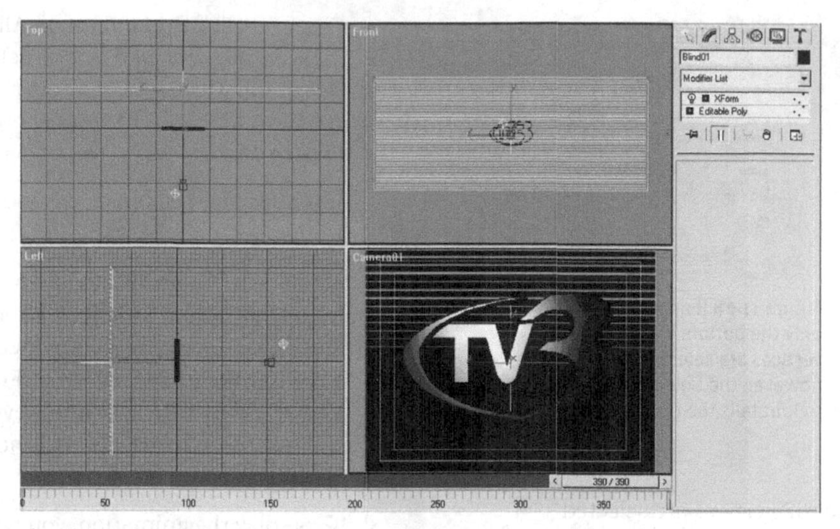

Figure 11.30 The blinds are in their final, closed, position.

Right now the blinds are facing you straight on. John's storyboard shows the blinds at more of an angle to the camera. Make sure you orient the blinds correctly.

9. Activate the Select and Rotate tool (View Z-axis) and in the Top view, rotate the Blind01 object Z: **−30** degrees (as shown in **Figure 11.31**).

   The Blind01 object is animated and in the correct orientation. You'll need to save your work and then apply the material.

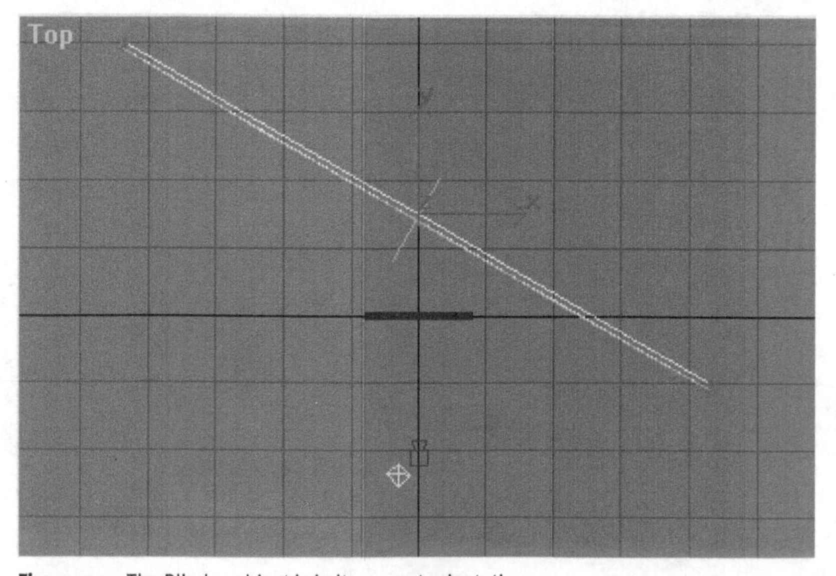

Figure 11.31 The Blind01 object is in its correct orientation.

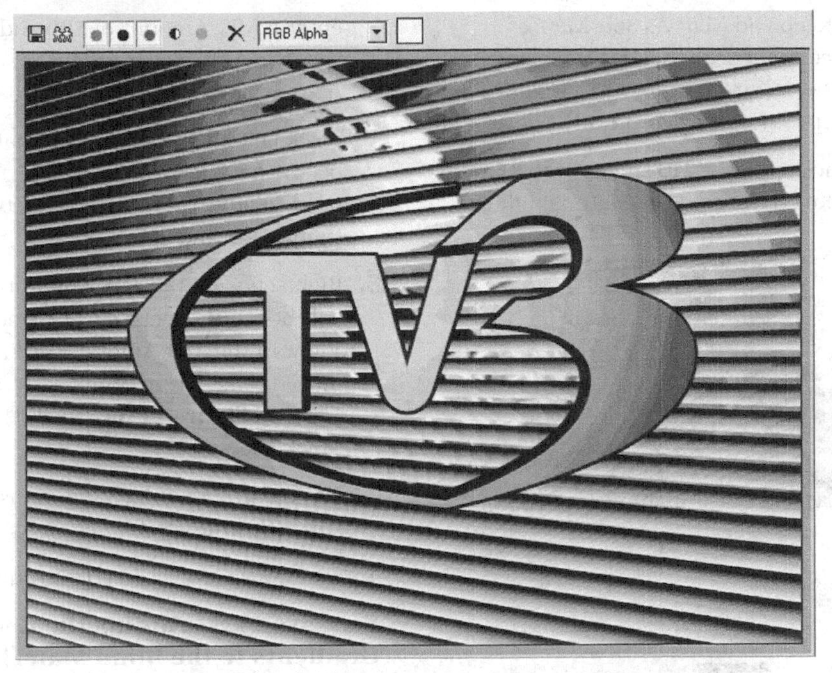

Figure 11.32 Camera01 rendered at frame 320.

10. Save your work as **11TV05.max**.

Add the linear gradient to the blinds, and you will better understand what the material will do.

11. With **11TV05.max** open, advance to frame 320 and open the Material Editor. Select the third material preview slot in the first row, name the material **Blinds**, and assign the material to the Blind01 object. In the Blinn Basic Parameters rollout, change the Self-Illumination amount to **100**. Click the Diffuse map button to open the Material/Map Browser. Choose Gradient and click OK to load the gradient into the Diffuse map channel. Name the map **Blinds-dif** and render the Camera01 view (see **Figure 11.32**).

You can see how the linear gradient visually separates each individual blind from the next.

Animating the Environment Background

Before you add the screen mapped gradients to the blinds, animate the environment background image to fade to black so you can accurately view the blinds. Because the animation in the environment background ends by frame 210, you need to dissolve it out by then. To create the dissolve, you will use a Mix material and animate it to transition from the animation to black between frames 145 and 210.

Exercise 11.7 Creating a Dissolve

Here you'll set up the dissolve in the Env map so that the environment background fades to black.

1. In the Material Editor, select the Env map. Click the Bitmap button to open the Material/Map Browser. Choose Mix and click OK. In the Replace Map dialog, leave Keep Old Map As Sub-Map? selected and click OK. Drag the black color swatch from Color #1 to Color #2 and copy it (see **Figure 11.33**).

2. Advance to frame 210 and activate the Auto Key button. In the Material Editor, enter a Mix Amount of **100** and deactivate the Auto Key button.

   You've mixed from the animation to the black color. However, the animation occurs between frames 0 and 210, so you need to adjust it to animate between frames 145 and 210.

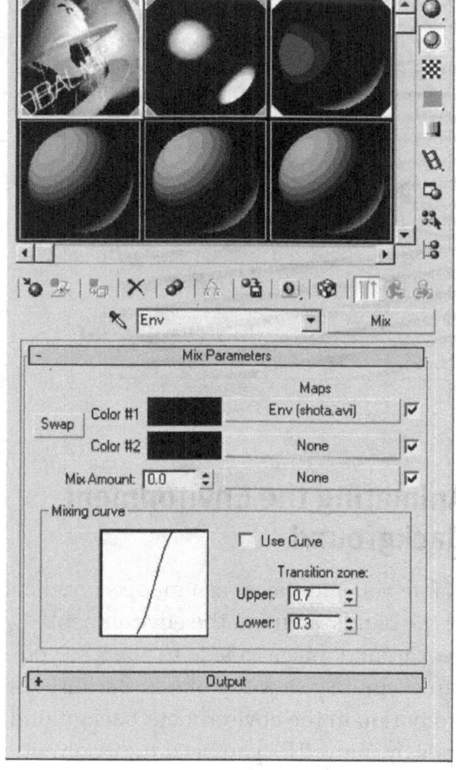

Figure 11.33 The Env map is in the Color #1 slot, and the black color is copied to Color #2.

3. Right-click on the Mix Amount spinner edit box and select Show in Track View. In the Mix Amount track, move the key from frame 0 to frame 145 (see **Figure 11.34**). Close the Track View.

   The environment background is now correctly animated.

4. Save your work as **11VT06.max**.

Exercise 11.8 Adding the Radial Gradients to the Blind Material

You can now continue to create the blind's material. First, add the first screen mapped radial gradient.

1. With **11VT06.max** open, return to the Blinds-dif map in the Material Editor. In the Gradient Parameters rollout, click the Color #2 button to open the Material/Maps Browser. Choose Gradient Ramp and click OK to load the gradient ramp. In the Gradient Ramp Parameters rollout, change the Gradient Type to Radial and deactivate the Show End Result button

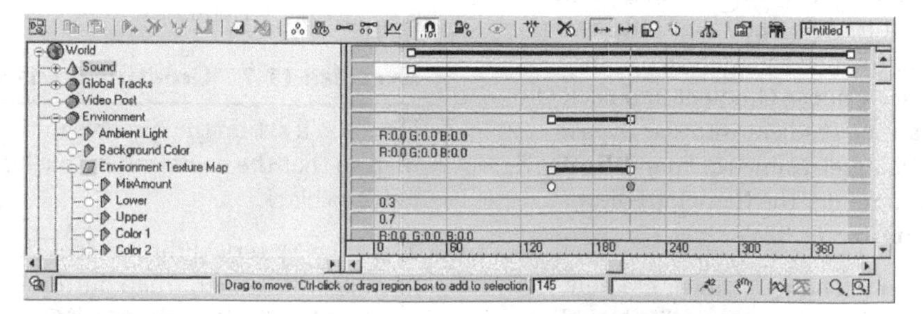

Figure 11.34 The Track View with the MixAmount keys in the correct locations.

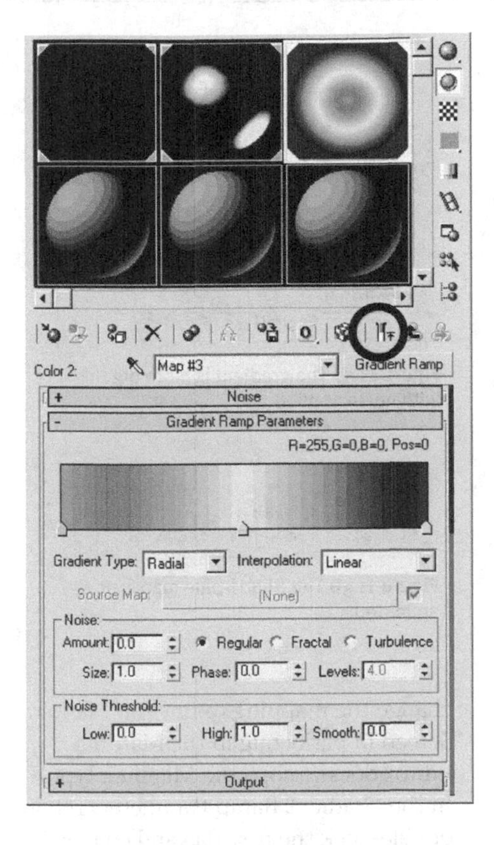

Figure 11.35 The Radial Gradient in the Material Editor with Show End Result deactivated.

(see **Figure 11.35**). Name this material **Blinds-blue**.

Change the colors of the gradient to better reflect those on the storyboard.

2. Double-click the leftmost flag of the gradient (refer to **Figure 11.35**) and change its color to RGB: **50, 120, 255**. Click the middle flag and change its color to RGB: **30, 60, 190**. Finally, click the last flag and change its color to RGB: **0, 0, 0**.

The radial gradient better matches what John has illustrated on his storyboard. However, the gradient on the storyboard is brightest in the lower-left corner. Position the gradient into the correct spot.

3. In the Coordinates rollout, change the Mapping to Environ(ment) Mapping: Screen, locking the gradient to the screen so that no matter where the camera is, the gradient will always be the way it appears in the preview window. To prove the point, advance to frame 320 and render it through the Camera01 view.

It may be hard to see because the radial gradient is only the middle color of the linear gradient. But if you look hard enough, you can see the blue radial gradient in the center of the screen, mapped on the blinds.

Okay, back to moving the gradient to match the storyboard.

4. In the Coordinates rollout, change the U Offset to **−.25** and V Offset to **−.35**. To make the gradient larger, change the U Tiling to **.4** and V Tiling to **.8** (as shown in **Figure 11.36**).

The gradient is in the correct position. You should be able to see a little of the tiled gradient peaking in from the top. That's okay, it will add to the whole randomness of the material.

Speaking of randomness, add a little noise to the gradient.

5. In the Noise group of the Gradient Ramp Parameters rollout, change the Amount to **.5** and change the Size to **3.5** (see **Figure 11.37**).

The noise is a nice touch to the gradient; it provides a nice random feel. While you're at it, go ahead and animate it.

6. Advance to frame 390 and activate the Animate button. Change the Phase to **15** and deactivate the Animate button

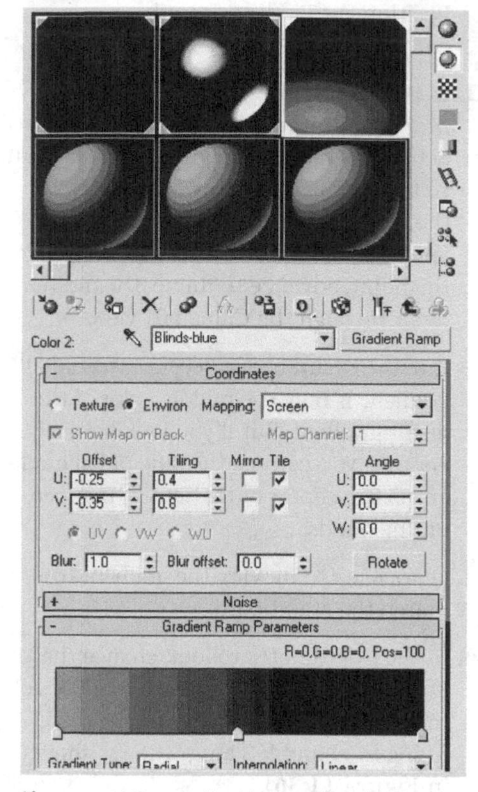

Figure 11.36 The gradient is now placed correctly.

(see **Figure 11.38**). Click the Make Preview button and in the Create Material Preview dialog, click OK to create the preview. After the preview renders, it will play, showing the slow undulation of the noise.

The Blinds-blue map is finished. Copy it to the first color channel of the Blinds-dif map and change its parameters to make it darker.

7. Click the Go to Parent button to return to the Blinds-dif map. In the Gradient Parameters rollout, copy the Blinds-blue map to the Color #1 button and open its parameters. Name the map **Blinds-purple**. In the Coordinates rollout,

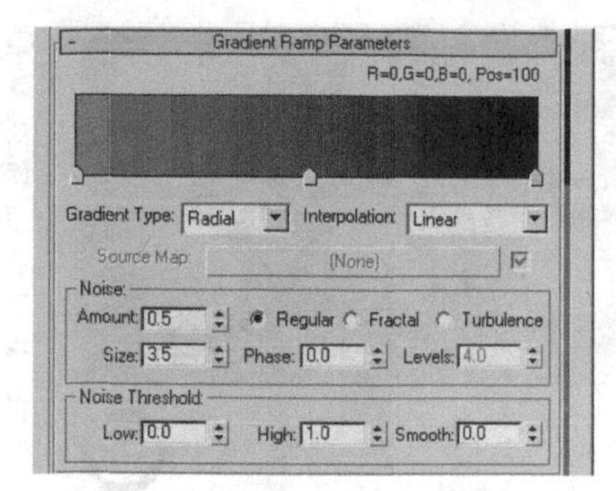

Figure 11.37 The gradient is more organic with noise applied.

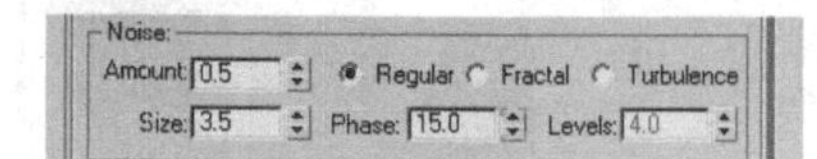

Figure 11.38 The Blinds-blue map is now animated

change the mapping to Environ Mapping: Screen (a pesky bug in the Material Editor doesn't copy the Mapping type). In the Gradient Ramp Parameters rollout, double-click the first flag and change its color to RGB: **120, 25, 190**. Click the second flag and change its color to RGB: **85, 15, 140**.

Because you copied this gradient, its animation copied as well. You don't want both gradients to have the same noise pattern. Therefore, to offset their patterns, you can simply change the Phase value. Currently the Phase of the Blinds-purple map animates from 0 to 15 between frames 0 and 390. If at frame 390 you changed the Phase value to 30 without activating the Auto Key button, the Phase value would animate from 15 to 30 between frames 0 and 390. Go ahead and do that.

8. Make sure you are still at frame 390, and in the Gradient Ramp Parameters rollout, change the Phase value to **30**.

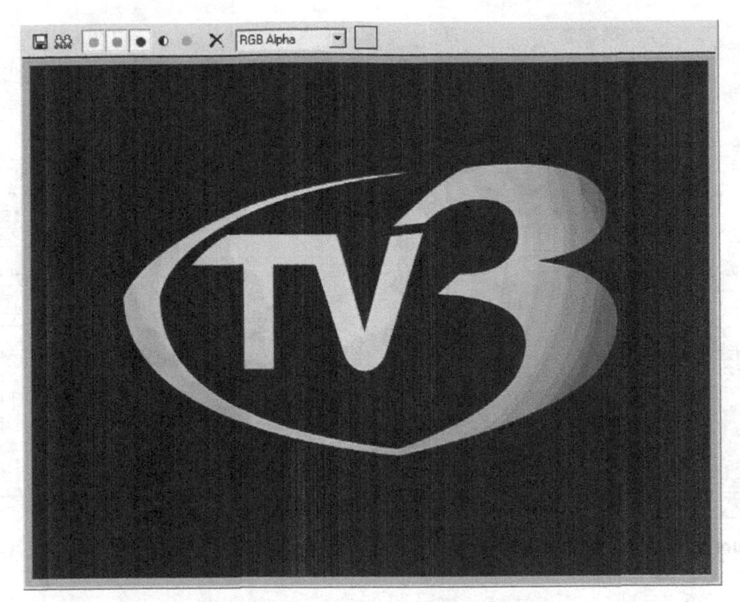

Figure 11.39 The finished Blinds material rendered through the Camera01 view at frame 320.

The Phase now animates from 15 to 30 between frames 0 and 390. Now instance the Blinds-purple map to the Color #3 slot of the Blinds-dif map.

9. Click Go to Parent to view the Blinds-dif map's parameters. In the Gradient Parameters rollout, drag the Blinds-purple map button over Color #3's map button and release the mouse. In the Copy (Instance) Map dialog, choose Instance and click OK.

   The Blinds-purple map is instanced into the Color #3 map. The Blinds material is finished. Render a frame and check it out.

10. Render frame 320 through the Camera01 view (as shown in **Figure 11.39**).

    The Blinds material looks fantastic.

11. Save your work as **11TV07.max** and close the Material Editor.

Adding a Strip of Text

You are now going to create the final object you need to complete this animation: a strip of type. John's storyboard shows one strip in the foreground and three in the background. In this animation, you will create only one behind the logo. If, after you add the first strip of text and animate it, you feel there should be more, you can add one or more on your own.

Exercise 11.9 Mapping Text on a Plane Object

To create the strip of text, you will opacity map the text on a plane object.

1. With **11TV07.max** open, open the Create > Geometry panel and click the Plane button. In the Front view, create a plane object with a Length of **30** and a Width of **1000**. Name the

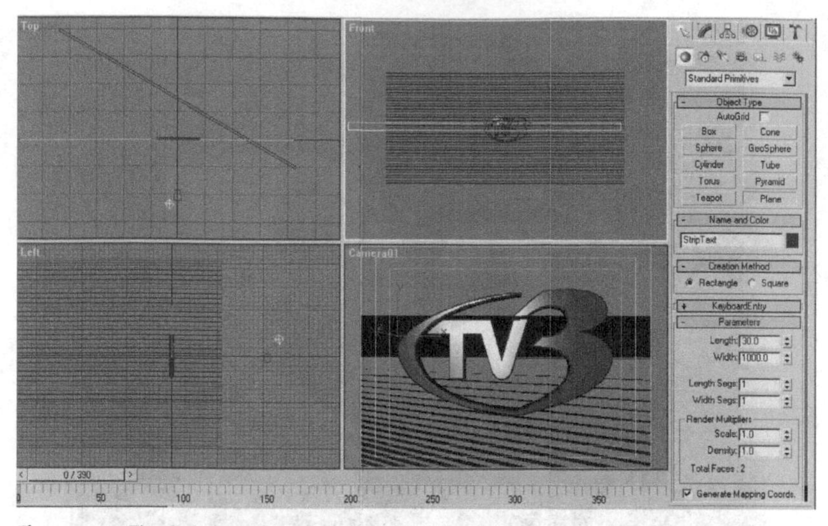

Figure 11.40 The StripText object was created in the Front view.

object **StripText** (as shown in **Figure 11.40**).

Now move the object into the correct orientation.

2. Move the StripText object to XYZ: **320, −95, −41**. Using the Select and Rotate tool (View Z-axis) in the Top view, rotate the StripText object Z: **−30** (see **Figure 11.41**).

Now you can apply the material to the StripText object.

3. Open the Material Editor and select the first preview slot of the second row. Name this material **StripText** and apply

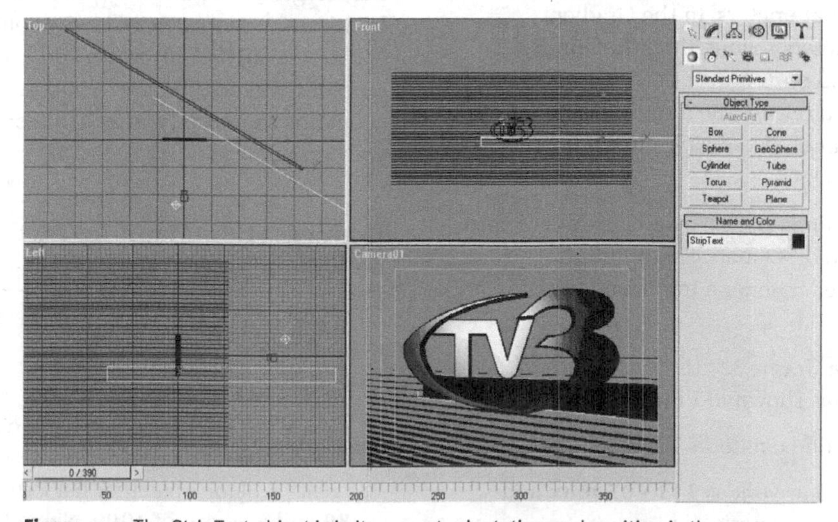

Figure 11.41 The StripText object is in its correct orientation and position in the scene.

the material to the StripText object.
In the Blinn Basic Parameters rollout, change the Self-Illumination value to **100**. Click the Diffuse color swatch and change its color to RGB: **255, 255, 255.**

Now you can add the opacity map to the material to cut out the type.

4. Click the Opacity map button to open the Material/Map Browser. Choose Bitmap and click OK to open the Select Bitmap Image File dialog. Choose **Project1\maps\GlobalNewsBlur.jpg** and click Open to open the image. Rename the map **StripText-opc** and click Show Map in Viewport. Render frame 320 through the Camera01 view (see **Figure 11.42**).

The type on the StripText object is a little too bright. You can adjust the output level of the GlobalNewsBlur.jpg image in the material to make the type more transparent.

5. In the Material Editor, expand the Output rollout. Check Enable Color Map, and the graph becomes active. Select the right graph point and move it to 1.0/.5 (as shown in **Figure 11.43**). Then close the Material Editor.

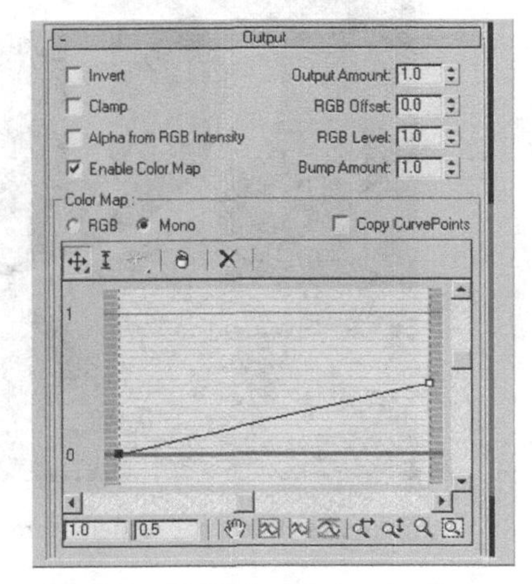

Figure 11.43 The Color Map's output is reduced by half.

Figure 11.42 Frame 320 rendered through the Camera01 view.

Figure 11.44 Frame 320 rendered through the Camera01 view.

By lowering the point from 1 to .5, you reduce the output of the map by half.

6. Render frame 320 again (see **Figure 11.44**).

   The type looks like it belongs there now. You are finished creating all the objects and adding their materials. Cool!

7. Save your work as **11TV08.max**.

Animating the TV 3 Logo

Looking at John's storyboard, you can see that the TV 3 logo matches the perspective of the blinds when you first see it, and as the animation reaches its end, the TV 3 logo turns to face forward. Because the camera will be dollying backward through the scene, you will see the blinds first and then the TV 3 logo.

Exercise 11.10 Setting Up the Rotation of an Object

Earlier, when you analyzed the music, you decided you would see the logo at approximately frame 180 during the beginning of the fourth measure of music. Because you want the viewer to see the TV 3 logo in the canted perspective before it starts to turn, you will start its rotation at frame 200 and end it in its forward orientation at frame 300 as the music hits its final crescendo.

1. With **11TV08.max** open, select the TV3 object. Advance to frame 200 and activate the Auto Key button. Use the Select and Rotate tool (Local Y-axis) to rotate the TV3 object Y: **−30** degrees (as shown in **Figure 11.45**).

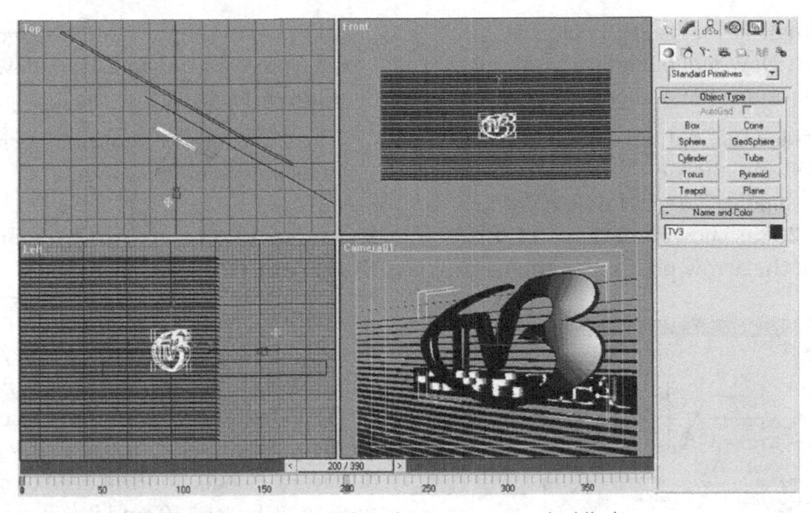

Figure 11.45 The TV3 object now matches the same cant as the blinds.

You just created a key at frame 200, but 3ds max also created a key at frame 0 that you do not need. You can delete it.

2. On the track bar, right-click the key at frame 0 and choose Delete Key > TV3: Rotation.

Now you're ready to animate the TV3 object into its end orientation.

3. Advance to frame 300 and, using the Select and Rotate tool (Local Y-axis), rotate the TV3 object Y: **30** degrees to face forward again (as shown in **Figure 11.46**). Deactivate the Auto Key button.

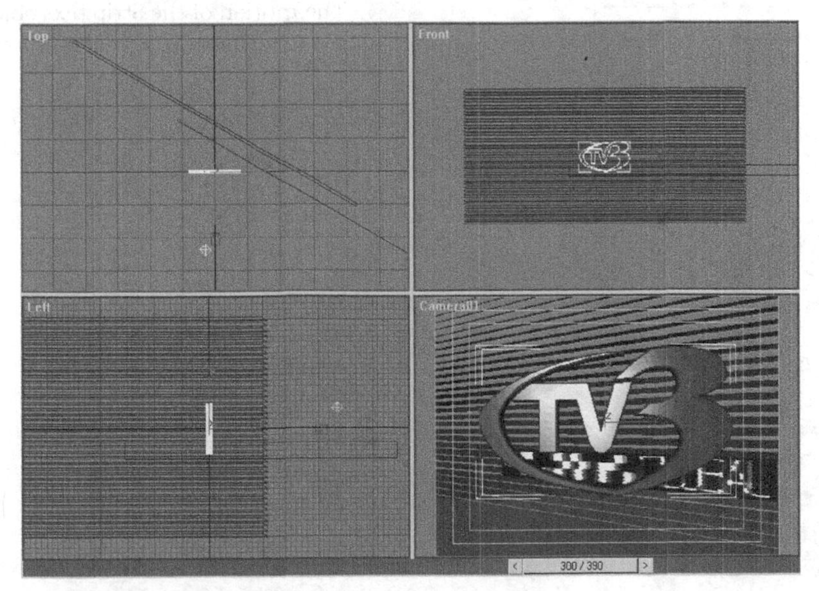

Figure 11.46 The TV3 object faces the camera at frame 300.

The animation for the TV3 object is complete. Now pull out all the stops and ease the rotation in and out.

4. On the track bar, right-click the key at frame 200 and choose TV3: Rotation to open its dialog. Change the Ease From: value to **25** (as shown in **Figure 11.47**) and click the arrow pointing to the right to move to the next key. Change the Ease To: value of key 2 to **25** (as shown in **Figure 11.48**). Close the dialog.

   The TV3 object's rotation now starts and ends smoothly. Nice touch!

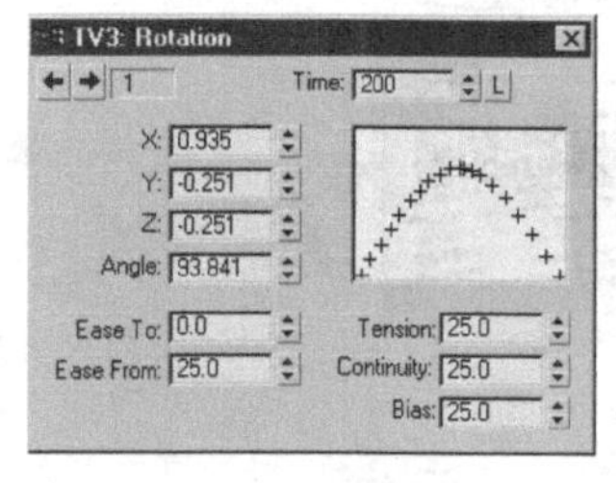

Figure 11.47 The Ease From value for key 1 is 25.

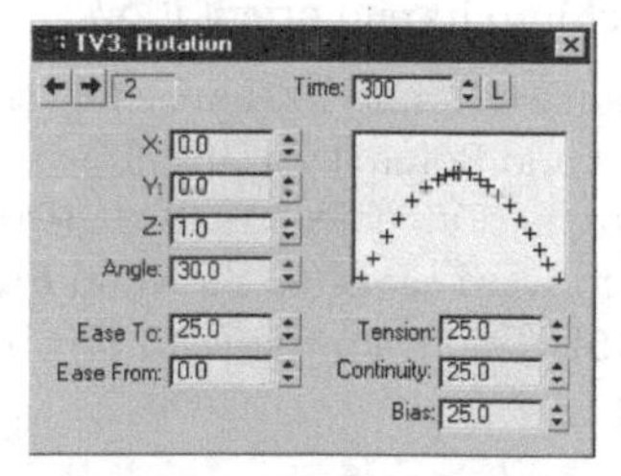

Figure 11.48 The Ease To value for key 2 is 25.

Exercise 11.11 Animating the StripText Object

Animating the StripText object is going to be simple. All you need to do is key the object's motion from right to left. Because the StripText object is layered closely to the blinds, you will see it much sooner than you do the TV 3 logo. You will need to start its motion at frame 150, and it will continue to the end of the animation at frame 390. Animate it now.

1. Select the StripText object and activate the Select and Move tool (Local X-axis). Advance to frame 390 and activate the Auto Key button. Move the StripText object roughly X: **−1000** units and deactivate the Auto Key button (see **Figure 11.49**).

   The motion of the Strip text object is correct. However, it animates between

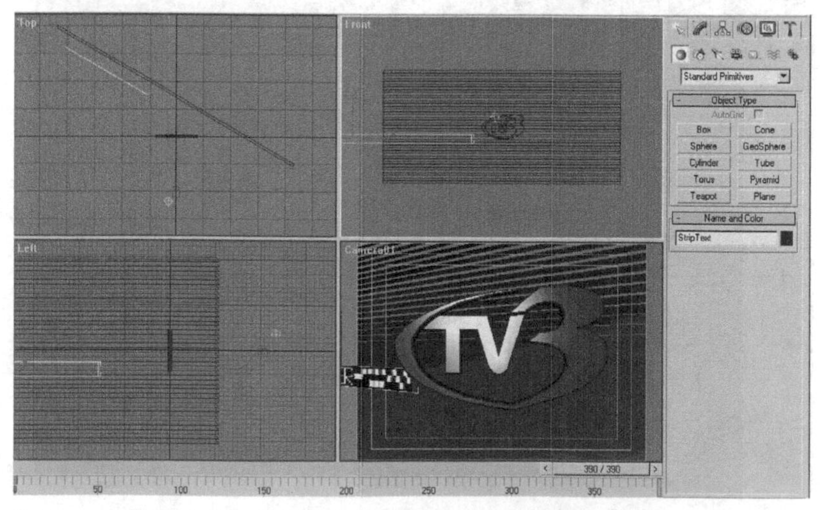

Figure 11.49 The StripText object's position at frame 390.

frames 0 and 390. You need to move the key at frame 0 to frame 150.

2. In the track bar, move the key from frame 0 to frame 150.

   The animation for the Strip Text object is complete.

3. Save your work as **11TV09.max**.

Exercise 11.12 Animating the camera

Life couldn't be simpler; all you have left to do is create linear camera motion between frames 130 and 230. You will be dollying backward through the blinds and through the TV 3 logo, and then the camera will stop in its ending location. Go on and get started.

1. With **11TV09.max** open, select Camera01 and advance to frame 230. Because the camera is located where you want it to end, you need to create a key for it at frame 230. Open the Motion panel and in the PRS Parameters rollout, click Position in the Create Key group. The button becomes ghosted, indicating a key has been created (see **Figure 11.50**).

   Now you need to create a start key for the camera.

2. Advance to frame 130 and activate the Auto Key button. Move the camera to XYZ: **33, 150, 0** (shown in **Figure 11.51**). Scrub through the animation to make sure the camera doesn't accidentally intersect with any objects. If it does, readjust the start position until it doesn't. Deactivate the Auto Key button.

   When the camera path is correct, add an ease to the position key at frame 230 so the camera will slowly come to a halt.

3. On the track bar, right-click the key at frame 230 and choose Camera01: Position to open its dialog. Change the In tangent to Slow (as shown in **Figure 11.52**) and close the dialog. Check the animation again for any accidental camera collisions and fix them if necessary.

4. Save your work as **11TV10.max**.

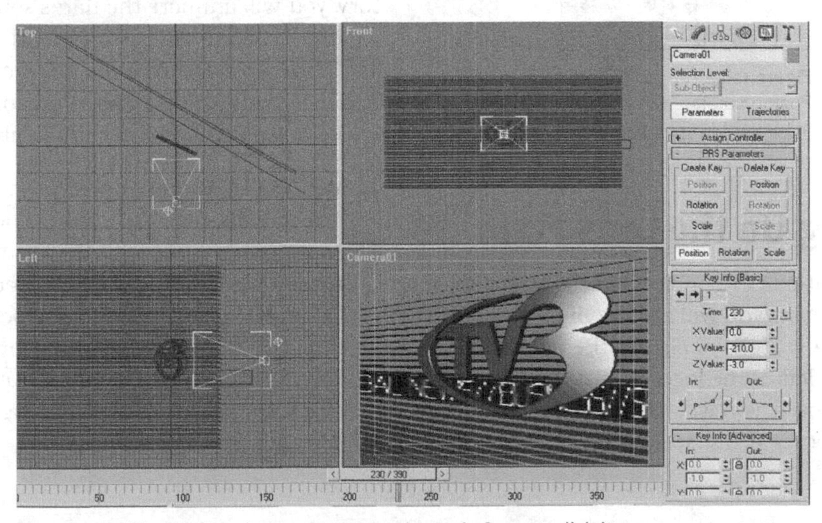

Figure 11.50 The Position button becomes ghosted after you click it.

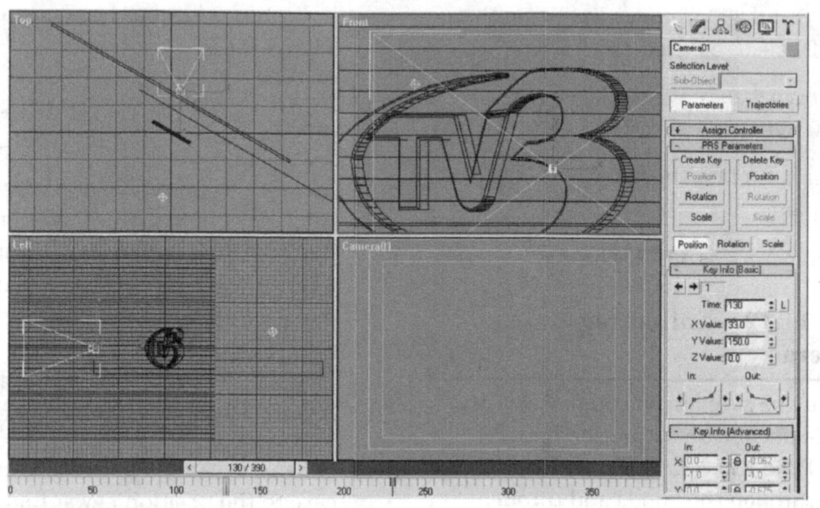

Figure 11.51 The camera is in its starting position.

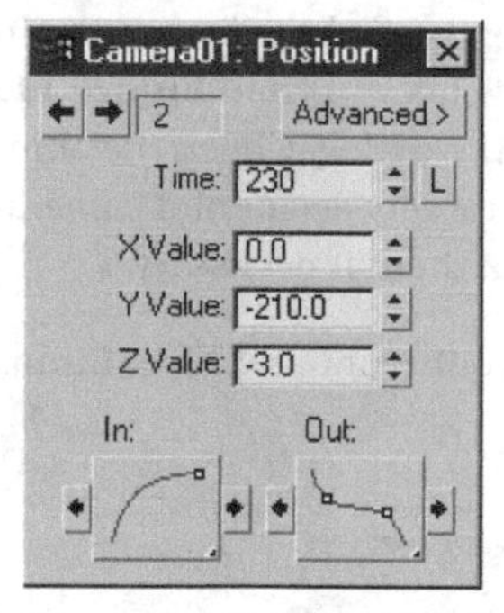

Figure 11.52 The Camera01: Position dialog with a Slow In tangent.

Setting Up the Lens Flare

The animation of the objects in the scene is complete. Now you will add one final touch: a lens flare. Instead of placing the flare high and to the left of the logo, as indicated on the storyboard, you will "trace" the upper half of the crescent shape on the logo.

Exercise 11.13 Creating a Segment of a Shape

Before you create the lens flare, you need to determine how you are going to animate the flare's trajectory around the perimeter of the crescent shape. To animate the flare's trajectory, you will animate the flare's source along a path. To create the path, you will copy the TV 3 logo object, delete the Bevel modifier, and delete most of the shape except for the area you want to trace with the flare.

1. With **11TV10.max** open, select the TV3 object. Choose Edit > Clone and create a copy of the object with the name **TV3-trace.** Advance to frame 330 and click Zoom Extents All Selected. Open the Modify panel and delete the Bevel modifier. Activate Segment sub-object level and select the upper-left crescent segment (see **Figure 11.53**).

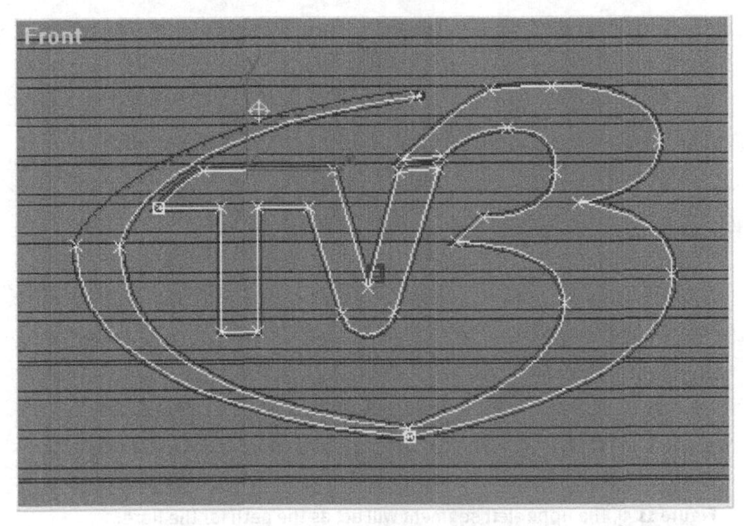

Figure 11.53 The upper-left crescent segment is selected.

2. Choose Edit > Select Invert to invert the selection (see **Figure 11.54**).
3. Press the Delete key to delete the selected segments, leaving only the upper-left crescent shape (as shown in **Figure 11.55**). Return to the Top-Level of the TV3-trace shape.

If you look in the Top view at the selected TV3-trace shape, you can see that it's behind the logo. You need to move it in front of the logo.

4. Activate the Select and Move tool (View Y-axis) and in the Top view, move the TV3-trace shape in front of the TV3

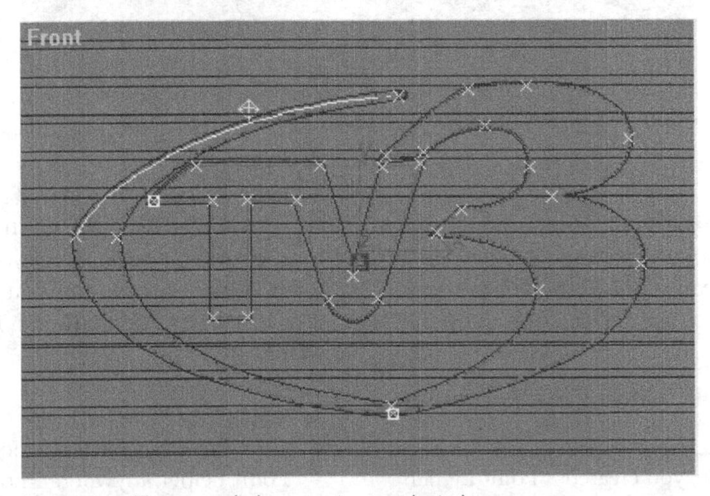

Figure 11.54 The unneeded segments are selected now.

Figure 11.55 The upper-left segment will act as the path for the flare.

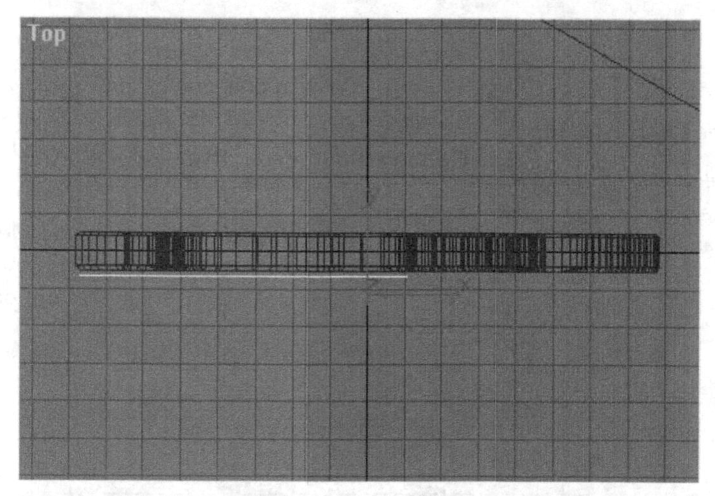

Figure 11.56 The TV3-trace shape is in front of the TV3 object.

object (see **Figure 11.56**). The TV3-trace shape is no longer obscured by the logo object. You can now add the Point helper that will act as the source of the flare to the scene.

Exercise 11.14 Adding an Animated Point Helper

In the first scene, you created a Point helper to act as the source for the flare. You need to create another Point helper in this scene for the same purpose. After you add the Point helper to the scene, you will animate it on a path constraint to the TV3-trace shape.

1. Open the Create > Helpers panel and click the Point button. Click to create a Point helper anywhere in the Top view and leave the name **Point01**.

Now you will animate the Point helper along the TV3-trace shape.

2. With the Point01 helper selected, open the Motion panel. Expand the Assign Controller rollout, select the Position track, and click the Assign Controller button (see **Figure 11.57**). In the Assign Position Controller dialog, choose Path Constraint (see **Figure 11.58**) and click OK to add the constraint.

3. In the Path Parameters rollout, click the Add Path button and click the TV3-trace shape. Its name then appears in the Target column (as shown in **Figure 11.59**). Deactivate the Add Path button.

   The Point01 helper now animates along the path from frame 0 to 390. Feel free to play the animation and examine the motion. You will see the flare only between frames 220 and 330, so adjust the Point01 helper's keys accordingly.

4. With the Point01 object selected, drag the key on the track bar at frame 0 to frame 220. Drag the key on the track bar at frame 390 to frame 330 (see **Figure 11.60**).

   If you play the animation again, you will see the Point01 helper tracing the edge of the upper-left crescent between frames 220 and 330. You are now ready to add the lens flare to scene.

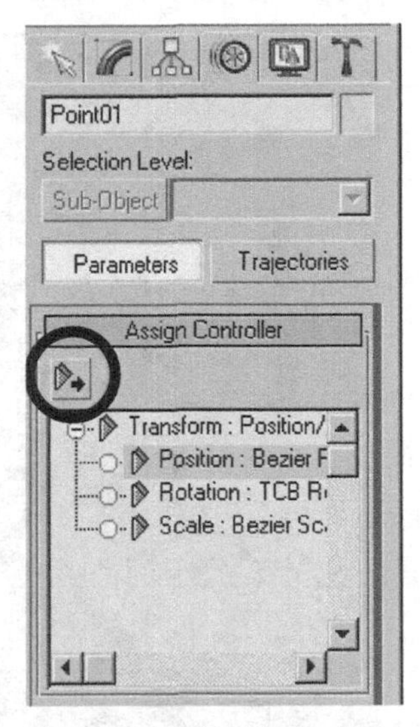

Figure 11.57 Select the Position track and click the assign Controller button.

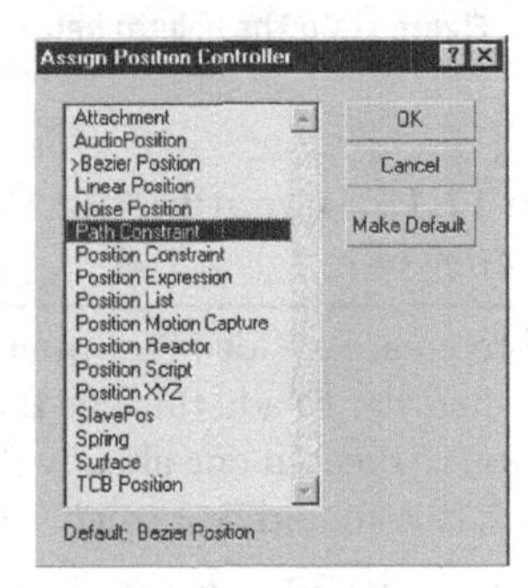

Figure 11.58 Path Constraint is selected in the Assign Position Controller dialog.

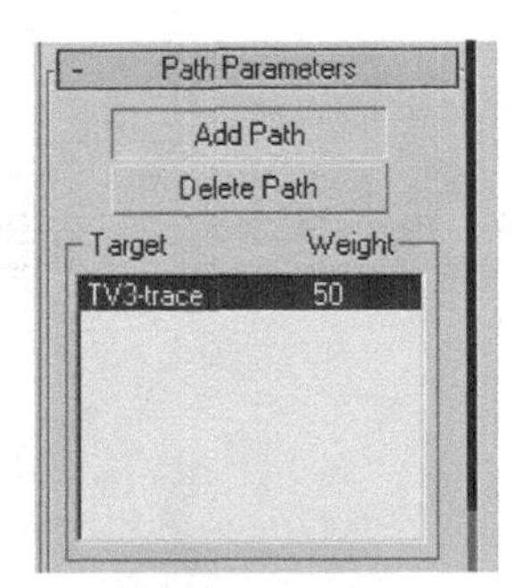

Figure 11.59 The TV3-trace shape has been added to the Target column.

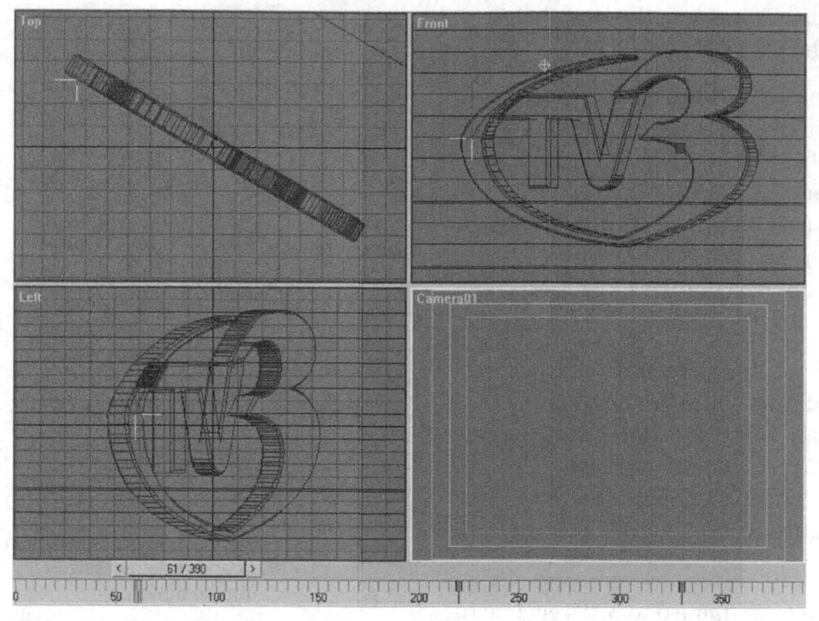

Figure 11.60 The Point01 helper's keys are now in the correct locations.

Exercise 11.15 Creating the Video Post Queue

You need to create a Video Post queue for this scene in order to add the lens flare. Because you've created one already (for the first scene), this should be a cinch.

1. Open the Video Post dialog. Click the Add Scene Event button and click OK to accept its default settings. Click the Add Image Filter Event button, choose Lens Effects Flare, and click OK to add it to the queue. Click the Add Image Output Event button and choose an output path and file name (I used Project1\images\TV-Done.mov). Then click OK to add it to the queue (see **Figure 11.61**).

2. Save your work as **11TV11.max**.

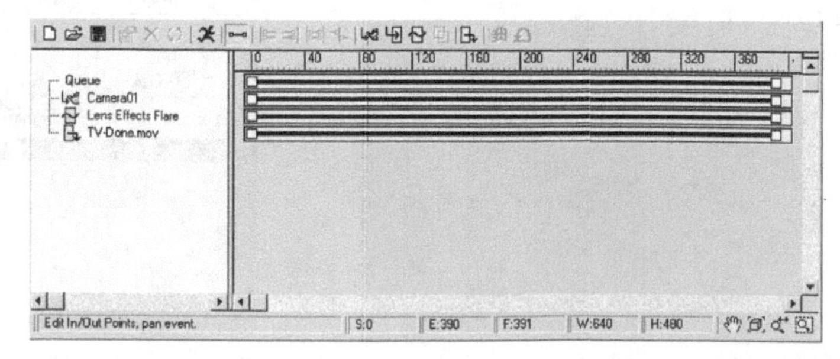

Figure 11.61 The complete Video Post queue.

Figure 11.62 The Lens Flare preview.

Figure 11.63 The glow becomes smaller and appears in front of the logo object.

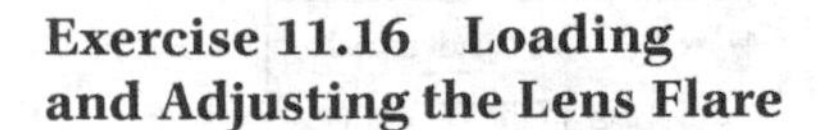

Exercise 11.16 Loading and Adjusting the Lens Flare

You can now load the flare you created for the first scene and see how it looks with your logo.

1. With **11TV10.max** open, advance to frame 280. In the Video Post queue, double-click the Lens Effects Flare event to open the Edit Filter Event dialog. Click the Setup button to open the Lens Effects Flare dialog. Click the Load button and load the flare you created in the first scene (Project1\flare01.lzf). Activate the VP Queue and Preview buttons to render a test frame (see **Figure 11.62**).

   The logo looks like it's on fire—not a good thing. You'd better can the Inferno effect.

2. Click the Prefs tab and deselect Inferno in the Glow column.

   That looks better, but the glow is far too large. Make it smaller.

3. Click the Glow tab and change the Size to **50**. Deselect Hide Behind Geometry so that the flare plays in front of the logo (see **Figure 11.63**).

   The glow looks much better. However, it's a little too bright. To fix that, adjust the Radial Transparency.

4. Right-click the middle flag of the Radial Transparency gradient and click Delete to delete the flag. Double-click the left flag of the Radial Transparency gradient and change the color to RGB: **150**, **150**, **150** (see **Figure 11.64**).

   The flare looks fantastic now. You're ready to animate it.

5. Click OK to close the Lens Effects Flare dialog.

Figure 11.64 The finished flare.

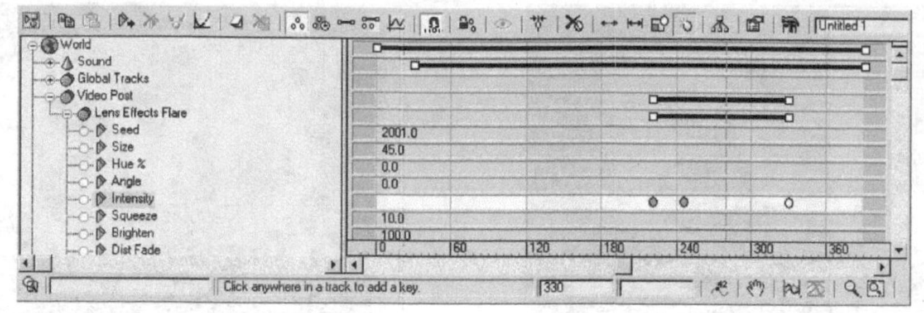

Figure 11.65 In the Intensity track, create keys at frames 220, 245, and 330.

Exercise 11.17 Animating the Lens Flare

Now that the flare is perfect, you can animate a few of its parameters to add a little spice to the effect. You will start by animating the intensity of the flare so it will appear at frame 220 and disappear at frame 330.

1. Open the Track View and expand the Video Post > Lens Effects Flare track. Activate the Add Keys tool and click in the Intensity track to create keys at frames 220, 245, and 330 (as shown in **Figure 11.65**).

   The Intensity should be 0 at frames 220 and 330.

2. Right-click the key at frame 220 to open the Intensity dialog. Change the Value to **0** and click the arrow pointing to the right twice to access key 3's parameters. Change its value to **0** (as shown in **Figure 11.66**). Close the dialog.

   The intensity is animated to be 0 at frame 220, 100 at frame 245, and 0 at frame 330. This will cause the flare to dissolve on and off between frames 220 and 330.

   You will now make the flare's manual secondaries "burst" by animating their Plane

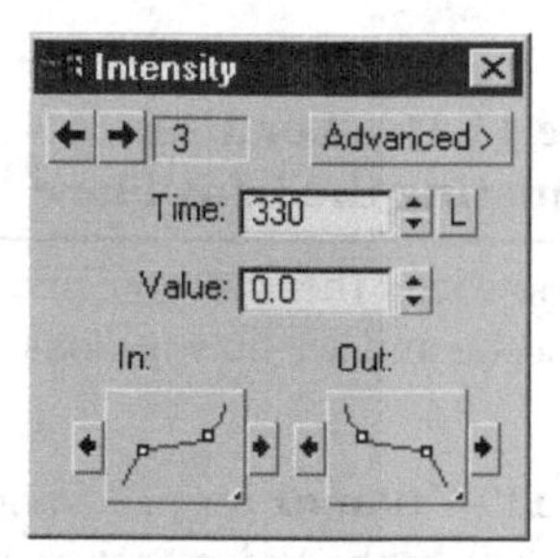

Figure 11.66 The intensity at frame 330 is 0.

   Scale values. The plane is the line on which the secondaries are created. A plane value of 0 will put the secondaries at the source of the flare; a larger plane value will move the secondaries further from the source. When you animate the Plane Scale values, the secondaries travel from the source of the flare outward.

3. Expand the Man Secondaries track in the Track View. With the Add Keys tool active, add keys to the Plane Scale track at frames 220 and 330 (see **Figure 11.67**).

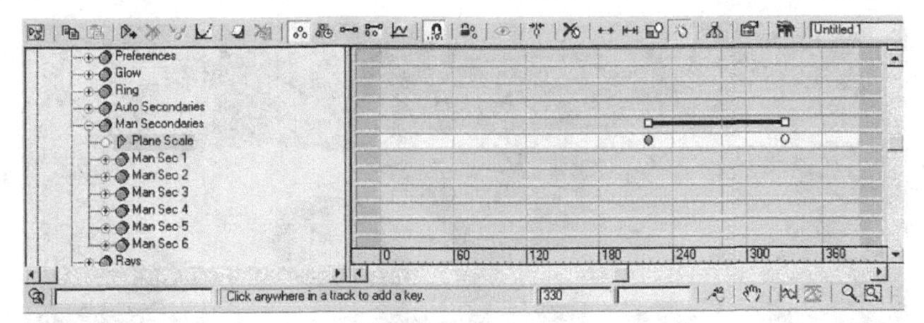

Figure 11.67 On the Plane Scale track create keys at frames 220 and 330.

4. Right-click the key at frame 220 to open the Plane Scale dialog and change its Value to **0**. Click the arrow pointing to the right to advance to the second key at frame 330 and change its Value to **2**. Close the dialog.

   The manual secondaries will now burst from the flare as it dissolves at frame 220 and will continue to grow until the flare disappears.

   You need to animate one last parameter before you can stick a fork in this animation. You need to animate the Rays angle, just like you did in the first scene.

5. Expand the Rays track in the Track View and click to create keys at frames 220 and 330 in the Angle track (see **Figure 11.68**).

   Now animate a slow counterclockwise rotation.

6. Right-click the key at frame 330 to open the Angle dialog. Change the Value to **−90** and close the dialog and the Track View.

   That's it—the animation is finished!

7. Save your work as **11TV12.max**.

8. When you are ready to render your animation, click the Execute Sequence button in the Video Post dialog. In the Execute Video Post dialog, choose your preferred output size (320×240 is suggested) and click Render. **Figure 11.69** shows the final result.

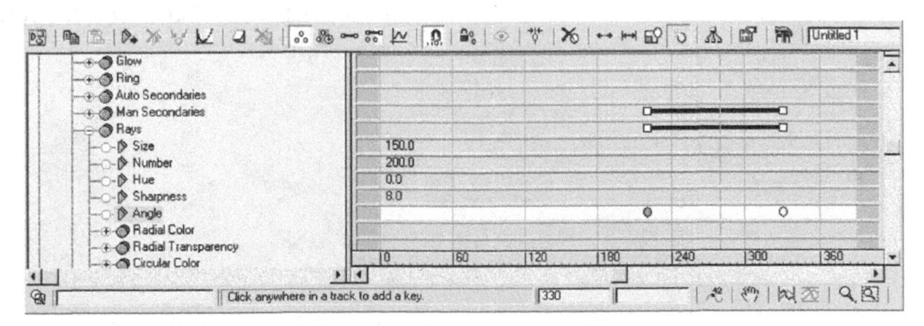

Figure 11.68 The Angle track has keys at frames 220 and 330.

Figure 11.69 The final render.

When the animation finishes rendering, you call Mr. Boss and John over to see the result of all your hard work. They are thrilled with it. Feeling good about yourself, you lean back in your chair and allow yourself to be hypnotized by the looping animation. You certainly deserve a good trance after all the hard work you've put in.

In Conclusion

It has been my pleasure to share in your journey through the exciting world of media animation. I hope you enjoyed the projects Vince, Victor, John, Gordon, and myself put together for this release. More important, I hope you've learned valuable information to help you perform and excel in your job as an animator. It has been wonderful sharing my time with you. Thank you for your continued support.

PART IV

INTEGRATING FOOTAGE

12 Rendering Project 1 for Compositing

Project 1 demonstrated how to create an entire media spot within 3ds Max. It is time to integrate the media graphic production process. The approach here is more like what would happen in a real production environment. Take the techniques in Part 3 of this book and apply them to Project 1. The technique is to generate render passes or elements within 3ds Max so that the elements can be composited in After Effects. 3ds Max will become the footage and element generator, while After Effects will composite all the elements together, create the transitions, and generate the effects (such as those completed in 3ds Max's video post).

The Fundamentals of Scanline Rendering

Working with 3ds max is all about producing images, either still images or animations. Images are created by rendering the 3D scenes you have created.

In this chapter, you learn about creating rendered images using the tried-and-true Scanline render engine that has been the standard renderer in 3ds max since version 1.

The main advantage of using the Scanline renderer is speed. It calculates the rendering through a top-down pass of rows of pixels, and through careful use of lighting and materials, you can create stunning images in a cost-effective manner:

- **The rendering process**—You learn to set up a scene to animate a still image and an animation sequence using the default Scanline renderer.
- **Render engines**—You learn about the different render engines or renderers in 3ds max.
- **Image resolution**—You learn to set image resolution for different scenarios.
- **File types**—You learn about some of the commonly used file types in 3ds max.
- **Network rendering**—You learn about the process involved in rendering a scene with multiple computers.

Key Terms

- **Renderer**—In 3ds max, you have several renderers available that process the modeling, lighting, materials, and effects into 2D images. They are Scanline, Radiosity, Light Tracer, and mental ray.
- **Resolution**—Images rendered from 3ds max must be sized appropriately for their intended use. The resolution is the image size as measured horizontally and vertically by the number of pixels or points of color of an image.
- **Scanline**—The default Scanline renderer processes information in the scene and creates a 2D image one line at a time, progressing from top to bottom. It is known for its rendering speed.
- **Rendered Frame Window (RFW)**—When you render an image in 3ds max, the image is displayed in the viewports with the Rendered Frame Window. This is independent of any image you might save as a separate file.
- **Delta compression**—This is a typical method of creating animation sequences where a frame is calculated completely and stored, and then the subsequent frames are compared against the stored frame and only the changed pixels are stored. This makes smaller file sizes and faster playback possible.
- **Codec**—A codec is computer code that tells 3ds max how to process and store a particular file format when rendered. Both the creator and the client viewing the files must have the same codec installed.
- **Network rendering**—This enables you to use multiple computers to calculate still images or animation sequences.

The Renderers

As mentioned in the introduction to this chapter, 3ds max offers you several renderers or rendering engines, and each processes objects, materials, lights, and effects in a different manner. Each has its advantages and disadvantages, but having a wide choice of industry-accepted renderers makes you, the user, more productive and marketable.

The renderers available to you in 3ds max are as follows:

- **Scanline**—This is the default renderer that processes the scene in horizontal lines from top to bottom. The Scanline render is one of the fastest in the industry, and the output can be used in a wide range of output needs.
- **Advanced lighting with Scanline**—Although not a standalone renderer, the Advanced Lighting options within the Scanline renderer—Radiosity and Light Tracer—add the calculation of bounced light and physically based lighting control to your scene. The scenes have a richer look because of the bounced light, but can take much longer to render.
- **Mental ray**—The mental ray rendering extensions built in to 3ds max offer raytracing options that are an industry standard in the feature film world. Mental ray can work with an 3ds max material and light, but also have special lights and shaders (materials) for specific effects such as caustics, or the effect of light diffused through glass or water, which are impossible with the other renderers. Setup time and rendering can be much longer with mental ray.

✔ Note

Other third-party renderers are available on the market that can be integrated into 3ds max and offer different levels of quality and control and special effects such as flat cartoon-type rendering.

A search on the Internet and the 3ds max newsgroups will turn up more up-to-date specific information.

The Rendering Process

You can use the Quick Render button to see a rendering of your scene in the Rendered Frame Window (RFW) on the screen. This does not save any image that you can access to the hard drive, although you have a Show Last Rendering option in the Rendering pull-down menu, which allows you to view the last rendered image of the current work session.

In this chapter, you perform exercises to render a scene in 3ds max for a high-resolution still image and for two animation sequences, one a delta compression animation file and the other a series of numbered still images.

The basic process is simple enough: You activate the viewport you want to render, usually a Camera viewport, and then choose the image resolution you need, the file type you want, and choose a folder on the hard drive to store it. The software and computer handle the rest of the work for you.

The Render Scene dialog is called by going to the Rendering pull-down menu and choosing Render (see **Figure 12.1**). You also can use the F10 function key as a keyboard shortcut or the Render Scene teapot button in the main toolbar.

The Render Scene dialog has five tabs with a variety of settings:

- **Common**—The Common tab enables you to set parameters such as the number of frames you want to render, the resolution, and the file type and locations to save the files. Within this tab, you also can assign which renderer will be used.
- **Renderer**—In the Renderer tab, you can set specific parameters of the currently active renderer, such as filtering and motion blurring.
- **Render Elements**—The Render Elements tab enables you to break out various components of a rendered image (for example, the lighting, reflections, or

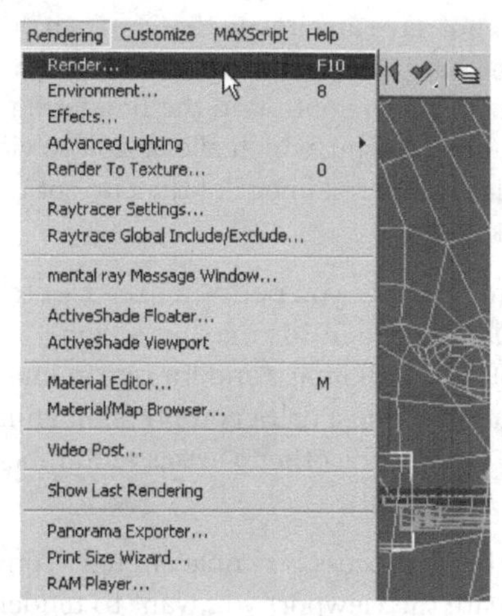

Figure 12.1 Choosing Render from Rendering pull-down menu or pressing the F10 function key opens the Render Scene dialog.

shadows) to separate files for post-processing with other software.

- **Raytracer**—You can adjust speed and quality parameters globally for raytracing in materials in this tab.
- **Advanced Lighting**—This tab has settings to choose and adjust the advanced Radiosity and Light Tracer rendering options.

In this chapter, you learn about the parameters in the Common tab for setting up the initial rendering process. You learn to set the resolution for printing and video output and to choose file types appropriate for those uses by rendering an outdoor animated scene.

Setting the Output Parameters for Print

One of your first decisions when rendering is the size, or resolution, of the rendered image that you will be saving to the hard drive. The resolution is the number of points in the mosaic that, viewed as a whole, create the image. You need sufficient resolution to contain the detail, but you must not use higher resolution than is efficient for your needs.

More resolution means larger file sizes and less efficiency, especially when playing back animations.

In Exercise 12.1, you learn to set up a scene for printing resolution and to save the settings as a preset for later retrieval.

Exercise 12.1 Setting Rendering Resolution and Presets for Print

1. Open the file called Ch12_Iceberg01.max on the CD-ROM. From the File pull-down menu, choose Save As, point to an appropriate subdirectory on your hard drive, and use the plus sign button to save a new file with the name incremented to Ch12_Iceberg02.max. This is the outdoor scene with the ship that has a few materials applied and has been animated to move across the camera view in an arctic scene (see **Figure 12.2**).
2. From the Rendering pull-down menu, choose Render or press F10. In the Common tab, you will see, in the Time Output area, rendering is set to a Single frame. This is the frame that the Time slider below the viewports is set on. Drag the Time slider to frame 19 for a full view of the ship in the Camera01 viewport.

✔ Tips

- One aid to learning 3ds max is to dissect other artists' scenes to try and discover what they used to create it. One hint is to select the dummy in the middle of the large iceberg on the left and go to the Motion panel. There has been an Attachment controller that uses the animated surface of the water for its position. The iceberg is linked to the dummy and tips and rolls as the wave passes through it.

Figure 12.2 The Ironclad glides silently past massive ice flows.

- The other object is an Atmospheric Apparatus Helper object with Volume fog to create looming clouds over the horizon and layered fog to create a hazy water surface in the background.
- Use the online Help file in the pull-down menus to investigate these features.

3. In the Output Size area, enter 3000 in the Width field and 2400 in the Height field. This is the resolution of the image that will be saved to the hard drive. The Pixel Aspect should be set to 1.0 for most printed images (see **Figure 12.3**). This means that there will be 3000 square pixels horizontally and 2400 square pixels vertically in the final image that is written to disk.
4. Scroll the Common Parameters rollout up and in the Render Output area click the Files button. In the Render Output File dialog, click the Save As Type: All Formats list and choose .jpg in the list

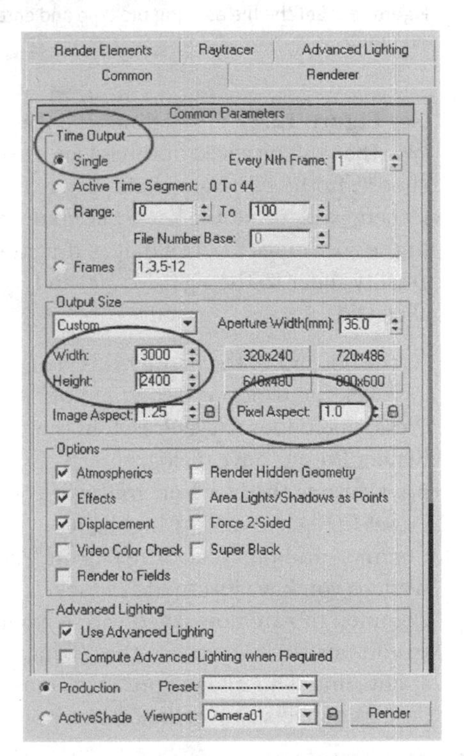

Figure 12.3 To set the output size of the rendered image for printing, enter the Width and Height in pixels and make sure Pixel Aspect is set to 1.0.

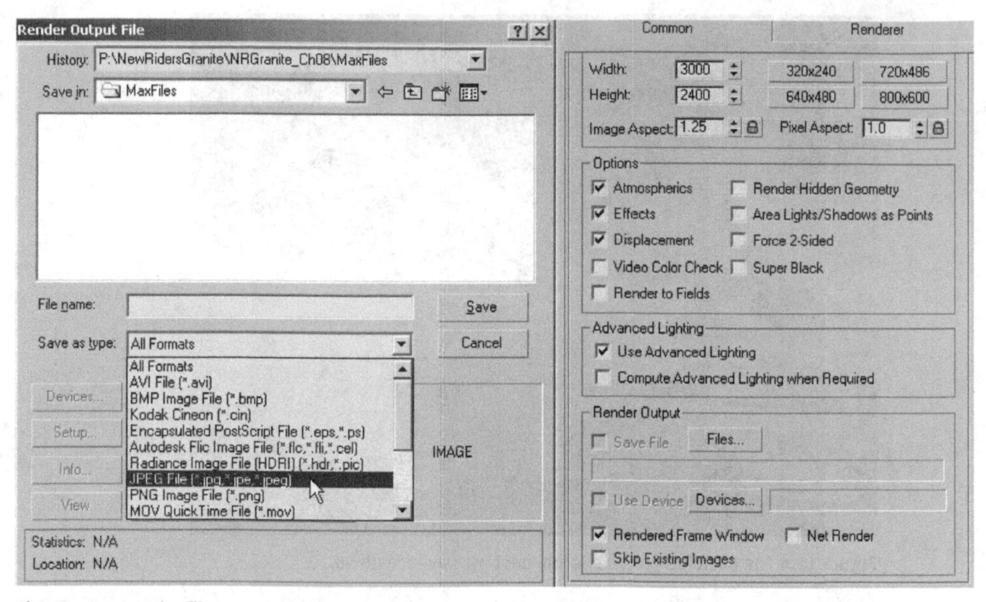

Figure 12.4 Set the file as a .jpg file type and enter Iceberg_still_print as the name with the .jpg quality set to 100.

(see **Figure 12.4**). This defines the file type that will be saved in the folder you choose. In the File Name field, enter Iceberg_still_print. Click the Save button. In the .jpg Image Control dialog, drag the Quality slider to the right for 100 and click OK.

5. At the bottom of the Render Scene dialog, click the window to the right of Preset and choose Save Preset. In the Render Presets Save dialog, enter print_test as the filename. In the Select Preset Categories dialog, highlight Common and press the Save button. The settings you have just made in the Common tab are now saved with a name, so you can quickly retrieve the settings at any time. This allows consistent renderings, especially in collaborative work.

6. Always check that you are rendering the correct viewport in the window to the left of the Render button. In the Render Scene dialog, click the Render button at the lower-right corner. Have patience; the scene will take a while to render because of the higher resolution. As you increase the resolution, the file sizes can grow exponentially. For example, a 320×240 image only contains 25 percent of a 640×480 image.

✔ Tip

- The images in the RFW might not be the same resolution as you have set because it is limited by the graphics card and monitor size. It is only intended as a preview.

7. In the Rendering pull-down menu, choose Print Size Wizard. You must know two pieces of information: the paper size (if the default setting is metric, switch to inches, if necessary) and the printer's DPI (dots per inch) setting. Enter those in the appropriate fields of the Print Size Wizard dialog, and then choose a file type and location to render to.

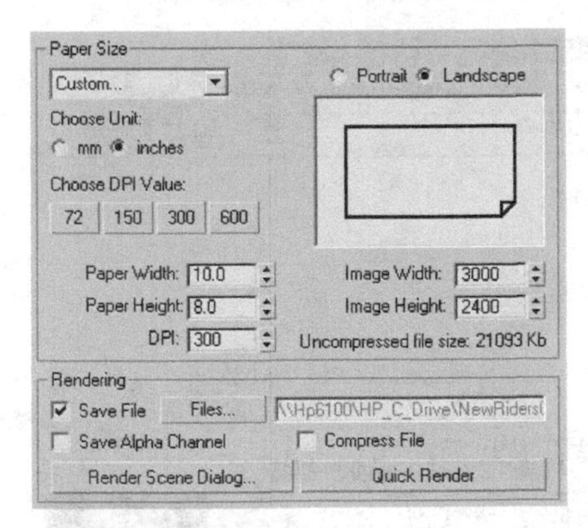

Figure 12.5 Click the Rendering pull-down menu and choose Print Size Wizard to determine the necessary resolution for paper size and printer dpi settings.

In this case, you are rendering to 10-inch by 8-inch paper in landscape format on a printer set to 300 dpi (see **Figure 12.5**). You do not need to render this image again.

✔ Note

What, you might ask, is the reasoning behind choosing a resolution of 3000×2400 for print? It was random in his case, but in production, it will depend mostly on the printer and the size of the indended print. The entire decision process can be a source of conflict and theory. However, 3ds max has a tool that helps you make the decision: the Print Wizard.

✔ Tip

- This is to be used as a rule-of-thumb starting point, Printing is a complex blend of art and science, and you must experiment with various printer settings, paper and ink combinations, and resolution settings before committing to a final image. Always render at the lowest resolution you need for the quality you want.

8. Close all windows and dialogs and save the file. It should already be called Ch12_Iceberg02.max.

Setting the Output Parameters for Video

In Exercise 12.2, you determine basic presets for rendering for typical video playback. Here, the device that will record the images onto videotape determines the resolution. Each device is different, so you have to check the manufacturer's data for the device you use. This hardware resizing must be compensated for in the rendered image. The pixel aspect must also match this resizing so that the spheres in the scene do not render as ovals.

Exercise 12.2 Rendering for Videotape

1. Open the file called Ch12_Iceberg02.max on the CD-ROM or from the preceding exercise. From the File pull-down menu, choose Save As, point to an appropriate subdirectory on your hard drive, and use the plus sign button to save a new file with the name incremented to Ch12_Iceberg03.max.
2. From the Rendering pull-down menu, choose Render. In the Common tab of the Render Scene dialog, check the radio button in the Time Output area called Active Time Segment: 0 to 44. In the Output Size area, click the Custom window and choose NTSC D-1(video) option in the list. This is a typical video format setting. Notice it is 720×486 resolution with a pixel aspect of 0.9 (see **Figure 12.6**). Again, always check your equipment before entering this information.
3. Click the field to the right of Preset at the bottom of the dialog and choose Save Presets. Name this new file video_test, and choose the Common option in the dialog list.

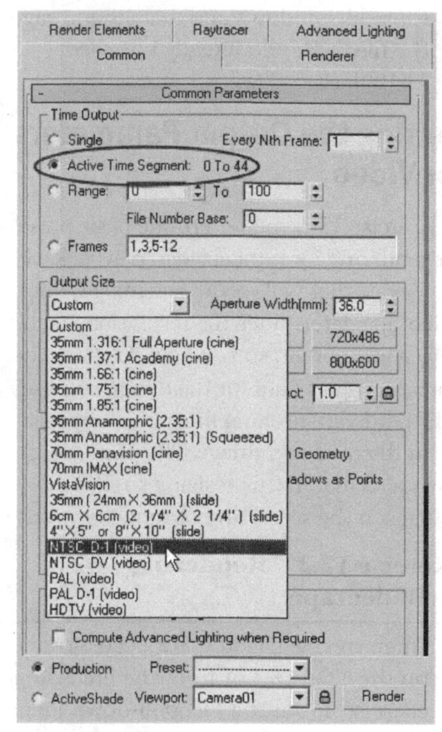

Figure 12.6 You can set the rendering to the Active Time Segment and choose from a list of typical output sizes that might match your equipment.

✔ Tip

- Pressing the Escape key eventually stops the rendering. It might not stop immediately if processes are being calculated in the background.

4. At the bottom of the Common Parameters rollout, click the Files button in Render Output area, change the filename to Iceberg_video, and choose .avi in the list of file types in the Render Output File dialog (see **Figure 12.7**). Click the Save button in the .avi File Compression Setup dialog, and click OK to accept the default Cinepack codec. In the Render Scene dialog, click the Render button.

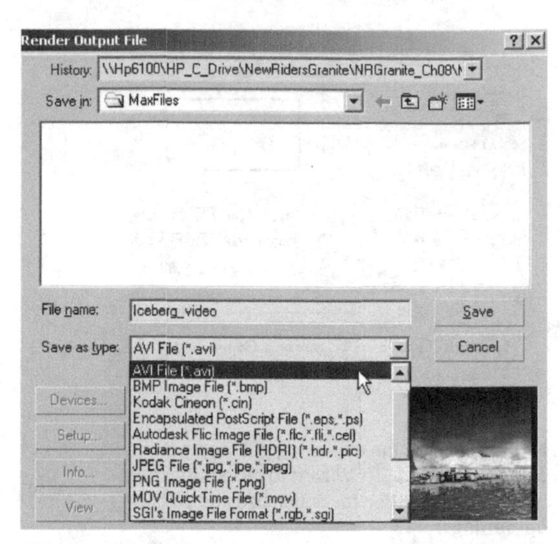

Figure 12.7 In the Render Output File dialog, you find a list of available file types in the Save As Type list. Choose .avi from the list.

✔ Tip

- You can play the .avi animation back by finding it with Windows Explorer and double-clicking the filename or, in the Rendering pull down menu, choose RAM player and open the file from there.

  You can also go the File pull down menu and choose View Image File to view images or animations.

5. The first frame renders, and the second frame (of 45 total frames, 0 to 44) starts. The Rendering progress dialog gives you the Last Frame Time and the best-guess time remaining and continues the process until all frames are finished.

6. Close all windows and dialogs and save the file. It should already be called Ch12_Iceberg03.miax.

Choosing File Types for Stills and Animations

So far in this chapter, you have rendered both a still image and an animation. For the still image, you chose a .jpg file type with highest quality as the rendering output and, for the animation, you chose an .avi file with a Cinepak codec.

Those were random choices for both the still and animation because you do not have a specific use in mind for the end results. In production situations, the choice of output file type can be a critical balance of quality, compression, and usability in post-processing or client viewing.

In this section, you learn some of the more common file types in use and some of the reasons why you might choose one or the other.

- For still images, the commonly used file types tend to be .jpg, .png, .tga, .tif, and .rpf.
- For animations, the commonly used file types tend to be .avi, .mov, and image sequence files.

A discussion of the various file types wouldn't be complete without a basic understanding of something called alpha channel.

Most images today are created at a color level of 24 bits. A *bit* is two pieces of computer information that define colors. The number of colors possible is calculated by 2 to the power of 24 or a maximum of 16.7 million colors in your palette.

The human eye can detect differences for only about 65,000 colors, so a large palette means that a complex image with lots of color gradients from dark to light will not show signs of banding because of lack of available colors.

Computer monitors are made of points of light. If a display shows a diagonal line across those points, a certain amount of stair-stepping effect is introduced. Computers use antialiasing to blend the diagonal boundary colors (see **Figure 12.8**).

The computer is mixing the white of the iceberg and the blue of the sky to smooth the edge with varying bluish-white pixels. If you were to lift this iceberg from the blue

Figure 12.8 In a close-up of the upper left edge of the iceberg, where it meets the sky, you can see the effects of antialiasing to smooth the stair-steeping effect on the pixels in a diagonal line.

background and place it on a red background, the edge would look terrible because of all the bluish pixels.

Some image types can be 32-bit images (.tga, .tif, and .png from the preceding list, for example). They have the same number of colors, but have an additional 8 bits of transparency information called alpha channel. Instead of mixing the edge colors, alpha channel uses transparency to smooth the boundary. When you place this information on a new background color, it matches perfectly.

Alpha channel files are used in 3ds max specifically for masking and compositing in the materials and when rendering images that will be processed with new background images in compositing software such as Discreet combustion. In the animation file types previously listed, only the image sequence files—which would be still images of .png or .tga, for example—can have alpha channel.

Here, you learn a little about each file type and some of the pros and cons of using them.

Still Images File Types

Although these are not the only file types available for rendering still images, they are the more commonly used and will usually be accessible by your coworkers and clients:

- **.jpg**—These files were some of the first compressed files available for rendering still images, which accounts for their popularity. Everyone can access them, and all software can read and write them. The compression, however, is called "lossy," which means information is discarded to make the file smaller. This leads to a degradation of the image that can show as blocky areas of color, especially in sky areas or others with large expanses of similar colored pixels. There is no alpha channel.
- **.tga**—.tga files are not highly compressed and do not degrade in quality. The file sizes can be quite large as the resolution increases, but they are commonly used. .tga can have an alpha channel or not.
- **.tif**—These exhibit similar quality and size to .tga, but are often preferred by commercial printers. They may or may not have alpha channel.
- **.png**—A relative newcomer to the scene, .png files have a quality as high as 48-bit color with optional alpha channel, but are compressed to a size similar to .jpg. Unlike .jpg, the compression is lossless with no degrading of quality. Most programs today read and right .png files.
- **.rpf**—This file type is not so commonly used but merits mentioning because of its integration with the Discreet Combustion compositing software. It allows the storage of extra information that allows a 2D image to appear to be 3D when imported into Combustion. The files can be very large.

The file type you choose for your work depends on many factors relating to how it will be used and by whom, and you might find that other file types might be better for you. In any case, the important common element to study further is alpha channel and how it can work for you.

Animation Image File Types

Not only do you have to be concerned with the file type itself in animation rendering, you also must carefully choose one of the many codecs or compressors available within the file type.

Some of the criteria you need to include in your decision are compression amounts, color quality, playback speed, resolution, and compatibility with the viewer's computer.

The decision of which file type to use is further complicated by the fact that the codecs are being modified and developed almost on a daily basis.

The codecs are known as delta compressors. They save the first frame completely, and then render and save only the changed pixels of the following frames, hence the compression. This makes it difficult to edit the animations after rendering, and it is impossible to take advantage of 3ds max built-in network rendering because it can't piece the changed pixel files together in the correct order.

In any case, it is highly recommended that you do not render directly to an animation codec. Always render to a series of sequential .png or .tga files and convert those to animation files later by using the RAM Player in 3ds max or some other available software.

When you choose to render a series of frames in 3ds max and choose a still image file type, max automatically saves each frame with sequential names (for example, Test0001.png, Test0002.png, and so on).

This allows for more flexible post-processing in other software and makes it easier for you to rerender any number of frames for areas that need to be fixed or changed. Converting to animation files is always quicker than rerendering scenes.

Network Rendering

One of the absolute best features of 3ds max has always been the free built-in network rendering capability. This enables you to distribute individual frames of an animation or, now in 3ds max, portions of a still image over any number of computers to be compiled back on a single machine.

✔ Caution

Make sure you have a clean network with the proper permissions so that each machine can access the machine that is managing the rendering. You need administrator access for the initial setup.

✔ Tip

- The rendering machine can be used both as manager and sever by starting each component. After the manager process is complete, the server process can be used in the backburner network rendering.

The rendering machines, called servers, do not need to be licensed copies of 3ds max, but only need a core of the program installed on the machine, and each machine needs to be on a TCP/IP network.

Network rendering is called by 3ds max, but the rendering management is handled by backburner, which is included on the CD-ROM that max ships on.

The server computers that do the rendering must have a system component called Server started, and the rendering machine must have a component called Manager started.

After the manager and server components have started, you need to specify a range of frames in the renderer, save to a still image format, and check the Net Render option in Common Parameters rollout (see **Figure 12.9**).

By opening the Queue Monitor component included in backburner, you can manage which jobs are sent to which machines on the network and you can view the progress of the rendering (see **Figure 12.10**).

✔ Caution

Network rendering does not directly support the mental ray renderer in 3ds max. You must have licenses for each machine on the network you want to use.

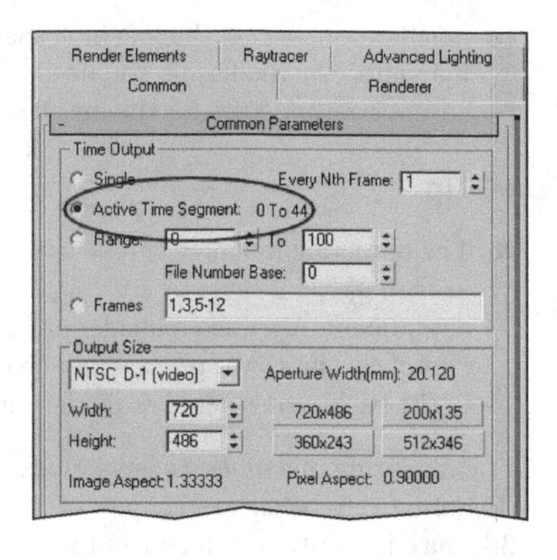

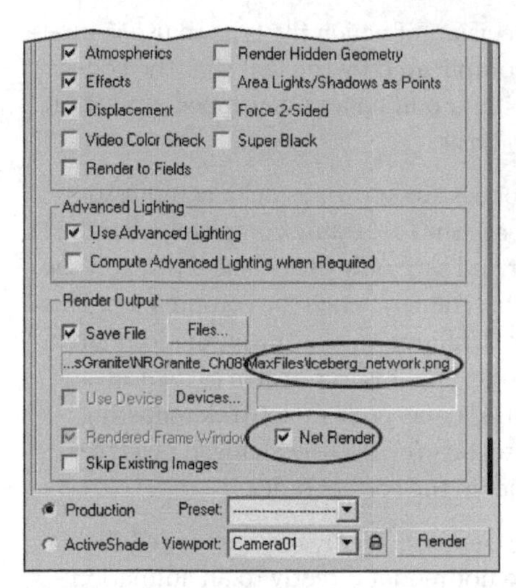

Figure 12.9 Network rendering must be to still image file types, and you must check the Net Render option in the Render Scene dialog. Backburner must be installed, and the manager and server components must be running on the appropriate machines.

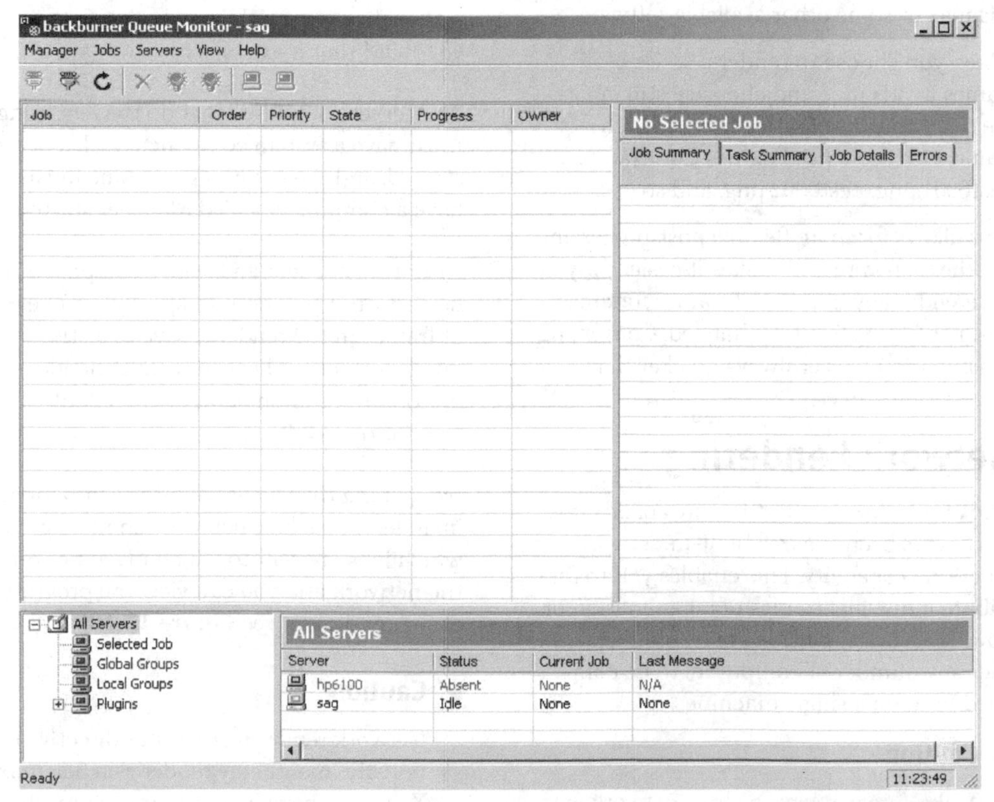

Figure 12.10 When rendering begins, you can use backburner Queue Monitor to assign jobs to machines and track the progress of the rendering.

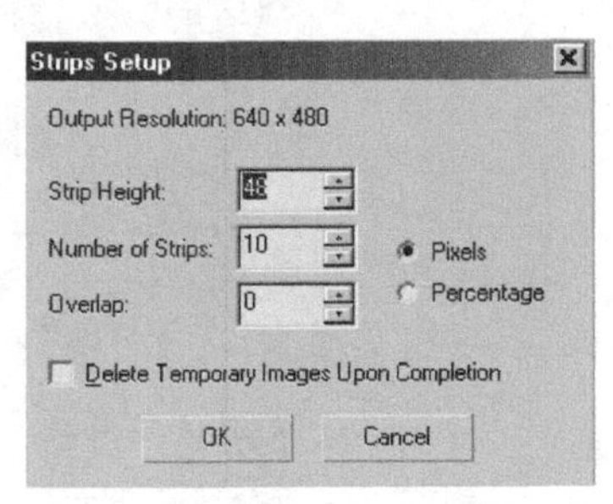

Figure 12.11 when you net render a single frame with Split Scan Lines turned on, you can set the distribution based on the image resolution and number of available machines.

Use the online Help file in 3ds max for a complete guide to setting up and using the network rendering capabilities, but be sure you are using it to increase production where applicable.

To distribute the rendering of parts of a still image over the network, you need to choose Single in the Render Scene dialog and choose the Split Scan Lines option presented when you click the Render button, then pick the Define button. In the Strips Setup dialog, you choose the number of strips based on the resolution and number of machines available on the network, and the image file will be reassembled on completion.

13

Render Elements

Multi-Pass Rendering

The technique of rendering multiple passes comes from the world of film-based special effects, where elements of a live-action scene are filmed separately and assembled in a darkroom to create a composite image. This method has been adopted and expanded by digital media. Many 3D renders use a multitiered hierarchy of passes in which scenes are broken down and objects are rendered separately from one another and their environments. This process allows further adjustment to those elements independently of other objects in the scene.

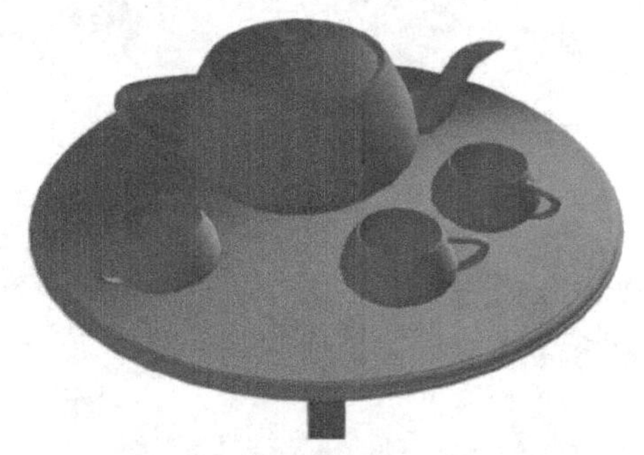

Figure 13.1 The diffuse pass contains color and shading.

To take this to the next level of quality, each of those passes can be further broken into elements. For instance, a single object in a scene might be composed of three or more passes: a diffuse pass, which contains color and shading; a specular pass, which has the object's specular highlights; and a reflection pass, which has reflections that appear on the surface of the object. The result of rendering those passes is a level of control over the final image quality that would be extremely difficult to achieve otherwise.

Figures 13.1 through **13.5** show examples of the passes that make up a typical multi-pass rendering.

Another benefit of rendering in passes is that if you need to make changes to specific characters or objects in an animation, you do not necessarily have to re-render the entire piece.

Multiple passes are also used to create the special effects for things such as iridescent

Figure 13.2 The reflection pass for the tray was rendered separately from other reflections in the scene, to allow it to be adjusted individually.

Figure 13.3 The cups were also rendered separately, to allow their reflections to be adjusted separate from the tray.

Figure 13.4 The shadow pass casts shadows where appropriate.

and translucent objects. To create the effects in the movie *Hollow Man*, artists used many separately rendered layers of computer graphics to create a see-through character.

Rendering Multiple Passes

Previously, the way to render multiple-pass renders in 3ds max was to create a different MAX file for each pass and render each element separately. To say the least, this was tedious and time-consuming.

A new feature of 3ds max, called Render Elements, is aimed at making the process of creating multiple-pass renderings more efficient and easier. Render Elements renders a full image and breaks it into multiple passes that you can specify and customize to meet your rendering requirements.

In Exercise 13.1, you will use the Render Elements feature to set up multi-pass renders.

✔ Note

Each rendering task is a different problem. The best way to begin is to render the Camera viewport and evaluate a frame or animated sequence to see whether the scene changes dramatically. In many instances, this also means working closely with the compositor to determine what elements he will need for the compositing process.

Here is a list of the different passes that you will need for compositing:

- You will render the diffuse passes for the Jester and truck as one pass. The diffuse

Figure 13.5 The passes have been combined to make a final composite. Note that the reflection and shadow passes were used at a fraction of their full strength.

pass will also contain the Alpha Channel, which will be used in compositing to matte the computer graphic elements over the video background.

- You will need a separate pass for the confetti particles so that they can be adjusted independently from the rest of the scene.
- You will need to render an effects pass of the particles emitted by the SuperSpray objects in the scene, to provide control over the level of the effect applied to the particles.
- You will need to render a shadow pass that will contain only the shadows cast by objects in the 3D scene. Because the lighting in the backplate is fairly uniform, you can render the shadows for all objects in the scene in one pass.
- You will need to render a reflection pass for the toy truck and a separate reflection pass for the tablecloth, providing individual control over the reflective properties of each object.
- You will need to render a specular pass, which will contain the scene object's highlights.

Diffuse Pass

The diffuse pass will contain the color information and shading for objects in the scene. Having color information as a separate pass is necessary to adjust color balance so that it blends with the background lighting. This is important when trying to match known colors such as skin tones with live-action backplates.

Sometimes, if the ambient lighting in a scene varies, it is helpful to render diffuse passes for each object or specific areas where the light is varied. In this scene, the ambient lighting is uniform throughout the scene, so you can render the diffuse pass for the entire scene.

In this next exercise, you set up the scene to render the individual passes needed to create the final composite.

Exercise 13.1 Setting Up the Passes

1. Open the file 13_01.max.
2. Go to frame 131. Render a single frame of the Camera viewport at 720 × 480 resolution with mapping, anti-aliasing, shadows, and the live-action back-plate.

   The following steps require that your PC be either connected to a network or have the loopback adapter installed.
3. Go to the Display panel and check Particle Systems in the Hide by Category rollout. You will be creating separate diffuse passes for the particles.
4. Click the Render Scene button to open the Render Scene dialog box.
5. In the Render Scene dialog box under the Render Output group, click the Files button and select My Network Places. Navigate to the name of the networked machine where you will be saving the renders (see **Figure 13.6**). Click the drive name where the project is stored, and create a new folder named Renders. This directory will hold the Render Elements.

✔ Note

Regardless of whether you are connected to a network, you should use this method of choosing the destination for renders even when rendering to your local machine. This way, if you are working on

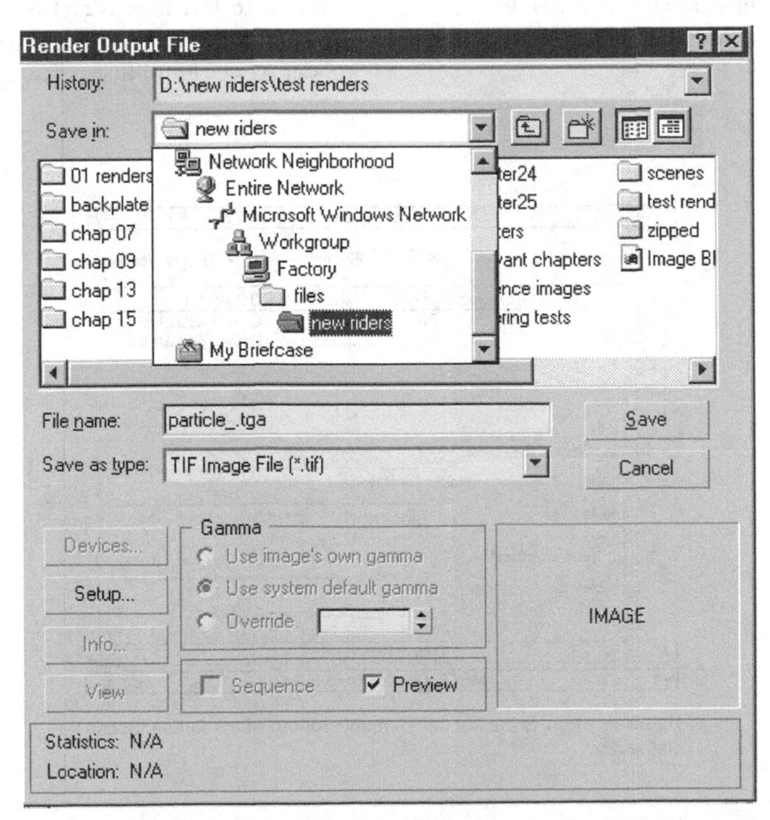

Figure 13.6 The Render Output File dialog box is used to specify a UNC path.

a network and decide that you want to render on multiple machines, all the machines will be capable of accessing the destination. Even if you are working on a standalone PC, this is a good workflow habit to develop.

6. In the Render Scene dialog box, click the Render Elements rollout, as seen in **Figure 13.7**.
7. In the Material Editor, open the material called cm_shadow. These are Matte Shadow materials.
8. In the Matte group, make sure that Opaque Alpha is unchecked.
9. In the Shadow group, uncheck Receive Shadows and Affect Alpha.
10. Click on the Add button in Render Elements, choose Diffuse from the options presented, and press OK to close the dialog box.

    If you look in the Render Elements list, you can see that a diffuse pass has been added to it.
11. Check to make sure that the pass has the Enabled option checked and that Display Elements is checked. Now render a single test frame from the Camera view.

    The result should be two images: one labeled Camera01, and the other labeled Diffuse (as seen in **Figure 13.8**).
12. Save the file as **13_render elements.max.**

Now that you've learned how to implement Render Elements to create a diffuse pass and how to save files using the Universal Naming Convention (UNC), you're ready to render passes for diffuse particles.

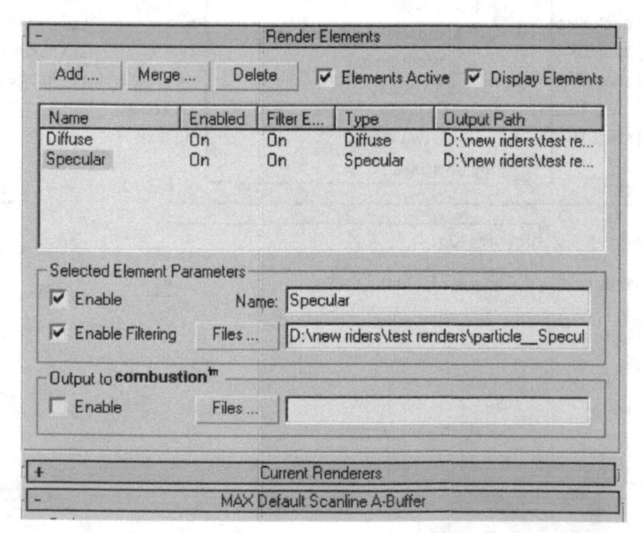

Figure 13.7 Here is the Render Elements rollout of the Render Scene dialog box.

Figure 13.8 This is the diffuse pass.

Exercise 13.2 Rendering Passes for Diffuse Particles

In this exercise, you will render separate passes for each of the two types of particles. The only thing you will be interested in doing with the particle passes is adjusting the color and compositing of each particle type separately. Both particle passes will be rendered without Render Elements because they do not have any specular or reflective properties that need to be adjusted.

1. Some of the passes will have to be set up in their own 3ds max file, so open the file 13_Render Elements.max. You will make changes to the previous file and save them under new names.

2. Go to frame 80, and select and hide the following objects: the particle systems called PArray01 and PArray02, the objects that make up the jester, and the toy truck.

3. Render a test frame to make sure that the only thing visible is the confetti particles (see **Figure 13.9**).

4. Save the MAX file as **confetti.max**.

5. Select and hide the particle system called SuperSpray01.

6. Unhide the particle systems called PArray01 and PArray02.

7. Render a test frame. Make certain that the Render Effect is enabled in the Render Effects dialog box. The result should be a rendering of only the pixie dust particles with a glow effect (see **Figure 13.10**).

8. Go to the Render Scene dialog box and disable Render Elements. Name the rendered files **pixie.tga**.

9. Save the MAX file as **pixie.max**.

To recap, you saved two files—one with the confetti visible, and the other with the pixie dust visible—so that they can be rendered as separate passes. Now you're ready to apply specular highlights.

Figure 13.9 These are the confetti particles.

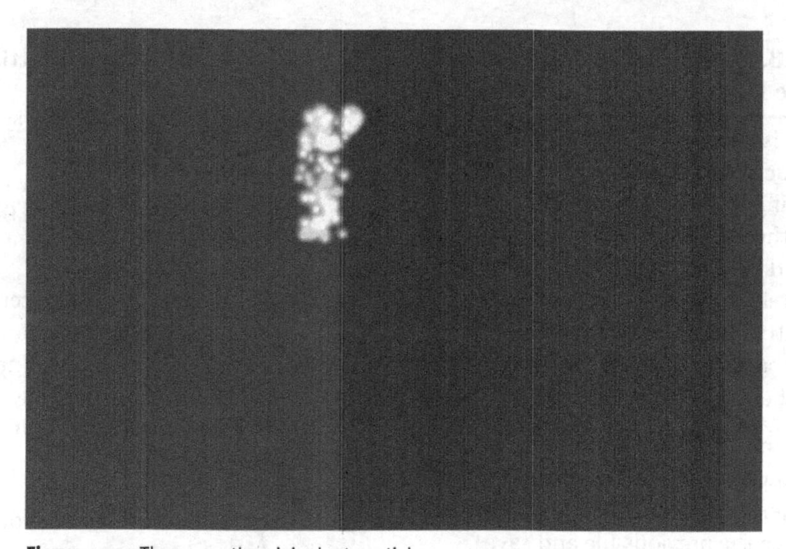

Figure 13.10 These are the pixie dust particles.

Exercise 13.2 Applying Specular Highlights

Specular highlights help you visually determine the smoothness of a surface. A highly polished or smooth surface such as glass will exhibit a highlight that is concentrated on a small area of the surface. This differs from a rough surface that is full of scratches or bumps that diffuse the highlights over a large area of the surface. Specular highlights respond less effectively to tweaking in the composite than the other layers, so you will render one specular pass for all the objects in the scene. Being able to make adjustments to the specular layer allows the levels and contrast of specular highlights to be adjusted to match the specular attributes of the backplate.

1. Open the file 13_Render Elements.max, and click the Render Scene button.
2. Click the Add button in the Render Elements area, and choose Specular.
3. Make sure that the specular element is enabled, and render the Camera 01 viewport at frame 130 (see **Figure 13.11**).

✔ Note

The resulting render will include a render of all elements in the scene together, and a render that has the specular attributes of the image separated from the rest. If any other Render Elements are enabled in the Render Elements queue, they will also be separated and displayed.

4. Save the file as **13_Render Elements.max**.

Now that you've added a specular pass to the Render Elements, you're ready to add a shadow pass.

Exercise 13.2 Creating a Shadow Pass

The shadow pass describes the areas of the scene in which a shadow-casting light is being blocked by an object with shadow-casting properties activated. Having the shadows isolated from the rest of the image enables you to adjust the density and sharpness of the shadows to match the characteristics of the shadows in the backplate. As with the diffuse pass, when the scene is evenly illuminated, you can render one shadow pass for all the objects in the scene at once.

The procedure for creating the shadow pass is different from the previous passes you have set up. Because of a flaw in the Render Elements process, objects that use Shadow Matte material do not display shadows correctly when the Shadow Render Element is rendered.

Figure 13.11 This is the specular pass.

You start by changing the Shadow Matte parameters so that the Shadow Matte material will display shadows that are cast on the matte objects in the scene.

1. In the Material Editor, use the Eyedropper tool to get the Matte Shadow material from any of the matte objects in the scene (these are objects with the cm_prefix on their names). In the Basic parameters, check the Receive Shadows and Affect Alpha options.
2. Now open the Render Scene dialog box. Go to the Render Elements section and add a Shadow Render Element to the queue. Also disable the Specular Render Element. Render the scene.

   The scene will render a Camera View window and a Shadow window. The Shadow window appears empty because the information for the Shadow Render Element appears in the Alpha Channel of the shadow pass.
3. At the top of the Shadow window is a series of icons. Click the one that is a circle that is half black and half white to view the Alpha Channel.

   The image that you see is actually a negative of the shadows cast in the scene. Areas that are black are areas with no shadow, the white regions are fully in shadow, and gray areas are partially in shadow. You see that the Shadow Matte objects are not showing any shadow at all; that is the bug.
4. To see how the Shadow Matte objects should appear, click the Camera window and view its Alpha Channel. In the Camera window, you see the shadows projected correctly on the Matte Shadow objects.

   You will work around the bug with the following steps.
5. Go to the Display menu and select Unfreeze All.
6. Click the icon for the Material Editor.
7. Create a new material and call it **Shadow Receiver**. Set the ambient color to black and the diffuse color to white.
8. Activate one of the other slots in the Material Editor, and use the Eyedropper tool to select the material from the cm_table object in the scene. Use the Select By Material button to select all objects that use the cm_shadow material.

✔ Note

Select By Material is a handy tool to use if you know what material the objects have but are not sure of the objects' names.

9. Go to the Material Editor, and make sure that the Shadow Receiver material is selected. From the Material Editor tool buttons, click the Assign Material to Selection button.
10. Open the Render Scene dialog box. Render the scene to see the result.

    The shadow pass information is visible in the Alpha Channel of the shadow window. The Matte Shadow objects should now have the shadows rendered on them. See **Figure 13.12**.
11. Save the scene as **Shadow Pass.max.**

Here you learned how to select by material and create a shadow pass without using Render Elements. Next, you'll apply a reflection pass.

Figure 13.12 This is frame 130 of the shadow pass.

Exercise 13.3 Applying the Reflection Pass

The reflection pass contains anything that is rendered as a reflection in the scene. Like specular passes, reflection passes tell you about the smoothness of a surface. Surfaces with scratches or pits diffuse and distort the scene reflected in them, and very smooth or polished surfaces reflect the scene more clearly. Because objects' surfaces can vary so greatly, it is very possible that you will need to break up the reflections for a scene into separate Render Elements for objects or areas of a scene that require different treatment.

When you look at the reflections in your scene, there are two major reflective objects. The truck has a glossy surface with defined reflections. In the backplate you see that the tablecloth reflects the objects that are sitting on top of it. The reflection is very subtle and reflects only the parts of the objects that are within half an inch of the tablecloth. As objects get farther away, the reflection quickly fades to nothing. Attention to how objects in the environment interact will help make your animation look as if it is really one with the backplate.

To make this reflection convincing, you will want to be able to adjust its intensity and softness later during the composite process without affecting the reflections on the Jester and the toy truck. To do this, you will create a reflection pass for the tablecloth that is separate from the other scene elements.

The first reflection pass will capture the reflections in the Jester and toy truck. You will render it as a straightforward Render Element pass.

1. Open the file 13_Render Elements.max, click the Render Scene button, and open the Render Elements section. Click Add and choose Reflection. Make sure that the reflection element is enabled, and render the Camera 01 viewport.

2. Render a test. It should be a render that has the reflection attributes of the image separated from the rest and the other Render Element passes that you have already set up. Save the file (see **Figure 13.13**).

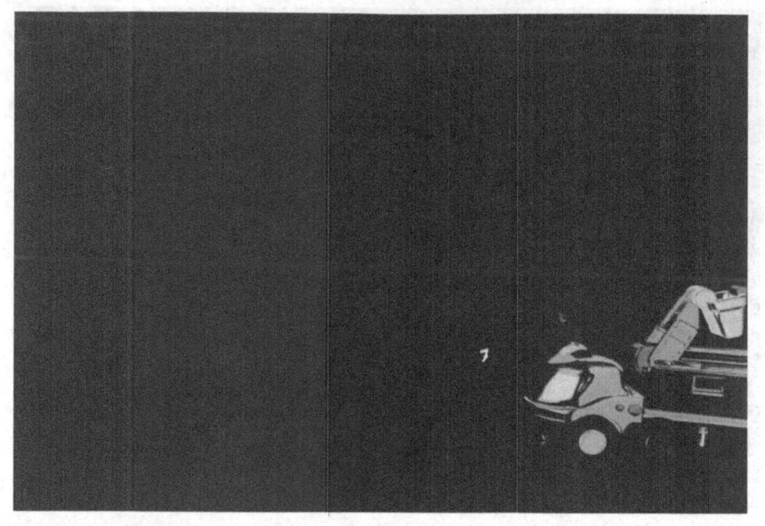

Figure 13.13 This is the Render Element reflection pass.

You will have to create a separate file that will contain the reflection on the tablecloth to create a reflection pass with the tablecloth only.

3. Open the Material Editor and create a new material called **Table Reflection**. Assign the material to the cm_table object.

4. Set the opacity and specular levels to **0**.

   You don't need to see the diffuse element of the object—just the reflections that it picks up.

5. Go to the Maps section of the Material Editor and click the Map button for reflection. Choose Raytrace from the Material/Map Browser. Open the Attenuation section (see **Figure 13.14**).

   Next you will set parameters that will cause the reflection to fade to 0 based on the distance of the geometry from the reflective surface.

6. Set the Fall-off Type to Exponential, and set the ranges to start at 0 and end at 6, with the exponent set to 3.

   The Exponential Fall-off Type will cause a greater reduction in reflectivity for geometry that approaches the extent of the ranges. This simulates the effect of the reflection in the tablecloth in which you see only the parts of the objects that are in contact with or very close to the surface of the tablecloth.

7. Assign the material to the cm_table object.

   In the second reflection pass, you will capture the reflections in the tablecloth. This will enable you to match the subtle effect of the reflections in the tablecloth in the video backplate.

8. Hide the toy truck.

   The truck sits on top of a napkin in the backplate, so it will not show up in the reflections on the tablecloth.

9. Select the Jester and bring up Properties. In the Rendering Control group, uncheck the Visible to Camera property.

   This causes only the reflection of the jester to appear in the rendering.

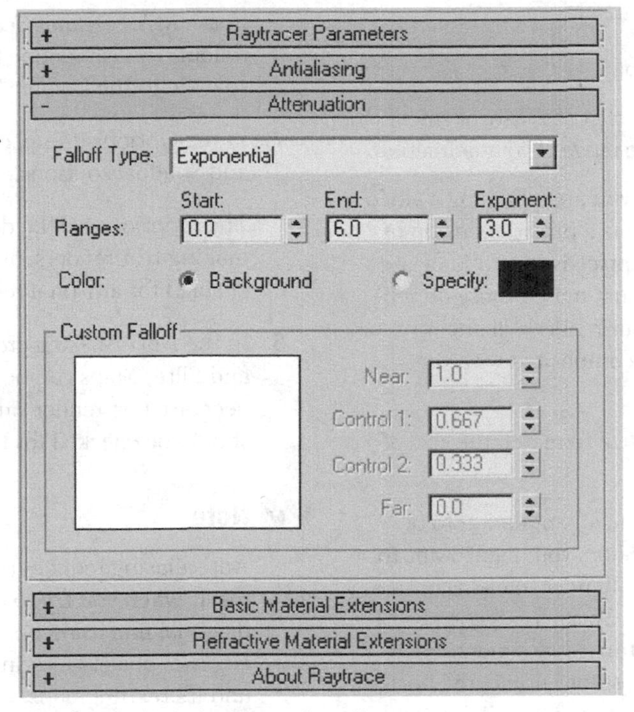

Figure 13.14 This is the Attenuation rollout.

10. Open the Render Scene dialog box and go to the Render Elements section. Disable all but the Reflection Render Element.
11. Under the Selected Element parameters, click Files and set the output name to **tableclothref_.tga.** Close the Render Scene dialog box and save the file as **tableclothref.max.**

In this exercise you created two separate passes for the reflections in the scene to have control over individual parts of the scene's reflections. Now you're ready to render the output.

Exercise 13.4 Rendering Output

To set up the final renders for the project, you need to know several pieces of information:

- What frame range do you need to render?
- What is the format to which you are rendering?
- What type of files do you need to render?
- Does a special naming convention need to be followed?
- Are you rendering with fields?
- Will motion blur be applied to objects in the scene?

When you know the answers to these questions, you can set up the render.

1. To set up your render, open the Render Scene dialog box.

   The first rollout, Common Parameters, is broken into four categories:

   - Time Output
   - Output Size

- Options
- Render Output

2. In Time Output, choose Active Segment to render the entire range of your animation.

   In Output Size, you are matching a video backplate that has a pixel dimension of 720×480 and a pixel aspect ratio of 0.900000. You must match those dimensions so that your render will line up correctly when composited with the backplate.

3. Set the output size to match the size of the backplate.

   If you are creating an animation to be viewed on television, you might want to render using the Render to Fields option, found under the Options category. NTSC television monitors display video by breaking an image into numbered horizontal lines called scan lines. Each field represents one 60th of a second. The two fields are put together in one frame in a process called *interlacing*.

4. For passes that use Render Elements, open the Render Elements rollout.
   All the elements that you created are displayed.

5. Make sure that all the Render Elements are enabled. Then check the Enable box for the Output to Combustion option.

   The Output to Combustion option creates a combustion file that contains all the enabled Render Elements, precomposited and ready for tweaking.

6. Click the Files button to enter the output path for the combustion file xox.

   In the MAX Default Scanline A-Buffer rollout, you can define the parameters specific to the Default Max renderer.

7. In the Options group, check the Mapping and Shadows options.

   These options can be disabled when making test renders, but they should be enabled for any final renders.

8. In the Anti-Aliasing group, Anti-Aliasing and Filter Maps can be turned off to decrease test render times, but both should be checked for final rendering.

✔ Note

Anti-aliasing reduces the jagged edges result when you try to create a curved or diagonal line using pixels by blurring the edges of objects filtering scene geometry and its texture maps.

The Filter drop-down menu contains 12 different anti-aliasing methods that can be used. An in-depth description would require an entire chapter in itself. The different filters are representative of a wide range of filters setups published in past SIGGRAPH papers. The differences between the filters are often subtle and can be affected by such variables as map detail and differences in geometry. A good starting point is the Sharp quadratic filter, which is a very high-quality filter. The Blend filter enables you to combine the attributes of the sharp Quadratic filters with softening. Cook Variable and Catmull Rom also produce good results.

14

Color Correction

I cannot pretend to be impartial about the colors. I rejoice with the brilliant ones, and am genuinely sorry for the poor browns.

–Winston Churchill

Color Correction

No skill is as essential for a compositor as the ability to authoritatively and conclusively take control of color, such that foreground and background elements seem to inhabit the same world, shots from a sequence are consistent with one another, and their overall look matches the artistic direction of the project.

The compositor, after all, is typically the last one to touch a shot before it goes into the edit. Inspired, artistic color work injects life, clarity, and drama into standard (or even substandard) 3D output, adequately (or even poorly) shot footage, and flat, monochromatic stills. It draws the audience's attention where it belongs, never causing them to think about the compositing at all.

Good compositors are credited with possessing a "good eye," but color matching is a skill that you can practice and refine even if you have no feel for adjusting images—indeed, even if you consider yourself color blind.

And despite that new color tools appear each year to refine your ability to dial in color, for color matching in After Effects, three color correction tools do most of the heavy lifting: Levels, Curves, and Hue/Saturation (and because Levels and Curves overlap in their functionality, in many cases you're just choosing one or two of the three). These endure (from the earliest days of Photoshop, even) because they are stable and fast, and they will get the job done every time—just learn how to use them, and keep practicing.

A skeptic might ask:

- Why these old tools with so many cool newer ones?
- Why not use Brightness & Contrast to adjust, you know, brightness and contrast, or Shadow and Highlight if that's what needs adjustment?
- What do you mean I can adjust Levels even if I'm color blind?

This chapter holds the answers to these and many more questions. First, we'll look at optimizing a given image using these tools, and then move into matching a foreground layer to the optimized background, balancing colors. The goal is to get you away from hacking away, to build skills that eliminate some of the guesswork and enable artistry.

This chapter introduces topics that resound throughout the rest of the book. Chapter 16, "32 Bit HDR Compositing and Color Management," deals specifically with HDR color, and then Chapter 17, "Light," focuses on specific light and color scenarios, while the rest of Section III describes how to create specific types of effects shots.

Optimized Levels

What constitutes an "optimized" clip? What makes a color corrected image correct? Let's look at what is typically "wrong" with source footage levels and the usual methods for correcting them, laying the groundwork for color matching. As an example, we'll balance brightness and contrast of a *plate* image, with no foreground layers to match.

✓ Note

The term *"plate"* stretches back to the earliest days of optical compositing (and indeed, of photography itself) and refers to the source footage, typically the background onto which foreground elements will be composited. A related term, "*clean plate*," refers to the background with any moving foreground elements removed; its usage is covered in the following chapter.

Levels

Levels may be the most-used tool in After Effects, and yet it's rare to find detailed descriptions of how best to use it. It consists of five basic controls—Input Black, Input White, Output Black, Output White, and Gamma—each of which can be adjusted in five separate contexts (the four individual image channels R, G, B, and A, as well as all three color channels, RGB, at once). There are two different ways to adjust these controls: via their numerical sliders or by dragging their respective carat sliders on the histogram. The latter is the more typical method for experienced users.

Contrast: Input and Output Levels

Four of the five controls—Input Black, Input White, Output Black and Output White (**Figure 14.1**)—determine brightness and contrast, and combined with the fifth, gamma, they offer more precision than is possible with the effect called Brightness & Contrast.

✓ **Note**

Two check boxes at the bottom of the Levels effect controls specify whether black and white levels "clip" on output. These are checked on by default, and until you work in HDR (Chapter 16), you might as well ignore their very existence; they handle values beyond the range that your monitor can display.

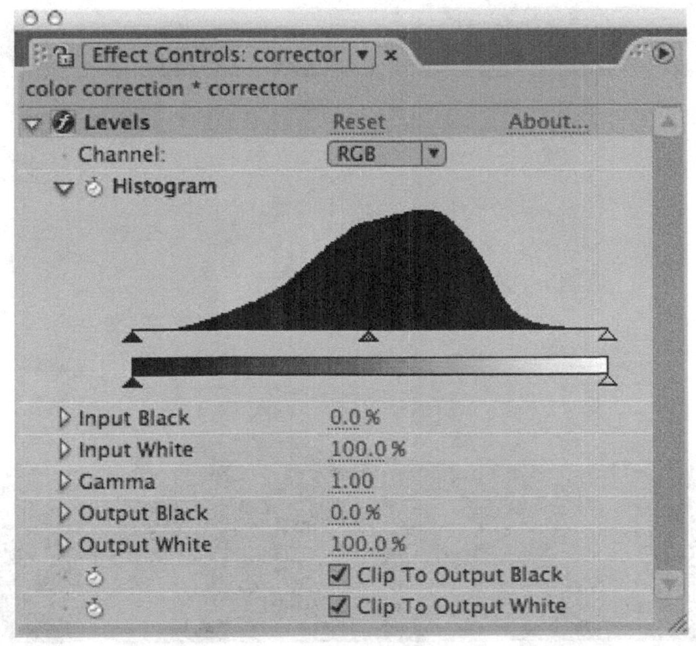

Figure 14.1 Possibly the most used "effect" in After Effects, Levels consists of a histogram and five basic controls per channel; the controls are typically adjusted using the triangles on the histogram, although the corresponding numerical/slider controls appear below.

Figures 14.2a and **b** show a Ramp effect applied to a solid using the default settings, followed by the Levels effect. Move the black caret at the lower left of the histogram—the Input Black level—to the right, and values below its threshold (the numerical Input Black setting, which changes as you move the caret) are pushed to black. The further you move the caret, the more values are "crushed" to pure black.

✓ Tip

- Compositing is science as well as art, and so this section employs a useful scientific tool: the control, which is a study subject that eliminates random or hidden variables. This control for the Levels effect is a grayscale gradient I generated with the Ramp effect. You can often set up similar experiments to clarify your understanding of computer graphics applications.

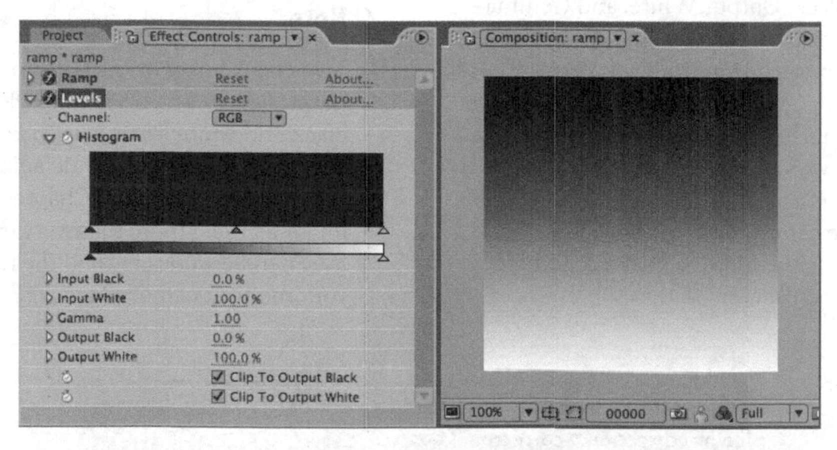

Figures 14.2a and b Levels is applied to a layer containing a Ramp effect at the default settings, which creates a smooth gradient from black to white (a); this will be the basis for understanding what the basic color correction tools do. You can create this for yourself or open 05_colorCorrection.aep, which also contains the image (b).

Move the Input White carat at the right end of the histogram to the left, toward the Input Black caret. The effect is similar to Input Black's but inverted: more and more white values are "blown out" to pure white (**Figure 14.3**).

✓ Close-Up

Why Not Brightness & Contrast? The Brightness & Contrast effect is like training wheels compared to Levels. It contains two sliders, one for each property. Raising the Contrast value above 0.0 causes the values above middle gray to move closer to white and those below the midpoint to move closer to black, in proportion. Lower it and pixels turn gray. The Brightness control offsets the midpoint of any contrast adjustment, allowing a result like that in Figure 14.4.

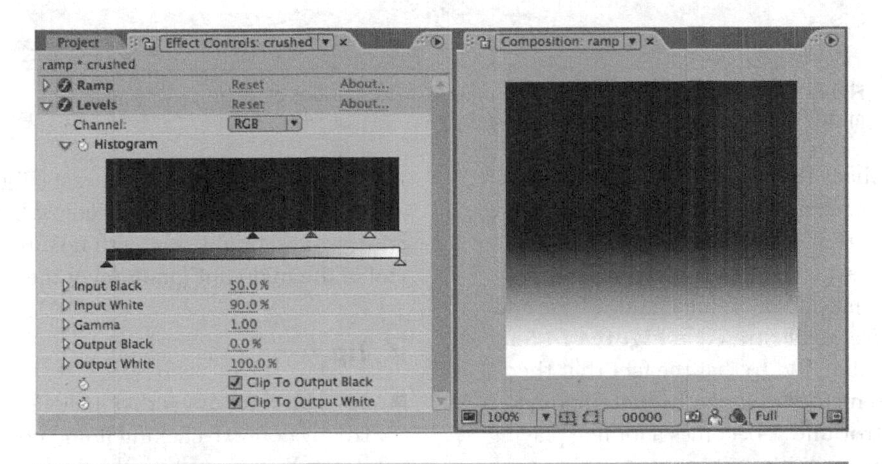

Figure 14.3 Raising Input Black and lowering Input White has the effect of increasing contrast at either end of the scale; at an extreme adjustment like this, many pixels are pushed to full white or black (in an 8-bpc or 16-bpc project).

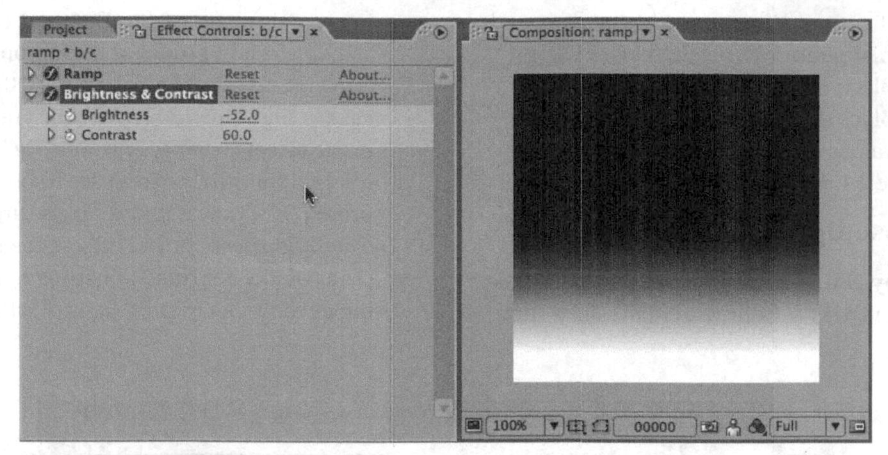

Figure 14.4 You can use Brightness & Contrast to match the look of Figure 14.3's gradient, mostly because it has no gamma adjustment.

So what's the problem? Almost any image needs black and white adjusted to a different degree, and Brightness & Contrast allows this only indirectly; this can make adjustment a game of cat and mouse, as illustrated in **Figures 14.5a, b,** and **c**. Add to that the fact that there is no histogram or individual Channel control, and it becomes a lot like playing the piano with mittens on.

Either adjustment effectively increases contrast, but note that the midpoint of the gradient also changes if one is adjusted further than the other. In Figure 14.3 Input Black has been adjusted more heavily than Input White, causing the horizon of the gradient to move closer to white and more of the image to turn black. You can re-create this adjustment with Brightness & Contrast (**Figure 14.4**), but to do so you must adjust both contrast and brightness, with no direct control of the midpoint (gamma) of the image.

✓ Tip

- You can reset any individual effect control by context-clicking it and choosing Reset. You know it's individual if it has its own stopwatch.

Reset Levels (click Reset at the top of the Levels effect controls) and try the same experiment with Output Black and Output White, whose controls sit below the little gradient. Output Black specifies the darkest black that can appear in the image; adjust it upwards and the minimum value is raised.

Figures 14.5a, b, and c The source (a) was balanced for the sky, leaving foreground detail too dark to make out. Raising Brightness to bring detail out of the shadows makes the entire image washed out (b); raising Contrast to compensate completely blows out the sky (c). Madness.

Similarly, lowering Input White is something like dimming the image, cutting off the maximum possible white value at the given threshold. Adjust both and you effectively reduce contrast in the image; with them close together, the gradient becomes a solid gray (**Figure 14.6**).

✓ Notes

Note that you can even cross the two carets; if you drag Output White all the way down, and Output Black all the way up, you have inverted your image (although the more straightforward way to do this typically is to use the Channel: Invert effect).

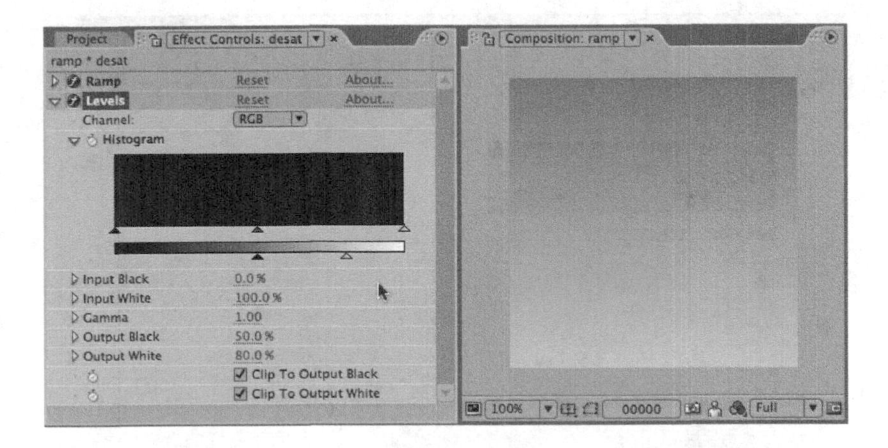

Figure 14.6 Raising Output Black and lowering Output White reduces contrast in the dark and light areas of the image, respectively; they will come into play in the Matching section.

Evidently the Input and Output controls have the opposite effect on their respective black and white values, when examined in this straightforward fashion. However, there are even situations where you would use them together.

As is the case throughout After Effects, the controls are operating in the order listed in the interface. In other words, raising the Input Black level first crushes the blacks, and then a higher Output Black level raises all of those pure black levels as one (**Figure 14.7**). It does not restore the black detail in the original pixels; the blacks remain crushed, they all just become lighter.

If you're thinking, "So what?" at this point, just stay with this—the controls are being broken down to build up an understanding.

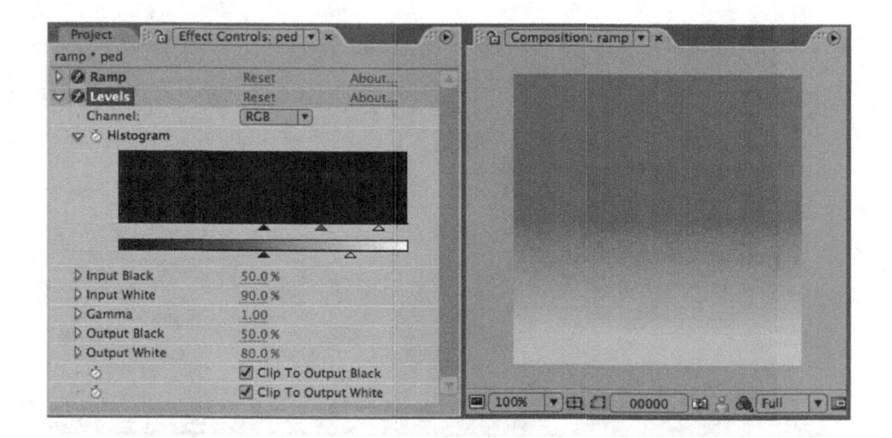

Figure 14.7 Black and white levels crushed by adjusting the Input controls aren't then brought back by the Output controls, which instead simply limit the overall dynamic range of the image, raising the darkest possible black level and lowering the brightest possible white.

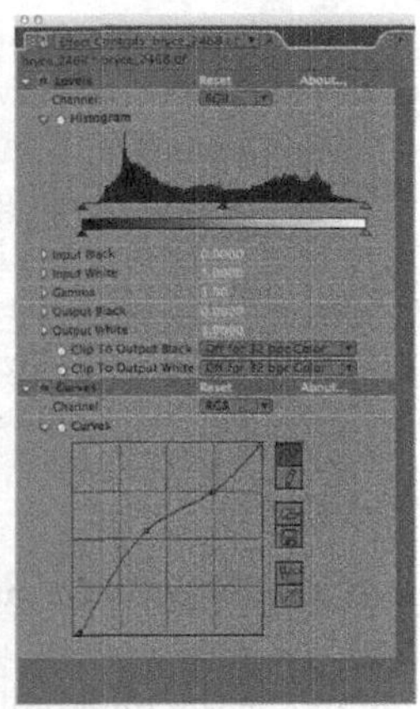

Figure 14.8 The image from Figure 5.2 is improved with a boost to gamma using Curves (explained ahead); the indication that this is a good idea comes not from the histogram, which looks fine, but from the image itself, which lacks foreground detail.

Brightness: Gamma

As you adjust the Input Black and White values, you may have noticed the third caret that maintains its place between them. This is the Gamma control, affecting midtones (the middle gray point in the gradient) at the highest proportion and black and white, not at all. Adjust it over the gradient and notice that you can push the grays in the image brighter (by moving it to the left) or darker (to the right) without changing the black and white levels.

Many images have healthy contrast, but a gamma boost gives them extra punch. Similarly, an image that looks a bit too "hot" may be instantly adjusted simply by lowering gamma. As you progress through the book, you will see that it plays a crucial role not only in color adjustment but also in the inner workings of the image pipeline itself (more on that in Chapter 16).

In most cases, the histogram won't itself offer much of a clue as to whether the gamma needs adjusting, or by how much (see "Problem Solving using the Histogram," for more on the topic). The image itself provides a better guide for how to adjust gamma (**Figure 14.8**).

So what is your guideline for how much you should adjust gamma, if at all? I first learned to adjust too far before dialing back, which is especially helpful when learning. An even more powerful gamma adjustment tool that scares most novice artists away is Curves (more on this later).

By mixing these five controls together, have we covered everything there is to know about using Levels? No—because there are not, in fact, five basic controls in Levels (Input and Output White and Black plus Gamma), but instead, five times five (RGB, Red, Green, Blue, and Alpha).

Individual Channels for Color Matching

In baseball, most hitters are "hackers," unable to discern when to swing at a pitch in the fraction of a second when it approaches the plate. A very few gifted hitters, even at the professional level, can actually discern a pitch as it approaches the plate at 90+ miles per hour; Barry Bonds is the ultimate example, and I say that not only as a beleaguered Giants fan. If you color correct images without looking at individual color channels, you're only hacking, but if you develop the habit of adjusting on individual color channels, you'll swing like Barry (with or without the stimulants).

✓ Close-Up

Geek Alert: What Is Gamma, Anyway? It would be so nice simply to say, "gamma is the midpoint of your color range" and leave it at that. The more accurate the discussion of gamma becomes, the more obscure and mathematical it gets. There are plenty of artists out there who understand gamma intuitively and are able to work with it without knowing the math behind it or the way the eye sees color midtones, but here's the basic math, just in case.

Gamma adjustment shifts the midpoint of a color range without affecting the black or white points. This is done by taking a pixel value and raising it to the inverse power of the gamma value, like so:

$$\text{newPixel} = \text{pixel}^{(1/\text{gamma})}$$

You're probably used to thinking of pixel values as being 0 to 255, but this formula works only if they are *normalized* to 1. In other words, all 255 values occur between 0 and 1, so 0 is 0, 255 is 1, and 128 is .5—which is the "normal" way the math is done behind the scenes.

Why does it work this way? Because of the magic of logarithms: Any number to the power of 0 is 1, any number to the power of 1 is itself, and any fractional value (less than 1) raised to a higher power approaches 0 without ever reaching it. Lower the power closer to 0 and the value approaches 1, again without ever reaching it. Not only that, but the values distribute proportionally, along a curve, so the closer an initial value is to pure black (0) or pure white (1) the less it is affected.

To try this for yourself, all you need is After Effects and a Web browser. Create a 255×255 comp and switch the Info panel to Decimal values (in the panel menu). Enter a Gamma value of .25, divide that value into 1 (result is 4) and at www.google.com search on .5^4, then check to see if the result matches the value you see by placing your cursor over the center of frame. Now try a gamma value of 2.0; divide it into 1 and you get .5, go to Google and try searching on .5^.5. The values will line up.

Many After Effects artists completely ignore that pull-down menu at the top of the Levels control that isolates red, green, blue, and alpha adjustments, and even those who do use it once in a while may do so with trepidation; how can you predictably understand what will happen when you adjust the five basic Levels controls on an individual channel? The gradient again serves as an effective learning tool to ponder what exactly is going on.

Reset the Levels effect applied to the Ramp gradient once more. Pick Red, Green, or Blue in the Channel pull-down of Levels and adjust the Input and Output carets. Color is introduced into what was a purely grayscale image. With the Red channel selected, by moving Red Output Black inward, you tint the darker areas of the image red. If you adjust Input White inward, the midtones and highlights turn pink (light red). If, instead, you adjust Input Black or Output White inward, the tinting goes in the opposite direction—toward cyan, in the corresponding shadows and highlights. As you probably know, on the digital wheel of color, cyan is the opposite of red, just as magenta is the opposite of green and yellow is the opposite of blue (a sample digital color wheel and a visual guide to how levels adjustments operate on individual channels are included on the book's disc).

Gradients are one thing, but the best way to make sense of this with a real image is to develop the habit of studying footage on individual color channels as you work. This is the key to effective color matching, detailed ahead.

Along the bottom of the Composition panel, all of the icons are monochrome by default save one: the Show Channel pulldown. It contains five selections: the three color channels as well as two alpha modes. Each one has a shortcut that, unfortunately, is not shown in the menu: **Alt+1** through **Alt+4** (**Option+1** through **Option+4**) reveal each color channel in order. These shortcuts are toggles, so reselecting the active channel toggles RGB. A colored outline around the edge of the composition palette reminds you which channel is displayed (**Figure 14.10**).

✓ Close-Up

Same Difference: Levels (Individual Controls) Both Levels and Levels (Individual Controls) accomplish the exact same task. The sole difference is that Levels lumps all adjustments into a single keyframe property, which expressions cannot use. Levels (Individual Controls) is particularly useful to

- Animate and time Levels settings individually
- Link an expression to a Levels setting
- Reset a single Levels property (instead of the entire effect)

Levels is more commonly used, but Levels (Individual Controls) is sometimes more useful.

Try adjusting a single channel of the gradient in Levels while displaying only that channel. You are back on familiar territory, adjusting brightness and contrast of a grayscale image. This is the way to work with individual channel adjustments, especially when beginning or if at all color blind. As you work with actual images instead of gradients, the histogram can show you what is happening in your image.

The Levels Histogram

You might have noticed the odd appearance of the histogram applying Levels to a default Ramp. If you were to try this setup on your own, depending on the size of the layer to which you applied Ramp, you might see a histogram that is flat along the top with spikes protruding at regular intervals (**Figures 14.9a** and **b**).

✓ Tip

- An often overlooked feature of Levels is that it allows direct adjustment of brightness, contrast, and gamma of the grayscale transparency channel (Alpha Channel).

The histogram is exactly 256 pixels wide; it is effectively a bar chart made up of 256 single pixel bars, each corresponding to one of the 256 possible levels of luminance in an 8-bpc image (these levels are displayed below the histogram, above the Output controls). In the case of a pure gradient, the histogram is flat because luminance is evenly distributed from black to white; if spikes occur in that case, it's because the image is not exactly 255 pixels high (or some exact multiple of 256, minus one edge pixel because the Ramp controls default to the edges of the layer), making it slightly uneven at 8 bits per channel.

✓ Tip

- Moving Input White and Input Black to the edges of the histogram is similar to

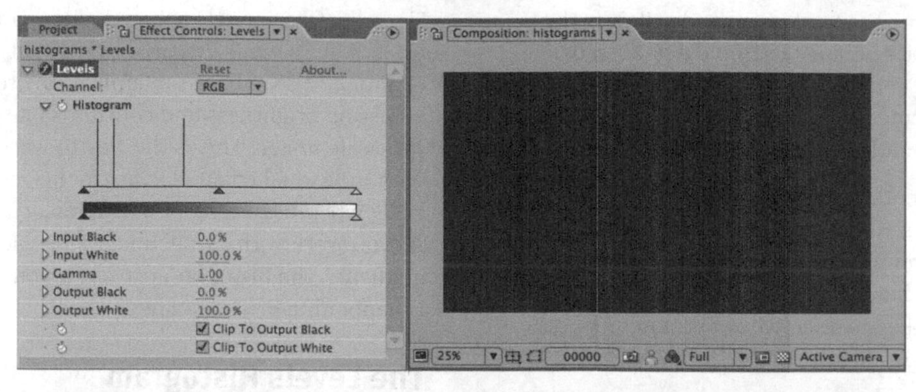

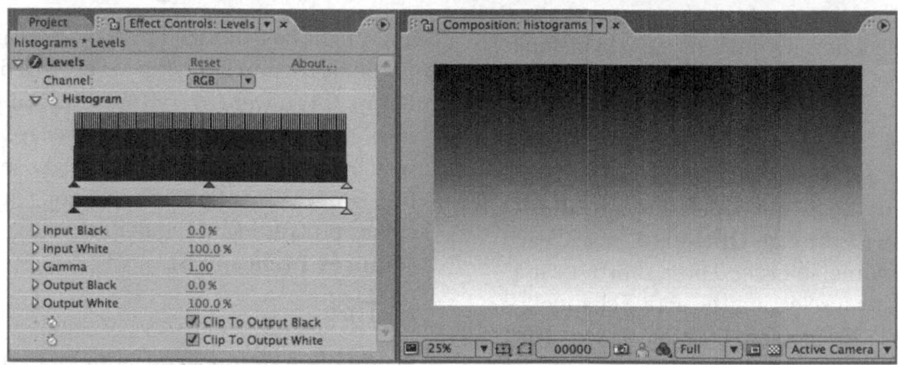

Figures 14.9a and b Strange-looking histograms. A colored solid (a) shows three spikes, one each for the red, green, and blue values, and nothing else. With Ramp (b) the distribution is even, but the spikes at the top are the result of the ramp not being an exact multiple of 255 pixels, causing certain pixels to recur more often than others.

what the Auto Levels effect does. If that by itself isn't enough to convince you to avoid using Auto Levels, or the "Auto" correctors, consider also that they are processor intensive (slow) and resample on every frame (so the result is not consistent from frame to frame, which isn't generally what you want).

In any case, it's more useful to look at real-world examples, because the histogram is useful for mapping image data that isn't plainly evident on its own. Its basic function is to help you assess whether any color changes are liable to help or harm the image. There is in fact no one typical or ideal histogram—they can vary as much as the images themselves, as seen back in Figure 14.8.

Despite that fact, there's a simple rule of thumb for a basic contrast adjustment. Find the top and bottom end of the RGB histogram—the highest and lowest points where there is any data whatsoever—and bracket them with the Input Black and Input White carets. To "bracket" them means to adjust these controls inward so each sits just outside its corresponding end of the histogram (**Figure 14.10**).The result stretches values closer to the top or bottom of the dynamic range, as you can easily see by applying a second Levels effect and studying its histogram (**Figure 14.11**).

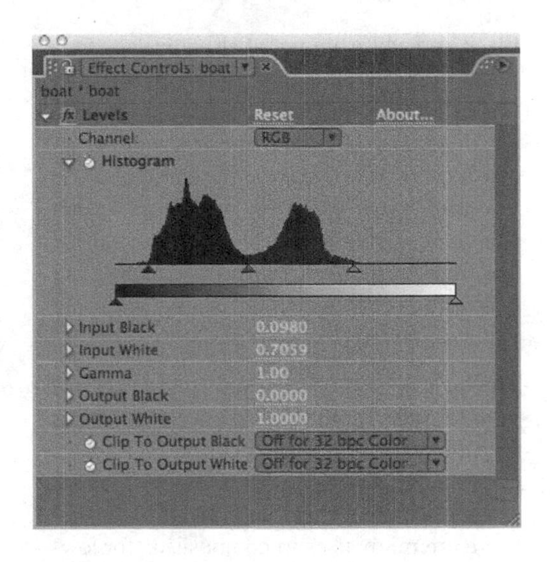

Figure 14.10 Here is a perfect case for bringing the triangle controls corresponding to Input Black and Input White in to bracket the edges of the histogram, increasing contrast and bringing out vibrant colors without losing detail.

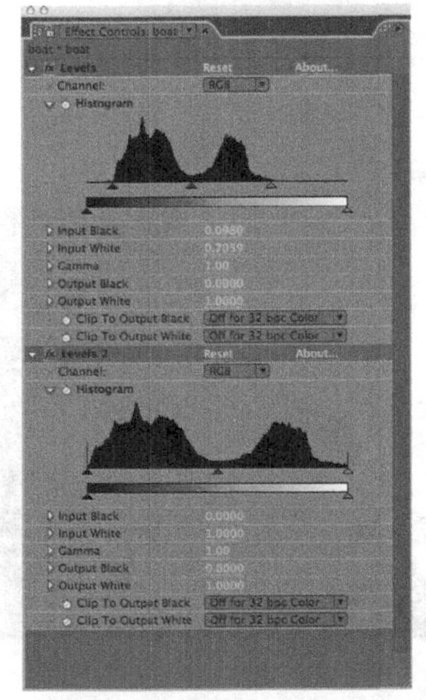

Figure 14.11 Adding a second Levels effect to this image's histogram only reveals the result of the prior adjustment; levels now extend to each end of the contrast spectrum.

✓ Tip

- Footage is by its very nature dynamic, so it is a good idea to leave headroom for the whites and foot room for the blacks until you start working in 32 bits per channel. Headroom is particularly important when anything exceptionally bright—such as a sun glint, flare, or fire—enters frame.

Try applying Levels to any image or footage from the disc and see for yourself how this works. First crush the blacks (by moving Input Black well above the lowest black level in the histogram) and then blow out the whites (moving Input White below the highest white value). Don't go too far, or subsequent adjustments will not bring back that detail—unless you work in 32-bpc HDR mode (Chapter 16). Occasionally a stylized look will call for crushed contrast, but generally speaking, this is bad form.

Black and white are not at all equivalent, in terms of how your eye sees them. Blown-out whites are ugly and can be a dead giveaway of an overexposed digital scene, but your eye is much more sensitive to subtle gradations of low black levels. These low, rich blacks account for much of what makes film look like film, and they can contain a surprising amount of detail, none of which, unfortunately, would be apparent on the printed page.

The occasions on which you would optimize your footage, making it look best, by raising Output Black or lowering Output White controls are unusual, as this lowers dynamic range and the overall contrast. However, there are many uses in compositing for lowered contrast, to soften overlay effects (say, fog and clouds), high-contrast mattes, and so on. More on that later in this chapter and throughout the rest of the book.

Problem Solving using the Histogram

As you've no doubt noticed, the Levels histogram does not update as you make adjustments. After Effects lacks a panel equivalent to Photoshop's Histogram palette, but you can, of course, apply a Levels effect just for the histogram, if only for the purposes of learning (as was done in Figure 14.11).

✓ Notes

> Many current displays, and in particular flat-panels and projectors, lack the black detail that can be produced on a good CRT monitor or captured on film. The next time you see a projected film, notice how much detail you can see in the shadows and compare.

The histogram reveals a couple of new wrinkles in the backlit shot from Figure 14.5, now adjusted with Levels to bring out foreground highlights (**Figures 14.12a** and **b**). At the top end of the histogram the levels

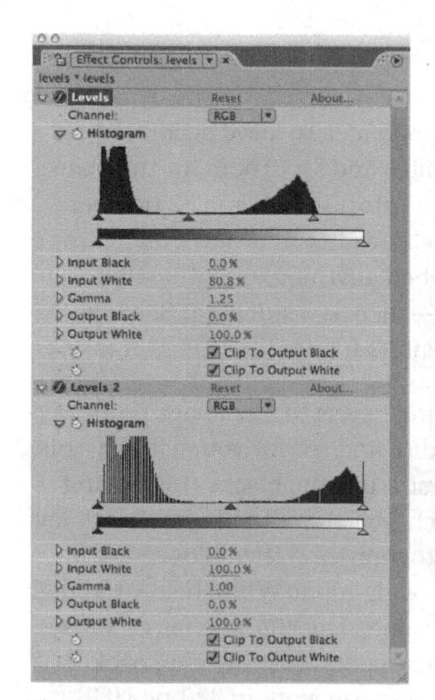

Figures 5.12a and b In the first instance of Levels (a), Gamma is raised and the Input White brought in to enhance detail in the dark areas of the foreground (b). The second instance is applied only to show its histogram.

peak into a spike. This may indicate clipping and a loss of image detail.

At the other end of the scale is the common result of a Gamma adjustment: a series of spikes rising out of the lower values like protruding hash marks, even though a 16-bpc project prevents quantization. Raising Gamma stretches the levels below the midpoint, causing them to clump up at regular intervals. As with crushing blacks and blowing out highlights—the net effect is a loss of detail, although in this case, the spikes are not a worry because they occur among a healthy amount of surrounding data. In more extreme cases, in which there is no data in between the spikes whatsoever, you may see a prime symptom of overadjustment, *banding* (**Figure 14.13**).

Figure 14.13 Push an adjustment far enough and you may see quantization, otherwise known as banding in the image. Those big gaps in the histogram are expressed as visible bands on a gradient. Switching to 16 bpc from 8 bpc is an instant fix for this problem in most cases.

Banding is typically the result of limitations of 8-bit color, and 16-bit color mode was added to After Effects 5.0 specifically to address that problem. You can switch to 16 bpc by Alt-clicking (Option-clicking) on the bit-depth identifier along the bottom of the Project panel (**Figure 14.14**) or by changing it in File > Project Settings. Chapter 16 explains more.

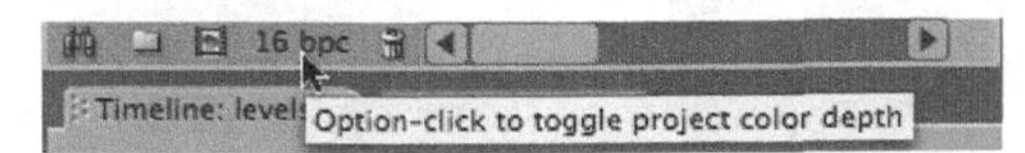

Figure 14.14 An entire project can be toggled from the default 8-bit color mode to 16-bit mode by Alt-clicking (Option-clicking) the project color depth toggle in the Project panel; this prevents the banding seen in Figure 14.13.

Perfecting Brightness with Curves

Curves rocks. I heart curves. The Curves control is particularly useful for gamma correction, because

- Curves lets you fully (and visually) control how adjustments are weighted and roll off.
- You can introduce multiple gamma adjustments to a single image or restrict the gamma adjustment to just one part of the image's dynamic range.
- Some adjustments can be nailed with a single well-placed point in Curves, in cases where the equivalent adjustment with Levels might require that you coordinate three separate controls.

It's also worth understanding Curves controls because they are a common shorthand for how digital color adjustments are depicted; the Curves interface recurs not only in all of the other effects compositing packages but also in more sophisticated tools within After Effects, such as Color Finesse (discussed briefly later in this chapter).

Curves does, however, have drawbacks, compared with Levels:

- It's not immediately intuitive, it can easily yield hideous results if you don't know what you're doing, and there are plenty of artists who aren't comfortable with it.
- Unlike Photoshop, After Effects doesn't offer numerical values corresponding to curve points, making it a purely visual control that can be hard to standardize.
- Without a histogram, you may miss obvious clues about the image (making Levels more suitable for learners).

The most daunting thing about Curves is clearly its interface, a simple grid with a diagonal line extending from lower left to upper right. There is a Channel selector at the top, set by default to RGB as in Levels, and there are some optional extra controls on the right to help you draw, save, and retrieve custom curves. To the novice, the arbitrary map is an unintuitive abstraction that you can easily use to make a complete mess of your image. Once you understand it, however, you can see it as an elegantly simple description of how image adjustment works. You'll find the equivalent Curves graph to the Levels corrections on the book's disc.

Figure 14.15 shows the more fully featured Photoshop Curves, which illustrates a little better how the controls work.

Figures 14.16a through **d** show some basic Curves adjustments and their effect on an image. **Figures 14.17a** through **f** use linear gradients to illustrate what some common Curves settings do. I encourage you to try these on your own.

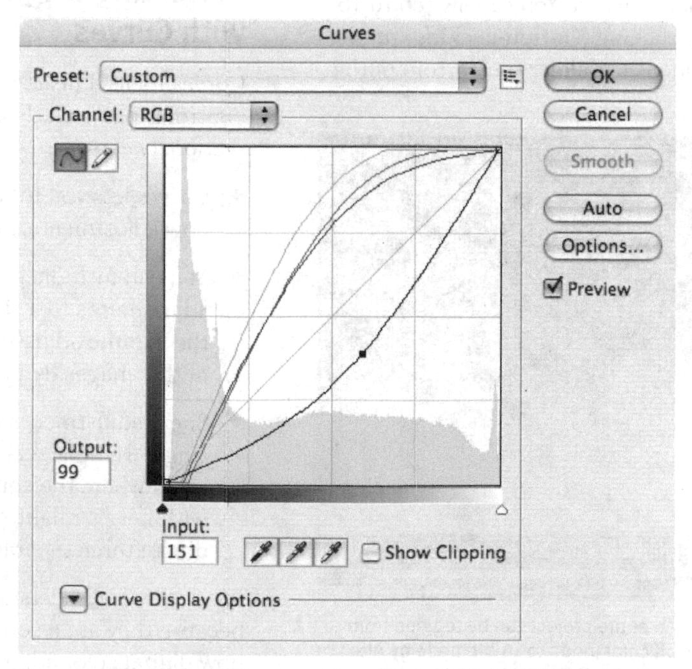

Figures 14.15 Photoshop's more deluxe Curves includes a histogram, built-in presets, displays of all channels together, and fields for input and output values for a given point on the curve.

Figure 14.16a The source image.

Figure 14.16b An increase in gamma above the shadows.

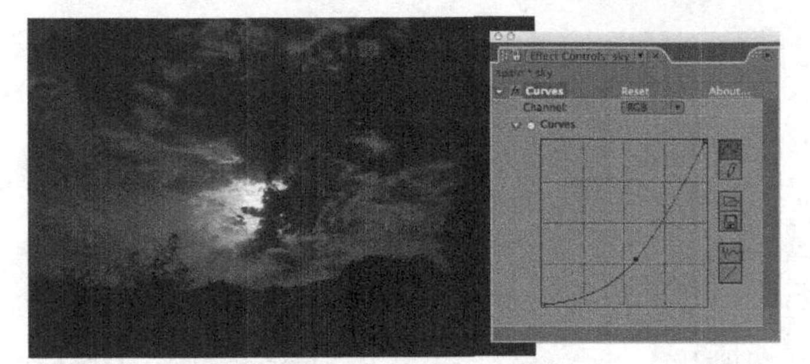

Figure 14.16c A decrease in gamma.

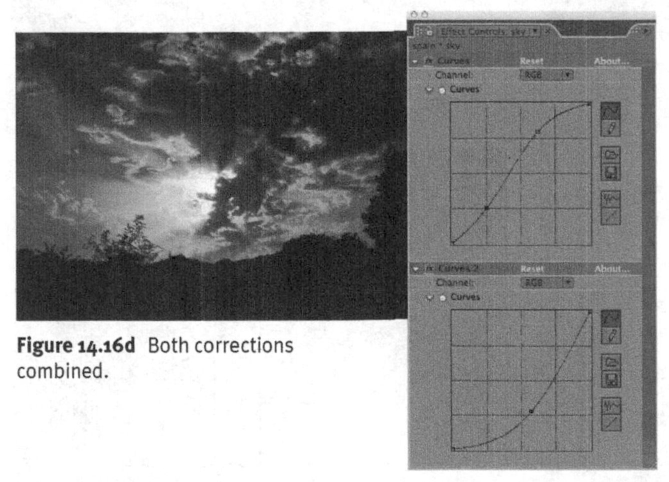

Figure 14.16d Both corrections combined.

Figures 14.16a through d What you see in an image can be heavily influenced by gamma and contrast.

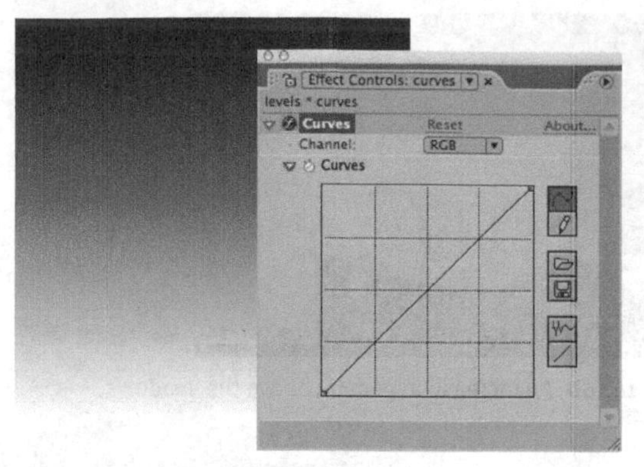

Figure 14.17a The default gradient and Curves setting.

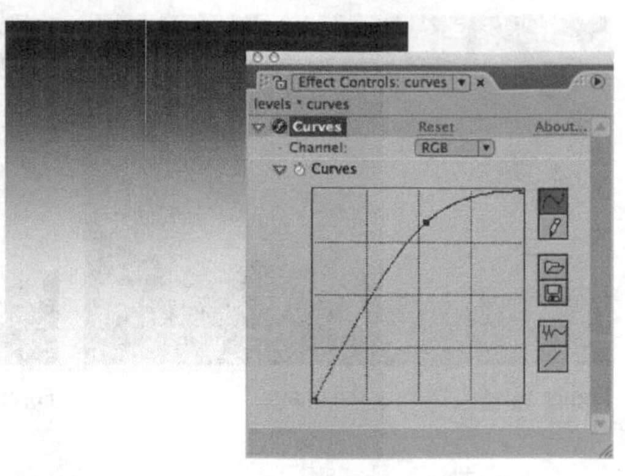

Figure 14.17b An increase in gamma.

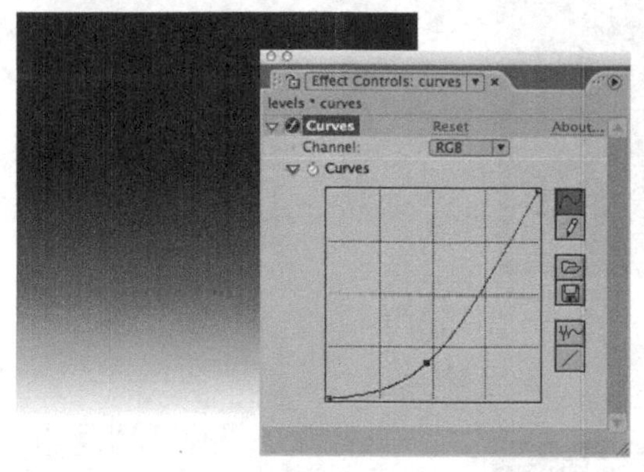

Figure 14.17c A decrease in gamma.

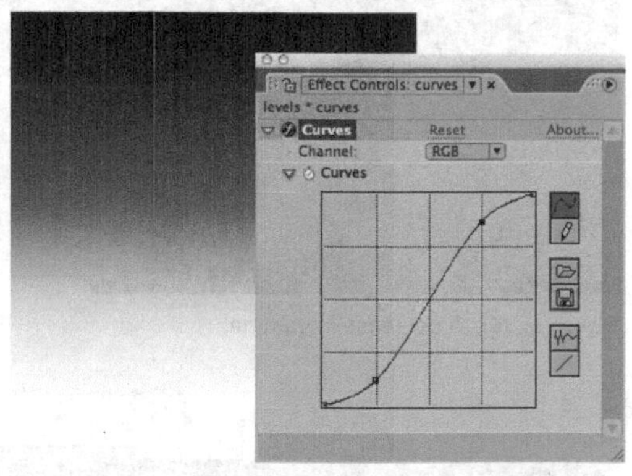

Figure 14.17d An increase in brightness and contrast.

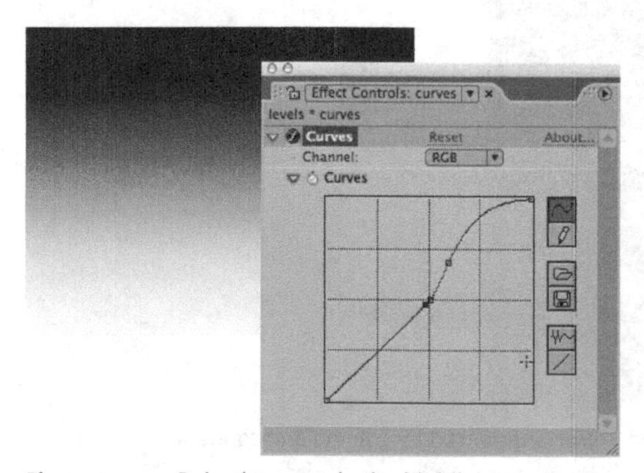

Figure 14.17e Raised gamma in the highlights only.

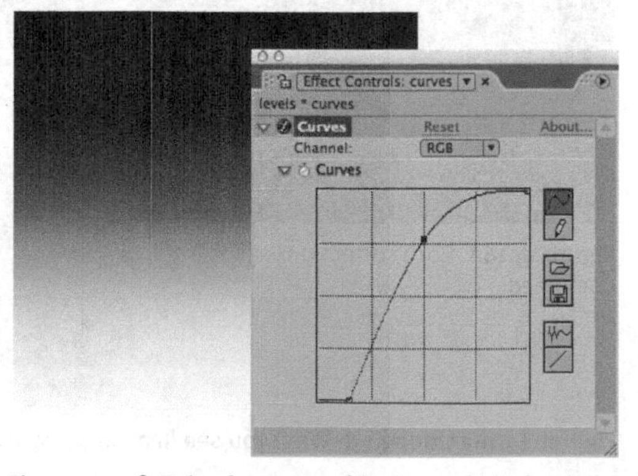

Figure 14.17f Raised gamma with clamped black values.

Figures 14.17a through f This array of Curves adjustments applied to a gradient shows the results of some typical settings.

More interesting are the types of adjustments that only Curves allows you to do—or at least do easily. I came to realize that most of the adjustments I make with Curves fall into a few distinct types that I use over and over, and so those are summarized here.

The most common adjustment is to simply raise or lower the gamma with Curves, by adding a point at the middle of the RGB curve and then moving it upward or downward. **Figure 14.18** shows the result of each. This produces a subtly different result from raising or lowering the Gamma control in Levels because of how you control the roll-off (**Figure 14.19**).

Figure 14.16b weights the gamma adjustment to the high end by adding a point to hold the shadows in place. The classic S-curve adjustment, which enhances brightness and contrast and introduces roll-offs into the highlights and shadows (**Figure 14.20**) is an alternative method to get the result of the double curves in Figure 14.16d.

Some images need a gamma adjustment only to one end of the range—for example, a boost to the darker pixels, below the midpoint, that doesn't alter the black point and doesn't brighten the white values. Such an adjustment requires three points (**Figure 14.21**):

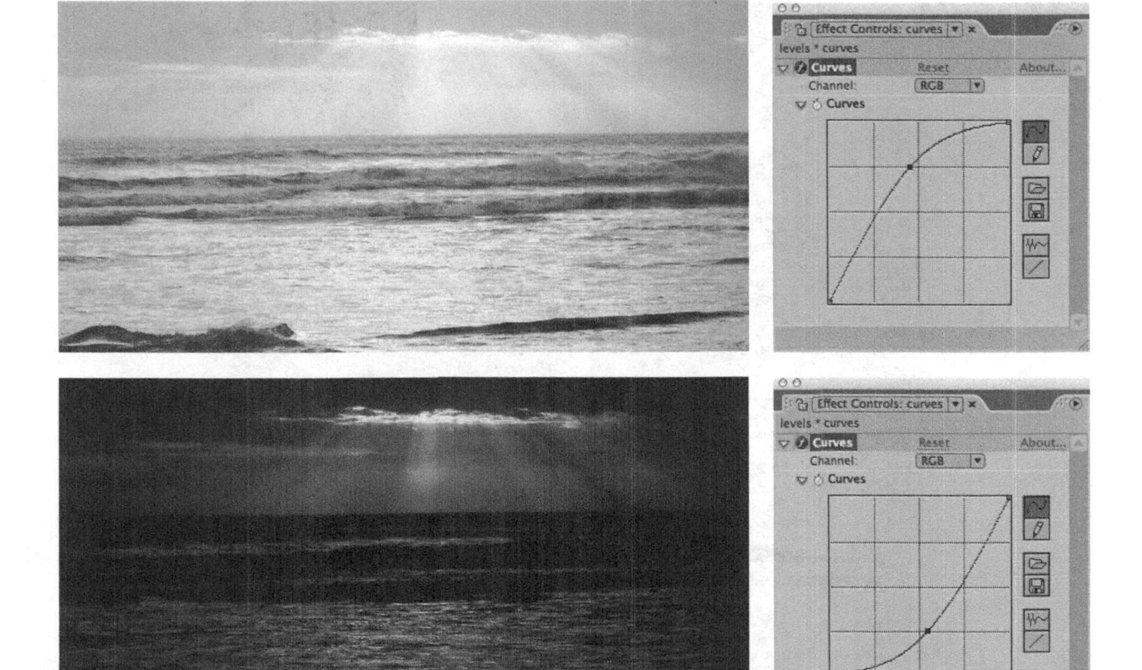

Figure 14.18 Two equally valid gamma adjustments employ a single point adjustment in the Curves control. Dramatically lit footage particularly benefits from the roll-off possible in the highlights and shadows.

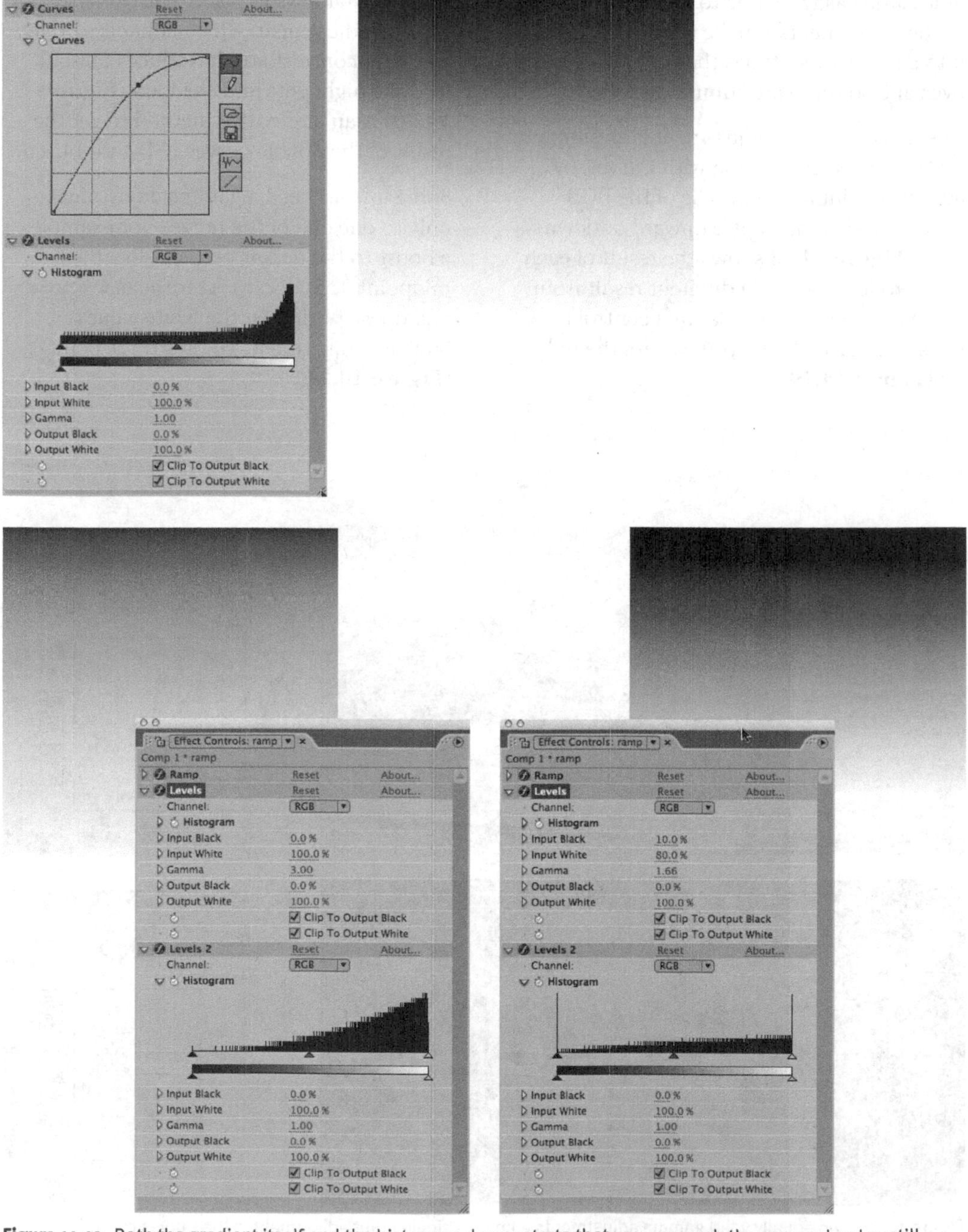

Figure 14.19 Both the gradient itself and the histogram demonstrate that you can push the gamma harder, still preserving the full range of contrast, with Curves rather than with Levels, where you face a choice between losing highlights and shadows somewhat or crushing them.

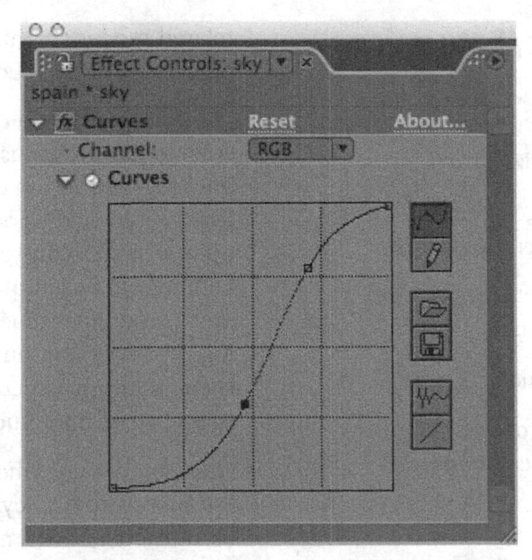

Figure 14.20 The classic S-curve adjustment: The midpoint remains the same, but contrast is boosted.

Figure 14.21 The ultimate solution to the backlighting problem presented back in Figure 14.5: Adding a mini-boost to the darker levels while leaving the lighter levels flat preserves the detail in the sky and brings out detail in the foreground that was previously missing.

- One to hold the midpoint
- One to boost the low values
- One to flatten the curve above the midpoint

A typical method for working in Curves is to begin with a single point adjustment to adjust gamma or contrast, then modulate it with one or two added points. More points quickly become unmanageable, as each adjustment changes the weighting of the surrounding points. Typically, I will add a single point, then a second one to restrict its range, and a third as needed to bring the shape of one section back where I want it. The images used for the figures in this section are included as single stills on the book's disc for your own experimentation; open 05_colorCorrection.aep to find them.

Just for Color: Hue/Saturation

The third of three essential color correction tools in After Effects is Hue/Saturation. This one has many individualized uses:

- Desaturating an image or adding saturation (the tool's most common use)
- Colorizing images that were created as grayscale or monochrome
- Shifting the overall hue of an image
- De-emphasizing, or knocking out completely, an individual color channel

✓ Notes

Chapter 17 details why Tint, not Hue/Saturation, is the right tool to convert an entire image to grayscale.

The Hue/Saturation control allows you to do something you can't do with Levels or Curves, which is to directly control the hue, saturation, and brightness of an image. The HSB color model is merely an alternate slice of RGB color data. All real color pickers, including the Apple and Adobe pickers, handle RGB and HSB as two separate but interrelated modes that use three values to describe any given color.

In other words, you could arrive at the same color adjustments using Levels and Curves, but Hue/Saturation gives you direct access to a couple of key color attributes that are otherwise difficult to get at. To desaturate an image is essentially to bring the red, green, and blue values closer together, reducing the relative intensity of the strongest of them; a saturation control lets you do this in one step, without guessing.

Often is the case where colors are balanced but merely too "juicy," and lowering the Saturation value somewhere between 5 and 20 can be a direct and effective way to make an image adjustment come together (**Figure 14.22**). It's essential to understand the delivery medium as well, because film is more tolerant and friendly to saturated images than television.

The other quick fix that Hue/Saturation affords you is a shift to the hue of the overall image or of one or more of its individual channels. The Channel Control menu for Hue/Saturation includes not only the red,

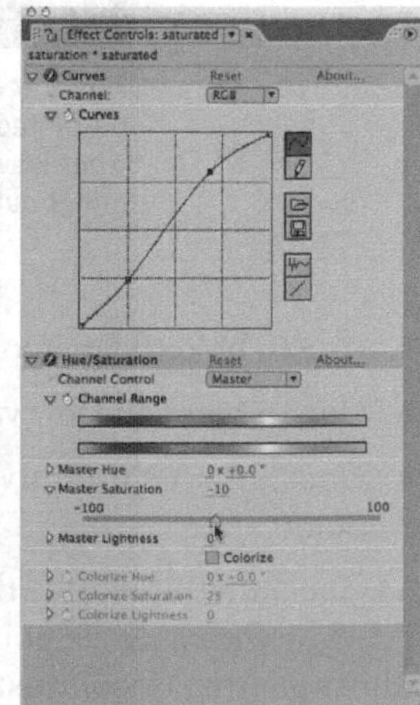

Figure 14.22 For footage already saturated with color, even a subtle boost to gamma or contrast can send saturation over the top. There's no easy way to control this with RGB tool, such as Levels and Curves, but moving over to the HSB model allows you to single out saturation and dial it back.

green, and blue channels but also their chromatic opposites of cyan, magenta, and yellow. When you're working in RGB color, these secondary colors are in direct opposition, so that, for example, lowering blue gamma effectively raises the yellow gamma, and vice versa.

✓ Tip

- When in doubt about the amount of color in a given channel, try boosting its Saturation to 100%, blowing it out—this makes the presence of that tone in pixels very easy to spot.

The HSB model includes all six individual channels, which means that if a given channel is too bright or over-saturated, you can dial back its Brightness & Saturation levels, or you can shift Hue toward a different part of the spectrum without unduly affecting the other primary and secondary colors. This is even an effective way to reduce blue or green spill.

More Color Tools and Techniques

This section has laid the foundation for color correction in After Effects using its most fundamental tools. The truth, of course, is that there are lots of ways to adjust the color levels of an image, with new ones emerging all the time. Alternatives used to create a specific look—layering in a color solid, creating selections from an image using the image itself along with blending modes, and more—are explored in Section III of this book.

✓ Tip

- One alternative usage of these basic color correction tools is to apply them via an adjustment layer, because you can then dial them back simply by adjusting the layer's opacity, or hold them out from specific areas of the image using masks or track matte selections.

Color Finesse

Color Finesse is a sophisticated color correction system included with After Effects Professional; unfortunately, it runs as a separate application, and does not allow you to see your corrections in the context of a composite, making it more suitable for overall color adjustments. Furthermore, it is made up mostly of tools that resemble the ones described in the preceding section, so you'd still want to master them. And although I love the way it allows easy isolation and adjustment of specific secondary color ranges, I rarely use it for compositing because of how separate it is from the After Effects workflow.

✓ Tip

- The previous edition of this book mentioned that Adobe Premiere Pro includes a Three-Way Color Corrector that is supported with an equivalent effect in After Effect. This effect appears only if applied in a Premiere Pro project that you then import into After Effects, however, where it then lacks the color wheel UI. This effect is still not directly available in After Effects CS3.

Three-Way Color

What has been sorely missing from After Effects is a three-way color corrector, typically featuring color wheels to adjust three distinct color ranges: shadows, midtones, and highlights. Look at any contemporary feature film or major television show and you're likely to find strong color choices that strongly deviate from how the original scene must have looked: In an ordinary day-lit scene the shadows might be bluish, the midtones green, and the highlights orange.

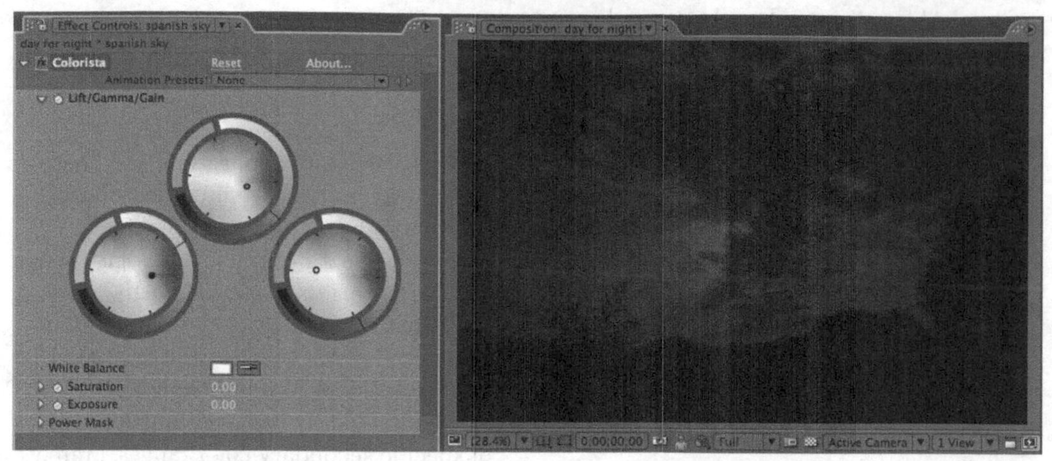

Figure 14.23 The hot After Effects plug-in for color work as of this writing is Colorista; the simple and intuitive color wheels make it easy to perform radical color surgery such as this day-for-night effect (detailed in Chapter 17).

✓ Notes

Chapter 17 includes a "roll your own" recipe and Animation Preset for cheap and cheerful three-way color correction.

A third-party tool, Magic Bullet Colorista, has recently been released by Red Giant Software to make this type of correction quick and intuitive in After Effects (**Figure 14.23**); a demo version is included on the book's disc. This type of tool can be essential to finish the color look of a project, although the more tried-and-true tools will work every time when matching colors, discussed next.

Color Matching

Having examined the color correction tools in depth, it's now time for the bread and butter of compositing: to match foreground and background elements so that the scene appears to have been taken with the same basic light conditions.

Although it requires artistry to do well, this is a learnable skill with measurable objective results. The process obeys such strict rules that you can do it without an experienced eye for color. Assuming the background (or whatever source element you're matching) has already been color-graded, you even can satisfactorily complete a shot on a monitor that is nowhere near correctly calibrated.

How is that possible?

As with so much visual effects work, the answer is derived by correctly breaking down the problem. In this case, the job of matching one image to another obeys rules that can be observed channel by channel, independent of the final, full-color result.

Of course, effective compositing is not simply a question of making colors match; in many cases that is only the first step. You must also obey rules you will understand from the careful observation of nature described in the previous chapter. And even if your colors are correctly matched, if you haven't interpreted your edges properly or pulled a good matte, or if such essential elements as lighting, the camera view, or motion are mismatched, the composite will not succeed.

These same basic techniques will work for other situations in which your job is to match footage precisely—for example, color correcting a sequence to match a *hero* shot (the one determined to have the right color juju), a process also sometimes known as *color timing.*

The Fundamental Technique

Integration of a foreground element into a background scene often follows the same basic steps:

1. First match overall contrast without regard to color, using Levels. When matching the black and white points, pay attention to atmospheric conditions.
2. Next, study individual color channels and use Levels to match the contrast of each channel (as needed—not all images contain so fundamental a color imbalance).
3. Match the color of the midtones (gamma), channel by channel, using Levels or Curves. This is sometimes known as *gray matching* and is easiest when an object in the background scene is known to be colorless gray (or something close).
4. Evaluate the overall result for other factors influencing the integration of image elements—lighting direction, atmospheric conditions, perspective, grain or other ambient movement, and so on (all of which and more are covered in this book).

The overall approach, although not complicated or even particularly sexy, can take you to places your naked eye doesn't readily understand when looking at color. Yet, when you see the results, you realize that nature beats logic every time.

The sad truth is that even an experienced artist can be completely fooled by the context of the image. **Figures 14.24a**, **b**, and **c** show an example in which seeing is most definitely not believing. Therefore you should not feel that working channel by channel is some kind of crutch. The results of your color adjustments will undoubtedly be challenged by other members of your production team, and when it comes time to review them channel by channel, it's pretty cool to be able to say you got it right.

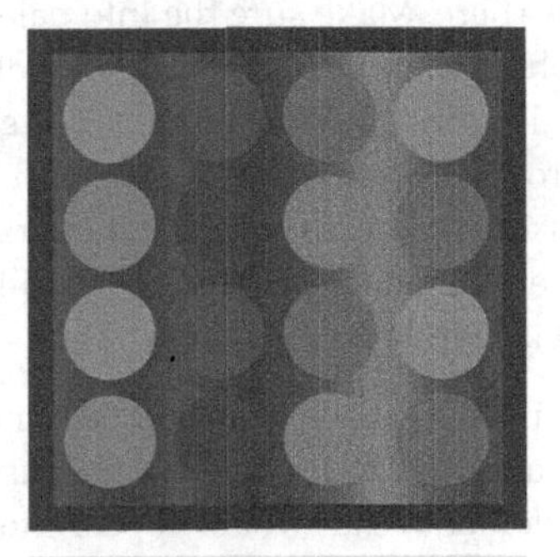

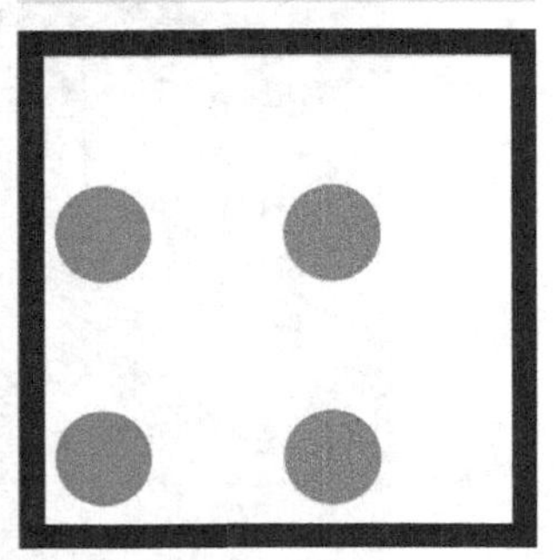

Figures 14.24a, b, and c There are no yellow dots in 14.24a, and no blue dots in 14.24b; the four dots shown in 14.24c are identical to their counterparts in the other two images.

Ordinary Lighting

We begin with a simple example: inserting a 3D element lit with ordinary white lights into a daylight scene. As you can see in **Figure 14.25**, the two elements are close enough in color range that a lazy or hurried compositor might be tempted to leave it as is.

With only a few minutes of effort, you can make the plane look as though it truly belongs there. Make sure the Info palette is somewhere that you can see it, and for now, choose Percent (0–100) in that palette's wing menu to have your values line up with the ones discussed here (you can, of course, use whatever you want, but this is what I'll use for discussion in this section).

This particular scene is a good beginner-level example of the technique because it is full of elements that would appear monochromatic under white light; next we'll move on to scenes that aren't so straightforward.

The background is dominated by colorless gray concrete, and the foreground element is a silver aircraft.

Begin by looking for suitable black and white points to use as references in the background and foreground. In this case, the shadow areas under the archways in the background, and underneath the wing of the foreground plane, are just what's needed for black points—they are not the very darkest elements in the scene, but they contain a similar mixture of reflected light and shadow cast onto similar surfaces, and you can expect them to fairly nearly match. For highlights, you happily have the top of the bus shelter to use for a background white point, and the top silver areas of the plane's tail in the foreground are lit brightly enough to contain pure white pixels at this point.

Figure 14.26 shows the targeted shadow and highlight regions and their corresponding readings in the Info palette. The shadow levels in the foreground are lower (darker)

Figure 14.25 An unadjusted foreground layer (the plane) over a day-lit background.

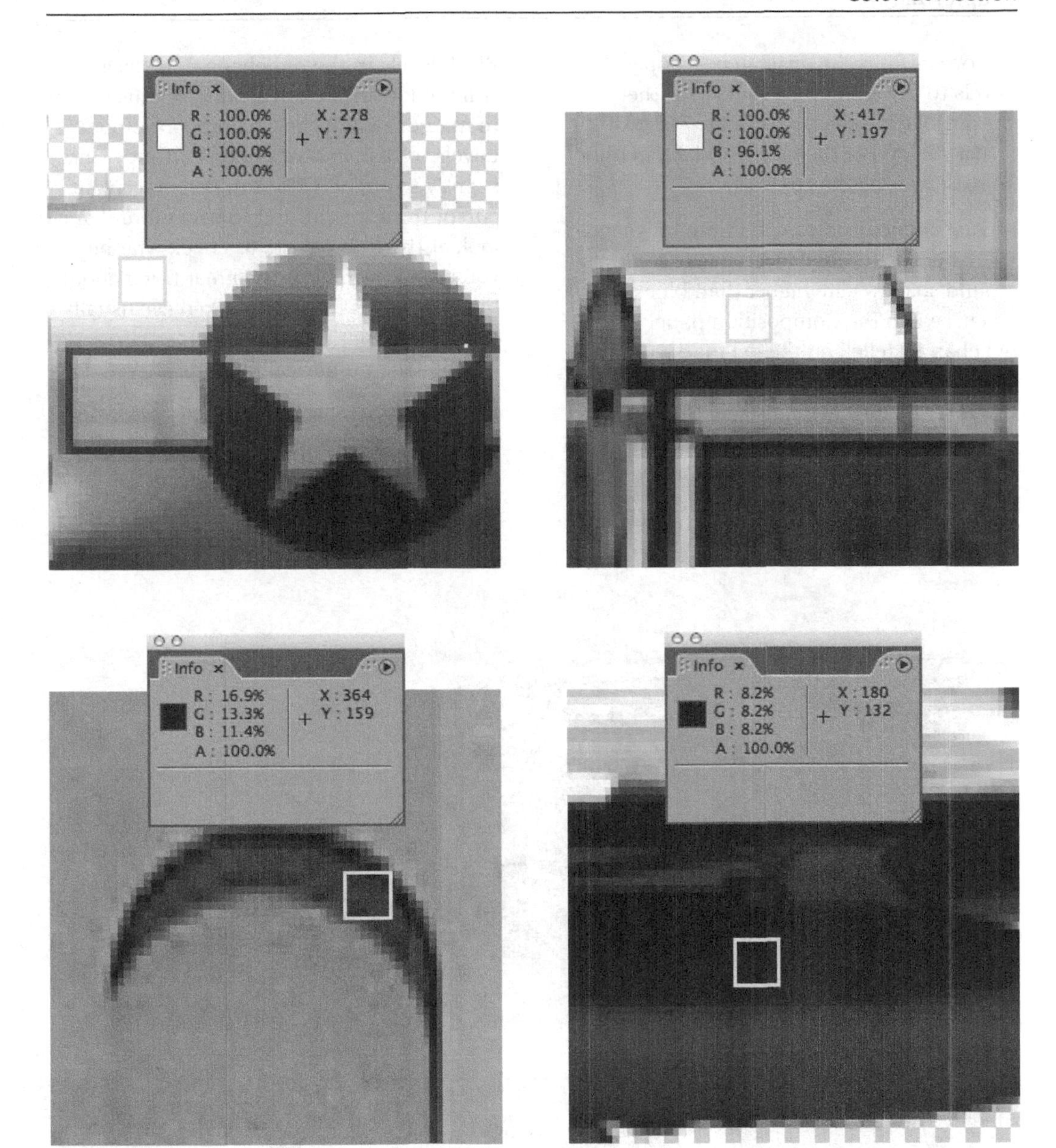

Figure 14.26 The target highlight and shadow areas for the foreground and background are outlined in yellow; levels corresponding to each highlight (in Percent values, as set in the panel menu) are displayed in the adjacent Info palette.

than those in the background, while the background shadows have slightly more red in them, giving the background warmth absent from the unadjusted foreground. The top of the plane and bus shelter each contain levels at 100%, or pure white, but the bus shelter has lower blue highlights, giving it a more yellow appearance.

To correct for these mismatches, apply Levels to the foreground and move the Output Black slider up to about 7.5%. This raises the level of the blackest black in the image, lowering the contrast.

Having aligned contrast, it's time to balance color. Because the red levels in the background shadows are higher than blue or green, switch the Composition panel to the red channel (click on the red marker at the bottom of the panel or use the **Alt+1/ Option+1** shortcut), causing a thin red line to appear around the viewer. You can now zoom in on an area that shows foreground and background shadows (**Figure 14.27**).

Black levels in the red channel are clearly still too low in the foreground, so raise them to match. Switch the Channel pop-up in Levels to Red, and raise Red Output Black slightly to about 3.5%. You can move your cursor from foreground to background and look at the Info palette to check whether you have it right, but the great thing about this method is that your naked eye usually evaluates variations in luminance correctly without the numerical reference.

Now for the whites. Because the background highlights have slightly less blue in them, switch to the blue channel (clicking the blue marker at the bottom of the Composition

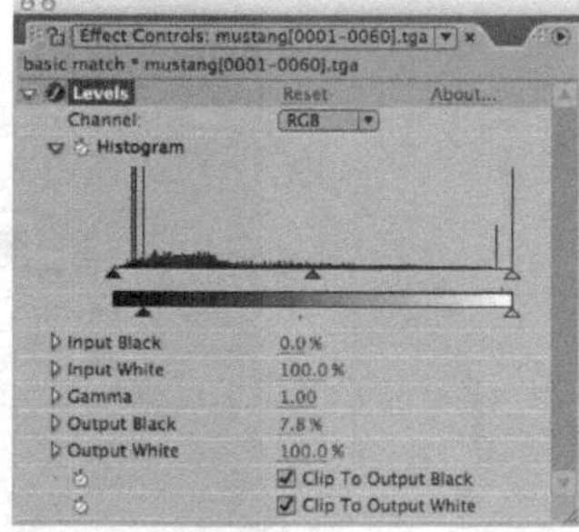

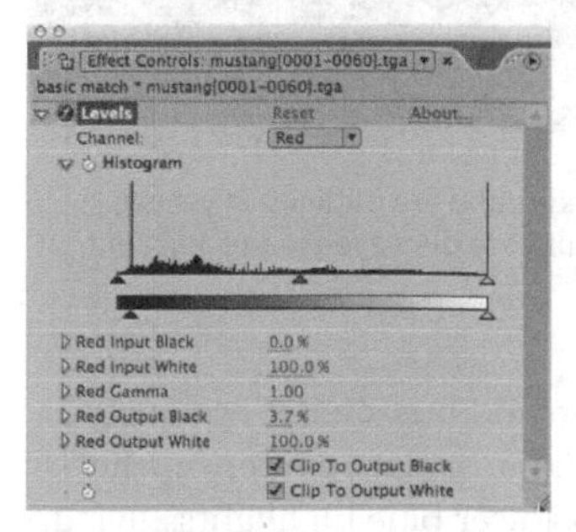

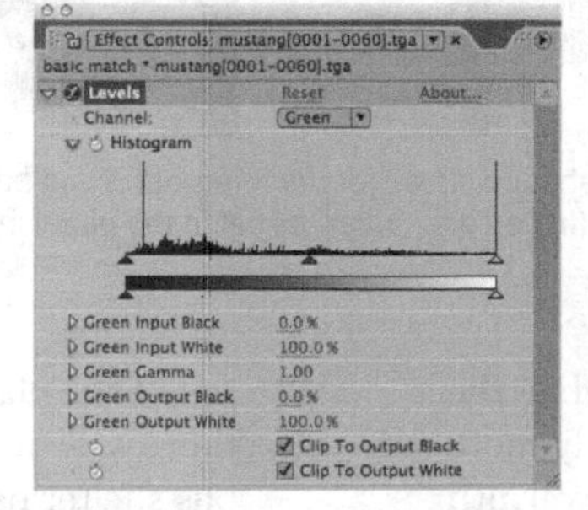

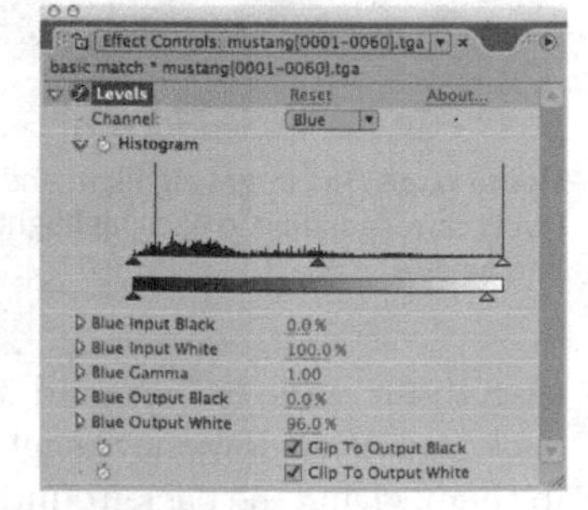

Figure 14.27 Evaluate and match black and white levels; start with RGB and then work on each color channel individually. In this case the image is "green matched:" The RGB adjustment is all that is needed for the green channel (often the best channel to match using RGB instead of its individual channel).

panel or using **Alt+3/Option+3**). Pull back slightly to where you can see the top of the bus shelter and the back of the plane. Switching Levels to the blue channel, lower the Blue Output White setting a few percentage points to match the lower blue reading in the background. Back in RGB mode (**Alt+3/Option+3** toggles back from blue to RGB), the highlights on the plane take on a more sunlit, yellow quality. It's subtle, but it seems right.

✓ Tip

The human eye is more sensitive to green than red and blue. Often, when you look at a shot channel by channel, you will see the strongest brightness and contrast in the green channel. For that reason, a sensible approach to matching color may be to get the overall match in the ballpark so that the green channels match perfectly, and then adjust the other two channels to make green work. That way, you run less risk of misadjusting the overall brightness and contrast of your footage.

What about the midtones? In this case, they're taking care of themselves because both the foreground and background are reasonably well balanced and these corrections are mild.

Figure 14.28 displays the result, with the same regions targeted previously, but with the levels corrected. To add an extra bit of realism, I also turned on motion blur, without yet bothering to precisely match it. You see that the plane is now more acceptably integrated into the scene.

Work on this composite isn't done either; besides matching the blur, you can add some sun glints on the plane as it passes, similar to those on the taxi. On the other hand, you can tell that the blur on the plane is too heavy for the pilot's absence from the cockpit to be noticeable, a good example of how an initial pass at a composite can save a lot of extra work.

Figure 14.28 This is a better match, particularly in the shadow areas; motion blur helps sell the color adjustment as well.

Dramatic Lighting

Watch a contemporary feature film objectively for color and you may be shocked at how rare ordinary day-lit scenes such as the plane example are. Dramatic media—not just films but television and theater—use color and light to create mood, to signify key characters and plot points, and more.

Therefore a scene dominated by a single color, such as **Figure 14.29**, is much more commonly found in dramatic films than it is in your everyday family snapshots. One of the main reasons films take so long to shoot is that the cinematographer and lighting director require the time and resources to get the lighting the way it needs to be to create an image that is both beautiful and serves the story.

✓ **Notes**

This section discusses colors expressed as percentages; to see the same values in your Levels effect, use the wing menu of the Info palette to choose Percent for the Color Display.

The foreground element added in **Figure 14.30** clearly does not belong in this scene; it does not even contain the scene's dominant color, and is white-lit. That's fine; it will better demonstrate the effectiveness of this technique.

Note that both the foreground and the background elements have some areas that you can logically assume to be flat gray. The bridge has concrete footings for the steel girders along the edges of the road, while the can has areas of bare exposed aluminum.

To play along with this game, open the project 05_colorMatching2.aep and apply Levels to the foreground layer in the "before" composition ("after" is the final comp to which you can refer as needed once you've tried this on your own).

Switch both your Composition view (**Alt+1/Option+1**) and the Channel pull-

Figure 14.29 This is the unembellished source lighting of this shot. (Image courtesy Shuets Udono via Creative Commons license.)

Figure 14.30 Not only is it clear that the can does not belong in the color environment of the background, the mismatch is equally apparent on each color channel.

down in Levels to Red. I'll warn you now that the most challenging thing about this technique will be remembering to keep both settings on the same color channel, which is why using a four-up setup as shown in Figure 14.33 is probably worth the trouble.

Now, let's pretend that the red channel is a black-and-white photograph in which you're using the red channel of the Levels effect to match the foreground to the background. Clearly, the foreground element is far too bright for the scene. Specifically, the darkest silver areas of the can are way brighter than the brightest areas of the concrete in the background. Therefore, adjust the gamma down (to the right) until it feels more like they inhabit the same world; in my example, I've adjusted Red Gamma way down to 0.67. Now cut down the red highlights a little; bring Red Output White down to about 92.5% or whatever looks right to you. The end result should look like a black-and-white photo whose elements match (**Figure 14.31a**).

Now move the Levels Channel and Composition view (**Alt+2/Option+2**) over to green. Green is the dominant color here, and its black contrast and brightness are much higher in the background. Therefore, raise Green Input Black to about 12.5% (for the contrast) and Green Gamma to something like 1.3 (**Figure 14.31b**). Better than copying my levels, try to find these on your own.

Finally, switch Levels and the Composition viewer (**Alt+3/Option+3**) to the Blue channel. Whoa; there is almost no match here. The can is way brighter and more washed out than the background. Again the Input Blue Level must come up, to about 17.5%, but this time gamma has to come way

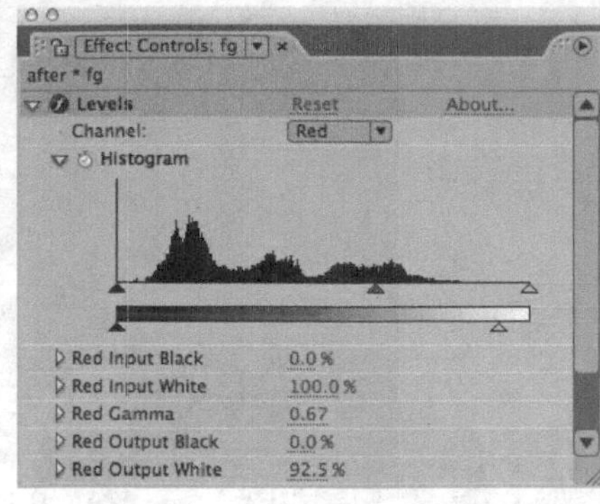

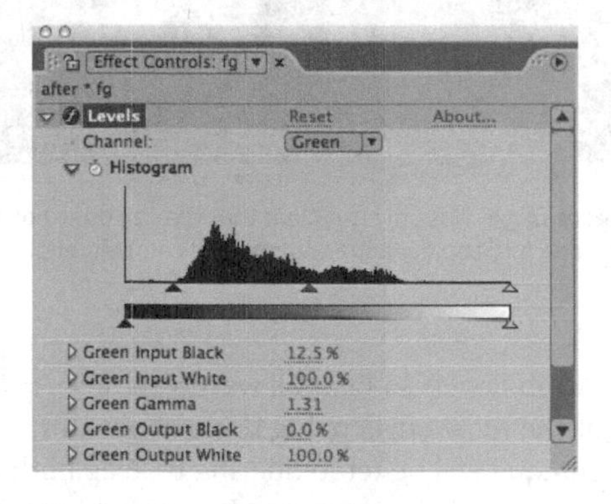

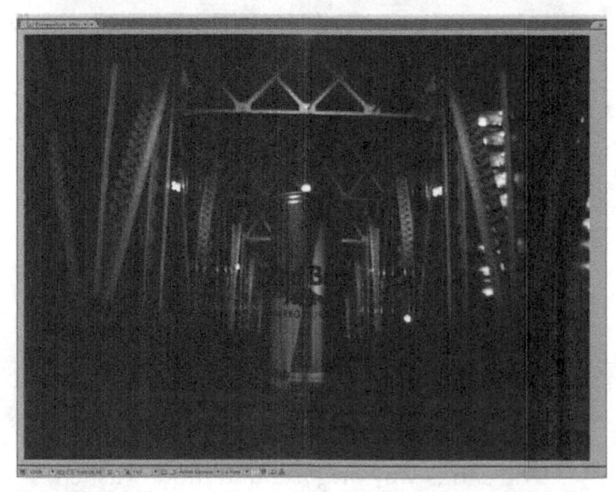

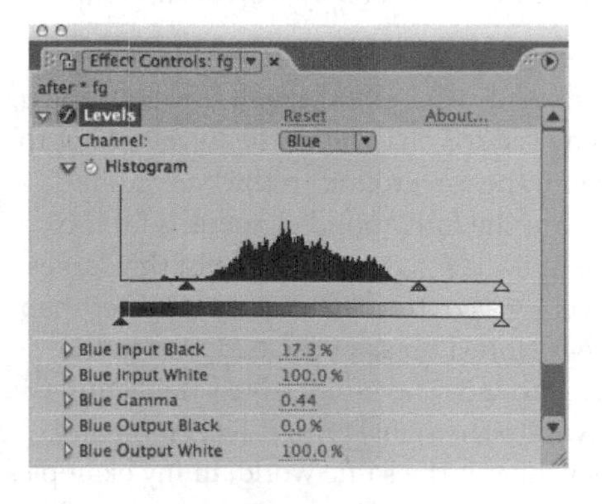

Figures 14.31a, b, and c It's actually fun to pull off an extreme match like this channel-by-channel. The Levels settings used were not really derived from the histogram, but by a mixture of looking for equivalent black/white/ midpoints in the image, as well as just analyzing whether the result looks like a convincing black and white image on each channel.

down, ending up at about 0.45%. Now the can looks believably like it belongs there (**Figure 14.31c**).

It's strange to make all of these changes without ever looking at the result in full color. So now, go ahead and do that. Astoundingly, that can is now in range of looking like it belongs in that scene; defocus it slightly with a little fast blur and add a shadow and you start to believe it. Make any final contrast adjustments on the Levels RGB Channel, and you have an impressive result that required no guesswork whatso ever (**Figure 14.32**).

When There's No Clear Reference

The previous examples have contained fairly clear black, white, and gray values in the foreground and background elements. Life, of course, is not always so simple.

Figure 14.33 is a scene that lacks any obvious gray values to match; the lighting is so strong, it's hard to tell what color anything in the scene was originally, or whether there were any neutral black, white or gray items in the scene.

✓ Notes

It's often a good idea to take a break when trying to finalize fine color adjustment. When you come back, even to a labored shot, you regain an immediate impression that can save you a lot of noodling.

The technique still works in this case, but it may require more in the way of trial and error, or artist's intuition. Looking at each individual color channel, only green is even close to a plausible match right off the bat; the red channel contains blown-out whites, and the blue channel is so dark (and grainy) it hardly exists.

Once again, just try to get the brightness and contrast adjusted, working channel by channel, and you get an initial result something like **Figure 14.34**. Considering how subjective the adjustments are by necessity in this case, this isn't half bad; and fine

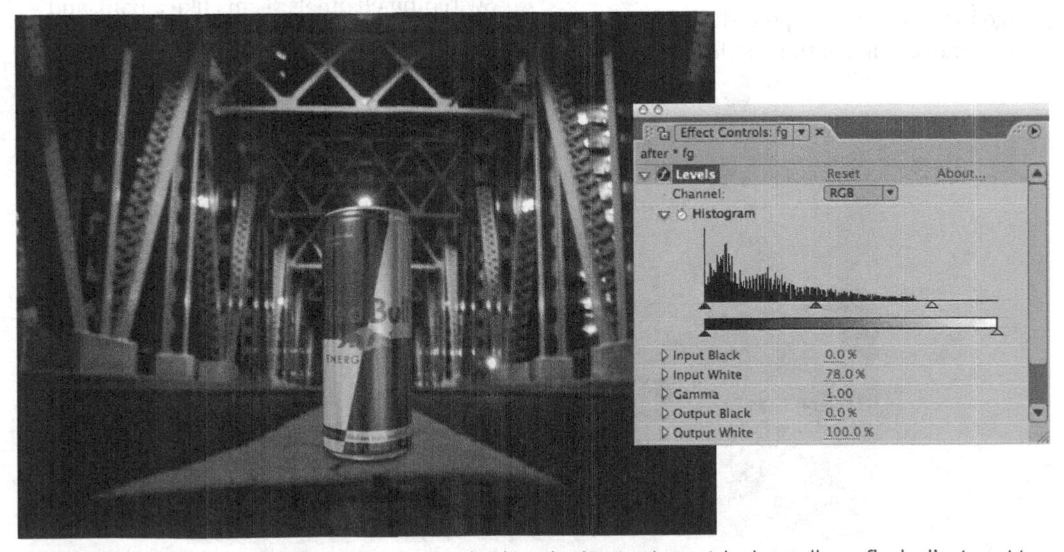

Figure 14.32 The result includes a subtle shadow that has also been color matched as well as a final adjustment to the white contrast.

Figure 14.33 What the heck is going on here? Again, the source image is as it was shot. Examine some of your favorite films and you may find scenes lit this dramatically; the eye quickly becomes accustomed to strong shifts of color, but the color can also be used to strike a subconscious chord. (Image courtesy Jorge L. Peschiera via Creative Commons license.)

adjustments to the RGB channel can bring it where it needs to go.

The ability to match color without seeing an image in full color is so powerful that it can seem almost magical the first few times you try it. Why, then, do so few artists work this way? I would have to say that laziness and ignorance are the main culprits here. Switching channels seems like a pain, and few untrained artists clearly realize that color works like this.

Figure 14.34 This one requires as much intuition as logic, but adjusting it channel by channel still yields a striking result.

Gamma Slamming

Maybe you've seen an old movie on television—the example I think of first is *Return of the Jedi* (before the digital re-release)—in which you see black rectangular garbage mattes dancing around the Emperor's head, inside the cloak, that you obviously shouldn't be seeing. *Jedi* was made prior to the digital age, and some of the optical composites worked fine on film, but when they went to video, subtleties in the black levels that weren't previously evident suddenly became glaringly obvious.

Don't let this happen to you! Now that you know how to match levels, put them to the test by slamming the gamma of the image. To do this, you need to make a couple of adjustment layers. I usually call one slam up and the other slam down, as in the examples. Be sure that both of these are guide layers so that they have no possibility of showing up in your final render.

To slam up, apply Curves with the gamma raised significantly (**Figure 14.35**). This exposes any areas of the image that might have been too dark to distinguish on your monitor; if the blacks still match with the gamma slammed up, you're in good shape.

Similarly, and somewhat less crucial, you can slam down by lowering the gamma and bringing the highlights more into the midrange (**Figure 14.36**). All you're doing with these slams is stretching values that may be difficult for you to distinguish into a range that is easy for you to see.

This method is useful anywhere that there is a danger of subtle discrepancies of contrast; you can use it to examine a color key, or a more extreme change of scene lighting.

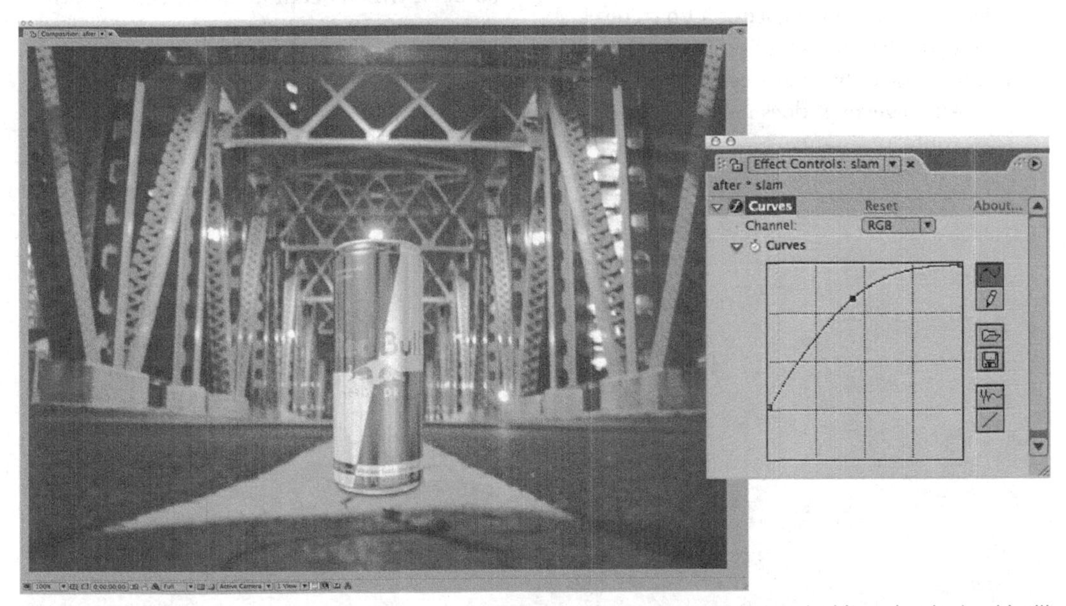

Figure 14.35 Slamming gamma is like shining a bright light on your scene. Your black and midtone levels should still match when viewed at these extremes.

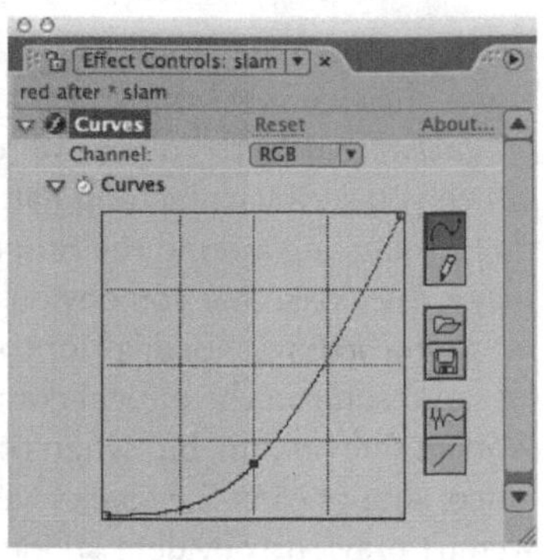

Figure 14.36 If in doubt about the highlights in your footage, you can also slam the gamma downward. Here, the slam makes it clear that the highlight reflected in the can is not as bright or bloomed as the overhead lights, and a lack of grain in the foreground becomes apparent. Grain matching is detailed in Chapter 15, "The Camera and Optics."

✓ Notes

You can try the Exposure control found at the lower right of every viewer window to slam the image and check levels; just scrub the numerical setting up and down, clicking the adjacent icon to reset when you're done. This approach requires no additional steps and does not render; however, it does not affect contrast, only luminance.

Beyond the Basics

This chapter has covered some of the basics for adjusting and matching footage. Obviously there are exceptional situations, some of which occur all of the time: depth cueing, changes in lighting during the shot, backlighting, interactive light and shadow. There are even cases in which you can, to some degree, relight a shot in After Effects, introducing light direction, exchanging day for night, and so on. These topics and more are covered in depth in Chapter 17.

PART V

ADVANCED TOPICS

15

THE CAMERA AND OPTICS

A film is never really good unless the camera is an eye in the head of a poet.

–Orson Welles

The Camera and Optics

It seems as if visual effects is all about simulating the look of the real world, but that's not quite the goal; as a visual effects compositor, your actual job is to simulate the real world *as it appears through the lens of a camera.* The distinction is critical, because when photographed the world looks different—more or less real, and possibly both.

It's not too grandiose to say that cinematography is essential to compositing, because After Effects offers the opportunity to re-create and even change essential shooting decisions long after the crew has struck the set and called it a wrap. Your shot may be perfectly realistic on its own merits but it will only belong in the story if it works cinematically. Factors in After Effects that contribute to good cinematography include

- Field of view
- Depth of focus
- The shooting medium and what it tells about the storyteller
- Planar perspective and dimensionality
- Camera motion (handheld, stabilized or locked) and what it implies about point of view

These seemingly disparate points all involve understanding how the camera sees the world and how film and video record what the camera sees. All of them transcend mere aesthetics, influencing how the viewer perceives the story itself.

Cameras: Virtual and Real

We begin our exploration of virtual cinematography with the After Effects camera, which relates closely to an actual motion picture camera without actually being anything like one. Following is an examination of how 3D operates in After Effects and how the application's features—not only the camera, but also lights and shading options—correspond to real world counterparts.

See with the Camera

Toggle a layer to 3D and *voila*, its properties contain three axes instead of two—but enabling 3D without a camera is a little bit like racing a car with automatic transmission: You can't really maneuver, and before long you're bound to slam into something.

The Camera Settings dialog (**Figure 15.1**) uniquely includes a physical diagram that helps tell you what you need to know about how settings in the 3D camera affect your scene.

Lens Settings

Although it is not labeled as such, and although After Effects displays previous camera settings by default, the true default lens preset in Camera Settings is 50 mm. This setting (**Figure 15.2**, see next page) is neither wide (as with lower values, **Figure 15.3**, see next page) nor long (as with higher values, **Figure 15.4**, see next page); and it introduces no shift in perspective.

"50 mm" is a virtually meaningless term because virtual space doesn't contain millimeters any more than it contains kilograms, parsecs, or bunny rabbits. This is the median lens length of a 35 mm SLR camera, the standard professional still image camera.

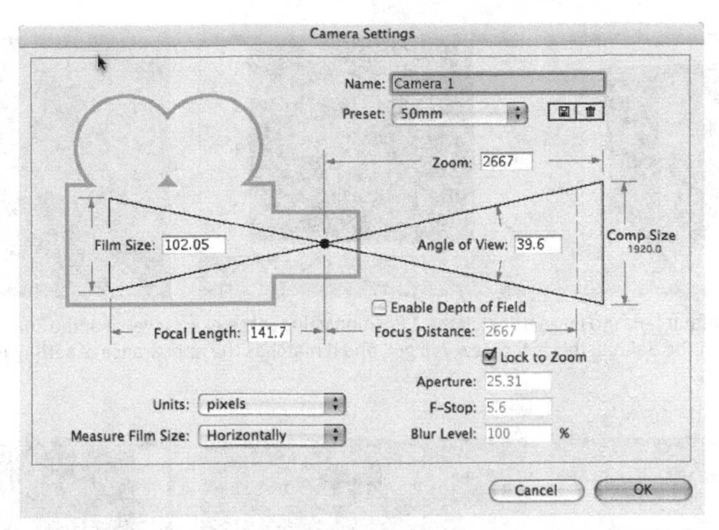

Figure 15.1 Artists love a visual UI, and the Camera Settings dialog provides one to help elucidate settings that might otherwise seem a bit abstract. The 50 mm preset is the neutral (default) setting.

Motion picture cameras are not so standardized. The equivalent lens on a 35 mm film camera shooting Academy ratio itself has a 35 mm length. A miniDV camera, on the other hand, has a tiny neutral lens length of around 4 mm. The length corresponds directly to the size of the backplate or video pickup, the area where the image is projected inside the camera.

Lens length, then, is a somewhat arbitrary and made-up value in the virtual world of After Effects. The corresponding setting that applies universally is Angle of View, which can be calculated whether images were shot in IMAX or HDV or created in a 3D animation package.

Real Camera Settings

To understand the relationship of the After Effects camera to those of a real-world camera, look again at the Camera Settings diagram (Figure 15.1). Four numerical fields—Film Size, Focal Length, Zoom, and Angle of View—surround a common hypotenuse.

A prime (or fixed) lens would have static values for all four. A zoom lens would of course work with a fixed Film Size, but would allow Zoom and Focal Length to be adjusted, changing the Angle of View. These four settings, then, are interrelated and interdependent, as the diagram implies, and the relationship is just the same as with a real camera, which the Film Size can even help emulate. Lengthen the lens by increasing Focal Length and you decrease Angle of View.

The settings you actually use are Zoom (to animate) and Angle of View (to match real-world source).

Angle of View is the actual radius, in degrees, that fit in the view. If you're matching it, note that Camera Settings lets you specify a horizontal, vertical, or diagonal measurement in the Measure Film Size pulldown.

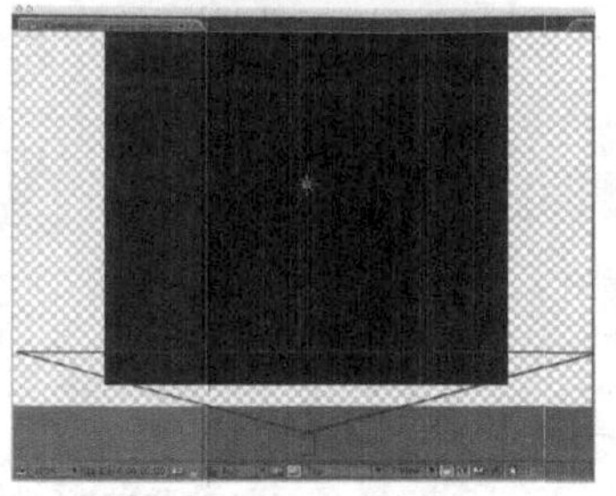
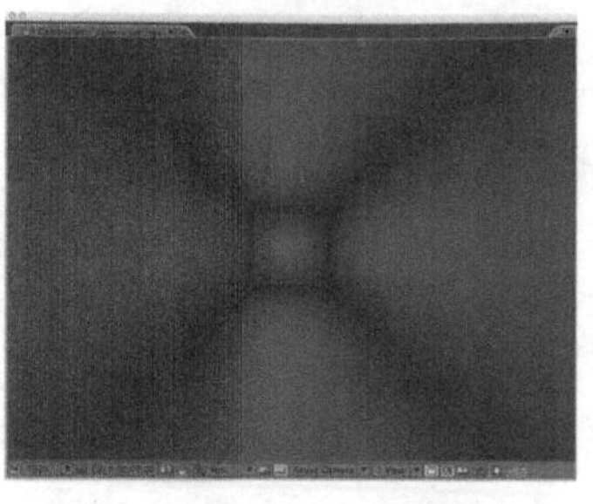

Figure 15.2 The default lens (50 mm setting). If the Z Position value is the exact inverse of the Zoom value, and all other settings are at the default, this is the view you get, and it matches the appearance of setting no After Effects camera whatsoever.

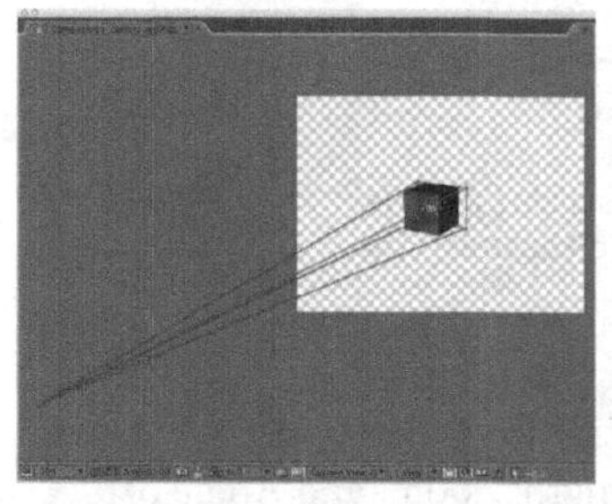
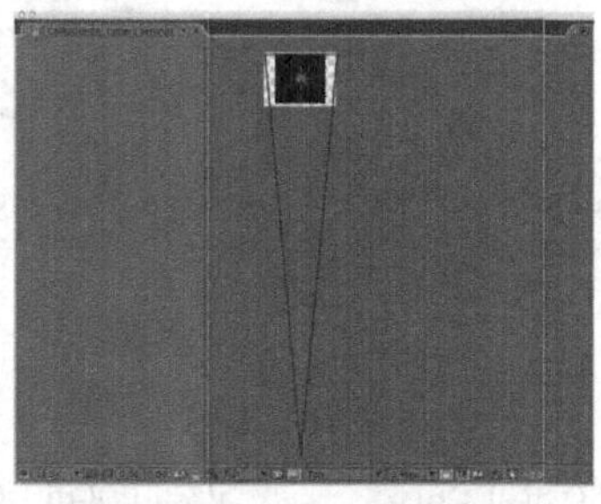
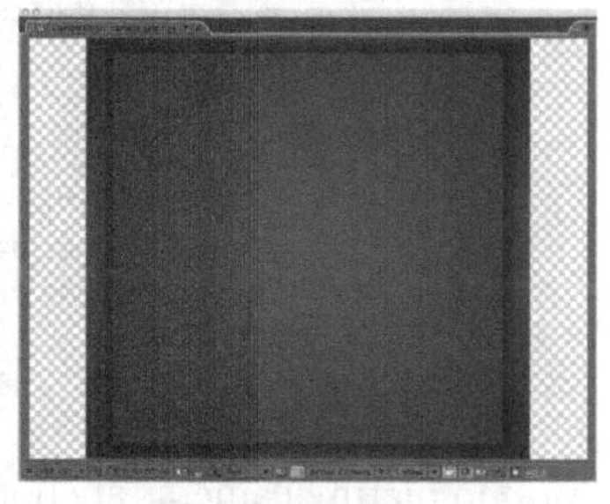

Figure 15.3 The extreme wide or fisheye lens pointed inside an evenly proportioned 3D box. Note that the "long" look of the box is created by this "wide" lens, which tends to create very strange proportions at this extreme. A physical lens with anything like this angle would include extremely distorted lens curvature.

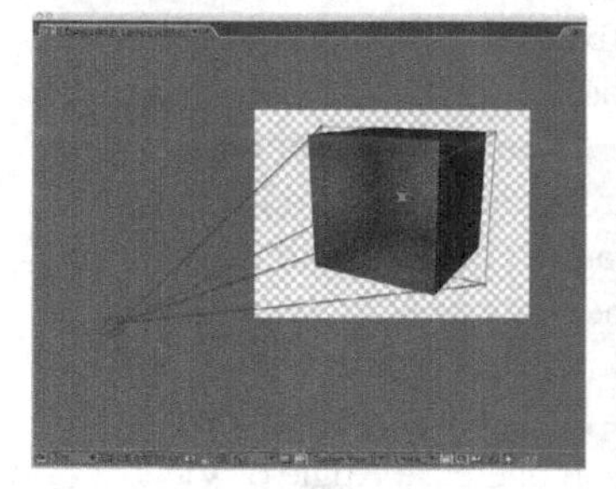
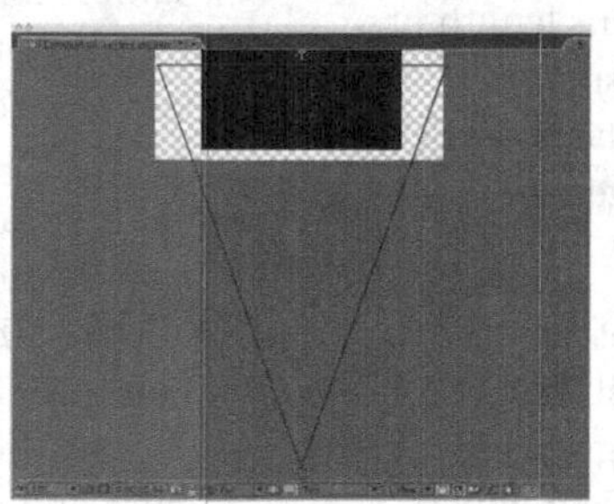

Figure 15.4 A telephoto lens (using the 200 mm setting) pushes items together in depth space, shortening the distance between the front and back of the box dramatically.

✔ Note

A fifth numerical field in Camera Settings, Focus Distance, is enabled by checking Enable Depth of Field; it corresponds to a camera's aperture setting, covered here separately.

In After Effects, the Zoom value is the distance of the camera, in pixels, from the plane of focus. Create a camera and its Z Position is the inverse of the Zoom value, perfectly framing the contents of the comp with a Z position of 0.0 (**Figure 15.5**). This makes for easy reference when measuring

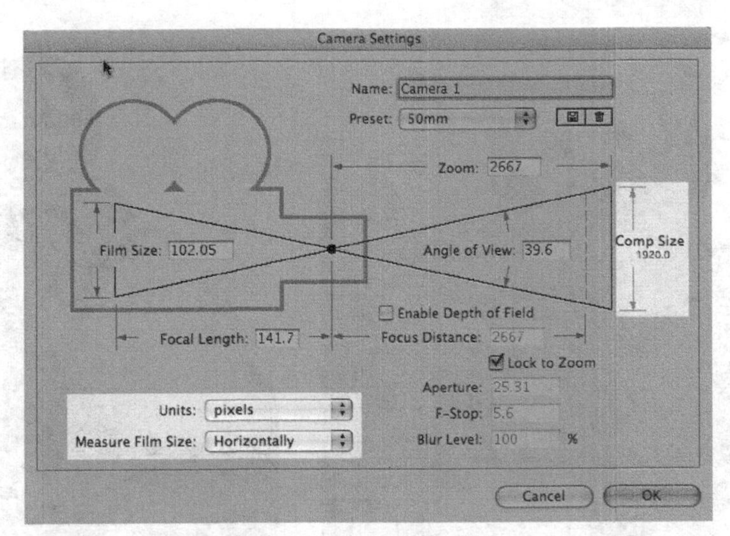

Figure 15.5 Comp Size (at the right) is the horizontal size, in pixels (although it always appears vertical in the diagram); orientation changes according to the Measure Film Size settings (left). Instead of pixels, you can measure in inches or millimeters, helpful when matching a physical camera (process described ahead).

depth of field effects, and it allows you to link camera position and zoom together via expressions (for depth of field and multiplane effects, discussed later).

Emulate a Real Camera

Other considerations when matching a real-world camera include

- **Depth of field:** This is among the most filmic and evocative additions you can make to a scene. It doesn't exist by default in After Effects the way it does with real-world optics, so you have to re-create it.
- **Zoom or push:** A move in or out is used for dramatic effect, but which type is it?
- **Motion blur and shutter angle:** These are composition (not camera) settings; introduced in Chapter 5, they are further explored here.
- **Lens angle:** The perspective and parallax of layers in 3D space change according to the angle of the lens used to view them.
- **Lens distortion:** Real lenses introduce *lens distortion*, curvature most apparent with wide-angle or "fisheye" lenses. An After Effects camera has no lens, hence, no distortion, but you can re-create it (see "Lens Distortion").
- **Exposure:** Every viewer in After Effects now includes an Exposure control (look for the aperture icon, lower right); this (along with the effect with the same name) is mathematically similar but practically different from a physical camera. Usage of these tools is detailed in Chapter 16, "32 Bit HDR Compositing and Color Management."
- **Boke, halation, flares:** All sorts of interesting phenomena are generated by

Figures 15.6a and b Camera movement generates motion blur (a); even on a stationary layer provided motion blur is active for the comp and layer (b). New in CS3, zooming the camera can also generate motion blur.

light interacting with the lens itself. These are subjective and almost abstract in reality, yet I think they offer a unique and beautiful aesthetic if grounded in realism.

A *camera report* is a record of the settings used when the footage was taken, usually logged by the camera assistant (or equivalent).

✔ Note

The movement of the camera itself can generate motion blur (**Figures 15.6a and b**). The key is that any layers to be blurred by the motion of the camera have Motion Blur toggled on.

The Camera Report

With accurate information on the type of camera and the focal length of a shot, you know enough to match the lens of that camera with your After Effects camera.

Table 15.1 details the sizes of some typical film formats. If your camera is on the list, and you know the focal length, use these to match the camera via Camera Settings. The steps are

1. Set Measure Film Size to Horizontally. (Note that hFilmPlane below stands for "Horizontal Film Plane.")
2. Set Units to Inches.
3. Enter the number from the Horizontal column of the chart that corresponds to the source film format.
4. Set Units to Millimeters.
5. Enter the desired Focal Length.

Once the Angle of View matches the footage, any objects that you track in maintain position in the scene as the shot progresses. It's vital to get this right when the camera moves during the shot, and especially if a wide or long lens was used.

Table 15.1 Typical Film Format Sizes

Format	Horizontal	Vertical
Full Aperture Camera Aperture	0.980	0.735
Scope Camera Aperture	0.864	0.732
Scope Scan0.825	0.735	
2:1 Scope Projector Aperture	0.838	0.700
Academy Camera Aperture	0.864	0.630
Academy Projector Aperture	0.825	0.602
1.66 Projector Aperture	0.825	0.497
1.85 Projector Aperture	0.825	0.446
VistaVision Aperture	0.991	1.485
VistaVision Scan	0.980	1.470
16 mm Camera Aperture	0.404	0.295
Super-16 Camera Aperture	0.493	0.292
HD Full 1.78	0.378	0.212 (Full Aperture in HD 1.78)
HD 90% 1.78	0.340	0.191 (90% Safe Area used in HD 1.78)
HD Full 1.85	0.378	0.204 (Full Aperture in HD 1.85)
HD 90% 1.85	0.340	0.184 (90% Safe Area used in HD 1.85)
HD Full 2.39	0.3775	0.158 (Full Aperture in HD 2.39)
HD 90% 2.39	0.340	0.142 (90% Safe Area used in HD 2.39)

Courtesy Stu Maschwitz / The Orphanage

✔ Tip

- A potentially easier alternative to the listed steps, for those who like using expressions, is to use the following expression on the camera's Zoom property:

```
FocalLength = 35 //
➥change to your value,
➥in mm
hFilmPlane = 24.892
➥//change to your film size, in mm
(horizontal measurement)
this_comp.width*(Focal
➥Length/hFilmPlane)
```

✔ Note

Included on the book's disc is a 12 minute video tutorial (courtesy fxphd.com) in which Mike Seymour shows how information including viewing angle and focus distance can be derived even if these were not recorded when the image was shot.

Lens Distortion

If a virtual camera is set with a wide-angle lens, as in Figure 15.2, it dramatically changes the perspective of 3D space, but it does not actually distort objects the way a real camera lens does because a digital camera uses no lens. A virtual camera can widen the view area and still scan it in a linear fashion, because all the imagery travels to a single point.

A lens curves light to project it properly across the camera backplate with physical width and height, no matter how small. To show up properly the reflected imagery must be perpendicular to the surface of the lens glass, so a wide-angle view requires not only a short lens length but also a convex lens in order to gather the full range of view.

At the extremes, this causes easily visible lens distortion; items in the scene known to contain straight lines don't appear straight at all, but bent in a curve (**Figure 15.7**). In a fisheye lens shot, it's as if the screen has been inflated like a balloon.

As you refine your eye, you may notice that many shots that aren't as extreme as a fisheye perspective contain a degree of lens distortion. Or you might find that motion tracks that are accurate on one side of the frame don't seem to apply equally well at the other side of the frame, proportions go out of whack, and things don't quite line up as they should (**Figures 15.8a** and **b**).

There's no way to introduce lens distortion directly to a 3D camera, but the Optics Compensation effect (Professional version only) is designed to add or remove it in 2D. **Figures 15.9a** and **b** shows this effect in action. Increasing the Field of View makes the affected layer more fish-eyed in appearance; to correct a shot coming in with lens distortion, check Reverse Lens Distortion and raise the Field of View (FOV) value.

This process is not exactly scientific, instead requiring eye-match because the Field of View settings don't correspond to measurable items in the camera report, such as the Lens Angle. Specifically

1. Having identified lens distortion in a background plate (as in Figure 15.8a), precomp the background into a new composition that is at least 20% larger than the plate to accommodate distortion.

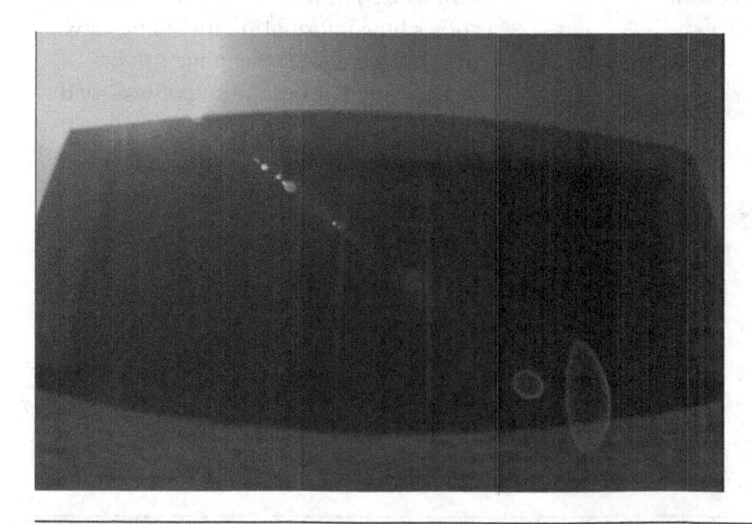

Figure 15.7 The almost psychedelic look of lens distortion at its most extreme; the lens flare itself is extremely aberrated. You can create just as wide a lens with the 3D camera, but there would be no lens distortion because there is no lens.

Figures 15.8a and b It is simply not possible to make all four corners and edges of a yellow solid line up properly with the side of a distorted building (a). Grid lines over footage of the bus clearly show distortion (b). (Building examples courtesy Stu Maschwitz; bus footage courtesy Pixel Corps.)

Figures 15.9a and b Optics compensation takes place in a composition larger than the source; the padding gives the corners of the image space. The Beam effect can serve as a virtual plumb line (a) or it can be clear from the grid that distortion has been corrected (b).

2. Add an adjustment layer above the plate layer, and apply Optics Compensation to that layer. Check Reverse Lens Distortion and raise the Field of View (FOV) setting until all straight lines appear straight.

3. Add a Beam effect to the adjustment layer (below the Optics Compensation effect, unaffected by it). To get away from the light saber look, match Inside Color and Outside Color to some easily visible hue, then align the Starting Point and Ending Point along an apparently straight line near the edge of frame. Fine-tune the Field of View setting a little more until the line is plumb (Figures 15.9a and b).

4. Precompose all of these layers and set this new composition as a guide layer. In **Figure 15.10**, you can see that the corner pin is now successful.

5. To complete the shot, restore the original field of view, including distortion. First create a new comp with the original background plate (no Optics Compensation) and the precomp with the assembled foreground elements.

Figure 15.10 Over the undistorted background plate, you can freely position, animate, and composite elements as if everything were normal. Note that the perspective is still that of a very wide-angle lens, but without the curvature.

6. Copy Optics Compensation with the settings added in step 2 and paste it to the foreground element. Toggle Reverse Lens Distortion off. The Field of View of the background is restored, but the foreground elements match (**Figure 15.11**).

Here is an original haiku (Stu Maschwitz gets the writing credit) to sum up the process:

undistort, derive
reunite distorted things
with an untouched plate

Figure 15.11 The Optics Compensation effect with Reverse Lens Distortion unchecked adds the original distortion to the foreground; features now line up properly.

2D and 3D

The point of matching 3D lens angles (and correcting any distortion) is most often to place elements in 3D space over a 2D plate background. This is so effortlessly possible in After Effects as to seem like no big deal:

- A 2D background layer remains in place (usually simply filling the frame) no matter how you move the camera.
- 2D adjustment layers set to comp size and default position affect the whole composition, including 3D layers.
- 3D layers can use vital features unique to 2D compositing, such as blending modes (over 2D elements, they obey layer order, and with other 3D elements, z-space depth).

Here are special cases that require extra care:

- It's rarely a good idea to combine a 3D track matte and a 3D layer. A 3D layer can use a 2D layer as a track matte; it is applied just as it would be to a 2D layer. A 2D layer can use a 3D layer as a track matte; the 3D perspective of the track matte renders first and is then applied. But combine two 3D layers in this manner and the matte is first translated by the camera perspective once, then applied, and then effectively translated again as the affected layer also obeys camera perspective.
- Paradoxically, the only layers in After Effects that themselves can contain true 3D data are 2D layers (which may nonetheless make use of the 3D camera perspective, **Figure 15.12**).
- A precomped set of 3D layers behaves like a single 2D layer unless Collapse Transformations is enabled on that layer. This toggle passes through all 3D data from the precomp as if those layers lived right in the master composition.

Every one of these has potential advantages provided you understand how the image pipeline works.

Figure 15.12 Incredibly, particles generated by Trapcode Particular occupy true 3D space, as is evident in a perspective view. Paradoxically, the effect is applied to a 2D layer. It calculates 3D data internally using the After Effects camera as a reference, an elegant workaround for the fact that 3D layers in After Effects are always flat planes.

Storytelling and the Camera

Locked-off shots have been used to great dramatic effect in landmark films by Welles, Hitchcock, Kubrick, and Lucas, among others, but they're the exception, not the norm, particularly in contemporary films, in which the camera point of view often can itself be a character.

In the bad old days of optical compositing, it was scarcely possible to move the camera at all. Nowadays, most directors aren't satisfied with a locked-off effects shot, yet the decision to move the camera might not happen on set, or it might have to be altered in post-production. This is no big deal; you can bend the rules, just don't break them.

Specifically, create a rough assemble with animation as early in the process of creating your shot as possible, because it will tell you a lot about what you can get away with and what needs dedicated attention. The audience should instead be focused on watching the lead character walk through the lobby, wondering what he has in his briefcase; if not, the film has more problems than can be fixed with more elaborate visual effects elements.

✔ Tip

- Always keep in mind where the audience's attention is focused—you can employ the magician's technique, misdirection, to get away with something you shouldn't. As is detailed in the fun book *Rebel Without a Crew* (Plume, 1996), El Mariachi got completed with meager funds only because Robert Rodriguez was willing to let massive continuity errors go. He was confident that if the audience was watching for those, the story had failed.

Figure 15.13 Prominent though it may appear in this still image, the audience isn't focused on that San Francisco skyline outside the window. There's no multiplaning as the camera moves because the background skyline is a still image; no one notices because viewer attention is on the foreground character. (Image courtesy The Orphanage.)

Camera Animation

The most common confusion about the After Effects camera stems from the fact that by default, it includes a *point of interest*, a point in 3D space at which the camera always points, for auto-orientation. The point of interest is *fully optional*, yet the setting is among the least discoverable in After Effects. To clarify

- Disable auto-orientation and the point of interest (making the camera a *free* camera) by context-clicking on the camera and choosing Transform > Auto-Orient (**Ctrl+Alt+O/Cmd+Option+O**) (**Figure 15.14**).

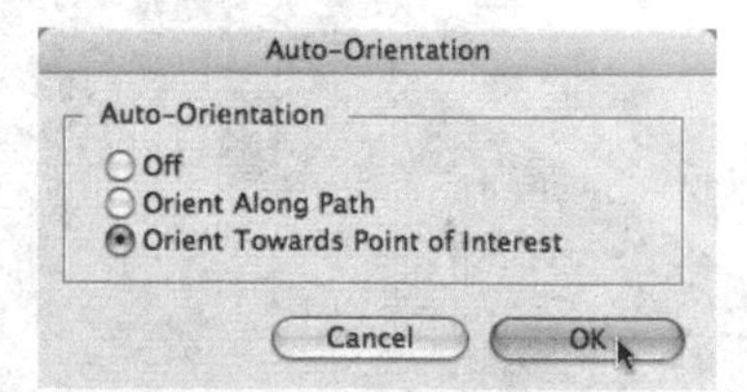

Figure 15.14 So many After Effects 3D camera tragedies could have been avoided if more users knew about this dialog box (**Ctrl+Alt+O/Cmd+Option+O**). By disabling auto-orientation, you are free to move the camera anywhere without changing its direction.

- In that same dialog, you can instead orient the camera along its path of camera motion, so that its rotation maintains tangency; in other words, it is angled the same direction as the path itself.
- You might want to use the point of interest but also move it and the camera together. To do this, don't attempt to match keyframes for the two properties—this is sheer madness! You can parent the camera to a null and translate that instead.
- Orientation works differently depending on whether auto-orientation is on (causing it to revolve around the point of interest) or not (in which case it rotates around its center, **Figure 15.15**).
- The auto-oriented camera always maintains an upright position; cross over the X/Y plane above the center and the camera flips. To avoid this behavior, use a free camera.

The above points come into play only with more elaborate camera animations; more modest use of the 3D camera, such as a simple camera push, raises other questions.

#	Source Name	
3	Camera 1	
	Transform	Reset
	Point of Interest	360.0, 270.0, 0.0
	Position	360.0, 270.0, -480.0
	Orientation	0.0°, 0.0°, 0.0°
	X Rotation	0x +0.0°
	Y Rotation	0x +0.0°
	Z Rotation	0x +0.0°

Figure 15.15 Just in case you've never taken a close look, a camera layer contains no anchor point, but includes two sets of rotation data: the Orientation (its basic angle), as well as separate X, Y, and Z Rotation values (to avoid problems with complex 3D rotations). The point of interest appears only when the default Orient Towards Point of Interest option is active (Figure 15.14).

✔ Tip

- Cycle through the camera animation tools using the **C** key to orbit, track X/Y, and track Z in the active view.

✔ Note

The Y axis is upside down in After Effects 3D, just as in 2D; increasing the Y value moves a layer downward. The 0,0 point in After Effects space was placed at the upper-left corner of the frame when it was 2D only, and so it remains for consistency's sake.

Push and Zoom

A camera *push* moves the camera closer to the subject; a *zoom* lengthens the lens while the camera remains stationary. **Figures 15.16a** and **b** demonstrate the difference, which is just as noticeable in After Effects as in the real world. The zoom has a more extreme effect on the foreground/background composition of the shot—often too extreme, calling too much attention to the camera itself.

Dramatic zooms for the most part had their heyday in 1960's-era Sergio Leone movies, while the push is a dramatic staple. The question is, to create one do you need a 3D camera, or can you simply scale 2D layers?

Scaling a 2D layer (or several parented to a null) works for a small move; however, to recreate progression through Z space the rate of scaling must increase logarithmically, which makes everything more complicated. Not only does a 3D camera move provide this type of scaling naturally, it makes it easier to add eases, stops and starts, a little bit of destabilization—whatever works.

✔ Note

The zoom may merely be out of fashion and ready to make a comeback, but it calls attention to the camera because the

Figures 15.16a and b Frame a similar shot with a long (a) and a wide (b) lens and you get an idea of the difference between a zoom and a push. A zoom merges the relative scale of objects at various depths, lowering apparent perspective.

human vision system has no equivalent; our eyes can only push as we progress through space—they can't zoom.

Natural camera motion will contain keyframe eases (Chapter 5), for the human aspect. A little bit of irregularity lends the feeling of a camera operator's individual personality (**Figure 15.17**), or even dramatic interest (hesitation, caution, intrigue, a leap forward—the possibilities are many).

✔ Note

Animation > Keyframe Assistant > Exponential Scale is the old-school, pre-3D way to fake the illusion of a camera move in on a 2D layer. There is no good reason to employ this feature when you can instead animate a 3D camera.

A move in or out of a completely 2D shot can easily look wrong due to the lack of parallax. Likewise, tracking and panning shots, crane-ups, and other more elaborate camera moves will blow the 2.5D gag unless minute. You can, however, get away with more layering soft, translucent organic shapes, such as clouds, fog, smoke, and the like.

✔ Tip

- When pushing in on multiple overlapping coplanar 3D layers, precompose

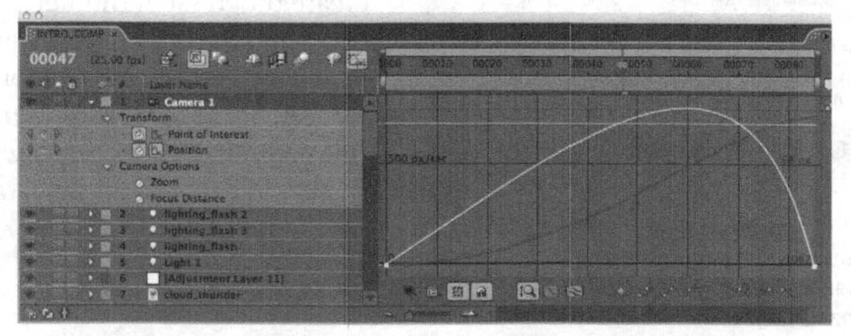

Figure 15.17 A simple camera animation can be finessed simply by applying Easy Ease (highlight keyframes and press F9), but why stop there? Lengthening the curve of the first keyframe gives the camera added (realistic) inertia transitioning from a static position.

before adding the camera animation and leave Collapse Transformations off. Coplanar 3D layers respect layer order, but an animated camera can easily cause rounding errors in floating point position calculation.

Camera Projection

Camera projection (or *camera mapping*) typically begins with a still photo, which is then projected onto 3D objects that match the dimensions and placement of objects in the photo, and then moving the camera—typically only along the Z axis—providing the illusion that the photo is fully dimensional (right up until the camera move goes too far, revealing some area of the image that wasn't part of the photograph).

Figures 15.18a, b, and c show a camera projection that ambitiously features two parked military vehicles in the foreground. A dozen separate white solids with masks were created to form a crude 3D model, ready to receive a projected image (**Figure 15.19**). This example shows both the magic of this technique—deriving perspective shifts from a flat, still image—and the associated problems of image tearing when an area of the frame is revealed that had previously been obscured in the source photo.

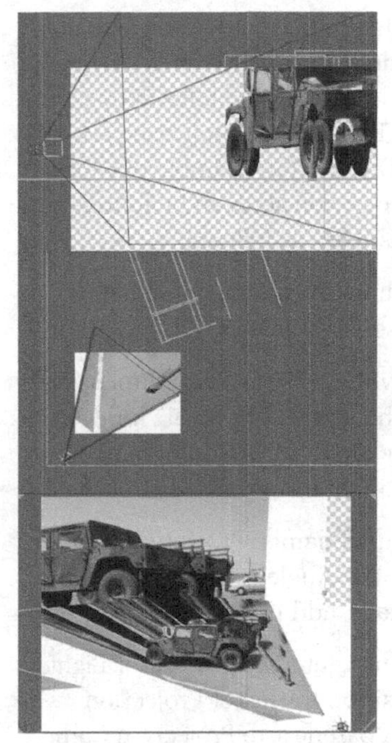

Figure 15.19 The rather complicated setup for this effect: from the top and side views you can see the planes that stand in for the vehicles and orange cone, which appears stretched along the ground plane.

The key to this effect is the setup: How is it that the one "texture" of the image (the photo) sticks to the 3D objects? The fundamental concept is actually relatively simple; getting it right is a question of managing

Figures 15.18a, b, and c The progression from the source image (a) through the camera move. By the final frame (c), image warping and tearing are evident, but the perspective of the image is essentially correct for the new camera position. The tearing occurs simply because as the camera moves it reveals areas of the image that don't exist in the source.

details, and that part is fairly advanced and not for the faint of heart (which is why mention of a third-party option follows this description). The steps to projecting any still image into 3D space (an example of which, 09_cameraProjection.aep, can be found on this book's disc) are as follows:

1. Begin with an image that can be modeled as a series of planes.
2. Create a white solid for each dimensional plane in the image. Enable 3D for each, and under Material Options, change the Accepts Lights option to Off.
3. Add a camera named Projection Cam; if you know the Angle of View of your source image, add that value.
4. Add a Point light called Projector Light. Set its position to that of Projection Cam, then parent it to Projection Cam. Set Casts Shadows to On.
5. Duplicate the source image, naming this layer Slide. Enable 3D, and in Material Options, change Casts Shadows to Only and Light Transmission to 100%.
6. Slide not located properly? Add a null object called Slide Repo; set its position to that of Projection Cam, and parent it to Projection Cam. Now parent Slide to it, and adjust its scale downward until the image is cast onto the white planes, as if projected.
7. Now comes the painful part: masking, scaling, and repositioning those white solids to build the model, ground plane, and horizon onto which the slide is projected. Toggle on the reference layer and build your model to match that, checking it with the slide every so often.
8. If planes that you know to be at perpendicular 90 degree angles don't line up, you need to adjust the Zoom value of the Projection Cam, scaling the model and slide as needed to match the new Zoom value. The example file includes an expression applied to the Scale value of the Slide layer so that the slide scales up or down to match however you adjust the Zoom of the camera, which is not necessary but is helpful.
9. Once everything is lined up, duplicate Projection Cam, and rename the duplicate (the one on the higher layer) Anim Cam. Freely move this camera to take advantage of the new dimensional reality of the scene (**Figure 15.20**).

Figure 15.20 Better than relying only on projection, which can lead to the tearing seen in Figure 9.18, is to position specific foreground layers. Here all of the people in the street are actually matted layers positioned in 3D space.

The best way to learn about this is probably to study the example file included on this book's disc; if it seems enticing rather than aggravating, feel free to give it a whirl.

Camera Blur

Camera blur is the result of objects positioned outside the camera's depth of field, whether because the lens was intentionally defocused or simply because the focal range was too shallow to capture everything sharply.

✔ Note

Buena Software offers a set of plug-ins known as Depth Cue, which includes Camera Mapper, a plug-in that controls this process and makes it easy to clean up such tearing and stretching errors as those seen in Figure 15.18c.

Ironically, the high-end medium of film naturally has a shallower depth of field than any video camera, and even more ironically, shallow depth of field and the aesthetic of camera blur is what you would call "cinematic" and thus largely desirable. A shallow focal range literally focuses the viewer's attention; moving areas of a shot in and out of focus, meanwhile, can create dramatic anticipation and a beautiful aesthetic.

It can be a lot of work to re-create depth of field effects in After Effects; it's better to get them in camera if possible. Nonetheless you can create specific cinematic blur effects such as a *rack focus* shot, in which the focus changes from a subject at one distance from the camera to another.

Limited focal range is a natural part of human vision, but camera lenses contribute their own unique blur characteristics that in the contemporary era are often considered aesthetically pleasing the world over. There is even a Japanese term (literally meaning "fuzzy") to describe the quality of out-of-focus light as viewed through a lens, *boke* (also *bokeh*, more phonetic but clunkier).

You can create these effects and more in After Effects. It's not automatic the way it is with the camera lens itself, and it can require patience and careful observation of nature, but if you're a compositor you have those already.

✔ Note

A solid description of boke with links lives on the Web at http://en.wikipedia.org/wiki/Bokeh.

Image Planes and Rack Focus

Any time you can divide a shot into distinct planes of depth with each plane as its own layer, you can rack focus. All you need is a focal point to animate and a depth of field narrow enough to create blur everywhere but the immediate plane of focus.

Narrow depth of field is created on a real camera by lowering the f-stop value, which lowers exposure as well. Not so with the After Effects 3D camera. Its Aperture and F-Stop settings (**Figure 15.21**) affect only focal depth, not exposure or motion blur. The two settings have an inverse relationship. F-Stop is the setting more commonly referenced by camera operators, and yet only Aperture appears as a property in the Timeline.

After Effects depth of field settings can be matched to a camera report, provided that it includes the f-stop setting used when the footage was shot. If so, open up the Camera Settings dialog (**Ctrl+Shift+Y/Cmd+Shift+Y**, or double-click on the Camera in the

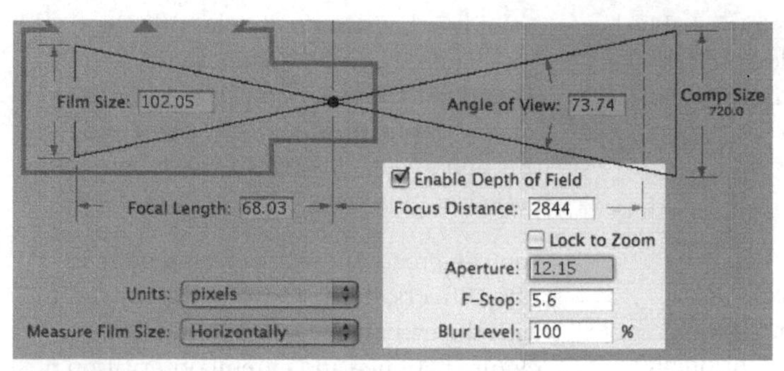

Figure 15.21 Check Enable Depth of Field in Camera Settings to activate Focus Distance (the distance in pixels of the focal point, which can be toggled to Lock to the Zoom). A low F-Stop (or high Aperture) with a Blur Level of 100% creates a shallow focal effect.

Timeline panel), check the box labeled Enable Depth of Field, and enter the value.

The key here is to offset at least one layer in Z space so that it falls out of focal range. Now, in the Top view, set the Focus Distance (under Options) to match the layer that will be in focus at the beginning of the shot, add a keyframe, then change the Focus Distance at another frame to match a second layer later in the shot (**Figure 15.22**).

A static focus pull doesn't look quite right; changing focus on a real camera will change the framing of the shot slightly. To sell the example shot, which starts on a view of the city and racks focus to reveal a sign in the foreground, I add a slight camera pull-back, which takes advantage of the nice shift in planes of motion from the offset layers (**Figure 15.23**).

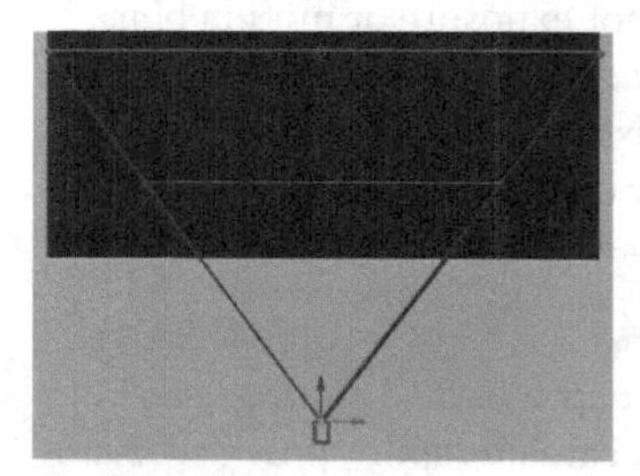

Figure 15.22 With Enable Depth of Field on, the Focus Distance is denoted by a red boundary line, easily viewed and animated in isometric views.

Figure 15.23 The final shot combines a rack focus with a gentle pull-back, using ease keyframes to animate Position and Focus Distance.

Boke Blur

Racking focus in this manner generates camera blur that is accurate relative to the plane of focus, but it does not truly create the look of a defocused lens.

Boke connotes the phenomenon whereby points of light become discs of light (also called *circles of confusion*) that take on the character of the lens itself as they pass through the camera lens and aperture. Like lens flares (covered in Chapter 17) these are purely a phenomenon of the camera lens, not human vision; they can add beauty and suspense to a shot.

Illuminated out of focus elements in a shot are, after all, mysterious. Visual intrigue is created as the shot resolves in or out of a wash of color and light (**Figure 15.24**).

A perfect lens passes a defocused point of light to the back of the camera as a soft, spherical blur. A bright point remains bright, but is larger and softer. Ordinary blur in 8 or 16 bit per channel color mode instead merely dims the highlights (**Figures 15.25a**, **b**, and **c**).

Most camera lenses are not perfect, so instead of perfect blurred spheres, boke spheres may be brighter toward the edges than in the middle. An anamorphic lens will show squashed spheres, and as with lens flares, the shape of the aperture itself may be visible in the circles, making them hexagonal (or pentagonal, and so on, depending on the number of blades in the opening).

Go for Boke

To accurately create the bloom of highlights as they are blurred requires 32 bit per channel color and source highlights that are brighter than what would be called full white in 8 or 16 bpc. This is explored and explained in Chapter 16.

Figure 15.24 Even in the very first, most blurred frame of this pull-back shot, you may recognize the image content, yet its appearance is strange and compelling. With shallow depth of field, highlights in the foreground retain blur even in a focused shot.

The Lens Blur effect does not operate in 32 bpc—it instead mimics the behavior of bright highlights through a lens. It's more or less a direct port from Photoshop; as such, it can be slow and cumbersome in After Effects. It won't blur beyond 100 pixels, and it does not understand non-square pixels (instead creating a perfect circle every time).

Instead of 3D camera or layer data, Lens Blur can use a Depth Map Layer, using pixel values (brightness) from a specified Depth Map Channel. You can rack focus by

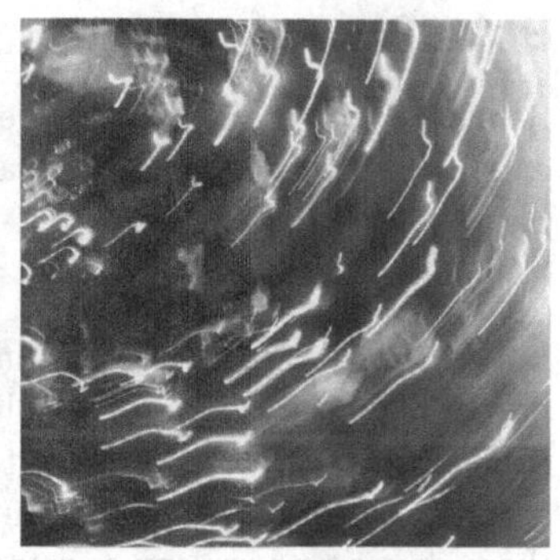

Figures 15.25a, b, and c Motion blur generated the standard way (a and b) literally pales in comparison to true motion blur on illuminated elements created by a moving camera (or objects) while the shutter is open (c).

adjusting Blur Focal Distance. Iris Shape defines polygons around the highlights, corresponding to the number of blades in the iris; these can also have a specified Iris Blade Curvature and Iris Rotation (this rotates the polygon).

✔ Note

The most respected third-party tool for lens blurs is Frischluft's Lenscare. The default settings are not reliable, but with adjustments and depth maps (for 3D footage), you can derive some lovely results (www.frischluft.com and on the book's DVD).

The actual amount of blur is determined by Iris Radius, the bloom by Specular Threshold (all pixels above this value are highlights) and Specular Brightness, which creates the simulation of highlight bloom. These are the controls you'll tweak most (**Figure 15.26**).

The Noise controls are designed to restore noise that would be removed by the blur operation; they don't relate to the blur itself and can be ignored in favor of grain techniques described in the following section.

By no means do the settings in Lens Blur (or for that matter, third-party alternatives such as Lenscare from Frischluft) exhaust the possibilities for how defocused areas of an image might appear, especially when illuminated. Keep looking at reference and thinking of ways to re-create what you see in it (**Figure 15.27**).

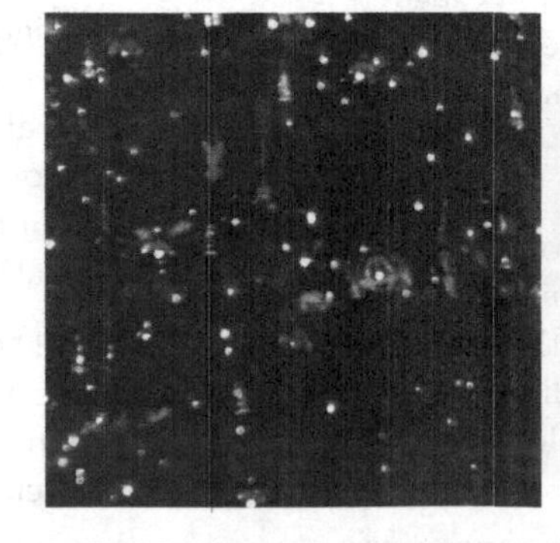

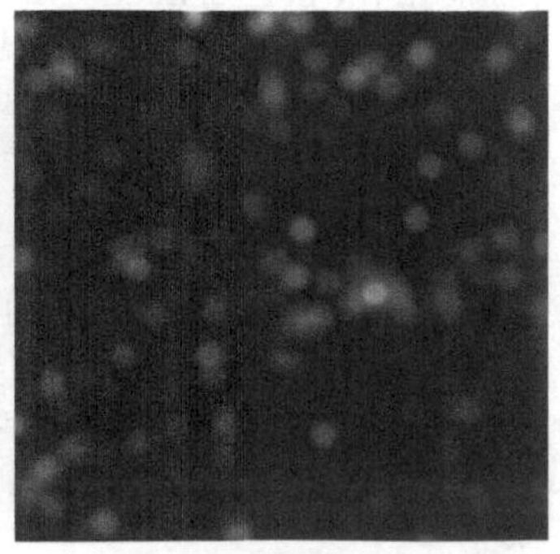

Figure 15.26 Lens Blur doesn't yield a perfect result when cranked up this high, but it does generate the disk shapes around specular highlights characteristic of Boke blur (here, set as hexagons). The result on the larger specular area of the lamp is odd (due to a low threshold of 90%), and there is no repeat edge pixel option, leading to a translucent fringe.

Figure 15.27 Now that you know a little more about the phenonemon of boke and how defocused images look, study up. Does an image with shallow depth of field look more cinematic? What do you see happening in the defocused background?

The Role of Grain

Once the image passes through the lens and is recorded, it takes on another characteristic: grain. Grain is essentially high-frequency noise readily apparent in each channel of most recorded footage, although with progress in image gathering technology has come a reduction of grain. Grain can however be your friend, adding life to static imagery and camouflaging edge detail.

Grain management is an essential part of creating high-quality moving images; properly done, it is not simply switched on or off, but requires careful per-channel adjustment. There are two basic factors to consider:

- Size of the grain, per channel
- Amount of grain, or amount of contrast in the grain, per channel

✔ Note

The day may come when digital cameras can deliver moving footage with no grain whatsoever. Already, all-digital movies that use no footage, such as those by Pixar, also do not use grain in the master.

The emphasis here is that these factors typically vary from channel to channel. Blue is almost universally the channel likeliest to have the most noise; happily the human eye is less sensitive to blue than red or green, but it can be bad news for blue-screen mattes.

How much grain is enough? As with color in Chapter 14, "Color Correction," the goal is typically to match what's there already. If your shot has a background plate with the proper amount of grain in it, match foreground elements to that. A fully computer-generated scene might have to be matched to surrounding shots.

✔ Note

Excessive grain is often triggered by a low amount of scene light combined with a low-quality image-gathering medium, such as miniDV, whose CCD has poor light-gathering abilities.

Grain Management Strategies

After Effects Professional includes a suite of three tools for automated grain sampling, grain reduction, and grain generation: Add Grain, Match Grain, and Remove Grain. Add Grain relies on your settings only, but Match Grain and Remove Grain can generate initial settings by sampling a source layer for grain patterns.

I often caution against the automated solution, but not in this case. Match Grain is not even appreciably slower with grain sampling than Add Grain, which does not sample but includes all of the same controls. Match Grain usually comes up with a good first pass at settings. In either case

1. Look for a section of your source footage with a solid color area that stays in place for 10 to 20 frames. Most clips satisfy

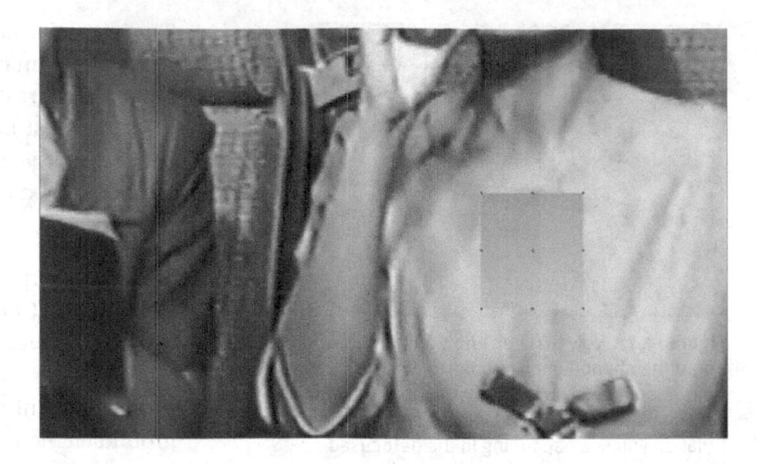

Figure 15.28 Insert a small solid and add a Ramp effect, then use the eyedropper tools in Ramp to sample the brightest and darkest areas of the background. This offers a clear evaluation of a grain match once Match Grain or Add Grain is applied.

these criteria, and those that don't tend to allow less precision anyhow.

2. Zoom to 200% to 400% on the solid color area, and create a Region of Interest around it. Set the Work Area to the 10 or 20 frames with little or no motion.

3. Add a solid small enough to occupy part of the Region of Interest. Apply a Ramp effect to the solid, and use the eyedropper tools to select the darkest and lightest pixels in the solid color area of the clip. The lack of grain detail in the foreground gradient should be clearly apparent (**Figure 15.28**).

4. Apply the Match Grain effect to the foreground solid. Choose the source footage layer in the Noise Source Layer pulldown. As soon as the effect finishes rendering a sample frame, you have a basis from which to begin fine-tuning. You can RAM Preview at this point to see how close a match you have. In most cases, you're not done yet.

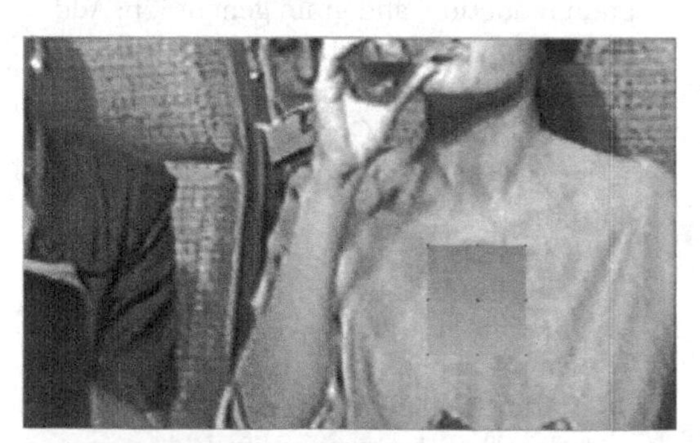

Figure 15.29 As with color matching, proper grain matching requires channel-by-channel examination. Match Grain includes the best kind of automation, enabling you easily to improve upon the initial result.

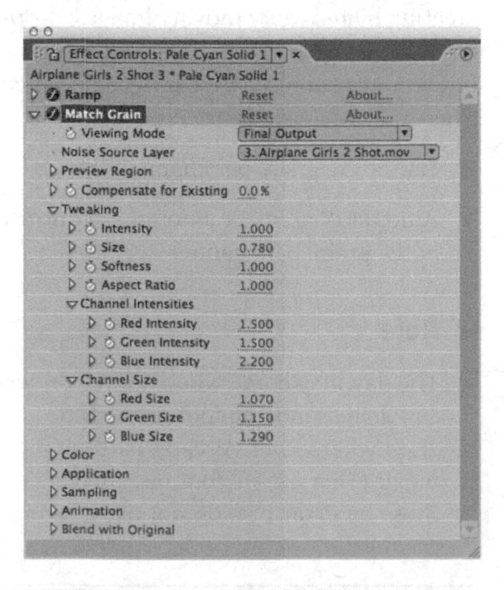

5. Twirl down the Tweaking controls for Match Grain, and then twirl down Channel Intensities and Channel Size. You can save yourself a lot of time by doing most of your work here, channel by channel.
6. Activate the red channel only in the Composition window (**Alt+1/Option+1**) and adjust the Red Intensity and Red Size values to match the foreground and background (**Figure 15.29**). Repeat this process for the green and blue channels (**Alt+2/Option+2** and **Alt+3/ Option+3**). RAM Preview the result.
7. Adjust Intensity, Size, or Softness controls under Tweaking according to what you see in the RAM Preview. You may also find it necessary to reduce Saturation under Color, particularly if your source is film rather than video.

✔ Close-Up

Use Noise as Grain Prior to the addition of Add Grain and Match Grain to version 6.5 Professional, the typical way to generate grain was to use the Noise effect. The main advantage of the Noise effect over Match Grain is that it renders about 20x faster. However, After Effects doesn't make it easy for you to separate the effect channel by channel, and scaling it requires a separate effect (or precomping).

You can employ three solid layers, with three effects applied to each layer: Shift Channels, Noise, and Transform. You use Shift Channels to set each solid to red, green, or blue, respectively, set Blending Modes to Add, and set their Opacity very low (well below 10%, adjusting as needed). Next, set the amount of noise and scale it via the Transform effect.

If the grain is meant to affect a set of foreground layers only, hold them out from the background plate either via precomping or track mattes. If this sounds complicated, it is, which is why Match Grain is preferable unless the rendering time is really killer.

In most cases, these steps yield a workable result; the example project (09_grainMatch.aep) used for these figures is included on your disc. The effect can then be copied and pasted to any foreground layers that need

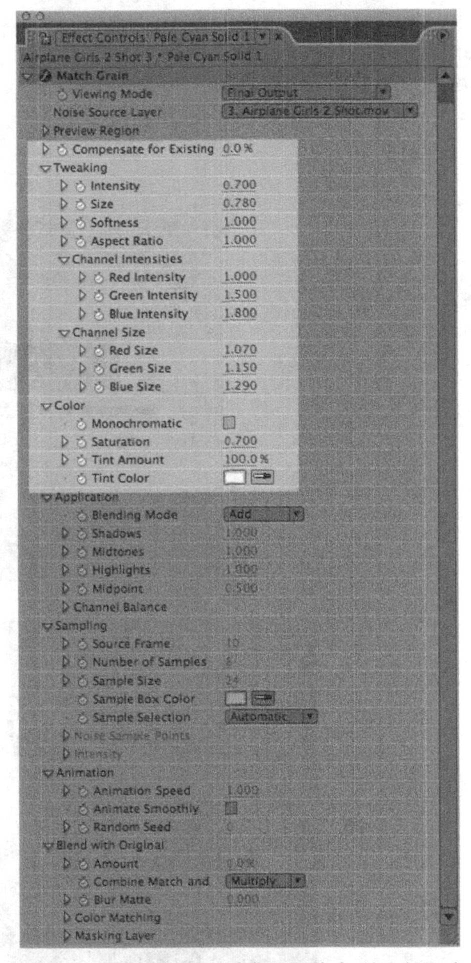

Figure 15.30 The essential controls in Match Grain contain a lot of properties, with the broadest and most used at the top: Intensity, Size, and Softness, then refining the individual Channel Intensities and Channel Size (as in Figure 15.28).

grain. If the foreground layer already contains noise or grain, you may need to adjust the Compensate for Existing Noise percentage for that layer.

Obviously, whole categories of controls are untouched with this method (**Figure 15.30**); the Application category, for example, contains controls for how the grain is blended and how it affects shadows, midtones, and highlights individually. Typically these are overkill, as are the Sampling and Animation controls, but how far you go in matching grain before your eye is satisfied is, of course, up to you and your team. This is one more case in which slamming the result can help ascertain its effectiveness (**Figure 15.31**).

Grain Removal

Removing grain, or sharpening an image in general, is an entirely different process from adding grain. On a well-shot production, you'll rarely have a reason to reach for the Remove Grain tool.

If you do, the reason for doing so may be unique to your particular footage. In such cases, you may very well find that Remove Grain at the default settings gives you a satisfactory result. If not, check into the

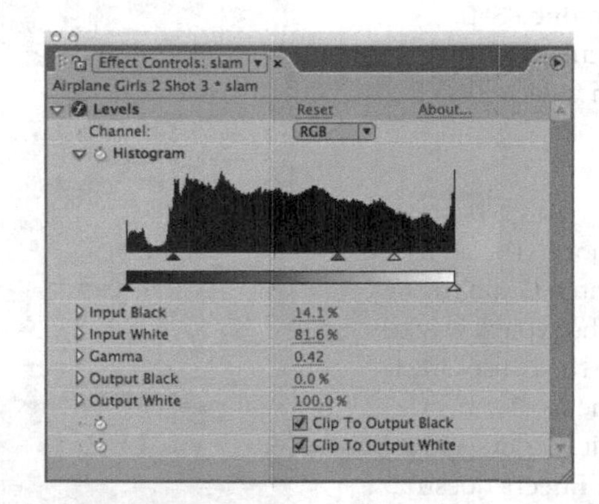

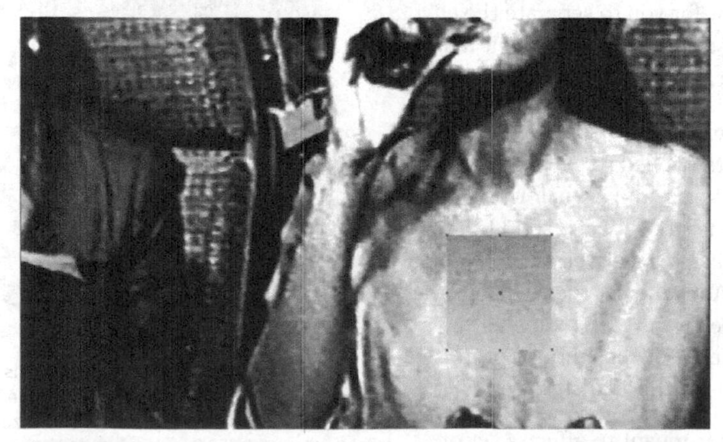

Figure 15.31 Slam the result, bringing out contrast in the grain and revealing the effectiveness of the match.

Fine Tuning and Unsharp Mask settings to adjust it.

✔ Tip

- If you're using Remove Grain to improve the likelihood of a clean blue-screen or green-screen key, apply the resulting matte back to your source footage as an alpha track matte. This offers the best of both worlds: a clean matte channel and realistic grain on the source color layer.

Remove Grain is often best employed "behind the scenes"—not across the entire frame (**Figure 15.32**) or intermediately in combination with other effects. It is, however, a fairly sophisticated solution that can really help in seemingly hopeless situations; this book's technical editor reports having used it extensively on a feature film on which the aging lead actor needed a lot of "aesthetic" facial work done (removing wrinkles and so on).

When to Manage Grain

The most obvious candidates for grain addition are computer-generated or still image layers that lack the moving grain found in film or video footage. As soon as your shot has to match anything that came from a camera, and particularly in a large format such as HD or film, you must manage grain.

Blurred elements may also need grain addition, even if they originate as source footage. Blurry source shots contain as much grain as focused ones because the grain is an artifact of the medium recording the image, not the subject itself. Elements that have been scaled down in After Effects contain scaled-down grain, which may require restoration. Color keying can also suppress grain in the channel that has been keyed out.

Other compositing operations will instead enhance grain. Sharpening, unless performed via Remove Grain, can strongly emphasize grain contrast in an element, typically in a not-so-desirable manner. Sharpening also brings out any nasty compression artifacts that come with footage that uses JPEG-type compression, such as miniDV video.

Lack of grain, however, is one of the big dead giveaways of a poorly composited shot. It is worth the effort to match the correct amount of grain into your shot even if the result isn't apparent as you preview it on your monitor.

Figure 15.32 It may suit a still figure in a book (applied at the right side of this image), but Remove Grain on an entire shot with the default settings is rarely desirable. In full motion the grain-reduced shot looks a bit strange and retains a certain soft lumpiness.

Film and Video Looks

If you flipped to this section intentionally, you may be trying to do one of two things with a given shot or project:

- Alter the viewer's impression of how footage was shot, stylizing the footage so that a shot you took with your HDV camera looks like old Super8 film, or has a bleach bypass look. Or maybe you're trying to degrade a clean computer graphics animation so it looks like it was shot with someone's handicam.
- Shoot your own movie for as little as possible and maximize the production value—that is, the quality of the imagery itself.

There are so many issues connected to the second one above and beyond what you can achieve in an After Effects comp that Stu Maschwitz went and wrote a whole book about it. *The DV Rebel's Guide: An All-Digital Approach to Making Killer Action Movies on the Cheap* (Peachpit Press, 2006) is an excellent resource, not only for After Effects knowledge, but for the whole process of low-budget digital filmmaking. The first chapter lists the major factors that influence production value. Many of these, including image and sound quality, location and lighting, cannot entirely be created in After Effects, which must be why Stu's book includes a bunch of information on how to actually shoot.

The first item, however, is closer to the realm of tricks you can pull off consistently in After Effects, including the following:

- **Lens artifacts**—In addition to those already discussed in this chapter, such as boke and chromatic aberration, are such filmic visual staples as the vignette and the lens flare.
- **Frame rate:** Change this and you can profoundly alter the viewer's perception of footage.
- **Aspect ratio:** The format of the composition makes a huge perceptual difference as well, although it's not so simple as "wider = better."
- **Color palette:** Nothing affects the mood of a given shot like color and contrast. It's a complex subject further explored in Chapter 17.

✔ Close-Up

Garbage In, Garbage Out You don't need me to tell you how difficult it is to bring a poorly shot image back from the dead, but check "The DV Rebel's Guide" for a thorough rundown of factors that go into a well-shot image, and if possible go on set to offer supervision and help eliminate flaws that will be difficult to fix in post. Among the less obvious points from the book

- When shooting digitally, keep the contrast low and overall light levels well below maximum; you are shooting the negative, not the final (**Figures 15.33a and 15.33b**).
- If using a small, light camera, mount it to something heavy to move it; that weight reads to the viewer as more expensive and more natural motion.

Lens Artifacts Aren't Just Accidents

Because this chapter is all about reality as glimpsed by the camera lens, several types of lens artifacts, visual phenomena that occur only through a lens, have already appeared in this chapter, including lens distortion and lens blur (or boke).

Figure 15.33 The low contrast source (a) of this digital image doesn't look too hot, yet because it has preserved all color, including the brightest areas of the sky, without clipping, it is possible to recover a good deal of color detail and dynamic range (b).

You won't be surprised to hear that this isn't all: potentially in your palette are more phenomena of the type that professional cinematographers tended to avoid until the 1970s (when they started to be considered cool). These include lens flares, vignettes, and chromatic aberration. None of these occur with the naked eye, but remember, your target is the look of the real world as seen through the camera.

Lens Flares

Lens flares are caused by secondary reflections bouncing around between the camera elements. Because they occur within the lens, they appear superimposed over the image, even when partially occluded by objects in the foreground.

Unlike your eye, which has only one very flexible lens, camera lenses are made up of a series of inflexible lens elements; the longer the lens, the more elements within. Each element is coated to prevent reflection under normal circumstances, but with enough light flooding directly in, reflection occurs.

Artists sometimes like to get goofy and creative with lens flares; how many of us, after all, are experts in how they should look? And yet this is one more area where seemingly unsophisticated viewers can smell something fake under their noses, so certain rules apply.

Zoom lenses contain many focusing elements and tend to generate a complex-looking flare with lots of individual reflections. Prime lenses generate fewer reflections and a simpler flare.

Just as with boke, aperture blades within the lens can contribute to the appearance of flares. Their highly reflective corners often result in streaks, the number corresponding to the number of blades. The shape of the flares sometimes corresponds to the shape of the aperture (a pentagon for a five-sided aperture, a hexagon for six). Dust and scratches on the lens also reflect light.

You can create a lens flare look by hand using solids and blending modes, but most people don't have the time for this. The Lens Flare effect that ships with After Effects is a rather paltry offering and includes little in the way of customization; you're best off with Knoll Light Factory (**Figure 15.34**), which is highly customizable and derived from careful study of lens behaviors, although if you already own Tinderbox 2 from The Foundry, the T_LensFlare is still a vast improvement over the After Effects default.

More about the behavior and application of lens flares appears in Chapter 17.

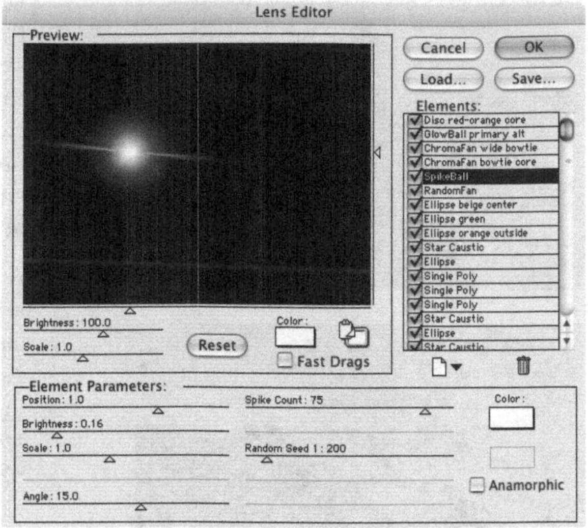

Figure 15.34 Knoll Light Factory is controlled via a custom interface launched from an Options button in the Effect Controls. Presets such as this one, called "Monkey Planet," may include dozens of individually adjustable elements, listed right.

Vignettes

Vignetting is a reduction in image brightness around the edges of an image. It's generally an undesired by-product of certain lenses (particularly wide-angle fisheyes), but it is sometimes deliberately chosen because of how it helps focus attention on the center of frame. I can say with authority that several underwater shots from *Pirates of the Caribbean: At World's End* contain vignettes, because I added them myself.

It's an easy effect to create:

1 Create a black solid the size of your frame as the top layer and name it Vignette.

2 Double-click the Ellipse tool in the toolbar; an elliptical mask fills the frame.

3 Highlight the layer in the Timeline and press **F** to reveal Mask Feather.

4 Increase the Mask Feather value a lot—somewhere in the triple-digits is probably about right.

5 Lower the Opacity value (**T**) until the effect looks right; you might prefer a light vignette (10 to 15%) or something heavier (40 to 50%).

Note that the vignette is elliptical, not perfectly round, and if your project is to be seen in more than one format (see below) you'll have to decide which is the target (**Figure 15.35**). There would be no reason for a realistic vignette to appear offset.

Chromatic Aberration

Even further down the road of questionably aesthetic visual phenomena is chromatic aberration, a fringing or smearing of light that occurs when a lens cannot focus various colors on the spectrum to a single point, because of the differing wavelengths. The effect is similar to that of light passing through a prism and dispersing into a rainbow of colors.

Like vignettes, and optically related to lens flares and boke, chromatic aberration is something higher-end lenses are designed to avoid, yet it can occur even under relatively expensive and high-end shooting circumstances, particularly if there is any type of lens conversion happening.

Figure 15.35 A vignette is created with a feathered mask applied to a solid (a). If the image is reframed for display in another format, such as anamorphic, you may have to use that framing instead of the source (b).

Unlike the others, it can really look like a mistake, so it's not the kind of thing you would probably add to a clip in order to make it look cool; instead you might add it to a shot or element to match another shot or background plate in which it appears. My recommendation in such a case?

1 Duplicate the layer twice and precompose all three.

2 Use the Shift Channels effect to leave only red, green or blue on for each layer (so you end up with one of each).

3 Set the top two layers to Add mode.

4 Scale the green channel to roughly 101% and the blue channel to roughly 102%.

5 Add a small amount of Radial Blur (set to Zoom, not the default Spin).

A before and after comparison appears in **Figure 15.36**.

Frame Rate Isn't Just Speed

One could probably write a whole book or thesis on this one topic alone, but it's no accident that film images are displayed at 24 frames per second and that newer digital formats, which could theoretically be optimized for just about any frame rate, also aim for this rate (despite how difficult it is to find a low-end camera that shoots 24p natively, with no interlacing).

The question that would generate all of the chatter is "why?" There is no logical answer, and many attempts have been made to explore alternatives. The simple truth seems to be that frame rates of 30 fps and higher feel more like direct reality, but 24 fps is just above the threshold where persistence of vision breaks down, giving it a more

Figure 15.36 A normal (a) and chromatically aberrated (b) image. Chromatic aberration is caused when different wavelengths of light have different focal lengths; most lenses attempt to correct for it with an added diffractive element.

ephemeral and dream-like quality, just as do other cinematic conventions such as light bloom and shallow depth of field.

If you have a choice on a given project and you want it to have a cinematic look, try creating it at 24 fps and judge for yourself. After Effects is quite forgiving about letting you change frame rates mid-stream compared with most video applications; details on how the conversion actually works appeared back in Chapter 5.

If you have no choice but to work at 29.97, you still have a choice: progressive versus interlaced. It's not necessarily an error to render animation without adding interlacing; in fact, step through your favorite animated series on television and you may find that it's animated at 15 fps or less (and basically never at 59.94 fps, which is effectively what 29.97 fps interlaced means in animation terms). *South Park* doesn't count.

✔ Close-Up

The Videotape Revolution The debate between using 24 fps film and 29.97 fps videotape in the U.S. and other countries with NTSC has been raging since long before the digital era. It began with the advent of videotape in the 1950s, when tape was cheap and fast, if cumbersome by today's standards.

One particular experiment from this era stands out. For six episodes the producers of *The Twilight Zone* tried tape before they evidently realized it was ruining the show's mystique.

Video's higher frame rate and harder look instantly turned one of the most intriguing and ironic series of all time into something that looked more like a soap opera. To judge for yourself, rent DVDs from Season 2 that include the following videotaped episodes: "Static," "Night of the Meek," "The Lateness of the Hour," "The Whole Truth," "Twenty-Two," or "Long Distance Call."

✔ Note

The numbers "1.85" and "2.35" give the width, relative to a height of 1, so it's like saying 1.85:1 or 2.35:1. The 16:9 format, which has become popular with digital video and HD, is equivalent to a 1.77:1 ratio, slightly narrower than Academy, but wide compared to the standard television format of 4:3 (1.33:1).

Format Isn't Just Display Size

As the world transitions from standard-definition to high-definition broadcast television, formats are undergoing the same

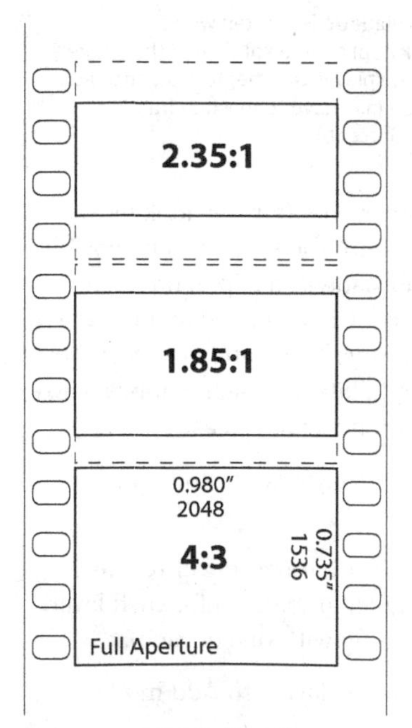

Figure 15.37 The "wider" film formats might more accurately be called "shorter" because they typically involve cropping the original 4:3 image.

transition that they made in film half a century ago. The nearly square 4:3 aspect is being replaced as standard by the wider 16:9 format, but 1.85 Academy aperture and 2.35 Cinemascope also appear as common "widescreen" formats.

A lot of artists (students, particularly) fall in love with the widescreen look for how it conjures *Star Wars* and *Lawrence of Arabia*, but if these formats aren't shown at 24 fps and don't obey other cinematic conventions outlined here, the result tends to appear a bit cheesy. So remember, it's a convention we associate with film, whether or not we know the following history.

In response to the growing popularity of television in the 1950s, Hollywood conjured up a number of different widescreen formats through experiments with anamorphic lenses and film stocks as wide as 70 mm. These systems—CinemaScope, VistaVision, Panavision, and so on—haven't completely faded away, but their presence in the modern era is mostly felt in the way that films are displayed, not how they are shot. 35 mm is once again the most popular shooting format, specifically the full-aperture version known as Super 35 mm.

Standard 35 mm film has an aspect ratio of 4:3, which is not coincidentally the same as a television. Almost all current movies are filmed in this format as if originally intended for the small screen. When shown in a theater using a widescreen aspect of 1.85:1 (also known as 16:9, the HDTV standard) or 2.35:1 (CinemaScope/Panavision), the full 4:3 negative is cropped (**Figure 15.37**). Theater patrons actually pay $10 to see less than if

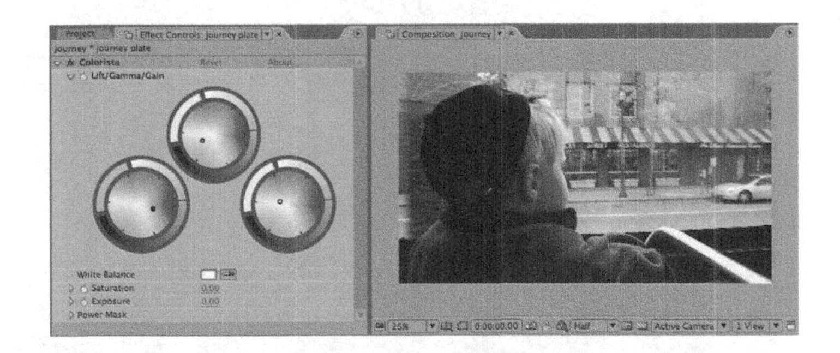

Figure 15.38a and b Two plug-ins from Red Giant Software aim to let you add color looks like a pro. Colorista (a) is a three-way color corrector superior in fundamental ways to those found in most nonlinear editing packages including Premiere Pro. Magic Bullet Looks 3 opens up a separate user interface and can deliver looks that go beyond just color, such as a diffusion effect (b).

they waited for the movie to get broadcast full screen on cable!

Color Can Be Much More than Pretty

The influence of color decisions on the final shot, and by extension on the story being told in the shot, is an immense topic, hashed over by cinematographers and colorists the world over. Any attempt to distill this into a few pithy paragraphs would be a disservice.

Thus, if you're new to the idea of developing a color look for a film or sequence, look at references. Study other people's work for the effect of color on the mood and story in a shot, sequence, or entire film. **Figures 15.38a** and **b** show a couple of third-party tools designed specifically to give a particular look or mood to your shot.

Conclusion

And really, you've just scratched the surface of what's possible. The inventive compositor can and should always look for new methods to replicate the way that the camera sees the world, going beyond realism to present what we really want to see—realism as it looks through the lens.

32 Bit HDR Compositing and Color Management

True realism consists in revealing the surprising things which habit keeps covered and prevents us from seeing.

–Jean Cocteau (French director, painter, playwright, and poet)

HDR Compositing and Color Management

You may already be aware that although After Effects by default matches the 8 bit per channel color limitation of your monitor, this is hardly the way to create the optimal image. Thus other modes and methods for color are available, including high bit depths, alternate color spaces and color management. Few topics in After Effects generate as much curiosity or confusion as these. Each of the features detailed here improves upon the standard digital color model you know best, but at the cost of requiring better understanding on your part.

In After Effects CS3 the process centers around Color Management, which is no longer a feature that can safely be ignored; operations essential to input and output now rely on it. The name "Color Management" would seem to imply that it is an automated process to manage colors for you, when in fact it is a complex set of tools allowing (even requiring) you to effectively manage color.

On the other hand, 32 bit High Dynamic Range (HDR) compositing is routinely ignored by artists who could benefit from it, despite that it remains uncommon for source files to contain over-range color data, which are pixel values too bright for your monitor to display.

Film can and typically does contain these over-range color values. These are typically brought into After Effects as 10 bit log Cineon or DPX files, and importing, converting, and writing this format requires a bit of special knowledge. It's an elegant and highly standardized system that has relevance even when working with the most up-to-date high-end digital cameras.

CS3 Color Management: Why Bother?

It's normal to wish Color Management would simply go away. So many of us have produced footage with After Effects for years and devised our own systems to manage color through each stage of production. We've assumed, naively perhaps, that a pixel is a pixel and as long as we control the RGB value of that pixel, we maintain control over the appearance of the image.

The problem with this way of thinking is that it's tied to the monitor. The way a given RGB pixel looks on your monitor is somewhat arbitrary—I'm typing this on a laptop, and I know that its monitor has higher contrast than my desktop monitors, one of which has a bluer cast than the other if I don't adjust them to match. Not only that, the way that color operates on your monitor is nothing like the way it works in the real world, or even in a camera. Not only is the dynamic range far more limited, but also an arbitrary gamma adjustment is required to make images look right.

Color itself is not arbitrary. Although color is a completely human system, it is the result of measurable natural phenomena. Because the qualities of a given color are measurable to a large degree, a system is evolving to measure them, and Adobe is attempting to spearhead the progress of that system with its Color Management features.

Completely Optional

The Color Management feature set in After Effects is completely optional and disabled by default. Its features become necessary in cases including, but not necessarily limited to, the following:

- A project relies on a color managed file (with an embedded ICC Profile). For example, a client provides an image or clip with specific managed color settings and requires that the output match.
- A project will benefit from a linearized 1.0 gamma working space. If that means nothing to you, read on; this is the chapter that explains it.
- Output will be displayed in some manner that's not directly available on your system.
- A project is shared and color adjusted on a variety of workstations, each with a calibrated monitor. The goal is for color corrections made on a given workstation to match once the shot moves on from that workstation.

To achieve these goals requires that some old rules be broken and new ones established.

Related and Mandatory

Other changes introduced in After Effects CS3 seem tied to Color Management but come into play even if you never enable it:

- A video file in a DV or other Y'CrCb (YUV) format requires (and receives) automatic color interpretation upon import into After Effects, applying settings that would previously have been up to you to add. This is done by MediaCore, a little known Adobe application that runs invisibly behind the scenes of Adobe video applications (see "Input Profile and MediaCore," below).
- QuickTime gamma settings in general have become something of a moving target as Apple adds its own form of color management, whose effects vary from codec to codec. As a result, there are situations in which imported and rendered QuickTimes won't look right. This is not the fault of Color Management, although you can use the feature set to correct the problems that come up (see "QuickTime," below).
- Linear blending (using a 1.0 gamma only for pixel-blending operations without converting all images to linear gamma) is possible without setting a linearized Project Working Space, and thus without enabling Color Management whatsoever (see the last section of this chapter).

Because these issues also affect how color is managed, they tend to get lumped in with the Color Management system when in fact they can be unique from it.

A Pixel's Journey through After Effects

Join me now as we follow color through After Effects, noting the various features that can affect its appearance or even its very identity—its RGB value. Although it's not mandatory, it's best to increase that pixel's color flexibility and accuracy, warming it up to get it ready for the trip, by raising project bit depth above 8 bpc. Here's why.

16 Bit per Channel Composites

A 16 bit per channel color was added to After Effects 5.0 for one basic reason: to eliminate color quantization, most commonly seen in the form of banding where subtle gradients and other threshold regions appear in an image. In 16 bpc mode there are 128 extra gradations between each R, G, B, and A value contained in the familiar 8 bpc mode.

Those increments are typically too fine for your eye to distinguish (or your monitor to display), but your eye easily notices banding, and when you start to make multiple adjustments to 8 bpc images, as may be required by color management features, banding is bound to appear in edge thresholds and shadows, making the image look bad.

You can raise color depth in your project by either Alt/Option-clicking on the color depth setting at the bottom of the Project panel, or via the Depth pull-down menu in File > Project Settings. The resulting performance hit typically isn't as bad as you might think.

✔ Note

Many but not all effects and plug-ins support 16 bpc color. To discern which ones do, with your project set to the target bit depth (16 bpc in this case), choose Show 16 bpc-Capable Effects Only from the Effects & Presets panel menu. Effects that are only 8 bpc aren't off-limits; you should just be careful about where you apply them—best is typically either at the beginning or the end of the image pipeline, and watch for banding.

Most digital artists prefer 8 bpc colors because we're so used to them, but switching to 16 bpc mode doesn't mean you're stuck with incomprehensible pixel values of 32768, 0, 0 for pure red or 16384, 16384, 16384 middle gray. In the panel menu of the Info panel, choose whichever numerical color representation works for you; this setting is used everywhere in the application, including the Adobe color picker (**Figure 16.1**). The following section refers to 8 bpc values in 16 bpc projects.

Monitor Calibration

Sometimes it becomes obvious that RGB values alone cannot describe pure colors; if you don't know what I'm talking about, find a still-working decade old CRT monitor and plug it in.

Assuming your monitor isn't that far out of whack, third-party color calibration hardware and software can be used to generate a profile which is then stored and set as a system preference. This monitor profile accomplishes two things:

- Defines a color space for compositing unique from what is properly called monitor color space

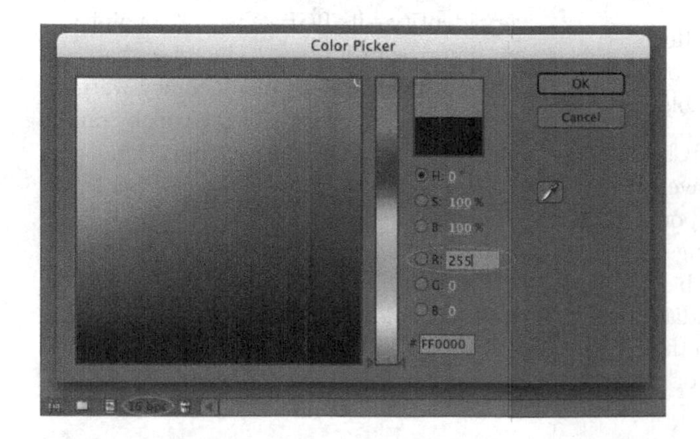

Figure 16.1 If you hesitate to work in 16 bpc simply because you don't like the unwieldy color numbers, consider setting the Info panel to display 8 bpc while you work in 16 bpc; this change will be rippled throughout the application, including the Adobe color picker.

- Offers control over the color appearance of the composition. Each pixel has not only an RGB value but an actual precise and absolute color.

In other words, the color values and how they interrelate change, as does the method used to display them.

✔ Note

Is there an external broadcast monitor attached to your system (set as an Output Device in Preferences > Video Preview)? Color Management settings do not apply to that device.

Color Management: Disabled by Default

Import a file edited in another Adobe application such as Photoshop or Lightroom and it likely contains an embedded ICC color profile. This profile can tell After Effects how the colors should be interpreted.

A file called sanityCheck.tif can be found on the book's disc; it contains data and color gradients that will be helpful later in the chapter to help understand linear color. Import this file into After Effects and choose File > Interpret Footage > Main (**Ctrl+F/Cmd+F**, or context-click instead). The familiar Interpret Footage dialog opens, with something new to CS3, a Color Management tab.

Figure 16.2 shows how this tab appears with the default settings. Assign Profile is grayed out because, as the Description text explains, color management is off and color values are not converted. You enable Color Management by assigning a Working Space.

Project Working Space

The proper choice of a working space is the one that typically matches the "output intent," the color space corresponding to the target device. The Working Space pull-down menu containing all possible choices is located in File > Project Settings (**Ctrl+Alt+K/Cmd+Opt+K**). Those above the line are considered by Adobe to be the most likely candidates. Those below might include profiles used by such unlikely output devices as a color printer (**Figure 16.3**).

By default, Working Space is set to None (and thus Color Management is off). Choose

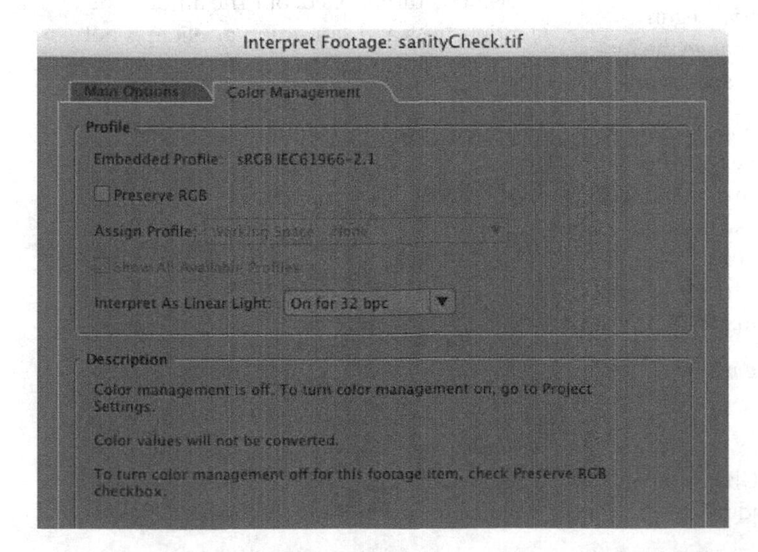

Figure 16.2 Until Color Management is enabled for the entire project, the Embedded Profile of a source image is recognized but not used to convert colors.

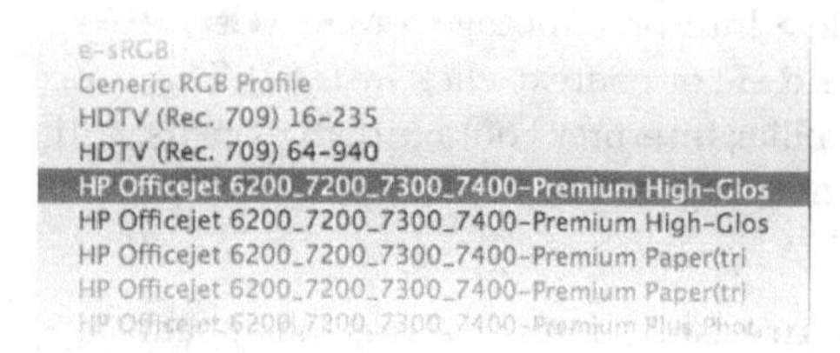

Figure 16.3 For better or worse, all of the color profiles active on the local system are listed as Working Space candidates, even such unlikely targets as the office color printer. To do a local housecleaning search for the Profiles folders on either platform—but you may need some of those to print documents!

a Working Space from the pull-down menu and Color Management is enabled, triggering the following:

- Assigned profiles in imported files are activated and displayed atop the Project panel when it's selected.
- Imported files with no assigned profile are assumed to have a profile of sRGB IEC61966-2.1, hereafter referred to as simply *sRGB*.
- Actual RGB values can and will change to maintain consistent color values.

Choose wisely; it's a bad idea to change working space mid-project, once you've begun adjusting color, because it will change the fundamental look of source footage and comps.

Okay, so it's a cop-out to say "choose wisely" and not give actual advice. There's a rather large document, included on the disc and also available at www.adobe.com/designcenter/aftereffects/articles/aftereffectscs3_color_mgmt.pdf, that includes a table itemizing each and every profile included in After Effects.

We can just forego that for the moment in favor of a concise summary:

- For HD display, HDTV (Rec. 709) is Adobe-sanctioned, but sRGB is similar and more of a reliable standard.
- For monitor playback, sRGB is generally most suitable.
- SDTV NTSC or SDTV PAL theoretically let you forego a preview broadcast monitor, although it's also possible to simulate these formats without working in them ("Display Management and Output Simulation," below).
- Film output is an exception, discussed later in this chapter.

To say that a profile is "reliable" is like saying that a particular brand of car is reliable: It has been taken through a series of situations and not caused problems for the user. I realize that with color management allegedly being so scientific and all, this sounds squirrelly, but it's just the reality of an infinite variety of images heading for an infinite variety of viewing environments. There's the scientifically tested reliability of the car and then there are real-world driving conditions.

Gamut describes the range of possible saturation, keeping in mind that any pixel can be described by its hue, saturation and brightness as accurately as its red, green, and blue. The range of hues accessible to human vision is rather fixed, but the amount of brightness and saturation possible is not—32 bpc HDR addresses both. The idea is to match, not outdo (and definitely not to undershoot) the gamut of the target.

✔ Note

A small yellow + sign appears in the middle of the Show Channel icon to indicate that Display Color Management is active (**Figure 16.4**).

Working spaces change RGB values. Open sanityCheck.tif in a viewer and move your cursor over the little bright red square; its values are 255, 0, 0. Now change the working space to ProPhoto RGB. Nothing looks dif-

Figure 16.4 When Use Display Color Management is active in the View menu (and after you set a Working Space) this icon changes in any viewer panel being color managed.

ferent, but the values are now 179, 20, 26, meaning that with this wider gamut, color values do not need to be nearly as large in order to appear just as saturated, and there is headroom for far more saturation. You just need a medium capable of displaying the more saturated red in order to see it properly with this gamut. Most film stocks are capable of this, but your monitor is not.

Input Profile and MediaCore

If an 8 bpc image file has no embedded profile, sRGB is assigned (**Figure 16.5**), which is close to monitor color space. This allows the file to be color managed, to preserve its appearance even in a different color space. Toggle Preserve RGB in the Color Management tab and the appearance of that image can change with the working space—not, generally, what you want, which is why After Effects goes ahead and assigns its best guess.

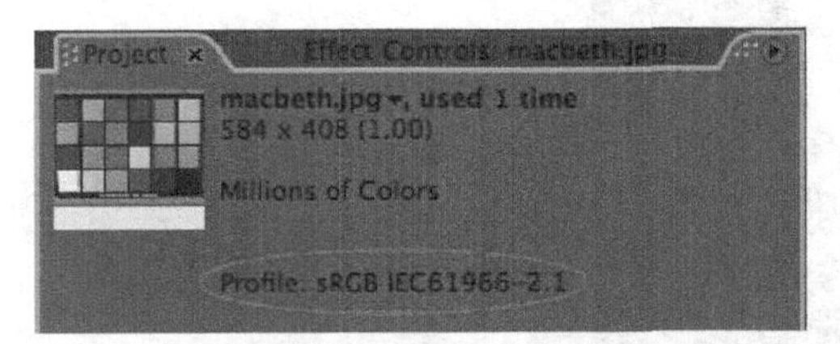

Figure 16.5 If an imported image has no color profile, After Effects assigns sRGB by default so that the file doesn't change appearance according to the working space. You are free to override this choice in the Interpret Footage dialog.

Video formats, (QuickTime being by far the most common) don't accept color profiles, but they do require color interpretation based on embedded data. After Effects CS3 uses an Adobe application called MediaCore to interpret these files automatically; it runs completely behind the scenes, invisible to you.

You know that MediaCore is handling a file when that file has Y'CbCr in the Embedded Profile info, including DV and YUV format files. In such a case the Color Management tab is completely grayed out, so there is no option to override the embedded settings.

✔ Note

In many ways, MediaCore's automation is a good thing. After Effects 7.0 had a little checkbox at the bottom of Interpret Footage labeled "Expand ITU-R 601 Luma Levels" that obligated you to manage incoming luminance range. With MediaCore, however, you lose the ability to override the setting. Expanded values above 235 and below 16 are pushed out of range, recoverable only in 32 bpc mode.

Display Management and Output Simulation

Are we having fun yet? Output Simulation is about the most fun you can have with color management; it simulates how your comp will look on a particular device. This "device" can include film projection, which actually works better than you might expect.

✔ Close-Up

Interpretation Rules A file on your system named interpretation rules.txt defines how files are automatically interpreted as they are imported into After Effects. To change anything in this file, you should be something of a hacker, able to look at a line like

```
# *, *, *, "sDPX", * ~ *, *, *, *,
"ginp", *
```

and, by examining surrounding lines and comments, figure out that this line is commented out (with the # sign at the beginning) and that the next to last argument, "ginp" in quotes, assigns the Kodak 5218 film profile if the file type corresponds with the fourth argument, "sDPX"–if this makes you squirm, don't touch it, call a nerd. In this case, removing the # sign at the beginning would enable this rule so that DPX files would be assigned a Kodak 5218 profile (without it, they are assigned to the working space).

Figure 16.6 shows HDTV footage displayed with the sRGB working space (or, if you prefer doing it the Adobe-sanctioned way, an HDTV Rec. 709 working space). This clip is also going to be broadcast on NTSC and PAL standard definition television, and you don't have a standard def broadcast monitor to preview it.

No problem. With the viewer selected choose View > Simulate Output > SDTV NTSC. Here's what happens:

- The appearance of the footage changes to match the output simulation. The viewer displays After Effects' simulation of an NTSC monitor.
- Unlike when you change the working space, color values do not change with output simulation.
- The image is actually assigned two separate color profiles in sequence: a scene-referred profile to simulate the output profile you would use for NTSC (SDTV NTSC) and a second profile that actually simulates the television monitor that would then display that rendered output (SMPTE-C). To see what these settings are, and customize them, choose View > Simulate Output > Custom to open the Custom Output Simulation dialog (**Figure 16.7a**).

Figure 16.6 The source image is set with a working space for HDTV output (not that you can evaluate the true color in a printed figure in a book).

Figures 16.7a and b The two-stage conversion in Custom Output Simulation does not change the actual RGB values but, in the case of a film projection simulation, dramatically changes the look of the footage, taking much of the guesswork out of creating a file destined for a different viewing environment.

✔Tip

- Having trouble with View > Simulate Output appearing grayed-out? Make sure a viewer window is active when you set it; it operates on a per-viewer basis.

This gets really fun with simulations of projected film (**Figure 16.7b**)—not only the print stock but the appearance of projection is simulated, allowing an artist to work directly on the projected look of a shot instead of waiting until it is filmed out and projected.

Here's a summary of what is happening to the source image in the example project:

1. The source image is interpreted on import (on the Footage Settings > Color Management tab).
2. The image is transformed to the working space; its color values will change to preserve its appearance.
3. With View > Simulate Output and any profile selected
   a. Color values are transformed to the specified Output Profile.
   b. Color appearance (but not actual values) is transformed to a specified Simulation Profile.
4. With View > Display Color Management enabled (which is required for step 3) color appearance (but not actual values) is transformed to the monitor profile (the one that lives in system settings, that you created when you calibrated your monitor, remember?)

And that's all just for simulation. Let's look now at what happens when you actually try to preserve those colors in rendered output (which is, after all, the whole point, right?).

Output Profile

By default, After Effects uses Working Space as the Output Profile, and that's most often correct. Place the comp in the Render Queue and open the Output Module; on the Color Management tab you can select a different profile to apply on output. The pipeline from the last section now looks like this:

1. The source image is interpreted on import (on the Footage Settings > Color Management tab).
2. The image is transformed to the working space; its color values will change to preserve its appearance.
3. The image is transformed to the output profile specified in Output Module Settings > Color Management.

✔ Tip

Suppose you wish to render an output simulation (to show the filmed-out look on a video display in dailies, for example). To replicate the two-stage color conversion of output simulation, apply the Color Profile Converter effect, and match the Output Profile setting to the one listed under View > Simulate Output > Custom. Change the Intent setting to Absolute Colorimetric. Now set a second Color Profile Converter effect, and match the Input Profile to the Simulation Profile under View > Simulate Output > Custom (leaving Intent as the default Relative Colorimetric). The Output Profile in the Render Queue then should match the intended display device.

If the profile in step 3 is different from that of step 2, color values will change to preserve color appearance. If the output format supports embedded ICC profiles (presumably a still image format such as TIFF or PSD), then a profile will be embedded so that any other application with color management (presumably an Adobe application such as Photoshop or Illustrator) will continue to preserve those colors.

In the real world, of course, rendered output is probably destined to a device or format that doesn't support color management and embedded profiles. That's okay, except in the case of QuickTime, which may further change the appearance of the file, almost guaranteeing that the output won't match your composition without special handling.

QuickTime

At this writing, QuickTime has special issues of its own separate from, but related to Adobe's color management. Because Apple constantly revises QuickTime and the spec has been in some flux, the issues particular to version 7.2 of QuickTime and version 8.01 of After Effects may change with newer versions of either software.

The current problem is that Apple has begun implementing its own form of color management, one that manages only the gamma of QuickTime files by allowing it to be specifically tagged. This tag is then interpreted uniquely by each codec, so files with Photo-JPEG compression has a different gamma than files with H.264 compression. Even files with the default Animation setting, which are effectively uncompressed, display an altered gamma.

If color management is enabled, an RGB working space and output profile is a close match to the 2.2 gamma that is written to QuickTime files, so there should be little or no mismatch.

Otherwise, for QuickTime to behave as in previous versions of After Effects, toggle Match Legacy After Effects QuickTime Gamma Adjustments in Project Settings. This prevents any gamma tag from being added to a QuickTime file.

Why was the tag added in the first place? Untagged QuickTime files don't look or behave the same on Mac and Windows; the gamma changes to match the typical gamma of each platform (1.8 for Mac, 2.2 for Windows), causing problems when you render from one platform to the other using common compression formats such as Photo-JPEG or DV.

However, tagged QuickTime files rendered by After Effects 8.0.1 exhibit inconsistencies even between After Effects, QuickTime Player, and Final Cut Pro, so until the issue is solved—possibly by an update to QuickTime 7.2, or possibly by an After Effects revision—untagged QuickTimes will behave more reliably when displayed in various applications.

✔ Close-Up

QuickTime Is Only a Container The funny thing about QuickTime is that it isn't a format like TIFF or JPEG; instead, it's more like a container for such formats as TIFF and JPEG (specifically, the Animation and Photo-JPEG codecs, respectively). To create a QuickTime file you must choose a Compression Type, which is more like what we are used to calling a format. QuickTime stores this as a track in the movie (**Figure 16.8**).

These files contain tags to specify characteristics, such as frame rate and pixel aspect ratio, so that when they are imported into After Effects, even though you can adjust these settings manually, it knows how to handle them automatically. For the most part that is a good thing, but different applications interpret these settings differently and the gamma tag seems to yield results that are inconsistent with After Effects in some of the more popular applications that heavily use QuickTime, including Apple's own Final Cut Pro.

To Bypass Color Management

Headaches like that make many artists long for the simpler days of After Effects 7.0 and opt to avoid Color Management altogether, or to use it only selectively. To completely disable the feature and return to 7.0 behavior:

- In Project Settings, set Working Space to None (as it is by default).
- Enable Match Legacy After Effects QuickTime Gamma Adjustments.

Being more selective about how color management is applied—to take advantage of some features while leaving others disabled for clarity—is really tricky and tends to stump some pretty smart users. Here are a couple of final tips that may nonetheless help:

- To disable a profile for incoming footage, check Preserve RGB in Interpret Footage (Color Management tab). No attempt will be made to preserve the appearance of that clip.

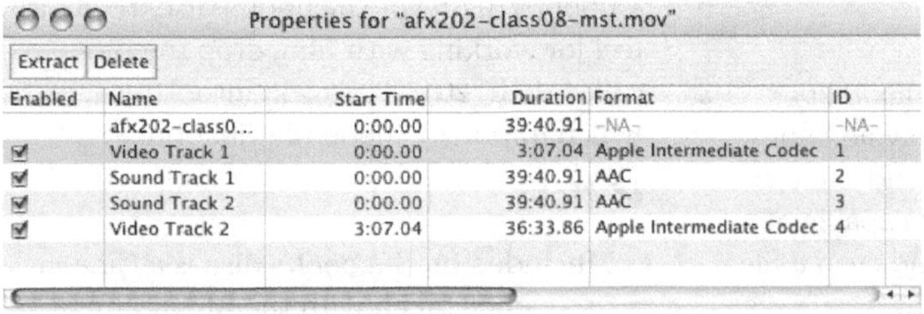

Properties for "afx202-class08-mst.mov"

Extract | Delete

Enabled	Name	Start Time	Duration	Format	ID
	afx202-class0...	0:00.00	39:40.91	-NA-	-NA-
✔	Video Track 1	0:00.00	3:07.04	Apple Intermediate Codec	1
✔	Sound Track 1	0:00.00	39:40.91	AAC	2
✔	Sound Track 2	0:00.00	39:40.91	AAC	3
✔	Video Track 2	3:07.04	36:33.86	Apple Intermediate Codec	4

Figures 16.8 Open a QuickTime .mov file in QuickTime Player and its Properties show that it's not an image file format but is instead a container for various tracks, each with its own potentially unique format.

- To change the behavior causing untagged footage to be tagged with an sRGB profile, in interpretation rules.txt find this line

  # soft rule: tag all untagged footage with an sRGB profile

  `*, *, *, *, * ~ *, *, *, *, "sRGB", *`

  and add a # at the beginning of the second line to assign no profile, or change "sRGB" to a different format (options listed in the comments at the top of the file).
- To prevent your display profile from being factored in, disable View > Use Display Color Management and the pixels are sent straight to the display.
- To prevent any file from being color managed, check Preserve RGB in Output Module Settings (Color Management tab).

Note that any of the above steps is bound to lead to unintended consequences. Leaving a working space enabled and disabling specific features is tricky and potentially dangerous to your health and sanity.

Film and Dynamic Range

The previous section showed how color benefits from precision and flexibility. The precision is derived with the steps just discussed; flexibility is the result of having a wide dynamic range, because there is a far wider range of color and light levels in the physical world than can be represented on your 8 bit per channel display.

However, there is more to color flexibility than toggling 16 bpc in order to avoid banding, or even color management, and there is an analog image medium that is capable of going far beyond 16 bpc color, and even a file format capable of representing it.

Film and Cineon

Reports of film's death have been greatly exaggerated, and the latest and greatest digital capture media, such as the Red camera, can make use of much of what works with film. Here's a look at the film process and the digital files on which it relies.

After film has been shot, the negative is developed, and shots destined for digital effects work are scanned frame by frame, usually at a rate of about 1 frame per second. During this, the Telecine process, some initial color decisions are made before the frames are output as a numbered sequence of Cineon files, named after Kodak's now-defunct film compositing system. Both Cineon files and the related format, DPX, store pixels uncompressed at 10 bits per channel. Scanners are usually capable of scanning 4 K plates, and these have become more popular for visual effects usage, although many still elect to scan at half resolution, creating 2 K frames around 2048 by 1536 pixels and weighing in at almost 13 MB.

Working with Cineon Files

Because the process of shooting and scanning film is pretty expensive, almost all Cineon files ever created are the property of some Hollywood studio and unavailable to the general public. The best known free Cineon file is Kodak's original test image, affectionately referred to as Marcie (**Figure 16.9**) and available from Kodak's Web site (www.kodak.com/US/en/motion/-support/dlad/) or the book's disc. To get a feel for working with film, drop the file called dlad_2048X1556.cin into After Effects, which imports Cineon files just fine.

✔ Note

Included on the book's disc is a Cineon sequence taken with the RED Camera,

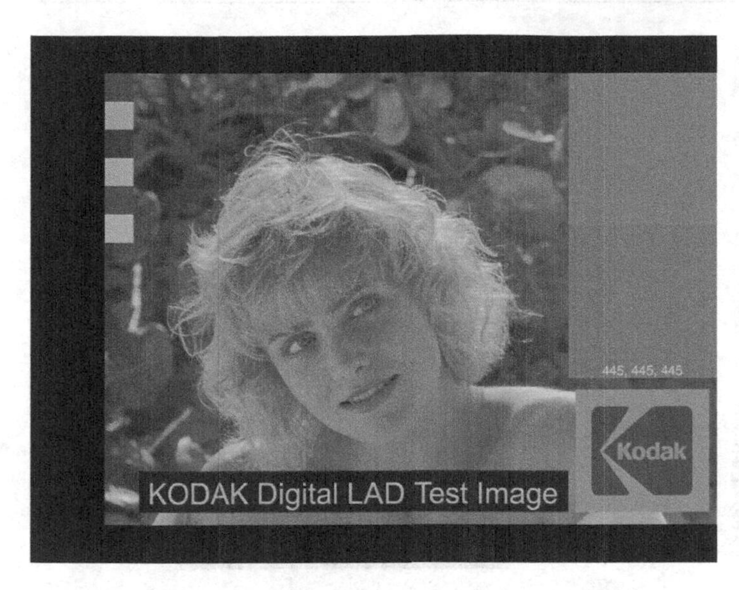

Figure 16.9 For a sample of working with film source, use this image, found on the book's disc.

showing off that digital camera's high dynamic range and overall image quality, and provided courtesy fxphd.com. A 32 bpc project with this footage set properly to display over-range pixels is also included.

The first thing you'll notice about Marcie is that she looks funny, and not just because this photo dates back to the '80s. Cineon files are encoded in something called log color space. To make Marcie look more natural, open the Interpret Footage dialog, select the Color Management tab, click Cineon Settings and choose the Over Range preset (instead of the default Full Range). The log image has been converted to the monitor's color space.

It would seem natural to convert Cineon files to the monitor's color space, work normally, and then convert the end result back to log; you can reverse the Interpret Footage setting on the Color Management tab of the Output Module, but you can even preview the operation right in After Effects by applying the Cineon Converter effect and switching the Conversion Type to Linear to Log. But upon further examination of this conversion, you see a problem: With an 8 bpc (or even 16 bpc) project, the bright details in Marcie's hair don't survive the trip (**Figures 16.10a**, **b**, and **c**).

What's going on with this mystical Cineon file and its log color space that makes it so hard to deal with? And more importantly, why? Well, it turns out that the engineers at Kodak know a thing or two about film and have made no decisions lightly. But to properly answer the question, it's necessary to discuss some basic principles of photography and light.

✔ Note

As becomes evident later in the chapter, the choice of the term "linear" as an alternative to "log" space for Cineon Converter is unfortunate, because "linear" specifically means neutral 1.0 gamma; what Cineon Converter calls "linear" is in fact gamma encoded.

Figures 16.10a, b, and c When you convert an image from log space (a) to linear (b) and then back to log (c), the bright details are lost.

Figure 16.11 Different exposures of the same camera view produce widely varying results.

Dynamic Range

The pictures shown in **Figure 16.11** were taken within a minute of each other from a roof on a winter morning. Anyone who has ever tried to photograph a sunrise or sunset with a digital camera should immediately recognize the problem at hand. With a standard exposure, the sky comes in beautifully, but foreground houses are nearly black. Using longer exposures you can bring the houses up, but by the time they are looking good the sky is completely blown out.

The limiting factor here is the digital camera's small dynamic range, which is the difference between the brightest and darkest things that can be captured in the same image. An outdoor scene has a wide array of brightnesses, but any device will be able to read only a slice of them. You can change exposure to capture different ranges, but the size of the slice is fixed.

Our eyes have a much larger dynamic range and our brains have a wide array of perceptual tricks, so in real life the houses and sky are both seen easily. But even eyes have limits, such as when you try to see someone behind a bright spotlight or use a laptop computer in the sun. The spotlight has not made the person behind any darker, but when eyes adjust to bright lights (as they must to avoid injury), dark things fall out of range and simply appear black.

White on a monitor just isn't very bright, which is why our studios are in dim rooms with the blinds pulled down. When you try to represent the bright sky on a dim monitor, everything else in the image has to scale down in proportion. Even when a digital camera can capture extra dynamic range, your monitor must compress it in order to display it.

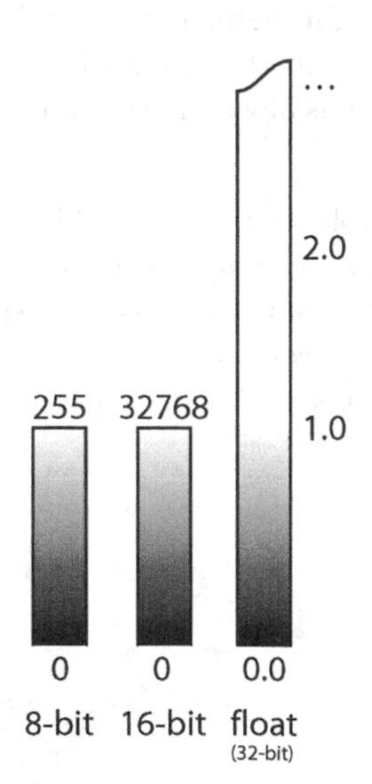

Figure 16.12 Monitor white represents the upper limit for 8-bit and 16-bit pixels, while floating point can go beyond. Floating point also extends below absolute black, 0.0, values that are theoretical and not part of the world you see (unless you find yourself near a black hole in space).

A standard 8-bit computer image uses values 0 to 255 to represent RGB pixels. If you record a value above 255—say 285 or 310—that represents a pixel beyond the monitor's dynamic range, brighter than white or overbright. Because 8-bit pixels can't actually go above 255, overbright information is stored as floating point decimals where 0.0 is black and 1.0 is white. Because floating point numbers are virtually unbounded, 0.75, 7.5, or 750.0 are all acceptable values, even though everything above 1.0 will clip to white on the monitor (**Figure 16.12**).

In recent years, techniques have emerged to create high dynamic range (HDR) images from a series of exposures—floating point files that contain all light information from a scene (**Figure 16.13**). The best-known paper on the subject was published by Malik and Debevec at SIGGRAPH '97 (www.debevec.org has details). In successive exposures, values that remain within range can be compared to describe how the camera is responding to different levels of light. That information allows a computer to connect bright areas in the scene to the darker ones and calculate accurate floating point pixel values that combine detail from each exposure.

But with all the excitement surrounding HDR imaging and improvements in the dynamic range of video cameras, many forget that for decades there has been another medium available for capturing dynamic range far beyond what a computer monitor can display or a digital camera can capture.

That medium is film.

✔ Note

Photoshop's Merge to HDR feature allows you to create your own HDR images from a series of locked-off photos at varied exposures.

Figure 16.13 Consider the floating point pixel values for this HDR image.

Cineon Log Space

A film negative gets its name because areas exposed to light ultimately become dark and opaque, and areas unexposed are made transparent during developing. Light makes dark. Hence, negative.

Dark is a relative term here. A white piece of paper makes a nice dark splotch on the negative, but a lightbulb darkens the film even more, and a photograph of the sun causes the negative to turn out darker still. By not completely exposing to even bright lights, the negative is able to capture the differences between bright highlights and really bright highlights. Film, the original image capture medium, has always been high dynamic range.

If you were to graph the increase in film "density" as increasing amounts of light expose it, you'd get something like **Figure 16.14**. In math, this is referred to as a logarithmic curve. I'll get back to this in a moment.

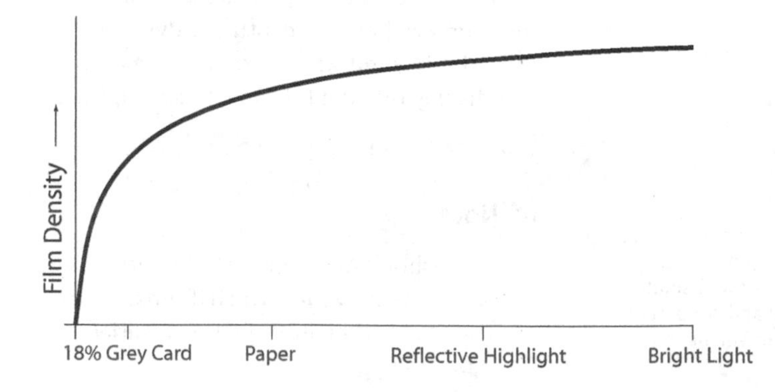

Figure 16.14 Graphing the darkening of film as increasing amounts of light expose it results in a logarithmic curve.

Digital Film

If a monitor's maximum brightness is considered to be 1.0, the brightest value film can represent is officially considered by Kodak to be 13.53 (although using the more efficient ICC color conversion, outlined later in the chapter, reveals brightness values above 70). Note this only applies to a film negative that is exposed by light in the world as opposed to a film positive, which is limited by the brightness of a projector bulb and is therefore not really considered high dynamic range. A Telecine captures the entire range of each frame and stores the frames as a sequence of 10-bit Cineon files. Those extra two bits mean that Cineon pixel values can range from 0 to 1023 instead of the 0 to 255 in 8-bit files.

Having four times as many values to work with in a Cineon file helps, but considering you have 13.53 times the range to record, care must be taken in encoding those values. The most obvious way to store all that light would simply be to evenly squeeze 0.0 to 13.53 into the 0 to 1023 range. The problem with this solution is that it would only leave 75 code values for the all-important 0.0 to 1.0 range, the same as allocated to the range 10.0 to 11.0, which you are far less interested in representing with much accuracy. Your eye can barely tell the difference between two highlights that bright—it certainly doesn't need 75 brightness variations between them.

A proper way to encode light on film would quickly fill up the usable values with the most important 0.0 to 1.0 light and then leave space left over for the rest of the negative's range. Fortunately, the film negative itself with its logarithmic response behaves just this way.

Cineon files are often said to be stored in log color space. Actually it is the negative that uses a log response curve and the file is simply storing the negative's density at each pixel. In any case, the graph in **Figure 16.15** describes how light exposes a negative and is encoded into Cineon color values according to Kodak, creators of the format.

One strange feature in this graph is that black is mapped to code value 95 instead of 0. Not only does the Cineon file store whiter-than-white (overbright) values, it also has some blacker-than-black information. This is mirrored in the film lab when a negative is printed brighter than usual and the

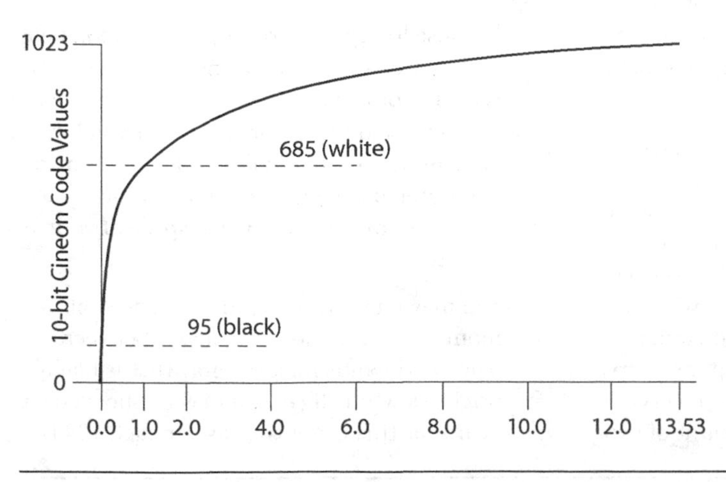

Figure 16.15 Kodak's Cineon log encoding is expressed as a logarithmic curve, with labels for the visible black and white points that correspond to 0 and 255 in normal 8-bit pixel values.

blacker-than-black information can reveal itself. Likewise, negatives can be printed darker and take advantage of overbright detail. The standard value mapped to monitor white is 685, and everything above is considered overbright.

Although the Kodak formulas are commonly used to transform log images for compositing, other methods have emerged. The idea of having light values below 0.0 is dubious at best, and many take issue with the idea that a single curve can describe all film stocks, cameras, and shooting environments. As a different approach, some visual effects facilities take care to photograph well-defined photographic charts and use the resultant film to build custom curves that differ subtly from the standard Kodak one.

✔ Close-Up

All About Log You may first have heard of logarithmic curves in high school physics class, if you ever learned about the decay of radioactive isotopes.

If a radioactive material has a half-life of one year, half of it will have decayed after that time. The next year, half of what remains will decay, leaving a quarter, and so on. To calculate how much time has elapsed based on how much material remains, a logarithmic function is used.

Light, another type of radiation, has a similar effect on film. At the molecular level, light causes silver halide crystals to react. If film exposed for some short period of time causes half the crystals to react, repeating the exposure will cause half of the remaining to react, and so on. This is how film gets its response curve and the ability to capture even very bright light sources. No amount of exposure can be expected to affect every single crystal.

As much as Cineon log is a great way to encode light captured by film, it should not be used for compositing or other image transformations. This point is so important that it just has to be emphasized again:

Encoding color spaces are not compositing color spaces.

To illustrate this point, imagine you had a black pixel with Cineon value 95 next to an extremely bright pixel with Cineon's highest code value, 1023. If these two pixels were blended together (say, if the image was being blurred), the result would be 559, which is somewhere around middle gray (0.37 to be precise). But when you consider that the extremely bright pixel has a relative brightness of 13.5, that black pixel should only have been able to bring it down to 6.75, which is still overbright white! Log space's extra emphasis on darker values causes standard image processing operations to give them extra weight, leading to an overall unpleasant and inaccurate darkening of the image. So, final warning: If you're working with a log source, don't do image processing in log space!

Video Gamma Space

Because log space certainly doesn't look natural, it probably comes as no surprise that it is a bad color space to work in. But there is another encoding color space that you have been intimately familiar with for your entire computer-using life and no doubt have worked in directly: the video space of your monitor.

You may have always assumed that 8-bit monitor code value 128, halfway between black and white, makes a gray that is half as bright as white. If so, you may be shocked to hear that this is not the case. In fact, 128 is much darker—not even a quarter of white's brightness on most monitors.

A system where half the input gives you half the output is described as linear, but monitors (like many things in the real world) are nonlinear. When a system is nonlinear, you can usually describe its behavior using the gamma function, shown in **Figure 16.16** and the equation

$\text{Output} = \text{input}^{\text{gamma}} \quad 0 <= \text{input} <= 1$

✔ Note

The description of gamma in video is oversimplified here somewhat because the subject is complex enough for a book of its own. An excellent one is *Charles Poynton's* Digital Video and HDTV Algorithms and Interfaces (*Morgan Kaufmann*).

In this function, the darkest and brightest values (0.0 and 1.0) are always fixed, and the gamma value determines how the transition between them behaves. Successive applications of gamma can be concatenated by multiplying them together. Applying gamma and then 1/gamma has the net result of doing nothing. Gamma 1.0 is linear.

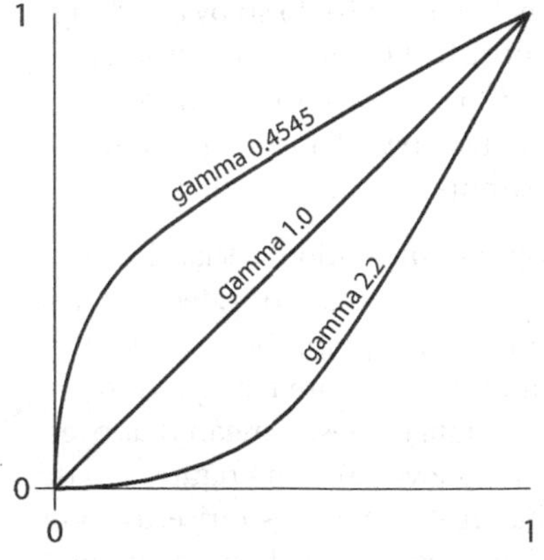

Figure 16.16 Graph of monitor gamma (2.2) with file gamma (0.4545) and linear (1.0). These are the color curves in question, with 0.4545 and 2.2 each acting as the direct inverse of the other.

✔ Close-Up

Gamma-rama In case all this gamma talk hasn't already blown your mind, allow me to mention two other related points.

First, you may be familiar with the standard photographic gray card, known as the 18% gray card. But why not the 50% gray card?

Second, although I've mentioned that a monitor darkens everything on it using a 2.2 gamma, you may wonder why a grayscale ramp doesn't look skewed toward darkness—50% gray on a monitor looks like 50% gray.

The answer is that your eyes are nonlinear too! They have a gamma that is just about the inverse of a monitor's, in fact. Eyes are very sensitive to small amounts of light and get less sensitive as brightness increases. The lightening in our eyeballs offsets the darkening of 50% gray by the monitor. If you were to paint a true gradient on a wall, it would look bright. Objects in the world are darker than they appear.

Getting back to the 18% card, try applying that formula to our gamma 0.4 eyes:

$$0.18^{0.4} = 0.504$$

Yep, middle gray.

Mac monitors have traditionally had a gamma of 1.8, while the gamma value for PCs is 2.2. Because the electronics in your screen are slow to react from lower levels of input voltage, a 1.0 gamma is simply too dark in either case; boosting this value compensates correctly.

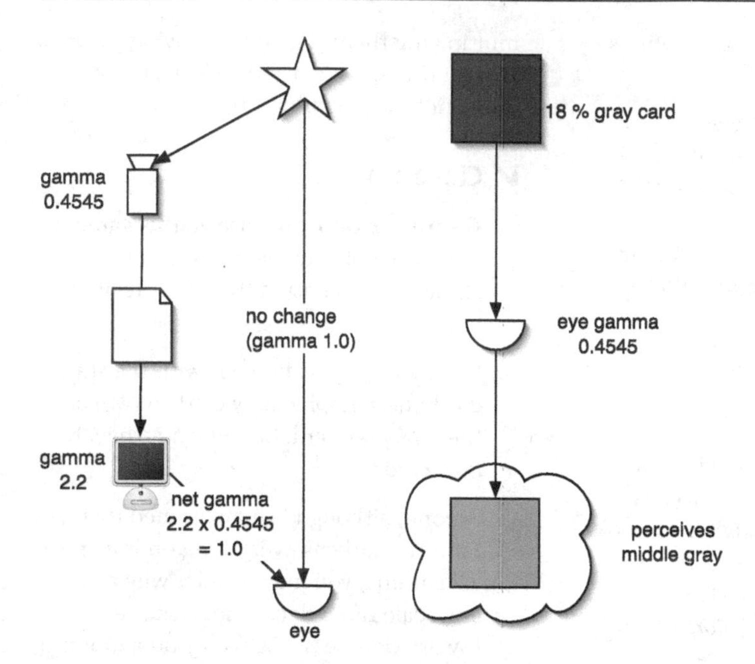

Figure 16.17 Offsetting gammas in the file and monitor result in faithful image reproduction.

The reason digital images do not appear dark, however, is that they have all been created with the inverse gamma function baked in to pre-brighten pixels before they are displayed (**Figure 16.17**). Yes, all of them.

Because encoding spaces are not compositing spaces, working directly with images that appear on your monitor can pose problems. Similar to log encoding, video gamma encoding allocates more values to dark pixels, so they have extra weight. Video images need converting just as log Cineon files do.

Linear Floating-Point HDR

In the real world, light behaves linearly. Turn on two lightbulbs of equivalent wattage where you previously had one and the entire scene becomes exactly twice as bright. A linear color space lets you simulate this effect simply by doubling pixel values. Because this re-creates the color space of the original scene, linear pixels are often referred to as scene-referred values, and doubling them in this manner can easily send values beyond monitor range.

The Exposure effect in After Effects converts the image to which it is applied to linear color before doing its work unless you specifically tell it not to do so by checking Bypass Linear Light Conversion. It internally applies a .4545 gamma correction to the image (1 divided by 2.2, inverting standard monitor gamma) before adjusting.

A common misconception is that if you work solely in the domain of video you have no need for floating point. But just because your input and output are restricted to the 0.0 to 1.0 range doesn't mean that overbright values above 1.0 won't figure into the images you create. The 11_sunrise.aep project included on your disc shows how they can add to your scene even when created on the fly.

Table 16.1 Comparison of Adjustments in Native Video Space and in Linear Space

	Brighten One Stop	Lens Defocus	Motion Blur
Original Image			
Filtered in Video Space			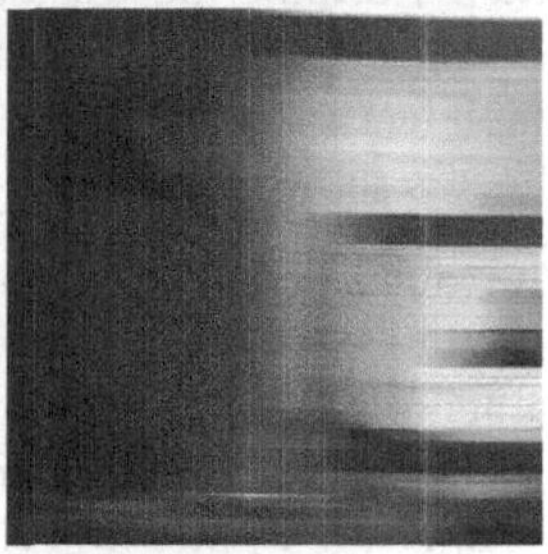
Filtered in Linear Space			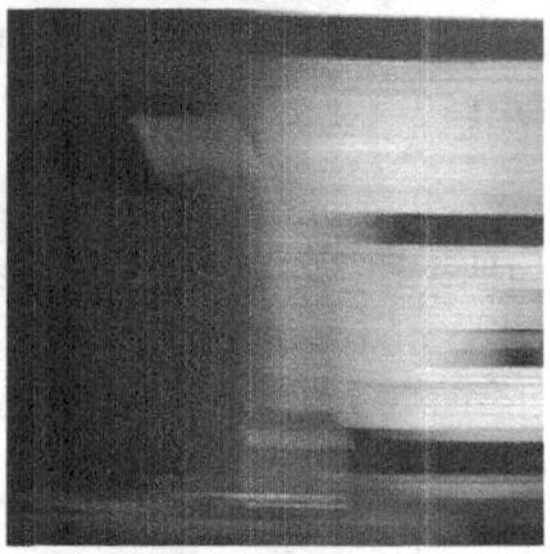
Real-World Photo			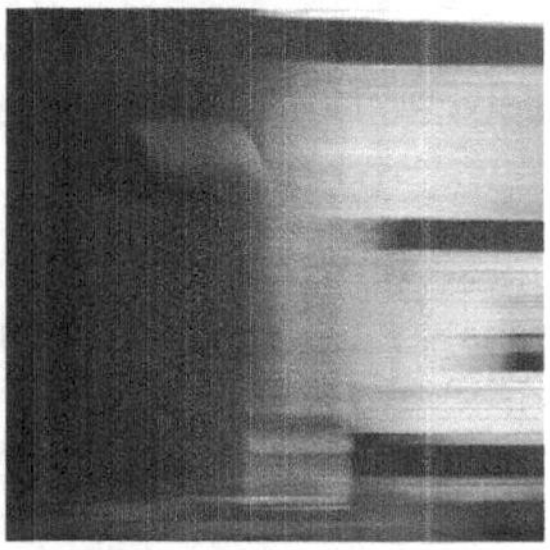

✔ Note

To follow this discussion, choose Decimal in the Info panel menu. 0.0 to 1.0 values are those falling in Low Dynamic Range, or LDR–those values typically described in 8 bit as 0 to 255. Any values outside this range are HDR, 32 bpc only.

The examples in **Table 16.1** show the difference between making adjustments to digital camera photos in their native video space and performing those same operations in linear space. In all cases, an unaltered photograph featuring the equivalent in-camera effect is shown for comparison.

The table's first column contains the images brightened by one stop, an increment on a camera's aperture, which controls how much light is allowed through the lens. Widening the aperture by one stop allows twice as much light to enter. An increase of three stops brightens the image by a factor of eight ($2 \times 2 \times 2$, or 2^3).

To double pixel values in video space is to quickly blow out bright areas in the image. Video pixels are already encoded with extra brightness and can't take much more. The curtain and computer screen lose detail in video space that is retained in linear space. The linear image is nearly indistinguishable from the actual photo for which camera exposure time was doubled (another practical way to brighten by one stop).

The second column simulates an out-of-focus scene using Fast Blur. You may be surprised to see an overall darkening with bright highlights fading into the background—at least in video space. In linear, the highlights pop much better. See how the little man in the Walk sign stays bright in linear but almost fades away in video because of the extra emphasis given to dark pixels in video space. Squint your eyes and you notice that only the video image darkens overall. Because a defocused lens doesn't cause any less light to enter it, regular 8 bpc blur does not behave like a true defocus.

The table's third column uses After Effects' built-in motion blur to simulate the streaking caused by quick panning as the photo was taken. Pay particular attention to the highlight on the lamp; notice how it leaves a long, bright streak in the linear and in-camera examples. Artificial dulling of highlights is the most obvious giveaway of nonlinear image processing.

Artists have dealt with the problems of working directly in video space for years without even knowing. A perfect example is the Screen transfer mode, which is additive in nature but whose calculations are clearly convoluted when compared with the pure Add transfer mode. Screen uses a multiply-toward-white function with the advantage of avoiding the clipping associated with Add. But Add's reputation comes from its application in bright video-space images. Screen was invented only to help people be productive when working in video space, without overbrights; Screen darkens overbrights (**Figures 16.18a**, **b**, and **c**). Real light doesn't Screen, it Adds. Add is the new Screen, Multiply is the new Hard Light, and many other blending modes fall away completely in linear floating point.

HDR Source and Linearized Working Space

Should you in fact be fortunate enough to have 32 bit source images containing overrange values for use in your scene, there are indisputable benefits to working in 32 bit linear, even if your final output uses a plain old video format that cannot accommodate these values.

Figures 11.18a, b, and c Adding in video space blows out (a), but Screen in video looks better (b). Adding in linear is best (c).

In the **Figures 16.19a**, **b**, and **c**, each of the bright Christmas tree lights is severely clipped when shown in video space, which is not a problem so long as the image is only displayed, not adjusted. Figure 16.19b is the result of following the rules by converting the image to linear before applying a synthetic motion blur. Indeed, the lights create pleasant streaks, but their brightness has disappeared. In Figure 16.19c the HDR image is blurred in 32 bit per channel mode, and the lights have a realistic impact on the image as they streak across. Even stretched out across the image, the streaks are still brighter than 1.0. Considering this printed page is not high dynamic range, this example shows that HDR floating point pixels are a crucial part of making images that simulate the real world through a camera, no matter the output medium.

The benefits of floating point aren't restricted to blurs, however; they just happen to be an easy place to see the difference most starkly. Every operation in a compositing pipeline gains extra realism from the presence of floating point pixels and linear blending.

Figures 16.20a, **b**, and **c** feature an HDR image on which a simple composite is performed, once in video space and once using linear floating point. In the floating point version, the dark translucent layer acts like sunglasses on the bright window, revealing extra detail exactly as a filter on a camera lens would. The soft edges of a motion-blurred object also behave realistically as bright highlights push through. Without floating point there is no extra information to reveal, so the window looks clipped and dull and motion blur doesn't interact with the scene properly.

✔ Close-Up

Terminology Linear floating-point HDR compositing uses *radiometrically linear*, or *scene-referred*, color data. For the purposes of this discussion, this is perhaps best called "linear light compositing," or "linear floating point," or just simply, "linear." The alternative mode to which

Figures 16.19a, b, and c An HDR image is blurred without floating point (a) and with floating point (b), before being shown as low dynamic range (c). (HDR image courtesy Stu Maschwitz.)

Figures 16.20a, b, and c A source image (a) is composited without floating point (b) and with floating point (c). (HDR image courtesy Stu Maschwitz.)

you are accustomed is "gamma-encoded," or "monitor color space," or simply, "video."

32 Bits per Channel

Although it is not necessary to use HDR source to take advantage of an HDR pipeline, it offers a clear glimpse of this brave new world. Open 11_treeHDR_lin.aep; it contains a comp made up of a single image in 32 bit EXR format (used to create Figures 16.19a, b, and c). With the Info panel clearly visible, move your cursor around the frame.

✔ Note

Included on the disc are two similar images, sanityCheck.exr and sanityCheck.tif. The 32 bpc EXR file is linearized, but the 8 bpc TIFF file is not. Two corresponding projects are also included, one using no color profile, the other employing a linear profile. These should help illustrate the different appearances of a linear and a gamma-encoded image.

As your cursor crosses highlights—the lights on the tree, specular highlights on the wall and chair, and most especially, in the window—the values are seen to be well above 1.0, the maximum value you will ever see doing the same in 8 bpc or 16 bpc mode. Remember that you can quickly toggle between color spaces by Alt/Option-clicking the project color depth identifier at the bottom of the Project panel.

Any experienced digital artist would assume that there is no detail in that window—it is blown out to solid white forevermore in LDR. However, you may have noticed an extra icon and accompanying numerical value that appears at the bottom of the composition panel in a 32 bpc project (**Figure 16.21**). This is the Exposure control; its icon looks like a camera aperture and it performs an analogous function—controlling the exposure (total amount of light) of a scene the way you would stop a camera up or down (by adjusting its aperture).

Drag to the left on the numerical text and something amazing happens. Not only does the lighting in the scene decrease naturally, as if the light itself were being brought down, but at somewhere around -10.0, a gentle blue gradient appears in the window (**Figure 16.22a**).

Drag the other direction, into positive Exposure range, and the scene begins to look like an overexposed photo; the light proportions remain and the highlights bloom outward (**Figure 16.22b**).

The Exposure control in the Composition panel is a preview-only control (there is an effect by the same name that renders); scan with your cursor and Info panel values do not vary according to its setting. This control offers a quick way to check what is happening in the out-of-range areas of a composition. With a linear light image, each integer increment represents the equivalent of one photographic stop, or a doubling (or halving) of linear light value.

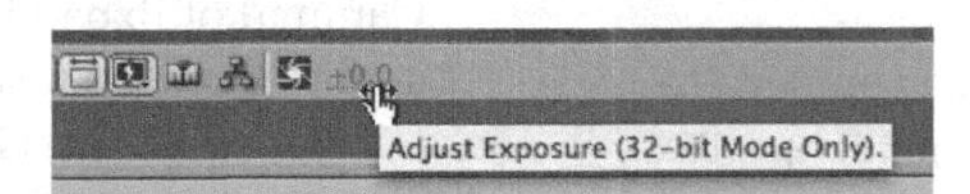

Figure 16.21 Exposure is an HDR preview control that appears in the Composition panel in 32 bpc mode.

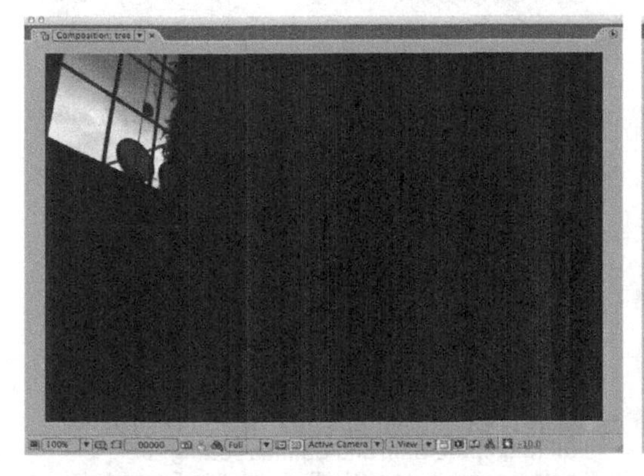

Figures 16.22a and b At -10 Exposure (a), the room is dark other than the tree lights and detail becomes visible out the window. At +3, the effect is exactly that of a camera that was open 3 stops brighter than the unadjusted image (b).

✔ Notes

Keep in mind that for each 1.0 adjustment upward or downward of Exposure you double (or halve) the light levels in the scene. Echoing the earlier discussion, a +3.0 Exposure setting sets the light levels 8x (or 2^3) brighter.

Incompatible Effects and Compander

Most effects don't, alas, support 32 bpc, although there are dozens that do. Apply a 16 bpc or (shudder) 8 bpc effect, however, and the overbrights in your 32 bpc project disappear—all clipped to 1.0. Any effect will reduce the image being piped through it to its own color space limitations. A small warning sign appears next to the effect to remind you that it does not support the current bit depth. You may even see a warning explaining the dangers of applying this effect.

Of course, this doesn't mean you need to avoid these effects to work in 32 bpc. It means you have to cheat, and After Effects includes a preset allowing you to do just that: Compress-Expand Dynamic Range (contained in Effects & Presets > Animation Presets > Image – Utilities; make certain Show Animation Presets is checked in the panel menu).

✔ Close-Up

Floating Point Files As you've already seen, there is one class of files that does not need to be converted to linear space: floating point files. These files are already storing scene-referred values, complete with overbright information. Common formats supported by After Effects are Radiance (.hdr) and floating point TIFF, but the newest and best is Industrial Light + Magic's OpenEXR format. OpenEXR uses efficient 16-bit floating point pixels, can store any number of image channels, supports lossless compression, and is already supported by most 3D programs thanks to being an open source format.

If the knowledge that Industrial Light + Magic created a format to base its entire workflow around linear doesn't give it credence, it's hard to say what will.

This preset actually consists of two instances of the HDR Compander effect, which was specifically designed to bring floating point values back into LDR range. The first instance is automatically renamed Compress, and the second, Expand, which is how the corresponding Modes are set. You set the Gain of Compress to whatever is the brightest overbright value you wish to preserve, up to 100. The values are then compressed into LDR range, allowing you to apply your LDR effect. The Gain (as well as Gamma) of Expand is linked via an expression to Compress, so that the values round-trip back to HDR. (**Figure 16.23**).

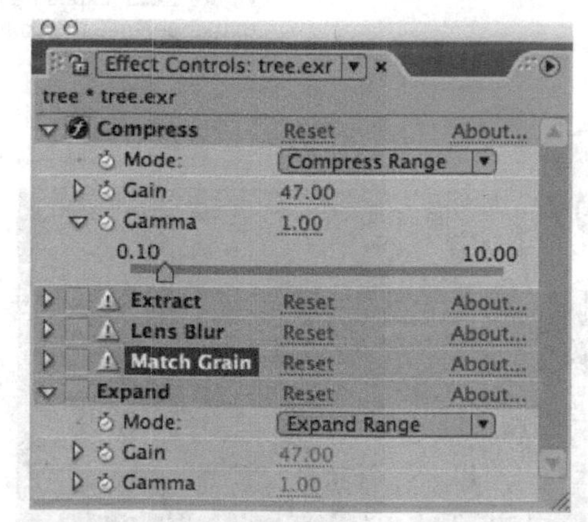

Figure 16.23 The Compress-Expand Dynamic Range preset round-trips HDR values in and out of LDR range; the Gain and Gamma settings of Compress are automatically passed to Expand via preset expressions. Turn off Expand and an image full of overbright values will appear much darker, the result of pushing all values downward starting at the Gain value.

If banding appears as a result of Compress-Expand, Gamma can be adjusted to weight the compressed image more toward the region of the image (probably the shadows) where the banding occurs. You are sacrificing image fidelity in order to preserve a compressed version of the HDR pipeline.

Additionally, there are smart ways to set up a project to ensure that Compander plays the minimal possible role. As much as possible, group all of your LDR effects together, and keep them away from the layers that use blending modes, where float values are most essential. For example, apply an LDR effect via a separate adjustment layer instead of directly on a layer with a blending mode. Also, if possible, apply the LDR effects first, then boost the result into HDR range to apply any additional 32 bpc effects and blending modes.

Blend Colors Using 1.0 Gamma

After Effects CS3 adds a fantastic new option to linearize image data only when performing blending operations: the Blend Colors Using 1.0 Gamma toggle in Project Settings. This allows you to take advantage of linear blending, which makes Add and Multiply blending modes actually work properly, even in 8 bpc or 16 bpc modes.

The difference is quite simple. A linearized working space does all image processing in gamma 1.0, as follows:

```
footage —> to linear PWS ->
   Layer ->
      Mask -> Effects -> Transform ->
         Blend With Comp ->
   Comp -> from linear PWS to
         OM space ->
output
```

whereas linearized blending performs only the blending step, where the image is combined with the composition, in gamma 1.0:

```
footage -> to PWS ->
   Layer ->
      Mask -> Effects -> Transform ->
         to linear PWS ->
         Blend With Comp -> to PWS ->
   Comp -> from PWS to OM space ->
output
```

Special thanks to Dan Wilk at Adobe for detailing this out.

Because effects aren't added in linear color, blurs no longer interact correctly with over-brights (although they do composite more nicely), and you don't get the subtle benefits to Transform operations; After Effects' much maligned scaling operations are much improved in linear floating point. Also, 3D lights behave more like actual lights in a fully linearized working space.

I prefer the linear blending option when in lower bit depths and there is no need to manage over-range values; it gives me the huge benefit of more elegant composites and blending modes without forcing me to think about managing effects in linear color. Certain key effects, in particular Exposure, helpfully operate in linear gamma mode.

Output

Finally, what good is it working in linear floating point if the output bears no resemblance to what you see in the composition viewer? Just because you work in 32 bit floating point color does not mean you have to render your images that way.

Keeping in mind that each working space can be linear or not, if you work in a linearized color space and then render to a format that is typically gamma encoded (as most are), the gamma-encoded version of the working space will also be used. After Effects spells this out for you explicitly in the Description section of the Color Management tab.

To this day, the standard method to pass around footage with over-range values, particularly if it is being sent for film-out, is to use 10 bit log-encoded Cineon/DPX. This is also converted for you from 32 bpc linear, but be sure to choose the Working Space as the output profile and that in Cineon Settings, you use the Standard preset.

The great thing about Cineon/DPX with a Standard 10-bit profile is that it is a universal standard. Facilities around the world know what to do with it even if they've never encountered a file with an embedded color profile. As was detailed earlier in the chapter, it is capable of taking full advantage of the dynamic range of film, which is to this day the most dynamic display medium widely available.

Conclusion

This chapter focused on the most fundamental techniques of effects compositing. In the next chapter, you'll apply those techniques. You'll also learn about the importance of observation, as well as some specialized tips and tricks for specific effects compositing situations that re-create particular environments, settings, conditions, and natural phenomena.

17

LIGHT

Image courtesy of 4charros

There are two kinds of light: the glow that illuminates and the glare that obscures.

–James Thurber

Light

Light is the most complex phenomenon for a compositor to understand. By "understand" I mean not only scientifically but intuitively, like a painter or cinematographer.

The world of the compositor is less pure and scientific than other areas of digital production, which rely on elaborate models to simulate the way light works in the physical world. Like a painter, you observe the play of light in the three-dimensional world to re-create it two-dimensionally. Like a cinematographer, you succeed with a feeling for how lighting and color decisions affect the beauty and drama of a scene, and how the camera gathers them.

Several chapters in this book touch upon principles of the behavior of light. Chapter 14, "Color Correction," was about the bread and butter work of the compositor, matching brightness and color of a foreground and background. Chapter 15, "The Camera and Optics," was all about how the world looks through a lens. Chapter 16, "32 Bit HDR Compositing and Color Management," explored less straightforward ways in which After Effects can re-create the way color and light values behave.

This chapter is dedicated to practical situations involving light that you as a compositor must re-create. It's important to distinguish lighting conditions you can easily emulate and those that are essentially out of bounds—although, for a compositor with a good eye and patience, the seemingly "impossible" becomes a welcome challenge and a favorite war story.

Source and Direction

In many scenes, however, there is clearly more involved with light than matching brightness and contrast channel per channel. Light direction is one fundamental factor, especially where the quality of the light is *hard* (direct) rather than *soft* (diffuse).

Such a huge variety of light situations are possible in a shot, and in an infinite array of combinations, that it becomes difficult to make any broad statements stand up about lighting. This section, however, tries to pin down some general guidelines and workflows for manipulating the light situation of your scene.

Location and Quality

You may have specific information about the lighting conditions that existed when your plate footage was shot. On a set, you can easily enough identify the placement and type of each light; this information is contained to some extent in a camera report also. If the source shot was taken only with natural lighting, you only need determine the position of the sun relative to the camera (**Figure 17.1**).

Figure 17.1 Sometimes light direction and quality is plainly evident, sometimes ethereally mysterious.

Figure 17.2 Multiple lights create unpredictable overlapping light and shadow areas. (Image courtesy Pixel Corps.)

Sometimes the location and direction of light is readily apparent, but not as often as you might think. Hard, direct light casts clear shadows and raises contrast, and soft, diffuse light lowers contrast and casts soft shadows (if visible at all). That much seems clear enough.

These, however, are broad stereotypes, which do not always behave as expected in the real world. Hard light aimed directly at a subject from the same direction as the camera actually flattens out detail, effectively decreasing contrast. And artificial lighting usually involves more than one light source, diffusing hard shadows (**Figure 17.2**).

Neutralize Direction and Hotspots

When the direction or diffusion of light on a foreground element doesn't match the target background environment, that's potentially a big problem. The solution is generally to neutralize the mismatch by isolating and minimizing it, rather than actually trying to fix the discrepancy by attempting to simulate relighting the element in 2D.

Every shot in the world has unique light characteristics, but a couple of overall strategies apply. Assuming you've considered the simple solutions such as flopping the shot (where lighting is off by 180 degrees), you can

- Isolate and remove directional clues around the element, such as cast shadows (typically by matting or rotoscoping them out).
- Isolate and reduce contrast of highlights and shadows in the element itself, typically with a Levels or Curves adjustment (potentially aided by a luma matte, described below).
- Specifically invert the highlights and shadows with a counter-gradient.

The simple way to undo evidence of too strong a key light in a scene is to create a counter-gradient as a track matte for an adjustment layer; a Levels or Curves effect on this layer affects the image proportionally to this gradient. The Ramp effect can be set and even animated to the position of a key light hotspot (**Figure 17.3**).

A radial ramp is merely linear, which is not the correct model for light falloff. Light's

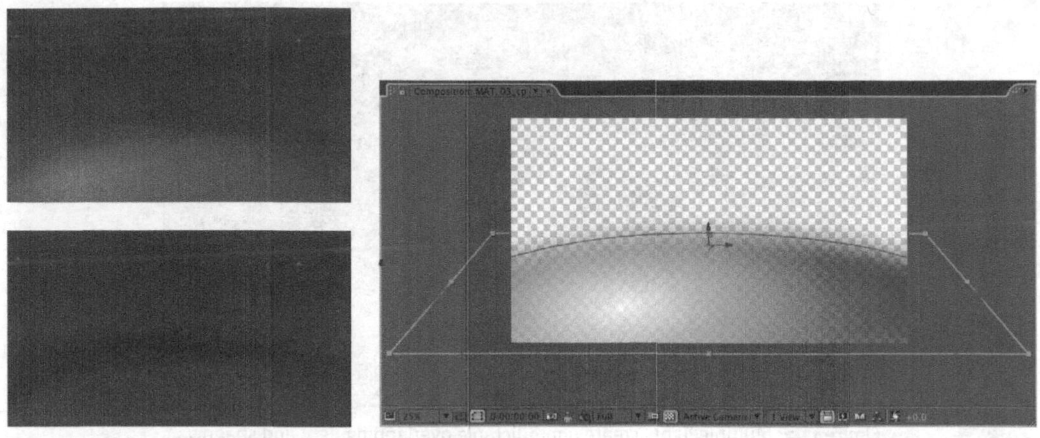

Figure 17.3 A counter-gradient is created with the Ramp effect on a solid, which in this case has been repositioned in 3D space to match the hot spot on the floor. This is then used as a track matte for an adjustment layer that lowers the brightness and contrast in the hotspot region.

intensity diminishes proportionally to its distance from the source squared, according to the *inverse square law*. An object positioned twice as far from a single light source is illuminated by one-quarter the amount of light. To mimic this with a gradient, precomp it, duplicate the radial gradient layer, and set the upper of the two layers to a Multiply blending mode (**Figures 17.4a, b**, and **c**).

Figure 17.4a, b, and c A simple gradient is linear (a), but light falls off in an inverse-square proportion, which can be re-created by multiplying a second gradient with linear blending enabled (b). Remember that, as explained in the previous chapter, in After Effects CS3 you can blend with a 1.0 gamma (giving you a precise inverse-square relationship) even without a linearized working space (c).

Color Looks

Have you ever seen unadjusted source clips or behind-the-scenes footage from a movie you consider visually compelling? It's a great way to learn the bold and deliberate use of color in modern films. Look at the work prints included with a heavily color-corrected film—the magic more or less disappears.

In older films this transformation was often accomplished via physical elements such as lens filters or photochemical processes, such as the well-known bleach bypass method, but nowadays it tends to happen on such computer-driven systems as the DaVinci.

After Effects has a big advantage over a system like a DaVinci in that it is a true compositing system; the controls over image selection are much finer. The main disadvantage is that After Effects was not created solely with color timing in mind, so its principal color tools (as described in Chapter 14) are simpler and less interactive. Third-party solutions such as Colorista and Magic Bullet Looks, both from Red Giant, aim to bridge some of this gap.

Keeping in mind that your job as a compositor is to emulate the world as it looks when viewed with a camera, it can be effective to begin by emulating physical lens elements.

Use a Layer as a Lens Filter

Suppose a shot (or some portion of it) should simply be "warmer" or "cooler." With only a camera and some film, you might accomplish this transformation by adding a lens filter. It could be a solid color (blue for cooler, amber to warm things up) or a gradient (amber to white to change only the color of a sky above the horizon).

Add a colored solid and set its blending mode to Color. Choose a color that is pleasing to your eye, with brightness and saturation well above 50%. Use blue or green for a cooler look, red or yellow for a warmer one (**Figure 17.5**).

At 100%, this is the equivalent of a full-color tint of the image, which is too much. Dial Opacity down between 10% and 50%, seeking the threshold where the source colors remain discernable, filtered by the added color to set the look.

To re-create a graded filter, typically used to affect only the sky, apply the Ramp effect to the solid and change the Start Color to your tint color; an amber filter adds the look of a heavily smoggy urban day. This is best applied with an Add or Screen mode instead of Color because the default End Color, white, desaturates the lower part of the

Figure 17.5 This saturated source image has four color filters applied to it as a test (you would normally choose just one to apply full frame, of course): yellow, green, blue/green, and blue. Linear blending is again enabled, so these solids applied with a Color blending mode behave a lot like lens filters of an equivalent color, but you control the opacity.

Figures 17.6a through c This Flag of Mars image (a) is made up of three fields of pure red, green, and blue. You can convert it to grayscale accurately with Tint (b), or a monochrome solid set to the blending mode Color (same result). Hue/Saturation (c) is mathematically correct but does not adjust for the perceptual differences in human color vision.

image. Sometimes, however, this might be just what you want.

✔ Notes

The flag of Mars is a red, green, and blue tricolor selected by the Mars Society and flown into orbit by the Space Shuttle Discovery. Seriously. It bears no apparent resemblance to the one Marvin the Martian used to claim Planet X.

Black and White

When removing color from an element entirely, there is a huge difference between using the Hue/Saturation effect and the likely alternatives. Counter-intuitively, Hue/Saturation is typically not the best choice to create a black-and-white image, because it maintains luminance proportions. **Figures 17.6a** through **c** visually illustrate the difference.

✔ Tip

- Hue/Saturation is great for more subtle saturation adjustments. Use it when you're focused only on brightness and contrast (using Levels), and overall saturation is a little hot, making the element appear a little too juicy.

Even if converting an image to black and white is only an intermediate step, you're best off doing so either using the Tint effect at the default settings or a fully desaturated solid (black, white, or gray, it doesn't matter) with a Color blending mode. To really get the conversion right may involve adjusting or shifting color channels prior to the color-to-black-and-white conversion, as shown in the chapter opener images.

Day for Night

Stronger optical effects are even possible, such as making a daytime scene appear as if shot on a moonlit night. Known in French as *la nuit américaine* (and immortalized in Francois Truffaut's ode to filmmaking of the same name), this involves a simple trick. Shoot an exterior scene under ordinary daylight with a dark blue lens filter to compensate for the difficulty of successful low light night shoots. If there is direct sunlight, it's meant to read as moonlight.

Lighting techniques and film itself have improved since this was a common convention of films, particularly westerns, but digital cameras retain a low signal to noise ratio under low light, hence the Nightshot feature on many consumer video cameras.

Figure 17.7 shows the difference between a source image that is blue and desaturated and an actual night look; if instead you're starting with a daylight image, look at the

Figure 17.7 An ordinary twilight shot of a house at dusk is converted to a spooky Halloween mansion. Note that the overall hue remains slightly blue, not monochrome, illuminated by its color opposite, a yellow moon. Other colors will not easily register in true low light, although this scene is much better lit than an actual moonlight shot would likely be if shot realistically. (Images courtesy Mars Productions.)

images on the book's disc, which take the image more in that direction. Overall, remember that the eye cannot see color without light, so only areas that are perceived to be well illuminated should have a hue outside the range between deep blue and black.

Color Timing Effects

Digital tools can of course go far beyond what is possible with lens filters. The industry standard tools rely on a *three-way color corrector*, which allows you to tint the image in three basic luminance ranges, highlights, midtones, and shadows, adjusting each separately via wheels which control hue and brightness. Premiere Pro has such an effect, which is retained if you import a project from that application despite that there is no such actual plug-in native to After Effects.

Even many Premiere Pro editors eschew this effect, however, instead using Colorista, a relatively inexpensive Red Giant plug-in (**Figure 17.8**). This effect is a lot like adding three color solids instead of one, and it lets you emulate the complex color look that is all the rage these days: blue shadows, green midtones, and orange highlights, anyone?

Figure 17.8 Colorista enables a subtle (or radical) mixture of individual Lift, Gamma, and Gain (low, medium, high) color wheel controls. The result uses Output Simulation to show how these changes will look on film (covered in the previous chapter).

✔ Tip

- If you don't like the idea of adding a third-party plug-in to your workflow, there is even a free alternative wired to a Color Balance (HLS) effect included in *The DV Rebel's Guide* (Stu Maschwitz, Peachpit Press) as RebelCC.

Source, Reflection, and Shadow

Scenes with strong prominent light sources are something of a gift to a compositor by offering a clear target. You can also make strong light choices confidently by referring to a shot that matches the target look. Either way, the message is simple: Use reference. You will be surprised how much bolder and more fascinating nature's choices are than your own, especially if you are still building your skills (and aren't we all continually doing that?).

✔ Notes

"Kiss of love" is a term Stu Maschwitz invented supervising *Star Wars, Episode One: The Phantom Menace* at Industrial Light + Magic. "I still use that term today," he says. "It's a great way to get an artist to think of a shot as theirs. Examples of kisses of love are reflections in things that might not strictly need it, aperture flares for lights leaving the frame (carefully matched to reference), or animating a starfighter pilot's head to turn as he banks."

You get the proverbial gold star for finding an unexpected surprise that works, and the play of light and shadow in the scene offers uniquely challenging and rewarding opportunities to do so. Such details can be the *kiss of love*, that something extra that nobody requested but everyone who is paying attention appreciates.

Big, bold, daring choices about light can and should become almost invisible if they are appropriate to a scene, adding to the dramatic quality of the shot instead of merely showing off what you as an artist can do.

Backlighting and Light Wrap

The conditions of a backlit scene are a classic example where the compositor often does not go far enough to match what actually happens in the real world.

✔ Notes

You can buy a light wrap plug-in for After Effects, but this is a case where "roll your own" works just as well, if not better.

This technique is designed for scenes that contain backlighting conditions and a foreground that, although it may be lit to match those conditions, lacks light wrapping around the edges (**Figure 17.9**).

Set up a light wrap effect as follows:

1. Create a new composition that contains the background and foreground layers, exactly as they are positioned and animated in the master composition. You can do this simply by duplicating the master comp and renaming it something intuitive, such as Light Wrap. If the foreground or background consists of several layers, it will probably be simpler to precompose them into two layers, one each for the foreground and background.
2. Set Silhouette Alpha blending mode for the foreground layer, punching a hole in the background (**Figure 17.10**).

Figure 17.9 The silhouetted figure has been color corrected to match the scene, but lacks any of the light wrap clearly visible around the figures seated on the beach.

3. Add an adjustment layer at the top, and apply Fast Blur.
4. In Fast Blur, check the Repeat Edge Pixels toggle on and crank up the blurriness (**Figure 17.11**).
5. Duplicate the foreground layer, move the copy to the top, and set its blending mode to Stencil Alpha, leaving a halo of background color that matches the shape of the foreground (**Figure 17.12** on the next page). If the light source is not directly behind the subject, you can offset this layer to match, producing more light on the matching side.

Figure 17.10 Using the alpha of the layer to which it's applied, Silhouette Alpha punches a hole through that layer and all underlying layers.

Figure 17.11 Heavy Fast Blur causes the background image color to bleed into the area of the underlying alpha channel.

6. Place the resulting comp in the master comp and adjust opacity (and optionally switch the blending mode to Add, Screen, or Lighten) until you have what you're after. You may need to go back to the Light Wrap comp to further adjust the blur (**Figure 17.13**).

When there is no fill light on the foreground subject whatsoever, most cameras are incapable of picking up as much detail in the foreground as your eye might see. In your reference photo, an unlit foreground subject might appear completely silhouetted. Because the foreground subjects are often the stars of the scene, you might have to compensate, allowing enough light and detail in the foreground that the viewer can see facial expressions and other important dramatic detail.

Figure 17.12 Stencil Alpha provides the inverse effect, preserving only the areas of the composition inside the alpha of the top layer to which it is applied. You have your light wrap.

Figure 17.13 The addition of light wrap causes the figure to appear as part of the scene.

In other words, this might be a case where your reference conflicts with what is needed for the story. Try to strike a balance, but remember, when the story loses, nobody wins.

Flares

For our purposes a "flare" is any direct light source that appears in shot, not just a cheesy 17-element lens flare whenever the sun pokes around the moon in some science fiction television show from the early 1990s. These don't come for free in After Effects; 3D lights don't even create a visible source if placed in shot until you add the Trapcode Lux effect (included on this book's disc).

✓ Close-Up

Three-Way Blur After Effects offers quite a few blur effects, but three are most common for general usage: Gaussian Blur, Fast Blur (which at best quality is no different but renders faster), and Box Blur, which can match the other two but offers more flexibility.

At the default Iterations setting (1), a Box Blur can seem crude and, well, boxy, but it can approximate the look of a defocused lens without all the more complex polygons of Lens Blur; you can also hold it out to the horizontal or vertical axis to create a nice motion blur approximation (where Directional Blur is actually too smooth and Gaussian).

Raising the Box Blur Iterations setting above 3 not only amplifies the blur but refines the blur kernel beyond anything the other two effects are capable of producing. What actually occurs is that the blur goes from a square appearance (suiting the name box blur) to a softer, rounder look. You're more likely to notice the difference working with over-range bright values in 32 bit HDR.

Fast Blur and Box Blur also each include a Repeat Edge Pixels checkbox; enable this to avoid dark borders when blurring a full frame image. The same setting with these two effects will not, alas, produce the same amount of blur even if Box Blur is set to 3 iterations (to match Fast Blur).

Real lens flares are never cheesy: Our eyes accept them as natural, even beautiful artifacts without necessarily understanding anything about what actually causes them (**Figures 17.14a**, **b**, and **c**).

Figure 17.14a, b, and c Figure 17.22a has no lens flare, when you might expect one; 17.22b has just the barest suggestion of a flare spiking out of the huge light source pouring in through the window, and 17.22c has a lens flare that is more natural but far less apparent than the flares you would get from the Lens Flare effect.

✔ Notes

Prior to the 1970s-era of Easy Rider and moon shots, flares were regarded as errors on the part of the cinematographer, and shots containing them were carefully noted on the camera report and retaken.

Therefore, to get lens flares or even simple glints right (not cheesy), good reference is often key. Only a tiny percentage of your viewers may know the difference between lens flares from a 50 mm prime and a 120 mm zoom lens, yet somehow, if you get it wrong, it reads as phony to a majority of viewers. Odd.

Here are some things you should know about lens flares:

- They are consistent for a given lens. Their angles vary according to the position of the light, but not the shape or arrangement of the component flares.
- The big complex flares with lots of components are created by long zoom lenses with many internal lens elements. Wider prime lenses create simpler flares.
- Because they are caused within the lens, flares beyond the source appear superimposed over the image, even over objects in the foreground that partially block the source flare.

Moreover, not every bright light source that appears in frame will cause a lens flare—not even the sun. (Look again at Figure 17.14a.)

✓ Close-Up

What Causes a Lens Flare? Unlike your eye, which has only one very flexible lens, camera lenses are typically made up of a series of inflexible lens elements. These elements are coated to prevent light reflecting off of them under normal circumstances. Extreme amounts of light, however, are reflected somewhat by each element.

Zoom lenses contain many focusing elements and tend to generate a complex-looking flare with lots of individual reflections. Prime lenses generate fewer.

Several other factors besides the lens elements also contribute to the look of a flare. Aperture blades within the lens cause highly reflective corners that often

Figure 17.15 This sequence shows the glint that plays off the chrome areas of the taxi as it passes a spot in the frame where the sun is reflected directly into the camera lens.

result in streaks, the number of streaks corresponding to the number of blades. The shape of the flares sometimes corresponds to the shape of the aperture (a pentagon for a five-sided aperture, a hexagon for six). Dust and scratches on the lens also reflect light.

Finally, lens flares look very different depending on whether they were shot on film or video, the excess light bleeding out in different directions and patterns.

The Lens Flare effect included with After Effects is rather useless as it contains only three basic settings. Knoll Light Factory, available from Red Giant Software, is much more helpful both because the presets correspond to real lenses and because the components can be fully customized in a modular fashion. The lens flare plug-in offered by The Foundry as part of Tinderbox also makes realistic-looking flares possible, although the included defaults are not so convincing.

Reflected Light

Reflected light is a common "kiss of love" opportunity for a scene; rarely is it prominently missing, but often a surface with some degree of specularity is added to a scene which will seem more palpably real with the addition of reflected light, from a glimmer or glint to a full window reflection.

Glints are specular flares that occur when light is reflected toward the camera from shiny parts of an element in scene, such as the chrome of the taxi in **Figure 17.15**, taken from the Chapter 5 color matching example.

There's no plug-in to create glints and no hard and fast rule about when they should appear; they are a near-pure kiss of love, although in this particular example you would expect a shiny metallic plane to cast glints just as the shiny taxi does. The glints on the taxi seem to occur just to the left of the frame's center, so you're looking for a specular hotspot on the plane that passes that point in the frame, and you get one on the tail.

By zooming in on your reference, you get the color and shape of a typical isolated glint (**Figure 17.16**). And behold, there's not much to it: a white blotch with six thin streaks coming off of it (which probably corresponds to a six-sided aperture). Looks like something you can paint rather quickly, no?

This is a perfect case in which it's best not to be a perfectionist. Close-up, the result of

Figure 17.16 There's not a whole lot to a glint when you look at it closely, especially at video resolution.

Figure 17.17 The plane passes by, hand-painted glints added to its tail.

my quickly painted glint looks most unimpressive indeed. But place it into a fast-moving shot that was never meant to be studied frame by frame, and I've just bought myself a good dose of extra realism for a few minutes' extra work (**Figure 17.17**).

Light Scattering and Volume

Light scatters as it encounters particles in the air, most dramatically causing the phenomena of volumetric light or God rays. Our atmosphere does not permit light to travel directly to the camera, uninterrupted. Instead, the light ricochets off tiny particles in the air, revealing its path.

The effect can be subtle. Lights that appear in the scene, casting their beams at the camera, tend to have a glowing halo around them. If the light traveled directly to the camera, the outline of the source light would be clear. Instead, light rays hit particles on their way to the camera and head off in slightly new directions, causing a halo (**Figure 17.18**).

Add more particles in the air (in the form of smoke, fog, or mist), and you get more of a halo, as well as the conditions under which volumetric light occurs. God rays are the result of the fact that light from an omnidirectional source, such as the sun, travels outward in a continuous arc (**Figure 17.19**).

The CC Light Rays effect is probably most helpful among those included with After Effects to re-create volumetric light effects, and even God rays. It not only boosts and causes halation around the source light, but also adds rays coming straight at camera. These rays can be made more prominent by boosting radius and intensity, but in order to create a God rays effect and not overwhelm an entire image with rays, it's usually best to make a target source and apply the effect to that. For example, you can

1. Add a solid of your preferred color.
2. Apply Fractal Noise (default settings are acceptable to begin).

Figure 17.18 You're so used to seeing halos around bright lights that it just plain looks wrong to lower the exposure so that the halos virtually disappear.

3. Mask the solid around the target God rays source area. Feather it heavily.
4. Apply CC Light Rays. Place the Center at the God rays target. Boost Intensity and Radius settings until the rays are prominent.
5. For rays only (no fractal noise) set Transfer Mode to None.
6. Set a Subtract mask or Alpha Inverted track matte to create occluded areas for the rays to wrap around, as in **Figure 17.20**.

Figure 17.19 The cathedral of light known to pious and pagan alike as God rays.

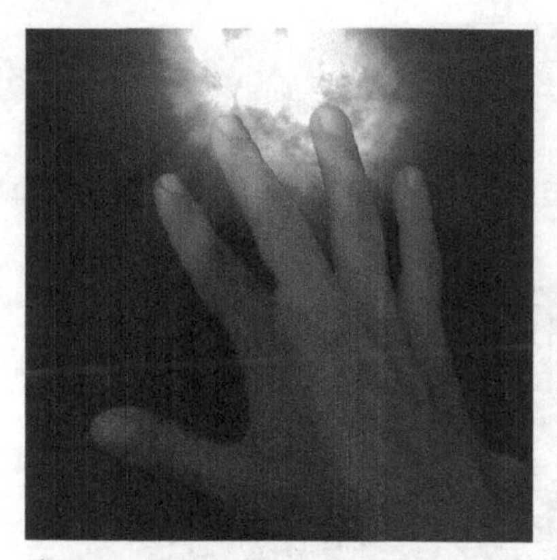

Figure 17.20 The included CC Light Rays effect is essential to creating your own volumetric light effects in After Effects. Masks or mattes can be used to occlude rays.

You can further hold out and mask out the rays as needed, even precomping and moving the source outside of frame if necessary. To make the rays animate, keyframe the Evolution property in Fractal Noise or add an expression such as time*60 causing it to undulate over time. Different Fractal Type and Noise Type settings will also yield unique rays.

Shadows

As there is light, so must there be shadows. Unfortunately, they can be difficult to re-create in 2D because they interact with 3D space and volume, none of which 2D layers have. The behavior of shadows can be unpredictable, but luckily, your audience typically doesn't know how they should look in your scene either.

You can certainly cast a shadow from a matted layer onto a plane by positioning each of them in 3D space and properly positioning a light. Be sure that you first change Casts Shadows for the matted layer from its default Off setting to On or Only (the latter option making it possible to create a precomp containing only the shadow).

You can instead corner pin the matte to the angle at which the shadow should fall and avoid the 3D setup altogether. In either case, the problem is that the illusion breaks if the light source is more than 10 degrees off-axis from the camera. The more you light a 2D element from the side, the more it just doesn't look right (**Figure 17.21**).

Figure 17.21 Compare the fake 3D shadow with the real thing and you instantly grasp the problem with this approach. You can cast a good shadow head-on, but not at this steep an angle.

There's also the possibility of cheating: if it's easy to add ground surface that would obscure a shadow (for example, grass instead of dirt), do so, and no one will even expect to see a shadow because it no longer belongs there.

Contact Shadows

For the most part, successful shading in a 2D scene relies on scaling back expectations. There are plenty of cases where a full cast shadow would be correct and no shadow at all clearly looks wrong, but a simple contact shadow will work.

A contact shadow is a lot like a drop shadow, basically just an offset, soft, dark copy directly behind the foreground. A drop shadow, however, is good only for casting a shadow onto an imaginary wall behind a logo, whereas a contact shadow is held out to only the areas of the foreground that have contact with the ground plane.

Figure 17.22 shows a good example based on a composite from Chapter 5. The foreground can layer is duplicated and placed behind the source. A mask is drawn around the base, and it is then offset downward. A blur is applied to soften the transparency channel. That gives you the matte.

You might now expect to simply darken the layer down to black and lower opacity to taste, but shadows are not simply cast pools of black, they are areas of obscured light, so there is a better way. Create an Adjustment layer just below the contact shadow layer and set an Alpha track matte. Add a Levels (or if you prefer, Curves) effect and adjust brightness and gamma downward to create your shadow. Treat it like a color correction, working on separate channels if necessary; the result is typically less bland and more accurate than a simple pool of blackness.

Figure 17.22 A simple contact shadow can make the difference between an object that appears to sit on a surface and an object that appears to float in space.

Indirect Light

It's easy to forget the actual physics of what gives an object a certain color; it is comprised entirely of the wavelengths of light that the surface does not absorb. All of the color in our world, save that of light sources such as the sun or your computer screen, is primarily the result of reflected light.

Most surfaces in the natural world are diffuse, and they reflect light softly in all directions (**Figure 17.23**). Thus in some subtle way, adjacent physical objects can color one another, but two layers composited together completely lack these light interactions, which occasionally would be quite prominent.

Computer software is becoming better at re-creating these types of interactions. Global illumination and radiosity features have been added to 3D rendering programs over the past decade to re-create the many effects of reflected light, enhancing the realism of completely synthesized scenes. For the compositor, of course, lighting remains more art than science. The 3D artist can be more like a sculptor, letting the light play

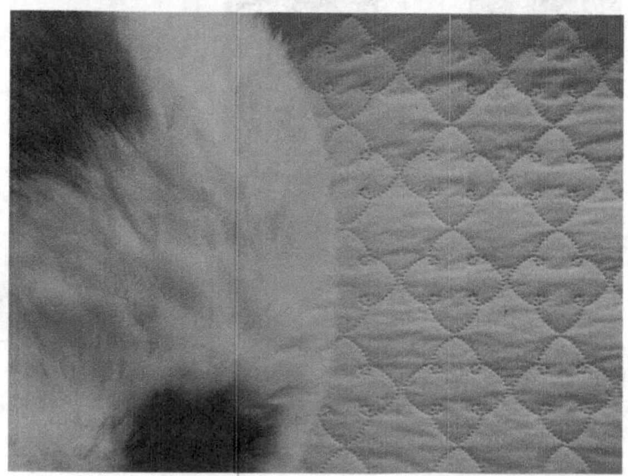

Figure 17.23 The color influence of indirect light is not always so evident as here, yet this phenomenon is always in play.

over the created work, but the compositor is more like a painter, observing and artistically interpreting the world without the benefit of realistic physics. Light that interacts directly between objects presents one more golden opportunity to make the scene feel real the way that a painter would.

Multipass 3D Compositing

Some artists, including a majority of those who work predominantly in 3D, labor under the delusion that you should finalize the look of a computer-generated element in one pass. Certainly, as it becomes more and more possible to adjust the look of a 3D model in real time (via the GPU, i.e., OpenGL) this becomes tempting.

However, it's possible to do better by dividing the render of a single element into multiple passes. This is different from rendering in layers, which while also useful for compositing is really only about separating foreground elements from the background. *Multipass rendering* is the technique of isolating individual surface qualities and creating a separate render for each. By surface qualities I mean things like specularity and wear and tear, also known as grunge. In his excellent book *Digital Lighting & Rendering, Second Edition* (Peachpit Press, 2006), Jeremy Birn calls out multiple benefits yielded by rendering a model on multiple passes, a few of which include

- **Changes** can be made with little or no re-rendering. If a shadow is too dark or a glow the wrong color, the adjustment can be made right in After Effects.
- **Integration** often requires multiple passes where the model interacts with the scene, casting a shadow on the ground or being reflected in water. If the cast shadow is simply part of a single render you lose all control over its appearance and cannot apply it as recommended in the previous section.
- **Reflections**, which often consume massive amounts of time to process, can be rendered at lower quality and blurred in After Effects.
- **Bump Maps** can be applied more selectively (held out by another pass such as a highlight or reflection pass).
- **Glows** can be created easily in 2D by simply blurring and boosting exposure of a specular pass.
- **Depth of Field** can be controlled entirely in 2D by using a Z pass as a matte for a blur adjustment layer.
- **Less render power and time** is required to render any one pass than the entire shaded model, so a lower powered computer can do more, and redoing any one element takes far less time than redoing the entire finished model.

Putting multiple passes to use is also surprisingly simple; the artistry is in all of the minute decisions about which combination of adjustments will bring the element to life. **Table 17.1** (on the next page) describes some common render passes and how they are typically used.

Other passes might include: a *Fresnel* (or *Incidence*) pass showing the sheen of indirect light and applied to an adjustment layer with a Luma Matte (raise Output Black in Levels to re-create sheen); a *Grunge* or *Dirt* map, applied as a Luma Inverted Matte, allowing you to dial in areas of wear and tear with Levels on an adjustment layer; a *Light* pass for any self-illuminated details; a *Normal* pass showing the direction of surface normals for relighting purposes. Many, many more are possible—really anything

Table 17.1

Ten Typical Multipass Render Layer Types

Type	Color/ Grayscale	Typical Blending Mode	Description	Use
Diffuse	Color	Normal	Full color render; includes diffuse illumination, color correction and texture, excludes reflections, highlights and shadows	Color basis for the element; main target for primary color
Specular	Color	Add or Screen	Isolated specular highlights	Control how highlights are rendered; can be reused to create a glow pass by simply blurring and raising exposure
Reflection	Color	Add or Screen	Self-reflections, other objects, environment	Control the prominence and color of reflections
Shadow and	Grayscale	Luma Inverted	Isolated translucent	Control appearance, color
		Matte	shadows in scene	softness of shadows; applied as a track matte to an adjustment layer with a Levels or Curves effect
Ambient	Color	Color	Color and texure maps without diffuse shading, specular highlights, shadows or reflections	Color reference, can be used to make the color/texture of an object more pure and visible
Occlusion	Grayscale	Luma Inverted Matte	Shadows that result from soft illumination, simulating light from an overcast sky or well-lit room	Adds natural soft shadows to an object; these can be tinted to reflect the color of reflected light
Beauty	Color	Normal	A render of all passes	Reference: this is how the object or scene would appear if rendered in a single pass
Global Illumination	Color	Add or Screen	Indirect light added to the scene by global illumination, potentially including raytraced reflections and refractions	Control intensity of indirect lighting in scene
Matte/ Mask/Alpha	Grayscale	Luma Matte	Can be used to contain multiple transparency masks for portions of the object or scene, one each on the red, green, blue and alpha channels	
Depth/Z-depth/ Depth Map	Grayscale or non-image floating point	Luma Matte	Describes the distance of surface areas from the camera	Can be used to control depth effects such as fog and lens blur, as well as light fall-off

you can isolate in a 3D animation program. **Figure 17.24a** through **i** show a robot set up for multipass rendering and a few of its component render layers.

Note that none of these passes necessarily requires a transparency (alpha) channel, and at the biggest old-school effects houses it is customary not to render them, since multi-

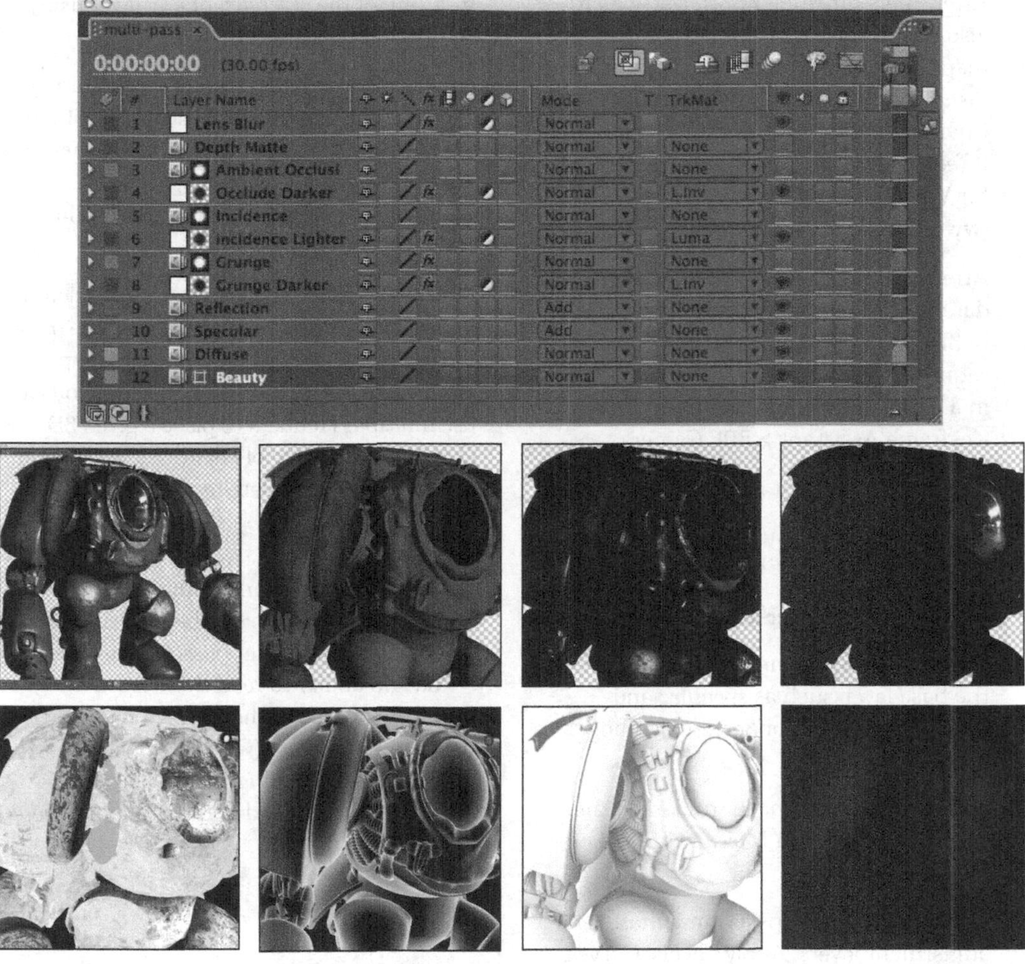

Figure 17.24a through i A basic multipass setup (a, above) with the beauty pass (b) as reference, and made up of the following color passes: diffuse (c), specular (d) and reflection (e) as well as grayscale passes applied as luma mattes to adjustment layers, each containing a Levels effect: grunge (f), incidence (g), and occlusion (h). A depth matte (i) can be applied in various ways; here it is used as reference to an adjustment layer containing a Lens Blur effect that utilizes it.

ple passes of edge transparency can lead to image multiplication headaches.

✓ Close-Up

RPF RPF files are an Autodesk update to RLA. After Effects offers limited native support for these files (via the effects in the 3D Channel menu) but more robust support for some of the finer features of RPF such as Normal maps is only available via third-party plug-ins. Commercially available plug-ins that can translate normal maps for use in

After Effects include ZBornToy (which also does amazing things with depth maps; a demo is available on this book's disc) from Frischluft and WalkerFX Channel Lighting, part of the Walker Effects collection. There is a free option for Windows only called Normality (www.minning.de/software/normality).

After Effects can also extract camera data from RPF files (typically generated in 3DS Max or Flame); place the sequence containing the 3D camera data in a comp and choose Animation > Keyframe Assistant > RPF Camera Import.

The general rules for multipass compositing are simple:

- Use the Diffuse layer as the base.
- Apply color layers meant to illuminate the base layer, such as specular and reflection, via Add or Screen blending modes.
- Apply color layers meant to darken the base layer, if any, via Multiply or Darken blending modes.
- Apply grayscale maps as luma mattes for adjustment layers. Apply Levels, Curves, Hue/Saturation to allow these mattes to influence the shading of the object or scene.
- Control the strength of any layer using that layer's Opacity.

Note that multipass renders present an excellent case to enable Blend Colors Using 1.0 Gamma in Project Settings, whether or not you assign a Working Space (and whether or not that working space is linearized).

Multipass rendering is only partially scientific and accurate; successful use of multiple passes is a highly individualized and creative sport. With the correct basic lighting setup you can use multipass renders to place a given 3D element in a variety of environments without the need for a complete re-render.

✔ Notes

An EXR image can contain multiple layers, each of which can be labeled to contain specific render passes. After Effects has no ability to read these extra layers until you install the ProEXR plug-in, free from Fnordware (www.fnordware.com/ProEXR). This plug-in also allows Photoshop to read and write multilayered EXRs.

INDEX

B

C

D

E

F

G

H

I

J

K

M

N

O

P

Q

R

S

U

V

W

X

Y

Z